Praise for
White House Ghosts

'Robert Schlesinger's meticulously researched *White House Ghosts* looks at the complicated relationship between speechwriters and the presidents they have served, from Franklin D. Roosevelt to George W. Bush. . . . Both historical and analytical, Schlesinger's narrative details the tension between style and substance, poetry and policy."

—Chuck Leddy, *The Boston Globe*

"A lively new history of White House speechwriters."

—Jack Rosenthal, *The New York Times Book Review*

"A president's words can frame an era or shape world history. That makes his speechwriters critical. Robert Schlesinger, son of one of the greatest, brings the flair of a storyteller and the insight of a scholar to the White House's obscure but glorious ghosts."

—Jonathan Alter, author of *The Defining Moment: FDR's Hundred Days and the Triumph of Hope*

"Robert Schlesinger knows a good story when he hears one. . . . *White House Ghosts* is a comprehensive account of the speechwriting process, from the relationships between presidents and their scribes to the origins of some of the most memorable words spoken by the nation's leaders. The insider's account offered by Schlesinger also allows the reader to examine the presidency from a new perspective—the prism of speechwriting."

—*Roll Call*

"Robert Schlesinger's *White House Ghosts* is a welcome addition to the literature on presidents from FDR to George W. Bush. His book not only adds a significant dimension to our understanding of how presidential speeches were constructed but also deepens our knowledge of the way in which major policies were developed. Schlesinger has given us an altogether delightful and informative study that will become essential reading for anyone interested in the modern presidency."

—Robert Dallek, author of *Nixon and Kissinger*

"Will delight history buffs and political junkies alike."

—Eric Fettmann, *New York Post*

"Thoroughly researched, smoothly written and frequently witty."

—John R. Coyne, Jr., *The Washington Times*

"It's no surprise that the men and women who have written speeches for our presidents have stories to tell! What is a surprise is that Robert Schlesinger has dug up so many of them. *White House Ghosts* flows along with one rich anecdote after the next. All the major speeches (and several minor ones) are dissected: how they evolved, were argued over, changed, vetted, rewritten. (Some presidents actually did some rewriting themselves. Imagine!) The book is fascinating. And funny. If you like reading American history, you'll love this book."

—Leslie Stahl, correspondent for *60 Minutes* and author of *Reporting Live*

"This book is insider heaven to the political junkie. Once you've read it, you never again will see a presidential address in the same light."

—Edward Cuddihy, *The Buffalo News*

"Here's a book about politics and presidents that says something new. Robert Schlesinger gives readers a captivating inside glimpse at the anonymous wordsmiths whose talent at crafting a president's speeches can make or break a presidency. Ted Sorensen. Peggy Noonan. Dick Goodwin. Bill Safire. James Fallows. Pat Buchanan. They are here, and many others, describing the often frustrating, sometimes heartbreaking, but ultimately rewarding process of framing the issues and passions of the moment in prose worthy of our great republic. From FDR's 'rendezvous with destiny' to JFK's stirring inaugural to Reagan's solemn tribute to the *Challenger* astronauts, Schlesinger shows us: the words matter."

—John A. Farrell, author of *Tip O'Neill and the Democratic Century*

"Those interested in learning about how presidential speeches are written will get a great deal out of reading *White House Ghosts* . . . a behind-the-scenes tour of White House speechwriting. . . . One of the biggest revelations in Schlesinger's book is how involved many presidents themselves have been in the writing and editing process. . . . Historical analysis—and some great backstage stories—make *White House Ghosts* a worthwhile book."

—Claude R. Marx, *St. Petersburg Times*

"Robert Schlesinger has given us an absorbing, detail-packed tour behind the scenes of some of the great defining moments of the modern presidency. His narrative is about the story of the speechwriters—those people in the shadows (and, increasingly, sharing the spotlight) of some of the most famous speeches in American history. In a larger sense, however, Schlesinger is writing not simply about speeches but about the

presidency itself. The ability to educate and persuade has always been the most important weapon in the presidential arsenal. The evolution of that power over recent decades, in a wildly changing political and media culture, is the theme of this first-rate history."
—John F. Harris, author of *The Survivor: Bill Clinton in the White House* and editor in chief of Politico.com

"Schlesinger confidently assesses the diverse contributions made by speechwriters toiling thanklessly on behalf of presidents from FDR to G.W. Bush. . . . Schlesinger lingers over particular speeches good and bad, thereby offering a revealing look at the making of history. Well-reasoned and capably constructed."

—*Kirkus Reviews*

"A snappy history, the first on its subject. . . . Administration by administration, the author takes us through a lively, often unforgettable cast of characters. . . . Schlesinger's coverage is wide, his research comprehensive, his pace fast, his prose light."

—*Publishers Weekly*

"Robert Schlesinger's entertaining *White House Ghosts* brings decades of presidential speechwriters back to life with fresh and revealing anecdotes about their most memorable achievements. He escorts Raymond Moley, Sam Rosenman and Malcoom Moos out from behind their typewriters to take a bow, alongside more familiar craftsmen—Ted Sorensen, William Safire, Peggy Noonan."

—A. J. Langguth, author of *Union 1812*

"A detail-packed volume chronologically covering presidents from Franklin D. Roosevelt through the current Bush administration, with extensive insight into how these leaders have had their messages crafted and packaged."

—*Library Journal*

"Schlesinger delivers in *White House Ghosts* an at-once comprehensive and breezily anecdotal book. . . . Schlesinger's 90-plus interviews and his wide reading yield a thought-provoking bundle of suggestions to what works and what doesn't work in the creation of presidential speeches—and all public communications by leaders."

—David Murray, *Speechwriter's Newsletter*

December 7, 1941.

PROPOSED MESSAGE TO THE CONGRESS

December 7, 1941, a date which will live in ~~world history~~ *infamy*

s of America was ~~simultaneously~~ *suddenly* and deliberately attacked

forces of the Empire of Japan ~~without warning~~

States was at the moment at peace with that nation and w

onversation with its Government and its Emperor looking

nance of peace in the Pacific. Indeed, one hour after

adrons had commenced bombing in ~~the American island of Oahu~~ *Oahu*

ssador to the United States and his colleague delivere

of State a formal reply to a ~~former~~ *recent American* message, ~~without~~

reply ~~contained a statement~~ *stated* that diplomatic negotiatio ~~*it seemed useless*~~

~~it seemed useless but~~ *it* contained no threat ~~and no~~ *or* hint of *war*

ecorded that the distance

WHITE HOUSE GHOSTS

Presidents and Their Speechwriters

Robert Schlesinger

SIMON & SCHUSTER PAPERBACKS

New York   London   Toronto   Sydney

*For Arthur M. Schlesinger, Jr., a student and teacher
of history, a writer of presidential speeches,
and most of all a wonderful father.*

SIMON & SCHUSTER PAPERBACKS
A Division of Simon & Schuster, Inc.
1230 Avenue of the Americas
New York, NY 10020

Copyright © 2008 by Robert Schlesinger

Illustration credits appear on page 579

First Simon & Schuster hardcover edition January 2009

SIMON & SCHUSTER PAPERBACKS and colophon are registered trademarks
of Simon & Schuster, Inc.

For information about special discounts for bulk purchases,
please contact Simon & Schuster Special Sales at
1-800-456-6798 or business@simonandschuster.com.

Designed by Dana Sloan

Manufactured in the United States of America

10 9 8 7 6 5 4 3 2 1

The Library of Congress has cataloged the hardcover as follows:
Schlesinger, Robert
White House ghosts: presidents and their speechwriters / Robert Schlesinger.
p. cm.
Includes bibliographic references and index.
1. Presidents—United States—History—20th century. 2. Presidents—United States—
Biography. 3. Rhetoric—Political aspects—United States—History—20th century.
4. Political oratory—United States—History—20th century. 5. Speechwriting—
United States—History—20th century. 6. Speechwriters—United States—Interviews.
7. Interviews—United States. 8. United States—Politics and government—1933–1945.
9. United States—Politics and government—1945–1989. 10. United States—
politics and government—1989–. I. Title.
E176.1 .S+   2008
2008003127

ISBN-13: 978-0-7432-9169-9
ISBN-10:   0-7432-9169-7
ISBN-13: 978-0-7432-9170-5 (pbk)
ISBN-10:   0-7432-9170-0 (pbk)

Contents

Introduction: The Coming of the "Literary Clerk" • 1

ONE
"Grace, Take a Law" • 5

TWO
"Missouri English" • 31

THREE
"Sometimes You Sure Get Tired of All This Clackety-Clack" • 69

FOUR
The Age of Sorensen • 101

FIVE
"Now That's What I Call a News Lead" • 145

SIX
"Concern for Image Must Rank with Concern for Substance" • 188

SEVEN
"Go Back and Give Me One Speech, Not Two Speeches" • 230

Contents

EIGHT

"Don't Give Any Explanation. Just Say I Cancelled the Damn Speech" • 268

NINE

The Musketeers • 312

TEN

"I'm Not Going to Dance on the Berlin Wall" • 362

ELEVEN

"No, No, No, This Is a Speech—I Just Want to Talk to People" • 402

TWELVE

"The Troika" • 456

Notes • 495

Acknowledgments • 559

Index • 562

Illustration Credits • 579

WHITE HOUSE GHOSTS

The Coming of the "Literary Clerk"

When George Washington considered retiring in 1792 after a single term as president, he asked James Madison to help him draft a farewell address. Four years later, when the general did leave the presidency, he passed the Madison draft, which Washington had augmented and edited, on to Alexander Hamilton. Washington then polished and added to Hamilton's effort. The result was the first and one of the best presidential farewell addresses. It was actually never orally delivered but rather was printed in Philadelphia's largest newspaper, the *American Daily Advertiser*. As a spoken speech could only reach its immediate audience, such documents were prepared with readers in mind more than listeners. Washington warned against "foreign alliances, attachments, and intrigues"; against "the necessity of those overgrown military establishments, which, under any form of government, are inauspicious to liberty, and which are to be regarded as particularly hostile to Republican Liberty"; against the party system; and in favor of the new federal government.

During his presidency, from 1829 to 1837, Andrew Jackson utilized Amos Kendall, a former newspaperman and a member of his "kitchen cabinet," for help in drafting his public statements—both written and spoken. Stooped, nearsighted, and poorly dressed, Kendall had a sallow complexion, a hacking cough, and prematurely white hair that made him look older than his forty-some years. Jackson would lie in his bed smoking and dictating thoughts. Kendall would smooth them out and read them back. Jackson would shake his head and try again, repeating the process until they arrived at a formulation that suited the president. One Jackson critic called Kendall "the President's thinking machine, and his writing machine, ay, and his lying machine."

The historian George Bancroft, the Secretary of the Navy, helped write President James K. Polk's message to Congress asking for a declaration of war against Mexico in 1846. Bancroft would later write messages to Congress for President Andrew Johnson.

As Abraham Lincoln was working on his first inaugural, he planned to close by telling his "dissatisfied friends" in the South that they had the choice between "peace or the sword." Incoming Secretary of State William Seward, who had vied with Lincoln for the Republican presidential nomination, suggested that the new president add a "note of fraternal affection." He supplied a few lines, including the hope that "the mystic chords which, proceeding from so many battlefields and so many patriot graves, pass through all the hearts and hearths in this broad continent of ours, will yet again harmonize in their ancient music when breathed upon by the guardian angel of the nation." Lincoln polished the thought into poetry for his inaugural address: "The mystic chords of memory, stretching from every battlefield and patriot grave, to every living heart and hearthstone, all over this broad land, will yet swell the chorus of the Union, when again touched, as they surely will be, by the better angels of our nature."*

If Judson Welliver, "literary clerk" to Presidents Warren Harding and Calvin Coolidge, was not the first aide to help a president compose a speech, he is recognized as the first ghostwriter in the modern sense—a White House staffer whose regular job description includes helping the president compose his remarks.

A snub-nosed, soft-spoken Illinois native, Welliver had been a well-known reporter, writing for the *Sioux City Journal*, the *Des Moines*

---

*We know that Lincoln consulted with Seward the night before he delivered the Gettysburg Address, but whether they discussed the speech remains a matter of historical conjecture. (Garry Wills, *Lincoln at Gettysburg: The Words That Remade America* [New York: Simon & Schuster, 1992], 31–32.)

Leader, the *Sioux City Tribune*, and the editorial page of *The Washington Times*, before joining the Harding presidential campaign. Welliver was described even by the acid-tongued H. L. Mencken as "a journalist of the highest skill and [who] knows how to write simply and charmingly." Mencken had no use for Harding, a former newspaperman himself. Harding, Mencken famously noted of the president's own inaugural address, "writes the worst English that I have ever encountered." He continued: "It reminds me of a string of wet sponges; it reminds me of tattered washing on the line; it reminds me of stale bean soup, of college yells, of dogs barking idiotically through endless nights. It is so bad that a sort of grandeur creeps into it. It drags itself out of the dark abysm . . . of pish, and crawls insanely up to the topmost pinnacle of posh. It is rumble and bumble. It is flap and doodle. It is balder and dash."

Is it any wonder that Harding sought help in drafting his public remarks? Welliver was not only speechwriter but press handler. During the campaign, he had written prepackaged news stories for reporters to send home. Harding died in August 1923, and Welliver stayed on with his successor, Calvin Coolidge, for more than two years, leaving on November 1, 1925, to become publicist for the American Petroleum Institute.*

Harding was the first president to have a full-time speechwriter, but it is no coincidence that only one president after him—Calvin Coolidge—forewent such an aide. When Harding was elected in 1920, the election results were for the first time broadcast on the radio, reaching a few thousand households in Pittsburgh. When the parties nominated their candidates four years later, there were nearly six hundred radio stations around the country and as many as 3 million receivers. The 1924 Republican and Democratic nominating conventions were the first to be broadcast.

Politics was on the cusp of a revolution. Radio supplanted print as the

---

*Welliver was succeeded by F. Stuart Crawford, but, as *Time* magazine noted, the position "went under a cloud when it was found that the Coolidge addresses, when dealing with geography and other indisputable facts, followed with a striking literalness the text of the International Encyclopaedia." ("Encyclopaedia," *Time*, April 8, 1929.)

dominant medium and was in turn replaced by television. Television evolved to include live, remote broadcasts, then fractionalized from three networks into a panoply of outlets, including twenty-four-hour news channels, a multiplication process that has grown exponentially with the Internet.

The rise of mass media allowed a new, more intimate kind of communication between president and populace. Using the radio, Franklin D. Roosevelt would practically invent this modern style of presidential communication. And as the opportunities for exposure multiplied, and with them competing entertainment alternatives, presidents responded by raising their own profiles. In his only term, from 1929 to 1933, Herbert Hoover made an average of a little more than eight public appearances a month; in less than a full term, John F. Kennedy averaged nearly nineteen such appearances; in his first term, Bill Clinton made more than twenty-eight. As the importance of public communications has grown, so has the importance of the aides who help presidents speak.

Presidential speechwriters are a group unique to the modern presidency, and as such they afford a unique lens through which to view the nation's modern chief executives. Looking at how presidents prepared their speeches, the care they put into them, and the people they chose to aid them, we can learn about their views of the modern presidency.

Clark Clifford, who helped write speeches for Harry S. Truman, used to talk about the speechwriters' code. Speechwriters, Clifford would say, tell the world that they go in to discuss with their president the upcoming speech in Pittsburgh, and the president gives an outline—points he wants to touch on—and from this the writers produce a draft. In fact, Clifford continued, the president would say: I've never carried Pittsburgh, they've always been against me, and who set up this goddamn thing anyway? The reality, more complicated and more fun, lies in the middle.

ONE

"Grace, Take a Law"

JULY 1, 1932

In Chicago, the Democratic Convention nominating speeches had given way to hours of seconding addresses. Around 3 am thunder rumbled and lightning crackled outside of Chicago Stadium. The first balloting did not start until 4:28 am and was bogged down by challenges.

At the Roosevelt estate in Hyde Park, New York, Judge Samuel Rosenman was wrestling with the conclusion to a speech he was not sure would be delivered.

He had passed the evening with Governor Franklin D. Roosevelt and some members of his family—wife Eleanor, mother Sara, twenty-two-year-old son Elliott—and Mrs. Dorothy Rosenman, listening on the radio to the party proceedings. By the time the storm raged over Chicago, Elliott was stretched asleep in a chair and Dorothy Rosenman dozed, slumped against her husband's seat. By morning the judge had sent to the closest delicatessen for hot dogs and retreated to a small, informal dining room to finish Roosevelt's acceptance speech.

Franklin Roosevelt and Rosenman had first met during FDR's 1928 gubernatorial run. Fifteen years removed from his last experience with New York legislative issues, Roosevelt had sought an aide to travel with him, reeducate him on what faced the state, and help him write speeches. Although his ghostwriting experience was limited, Rosenman, who had been a state legislator for five years and a member of the Bill Drafting Commission for three, otherwise qualified. Clean-shaven and slightly plump, Rosenman's fastidious appearance reflected an ordered mind. "He was a neat man," aide David Ginsburg recalled seven decades later. He "knew where things were and knew what he wanted."

When FDR won the 1928 election, Rosenman worked as his counsel, helping the governor deal with the New York City political machine and the state legislature, and aiding him in drafting speeches and political messages. For the last two years of Roosevelt's term, Rosenman lived in the governor's mansion—exposure that helped him learn the processes of his boss's mind, especially how he wrote and spoke. Rosenman had in March suggested to Roosevelt that he bring university professors to Albany to discuss national problems that he would face as president—what would become known as FDR's "Brains Trust."

Now, Rosenman was determined to finish the speech regardless of the outcome in Chicago: an incomplete project irked the ordered lawyer, and after all it only lacked a peroration. "I pledge you, I pledge myself, to a new deal for the American people," he wrote.

Like most such memorable political phrases, "New Deal" was not conceived in capital letters. When Rosenman handed FDR the new paragraphs, the governor glanced at them and apparently gave them little more thought. Like other memorable slogans, this one had antecedents and echoed ideas already floating through the public consciousness. The issue of *The New Republic* presently on newsstands had a cover story by economist Stuart Chase entitled "A New Deal for America." In 1933, FDR would tell a founder of the International Mark Twain Society that he had "obtained" the phrase from Twain's *A Connecticut Yankee at King Arthur's Court*. Rosenman would dismiss speculation that the phrase was designed to echo FDR cousin Theodore Roosevelt's "Square Deal" and FDR hero Woodrow Wilson's "New Freedom."

Raymond Moley, who had been the principal drafter of the acceptance speech (per custom he had not written a closing), later claimed credit for the phrase's origin, noting that he had first paired the words in a May 19 policy memo to the governor. But while his assertion is literally correct, he had used the words only in passing—"Reaction is no barrier to the radical. It is a challenge and a provocation. It is not a pledge of a new deal; it is a reminder of broken promises."*

Whether any of this entered into Rosenman's choice is unknowable. But the phrase would have been lost to history if another close FDR aide had had his way.

After Roosevelt forces secured the nomination on the fourth ballot on the evening of July 1, the candidate announced he would fly to Chicago to address the convention, a risky move—air travel was still a novelty—and a break with tradition. The throng that greeted Roosevelt's trimotored plane in the Windy City on the afternoon of July 2 included a mismatched pair of Roosevelt aides, each with designs on the nominee's speech.

One was Moley. A Columbia University professor of public law, he had an incisive mind and grounded sense that distinguished him as a realist among the ivory tower set. He had piercing eyes, and smoked a heavy, dark pipe. He had first met Roosevelt in 1928 when he helped the candidate prepare a plan and a speech on simplifying the state's justice system. In the 1920s, Moley had conducted studies of criminal justice in Cleveland, Ohio, and then in Missouri and Illinois. He had directed research for the New York State Crime Commission and had also done some work for a group called the National Crime Commission, of which FDR was a director.

After Roosevelt was elected governor, he appointed Moley to a committee that helped overhaul the state's parole system and to the Commission on the Administration of Justice in the State of New York. He also informally consulted with Moley on such matters, sometimes using him to help draft speeches. Rosenman had tapped Moley as the first member of the Brains Trust and he had become its leader, ferrying a stream of professors up to Hyde Park.

---

*When the *Saturday Evening Post* serialized Moley's administration memoir *After Seven Years* (1939), Rosenman clipped the article containing Moley's "new deal" claim and sent it to FDR. "If you have some idea that you had anything to do with making yourself President, you should read the attached modest, self-effacing account of the process by one Raymond Moley," Rosenman wrote in a cover note. "He now emerges in a new role, a master of—fiction!" (Rosenman, note to FDR and attached clipping, "Rosenman, Samuel: 1933–40" folder, President's Secretary's File, FDR Library.)

Also awaiting the candidate in Chicago was a former reporter, Louis McHenry Howe, an aide of longer standing than any other in FDR's orbit, having first met the young politician when Roosevelt was a one-term state senator more than two decades earlier. Sensing potential greatness, Howe had undertaken to teach him politics and had become an all-purpose political aide and confidant, acting as everything from surrogate to strategist to speechwriter. He stood five foot four inches tall, weighed less than one hundred pounds, and seemed chronically ill. His face cratered by a childhood bike accident, Howe was known as "the medieval gnome," an appellation that he embraced with grim humor. He was devoted to FDR, territorially jealous, snapping angrily at others who drew close to his Franklin.

As a trio, Rosenman, Moley, and Howe did not mesh, getting along only as their common cause required. Rosenman later described Moley as "very devious in some of his dealings" but "an excellent writer. . . . He was sort of a hypochondriac, was quite morose, had a very limited sense of humor, and for that reason, he was not easy to work with." Moley, in turn, viewed Rosenman as "patently on the smug side, a trifle obsequious if you were 'important,' a shade highhanded if you weren't." Roosevelt did not need them to get along so long as he could employ their talents.

When during the convention Howe saw a copy of the acceptance speech in Chicago, he flew into a rage. "Good God, do I have to do everything myself?" he exclaimed. "I see Sam Rosenman in every paragraph of this mess." By the time Roosevelt landed in Chicago, Howe had produced his own draft, to Moley's great alarm. The professor fought his way through the chaos to Rosenman. "You've got to do something about this," he told Rosenman, explaining Howe's intention to switch the speeches. "I have tried to tell him how foolish that would be, but it's no use; he is over there talking to the governor about it now."

Rosenman approached the open car that would carry Roosevelt to Chicago Stadium (already two and a half hours late, he had no time to rest) in time to hear Howe arguing with Roosevelt. "I tell you it's all right Franklin," Howe said. "It's much better than the speech you've got now—and you can read it while you're driving down to the convention hall, and get familiar with it."

"But Louis, you know I can't deliver a speech that I've never done any work on myself, and that I've never even read," Roosevelt responded. "It will sound stupid, and it's silly to think that I can."

Howe would not be put off. The governor agreed to peruse the alternative text en route to the convention hall. For years to come, FDR would recount with relish how, his car speeding through the crowd-lined streets of Chicago, he had smiled, waved, and tipped his hat to the crowd while sneaking glances at the Howe speech in his lap.

Standing in the back of the convention hall, Rosenman and Moley listened in horror as Roosevelt started reading Howe's speech. But after a minute he returned to words the pair knew well. FDR had torn the front page off Howe's speech and then gone back to the Albany draft, including the historic promise of a "new deal."

In campaigns and in the White House, speeches not only reflect policies but frequently act as a policy-forcing mechanism: The fact of a pronouncement focuses and curtails any lingering debates—most of the time. The central issue of the 1932 presidential campaign was the depression that had brought the country to the brink of material and psychological collapse. One component of the economic debate was the question of trade tariffs, an issue that had torn the Democratic Party for a generation.* In early September, Moley presented Roosevelt with a pair of tariff-focused speeches: one, inspired by Tennessee Democratic senator Cordell Hull, a free trader, advocated a 10 percent across-the-board cut in tariffs; the other, a response written by retired Army Brigadier General Hugh Johnson, argued against cutting the tariff in favor of bilateral "old-fashioned Yankee horse-trades."

Roosevelt seemed to scrutinize the two speeches before he looked up at his aide and told Moley to "weave the two together." It was of course an impossible order and Moley told him so. Roosevelt deferred a decision for weeks, before, in the Palace Hotel in San Francisco, finally shifting in favor of the Johnson approach. It would not be the last time

---

*Seventy-five years later, the Democratic Party remained split on the issue of trade.

FDR or other presidents would blithely expect his writers to execute the rhetorical equivalent of cognitive dissonance.

Of greater importance at the Palace on the evening of September 22 was Roosevelt and Moley's first discussion of an inaugural address. FDR removed his heavy leg braces and ordered the telephone cut off. Despite a long day of campaigning, he was at his best at night, and after briefly going over the next day's address, he and Moley turned their thoughts to what Roosevelt might say after being sworn in more than five months later.*

Moley always bristled at being characterized as a "speech writer" or—worse—a "ghost writer," both of which he interpreted to be something akin to a scriptwriter producing finished texts that pols would read verbatim. "My job from the beginning—and this continued for four years—was to sift proposals for him, discuss facts and ideas with him, and help him crystallize his own policy," he wrote in 1939.

This summation is a good starting definition for the position of presidential speechwriter. Implicit is the notion that policies and words are inextricably linked—the former cannot be conjured in the absence of the latter. It was a role Moley and others played for FDR in the White House, not mere wordsmiths but advisers who helped the president flesh out policy by putting it in words. The job of speechwriter has evolved as television eclipsed radio as the nation's medium, as the White House staff grew from a handful to a sprawling group of specialized cadres, and, of course, as each president has dealt with it in his own way. The rise of presidential speechwriters has also spurred philosophical questions involving whose words the president speaks. And these are issues that not only relate to questions of credit but can have real world consequences.

The topic of the inaugural speech was next broached on a train trip in early February from Warm Springs, Georgia, to Jacksonville, Florida. Moley then brought a draft to Hyde Park on Sunday, February 26, 1933—six days before FDR's inaugural.

---

*Prior to the Twentieth Amendment (ratified in 1933 but too late to affect Roosevelt's first term), which among other things set the date of the presidential inauguration at January 20, presidents were sworn in on March 4.

Around 9 pm the next evening, after dinner, Moley and the president-elect retired to the library, with its lit fireplace. Roosevelt, sitting at a folding card table, carefully read Moley's typed draft before remarking that he had better transfer it into his own longhand. Howe was arriving the following morning and would "have a fit" if he suspected any other hand but FDR's had composed the speech.

So, with Moley sitting on the long couch in front of the fireplace, Roosevelt rewrote the speech on a legal-size tablet of paper. The two men sipped whiskey and edited on the fly, reconsidering each sentence, sometimes each word, before FDR committed it to paper. "How do you spell foreclose?" Roosevelt asked at one point. There were occasional distractions and interruptions—calls from incoming cabinet members—as they worked through to the draft's end.

When they finished, Moley took his original and tossed it onto the still-glowing fireplace embers. "This is your speech now," he said.

But Roosevelt had in mind more than to fool Louis Howe. His handwritten copy of the speech, on file at the Franklin D. Roosevelt Library at Hyde Park, has a typewritten note dated March 25, 1933, signed by the president and explaining that it was "the Inaugural Address as written at Hyde Park on Monday, February 27, 1933. I started in about 9.00 P.M. and ended at 1.30 A.M. A number of minor changes were made in subsequent drafts but the final draft is substantially the same as this original." That account omits Moley, conjuring an image of FDR writing in solitude. A generation of historians recounted the scene before Moley—incensed by the Roosevelt deception—published his second New Deal memoir in 1966, correcting the record.

It was an unworthy and uncharacteristic ploy on Roosevelt's part, but illustrates the tension that often exists over ownership of a speech or phrase when a president uses a writer. Moley burned his draft of the speech because of "a keen sense that whatever might be the authorship, he and he alone would have to carry the responsibility of what was said on the fateful day of inauguration." The president has ownership of his words, if not always literal authorship.

And the authorship question is rarely clear-cut. In the case of the Roosevelt inaugural, the absence of any extant copy of Moley's original makes it impossible to pinpoint the parentage of most phrases. His draft was informed not only by discussions with Roosevelt but months of close contact. Whatever he had brought to Hyde Park was already FDR-sponsored, if not produced. And Roosevelt was a careful participant in the speechwriting process, a close editor who reworked material to fit his own needs.

Roosevelt's charade achieved its immediate goal: Howe believed the speech was FDR's alone. He edited it himself, dictating a shorter, tighter version, with a new first paragraph that contained the exhortation, "The only thing we have to fear is fear itself."

Several theories about the line's origin have been suggested over the years. Rosenman later remarked to Eleanor Roosevelt that it echoed Henry David Thoreau ("Nothing is so much to be feared as fear"), and she replied that her husband had had a volume of the American philosopher's works in his room in the Mayflower Hotel the night before the inaugural—an account Moley disputes.

Like the phrase "new deal," the concept of fearing fear was not new. It had echoes, from Epictetus to Cicero to Shakespeare to Daniel Defoe to Thoreau. A 1931 edition of *The New York Times* had a front-page story quoting U.S. Chamber of Commerce chairman Julius H. Barnes as saying, "In a condition of this kind, the thing to be feared most is fear itself."

Moley recalled the phrase appearing in, of all places, a February 1932 department store ad, but that advertisement has disappeared. Whether Howe saw the ad or the *Times* piece (possible), picked up the concept from classic literature (unlikely: his tastes ran almost exclusively to pulp detective novels), or arrived at the thought on his own will never be known.

Roosevelt had a keen sense of public psychology. He understood that what people needed was restored hope and a sense of order. As important was his insight that radio, the first live mass medium, lent itself to a previously unimagined oratorical intimacy. For the nation's first 150 years, political addresses were designed to be delivered to large, present audiences. Speeches had to be long enough to satisfy people who had traveled great distances to hear them, and delivery had to reach the peripheries of crowds. Radio flipped things: instead of aiming addresses at large public crowds, one could now visit individuals in the quiet of their homes. FDR's lower-key, more casual style supplanted formal rhetoric.

Yet under these apparently effortless performances existed a new political mechanism. Other presidents had had help with speeches, but the intersection of a new medium and a new governmental style under Roosevelt created a need that has not abated. Presidents could communicate instantaneously with greater numbers of their countrymen than ever before, but as the scope of the federal government and expectations of it grew starting with the New Deal, presidents would have less time to prepare their own communications.

While presidents and politicians have sought to mimic FDR's achievement by adopting his style—and later John F. Kennedy's and Ronald Reagan's—the successful communicators have found ways to match his success in finding collaborators who could help them develop and elevate their own rhetorical voices. No president after Roosevelt tried to serve without one, and more often several, speechwriters. Their political successes often reflected their ability to properly use these aides.

Like so much in the Roosevelt White House, the speechwriting system was not well ordered. FDR used a broad selection of friends and aides to draft speeches and written messages to Congress, often drawing them into the process through their policy portfolios. And as FDR experimented with different policies, he cycled through various advisers. Howe, appointed as Roosevelt's private secretary, continued to contribute to speeches to the end of his life in 1936. Other contributors included Donald Richberg, a Chicago labor lawyer before joining the administration; the diplomat William Bullitt; law professor Felix Frankfurter, who would continue to consult on speeches even after he joined the Supreme Court; retired Army Brigadier General Hugh Johnson, who was a key official in the National Recovery Administration and later the Works Progress Administration; Brains Trusters Rex Tugwell, an agriculture expert and Columbia professor, and Adolph Berle, a former child prodigy who graduated from Harvard as a teenager and was appointed to be counsel for the Reconstruction Finance Corporation.

Moley took a nominal position as Assistant Secretary of State, off the White House staff so as to avoid inflaming Howe, but that role was short-lived. Secretary of State Cordell Hull discovered at the 1933 World Economic Conference in London that Moley had been secretly sending negative reports to Roosevelt. So when he left the department in September 1933, he moved at once into preparation of a new weekly news and opinion magazine, *Today*.

Almost immediately, Moley was summoned by Roosevelt on October 22 to help prepare a fireside chat for that evening on commodity prices and the value of the dollar. Moley opposed FDR's plan but he answered the call because, "in this instance, I was merely a draftsman." Later he rejected suggestions that he was a mercenary pen who provided words without regard for their content. "I was no weaver of fancy phrases to fit whomever might call for such confections," he wrote in 1966. "If I had not believed in Roosevelt's objectives, I could not have participated."

But in October 1933, Moley was ready to weave. While loyalty and overall agreement with the New Deal quieted his discomfort, the fireside chat signaled a policy divergence between the two friends that would grow over the next three years. Five days later *Today* debuted,* with a Moley editorial saying that Roosevelt's character and heritage would prevent him from ever assuming dictatorial powers. If this seems oddly obvious seventy-five years later, it was not so at the time: that the president could assume extraordinary authority to battle depression was part of the political debate. But Moley was not being entirely truthful: his notes from his initial inaugural discussions with Roosevelt included ideas of "dictatorship" and "dictatorial powers." The inaugural address raised the notion that Roosevelt might ask for wartime powers if Congress did not act quickly.

Quiet invitations to the White House remained a regular part of Moley's life during FDR's first term. By his own reckoning, he made the train trip from New York to Washington no fewer than seventy-five times, spending 132 days in D.C., to consult on speeches and written

---

*In 1937 the magazine merged with rival publication *News-Week* to form *Newsweek*.

messages to Congress—and that did not include trips to Hyde Park. He would slip in a side entrance, through the Cabinet Room and the office of Marguerite "Missy" LeHand, FDR's personal secretary, thus avoiding the media (of which he, of course, was a member).* He stayed overnight in the executive mansion occasionally, but more often would check into a hotel. As he avoided the official White House calendar, his visits did not attract press attention.

The editor of a news weekly moonlighting as the president's top speechwriter would be a scandalous violation of journalistic ethics in present times. But the battle lines were then less distinct. In May 1932, for example, a small group of reporters picnicking with Roosevelt and LeHand were ribbing the governor about his speeches, so FDR jokingly challenged them to produce something better. The *Herald Tribune's* Ernest K. Lindley, with help from his colleagues, wrote a draft the candidate used at Oglethorpe University later that month. The speech's promise of "bold, persistent experimentation" became a neat summation of Roosevelt's governing philosophy.

In December 1933, Roosevelt asked Moley to oversee the drafting of a securities exchange bill for the following year. Moley called in a pair of young lawyers he knew, Tom Corcoran and Ben Cohen. Corcoran worked at the Reconstruction Finance Corporation while Cohen was a staffer at the Public Works Administration. Both disciples of Frankfurter, the two were an inseparable team. Corcoran—"Tommy the Cork"—was brash and blustery, unafraid to fight, threaten, or cajole. He played piano well and accordion better, singing along from a bottomless supply of Irish folk songs and sea shanties. Cohen was quieter, more cerebral, moodier. The pair complemented each other, and became presidential favorites as policy advisers and eventually speechwriters.

Moley got more assignments. "I'd be called in to put together ideas against which I had argued passionately," he wrote. "I was summoned, in such cases, as a technician at speech construction, just as I'd be called in if I were a plumber and a pipe needed fixing." He justified it to him-

*Until the Nixon administration, the White House did not have a press room, so the reporters would gather in the main lobby of the West Wing.

self as a chance to do good: "For every time I would be asked to put clarity into statements of which I thoroughly disapproved there would be two or three times when it was possible to modify or head off a step entirely," he stressed.

The disagreements became more frequent, and Moley's *Today* editorials were increasingly critical. The First New Deal, which emphasized government and business working cooperatively, was giving way to the Second New Deal, which had a more populist, anti-corporate tone. Moley was openly and approvingly suggesting that conservatism and big business would soon be back in public favor. The divergence crystallized at the White House five days before Christmas 1935 during a discussion of FDR's upcoming annual message to Congress.* Roosevelt, at just over 50 percent in the polls, said he wanted a "fighting speech" to kick off the campaign year.

"Whom are you going to fight?" Moley asked. "And for what?"

But while he opposed the idea, he played technician once again. The resulting speech evoked "battle" against the attempted return to power of "entrenched greed" and a "resplendent economic autocracy" that wanted "power for themselves, enslavement for the public." It turned Moley's stomach. He had never before realized "the extent to which verbal excesses can intoxicate not only those who hear them but those who speak them." For five more months he muddled along, trying to square the circle—either to extricate himself from Roosevelt's orbit or persuade the president to steer a more business-friendly course. His attitude became "Nunc dimittis—Now lettest thou thy servant depart in peace."

Roosevelt was already preparing for that eventuality. In May 1936, he invited the Rosenmans for a Memorial Day weekend Potomac cruise on the presidential yacht, the *Potomac*. Also aboard were Stanley High and his wife. A Chicago native, High held a doctorate in theology, had

---

*What is now called the State of the Union address was simply the "annual message" until well into the twentieth century. FDR's 1934 speech was the first to incorporate the title, but not until 1947 did it come into general usage. (Michael Kolakowski and Thomas H. Neale, "The President's State of the Union Message: Frequently Asked Questions," Congressional Research Service, March 7, 2006, available at www.senate.gov/reference/resources/pdf/RS20021.pdf.)

served as a Methodist minister in China and, while never ordained, was the pastor of a church in Stamford, Connecticut. And he was a Republican: He had actively opposed Roosevelt in 1932 and would return to the GOP fold in 1940, but for a brief season he was a New Dealer. He had started occasionally contributing to FDR's speeches in 1935.

Moley was well on his way to becoming the first in a line of publicly embittered former presidential speechwriters. And while the feeling was mutual—FDR thought Moley had swung too hard to the right to be an effective collaborator—it was not in Roosevelt's character to make a clean break with an old friend and comrade-in-political-arms. Moley allowed FDR to pull him back for his 1936 acceptance speech, reworking a monstrously long Corcoran draft that included the statement, "this generation of Americans has a rendezvous with destiny."

What Moley did not know was that FDR had also tapped Rosenman and High to write a draft. Such competing assignments were standard procedure in other areas of the Roosevelt White House, but rare in presidential speechwriting—and even then, usually happened only where Moley was concerned.

Three days before the speech was to be delivered, FDR invited the four writers to dine with him and Missy LeHand. The president and Moley quarreled at the dinner table. Roosevelt ribbed the writer about his "new, rich friends" and their influence on his editorials. Moley shot back that FDR's inability to take criticism was leading him to poor policy. The other guests were aghast—it was the only time, Rosenman later wrote, that he ever "saw the President forget himself as a gentleman." Moley downplayed the exchange as typical of the kind of informal relationship he had with the president, including a "habit of plain, even rough, talk," and said it was quickly forgotten.

Moley produced a draft that was, in his words, "Sweetness, if not Light," invoking faith, hope, and charity. The Rosenman-High effort, on the other hand, was closer to thunder and lightning, decrying "a new despotism" wrapped "in the robes of legal sanction." The result was a ragged stitch job that in one breath attacked "economic royalists" (a High contribution) and in the next waxed about giving government "the vibrant personal character that is the very embodiment of human charity."

As he had four years earlier, FDR hid the fact of other hands in the speech. But this time Moley was the deceived, as the president told him that he himself had made some changes to add "fire" to the talk.

Roosevelt and Moley went through the motions one last time in Hyde Park in September, on the writer's fiftieth birthday. As an absurd hide-and-seek went on—Rosenman, Corcoran, and High, who along with Cohen became the 1936 campaign speech team, were squirreled away on another part of the estate—Roosevelt made a halfhearted attempt at recruiting Moley. The writer declined. After Roosevelt's re-election he sent a polite telegram of congratulations. "And there the story of personal relations ends," Moley noted in 1939. "There was no 'break,' no trouble, no recriminations, no bitterness." The two friends met only once more, and Moley quickly became one of the president's most pungent and vocal critics.

During the first term, the Supreme Court had struck down various elements of the New Deal. In response, Roosevelt had made one of his few major political errors, proposing in February 1937 a "reorganiza-tion bill" that would, among other things have added a new justice to the Supreme Court for every one that had reached the age of seventy years and six months, with a total possible limit of fifteen. When the Senate Judiciary Committee convened its first hearings into the Court plan in 1937, Moley was the first witness to testify in opposition. Years later he told an interviewer that when he dreamed of FDR, it was always of their reconciling.

Roosevelt marked up no other speech as much as his second inaugural address. Richberg had written a first draft, but as he was a better lawyer than speechwriter, Rosenman and Corcoran reworked it before send-ing it to Roosevelt. Then the four men edited, tightened, worked, and reworked the speech to the president's satisfaction.

FDR's skill as an editor lay in his ability to pare sentences and punch up tired rhetoric. He would usually produce the sort of homely analogy that so often illustrated his public pronouncements. Between the sec-ond and third drafts, a section was inserted outlining the problems the country faced, each proceeded by "I see . . ." For example, "I see millions of families trying to live on incomes so meager that the pall of family disaster hangs over them day by day." FDR produced the capstone to this series, giving the speech its signature line. Rosenman had penciled a summary line into the text, but Roosevelt erased it and wrote: "I see one third of a nation ill-housed, ill-clad, ill-nourished."

This kind of moment was not uncommon. Roosevelt would stop, lean back in his chair, and stare up at the ceiling. Sometimes minutes passed in silence. Then he would dictate a passage that more often than not remained in the speech's final draft. He sometimes prefaced this by turning to his secretary, Grace Tully, and saying, "Grace, take a law"—a nod to a George M. Cohan Broadway musical, *I'd Rather Be Right*, in which Roosevelt, during the Hundred Days, would dictate laws to Congress.

Sometimes FDR's dictations would nail the point. At other times he would ramble, eventually losing steam and finally saying breezily, "Well—something along those lines—you boys can fix it up." Sometimes his inserts were never meant for the speech at all, but were simply an opportunity for the president to vent, confident that his aides would know better than to leave the bile in the next draft. If his writers were united in disagreement with him, he might turn to Tully or LeHand and say with mock plaintiveness, "They won't let me say anything of my own in my own speech." He often overruled his aides at these times, though he might tell them they could remove an offending section, adding, "I'll just ad-lib it"—and he would.

When a final text was produced, FDR marked it up for ease of reading—underlining words to emphasize or noting pauses. "Hard-headedness will not so easily excuse hard-heartedness," the second inaugural said, a neat bit of phraseology too easily transposed, as FDR did while reading the draft out loud to himself. To ensure that no such mistake occurred during his actual delivery, the president drew a small circle (the head) over "headedness" in his reading copy and a small heart over "heartedness."

The president's phone rang at around 3 am on Friday, September 1, 1939. Both the hour and the fact that the call went directly through to

Roosevelt indicated its gravity. It was William Bullitt, the U.S. ambassador to France, calling from Paris. He was relaying a message from Anthony Biddle, the U.S. ambassador to Poland, who had been unable to reach Washington directly. Biddle's message: German bombs and shells had started falling on Poland.

The years between the outbreak of war and the United States entry into the conflict presented special problems for Roosevelt, who had to lead an electorate that had competing opinions about how to handle the international situation. " 'Stay out of war.' 'Help England and France.' Anybody who wants to understand the American people today must take those two desires into full account," the pollster George Gallup wrote in *The New York Times* on April 30, 1939. The strains of these competing impulses found voice in increasingly vocal isolationist and interventionist movements, the former arguing that Europe's problems were of no concern to the United States, while the latter advocated U.S. aid to Britain and France—for example, by repealing the neutrality laws that forbade the United States from selling arms to belligerents.

The trick for Roosevelt during these years was to orient the country to resist the Fascist menace without getting so far ahead of public opinion as to lose it. It was a time of transition and tension in terms of his speechwriting: whether in building a new speechwriting staff or in pushing his own government rhetorically farther than its diplomats preferred.

On Sunday evening, September 3, Roosevelt was giving his first fireside address since June 1938.* He aimed to calibrate American reaction to the war, warning that an ocean separating the United States from the fighting did not place the nation beyond the conflict's reach, while also pledging that the country would remain officially neutral. "This nation will remain a neutral nation, but I cannot ask that every American remain neutral in thought as well," he said. "Even a neutral has a right to take account of facts. Even a neutral cannot be asked to close his mind or his conscience."

---

*Roosevelt's fireside chats took on such importance that in later years popular imagination had the president at the microphone monthly if not more often; in fact, after 1933, he never gave more than three fireside talks in any of his remaining peacetime years in office.

Roosevelt had himself added that qualification during the initial editing process of a draft that originated in the State Department. The occasion also illustrated a shift in FDR's speeches. From 1939 onward, his focus was increasingly international and war-related, away from domestic issues. And it would not be the last time that Roosevelt—or any president—punched up a State-drafted speech to point the country in the proper international direction.

When Roosevelt gave the commencement address at the University of Virginia on June 10, 1940—the day that Italy declared war on France and Great Britain—the State Department prepared a lengthy insert for his speech. But Roosevelt himself—picking language from a cable sent by French premier Paul Reynaud—again found a cutting image to dramatize the occasion. Under Secretary of State Sumner Welles argued that it would be diplomatically imprudent and got Roosevelt to remove the phrase. But the president reconsidered and on the train ride down to Charlottesville handwrote the line back into his speech: "On this tenth day of June, 1940, the hand that held the dagger has struck it into the back of its neighbor."

By the end of that summer, the list of former Roosevelt speechwriters well outnumbered the roster of available talent: Howe was dead; Moley had become an FDR critic, as had Hugh Johnson; High was expelled from the New Deal ranks in early 1937 after committing the cardinal sin of using his insider status and information for an article in the *Saturday Evening Post*; Corcoran had offended too many people to maintain his utility ("Nearly all the Democratic national political leaders in the country had become bitter at him," Rosenman later wrote); and while Cohen would occasionally contribute, he was not as effective without his partner. Rex Tugwell and Don Richberg had long since left the administration.

Bullitt contributed briefly during the summer and fall of 1940 but, preferring to work alone, was never part of a speechwriting team. Librarian of Congress Archibald MacLeish contributed occasionally, starting that year. Rosenman had been a fixture since the 1936 reelection campaign and would remain through the balance of Roosevelt's presidency.

But one key aide had joined the speechwriting group: Harry Lloyd Hopkins. Iowa-born, he had worked in New York State social services before joining the administration in March 1933 as head of federal relief efforts. He had moved into the president's inner circle (and for a time into the White House itself), and was for FDR's last five years his most important aide. He was in a sense a bookend to Howe, though whereas Howe had taught Roosevelt, it was the president who instructed Hopkins in the arts of politics. Like Howe, Hopkins was territorial about his boss and also almost constantly sick.

Hopkins had no truck with formality and relished cutting through ceremony or meandering chatter. Winston Churchill once told him that when the war was over, the British government planned to give him a noble title. When Hopkins responded that nobility was not something he sought, Churchill said, "We have already selected the title: You are to be named, 'Lord Root of the Matter.'"

Hopkins's greatest strength as a speechwriter lay in criticism: he had a keen eye for weaknesses in an argument, and would deftly tear up substandard drafts. But he had other duties, and the advent of the 1940 campaign prompted Rosenman and him to have an emergency meeting about their speechwriting. They needed one more collaborator—a liberal who could write and, as important, was sympathetic to the president's foreign policy. Their first choice, a radio commentator named Raymond Gram Swing, was unavailable, as was their second choice, a newspaper commentator who was on assignment in India.

They finally lit upon a choice with a touch of glamour: Robert Emmet Sherwood, the playwright, who had already won two Pulitzer Prizes. He had a bright wit and quick humor and was something of a bon vivant. An activist who had rallied aid for Great Britain, Sherwood had known Roosevelt at least casually for a number of years. "Those of us who voted against you have caused [sic] to be ashamed of ourselves," he wrote Roosevelt in May 1933.

Sherwood and his wife visited the Roosevelts in January 1940, and the president expressed an interest in a pair of speeches that Abraham Lincoln gives in Sherwood's *Abe Lincoln in Illinois*. The playwright sent these along with a note that said: "I saw Harry Hopkins and told him that I wish with all my heart to offer my services, for whatever they're worth, to you in this crucial year and to the cause which is yours as surely as it was Lincoln's."

Hopkins ran into Sherwood one Sunday that summer in Long Island. "What are you warmongers up to now?" Hopkins growled, referring to Sherwood's work with William Allen White's Committee to Defend America by Aiding the Allies, a pro-interventionist political group. Sherwood lost his temper when Hopkins called the playwright and his friends "pro-British fanatics" who were undermining the president by pushing too hard for U.S. aid to Britain. When Sherwood finished an impassioned defense of internationalism, Hopkins, no isolationist, grinned: "All right then—why do you waste your breath shouting all this at *me*?" he asked. "Why don't you get out and say these things to the people?"

Sherwood would get his chance to do more than that. Hopkins brought him to see Rosenman in early October at the judge's Central Park West apartment to discuss the president's speeches.* Rosenman and his wife shared an amused glance when the playwright said that the president must draft all of his speeches himself. "If there had been substantial assistance there would have been a mélange of style and quality which would have shown it right away," Sherwood said.

Talk turned to a foreign affairs speech the president was to give on Columbus Day, October 12. The men passed around and critiqued a draft that the State Department had produced. Satisfied not only that Sherwood's foreign policy ideas were in sync with FDR's but that he could express them with clarity and force, Rosenman slapped a pencil down on the table. "Boys, there comes a time in the history of every speech when it's got to get written—that time for this speech is *now*," he said. "So let's get to work."

He turned to Sherwood and suggested he put into writing some of the points he had been expounding. The playwright looked mystified, as if wondering, What in the world is the use of my writing a couple of paragraphs here in this apartment in New York City? How is that going to do any good in a speech the president is writing in Washington?

Roosevelt's final speechwriting team was now in place. Virtually

---

*It illustrates how relatively infrequently the president spoke then that for most of his first decade in office his principal speechwriters, Moley and later Rosenman, lived in New York City.

every major FDR speech over the next five years would be written by some combination of Rosenman, Hopkins, and Sherwood—usually all three.

Work on the speeches generally took place after the regular work day, a reflection of the informality retained even through the war years. Perhaps a half-dozen evenings a month, the writers gathered in the Oval Office at the cocktail hour, while the president mixed drinks and held court. He displayed more enthusiasm as a bartender than skill: his bourbon old-fashioneds were first rate, but his martinis—with two kinds of vermouth and, occasionally, absinthe*—were less well received.

Dinner—the White House kitchen was surprisingly mediocre—was served at seven forty-five and only afterwards would the real work commence. Roosevelt sat on a couch near the fireplace in his office, his feet propped up on a custom-built stool. He often pulled from his pockets little scraps of paper on which he had noted down ideas, phrases, or specific points to make.

The president would retire by eleven; the speechwriters then retreated to the Cabinet Room to finish the draft and often another. White House stenographers, security guards, and—perhaps most important—kitchen staff quickly became used to the odd hours. These late work nights often involved plates of sandwiches, pots of coffee, bottles of soda, beer, and bourbon: Rosenman drank Coca-Cola and coffee to keep himself up; Sherwood and Hopkins insisted that bourbon had the same effect on them.

The three men were gathered around Roosevelt's desk on such an evening preparing for the 1941 State of the Union address, which he was scheduled to give on January 6. It was coming at a critical moment: The Fascist plague had darkened most of Europe, with Great Britain barely holding out under Churchill's stalwart exhortation six months earlier that, "we shall fight on the beaches, we shall fight on the landing grounds, we shall fight in the fields and in the streets, we shall fight in the hills; we shall never surrender."

The truth was that Great Britain was rapidly running out of cash

---

*The fact that absinthe had been banned in the United States since 1912 apparently did not deter the mixologist-in-chief.

with which to pay for arms (Roosevelt had prevailed in 1939 in amending the neutrality laws to allow weapon sales). So, in mid-December 1940, Roosevelt had hit upon the idea of lending weapons to Britain, selling the plan (in a metaphor of his own creation) as being the equivalent of lending a length of hose to a neighbor whose house was on fire. "If he can take my garden hose and connect it up with his hydrant, I may help to put out his fire," Roosevelt told reporters on December 17. "Now, what do I do? I don't say to him before that operation, 'Neighbor, my garden hose cost me $15; you have to pay me $15 for it.' What is the transaction that goes on? I don't want $15—I want my garden hose back after the fire is over."

Twelve days later, Roosevelt gave a fireside chat on the subject ("This is not a fireside chat on war. It is a talk on national security"), telling his countrymen that the United States must be—in a phrase coined by French diplomat Jean Monnet—"the great arsenal of democracy."

The 1941 message, then, was the next crucial step in selling the plan, and in preparing the country for war. Hopkins, Rosenman, and Sherwood were revising the third draft with the president when he announced that he had a thought for the peroration. He leaned back in his swivel chair and stared at the ceiling. And stared. The silence became uncomfortable.

FDR's hesitation had less to do with an epiphany than phrasing and refinement. Speaking to the press in July, he had outlined what he called the five freedoms that were the objective of U.S. foreign policy—freedom of information, freedom of religion, freedom of expression, freedom from fear, and freedom from want. Now, merging freedom of information and expression, he was ready to introduce the concept on a broader stage.

He finally leaned forward. "Dorothy," he said to his secretary Dorothy Brady, who would sometimes relieve Tully during long speechwriting sessions, "take a law."

"The first is freedom of speech and expression everywhere in the world," his message would say.

The second is the freedom of every person to worship God in his own way everywhere in the world. The third is freedom from want—which trans-

lated into international terms means economic understandings which will secure to every nation everywhere a healthy peace time life for its inhabitants. The fourth is freedom from fear—which translated into international terms means a world-wide reduction of armaments to such a point and in such a thorough fashion that no nation anywhere will be in position to commit an act of physical aggression against any neighbor.

Roosevelt's "Four Freedoms" were a stirring expression of foreign policy ideals that both elevated the immediate argument and provided an enduring conception of U.S. policy. The Four Freedoms would become a central piece of Allied propaganda once the United States entered the war. Sixty years later, President George W. Bush's speechwriters would study the speech as they worked on their president's remarks to Congress in the wake of the September 11, 2001, terrorist attacks.

Harry Hopkins remained unconvinced. "That covers an awful lot of territory, Mr. President," he said. "I don't know how interested Americans are going to be in the people of Java."

"I'm afraid they'll have to be some day, Harry," Roosevelt replied. "The world is getting so small that even the people in Java are getting to be our neighbors now."

Indeed, the eyes of the United States would focus on the South Pacific sooner than even FDR likely anticipated.

Shortly before 5 pm on Sunday, December 7, 1941, Roosevelt summoned Grace Tully to his study. Reports had been coming in from a smoldering Pearl Harbor all afternoon and the president finally had a moment to reflect on the speech he would give the next day to Congress and the nation. Tully found him alone behind his desk. Two or three piles of notes were neatly stacked in front of him and he was lighting a cigarette. "Sit down, Grace," he said. "I'm going before Congress tomorrow. I'd like to dictate my message. It will be short."

He took a long drag on his cigarette.

"Yesterday—comma—December 7—comma—1941—comma—a date which will live in world history—comma—the United States of

America was simultaneously and deliberately attacked by naval and air forces of the Empire of Japan—period." Later, going over the draft, Roosevelt made a handful of changes, scratching out "world history," for example, for "infamy." He tacked "without warning" onto the end of the first sentence, but thought better of it and crossed it out.

He kept revising the speech the next morning, going over it with Hopkins and updating it with the latest news from the Pacific— through the war years, he would always strive to include the latest news from the front. "Last night Japanese forces attacked Hong Kong," he inserted. "Last night Japanese forces attacked Guam."

Reaching for an extra bit of symbolism, FDR asked Edith Wilson, Woodrow Wilson's widow, to sit with Eleanor in the House gallery.*

As he had used his speeches to lift the public spirit during the Great Depression, so too he would calibrate the public mood during the war: Not too dour in the early going when the enemy forces were advancing across the Pacific, and not too optimistic when the tides later turned.

War brought changes that ranged from mundane—blackout curtains now covered the Cabinet Room windows during the all-night writing sessions so as to avoid giving a target to potential enemy bombers—to frustrating—the ever present push to include news from the front in speeches.

The triumvirate stayed basically intact through the war years. Rosenman continued commuting from New York City to Washington—flying down after court and catching the 2 am sleeper train back— until March 1943. Over the course of four or five days that month, he went blind in one eye. He had optic neuritis, a rare condition resulting from overwork and nervous strain. Six weeks convalescence at Johns Hopkins Hospital brought back most of his vision, but his doctors gave him a choice: He could quit the court or quit the president. Continuing his current dual workload could result in permanent blindness. At FDR's request, Rosenman resigned the bench in October and moved down to Washington. For the first time in seven years working for President Roosevelt, he drew salary as a White House staffer.

---

*This presaged by more than four decades the Reagan-inspired tradition of strategically placing guests in the first lady's box.

Roosevelt had at first suggested that he create a position for Rosenman akin to the one he had held in Albany: counsel. But Attorney General Francis Biddle objected on the grounds that his position as the president's chief legal adviser made him the counsel. What to do? FDR decided that Rosenman would be *special* counsel. "Next week Biddle is going down to Mexico to make a speech," Roosevelt said. "While he's away I'll announce it and when he comes back it'll be a fait accompli."

Sherwood went to Britain in February 1944 as head of the Office of War Information's Overseas Branch. He stayed until the fall when, in September, he resigned his post to return home to work for Roosevelt's reelection. This did not mark the end of his official foreign work, however: In the spring of 1945, FDR sent him to the Pacific to sound out General Douglas MacArthur on the future governance of an occupied Japan.

Returning in late March, Sherwood reported directly to the president and, at his request, wrote a memo summarizing his findings.* He told his wife afterward that he had never seen the president in such poor shape: He had been uncharacteristically quiet and querulous and Sherwood was shaken.

Nevertheless, it scarcely occurred to him that he would never again see Roosevelt. Even when he got the news on April 12 of FDR's death, he could hardly believe it—expecting to learn it had been a hoax. He spoke to Hopkins—convalescing from one of his assorted bouts of illness at a hospital in Rochester, Minnesota—the next morning. They had something great they would take with them the rest of their lives, Hopkins told Sherwood, no sadness in his voice. "Because we know it's *true* what so many people believed about [FDR] and what made them love him," he said.

Hopkins was in and out of hospitals for the remainder of 1945 and

---

*"General MacArthur's intelligence service on the enemy and enemy-held territory is superb. . . . On the other hand, I was shocked by the inaccuracy of the information held by General MacArthur and his immediate entourage about the formulation of high policy in Washington. There are unmistakable evidences of an acute persecution complex at work." (Robert Sherwood, memorandum to the president, March 24, 1945, "Sherwood, Robert E." folder, President's Secretary's File, FDR Library.)

into 1946. He died of hemochromatosis on January 29, 1946, at the age of fifty-five.

Sherwood returned to his entertainment roots after the war, reaching a new peak in 1946 when he won an Oscar for best screenplay for *The Best Years of Our Lives*. In 1949, he won his fourth Pulitzer Prize for his memoir, *Roosevelt and Hopkins*. But beneath the success there was personal drift—the rest of his work, Rosenman later commented, consisted of unremarkable movies and television scripts. Sherwood told Rosenman that his years in Washington, living real drama, had dulled his ability to write the fictional variety. He died of a heart attack in New Rochelle, New York, on November 14, 1955.

"It was really best for him, in my opinion, that he finally went, rather than continuing along the path that he was going," Rosenman later said. "He never became disreputable or a matter of public scorn, but his friends knew that he was drinking too much. It was quite sad."

Rosenman lived until 1973. New generations of White House speechwriters periodically invited him down for a meal in the White House mess to pick his brain about how it had been at the beginning. Taken into the Cabinet Room in 1969 by Nixon speechwriter William Safire, Rosenman grew misty-eyed. "That's where Bobby Sherwood, Harry Hopkins and I used to work on speeches," he said. "It always seems so much smaller when you come back, from the way you remembered it."

Roosevelt left numerous legacies with which his successors could grapple and try to adjust, whether in governmental size or philosophy, in the style of his public pronouncements or the manner in which they were drafted. He was not the first chief executive to employ a speechwriter full time, but by institutionalizing the position, he revolutionized it—and presidential communications. And if too often FDR's successors reached for his speaking style—presidents through the 1970s would still try to give "fireside chats"—this often reflected a failure to achieve Roosevelt's skill in the hidden processes that lead up to a speech.

Roosevelt's gift—by design or by instinct—was to find people who could catch and augment his own style, aides who could, to use a sports metaphor, help the president elevate his own game. As the speechwriting was often part of the policy formulation process, these were men who could and did debate policies with their chief. And as he had the time and interest to engage deeply in the preparation process, these were for the most part men who knew their boss intimately.

As with trying to mimic FDR's speaking style, adopting the specifics of his preparation style would not necessarily make sense for his successors—especially given the growth of the government and White House staff, and their own predilections. But to the extent that succeeding presidents have managed to even approximate FDR's skill in using speechwriters to augment their own styles, they have succeeded in presidential communication. It has come naturally to some, while others have had to learn on the job. Those who failed to use this tool found their White House tenures curtailed.

"Missouri English"

APRIL 1945

If the activity was familiar, the experience was brand-new for Sam Rosenman. Once again he was sitting at the big table in the Cabinet Room writing a speech for the president of the United States—an address to the San Francisco conference that was creating the United Nations—but instead of working intimately with his boss and one or two others, Rosenman was one of at least nine. More talking than writing got done as paragraphs, phrases, or ideas were inserted with little thought of cohesion or continuity of style. The chaos and resulting mishmash of a speech rankled the orderly judge, who referred to the process as a "speechwriting convention."

As strange was the man who would give the speech. Through a dozen years of depression and war, Franklin D. Roosevelt had defined the presidency in the age of mass communications, reinventing how the nation's chief executive communicated with the voters. When he was elected in 1932, radio was still developing as a political communications tool. It had blossomed under FDR and he had mastered it. Now Harry S. Truman faced the challenge of following him not simply in terms of giving speeches but in preparing them.

Rosenman had not spoken ten words to Truman before FDR's death. In the days after Truman became president, Rosenman and the rest of the White House staff—no more than twenty people in total—submitted their resignations so that the new president could bring his own folks in to the administration. Hearing nothing for several days, and spurred by the untidy new speechwriting process, not to mention business opportunities he was starting to line up (which would have paid a great deal more than the $10,000 he received in annual White House wages), Rosenman went to see Truman. Stay until V-E Day, Truman asked. Rosenman argued briefly but acquiesced: He would stay until victory in Europe. He was struck by Truman's sociable humanity, in contrast to Roosevelt's majesty. FDR was always pleasant, but one never forgot that he was the president.

Rosenman was not the only one struck by such differences. On April 18, six days after FDR died, Truman paid his first visit to the White House Map Room, the top secret nerve center from which Roosevelt had overseen World War II. Carpetless so as to avoid entangling FDR's wheelchair, it was a small first-floor room that lay directly across from the elevator Roosevelt used to come to and from the residence each evening. It was outfitted with maps of the world that had grease pencil markings on clear plastic overlay denoting troop dispositions, and pins signifying Axis and Allied ships—blue for U.S. vessels, orange for Japanese, red for British, black for German, gray for Italian.* The area was so secure that Map Room personnel had to wheel Roosevelt around, as his valet was not cleared to enter. Truman had never seen it as vice president.

Truman was expected at 2 pm, but because Roosevelt was chronically late, the duty officers were startled when three loud raps announced his arrival at 1:48 pm. Such early arrivals would "scare the bejesus out of staff members," recalled George Elsey, a naval reservist who was working as assistant to the president's naval aide. Lanky and good-looking, Elsey was "very crisp and very precise and very logical,"

---

*More than fifty years later, George Elsey returned to the White House and the Map Room at the invitation of three George W. Bush speechwriters: John McConnell, Michael Gerson, and Matthew Scully. Asked how it looked during the war, Elsey described the room, walking over to a portrait hanging on the wall. The maps should be right back here, he said, and—much to his hosts' horror—yanked at the picture. Sure enough, there were the maps. (Author interview with Matthew Scully.)

one colleague recalled years later. He had been a graduate student in American history at Harvard before joining the Office of Naval Intelligence in December 1941. While working in the Map Room, he had helped Sherwood, Rosenman, and Hopkins with research for FDR's speeches, and on one occasion collaborated with Sherwood on a radio address praising Christopher Columbus.

On that first visit to the Map Room, Truman said that he wanted to meet the young watch officers—and then walked around the room introducing himself. Roosevelt would have let the officers come to him.

On May 8, 1945, the Allies achieved victory in Europe. Rosenman again went to Truman and asked that the president accept his resignation. Stay until V-J Day, Truman asked. Rosenman acquiesced. Writing in his diary the next month, Truman described Rosenman as "one of the ablest men in Washington, keen mind, a lucid pen, a loyal Roosevelt man and an equally loyal Truman man." By then, Rosenman had resolved to kill the speechwriting convention: He and press secretary Charlie Ross, a friend of Truman's since high school, went to the president and explained that it did not work, that the two of them had to be able to write the first draft themselves; then the convention, which was mostly composed of Truman's Missouri cronies, could have a crack at it. Truman gave them the okay. It was the first victory in Rosenman's campaign to eliminate the speechwriting group. And when on June 26 the president spoke to the closing session of the United Nations Conference, it was the first speech composed with what Rosenman viewed as any sense of order.

Having eliminated the convention from the preparation of the first draft, Rosenman set about dismantling it entirely. "It's very easy to sit around a table and smoke a cigar and say you ought to do this and you ought to say that," he recalled. "When that happened I would take a yellow pad and say, 'That's very good, take this pad and go into the next room and write me three paragraphs.' Usually that fellow disappeared because when it came to putting something on paper he couldn't."

In mid-July, Truman was scheduled to travel to Potsdam, Germany, to meet with Joseph Stalin and Winston Churchill to discuss postwar issues. Early that month, Admiral James K. Vardaman, his naval aide, brought a young officer in to the Oval Office to meet Truman. "Mr.

President, this is Lieutenant Clark Clifford, the 38-year-old naval officer I told you about," Vardaman said. "He is going to look after my office while we are gone." Truman's expression registered no change as he glanced up and quickly took in the officer, saying only: "Big fella, ain't he?"

"He was like a Greek god—way over six feet tall, and handsome," one Truman White House staffer later recalled. Clifford had spent sixteen years as a trial lawyer in St. Louis, starting out with pro bono work. "I handled fourteen of those and every client I had went up to the state penitentiary," he said. "But I was learning all the time." Looking back, Clifford ascribed his skills as a political infighter and White House aide to these tough courtroom lessons. Speaking in front of a jury trained him to organize facts and present them in as persuasive a manner as possible.

His ascent to the White House was brilliant luck. Joining the Naval Reserve in 1944, Clifford was stationed in San Francisco working on naval logistics. It was there that he got a call from an old client and friend, Vardaman, a naval reservist who had just been assigned to the White House. Why not come along? Vardaman asked. "He was energetic and highly capable, which could not be said of several of Truman's early appointees," Elsey later said of Clifford. Clifford quickly discovered that in the White House the naval aide had little to do—and his assistant less. But he also noticed that even when the rest of the building was quiet, Rosenman's office hummed with activity. Clifford and Rosenman, with a shared affinity for legal nuance, quickly hit it off, and the young naval officer soon ingratiated himself with the White House veteran, helping out the special counsel where he could.

On August 15, 1945, Emperor Hirohito announced his nation's surrender. With victory over Japan, World War II was concluded—but Rosenman's White House tenure was not. He again asked Truman for his release. Stay while the country reconverts to a peacetime footing, the president now asked. Again, Rosenman agreed.

By this time the two had gotten into a "groove," as Truman put it, in terms of preparing his speeches and messages. Returning from the Potsdam Conference in early August, Truman had observed to Rosenman that his presidency had focused almost exclusively on foreign affairs, and that he had to force his attention to domestic issues. Rosenman suggested that Truman lay out his political philosophy in a written message to the Congress detailing his domestic plans. The judge had talked to Truman's new aides and old Missouri friends like John Snyder, whom Truman would appoint Secretary of the Treasury in 1946. They were all conservative, and Rosenman supposed that Truman would depart from the liberal, New Deal path in favor of a more conservative course on domestic policies. So he was pleasantly surprised when Truman, talking to Rosenman about what he wanted in the message, laid out a strongly liberal agenda.

Rosenman, with Ross's help, wrote a pair of drafts of the message before sharing it with the other writers. A week of sometimes heated argument ensued, with Rosenman and Ross advocating for a liberal continuation of the New Deal while Snyder and others argued that the suggested program was communistic and would be a disaster for both the country and the Truman presidency. The message would be a blueprint for the nascent administration. "This was indeed the show-down for the President—the point of no return," Rosenman later noted. "It set President Truman on the path of the future which he was to follow." Truman's decision to follow the liberal course brought Snyder to tears.

On both speeches and written messages, Truman had a different collaborative approach from FDR. Rosenman later estimated that stylistically Truman did not contribute 20 percent of what Roosevelt did to the speech process. He would give detailed instructions about what he wanted to say, but would contribute little in terms of how to say it. This would change as Truman became more comfortable as president and learned to use his speechwriters not simply to echo Roosevelt but to amplify Truman. But it was a slow process.

When Rosenman ran into Robert Sherwood on an airplane toward the end of Truman's first term, they got to reminiscing. They laughed about how the playwright had been so sure that Roosevelt drafted his own speeches because of their stylistic consistency. "It's a strange thing about that continuity of style," Sherwood teased. "It not only stayed with Roosevelt all during his governorship and the presidency, but I've even noticed that it's lapsed over to his successor." Clifford too had noticed the similarity and resolved to help the president sound like Truman, not FDR.

Truman also paled in comparison to his predecessor when it came to delivering a speech. Roosevelt was a master with a prepared address, whether it was a fireside talk or a rally in front of thousands. Truman was a mess. Even with thick-lensed glasses compensating for his poor eyesight, he had trouble reading a text. He would lean so far over the page, straining to see the words, that his audience often saw more of the top of his head than his face. He would look up, trying to connect with the audience—and then back down, trying to relocate his place in the speech, which took a moment or two—and then back up, restarting the process. He sped through his texts, the words streaming steadily in what the press liked to call his "drone," the slightly nasal midwestern voice flat, as if he was concentrating so hard on getting the words out that he could expend no thought on which to emphasize. He gestured in a way that came to be derisively known as "chopping wood."

Truman and his staff tried various tricks to improve his delivery. He would read the speech out loud in the Cabinet Room or residence, record it, and then listen with Rosenman, radio adviser Leonard Reinsch, and other aides. This helped him slow down the pace. His secretary, Rose Conway, typed the speeches with natural pauses at the end of lines so that they would coincide with his eyes sweeping back to the start of the next. She left the bottom third of the page blank so that Truman would not have to tilt his head too far down to keep reading. And because she put relatively little of the speech on any one page, he had to turn them often, which also slowed him.

Truman did not always *want* to slow down. During the 1944 campaign, Reinsch had visited Truman in Independence and brought the transcript of a fifty-five-minute speech the senator had so rushed that parts of it were entirely unintelligible. When Reinsch asked why he had spoken so quickly, Truman replied: "Well, I didn't think it was very interesting and I wanted to get it over with." He had not cut the speech, he added, because everyone who had worked on it thought their contributions important and he did not want to hurt their feelings.

Rosenman approached Truman again about leaving in November

1945. He was pretty well broke, he told the president, and had to finally return to private practice in New York. This time Truman released him, allowing him to leave on February 1, 1946, on condition that he return when needed. Truman appealed to him that no one could take his place, but Rosenman replied, "Mr. President, you have a fine replacement sitting right here in the White House, and he even happens to be from Missouri. His name is Clifford." The assistant naval aide was too young and inexperienced to be special counsel, Truman replied. When he officially announced Rosenman's departure, he stated that with the end of the war there was no longer a need for a White House special counsel.

After Rosenman's departure, George Elsey noted to himself: "Comes the deluge, Lord knows who will have brains then. There is no one of ability near the President with a positive program, or even with any *ideas* on economic matters."

The first spring after World War II thawed labor problems that had been frozen by conflict. At the end of March 1946, 400,000 coal miners went on strike. And although Truman quickly moved to federalize the mines, bringing the workers back, 164,000 of them stayed away from their jobs. The situation reached a critical point on May 23, when the rail workers also struck. In the mid-1940s, the United States literally ran on coal and rails. More than half of industrial energy came from coal, as well as 62 percent of the nation's electrical power. Virtually all the railroads ran on coal—and they were the dominant medium of interstate commerce and travel. When the rail workers walked out, they ground the country to a halt. Of 24,000 freight trains that had been scheduled to run, fewer than 300 did. Roughly 175,000 men and women were scheduled to travel by rail, yet only around 100 could do so. Commuters were stranded across the country—in Washington, D.C., enterprising cab drivers charged $150 to drive to Boston and $100 for a trip to Atlanta, more than six hundred miles away.

Truman fumed. With the nation struggling to regain a peacetime footing, this was no time for labor unions or anyone else to put their own financial interests over the country's. Deciding to draft the rail workers into the armed forces, he called a cabinet meeting for the next day, Friday, May 24. He would address the nation on Friday evening and the Congress on Saturday to explain his move.

Truman handwrote his remarks to the nation over seven pages, his anger controlling the pen: Labor leaders had lied to him. Congress was "weak-kneed" and lacked "intestinal fortitude." The time had come for vilification and misrepresentation of government to end. A World War I combat veteran himself, he called upon "you men who fought the battles to save the nation just as I did twenty-five years ago," to help him "eliminate" the major labor leaders, as well as the "Russian Senators and Representatives and really make this a government of, by and for the people," he wrote in his jagged scrawl, assuring that he had no more regard for "the Wall Street crowd" than he did for the labor union leaders. He concluded: "Let us give the country back to the people. Let's put transportation and production back to work, hang a few traitors, make our own country safe for democracy, tell the Russians where to get off and make the United Nations work. Come on boys, let's do the job."

Hang a few traitors. Do the job indeed.

When Clifford first saw the proposed speech, he worried that the president had spun "perilously out of control." As Truman's biographer David McCullough later wrote: "It was as though somewhere deep within this normally fair-minded, self-controlled, naturally warm-hearted man a raw, ugly, old native strain persisted like the cry of a frontier lynch mob, and had to be released." Truman likely never meant for the speech to be delivered. Like FDR before him, he periodically indulged in what he called "long-hand spasms" where he committed his raw emotions to paper safe in the knowledge that his most trusted aides would intercept the verbal salvos before they reached public ears.*

Truman gave the draft to Ross, who then met with the president privately in the Oval Office and quickly convinced him that such a speech would backfire. They decided to have Clifford, who had replaced Var-

---

*The system did not always work. When *Washington Post* music critic Paul Hume savaged Margaret Truman's musical debut, the president personally mailed his outraged letter so his staff could not intercept it. "Some day I hope to meet you," Truman wrote. "When that happens you'll need a new nose, a lot of beefsteak for black eyes, and perhaps a supporter below!" (McCullough, *Truman*, 828.)

daman as naval aide in April, rewrite it. He got the assignment at 5 pm. The speech was scheduled to be delivered at 10 pm.

For Clifford, it was a decisive moment. In ten short months in the White House, he had been working his way into Truman's inner circle, doing various jobs for the president including shepherding Vardaman's nomination to the Federal Reserve through the Senate. Truman had come not only to appreciate the quality of Clifford's work and the incisiveness of his advice, but, perhaps more important, designated him to organize his regular poker games. After a short time, Clifford was even invited to play. He tackled it characteristically: He bought and studied a book on poker, eventually becoming a regular winner.

For Truman's speech to the nation regarding the labor crises, Clifford huddled in the Cabinet Room with Rosenman, who had been summoned from New York; John Steelman, who had been the point man on the labor negotiations; Ross and Snyder. With two hours to go before airtime, they had assembled a six-page draft.

His rage having cooled, Truman rewrote a first sentence describing the rail strike as "the greatest crisis in this country since Pearl Harbor."[*] But the speech retained some of the tough tone from his earlier draft: "The crisis of Pearl Harbor was the result of action by a foreign enemy," Truman told the nation that night. "The crisis tonight is caused by a group of men within our own country who place their private interests above the welfare of the nation." Clifford later confessed to embarrassment over the tone but the president liked it.

Clifford and company missed the 10 pm deadline for a final draft: Rose Conway was still typing the speech when Truman uttered "My fellow countrymen" to start the broadcast. The last page was tucked in front of him as he got about two thirds of the way through the address. He called for an end to the strike by 4 pm the following day or he would mobilize the army and do what was necessary to end the impasse. He held in reserve the possibility of drafting the workers into the armed forces.

---

[*]The Pearl Harbor comparison was itself a step down in tone for Clifford—in his original outline, he described the crisis as the most serious "in the history of this country." ("1946, May 24, Railroad Speech [re strike]" folder, Papers of Clark Clifford, HSTL.)

Clifford stayed up most of the night with Rosenman working up a draft of the speech to the joint session of Congress. The next day, the two men revised the draft as Steelman continued negotiations with the labor leaders at the Statler Hotel. An hour before the speech, Steelman called to report that a deal was close—possibly before Truman's address. Clifford and Rosenman wrote a few softer, alternate paragraphs just in case. But nothing was complete when Truman had to leave for the Hill and, alternate language in hand, Clifford ran to catch his car.

Shortly after 4 pm, wearing a dark blue summer suit and white shirt, a grim-faced Truman strode into the House chamber, receiving the most raucous greeting he had gotten there in his short presidency. As he started to speak, Clifford was in House Speaker Sam Rayburn's office near the House floor, on the phone with Steelman: a preliminary settlement had been reached, but it was still being typed up.

In the chamber, Truman reach the crux of his speech: He wanted emergency legislation that would authorize him to draft the striking workers into the armed forces. The assembled legislators—whom days earlier Truman had angrily called "Russian"—roared their approval for twenty-three seconds, long enough for Secretary of the Senate Les Biffle to dart in and hand Truman a slip of red paper, a note from Clifford.

"Word has just been received that the railroad strike has been settled, on terms proposed by the President," Truman said in his monotone. This time the applause lasted for thirty-two seconds and included whoops and hollers. The moment was so dramatic that at least one senator—Wayne Morse, a Republican from Oregon—publicly charged that it had been staged. Typically, after announcing that the strike had been settled, Truman drove right back into his text, motoring through as if nothing had happened. The House and Senate quickly passed his legislation.

Now the president would rectify a mistake. He summoned Captain Clifford to the Oval Office in early June and told him that it was time to return to civilian life—as White House special counsel. He announced the appointment at his press conference on June 27, not only resurrecting the position but formalizing Clifford's rise as one of his most important aides. In turn, Clifford's most trusted assistant was George Elsey. The pair had met in the Map Room on Clifford's first day in the White

House. They would remain close associates for the next two and a half decades.

Clifford and Elsey had bonded quickly and spoke frankly about the Truman White House staff. "There is no policy-making body," Clifford said, amazed and appalled by the haphazardness of it all. "It's just a collection of not-too-well-informed men, each one intent on his own job."

"We used to call George Elsey 'the man who did Clark Clifford's thinking for him,'" said Steve Spingarn, who would replace Elsey as Clifford's assistant in 1949. Indeed, while Clifford, who was always conscious of his image and assiduously cultivated the press, garnered much of the credit as Truman's speechwriter, he often acted as more of an editor than drafter, and on several notable occasions attached his name to what was substantially others' work. "He did not do a great deal of writing," his successor as special counsel, Charles Murphy, later said. "Clark Clifford is an excellent salesman of other men's ideas, but he's not an original thinker," Spingarn added.

Clifford and Elsey were Truman's key speechwriting team for the remainder of Clifford's White House tenure—though their duties were hardly limited to ghostwriting. As Clifford was Truman's top adviser on political and policy-related matters, they got into everything. Elsey's body of work ranged from redesigning the presidential seal* to surveying U.S. relations with the Soviet Union.

"President Truman's speeches and messages and the like were written not by 'writers,' but by lawyers and economists and public administration types who had picked up along the way a skill as generalists in government," Richard Neustadt, a second-term speechwriter, noted later. "This may not have meant the highest literary quality for Truman's public papers, but it certainly meant sensitive awareness of their potential as vehicles for making or influencing policy."

There were drawbacks, especially regarding literary quality. Rosen-

---

*In the press release announcing the new presidential flag and seal, Elsey noted that the head of the eagle in the seal had been turned to face right because it was the direction of the olive branches of peace clutched in one talon, as opposed to the arrows of war in the other. In fact, he had turned the eagle's head for obscure heraldic reasons—left indicated illegitimacy, while rightward was a direction of honor. (Elsey, *An Unplanned Life*, 93–94.)

man had written the 1946 State of the Union Address solo. Clifford and Elsey labored to produce the message for 1947. "Three years in the Map Room—that hadn't educated me to do political speeches for the president," Elsey said with a laugh. Nor did Clifford make any bones about having literary talent: "I wrote slowly and laboriously in long-hand, using a soft pencil, erasing and revising constantly," he recalled in his memoirs.

Truman himself was pleased with the speech, the first State of the Union to be televised.* His journal entry that evening said: "Read my annual message. It was good if I do say so myself. Clark Clifford did most of the work. He's a nice boy and will go places."

On February 21, 1947, the British government formally notified the United States that it could no longer afford to provide economic aid to Greece and Turkey, two countries that the United States and Britain had already determined were keys to preventing a Soviet tide from sweeping out of occupied Eastern Europe into the fragile but still free countries of Western Europe. If the two nations were going to hold, it would have to be with generous aid from the United States.

Truman consulted with congressional leaders and his own top aides. Republican senator Arthur Vandenberg of Michigan, the influential president pro tem of the Senate and chairman of the Senate Foreign Relations Committee, told Truman that he would support a massive foreign aid plan, provided that the president put the case in the proper context—explaining in stark terms the link between these discrete foreign aid cases and the broader global struggle that was unfolding against Soviet aggression. Truman moved decisively. He was willing, he told Clifford, to "lay it on the line" with the American people.

In July 1946, Truman had told Clifford to compile a list of the treaties and agreements that the Soviet Union had broken over the years. Clifford delegated the job to Elsey, who had more than passing

---

*Other State of the Union firsts: Calvin Coolidge's 1923 address first to be broadcast on radio; George W. Bush's 2002 address first to be Web-cast from the House Web site. (www.senate.gov/reference/resources/pdf/RS20021.pdf.)

familiarity with the issue because of his Map Room duties. He accompanied Truman on weekends on the presidential yacht *Williamsburg*, handling classified cables and reports for him. Reading the classified traffic, Elsey noted with rising alarm both aggressive Soviet actions and their apparent failure to make a strong impression upon the president. "I, for one, am afraid that Mr. Truman is not yet fully conscious of the aggressions the Soviet Union has in mind," Elsey noted to himself on March 10, 1946. "He keeps brushing aside reports on the events in Eastern Europe & the Near East & Asia with a phrase like 'That's not so good, is it?' and then he's on to the next matter."

Elsey resolved to provide more than a mere list of broken agreements. He spent the summer canvassing senior officials and produced a devastating eighty-one-page case against the Soviets. "The gravest problem facing the United States today is that of American relations with the Soviet Union," the report began. "The solution of that problem may determine whether or not there will be a third World War. Soviet leaders appear to be conducting their nation on a course of aggrandizement designed to lead to eventual world domination by the U.S.S.R."

Clifford wrote a cover letter and passed the report on to the president as "a report by the Special Counsel" (Elsey was not mentioned). Truman called him at seven o'clock the following morning. "Powerful stuff," he said, asking that Clifford immediately bring him all existing copies, which he planned to lock up. "It is very valuable to me—but if it leaked it would blow the roof off the White House, it would blow the roof off the Kremlin," Truman told his aide. "We'd have the most serious situation on our hands that has yet occurred in my administration."

The report disappeared for more than two decades, but its effects were felt both in a hardening of Truman's attitude toward the Soviets and in Elsey and Clifford's familiarity with the issues surrounding the European crisis.*

---

*The report was first made public in 1968 in Arthur Krock's *Memoirs*, where he credited Clifford with its authorship. Margaret Truman revealed Elsey's role in her *Harry S. Truman* (1973). "The report," Elsey wrote in his own memoirs, "is a good example of the old Washington adage: 'No one signs a paper that he writes, nor does he write a paper that he signs.'" (Elsey, *An Unplanned Life*, 144.)

A heavy-flaked, wet snow covered Washington on the evening of Saturday, March 1, 1947, eight days after the British had warned of the impending problem. In the State Department, Deputy Secretary of State Dean Acheson oversaw production of initial drafts of what would come to be known as the Truman Doctrine speech, with public affairs officer Joseph Jones writing three drafts, the last of which was sent to Clifford on Friday, March 7, the day that Truman decided that he would give a speech. His staff did not unanimously agree: That day Elsey had sent Clifford a letter arguing that this was not "the occasion for the 'All-out' speech." The message to Congress should be focused, he wrote, because the Soviets had not given an explicit pretext for such a confrontational message, because the public was not ready for such a stunning declaration, and because the administration would need more time to properly write the address. But Clifford, like Truman, thought that the moment had come to make the case. There were, he thought, always opportunities for delay in crises. "This speech must be the opening gun in a campaign to bring people to the realization that the war isn't over by any means," he told Elsey, who climbed on board.

Truman thought the State draft too wordy. Clifford agreed. These complaints were not surprising. Prose from the cabinet departments tended to be bureaucratic and cautious, and the State Department compounded these problems with overly flowery rhetoric—the kind particularly unsuited to a president from the Midwest who valued direct simplicity in his speeches.

Truman believed that the idea behind a speech was to say what you had to as simply as you could. Thanks to Clifford's efforts, and an increasing willingness on the part of Truman to assert himself over his own speeches, a distinct rhetorical style was starting to emerge. As Truman's White House tenure went on, speechwriters translated their prose into what they called "Missouri English"—plain, short, direct, sentences that suited his style. "Subjunctives, passives, polysyllabic words, foreign phrases, lengthy sentences and a unique language called 'State Departmentese' received a brutal blue penciling," Kenneth Hechler, a second-term ghost, noted later. "Anything that sounded like a diplomatic communiqué or an after-action report of military operations was immediately tossed out."

Once the writers had a sufficiently polished product to show the president he would make comments and edits, and they would eventually circulate it to the cabinet departments. Finally a "freezing session" would convene in the Cabinet Room, typically attended by the special counsel and any speechwriters involved, along with the press secretary, and administration officials with knowledge of the subject matter. Truman would read the speech aloud—not as if he were delivering it, but conversationally, to see how it struck his ear. Occasionally he asked Clifford to read it aloud, so that he could hear how it sounded. He would catch phraseology that might trip him up.

"What impressed me were the comments he made as he went along, alluding to certain historical references," Milton Kayle, another second-term speechwriter, recalled. "There was depth of understanding. It may have been the first time he saw the speech and people were theoretically putting words in his mouth, but they were putting words in his mouth only with his absolute and complete understanding of what he was saying."

For the Truman Doctrine speech, Clifford and Elsey met with Jones and Carl Hummelsine, the director of the State Department's executive secretariat on Saturday, March 8, four days before the speech was to be given, to suggest rewrites. The message needed to be restructured, Clifford said; the draft did not build toward a logical conclusion. He made specific suggestions as well: speaking from his own experience supervising logistics at the close of the war, Clifford suggested mentioning that U.S. administrators would closely supervise the funds to make sure none would be lost to graft. The resulting paragraph prompted one of only three interruptions for applause during Truman's speech.

Clifford jotted notes in his neat writing for the meeting with Jones. He listed several points to cover, including "Totalitarian regimes are born where people's hope dies, (Continuation of belief in democracy)." It presaged the final speech: "The seeds of totalitarian regimes are nurtured by misery and want. They spread and grow in the evil soil of poverty and strife. They reach their full growth when the hope of a people for a better life has died." Another passage was closer to full-born in his notes, which read: "It is a grim job with nothing to recommend it except that the alternative is grimer [*sic*]." Four days later, Truman declared: "This is a serious course upon which we embark. I would not recommend it except that the alternative is much more serious."

The revised State draft arrived at Clifford's office the next morning, Sunday, March 9, at nine thirty. A couple of dozen steps from the Oval, it was the nicest staff office in the West Wing (Rosenman had been a previous occupant), complete with its own fireplace and, more important, its own bathroom. Elsey and Clifford spent the rest of that Sunday sequestered there, trying to summon a Trumanesque talk from the wooden and dense State language. They made, by Clifford's count, more than a hundred changes to the speech.*

By Monday morning, March 10, Clifford and Elsey both still thought that the speech, the most important of Truman's presidency, had a hole—it still lacked a cogent, concise statement of principles. "I was worried by the absence of what would today be called a 'sound bite,'" Elsey later wrote. "Where were the two or three sentences that would convey the essence of the president's policy? Where were the highly quotable words that the press and the public would grasp at once and know that this was a policy that went far beyond $400 million of assistance for Greece and Turkey?"

He focused on a paragraph that Acheson had already rewritten once. "I believe it must be the policy of the United States to give support to free peoples who are attempting to resist subjugation by armed minorities or outside forces," the State draft read. "It is essential to our security that we assist free peoples to work out their own destiny in their own way, and our help must be primarily in the form of that economic and financial aid which is essential to economic stability and orderly political processes."

Elsey sensed that what he was looking for was buried in this verbiage. He needed to simplify it and make it stand out. Using "I believe"

---

*One change softened an early summation of the domino theory: "Collapse of free institutions and loss of independence would be disasters not only for them but for the world. Discouragement and possibly failure would quickly be the lot of neighboring peoples engaged in a struggle to maintain their freedom and independence. A chain reaction of this sort would very quickly undermine our national security." (Revised draft of President's Message to Congress, March 9, 1947, "1947, March 12, Speech to Congress on Greece [re aid to Greece and Turkey]" folder, Papers of Clark Clifford, HSTL.)

as a keystone, he created what he and Clifford called "the credo"—and what history knows as the Truman Doctrine.

> *I believe that it must be the policy of the United States to support free peoples who are resisting attempted subjugation by armed minorities or by outside pressures. I believe that we must assist free peoples to work out their own destinies in their own way. I believe that our help should be primarily through economic and financial aid which is essential to economic stability and orderly political processes.*

Planning for the 1948 political campaign began in earnest in November 1947. Clifford received a thirty-four-page election analysis from James Rowe, an FDR White House aide who argued that Truman could win by running an aggressively liberal campaign. Rowe was a law partner of Tommy Corcoran, the Roosevelt aide who had put off so many Democratic leaders—including Truman (whose dislike for the Cork was heightened by information FBI director J. Edgar Hoover sent the president from a tap on Corcoran's phone). Rowe's association with Corcoran had earned him a share of Truman's dislike as well, so Clifford updated and polished the document and then passed it on to Truman in November under his own name.

"The basic premise of this memorandum—that the Democratic Party is an unhappy alliance of Southern conservatives, Western progressive and Big City labor—is very trite," Clifford wrote. "But it is also very true. And it is equally true that the success or failure of the Democratic leadership can be precisely measured by its ability to lead enough members of these three misfit groups to the polls on the first Tuesday after the first Monday of November, 1948."

Truman and his staff decided to make the 1948 State of the Union speech the keynote to his campaign. It "must be controversial as Hell, must state the issues of the election, must draw the line sharply between Republicans and Democrats," Elsey argued to Clifford in a memorandum in late 1947.

Another writer joined the effort for the 1948 State of the Union: Charles Murphy, a new administrative assistant. Murphy—"Murph" to

Truman—was a soft-spoken North Carolinian, who had first gotten to know the president while working as a legislative aide in the Senate Counsel's office. It was Murphy who, at Truman's request, had drawn up the legislation that created the senator's panel to investigate waste and fraud during the war.

Balding and bespectacled—he "looks and acts like an amiable dentist," Spingarn later said—Murphy's long service on the Hill had left him with a judicious mind and somewhat diffident temperament. But it had prepared him well for speechwriting: The Senate Counsel's office takes legislative ideas and puts them into the legal wording needed for an actual bill. The requirements were less eloquence than the ability to translate mass amounts of data into clear prose. As Clifford once had, Murphy figured out that special counsel was the most interesting job in the White House. "It was the kind of work I wanted to do, and so I went and asked if I could help, and he said he would be glad to have me," Murphy recalled.

Murphy and Elsey toiled over a combative State of the Union draft—and Truman and Clifford both liked it. "Congress meets—Too bad too," Truman wrote in his diary on January 6, the day before the speech. "They'll do nothing but wrangle, pull phony investigations and generally upset the affairs of the Nation. I'm to address them soon. They won't like the address either." Indeed, Truman started by saying that on such an occasion Congress and the president should focus "not upon party but upon the country; not upon things which divide us but upon those which bind us together"—and then went on to give a campaign kickoff address that was aimed at reassembling the New Deal coalition and laid out his reelection platform.

It was, one White House intimate told *Time*, "the Bible for the Democratic Party." And as predicted, Congress did not like it. In forty-three minutes, Republicans in the crowd applauded twice. But Truman was so pleased with the speech that afterwards he invited Elsey and some others into the Oval Office, opened a desk drawer, and pulled out bottles of scotch and bourbon. Together they drank to "Success in '48!"

Despite the fighting spirit, Truman had delivered the State of the Union in his usual lifeless Missouri twang. Truman simply could not read a speech with passion or force. Clifford, Murphy, and Ross continued to wrestle with the problem of bringing out the interesting, informal Truman they knew in private but who disappeared behind the bland monotony that a written speech produced. In October 1947 Clifford had tried to have Truman read off giant cue cards, but his poor eyesight scuttled the idea.

Murphy now came up with the idea of having the president speak from an outline. The first try came on the evening of April 17, when Truman addressed the American Society of Newspaper Editors in a speech broadcast nationwide. The president droned through a prepared text on inflation that, as one ally noted, had "neither meat nor juices nor votes." The audience fidgeted. But after the broadcast portion of the speech ended, Truman kept talking, giving a twenty-minute, off-the-record, off-the-cuff talk about U.S.-Soviet relations. It was as if two Trumans had spoken. "He was suddenly a very interesting man of great candor who discussed the problems of American leadership with men as neighbors," his ally and biographer Jonathan Daniels recalled. "He spoke the language of them all out of traditions common to them all." The result, Truman recorded in his memoirs, was the most enthusiastic applause he had ever received from a predominately Republican crowd.

After a successful repeat performance on May 1 before the National Health Assembly, Clifford, Murphy, and Ross convinced the president to use the new technique in an early afternoon speech before the National Conference on Family Life—a speech that would be broadcast nationally. "The audience gave me a most cordial reception," Truman recorded in his diary afterward. "I hope the radio and television audiences were half as well pleased. I may have to become an 'orator.' I heard a definition of an orator once—'He is an honest man who can communicate his views and make others believe he is right.' Wish I could do that."

He could. "Returns from the radio on the family life speech are very satisfactory," he wrote the next day. "Look as if I'm stuck for 'off the cuff' radio speeches. It means a lot of hard work, and the head of 64 doesn't work as well as it did at 24."

The final piece of the 1948 campaign plan came in early June, when Truman took a fifteen-day train trip to California, where he was scheduled to give the commencement address at the University of California at Berkeley. He traveled across the country and back by train, making five major speeches and around forty minor ones—all ostensibly non-political addresses savaging what he started calling "the good-for-nothing, do nothing, Republican Eightieth Congress."

On June 11, Senator Robert A. Taft, speaking at the Union League Club in Philadelphia, assailed Truman for "black-guarding Congress at whistle-stops all across the country." The Ohio Republican should have known better—"whistle-stop" implied that a town was too small to merit a regular train stop (the phrase derived from the fact that when a stop was required at such a station, the conductor would alert the engineer by pulling a signal cord and the engineer would reply with two toots of the train's whistle).

The Democratic National Committee pounced on the blunder, cabling the mayors of the towns through which the presidential expedition had passed, asking for their reactions. "Must have the wrong city," the mayor of Eugene, Oregon, replied. "Very poor taste," came the answer from Gary, Indiana. Upon arriving in Los Angeles, Truman pronounced the City of Angels to be the biggest whistle-stop of them all. Taft had introduced a new phrase to the American political lexicon.

There were kinks in the Truman operation. A foul-up in Nebraska left 8,000 empty seats at a major address in a 10,000-seat venue. In the small hamlet of Carey, Idaho, Truman spoke movingly, dedicating the Willa Coates Airport, praising the young man for whom it was named for giving up his life for his country . . . only to have Coates's grieving mother explain that Willa was a girl who had perished in a civilian air crash. Then there was the "old Joe" gaffe, the most damaging of all. Speaking from the rear platform of his train in Eugene, Truman waxed sentimental about Soviet leader Stalin. "I like old Joe! He is a decent fellow," he said, stunning both reporters and aides.

The mistakes drove home that the off-the-cuff style worked, but only with sufficient preparation. Detailed outlined remarks were required to prevent Truman from either meandering into verbal mine fields or simply making stupid mistakes. But all the while, the crowds grew. Truman's new style—informal, irreverent, and entertaining—was a hit.

The president remained far behind in the polls. A sense of impending doom accompanied the Democrats to Philadelphia for their nominating convention in mid-July. "As the convention met, the depressing feeling of a coming defeat overhung the hall," Rosenman later recalled. The day the convention opened, *The New York Times* ran a piece capturing the mood of the town: delegates wandering deserted streets, one quoted as describing the scene as akin to a wake, while a cab driver quipped that "We got the wrong rigs for this convention. They shoulda given us hearses." How bad was the mood? "Even Texans whispered, probably for the first time in history."

The actual convention did little to improve the outlook. The passage of an historic civil rights plank prompted all twenty-three members of the Alabama delegation and thirteen members of the Mississippi delegation to walk out. They eventually supported Strom Thurmond's Dixiecrat presidential bid.

In Washington, confusion muddled the drafting process for Truman's acceptance speech, which he was to give on Thursday, July 15. Rosenman—quietly summoned from New York by the president—and Murphy had each prepared drafts. Truman expected the two to work with Clifford and Elsey to produce a unified speech. But with no clear guidance about who was in charge, the only thing that had been decided by Wednesday was that Truman would speak from an outline rather than a prepared text. The process did not start rolling until Murphy, back early from lunch, started sketching the address. When the others returned, they kept arguing before finally noticing that Murphy was writing. What have you got there? Rosenman asked. From there it flowed.

Almost the entire speech was put in outline form. Rosenman suggested that since the Republicans had adopted a surprisingly liberal platform at their convention in June, Truman should call them back into session to act on their campaign promises. They did, after all, control both chambers of Congress and so could enact the platform forthwith.

Truman's train arrived in Philadelphia at 9:15 pm on the evening of his nomination. A light rain was falling. He emerged wearing a white suit and white shirt with a dark necktie, proper attire for stultifying

Philadelphia heat made only worse by a Convention Hall that had no air-conditioning, but did have television lights. The heat in the arena was so bad that Truman and his running mate, Senator Alben Barkley of Kentucky, sat by a loading ramp to get what passed for fresh air while the convention went through the nominating motions.

But the processes dragged on. And on. Four hours later—at 1:42 am—Truman was nominated. Sam Rayburn, the House Democratic leader and convention chair, advised Truman to call it an evening and give his speech the next day. But the president insisted on going ahead.

Rayburn was introducing Truman when a "plump, powdered and behatted" older woman bustled up to the podium bearing a large Liberty Bell made of flowers and seized control of the microphone. She was Mrs. Emma Guffey Miller, a perennial committeewoman and the sister of a former senator from Pennsylvania. She called herself the Old Grey Mare. Her flower arrangement housed four dozen white pigeons ("doves of peace"), which had been caged in the stifling heat all evening. The birds that were still alive were suddenly freed and, maddened by the heat, went wild. "The dignitaries on the platform cringed and shrank away like troops before a strafing attack," *Time* reported. "If the President had not won his audience right away, the pigeons might have given him real competition. As [Truman] spoke, pigeons teetered on the balconies, on folds in the draperies, on overhead lights, occasionally launched on a quick flight to a more pigeonly position."

It was two o'clock in the morning when Truman took the rostrum, for the first time addressing his party as leader elected in his own right. He got to the point: "Senator Barkley and I will win this election and make these Republicans like it—don't you forget that!" As with most of his speech that night, Truman ad-libbed that line. The new Truman was in full effect: Where his regular delivery achieved metronomic flatness, his tone now rose and fell, his pace quickened and slowed. He projected energy to his audience.

"My duty as president requires that I use every means within my power to get the laws the people need on matters of such importance and urgency," Truman said. "I am therefore calling this Congress back into session July 26th. On the 26th day of July, which out in Missouri we call 'Turnip Day,' I am going to call Congress back and ask them to pass laws to halt rising prices, to meet the housing crisis—which they are saying they are for in their platform."

Of 2,622 words Truman spoke that early morning, roughly 1,031—40 percent—appeared in the reading outline the president brought to the stage. Using a technique that he would take on the train tracks in the fall, Truman used the talking points as jumping-off points and weaved in his own Trumanisms and style. "Turnip Day" was, not surprising, a Truman ad-lib, as were his admonitions that farmers and labor unions would be "the most ungrateful people in the world" if they failed to vote Democratic.

The speech was a smashing success.

"Entire speech was superb," William Batt, head of the Democratic National Committee's newly minted research division, cabled to Clifford. "Best yet you were 100 percent right on off the cuff decision special session idea electrified convention."

After a brief Labor Day swing to Michigan, the whistle-stop campaign of 1948 began in earnest on September 17. As Truman departed on a two-week swing that would take him to the west coast, Barkley and Secretary of State George C. Marshall saw him off at Washington's Union Station. "Mow 'em down, Harry!" yelled Barkley. "I'm going to give 'em hell," Truman shot back, smiling despite a sore throat.

The 1948 whistle-stop campaign has acquired political legend glamour, but for the participants, it was relentless and backbreaking. "I remember it as a miserable, ceaseless and exhausting treadmill," Clifford wrote in his memoirs. He told his collaborator: "I cannot remember any fun on the train at all."

First built as one of a series of half a dozen luxury train cars named for famous explorers, Truman's train, the *Ferdinand Magellan*, had been refitted in 1942 for presidential use. New three-inch thick bulletproof glass windows were installed and the car's entire body was plated with 5/8th-inch-thick nickel steel. It had two escape hatches. It retained its luxury heritage inside. Walking from front to back, one would pass through a galley, a pantry, servants' quarters, and the oak-paneled dining room. Around the table Truman conferred with his top aides, all sitting in matching chairs upholstered with gold-and-green damask. Continuing back, one would pass four bedrooms, A through D. Rooms B and C were the presidential suite, with the first lady staying in B. Finally came the observation lounge at the rear, opening onto the platform from which the president spoke.

The one thing the train lacked as it pulled out of Union Station that September day was a stock of speeches. One speech had been prepared ahead of time: the first major address, on farm policy, for the next day at Dexter, Iowa. The other 133 talks on the two-week swing were assembled on the fly, a pattern that held for all three of his whistle-stop trips during the campaign. At no point would Truman's staff get more than two days ahead of schedule in terms of preparation.

"It is surprising to me that these speeches were not conceived, drafted and polished weeks ago, so that they did not have to be whipped into shape on the midnight before mailing, without time for mature consideration and inspirational touches," Albert Z. "Bob" Carr, who was brought on board to bolster the speechwriting corps during the campaign, wrote in September.

Campaign speechwriting worked on two tracks. The major speeches that Truman gave in big cities, which were typically carried over the radio, were fully written out ahead of time. Murphy, working from the White House, produced first drafts of those, with help from David Lloyd, who was brought on from the Democratic National Committee (DNC), and David Bell, a Harvard-trained economist who had joined the White House staff from the Bureau of the Budget in late 1947. In the second term, Lloyd, who also had a flair for humor, specialized in foreign policy speeches. Bell, a tall ex-Marine, would take a lead role in economic speeches in the second term.

These drafts would be flown out to meet the campaign train, where Clifford would work them over with the president and others. "Never use two words when one will do best," Truman would admonish his writers, going over the major speeches as the landscape rolled by. Striking out language he did not like, he might say: "That's not the way I would say it," or, "Let's just say what we mean."

But Truman's rear-platform, off-the-cuff speeches were the heart of the campaign. These were the province of Elsey on the train and Bill

Batt in Washington. Batt and his DNC research team were holed up in a small house near Dupont Circle. They would write detailed briefs on every community where the president was scheduled to speak. They had a "secret weapon"—a complete set of Works Progress Administration guides for the country, which featured detailed descriptions of every city and town in a given state.* And Truman had his own store of facts about small towns across the country that he had visited while investigating defense contractor waste and fraud in the early 1940s.

Elsey had boarded the train with briefcases filled with thorough, Batt-profiles of the first few stops on the trip—and promises of daily updates. These files were complete and detailed: background and history of the town, its leaders, information about the congressional incumbent, including his voting record and data regarding his opponent; hot issues in the local race; suggested speaking topics for Truman. Elsey would start with two or three full sentences to get the president rolling, follow with bulleted topics from which he could extemporize, and close with full sentences. Sometimes Elsey handed the draft to Truman just as the train was stopping in the station.

The work was grueling. Truman would give eight, ten, twelve, in at least one case fifteen whistle-stop addresses in any given day, none repeated. Elsey tried to hit as many different issues over the course of a day as possible. But from outside the campaign bubble, the whistle-stop trips had the air of a carnival of the sort that used to meander from town to town, or an old-time political procession where a famous orator would come to town—popular entertainment in the days before radio and television.

The train's arrival stirred the waiting crowd, whose excitement rose as the president emerged. "Now, in 1946 just one-third of the people who were entitled to vote in this country elected that 'do-nothing,' good-for-nothing 80th Congress," he said in Efaula, Oklahoma, on

---

*Kenneth Hechler assumed the job of producing whistle-stop material during the 1950 and 1952 campaigns. "Truman told me to subscribe to the local weekly newspapers and find out what people are talking about," he recalled. "He said also put in a call to not only public officials of the town but see if you can get a hold of taxi drivers and beauty shop operators and if they have a statue in the town square, why is it there and what are the people proud of?" (Author interview with Hechler.)

September 28. "And see what you got. I won't feel a bit sorry for those people who stay at home and don't vote and then complain about what they're getting out of this Republican Congress. They haven't got a kick coming. Don't do that this time."

Little noticed by the crowd, a figure would step down from the train and wander amid the throng. Under most other circumstances, with his height and looks Clifford would be a center of attention. But on these occasions, sometimes accompanied by one-star General Wallace Graham, the president's personal physician, he would wander through the crowd and subtly pump up the enthusiasm (one reporter described the pair as a couple of "carnival shills")—not that Truman needed much help on that count.

"Truman was entertainment: He not only had something to say, but he always said it in a manner that the audience liked, even if they weren't going to vote for him, and even if they *knew* he was going to lose," Elsey recalled. "He was free entertainment."

He was also good copy for the newspaper reporters who scrambled out of the train, hoping not to miss anything the president might say. As a result, the next day's papers would have Truman's comments on a range of issues. The reporters were not the only ones scrambling. His writers would either listen live or get hold of transcripts to see what lines Truman had used on the stump and then write the good ones into the next speech or outline. "In this sense, I suppose he did more in writing his own whistle-stop speeches than anyone else because this was a standard technique," Murphy recalled. "I suppose you might call it an editing job."

Speaking from one of Elsey's outlines, Truman would lay into his favorite target, the "do-nothing Eightieth Congress," whipping the crowd up before asking if they would like to meet his family. Out would come "the Boss"—Mrs. Truman—followed by Margaret ("Miss Margaret," in the border states), whom he described as the one "who bosses the bosses." The president would then lean over the brass railing, grabbing an outstretched hand or two as the local band started to play again. A piercing toot would send reporters scrambling back on board. And slowly the train would start rolling down the tracks. As the *Ferdinand Magellan* trundled away, Margaret would toss a single red rose into the crowd.

They loved it: He was going to lose, but so what?

But ceaseless work for an apparently futile cause took its toll. Clifford suffered from an attack of boils during the course of the summer. "It was a real ordeal," he said of the campaign. "I don't know quite how I got through it except I was young at the time and strong and vigorous." For months after the election, Clifford woke in cold sweats, sure that he was still on the train, unable to escape.

Spared the stress—and none too pleased about it—was Sam Rosenman. Although he had worked on the acceptance speech and had cleared his fall schedule to travel with the president, he was not invited on the train trip. "I know it was not an oversight but a deliberate exclusion," Rosenman said sadly more than twenty years later. "It has always been a mystery to me . . . I make no secret of the fact that I resented it, was very angry about it—and still am." Rosenman did contribute to a handful of speeches late in the campaign, but he was mostly absent.

At times it seemed as if Truman was the least affected by the stress and pace. He drew energy from the growing and enthusiastic crowds. And they responded—especially when he savaged his favorite target, the GOP Congress. "And this Republican Congress never acted until it heard its master's voice—the chief lobbies for whatever bill was pending before the Congress," he told the crowd at Muskogee, Oklahoma, on September 29. "I make that charge advisedly, and if they want me to prove it and name names and give them the chapter and verse, I can give them that, too."

A typical speech started with praise for the crowd and community. "We had quite an experience this morning down at a little town called Oxford," Truman said in Des Moines on September 18. "They told me the town had 500 people in it, and there were 2,500 people on the platform. Now, that's a feat that I never have known a big city to do in the history of the country—to get five times the number of the people in the town on the platform to welcome the President of the United States."

He would site a piece of trivia or praise a local candidate before lighting into the Republicans, especially on issues important to farmers or union members, two of the groups targeted in his campaign.

"This 80th 'do-nothing' Republican Congress did its best to cut the ground from under the farmer, and I want to say to you that, if this Republican outfit had control of the government of the United States, the farmer would have been out the window right now," he said in Fort Worth, Texas, on September 27. Or in Ashland, Kentucky, on October 1: "Congressman Hartley proposed only a few days ago to bring the unions under the laws against monopolies. That's a typical Republican Party act. They want to put the laboringman, in his fight for good wages, in the same class with the billion-dollar corporation. They want to do that so they can cut down on the workingman's share of the national income."

Not everyone agreed with Truman's attack posture—his press secretary Charlie Ross thought that the president should use more dignified language. Even Clifford later conceded that some of the lines—that Republicans were "gluttons of privilege" who had "stuck a pitchfork in the farmer's back"—could have been moderated. But Truman loved it. "You remember back in Hoover's campaign, the slogan was: 'Two cars in every garage,'" he said in Wilmington, Delaware, on October 6. "Apparently, the Republican candidate is running on a slogan of two families in every garage."

One of the few Republicans he rarely mentioned was New York governor Thomas Dewey, his opponent. Starting with the "Turnip session," Truman ignored the moderate Dewey and instead ran hard against the villainous Congress. In two months of off-the-cuff campaign talks, he mentioned Dewey by name twice. By comparison, he mentioned Ohio Republican senator Robert Taft more than three dozen times.

He would occasionally refer to Dewey obliquely. "My opponent has talked a great deal too, but he said almost nothing about where he stands on the major issues facing the American people today," the president said in Garrett, Indiana, on October 25. "He just keeps on giving the people high-level platitudes. You know, that's what 'G.O.P.' means in this day and age—it means 'Grand Old Platitudes.'"

Truman was right. Comfortable in the certainty of victory, Dewey ran a bland, robotic campaign. Where Truman gave a new speech at as many as fifteen stops per day, Dewey repeated the same speech over and over again.* Reporters scrambled to hear Truman's talks but stayed on Dewey's train when he spoke. "Perhaps the best way to describe the atmosphere on the campaign train during this trip is to use the characterization of a newspaper man who rode with us," White House aide William Bray recalled. "On the Dewey train, he said, the newspapermen played bridge and drank martinis and manhattans. On the Truman train they played poker and drank scotch and bourbon."

An opportunity was about to be wasted, Elsey thought. Two weeks after Truman's stunning election victory, the president planned to send a written State of the Union message up to Congress, focusing his energy on his inaugural address.† Elsey dashed off a memo to Clifford, who was vacationing with Truman in Key West, Florida. The president should deliver the State of the Union in person, Elsey wrote, focusing it exclusively on his domestic agenda while devoting the inaugural address to foreign affairs.

His memo won Elsey a trip down to Key West to make the case personally. When Truman agreed to the idea, Murphy took the lead on writing the speech, with help from Lloyd, who had impressed with his contributions in the campaign. Three days before it was to be delivered, Truman, Clifford, and the rest of the writers were arrayed around the Cabinet Room table editing. Truman made only minor changes— scratching out the occasional word or inserting a clarifying phrase. His one major edit came in the conclusion. Crossing out a paragraph about the American people's desire that the president and Congress work together as "responsible partners," he scribbled an insertion that read, in part, "I expect to try to give every segment of our population a fair deal."

Historic phrases and slogans rarely come bidden. Like "new deal" seventeen years earlier, "fair deal" appeared organically as a lower-cased

---

*In this regard, he resembled modern presidential candidates.

†While modern presidents would not pass up what is oftentimes the only opportunity to speak to the entire nation, in-person delivery did not become a fixed tradition until 1934. All told, of 219 annual messages delivered by presidents through 2008, 75 were spoken. (www.senate.gov/reference/resources/pdf/RS20021.pdf.)

phrase before it became an upper-cased, agenda-defining slogan. Clifford quickly saw the potential of the phrase, however, and pointed it out to reporters in background discussions. Having broken free of Roosevelt's stylistic shadow in the campaign, Truman was now setting his programmatic mark.

After Truman gave the State of the Union address on January 5, 1949, he and his staff incredibly took a few days' breather before starting the serious work of the inaugural address. The development of the speech is striking first because substantial work on it was done in less than two weeks, a very short time, and second, the speech created a landmark foreign aid program almost from whole cloth, and almost entirely within the White House writing staff.

"The circumstances of the President's re-election thrilled the free world, and the dramatic occasion of his inauguration on January 20 will insure [sic] world-wide attention to what the President may say on that occasion," Elsey had written in November 1948. "No other occasion in the foreseeable future offers the President so great an opportunity to speak to the entire world. His election on November 2 confirmed his role as the leader of the free peoples of the world in their search for peace, and I believe his words on January 20 should match the dignity and responsibility of that role."

Clifford, Elsey, and Lloyd met at ten thirty in the morning on Monday, January 10, in Clifford's office—ten days before Truman would be sworn in—to outline the inaugural. They contemplated a half-dozen ideas, discarding a pair outright (one, according to Elsey's handwritten notes, was a discussion of what would happen if the Soviets and the United States "clashed"; the other was "Why clash . . . unnecessary").

On the list of ideas, along with references to the Marshall Plan, the North Atlantic Treaty Organization, and the United Nations, Clifford had added in pencil: "Hardy's idea." The first three items were well known and well developed, and formed the heart of a typically overwritten first draft that the State Department produced. That draft was a grand philosophical statement about the nature of democracy and the rights of man, containing decidedly non-Trumanesque rhetoric. ("Today we find world democracy, adding to its bright record of progressive achievement, not only challenged by tasks of sobering magnitude but also under calculated assault by doctrines dedicated to the proposition that men cannot be trusted to govern themselves.")

Enter Benjamin Hardy. A former reporter for the *Atlanta Journal*, Hardy had joined the State Department and, during the war, served in Brazil. The New Deal's accomplishments in his home state of Georgia having shown him new technologies' power to transform underdeveloped economies, he realized the same lessons could work abroad. At the midlevel in the department's public affairs division Hardy had seen a mid-November Clifford memorandum requesting new ideas for the inaugural. Hardy suggested to his superiors that the United States give technical aid to Third World countries to help their development. "This is the way to make the greatest psychological impact and to ride and direct the universal groundswell of desire for a better world," he wrote on November 23 to Francis Russell, the department's head of public affairs. The Department of State reacted in the classic bureaucratic manner: The proposal required more study.

And the idea likely would have disappeared into Foggy Bottom's musky innards but for Hardy's initiative. On December 15, he picked up the phone and called Elsey directly, asking to see him. Assuming that it was official, "in-channels" business, Elsey agreed. He was surprised when Hardy arrived in his White House office and launched into a passionate plea for his idea. Elsey liked it, as did Clifford. It was "a speech in search of an idea, and an idea in search of a speech," Elsey later said.

Grouped with the three familiar pillars of foreign policy, this program became known as "Point Four." Bureaucratic maneuvering ensued. In order to protect Hardy, Clifford and Elsey made a pretense of officially asking the department for suggestions on a technical assistance program for the address. Though at least five drafts of a response circulated inside the department, the only one Clifford or Elsey ever received was leaked to them by Hardy.

Despite State Department resistance, a draft of the inaugural, including Point Four, was ready for a presidential read-through on the afternoon of January 14. Truman immediately grasped the importance of the program, saying that he wanted to emphasize that it was not a sop to

Wall Street but that the development would be in the interests of the countries concerned.

"H.S.T." was "All for point 4," Elsey penciled in his notes. "But just don't play into hands of crackpots at home—no 'milk for Hottentots.'" This was a reference to Henry Wallace's 1942 comment as vice president that the object of the war was to "make sure that everybody in the world has the privilege of drinking a quart of milk a day." The remark had led to critics derisively referring to his aims as "Milk for Hottentots."

Told that neither State nor the Bureau of the Budget had signed off on the new program, Truman laughed. "I'll announce it and then they can catch up with me!" he responded. He gave the speech on a crisp, clear, cold January afternoon and was enthusiastically received. "We must embark on a bold new program for making the benefits of our scientific advances and industrial progress available for the improvement and growth of underdeveloped areas," Truman said. "More than half the people of the world are living in conditions approaching misery. Their food is inadequate. They are victims of disease. Their economic life is primitive and stagnant. Their poverty is a handicap and a threat both to them and to more prosperous areas. For the first time in history, humanity possesses the knowledge and skill to relieve suffering of these people."

The 1949 inaugural was the first to be broadcast on television, bringing 10 million more viewers than were present—the largest number of people who had ever watched any single event to that point in history. As David McCullough points out, more people would see Harry Truman take his oath of office that day than had witnessed all of his predecessors combined.

Point Four was widely acclaimed. *The Washington Post* called it a "Fair Deal" plan for the world. "Franklin D. Roosevelt, Woodrow Wilson, Theodore Roosevelt, Abraham Lincoln . . . could have applauded the principles upon which he dealt," enthused *The New York Times*.

A bureaucratic rearguard action by the State Department and intransigence in Congress delayed Point Four's implementation. When it finally became a reality in June 1950, it was badly underfunded. Nevertheless, by the time Truman left office in January 1953, 2,445 U.S. technicians were implementing the program in thirty-five countries, and 2,862 specialists had been sent from those countries primarily to the United States for training. "In its immediate and long-range effects," Truman wrote in his 1956 memoirs, "Point Four provided the strongest antidote to Communism that has so far been put into practice."

Ben Hardy left the State Department and joined the newly created Technical Cooperation Administration as its chief information officer. He was traveling with Dr. Henry Bennett, the agency's first administrator, and other officials in December 1953 when their plane crashed in Iran. All aboard were killed. Hardy was forty-five.

Truman's first full term brought the end of the Clifford-Elsey team. After the inauguration, Elsey left the White House for six months to return to active naval duty to help Samuel Eliot Morison write a history of World War II naval operations. Clifford was contemplating a departure as well, making a government salary that was less than half of what he had been earning before the war. He wanted to be U.S. Attorney General, and turned down an offer to become Under Secretary of State. During the summer, Truman asked if he had any interest in the Supreme Court. Clifford said that he did not.

Stephen Spingarn, who replaced Elsey as Clifford's assistant, thought that even though he was at the White House, Clifford already had plans to leave. "As far as I could see, if he was concentrating on White House matters (and I was his only professional assistant), I never saw it," Spingarn later said. "It is true that he sat in on the last rounds of the speech conferences and things like that, but that didn't amount to much." By the time Elsey returned to the White House in August 1949, Charles Murphy was substantially in charge of the speechwriting operation.

When he returned, Elsey did so as an administrative assistant, reporting directly to Truman. "Clifford's interest in my promotion was not entirely altruistic," Elsey later wrote. "He would [soon] set himself up in law practice in Washington, and he would count on me to help him stay in touch with White House goings-on. The higher my status, the better I could do so. In the remaining years of the administration, we kept in close contact, closer than would today be considered proper."

Clifford left at the end of January 1950. "It would be difficult to overstate the value of the services which you have rendered your country," Truman wrote him. But Clifford took special delight that Truman had noticed his judicial roots. "In the marshaling and presentation of facts your method reflected your days before the jury. Quick in the detection of spurious evidence and alert always in detecting the fallacious arguments of your opponents, your final opinions were always the models of brevity and accuracy as well as clarity and strength."

Clifford returned to private practice, keeping a hand in Democratic politics and becoming one of the éminences grises of Washington. In 1968, Lyndon Johnson appointed him Secretary of Defense, where he enlisted Elsey to join him. His career was tainted in the 1990s when he was involved in the scandal surrounding the Bank of Credit and Commerce International (BCCI). He died in 1998 and is buried in Arlington National Cemetery.

Murphy took over as special counsel. He cut a starkly different figure from the dashing Clifford. Murphy's shy-seeming, self-effacing demeanor tended to make the press—and historians—understate his importance. "For ease of turning out a speech, ability to craft one on his own, Charlie Murphy was probably the best," Elsey said. "And poor Charlie has never gotten the proper credit for his contributions to the Truman administration. . . . Charlie didn't leave a paper trail."

When Murphy died in 1983, James Sundquist, who contributed to the 1947 State of the Union and then joined the White House staff full time in the administration's last year, wrote that Murphy was "the pivot on which the White House turned. Murphy was not one of the president's bourbon-drinking and poker-playing cronies; he was, rather, the man on whom Truman leaned intellectually to keep the program of his administration consistent, liberal and honest. This Murphy did by controlling the flow of words from the presidential office. . . . By being in charge of the words that explained the president's program, Murphy became perforce the coordinator of program development as well."

He expanded the Special Counsel's office staff and did not "share Clifford's pretense that every speech from his office was solely his own product," Elsey later wrote. "Early in the second term Murphy had assembled a first-rate team of young assistants to whom he gave generous credit." With a larger staff, and thus a great ability to handle the workload, Murphy was able to bring a higher level of order to the speechwriting process than Clifford achieved.

That team included Bell and Lloyd—both veterans of the 1948 campaign; Kenneth Hechler, a Princeton professor who would take Elsey's role as producer of speech outlines in the 1950 and 1952 whistle-stop tours; and Richard Neustadt, a political scientist who also transferred from the Bureau of the Budget staff. The group went on to impressive careers. Murphy became an under secretary in the Kennedy and Johnson Departments of Agriculture and later chairman of the Civil Aeronautics Board; Bell became Kennedy's budget director; Neustadt became a Harvard professor and the nation's preeminent scholar of presidential power.

At around 4 am local time on the rainy morning of Sunday, June 25, 1950, the North Korean military started shelling South Korean army positions south of the 38th parallel. Infantry and armor soon followed. Truman quickly moved to aid the South Korean military. By the end of the month, General Douglas MacArthur had permission to deploy ground forces to the Korean peninsula.

Although he made a series of short statements about the Korean conflict, Truman did not address the nation until Wednesday, July 19, twenty-five days after it had begun. Murphy and Elsey started working on the speech on Monday, and, with help from Bell and others, had four drafts done by four o'clock on the day of the speech. Truman met with the writers and other senior staff in the Cabinet Room and read it through slowly, pausing at the end of each page to take comments and suggestions, but never reading it through without stopping.

Just before they finished freezing the speech, a message from MacArthur arrived. Elsey thought that word from the general would add drama to the address and, with Truman's permission, had sent him a draft via the White House Signal Center. They found a portion of MacArthur's reply to quote and inserted it. "That's a darn good speech," Truman said at the end, though Elsey doubted, given how he had read it, whether he could really tell.

"This attack has made it clear, beyond all doubt, that the international Communist movement is willing to use armed invasion to conquer independent nations," Truman told the nation.

> *An act of aggression such as this creates a very real danger to the security of all free nations. The attack upon Korea was an outright breach of the peace and a violation of the Charter of the United Nations. By their actions in Korea, Communist leaders have demonstrated their contempt for the basic moral principles on which the United Nations is founded. This is a direct challenge to the efforts of the free nations to build the kind of world in which men can live in freedom and peace. This challenge has been presented squarely. We must meet it squarely.*

Relations between the general and the president deteriorated over the following months as MacArthur issued his own foreign policy statements, including threatening to attack China. His repeated defiance finally prompted Truman to action in early April 1951. "So the staff won't have to read it in the papers, I'm going to tell you now that I fired MacArthur yesterday," Truman told his aides on the morning of April 10. "Frank Pace [the secretary of the army] is in Japan or Korea—I don't know exactly where—he is going to tell him. I'd kind of like to announce it myself."

What Truman did not know was that the order had been slow reaching Pace, which in turn delayed MacArthur hearing the news. Rumors shot around Washington that night that the *Chicago Tribune* would report that the general was about to resign, prompting Truman to wire MacArthur directly firing him and to order White House press secretary Joe Short to announce the resignation to the press at 1 am. "I wasn't going to let the SOB resign on me," Truman told Elsey the next day. "I wanted to *fire* him."

Murphy and the speechwriters worked all day April 11 on a radio address for an unpopular president—his approval rating in the 20s—to explain why he had sacked a widely admired general. Truman and his staff finished freezing the 10:30 pm speech shortly before ten. Truman went into correspondence secretary William Hassett's office, moved some books off his sofa, curled up, and took a short nap, rising in time to address the nation.

At 10:23 pm, presidential assistant Averell Harriman, a former ambassador to Russia and to Great Britain, and a foreign policy expert, asked Elsey if there was any mention in the speech of MacArthur's replacement, General Matthew Ridgway. There was not. The two men quickly wrote a sentence and at 10:26 walked it into the Oval Office. Elsey paper-clipped the handwritten insert to the speech.

The speech mostly focused on the reasons for the Korean conflict. The president mentioned MacArthur only at the end:

> *I believe that we must try to limit the war to Korea for these vital reasons: to make sure that the precious lives of our fighting men are not wasted; to see that the security of our country and the free world is not needlessly jeopardized; and to prevent a third world war. A number of events have made it evident that General MacArthur did not agree with that policy. I have therefore considered it essential to relieve General MacArthur so that there would be no doubt or confusion as to the real purpose and aim of our policy.*

The MacArthur incident had an unexpected side effect for Elsey. A little over a week after Truman fired the general, he ordered Elsey to leak to *The New York Times* confidential minutes of a meeting between the president and the general the previous October at Wake Island. This set Elsey afoul of Joe Short, who neither forgot nor forgave. For months he quietly sniped at Elsey until the longtime aide was on the verge being reassigned to active duty as naval historian in the Mediterranean. Instead, Elsey joined the staff of Averell Harriman in the Mutual Security Agency. After the Truman presidency ended, he joined the Red Cross. Except for a stint with Secretary of Defense Clark Clifford at the end of the Johnson administration, Elsey worked for the relief organization until retiring in 1990.

In June 1951, Kenneth Hechler was reporting to Truman on how the president had looked giving a speech on television. When he mentioned that the audience could see the president turning the pages of address, Truman mused that he had heard about a gadget that might be of use: "Say, I understand that the president of CBS has a new thing called a 'TelePrompter' which will bear some looking into." This was in keeping with Murphy's ongoing desire to improve Truman's delivery, including, as he put it in a September 1950 memorandum to Truman, using "improvements in the mechanical arrangements" for speeches. "Particularly, we should explore thoroughly the possibilities of reading from a screen for television purposes." But Truman never used the machine—it was not his style. "He was a little suspicious of any gimmick that made it appear that he was faking his sincerity of communication," Hechler later noted.

On January 19, 1953, as the administration was closing down, someone jokingly asked Hechler if he was going to come into work the next day. "Sure, why not?" Hechler said. So on the day that Dwight D. Eisenhower became the thirty-fourth president of the United States, Hechler went to his office. The officials of the new administration were too busy slapping each other—and him—on the back to question who he was or what he did.

When the White House personnel director circulated a memorandum restricting access to the White House mess, Hechler's name appeared on the cleared list, so he kept eating there until one day, sitting at the common staff table, someone asked who he worked for. The special counsel, Hechler replied—attracting the attention of a gentleman sitting at the end of the table. "I'm the special counsel," he said. "What do you do for me?"

Hechler, who would go on to serve nine terms in Congress and sixteen years as secretary of state of West Virginia, had been at the White House for long enough that he could not be fired without cause—and being a Democrat was not a sufficient cause. Finally after several more weeks he received a note telling him that his services were no longer required—he had "completed" his "assignment."

THREE

"Sometimes You Sure Get Tired of All This Clackety-Clack"

MARCH 4, 1953

The news electrified and quickly obsessed official Washington. "Stalin Gravely Ill After a Stroke; Partly Paralyzed and Unconscious; Moscow Discloses Concern for Him," *The New York Times*'s triple-decker headline read. Word the following day that the Soviet leader had succumbed spurred a flurry of activity and speculation. Stalin's death represented an opportunity: The Cold War was less than a decade old and his passing threw it into flux. Here was a chance to end the standoff before it became a hot war.

President Dwight Eisenhower convened his cabinet two days later, a meeting that speechwriter Emmet Hughes, listening from the staff seats, found "impossible to describe as inspiring."

Eisenhower himself summarized the problem his government faced. "Ever since 1946, I know that all the so-called experts have been yapping about what would happen when Stalin dies, and what we, as a nation, should do about it," Ike said. "Well, he's dead. And you can turn the files of our government inside out—in vain—looking for any plans laid. We have no plan. We're not even sure what difference his death makes."

One man trying to sort it out was C. D. Jackson, the president's top assistant for Cold War planning. A once-and-future *Time* reporter,

Jackson had, along with Hughes and others, worked on Eisenhower's campaign speeches. Cloistered in the Commodore Hotel in New York City, they had fired drafts off to the candidate's train. Now in the White House Jackson worked with the State and Defense departments through the Psychological Strategy Board to plan Cold War strategy.

Eisenhower had brought Jackson into the administration in part as a counterbalance to the staid, immovable Secretary of State, John Foster Dulles. "Granted that Dulles was a man of great moral force and conviction, he was not endowed with the creative genius that produces bold, new ideas to gain hitherto unattainable policy goals," White House chief of staff Sherman Adams later wrote. Ike hoped that Jackson might provide that spark.

Under Jackson's guidance, the board was working up a post-Stalin plan meant to capitalize on the uncertainty the dictator's death would bring in the Soviet bloc. An Eisenhower speech was its keystone. The wisdom of such an address was the subject of much debate within the administration. "It is difficult to see any great advantage in the present situation in a public message or speech by the President," Charles E. "Chip" Bohlen, Eisenhower's nominee to be ambassador to the Soviet Union, wrote to Emmet Hughes four days after Stalin's death.

As Hughes summarized in a memorandum to Eisenhower the next day, March 10, "All this resolves itself into a clear, simple conflict between two propositions: <u>A</u>. Presented a unique opportunity to exploit the deep and inherent weaknesses of the Soviet system, we cannot afford to fail to act affirmatively and quickly. <u>B</u>. Presented with a situation of unknown potentialities, we can well afford to give the internal stresses of the Soviet system time to become acute—and, in the meanwhile, nothing is better calculated to increase Soviet nervous strain than studied American silence."

Hughes leaned initially in the direction of inaction—there was little point, he believed, in saying something just for its own sake. He wished to avoid "verbal improvisation, in lieu of serious national policy." He knew that in this case the policy and the speech were inexorably linked—and that as the speechwriter, he was in a unique position to exercise influence at that nexus. "I now came to appreciate again the curiously strategic value of being the source of presidential words that must be persuaded, somehow, to flow," Hughes later wrote. "I resisted and evaded all exhortations to write some compelling rhetoric for the occasion."

Hughes, thirty-two, had joined the White House staff only reluctantly and with an understanding that his tenure would be brief. "Emmet was a loner. He wanted to do everything himself," recalled Robert Kieve, his assistant. "And he did it rather brilliantly." Quickwitted, ironic, and impatient, Hughes was a tall, lean, sharp-featured man, with dark hair. A former editor of *Life*, one friend recalled him as "a dashing fellow."

Eisenhower appreciated Hughes's ability to craft speeches, but they were an imperfect fit. Writing in his diary about the process of preparing his first inaugural address, Eisenhower said that Hughes "has been no help—he is more enamored with words than ideas. I don't care much about the words if I can convey the ideas accurately."

While Hughes was in many ways following in the tradition of Raymond Moley—especially—Samuel Rosenman, Clark Clifford, and Charles Murphy, he had the distinction of being the first presidential assistant to hold the official position of speechwriter. Hughes's predecessors all had broader portfolios that included speechwriting as a subset. But Hughes's job *was* speechwriter, though his one-on-one access and willingness to engage in policy debates meant that he and his successors also could play a key role in Ike's administration.

Late one afternoon more than a week after Stalin's death, Eisenhower walked a long, slow arc around the Oval Office addressing Hughes in measured, forceful tones. "Look, I am tired—and I think everyone is tired—of just plain indictments of the Soviet regime," he said. "I think it would be wrong—in fact, asinine—for me to get up before the world now to make another one of those indictments. Instead, just *one* thing matters: What have *we* got to offer the world?"

As Eisenhower spoke, it seemed to Hughes that his contemplation was drawing to a close. Ike's thoughts were now coalescing. The president stopped and, jaw set, stared out the window onto the South Lawn. The tiny speck of an F-86 Sabre buzzed across the sky.

In an instant his reverie broke, and he wheeled around: "*Here* is what I would like to say. The jet plane that roars over your head costs three quarters of a million dollars. That is more money than a man earning ten thousand dollars every year is going to make in his lifetime. What world can afford this sort of thing for long? We are in an armaments race. Where will it lead us? At worst to atomic warfare. At best, to robbing every people and nation on earth of the fruits of their own toil.

"Now, there could be another road before us—the road of disarmament. What does this mean? It means for everybody in the world: bread, butter, clothes, homes, hospitals, schools—all the good and necessary things for decent living. So let *this* be the choice we offer. If we take this second road, all of us can produce more of these good things for life—and we, the United States, will help them still more. . . . This is what I want to say. And if we don't really *have* anything to *offer*, I'm not going to make a speech about it."

The basics were set quickly: an appeal to the Soviets to seek security through trust rather than military might; a detailed explanation of the cost of the arms race; a call for signs of Soviet good faith—including a treaty settling the status of Austria, which was still occupied by both Western and Soviet troops;* a set of principles regarding disarmament; and finally a discussion of the fruits disarmament might bear. There was little new in the various offers and demands the speech would contain, but it expressed a nuanced understanding of the cost of war—cold or hot—in the atomic age as well as of the opportunities for peace.

Roughly a month remained before the speech was to be delivered to the American Society of Newspaper Editors on April 16—time to polish and refine, and also time for opponents within the administration to marshal their criticisms. One key adviser bound to be displeased was Dulles, the tall, dour arch conservative, who less than twenty-four hours earlier had told Hughes that peace in Korea would be undesirable until the U.S. military had given the Chinese "one hell of a licking."

Hughes pointed to the difference between what Ike was expressing and Dulles's views. Eisenhower paused before replying: "All right then. If Mr. Dulles and all his sophisticated advisers really mean that they can *not* talk peace seriously, then I am in the wrong pew. For if it's *war* we

---

*The 1955 Austrian State Treaty established Austria as an independent, neutral state.

should be talking about, I *know* the people to give me advice on that—and they're not in the State Department."

Dulles did not like the notion of the speech at all. New Soviet premier Georgi Malenkov had initiated a post-Stalin "peace offensive," as Dulles and the press described it. On March 15, when Eisenhower was sketching out his own speech for Hughes, Malenkov had in his inaugural address before the Supreme Soviet said there were no problems between the USSR and the United States that could not be decided by peaceful negotiations, a sentiment echoed by other Soviet leaders.

Dulles did not buy the peace overtures from Malenkov or any other Soviet leader and he feared a "real danger of our just seeming to fall in with these Soviet overtures" if Eisenhower gave his speech, he told Hughes. The way to retake the initiative in the face of a Soviet "peace offensive," Hughes countered without effect, was "not by turning to race in the opposite direction—but by publicly leaping several steps *ahead* of Soviet proposals, to a prepared position where we take *our* stand and summon the Soviets to come to *us*."

Secretary of Defense Charles Wilson, Hughes was told on April 10, wanted it "clearly indicated that while we <u>wish</u> we could devote to schools, roads, hospitals, etc. the money now going into U.S. rearmament, we <u>have</u> to keep on with our rearmament until the USSR make a <u>basic</u> change in its present policies and actions."

To protect the speech, Hughes kept the bureaucrats out of the loop. He worked directly with Eisenhower, going through more than a dozen drafts, each carefully read and edited by Ike. Only occasionally did he circulate updated versions to Dulles; his brother Allen Dulles, who was director of the CIA; and Jackson. He safeguarded the speech with the knowledge and endorsement of Eisenhower, who enjoyed the one-on-one act of creation rather than having language and substance cleared to insipidity.

On April 11, there was a threat to the speech from an unexpected quarter. Viewing the Soviet situation from the opposite perspective of Dulles, Prime Minister Winston Churchill had nevertheless arrived at the same conclusion. Because he was heartened by the Soviet moves, Churchill cabled that while he thought the speech "grave and formidable," Eisenhower would do better to "bide your time" to see if silence might draw further Communist concessions.

Hughes was summoned to a conference with the president's brother and close confidant Milton Eisenhower, who frequently consulted on speeches, and Under Secretary of State Bedell Smith, who had been Eisenhower's chief of staff during World War II. Hughes privately suspected that Churchill wanted to be the one to make any dramatic offers to the Soviets. Smith said that while the State Department supported the speech, Dulles still doubted the "need" for it. "Maybe Churchill's right," the president said with an air of resignation, "and we can whip up some other text for the occasion." Feeling a tingle of desperation, Hughes reminded the assembled group that he had initially been leery of a premature talk but that the time was right for such an address. The matter hung in the balance for long minutes until it was resolved in the way these things so often are—the conversation drifted from the question of whether to give the speech to issues of substance and content. Finally Eisenhower dictated a message to Churchill that he was going ahead with his speech because his official statement about the Soviet situation would need to convey a clear reaction and be "more than just a jumble of platitudes."

Eisenhower interrupted a golfing trip to Augusta, Georgia, to give the address on April 16. Arriving in Washington, he was seized with such a severe intestinal upset that Sherman Adams, his chief of staff, worried he would not be able to speak. He did, barely. He skipped passages he deemed of lesser import, struggling to read words that seemed to dance before his eyes. He later confided to Adams that he had no recollection whatsoever of what he had said toward the end.

It was no matter. The speech was acclaimed then and remains one of the underappreciated pieces of Cold War eloquence uttered by a president:

Every gun that is made, every warship launched, every rocket fired signifies, in the final sense, a theft from those who hunger and are not fed, those who are cold and are not clothed. This world in arms is not spending money alone. It is spending the sweat of its laborers, the genius of its scientists, the hopes of its children. The cost of one modern heavy bomber is this: a modern brick school in more than thirty cities. It is two electric power plants, each serving a town of 60,000 population. It is two fine, fully equipped hospitals. It is some fifty miles of concrete highway. We pay for a single fighter plane with a half million bushels of wheat. We pay for a single destroyer with new homes that could have housed more than 8,000 people. This, I repeat, is the best way of life to be found on the road the world has been taking. This is not a way of life at all, in any true sense. Under the cloud of threatening war, it is humanity hanging from a cross of iron.

Eisenhower had laid out two paths, and explained the grim costs of following the current course. He made an appeal to follow the second path, toward "a peace that is neither partial nor punitive." Word later reached the White House that listeners behind the iron curtain had wept upon hearing the speech. Churchill sent a personal message to Soviet foreign minister Vyacheslav Molotov praising the address.

Dulles, who had grumbled and questioned throughout the process, spoke at the same conference two days later. The speech, he told the newspaper editors, was "a planned stage in the evolution of the Eisenhower foreign policy."

Hughes, who had struggled with Dulles over the draft, left the administration that September, gladly returning to writing that appeared under his own name. He had never planned on staying in the White House more than "a few months," but privately he told Jackson in July that he had reached the end of his patience with Dulles's foreign policy.

Around the time that Eisenhower spoke to the world about the chance for peace, Jackson and Robert Cutler, the national security adviser, suggested to the president that he should educate the American people on the very real dangers presented by an atomic conflict. Within the White House, it was called "Operation Candor." The notion of having to explain the peril posed by nuclear war may seem odd today, but the exact nature of the threat was still unclear to large sections of the public. One Gallup poll showed that less than one third of those surveyed believed there was much danger of their city being destroyed in a Soviet attack.

Jackson produced several drafts between April and June 1953, each more depressing than the last. They came to be known as the "Bang!" papers because they described in too much detail the wounds the United States would suffer in a nuclear war. When Eisenhower read one May draft, he shuddered and turned away, saying, "We don't want to scare the country to death!"

Domestic politics were the focus when Eisenhower took to the television airwaves on June 3, appearing with Secretary of Health, Education and Welfare Oveta Culp Hobby,* Treasury Secretary George Humphrey, Agriculture Secretary Ezra Taft Benson, and Attorney General Herbert Brownell.† Eisenhower's speaking style worked on television—unpretentious, matter-of-fact, a plain sincerity that carried well over the airwaves. And while he appreciated the need for a president to communicate with the voters, he preferred to do it in settings like this, with cabinet secretaries answering his questions. "I keep telling you fellows I don't like to do" direct, solo addresses to the nation, he told his staff. "I can think of nothing more boring, for the American public, than to have to sit in their living rooms for a whole half hour looking at my face on their television screens."

Eisenhower had other issues with the medium. He had a skin pigmentation that made his face seem a dead, pasty white on television regardless of how ruddy or tanned he was. For much of his administration the actor Robert Montgomery served as a television coach, flying in on the day of a speech to help him prepare his delivery. Montgomery took the role very seriously, but was viewed with skepticism by some members of the staff. "His real role, it seemed to me,

---

*Eisenhower noted that Hobby was in charge of a brand-new government department. "It has to do with the welfare and the education and the health of our people," he said. "And so as you would imagine it is headed by a woman because that's the woman's job in the home."

†On this occasion Ike kicked the presentation off with a letter from a "housewife with four children" in Pawtucket, Rhode Island, asking about the problems of balancing the federal budget. "The sums are so huge I really find it almost impossible to grasp them," wrote Mrs. John Glover. What Eisenhower did not know—and remarkably no reporter thought to check—was that Mrs. Glover was fictitious. Stephen Benedict, who occasionally wrote speeches, had not been able to find a letter asking the right question among the thousands mailed daily to the White House, so he wrote one up himself. (Author interview with Benedict.)

was to stand as close to the president as he could in the minutes before the speech," Robert Kieve, Hughes's assistant, recalled, "and to point his finger at the president in a provocative way so that when the cameras clicked they would show Robert Montgomery instructing the president on how to speak English."

Montgomery introduced Eisenhower to the gadget that Truman had declined to try: the TelePrompTer. He had brought the device to Ike in France in 1951 and it "ran backwards and every way except properly," Eisenhower aide and speechwriter Kevin McCann recalled. After further foul-ups in the campaign, "it took years for anyone to get to talk about TelePrompTers to Dwight Eisenhower." He eventually did grudgingly use it on occasion, but he felt it confined him—forcing him to keep to a certain pace, and not skip paragraphs that he decided were extraneous. If you could control the movement yourself, he thought, it might work, but otherwise Eisenhower did not like the thing.

White House officials had the June 3 style Eisenhower-and-friends format in mind for Operation Candor. "The patent purpose is to engender a greater understanding of the nature of the fight for freedom or the struggle for existence (call it what you will) in which we are engaged—and appreciation of the enormity of the threat which faces us as a nation," James Lambie, the special assistant who headed the White House's advertising liaison office, wrote on June 9 to Claude Robinson of the Opinion Research Corporation, a polling group that had done some work for Eisenhower during the election. "Needless to say, this is conceived as a true Operation <u>Candor</u>, not Operation Politick or Operation Justifying Republican Maneuvers."

C. D. Jackson's next set of drafts, "Bang! BANG!", started circulating in July. "This leaves everybody dead on both sides, with no hope anywhere," the president told Jackson. "Can't we find some hope?" As Eisenhower later wrote to a friend, he wanted "to give our people and the world some faint idea of the size of the distance already traveled by this new science—but to do it in such a way as not to create new alarm."

Jackson was losing hope that the speech would ever be given. But on August 8 Malenkov announced to the world that the Soviet Union possessed the hydrogen bomb, a weapon with far greater firepower than the atomic bombs that had devastated Hiroshima and Nagasaki. Four days later the Soviet Union proved its claim, testing its first H-bomb. Eisenhower was vacationing in Colorado when word reached him.

Still searching for some hope, the president started thinking about how the threat of nuclear war had cast the atom as simply a force for destruction. He wanted to convey that not only was there another side to the matter, but it could benefit the other countries of the world. "The hope," he later wrote in his diary, "was to awaken in these small nations an understanding that there were steadily opening up new and promising opportunities for using these materials and these skills to the benefit rather than to the destruction of men." His idea was for the United States and the USSR to contribute isotopes to a United Nations–administered pool of nuclear material that could be used to demonstrate and share the positive side of the atomic equation.

The speech drafts remained grim. "The whole world for the first time in its history is faced with the possibility of the havoc of global atomic war," an August 24 draft read. It described how much of Washington, D.C., or St. Louis would be obliterated in a surprise Soviet attack, before adding: "Unfortunately for mankind, even these are not the limits of atomic destructiveness. We can foresee no ceiling to the power of atomic bombs either in terms of size or in variety or conditions of employment."

And the speech remained mired in bureaucratic muddle. "I am afraid that the Candor speech is slowly dying from a severe attack of Committee-itis," Jackson wrote in early September. It was his unhappy task to guide the speech and the proposal through the bureaucracy. During the fall a debate raged within the administration about when, where, and whether to give the speech—and what exactly it should say.

Leaks were one problem. Through September columnist brothers Joseph and Stewart Alsop published a series of articles detailing the internal debate over Operation Candor. "C. D. Jackson asks me to use this outworn method (rather than the more expeditious one of going directly to Stewart Alsop) to make sure you are are apprised of the following," Lambie started a September 28 memo.

October brought two important decisions. First, despite Eisenhower's desire not to be the focus of such public pronouncements, his advisers convinced him that his appearing with other officials was not a good idea. "The speech should be televised and the fact that you will read it will add rather than detract from its importance and solemnity," Jackson wrote to Eisenhower on October 2. "Other personalities or the use of props would detract."

The next day, Eisenhower convened a breakfast meeting at the White House that included Jackson, Dulles, Wilson, and Atomic Energy Commission chairman Lewis Strauss. The president finally asserted himself over the process. He wanted practical ideas of how to make his international atomic energy idea work, he told them. No more debate on the matter. Since the speech was taking on a new positive tone—no longer simply the dangers facing the world but the possibilities for progress—the project was given a new code name. It would now be Operation Wheaties because the decisive meeting had taken place over breakfast.

Administration hard-liners resisted. Jackson called Cutler on October 17 to complain that drafting "was getting off the rails again thanks to Foster [Dulles], who give[s] every appearance of deliberately side-tracking me." Dulles and other State Department officials were leery as to whether the Soviets could be successfully engaged in public, preferring quiet diplomacy. "The specific and simple terms desirable for a speech are not a good basis for beginning negotiations," Dulles wrote Eisenhower on October 23. "Either they seem to give away too much of our case or else they seem to be primarily propaganda, which would be likely to provoke only a propaganda response. I think, therefore, that when the time comes, the approaches should be primarily private."

Jackson persevered. "Big meeting in Foster Dulles' office" regarding the speech, Jackson noted in his daily log on November 25, 1953. "Red lights started blinking all over the place. Joint Chiefs and Defense have laid their ears back." Another meeting in Dulles's office two days later brought this entry: "Real problem is very deep and goes beyond any disagreements on wording or technical details. Real problem is basic philosophy—are we or are we not prepared to embark on a course which may in fact lead to atomic disarmament? Soldier boys and their civilian governesses say no. Foster Dulles doesn't say yes or no, but says any atomic offer which does not recognize ultimate possibility is a phoney and should not be made. Strauss and I say we won't be out of the trenches by Christmas, or the next Christmas or the next one, but let's try to make a start and see what happens. Foster considers this mentally dishonest (he should talk!)"

Draft after draft was circulated, with proposals and language added and dropped. One draft proposed to build nuclear plants "as quickly as possible for two cities which have a special right to know the force for good that man has found. Those two cities are Hiroshima and Nagasaki."

The speech had been tentatively scheduled to be delivered before the UN General Assembly on December 8. On Friday, December 4, Eisenhower flew to Bermuda for scheduled meetings with French and British leaders. Inside the American delegation, debate over the speech continued. It was not until Sunday, December 6, two days before the address, that the final decision was made to give it.

Three more drafts were produced in Bermuda, with a fourth edited on the silver four-propeller Lockheed Constellation *Columbine*, the president's personal plane, as it flew to New York City.* Eisenhower, Jackson, Dulles, and Strauss worked on the speech sitting in swivel chairs around the table in the president's compartment. As they made final tweaks, they handed the finished paragraphs to Marie McCrum, Jackson's secretary, who then read it aloud to Ann Whitman, the president's personal secretary, who was at the special typewriter that produced the oversized text suitable for reading copy. Another secretary, Mary Caffrey, typed the speech up for distribution, cutting mimeographed stencils of each page. As they were finished, the stencils were rushed to the rear of the airplane, where an army staff sergeant was producing five hundred copies on a hand-cranked machine.

As the *Columbine* arrived over Manhattan, the tedious work of collating and stapling was still going on, so the plane circled for fifteen minutes and then taxied slowly on the La Guardia Airport runway as its

---

*The term Air Force One had not yet entered common usage. The plane was named for the official flower of Mamie Eisenhower's home state, Colorado.

passengers scrambled to finish. The president sat quietly, underscoring lines of the jumbo copy for emphasis. Dulles wandered into the area where copies of the speech were being collated and stapled. "You can't sit there, Mr. Secretary—we're busy," Whitman snapped. And with that, even the starched Secretary of State lent a hand in the final push. The work continued in the limousine on the way into Manhattan, the ink still wet on the copies.

The speech retained some remnants from Operation Candor, describing the extent of U.S. nuclear testing, noting the threat of Soviet forces. But it had the hope Eisenhower wanted: If the United States and the Soviet Union each make contributions from their stockpiles of fissionable materials into a UN-established International Atomic Energy Agency, it could bring the virtues of nuclear power to developing parts of the world that lacked electricity.

"The United States would seek more than the mere reduction or elimination of atomic materials for military purposes," Eisenhower told the diplomats. "It is not enough to take this weapon out of the hands of the soldiers. It must be put into the hands of those who will know how to strip its military casing and adapt it to the arts of peace. The United States knows that if the fearful trend of atomic military buildup can be reversed, this greatest of destructive forces can be developed into a great boon, for the benefit of all mankind."

Uninterrupted as he spoke, Eisenhower was met with a thunderous applause the likes of which the United Nations had never before seen. As the historian Stephen Ambrose wrote later: "Eisenhower's proposal of Atoms for Peace was the most generous and the most serious offer on controlling the arms race ever made by an American President." Unfortunately, though Eisenhower's proposal was met with acclaim, the Soviet reaction was muted and long coming. By the time the International Atomic Energy Agency was created in 1957, the Cold War had moved to new levels.

Eisenhower selected Bryce Harlow, an Oklahoma native and former Hill staffer who had been working in the Congressional Liaison Office, to replace Hughes. Powered by a stream of cigarettes and coffee (lots of cream, one small pill sweetener), Harlow, a former captain of the University of Oklahoma tennis team, worked eleven or twelve hours a day, six days a week and half a day on Sunday. He was "short and walked very fast to make up for the length of his legs," recalled Stephen Benedict, who worked with him on the Eisenhower staff. "You had the impression that he was in motion all the time."

Harlow had resisted taking over the speechwriting shop, and only agreed on the condition that he get to spend a great deal of time around the president so as to best understand how Ike liked to express himself, what his concerns were, how to capture the man's voice.

In many ways, Hughes and Harlow were opposite images of each other. Where Hughes was tall and lean, Harlow was five foot four and slightly stocky. He was balding, and where Hughes had sharp features, Harlow had a round, cherubic face. "In manner they were so different, so very, very different," recalled Kieve, who worked for both men. Hughes was "impatient, insistent whenever he could be on doing things his way. Bryce was the exact opposite. He was courteous, very thoughtful about the feelings of other people and tried very, very hard to satisfy them."

And while Hughes wrote prose that soared—"humanity hanging from a cross of iron"—Harlow had a straightforward, meat-and-potatoes style that was more suited to the president. "His greatest aversion was the calculated rhetorical device," Hughes noted of Eisenhower. "This meant more than a healthy scorn for the contrived and effortful. It extended to a distrust of eloquence, of resonance, sometimes even of simple effectiveness of expression. All oratorical flourishes made the man uneasy, as if he feared the chance that some hearer might catch him *trying* to be persuasive."

As Harlow saw it, the president's voice had so much natural amplification that a ghost had to underwrite for him. "The president must understate his case, because the fact that he is saying it, in itself, overstates it," Harlow said. "He wanted the word to convey the thought and convey the substance of what he was saying but get lost," William Bragg Ewald, Harlow's assistant, said.

Harlow's writing and editing style was known as "Harlowizing"—writing "as though you're arguing with somebody." Interior Secretary

Fred Seaton once said that Harlowizing could result in "blood flowing in the gutters, virgins raped on every street corner, rockets fired off, purple in every sentence."

Arthur Larson, a second-term speechwriter in the administration, would write in his journal of Harlow: "He tries to sound like Hemingway, and ends by sounding like McGuffies' first reader. 'What is this? It's a house.'"

Harlow was "ardent Republican," Ewald recalled years later. "He would throw the knife all the time at the Democrats, all the time, and Ike didn't like that, really. It wasn't his style." Eisenhower was not interested in gut-fighting politics. Larson noted in May 1956 that "He is really not partisan at heart—doesn't want to paint Republicans all white and Democrats all black." In 1958, looking over a draft from Larson, Eisenhower struck out a line about the upcoming congressional campaign. "Frankly, I don't care too much about the congressional elections," he told Larson.

This partisan tension came to a head during the 1954 congressional campaign. As the *Columbine* cut through the September skies toward Los Angeles, Harlow and other top aides huddled on how to convince their boss to endorse his own political party. They were speeding to a September 23 rally at the Hollywood Bowl, which would feature not only Republican groups but "Democrats for Eisenhower." "Try to write your way down the middle of that one," Eisenhower had told his writers. But his continued partisan reticence had prompted some talk that, as former President Harry S. Truman put it, "President Eisenhower should be secretly wishing for a Democratic Congress." Harlow and other aides were determined to quash the talk.

There was precedent for swaying Eisenhower on political matters. During the 1952 campaign, he had been scheduled to give a speech in Wisconsin praising retired General George C. Marshall, an Eisenhower mentor, and a favorite target of the Red-baiting Senator Joe McCarthy, who was from the Badger State. The speech would have been a slap at McCarthy, but Eisenhower let himself be talked out of it.

On September 17, 1954—the same day that Truman made his remark about Eisenhower and the congressional contest—Harlow sent

Eisenhower two drafts of the Hollywood Bowl speech; one, as he put it, was "almost devoid of politics," while the other had "a dash of nonpartisan Republicanism." The biggest sponsor of the event was the National Federation of Republican Women, he wrote, so there might be a "need for more than perfunctory reference to the GOP."

Harlow had crafted an Eisenhower-approved, pro-GOP speech that still had a crucial hole: It lacked an explicit endorsement of a GOP Congress. White House lobbyist Jack Martin was selected by his colleagues to walk forward to the president's cabin. "Mr. President, I'll leave the door open so that you can throw me out," Martin said. "We think the speech ought to include an outright call for the election of a Republican Congress." He showed the president a draft insert that they had worked up, and, grumblingly, Ike accepted it: "If you want it in there, here's where it should go, not where you have suggested it."

"When, unfortunately, the Congress is controlled by one political party and the executive branch by the other, politics in Washington has a field day," Eisenhower told the crowd. "The conduct of government tends, under these conditions, to deteriorate into an endless round of contests for political advantage—an endless round of political maneuverings, of stagnation and inaction—of half measures or no measures at all. These are the reasons—the compelling reasons—why the completion of your great program requires the election of a Republican-led Congress."

As the campaign progressed, Eisenhower loosened up and became more comfortable stoking partisan fires, but his resentment at having to do so grew as well. After giving a radio address to the country on the eve of the election, he could be heard muttering, "By golly, sometimes you sure get tired of all this clackety-clack."

By the end of the 1954 campaign season Ike had given almost forty speeches, exhorting voters to return a Republican-controlled Congress to Washington. He had wearied of the whole process. And when he finally lost his temper, it was Harlow, the lusty partisan, who caught the brunt.

"I don't see how you write a goddamned thing with so many people telling you what to do," Eisenhower exploded at his aide toward the end of the campaign.* He was talking about Harlow's propensity for thoroughly and widely consulting on each draft of a speech. "I used to write speeches for MacArthur out in the Philippines," Eisenhower went on. "And one thing I know: If you put ten people to work on a speech, they'll kill anything in it that has any character. Now the next time you write something that has any character, you bring it right here. Don't you show it to anybody."

Leaving the Oval Office, an ashen Harlow walked back to his office in the East Wing and, crestfallen, relayed the story to Ewald, his assistant. "I've just been eaten alive," he said. It seemed to Ewald that Harlow never quite got over Ike's attack. It was years before he wrote another speech for Eisenhower.

Replacing Harlow was an old comrade-in-arms, Kevin McCann, who had first written for Eisenhower in the army in 1946. He had been brought into the White House as a part-time consultant in 1953 and joined the staff full time in 1954. "You know, Kevin, I'm like an old cat," Eisenhower told him years later. "I like familiar faces around. Strange faces scare me."

Tall, gaunt, gray, tense, Irish-born and Jesuit-educated, with, as Ewald wrote, "bright pig eyes," McCann among all of Eisenhower's speechwriters understood him best, knew him the longest, and shared his positive disposition. In his years at the White House he had a sign on his office door that said: "Both Southern and Yankee spoken here," an allusion to the fact that he could get along equally well with either of the president's two key aides, Alabama-born Wilton J. Persons and Sherman Adams, the former governor of New Hampshire. He liked to dictate or write in longhand—and would wander the corridors of the White House mumbling to himself whilst in the throes of composition.

---

*Eisenhower had a powerful temper. "You sometimes thought the varnish was going to peel off the desk, you know, he'd get so furious," recalled Malcolm Moos, Eisenhower's last chief speechwriter, who added that these outbursts would blow over quickly. Once, hours after blowing up at him, Eisenhower sent Secret Service agents to fetch Moos from bed. "Bring Malcolm down, I want him to have a couple of drinks with me," Ike said. (Malcolm Moos Columbia University oral history interview, November 2, 1972.)

But while Eisenhower liked his old friend, he and Sherman Adams thought him "neither technically nor emotionally up to the job," C. D. Jackson, now back at *Time*, wrote to publisher Henry Luce in April 1956. "Apparently anything outside of 'I Like Ike' gives him ulcers, and what he should really be doing is going back to Defiance College to be a good Christian college president." When Adams asked Eisenhower who he wanted as a collaborator for the campaign, his immediate one-word answer was "Emmet."

Although "I think that we do want to help get Eisenhower elected," Jackson wrote to Luce, he was concerned that allowing Hughes to return to speechwriting "would tie the sheets down on us even tighter in the Administration bed, which is something we are seriously worrying about." Jackson wrote Adams on April 20 that a Hughes reprise would be impossible, a conclusion with which Hughes apparently agreed.

For the convention acceptance speech, Eisenhower called in Arthur Larson, a former dean of the University of Pittsburgh's Law School who had served as Under Secretary of Labor and had written a book in 1956, *A Republican Looks at His Party*, in which he argued that Ike's GOP occupied the center of the American political spectrum. Eisenhower read the book and was sufficiently impressed to tap Larson for the big speech.*

Larson quickly learned that Ike had a set of rigid guidelines for his speeches. He liked to talk in such a way that "the words don't call attention to themselves," for example. In addition, "every speech must have a Q.E.D."—a point. He did not, he would tell Larson, "want to give a speech just to hear my voice." Also, he demanded brevity. Twenty minutes was the rule of thumb. Finally, Eisenhower had a strong sense of dignity in presidential speeches. He cited Lincoln as an example of a president who maintained an appropriate level of rhetorical style.

His edits ranged from structural—rearranging an entire draft—to word substitution. His admonitions could be pedantic and were exact-

---

*Eisenhower was in fact so impressed that at a meeting with local political leaders in Seattle, he suggested Larson might make a promising presidential candidate in 1960. (Hughes, *Ordeal*, 175.)

ing: Do not use the word "merit" as a verb; never use the pronoun "I" in consecutive sentences; do not use the phrase "warm best wishes"—either give warm wishes or best wishes, but not both. He tried to avoid the use of the phrase "foreign aid," opting instead for the perhaps more domestically appealing "mutual aid."

Writing speeches in the late 1930s for the flamboyant MacArthur—who constantly tossed off sweeping statements like "Never before in history has an operation of such magnitude . . ."—had instilled in Eisenhower a dislike for superlatives. He also wished to avoid unqualified statements of fact. He would, for example, take a draft that spoke of the American citizen as being "expected to understand everything from the effects of change in the Federal Reserve discount rate to a boundary dispute in the Sudan," and qualify it to read: "He is seemingly expected to understand . . ."

He had "the best American English–teacher kind of language," Stephen Benedict said. "A stickler on grammar. The correct syntax—he could spot anything right away that wasn't right." All of this added up to Ike's plainspoken, low-key speaking style. He was "very direct, very unflowered, very unornamented," Benedict recalled.

And he made sure his rules were followed—he was a careful, relentless editor. He would substitute "futile" for "fatuous," "devout" for "passionate," and "paternalistic regimentation" for "paternalistic wand-waving."*

Larson also learned that Eisenhower was not as moderate as he had believed. When on May 17, 1954, the Supreme Court—led by Eisenhower appointee Earl Warren—declared that segregated schools were unconstitutional, Eisenhower had maintained a studied silence. During their summer 1956 drafting sessions, Eisenhower and Larson fought a tug-of-war about how to handle the issue of civil rights. Larson's first draft had a reference to "that ugly complex of injustices called discrimi-

---

*Eisenhower's performance in press conferences gave him a reputation for linguistic ineptitude. Once, on the way into a press conference, Ike was warned by press secretary James Hagerty about a developing situation in the Formosa Strait. "Don't worry, Jim, if that question comes up, I'll just confuse them." Ike said with a laugh. He answered with syntax so mangled that years later he would still chuckle about Chinese and Russian intelligence analysts trying to translate the comments. (Ambrose, *Eisenhower*, 384.)

nation," a passage that Eisenhower eliminated. He did not like the word "discrimination," he said, and, it seemed to Larson, he was not wild about the word "racial." Ike explained that just as the *Brown v. Board of Education* case was based on the inner feelings of black children, so too must the inner feelings of southern whites also be considered. He wanted to make it clear that political and economic equality would not mean social equality—"or that a Negro should court my daughter."

Larson tried formulation after formulation. "Racial discrimination" became "equal justice," and eventually "social justice." The final speech contained exhortations regarding "various kinds of discrimination" and "all existing kinds of discrimination." The only reference to race came in the observation that the Republican Party "is again the rallying point for Americans of all callings, ages, races and incomes." And on October 1, a week after the president federalized the National Guard to integrate the Little Rock Central High School, he told Larson that he had been careful not to take a position on the merits of the 1954 Supreme Court decision. "As a matter of fact, I personally think the decision was wrong," the president said. (Eisenhower changed his tune in his memoirs, saying that he supported the decision.)

As Larson was helping draft Eisenhower's convention speech, Emmet Hughes was composing one for himself. On Friday, August 17, McCann made a frantic series of calls to Hughes to discuss the fall campaign. The next day, Adams called and said that Hughes should catch the next plane out to San Francisco, the site of the GOP national convention, which was convening in a few days—Eisenhower wanted his help redrafting Washington governor Arthur Langlie's keynote address. Hughes answered the summons.

The previous week, he had composed a speech to be given at the convention by a voter independent of the two parties, extolling Eisenhower. It was now suggested that Hughes give the speech. He and Jackson spoke on Monday, August 20. Jackson "expressed surprise at Emmet's being in San Francisco," according to Jackson's notes from the conversation, and suggested that his appearing at the GOP convention might not be a great idea. "I don't want to, and have no right to, say what you should do," Jackson said. "But my radar on this one indicates a collision course, and that if Emmet Hughes, no matter how billed, delivers this one, there will be a ruckus." Hughes agreed that it would require close scrutiny and then asked about the nature of the problem. It stemmed, Jackson explained, from "a carefully thought-through desire of [Time/Life] over the last several months to disengage from being a house organ, and a captive publisher."

By August 22, when he appeared before the GOP convention, Hughes had taken another leave of absence from journalism and was officially on Eisenhower's staff, where he remained through the second inauguration. He was drawn back by his diminished but lingering hope of helping Eisenhower forge a new, moderate Republican Party. Like Larson, he argued with Eisenhower about civil rights. "The text on civil rights signaled the playing of a kind of rhythmic game between us, accepted but unacknowledged—I toughening every reference, he softening it," Hughes later wrote. "I rephrasing upward, he rewording downward."

Hughes helped Eisenhower write his second inaugural and contributed to one other speech in the second term, but increasingly he felt that he was losing the battle for the president's political soul. Like Raymond Moley, he would publish a critical insider account of his White House experiences. (He would also go on to write a column for *Newsweek*—while Moley was still an editor there.)

"An indictment of Eisenhower . . . for allowing himself to be a meek creature of traditional Republican conservatism, rather than a bold creator of a new Republican liberalism, must start from the premise that Eisenhower was not, in fact, a conservative," Hughes wrote wistfully in *The Ordeal of Power* (1962). "The passage of years proved this premise largely false."

He added: Eisenhower's "purpose was the invigoration and rejuvenation of the Republican party. This purpose ended in defeat." On foreign policy, his assessment was as damning: "And so the years inscribed a record, not stained with the blots of many foolish or reckless acts, but all too immaculate. All the acts of omission signified a waste of something more than briefly enjoyed military superiority. The great waste could be measured only by the vastness of the unused political resources at the command of the most powerful and popular leader of any free nation in the world."

Hughes's books—*Ordeal* and his 1959 *America the Vincible*—widened the split between writer and president. Working on his memoirs years later, Eisenhower gleefully gave credit elsewhere for his dramatic 1952 campaign declaration, which Hughes had written, that a victorious Eisenhower would "go to Korea" to personally survey the situation there.

"My position is desperate," the president told Arthur Larson. It was nine o'clock in the morning on October 6, 1957. Two days earlier, the Soviet Union had electrified the globe, and shocked much of the free world, by launching a 183-pound, basketball-sized object into orbit around the earth. They called it Sputnik, and every ninety-eight minutes, as it circled the planet, terrestrial listeners could hear the shrill series of beeps that were its telemetry.

Eisenhower did not personally share the sense of crisis that Sputnik instilled in so many of his fellow countrymen, but he knew that as president he would have to react. He arranged for a series of four major speeches meant to address the issue, and needed someone to help write them. So he turned to Larson, whom he had appointed head of the United States Information Agency (USIA) in December 1956.

Larson had been thinking about presidential speeches—their preparation struck him as haphazard and reactive. He envisioned a television-age counterpart to FDR's fireside chats. Instead of waiting for a crisis—whether Sputnik or school integration problems—and then having to rush a response, Larson thought the president should take the initiative with a series of televised speeches planned far in advance, tackling issues before they matured into emergencies.

Larson drew upon his own experience producing television at USIA to sketch for Eisenhower a vision of televised addresses that used film clips, props, and other visuals to spice up the show.* Ike immediately

---

*Larson's love of props proved unintentionally comical when he arranged to bring in the nose cone from a Jupiter rocket that had successfully entered space and returned to earth—not realizing that the piece of machinery was bigger than the president's desk. "The object *here in my hand* is a nose cone that has been to outer space and back," Eisenhower read in the dry run of the speech. (Larson, *Eisenhower*, 155.)

agreed. Larson put together an ambitious agenda of thirteen speeches for 1958 on topics ranging from "Education" to "Achievement and Juvenile Delinquency" to "The Arts" to "Every Man a Capitalist."

Larson was the most hardheaded of Eisenhower's speechwriters, willing to push an argument well beyond the point anyone else would take it. "In my long hours of working the President in his Oval Room study, crouched over manuscripts with our heads practically touching, and usually working under considerable pressure against some deadline, I would soon forget that the man at my right elbow was the President of the United States and would insist on my own ideas of style and arrangement, and perhaps even sometimes of content, much longer than was seemly," he later wrote.

Larson recorded in his journal on November 4, 1957: "I had quite a few items on which I argued with the President today." And again the next day: "I had quite an argument on a number of things with the President—lost some, won others. Once he said 'Dammit Arthur, if you don't let me write this in, I'll extemporize it anyway.'" Three days later, Sherman Adams, Eisenhower's chief of staff, told Larson that the president enjoyed their collaboration but, Larson recorded in his journal, "the President wished I wouldn't argue so much with him. After all—it's <u>his</u> speech. I should try to get his ideas and incorporate them. I told Adams I realized that I got worked up and forgot I was talking to the President."

These sessions could sometimes be relaxing for the president—he might pull out foot-long desk shears and start trimming his nails. Age had caused his nails to get brittle and start to split, he once explained. "I've tried every vitamin there is, and the only thing that helps is ladies' clear nail varnish," he said. "I put on three coats."

As part of his plan to take a more structured approach to the president's public communications, Larson expanded his speechwriting staff. He considered the writer Gore Vidal and eventually did hire a Johns Hopkins University political scientist named Malcolm Moos. He also arranged for Frederic Morrow, who had been doing "special projects" on the White House staff, to move over to speechwriting. The grandson of a former slave, Morrow was the first African-American to serve in an executive position on a president's White House staff.

Now, in November 1957, he became the first black presidential speechwriter.

The son of a minister, Morrow had graduated from Bowdoin College and earned a law degree from Rutgers University. Before World War II, he had worked at the Urban League and at the NAACP, and in public affairs at CBS after the war. He found his White House colleagues to be "correct in conduct, but cold." But he was capable of wry humor: Asked to speak at a celebration honoring him at the White House mess, Morrow got up, said, "It's a great day for the Irish!" and sat down.

Morrow was torn about taking the job. "This opportunity of service to both a President and a race has never before come to a Negro American," he wrote in his diary on October 29. "It may be a long time coming again. To put personal difficulties above even a little good that might flow from this relationship is cowardice. But the real clincher in the decision is this—it was a struggle to get there and the opposition was severe. It is quite possible that if I resign, no similar appointment will be made. . . . For a minority member in this kind of a spot anywhere, there is always the haunting specter that to quit gives delight and comfort to your enemies and oppressors. It indicates that you could not take it."

He had enjoyed his special projects work and did not want to leave it, but was told "that it has been decided at the highest possible level that I will take the job," as he recorded in his diary on October 21. "I move into this new post with great trepidation, and can only hope that I will be pleasantly surprised by the outcome." It was not to be.

On November 26, Morrow noted in his diary: "This is an anxious day as we await the latest bulletin on the President's health. He suffered a chill on his return from meeting the King of Morocco at the airport yesterday, and his doctors ordered him to bed immediately."

In fact, Eisenhower did not have a chill. "The latest bulletin on the President's health has just confirmed our worst fears," Morrow wrote later that day. "He apparently suffered a slight stroke."

On the afternoon of November 25, 1957, Eisenhower had summoned Ann Whitman, his personal secretary, into the Oval Office and started speaking gibberish at her—recognizable words were coming out but not in any order that made sense. He would recover with remarkable speed and maintained a regular public speaking schedule, but

Larson's plan for a series of new-style fireside chats never regained the momentum it had that fall.

Larson met with Adams on December 12 to discuss a short draft of the 1958 State of the Union that he had put together. Ike did not like it very much but had not said what he wanted. "The process of preparing the President's speeches so as to reflect his ideas is rather like trying to construct a dinosaur skeleton out of a fragment of ankle bone," Larson later wrote in his journal. "If I get even a word as a clue—I can take it from there, but without that clue, I never know if I'm on the right track. . . . For the State of the Union message, all I have is the general idea that we as Americans do indeed have greater resources to bring to bear."

Larson asked Sherman Adams if Eisenhower had indicated any specific ideas he wanted in the speech. "Adams, with great tenderness, said, 'This man is not what he was,'" Larson related in his diary. "At almost this point I began to accept the idea of a sort of protectorate, an idea I have resisted until now." But he had become convinced that "we have on our hands the problem of maintaining the world's greatest figure of peace—although he is getting crotchety unpredictable [*sic*] and rather unsure of his footing."

Morrow was unsatisfied with the progress of the annual address for entirely different reasons. He had handled minor speeches, but since helping to sift through the various departmental State of the Union proposals in November had been left out of the process. Friends and staff members would daily ask him how the big speech was going, he noted in his journal on New Year's Eve, and "it is very embarrassing when I have to reply that I have no knowledge of its status."

"The performance on the part of Mr. Larson has been almost incredible," Morrow recorded on January 7, 1958. "This man went to great efforts to get me assigned to him as assistant, and yet at no time have I been taken into his confidence, or informed as to what was going on."

On his own, Larson kept working on the State of the Union. In an effort to spare Eisenhower from pressing too much in such a high-profile setting, the staff planned to keep the speech to no more than twenty minutes. Eisenhower had different ideas. He called Larson from his home at Gettysburg on New Year's Day, 1958, to talk about the economic and defense organization portions of the speech. "Don't tell the damn staff this, Art, but I don't mind if the speech goes to thirty-five or forty minutes," Ike said.

On January 9, Eisenhower gave his State of the Union address: it ran forty-four minutes, and while he stumbled a handful of times, it was not more frequent than usual. "When the President today finished reading to Congress his message on the State of the Union a heavy burden of proof rested on those who have called into question his will to lead the country, and his possession of the physical and mental vigor required," *The New York Times* reported. "So far as this occasion was concerned, he rose to it."

Five days after the speech, Jackson went to see Eisenhower and found him looking "extremely well, clear bright blue eyes, splendid color, full firm cheeks, and easy relaxed speech," as he recorded in his daily log. Conversation eventually turned to the stroke's lingering aftereffects. Jackson commented that he had not noticed any stuttering or stumbling. "It is not a question of stuttering, or even stoppage," Eisenhower told Jackson. "What happens is that the nerve in the brain that brings the right word to your mouth to express what you are thinking about doesn't work right, and sometimes a completely incorrect word shows up in your mouth."

The speechwriters did notice other problems. For example, Stephen Hess, who served as a speechwriter toward the end of Eisenhower's tenure, tried to write speeches that avoided *s* sounds, with which the president seemed to have trouble.

By March, Morrow had reached the end of his patience. When Larson "confided to me that things had not worked out as he had dreamed," Morrow wrote in his journal on March 10, 1958, it "seemed a masterpiece of understatement." Morrow asked out of the speech-writing job and was liberated from it the following month. Not until January 27, 1959, after nearly five years working in the White House, was he formally given his commission as a staffer. The president usually attends such ceremonies, but that would mean the press as well. "To handle this in the usual manner now could open a Pandora's box of questions and difficult answers," such as why it had taken so long, Morrow wrote in his diary.

Eisenhower did not attend the ceremony.

• • •

"By the way, Malcolm, I want to have something to say when I leave here, and I want you to be thinking about it," Eisenhower said. "I'm not interested in capturing headlines, but I want to have a message and I want you to be thinking about it well in advance."

The president and Malcolm Moos were chatting in the Oval Office in late 1958. Moos, recently promoted to the top speechwriting spot, had been showing Ike a book on great presidential speeches and George Washington's Farewell Address had spurred Ike's remark.

Moos had flitted through various aspects of public life, spending time as a political science professor at Johns Hopkins University starting in 1942, and as an editor at the *Baltimore Sun* from 1945 to 1948, where he befriended the legendary journalist H. L. Mencken. Moos first met Eisenhower at the 1952 Republican Convention. When the future president found out that Moos taught political science, he told the professor, "I am going to be one of your first students." From 1954 to 1958, Moos was chairman of the Maryland Republican central committee.

Wispy at five foot ten and only 130 pounds ("you'd think that a good puff of wind would blow him away—but he sure had a lot of character and a lot of strength," recalled one assistant), Moos was described by *Time* as "an energetic mixture of egghead author and practical politician." A self-described "full-blooded Bull Moose Republican" (referring to Teddy Roosevelt), Moos was viewed with suspicion by conservatives, one telling *The New York Post*, for example, that he was "no better than a Democrat, and a New Deal Democrat at that."

Nevertheless, under Moos's guidance, Ike's 1958 congressional campaign speeches took on a tough new tone. The reluctant partisan disappeared for the campaign season and the press started talking about a "new" Eisenhower whose speeches featured a punchier, staccato style. "The excitement in town this week has been provided by the 'new Eisenhower'—that gloves-off Republican partisan who talks about Democrats the way Harry S. Truman talks about Republicans," *The New York Times* reported in late October.

"Curiously, however, no one seems to attribute his new bellicosity to the President himself. Instead, the assumption is that he is only speaking words put in his mouth by someone else, and the question tantalizing the capitol [sic] is: Who really put them there? One suspect is Meade Alcorn, Republican national chairman. Another is Dr. Malcolm Moos, his new speech writer." This did not mean Moos had given up his liberal attitudes: During the Little Rock crisis of September 1957, for example, he had suggested to Milton Eisenhower that the president personally go down to Little Rock and walk with the black children into Central High. (The sound bite practically writes itself: "I will go to Little Rock.")

In at least one instance, it was Alcorn who supplied lines for the president. Campaigning in California in October, Eisenhower referred to his opposition as "the Democrat Party," a GOP epithet that dated to Thomas Dewey and had been popularized by Joseph McCarthy in the early part of the decade. Moos thought dropping the "ic" was "an insane notion," and for that matter Eisenhower had not used it before and did not again (asked in 1956 if he would use the shortened title, Ike said, "if they want to be known as the Democratic Party, it's all right with me"). But as he had done in 1952 regarding Marshall and McCarthy, and in 1954 on the question of endorsing a GOP Congress, Eisenhower—who disclaimed partisanship—deferred to the professionals on a political matter.*

Though he might be willing to bend on some partisan matters, Eisenhower remained a stringent editor. But whereas he had worked closely from the start on speech drafts during the early years of his administration, he entered the process somewhat later by the end. "He liked to have a draft that he could chew on," Moos said. Ike's editing had not lost its acuity. "Usually his first brush with a speech was a full-text version sent in by Mac [Moos]," speechwriter Ralph Williams recalled. "*Then* he would lock into it like a target-acquisition radar, throwing out paragraphs, changing sentences, fiddling with words, re-writing whole

---

*The "Democrat" epithet stayed on Republican tongues for decades, gaining renewed currency when the GOP, led by Newt Gingrich, who placed special emphasis on precisely polled words and phrases, took control of the House for the first time since the Eisenhower administration. It gained extra notoriety in January 2007 after Democrats retook control of the House, when President George W. Bush used it in his State of the Union address, enraging Democrats, who thought it a partisan swipe.

pages, until by the tenth draft he'd probably put more time into it than both of us combined."

Working in the East Wing, Moos had two assistants. Stephen Hess had been a Moos pupil at Johns Hopkins before being drafted into the army (and would later become a distinguished scholar of the American presidency). In later years he joked that he had gotten out of the army as Private First Class on a Friday and by Tuesday was a presidential speechwriter with a sergeant driving him around.

Ralph Williams, hired as the assistant to the naval aide, followed in the tradition of Clark Clifford and George Elsey: his real job was speechwriting. A Texas native, Williams had joined the navy in June 1941 and was stationed at Pearl Harbor on December 7 of that year. He was hired as the president's speechwriter around the same time that Moos was made chief speechwriter, in the late summer of 1958. After ten days on the job, Williams started hearing about "the other speech-writer." He sought Moos out, and calculating that the professor had more political pull, offered his services as an assistant.

Moos handled the speechwriting duties like a university professor with grad students. When a speech came up, he called in Williams and Hess to brainstorm. If he liked an idea, he would ask for a memo on it. "We're carpenters, not architects," Moos would say—hammering and nailing together bits of speech until it was ready for the president.

By the end of October 1960, Moos was thinking about something for Eisenhower to say before departing the White House. Data points had been rattling around his head: aerospace journals had caught his eye listing the thousands upon thousands of companies related to the new and burgeoning U.S. defense industry; a former student of Moos's had done some research into the number of officers who had left the military midcareer and gone to work for the defense industry.

On the morning of October 31, Moos and Williams had a brain-storming session for the 1961 State of the Union address, which would be given just days before either Vice President Richard Nixon or Senator John F. Kennedy succeeded Eisenhower in the White House. Moos liked a couple of Williams's ideas and asked for a memo outlining them. One was what Williams called "the problem of militarism." He noted that "for the first time in its history, the United States has a permanent war-based industry. Not only that but flag and general officers retiring at an early age take positions in a war based industrial complex shaping its decisions and guiding the direction of its tremendous thrust."*

Concerns about militaristic influence were not new to Eisenhower. As early as his April 1953 "Chance for Peace" speech, he had talked about the costs of the Cold War, not simply in dollars spent but in what they were not spent on. In May 1953, he warned that "it is fact that there is no such thing as maximum military security short of total mobilization of all our national resources. Such security would compel us to imitate the methods of the dictator. It would compel us to put every able-bodied man in uniform—to regiment the worker, the farmer, the businessman—to allocate materials and to control prices and wages—in short, to devote our whole nation to the grim purposes of the garrison state." Later that same summer, after signing the Korean armistice, Eisenhower had written to a friend that "there must be a balance between minimum requirements in the costly implements of war and the health of our economy."

Eisenhower had spent his two terms struggling—sometimes within his own administration—to keep defense spending from either spiking up and down or rising too quickly. Those efforts, combined with the detonation of the hydrogen bomb and the launch of Sputnik in 1957, led to rising criticism for letting the U.S. military fall behind the Soviets. The 1960 presidential election had turned in no small part on Kennedy's allegations that a "missile gap" had grown between the So-

---

*Williams's second point disappeared in the drafting process. "Over the past year there has been a world wide tendency for orderly societies to break down into mob ridden anarchies, e.g. student riots. It is easy to wave banners to riot, to protest, but the difficult thing is to work a constructive change so that society is strengthened rather than weakened and divided." Looking back decades later, Williams regretted the excision. In its stead, little remembered, Eisenhower's farewell address also warned about government domination of scientific research. "Considering what happened in the next decade, I feel that the latter warning was a good deal more prescient than the caveat about the scientific-technological elite," Williams said. (Ralph Williams memo to file, October 31, 1960, "Chronological [1]" folder, Williams, Ralph E.: Papers, 1958–60, Dwight Eisenhower Library; Ralph Williams letter to Patrick J. Haney, April 6, 1988, "Letters 1985–88" folder, Williams, Ralph E.: Papers, 1958–60, Dwight Eisenhower Library.)

viet forces and the American—though in reality U.S. estimates were wildly overblown.

During the first week of December, Moos gave Eisenhower a draft of the speech. It warned against a "military-industrial-scientific complex," a formulation that was later shortened at the suggestion of scientific adviser James Killian. A later draft discussed a "military-industrial-congressional" complex, but Eisenhower decided it was inappropriate to lecture Congress and dropped the legislative reference. "I think you've got something here," Eisenhower told Moos, slipping it into his desk. On December 14, Ike received a call from Norman Cousins, editor of the *Saturday Review*, urging him to "give a 'farewell address' to the country . . . reviewing your administration, telling of your hopes for the future. A great, sweeping document."

Addressing the nation at 8:30 pm three days before John F. Kennedy's inaugural, Eisenhower delivered his famous warning:

> *In the councils of government, we must guard against the acquisition of unwarranted influence, whether sought or unsought, by the military-industrial complex. The potential for the disastrous rise of misplaced power exists and will persist.*

Eisenhower had told Moos that he was not interested in capturing headlines, and in that regard the speech was a success. While Walter Lippmann noted that Ike's speech "will be remembered and quoted in the days to come," it in fact went largely unremarked.

Things began to change months later. "There is an interesting development, Mr. President, involving your 'Farewell Address,'" Harlow wrote to Eisenhower on March 17, 1961. "At least two vigorous young Republicans in the House (Bob Michel of Illinois and Brad Morse of Massachusetts) have interested themselves in your warning to America against excessive power being accumulated by the military-industrial complex and are girding their loins to raise a rumpus though the Congressional investigation route. . . . The point is, this part of the Address turns out to be curiously yeasty, and one can expect some fall-out from it in the Congressional-political area over the coming months."

Little appreciated at the time, Eisenhower's farewell warning about the dangers of such military-industrial concentrations is now ranked with George Washington's Farewell Address, warning against foreign alliances, as a classic in terms of valedictory remarks. It was a notable meeting of man and moment: As a lifelong military man and certified, venerated war hero, Eisenhower had special credibility regarding national security matters. And he spoke at a moment of transition: a new generation—"born in this century, tempered by war, disciplined by a hard and bitter peace,"* as its most visible representative would say three days later—was about to assume its leadership role.

When Eisenhower entered the White House, the Cold War and the incipient U.S. defense industry were still new developments; by the time he departed, both had existed for almost a full generation and had become apparently permanent parts of the geopolitical scene. This combination helped give the speech its enduring resonance. Almost fifty years later, Eisenhower's final words as president remain his best known.

---

*Born in 1890, Eisenhower was the last U.S. president who had lived in the nineteenth century.

FOUR

The Age of Sorensen

JANUARY 1953

The two quiet, serious young men huddled amid the bustle of a U.S. House office in transition. The congressman had been elected to the U.S. Senate, but his new suite of offices was not yet ready, and another legislator and staff were moving into his old digs.

In two five-minute sessions the new senator, occasionally tapping his fingers on his teeth and knee, sized up and accepted the prospective aide. The younger man, impressed by the Massachusetts scion's " 'ordinary' demeanor," satisfied himself about the congressman's politics (anti-McCarthy) and the nature of the position. Those ten minutes in January 1953 would change the lives of thirty-five-year-old John F. Kennedy and twenty-four-year-old Ted Sorensen.

Sorensen, of Lincoln, Nebraska, was not an obvious match for John F. Kennedy of Brookline and Hyannisport, Massachusetts, Palm Beach, Florida, and Washington, D.C. JFK was best known for his good looks and the amount of his family's money that had gone into his Senate race, and his liberal credentials were questionable. Sorensen was "not a Harvard man or an Easterner or a Catholic or an Irishman or a hereditary Democrat, or a political middler or culturally sophisticated or rich or an aristocrat or an urbanite or an intellectual dilettante or widely traveled or weak on the civil-liberties side or primarily interested in

Why England Slept type of foreign affairs or a master of the Ivy League casual style or anything at all of a playboy," William Lee Miller, a home-state friend, wrote. "He was instead, insofar as these things have opposites, somewhere near the opposite of all of them."

Theodore Chaikin Sorensen came from a politically active Nebraska family whose Republicanism was in the mold of Senator George Norris, a Progressive who had fought for reform in the U.S. House of Representatives, against arming U.S. merchant ships during World War I, and against Herbert Hoover in 1928 (stands that later earned him a chapter in Kennedy's *Profiles in Courage*).

Sorensen's father, C. A. Sorensen, had managed one of Norris's campaigns, and from 1929 to 1933 was Nebraska's attorney general. His mother, Annis Chaikin, the child of Russian Jews, was also a committed social activist, working for, among other things, women's suffrage. The couple had met when Sorensen defended Chaikin and other pacifists during World War I. (Young Ted himself registered as a conscientious objector during World War II.) The Sorensens were Unitarian, "that mid-western Unitarianism that is marked by its self-conscious rejection, in the name of Reason and Freedom, of orthodoxy."

C. A. Sorensen raised Ted in a serious-minded, public affairs–oriented household that was filled with national newsmagazines. Ted's older brother, Tom, who would serve in Kennedy's U.S. Information Agency, quizzed him about Attorneys General and the Sherman Anti-Trust Act. C. A. Sorensen offered his son a silver dollar if he achieved his twenty-first birthday without taking a drink or a smoke, a bet that he won. (Joseph P. Kennedy offered his son John $1,000 for the same feat—JFK did not collect.)

Ted attended Lincoln public schools and then the University of Nebraska, where he earned his undergraduate diploma and a law degree. He had a fierce commitment to racial justice, helping to found the Lincoln, Nebraska, chapter of the Congress of Racial Equality—they got the municipal swimming pool integrated, but their "skate-in" at the local roller rink faired less well. He testified in front of the state legislature in favor of a Fair Employment Practices Committee. And when the dean of the University of Nebraska opposed integrating the dorms,

Sorensen and his friends wrote letters of protest. Ted's was the most persuasive: shorter, more analytical, clearer.

"I arrived in Washington unbelievably green," he said later. "I knew not a soul. I had no legislative experience, no political experience. I'd never written a speech. I'd hardly been out of Nebraska. Whatever I was, it was Lincoln. Lincoln and Nebraska, that was me."

He worked briefly at the Federal Security Agency, and then at the Temporary Committee of the Congress on Railroad Retirement Legislation, before he found himself meeting with Senator-elect John Kennedy.

"Jack wouldn't hire anyone Joe Kennedy wouldn't tell him to hire—and, with the exception of Jim Landis, Joe Kennedy hasn't hired a non-Catholic in fifty years!" a friend warned Sorensen. Though the friend proved incorrect on both counts, Kennedy's father did tell Sorensen on their first meeting, "You couldn't write speeches for me. You're too much of a liberal. But writing for Jack is different." By 1954, Sorensen was one of Kennedy's top aides, and when the senator approved a speech draft for a St. Patrick's Day dinner, a speechwriting team was set.

When Kennedy was considered for the vice-presidential spot on former Illinois governor Adlai Stevenson's 1956 Democratic ticket, Sorensen was in the thick of the effort. After Eisenhower's reelection, Sorensen became his boss's chief political strategist and main traveling companion. For the next three and a half years, the two men traveled through all fifty states, collecting delegates and other political IOUs. Sorensen built up a card file of political contacts that reached 30,000 names. Asked in 2006 how a middle-class Nebraska Unitarian could so fully understand a monied New England Catholic, Sorensen pointed to the days spent in airplanes, hotel rooms, and cars, traversing the nation.

"Those three and a half years of traveling the country together made an enormous difference," he said. "There were all kinds of press stories—some of them exaggerations—about how I was inside his mind, could finish his sentences, knew what he was thinking before he said it. Well, I think maybe there is something to that. That's a tremendous advantage for a speechwriter to know his boss's mind as well as I did."

Their bond was well known around town. "When Jack is wounded, Ted bleeds," one observer told *The New York Times* in 1960. Kennedy himself used a different blood metaphor, calling Sorensen "my intellectual blood bank."

The journalist Theodore White described Sorensen as "self-sufficient, taut, purposeful, a man of brilliant intellectual gifts, jealously devoted to the President and rather indifferent to personal relations." Indeed, this indifference and his intense demeanor rubbed some of his colleagues the wrong way. "Even to this day he is unaware of the extent to which [other senior members of the White House staff] disliked him," Richard Goodwin, who wrote speeches for Kennedy in the campaign and for a little while in the White House, said in 2007. "That's an insensitivity he has."

Sorensen concedes that he may not have been the most pleasant person to work with. "Abrupt, cold, short," he told one interviewer. "That's probably true. From the day I went to work for the president, I was overcommitted, overscheduled, overprogrammed and sleep-deprived."

He was not without appeal. "Underneath the appearance of bluntness, taciturnity and, at times, sheer weariness, he was capable of great charm and a frolicsome satiric humor," Kennedy aide Arthur M. Schlesinger, Jr., wrote. "His flow of comic verse always enlivened festive occasions at the White House."

The abstemious Sorensen developed the habit of drinking an occasional Heineken or pre-dinner daiquiri—Kennedy's quaffs of choice. Sorensen even picked up JFK's verbal mannerisms and gestures—the senator sometimes had Sorensen impersonate him on the telephone.

The intellectual communion did not perfectly translate personally. "Of Sorensen and Kennedy themselves, two men could hardly have been more intimate and, at the same time, more separate," Schlesinger wrote. "They shared so much—the same quick tempo, detached intelligence, deflationary wit, realistic judgment, candor in speech, coolness in crisis—that, when it came to policy and speeches, they operated nearly as one. But there were other ranges of Kennedy's life, and of these Sorensen partook very little."

On November 8, 1960, Kennedy edged Vice President Richard M. Nixon, achieving a 120,000-vote plurality out of more then 68 million cast. Kennedy and Sorensen commenced work on his inaugural address in the weeks after this hairbreadth victory. They first spoke about the speech in November. Solicit suggestions, Kennedy said, and keep it short—"Make it the shortest since T.R. (except for FDR's abbreviated wartime ceremony in 1945)," Sorensen scrawled in a note to himself; make it forward-looking, JFK said, marking the generational change for which he had campaigned.

Read previous inaugurals, he instructed Sorensen, who concluded that they were an "undistinguished" body of work, with much eloquence coming from some of the nation's least accomplished presidents. Kennedy also assigned the Gettysburg Address, tasking Sorensen with ferreting out the secret of its genius. "My conclusion, which [Kennedy's] Inaugural applied, was that Lincoln never used a two- or three-syllable word where a one-syllable word would do, and never used three words where one word would do," Sorensen later wrote.

Once the election results were certain, John Kennedy had seventy-two days to construct his administration. As JFK's closest adviser and top aide, newly minted White House special counsel Ted Sorensen—the first appointee announced—was busy with that transition. Nevertheless, he pondered his inaugural assignment. On Thanksgiving, 1960, a little over two weeks after the election, Sorensen dined at the Ellicott Street NW home of his friend and deputy, Myer "Mike" Feldman. They chatted after dinner about the upcoming speech. Sorensen had gone over Library of Congress–assembled materials on previous inaugurals as well as other great speeches, such as Pericles' Funeral Oration. Retiring to Feldman's study, he made a first pass at the inaugural, emerging after three hours around two o'clock in the morning. Thirty-five years later, neither Feldman nor Sorensen could recall with any precision the content of that first product, and there is no known surviving copy.

Feldman read it—or a version of it—when they flew together down to Palm Beach to meet with Kennedy shortly before Christmas. Feldman later described it as a "stream of thoughts" that was "more than notes" and "more than an outline," but was "not a finished speech." In 2006, Feldman recalled how different that early document was from the speech Kennedy eventually gave in January. It did not have the "ask not" passage, for example.

"What was in it sounded like selections from—well, he liked Lincoln's second inaugural and he liked Pericles, and so you could see some of that in it," he said. "But not a lot of that was left in" the final version. It's pretty good, Feldman told his boss, but not good enough for an inaugural. Privately, he thought it too flowery.

Over the next month and a half, Sorensen worked on it in odd snatches of time. On December 23, he sent a Western Union telegram to ten people, including former Illinois governor Adlai Stevenson, who had been the Democratic standard-bearer in 1952 and 1956; economist John Kenneth Galbraith;* and three future Kennedy cabinet secre- taries—Secretary of State Dean Rusk, Secretary of Labor Arthur Gold- berg, and Secretary of the Treasury Douglas Dillon—soliciting their advice.

"The President-Elect has asked me to collect any suggestions you may have for the Inaugural Address," Sorensen wrote, asking for re- sponses before year's end. "We are particularly interested in specific themes and in language to articulate these themes whether it takes one page or ten pages. Many many thanks."

He got at least five replies, and countless other drafts as suggestions poured in to Kennedy and to Sorensen from around the country. On the down side, Sorensen had had to dip into JFK's inaugural file for his farewell address to the Massachusetts legislature on January 9, which had been an elegant, eloquent success. Kennedy fretted that they were "using up some of our best lines."

The president-elect flew down to Palm Beach on January 10 on board his Convair 240, twin-engine plane, dubbed *Caroline* after his daughter. Sorensen had given him a six-page typed draft of the inaugu- ral address. It contained the final basic structure and at least rough ver- sions of many of the memorable phrases of the inaugural address. "So let the word go forth to all the world—and suit the action to the word—

---

*That same afternoon, Galbraith had already submitted his own thirteen-page, presumably unsolicited, draft of the inaugural in a face-to-face meeting with Kennedy in Florida. (Tofel, *Sounding*, 41–48.)

that this generation of Americans has no intention of becoming soft instead of resolute, smug instead of resourceful, or citizens of a second-rate power," the draft read, as compared with the final version: "Let the word go forth from this time and place, to friend and foe alike, that the torch has been passed to a new generation of Americans—born in this century, tempered by war, disciplined by a hard and bitter peace, proud of our ancient heritage—and unwilling to witness or permit the slow undoing of those human rights to which this nation has always been committed, and to which we are committed today at home and around the world."

Several contributors' work was in this draft. Sorensen liberally borrowed from Stevenson and Galbraith (whose "We shall never negotiate out of fear. But we shall never fear to negotiate," became the more exhortative: "Let us never negotiate out of fear. But let us never fear to negotiate").*

Using Sorensen's draft as a starting point, Kennedy dictated to Evelyn Lincoln, his secretary, another version of the speech, which included important new material (a generation "born in this century—tempered by the war," and a willingness to "pay any price, bear any burden, meet any hardships, support any friend, oppose any foe"). He inserted several pages from the Sorensen draft, encompassing much of the body of the speech. He also added a new opening and a nautical metaphor that were ultimately dropped.

An early version of the famous "ask not" passage appeared in the six-page Sorensen draft. Like other timeless sentiments, variations of this phrase had been expressed before. Supreme Court Justice Oliver Wendell Holmes had said in 1884: "It is now the moment when by common consent we pause to become conscious of our national life and to rejoice in it, to recall what your country has done for each of us, and to ask our-

---

*Galbraith—an eager ghost here—had made his suggestions by way of a second proposed draft. Stevenson, whose relationship with Kennedy was complex and at times strained, had initially written Sorensen that "your wire arrives at most difficult time for me. I will do what I can"—and then provided ten pages of "hurried paragraphs" and another eight pages of explanation. (Tofel, *Sounding*, 43–50; Adlai Stevenson telegram to Ted Sorensen, December 28, 1960, "Inaugural Address, 1/20/61, Memoranda, Speech materials + correspondence, 12/10/60–5/23/61 + Undated" folder, Theodore C. Sorensen Papers, JFK Library.)

selves what we can do for our country in return." In 1916, Warren Harding, speaking to the Republican National Convention, had said: "we must have a citizenship less concerned about what the government can do for it, and more anxious about what it can do for the nation."

Kennedy had considered the idea at least as early as 1945, when, in a looseleaf notebook he kept, he jotted down Rousseau's quotation that "As soon as any man says of the affairs of state, What does it matter to me? the state may be given up as lost." He had tried different riffs on it during the presidential campaign: the New Frontier—the slogan summarizing his get-America-moving program—"sums up not what I intend to *offer* the American people, but what I intend to *ask* of them," he said, in accepting his party's nomination in Los Angeles on July 15. And on September 5, at Detroit's Cadillac Square, he had ad-libbed: "The new frontier is not what I promise I am going to do for you. The new frontier is what I ask you to do for your country." Speaking on national television on September 20, he said, "We do not campaign stressing what our country is going to do for us as a people. We stress what we can do for the country, all of us."

The inaugural address had other campaign antecedents. In his acceptance speech, Kennedy had noted that man "has taken into his mortal hands the power to exterminate the entire species some seven times over" (The inaugural: "For man holds in his mortal hands the power to abolish all forms of human poverty and all forms of human life"). And he had repeatedly spoken of how the time had come for "a new generation of Americans" to take charge of the country.

These rhetorical evolutions have been cited as evidence that Kennedy himself was responsible for "ask not" and other memorable phrases from the inaugural speech. This begs the question, though, of authorship of the campaign trail speeches—which were predominately the product of Sorensen and Richard N. Goodwin, with help from Feldman. But they in turn operated from an intimate knowledge of their boss's mind derived from discussions and observations and—in Sorensen's case—years in close quarters on the road.

Seeking the origin of a specific phrase, then, is akin to straining to find the source of the first noise in an echo chamber. It is unknowable— and while the search makes for interesting historical trivia, the answer is ultimately irrelevant. "It isn't all that important who wrote which word or which phrase in Kennedy's inaugural," Sorensen said in 2006. "What's important are the themes and the principles that he laid out."

He added that, as a pair of recent books on the speech's composition make clear, several people contributed, including Galbraith, Stevenson, and Walter Lippmann. "And some parts came from John F. Kennedy and some parts came from me," he said. "In other words, it was a mixture. And that's a correct verdict so that's where I would like to leave it."

Kennedy spent a week in Palm Beach at La Guerida, his father's sprawling beachfront Spanish Revival mansion. He relaxed while wrapping up the business of the transition, mixing in tanning and speechwork, rounds of golf with meetings and phone calls. He scribbled on a yellow legal pad while puffing on a small cigar. Some mornings he read selections to his wife, Jacqueline, who later described hearing the address "in bits and pieces" that week. Pages of his revisions and notes covered their bedroom floor and she would straighten them up when he left the room.

The drafting style was haphazard, with Kennedy in Florida and Sorensen in Washington. On the evening of January 11, for example, Alaska senator Ernest Gruening, a Democrat, sent Kennedy a telegram in Palm Beach asking that he include in his State of the Union message a call to develop Alaska's natural resources. Kennedy made no such mention, but Sorensen, given the telegram at Kennedy's written instruction, used it as handy scrap to jot down a revamped, almost finalized paragraph about the trumpet summoning once again.

Sorensen joined Kennedy in Florida on January 16 before flying back north with him on the *Caroline* the following day. Others on the plane included Washington senator Warren Magnuson, press secretary Pierre Salinger, Evelyn Lincoln, and *Time* correspondent Hugh Sidey. Once in the air, Kennedy summoned Sidey to his private compartment and, with the reporter watching, picked up a yellow legal pad, squinted out the compartment's square window, then started scratching out an apparent first draft of the inaugural. At one point Kennedy tossed the pad into the reporter's lap and asked his opinion. When Sidey said that he could not decipher the president-elect's notoriously poor handwriting, JFK, a little impatiently, took the pad back and read selections out loud.

"It's tough," Kennedy told Sidey. "The speech to the Massachusetts legislature went so well. It's going to be hard to meet that standard."

Sidey was stunned that only three days before his swearing-in, Kennedy was still working on a first draft of his speech. But the truth was that the speech was in almost final form: the performance was designed to illustrate to a leading reporter that the new president was his own writer.*

The ploy was undoubtedly motivated by a desire to establish authorship both for the contemporary audience and, as Roosevelt had done twenty-eight years earlier, for posterity. But unlike FDR, JFK was also driven by questions about what he had written himself. Rumors and accusations had circulated in Washington ever since the publication of his Pulitzer Prize–winning *Profiles in Courage*, angering Kennedy no end.†

A few more changes were made to the speech after his return from Florida. Lippmann, lunching with Sorensen, suggested that the word "enemy" in references to the Soviet Union be replaced with "adversary." Civil rights aides Harris Wofford and Louis Martin suggested that the words "at home and abroad" be inserted at the end of a sen-

---

* At another point in the flight, JFK noted to Sorensen that a recently discovered early draft of FDR's first inaugural had fetched close to $200,000 at auction. Months after he took office, the White House supplied a photograph of the first page of the handwritten draft for a book on Kennedy's first hundred days, along with a caption describing it as "The President's first draft of the inaugural address." Kennedy was copying Roosevelt more than he knew. Raymond Moley's involvement in drafting the address—and Roosevelt's transcribing their draft before Moley burned the original—did not become public until after JFK's death. (Clarke, *Ask Not*, 101; Sorensen, *Kennedy*, 243; Tofel, *Sounding*, 71.)

†Robert Dallek, who examined the supporting materials for *Profiles*, including audiotapes of Kennedy dictating chapters of the book, concluded: "The tapes of these dictations, which are available at the John F. Kennedy Library, provide conclusive evidence of Jack's involvement. Jack did more on the book than some later critics believed, but less than the term *author* normally connotes. *Profiles in Courage* was more the work of a 'committee' than of any one person." (Dallek, *An Unfinished Life*, 199.)

tence referring to human rights. An implicit nod to the U.S. civil rights struggle, it was the speech's only domestic policy reference.*

Like many presidents, even in their highest profile speeches, Kennedy kept editing as he delivered the address, making mostly small cuts and mild interpolations. Calling for the creation of a new world of law, for example, the reading copy contemplated a place in which "the strong are just and the weak are secure and the peace is preserved forever." Kennedy dropped the "forever." Asked forty-five years later if he could recall anything of which he was particularly proud that had not made it into a Kennedy speech, Sorensen identified that one word. Establishing such a world for eternity might have been an unrealistic expectation, Sorensen said, but, quoting the poet Robert Browning, he added: "For a man's reach must exceed his grasp or what's a heaven for?"

Shortly before 1 pm on January 20, 1961, as applause echoed against the marble pillars and walls of the Capitol, Kennedy shook the hands of Chief Justice Earl Warren, Vice President Lyndon Johnson, former Vice President Richard Nixon, and finally Dwight Eisenhower. Kennedy pivoted and took a half-step to his left, and they returned to the background. Alone now at the podium, he opened the binder that contained his address, and waited for the cheers to fade.

After a few seconds' pause, and then dispensing with the preliminaries (greeting his vice president; the speaker of the House—"Mr. Speekah," in his Boston accent—other VIPs; and his fellow citizens), he commenced:

We observe today not a victory of party, but a celebration of freedom, symbolizing an end as well as a beginning, signifying renewal as well as change. . . .

• • •

---

*A second, more dramatic insertion on race was rejected. It would have followed the call for a global alliance to combat tyranny, poverty, disease, and war itself with a challenge: "Are you willing to demonstrate in your own life—in your attitude toward those of other races and those here from other shores—that you hold these eternal truths to be self-evident?" (Undated "CHANGES IN INAUGURAL SPEECH—TO BE READ AND APPROVED BY SENATOR," "Inaugural Address, 1/20/61" folder, President's Office Files, Papers of President Kennedy, JFK Library.)

Moving into the White House, Kennedy and Sorensen continued the pattern that they had developed over the previous seven years. They would begin by discussing how Kennedy wanted to approach a topic and what conclusions he wished to reach. He would often have quotations ("Someone—was it Falkland?—gave the classic definition of conservatism which went something like 'When it is not necessary to change, it is necessary not to change.' Let's include the exact quotation and author"*), historical allusions, or obscure facts he wished to include.†

Having gotten Kennedy's direction, Sorensen would prepare a first draft. Speeches were not to exceed twenty or thirty minutes—when JFK spoke admiringly of Khrushchev's speechwriters, Schlesinger needled back that Kennedy's speechwriters "could do as well for him if he would only give two-hour speeches." "Words were regarded as tools of precision, to be chosen and applied with a craftsman's care to whatever the situation required," Sorensen noted. Soft words and phrases—"suggest," "perhaps," and "possible alternatives for consideration"—were avoided.

Short words and clauses were the order, with simplicity and clarity the goal. And while the summoning trumpets of the inaugural address have linked Kennedy in the public mind with flowery prose, he generally shunned rhetorical excess. "The inaugural was a special occasion

---

*Though correct about Falkland, JFK was an inveterate quote-mangler. Ralph Keyes has noted that "the young president launched any number of misworded, misattributed or completely mystifying quotations into the public conversation that have stuck around to this day." Perhaps most notably, JFK attributed to Edmund Burke the aphorism that "The only thing necessary for the triumph of evil is that good men do nothing," an elegant expression judged the most popular quotation of modern times by the editors of *The Oxford Dictionary of Quotations*. "Even though it is clear by now that Burke is unlikely to have made this observation, no one has ever been able to determine who did," Keyes noted. (Keyes, "Ask Not Where This Quote Came From," *The Washington Post*, June 4, 2006.)

†In September 1962 JFK asked Arthur Schlesinger, Jr., to prepare remarks for a dinner before the America's Cup sailing races and suggested including a fact that he had heard somewhere that human blood has the same percentage of salt as seawater. The historian was skeptical, but the president was correct. "All of us have in our veins the exact same percentage of salt in our blood that exists in the ocean, and, therefore, we have salt in our blood, in our sweat, in our tears," Kennedy said at the dinner. "We are tied to the ocean. And when we go back to the sea—whether it is to sail or to watch it—we are going back from whence we came." (Schlesinger, *A Thousand Days*, 691.)

and there was a special tone in that speech," Sorensen later explained. "It was more elevated language." A self-described "idealist without illusions," JFK preferred a cool, cerebral approach and had little use for florid expression and complex prose. He felt that his voice lacked the range of an Adlai Stevenson, who could give greater tonal inflection to his speeches. "JFK used to tease me about writing for Stevenson, because, he said, 'Sorensen has my voice and you have Stevenson's,'" Arthur M. Schlesinger, Jr., who occasionally wrote speeches for him, recalled. " 'You're too complicated for me.'"

He "valued pungent expressions," Schlesinger noted, and, Feldman said, liked "when the form of words was memorable." (This put JFK in direct contrast with his predecessor, who did not want his words to stand out.) He liked alliteration, "not solely for reasons of rhetoric but to reinforce the audience's recollection of his reasoning." His taste for contrapuntal phrasing—never negotiating out of fear but never fearing to negotiate—illustrated his dislike of extreme opinions and options. "He believed in retaining a choice—not a choice between 'Red and dead' or 'holocaust and humiliation,' but a variety of military options in the event of aggression, an opportunity for time and maneuver in the instruments of diplomacy, and a balanced approach to every crisis which combined both defense and diplomacy," Sorensen wrote.*

As an editor, Kennedy had an uncertain sense of structure, spelling, or grammar. But he had a knack for tightening phraseology and sharpening thoughts. Schlesinger gave him a draft for brief remarks for an April 29, 1962, dinner of Western Hemisphere Nobel Prize winners that started by doubting whether the White House had ever before seen such a concentration of genius and achievement. JFK scribbled on his copy, "except when Jefferson was here who combined <u>all</u>," and then told the gathering: "This is the most extraordinary collection of talent, of human knowledge, that has ever been gathered together at the

---

*Harry McPherson, a Johnson speechwriter, summed up the mixture of admiration and anxiety Sorensen's legend inspires in many White House ghosts: "I thought Sorensen, whom I admire enormously, was both a terrific writer and had poisoned the well for presidential speeches because he had sort of invented presidentialese. He sort of developed the antipodal sentence: You march up to the middle, you turn around and march back down." (Author interview with Harry McPherson.)

White House, with the possible exception of when Thomas Jefferson dined alone."

In March 1961, Schlesinger received complaints from friendly columnists and reporters about Kennedy's failure to use his speeches and other public statements to educate and sway the voters. "They all have a point," he wrote in his diary on March 16. "Everyone has been so busy finding his office and learning his job that they have not paid much attention to the public instruction needs. JFK himself in his press conferences speaks a kind of shorthand to the reporters, where FDR would have seized the opportunity to spell things out in words of one syllable, even if they were already amply evident to the immediate audience of reporters."

Schlesinger wrote a three-page memorandum to JFK that same day arguing in favor of not only the president but also his aides making a more concerted effort at public education. "Active government requires an active policy of presenting facts, alternatives and policies to the press and the people," Schlesinger noted, approvingly citing Roosevelt. The FDR comparison was on JFK's mind as well. In the fall, he asked Schlesinger for information on how often Roosevelt had in fact given his fireside chats. The answer was a handful—no more than four—per year. "All this shows the unreliability of memory," Schlesinger wrote the president. "Many of your critics seem to suppose that FDR took to the microphone every couple of weeks."

On Saturday, April, 15, 1961, eight B-26s bombed Cuban air fields in an attempt to disable Fidel Castro's air force. A land invasion by just under 1,500 men started on Monday, April 17. But a surprising Cuban air response and successive waves of ground troops quickly sent the plan awry. By Tuesday morning it was clear how the landing at the Bay of Pigs was going to end.

The operation had quietly been U.S.-sponsored, but Kennedy, who had inherited the plan from Eisenhower, had refused to openly commit U.S. troops. In his sole discussion with Kennedy about the invasion beforehand, Sorensen, who was not yet attending National Security Council meetings and did not know the details, had worried about rumors that the United States was going to participate in an invasion. "I know that everyone is worrying about" getting hurt, Kennedy had replied with irritation—using a more vulgar term than "hurt."

The bungled plan prompted domestic and international outrage. "In one stroke, it has dissipated the sense of wild and romantic expectation which greeted JFK everywhere in the world," Schlesinger recorded in his diary. "Cuba did not cause many people to turn against Kennedy; it induced rather a feeling of disenchantment, anticlimax and alienation. Kennedy still seemed better than any alternative, but the magic had gone."

JFK decided to use his scheduled speech to the American Society of Newspaper Editors to address the situation on Thursday, April 20. He spoke briefly with Sorensen about the speech on April 19. Sorensen then consulted with Attorney General Robert F. Kennedy, the president's closest adviser. The U.S. Attorney General and Sorensen then conferred with CIA chief Allen Dulles and members of the Joint Chiefs of Staff before Sorensen wrote a draft of the speech, with contributions from Dean Rusk as Secretary of State and Charles "Chip" Bohlen, who was the Special Assistant Secretary of State for Soviet Affairs. That group, Sorensen, and the two Kennedys then went over Sorensen's draft before he retired to revise it.

Finding the president still in his office late that night, Sorensen went over it with him again, before going back to his office and working on it through the night.

JFK told the newspaper editors, among other things, that while unilateral intervention in the Bay of Pigs would have run counter to both U.S. interest and traditions, his government would not fail to act in the face of "outside Communist penetration." (The day before the speech, Robert Kennedy had sent a letter to his brother warning that "If we don't want Russia to set up missile bases in Cuba, we had better decide now what we are willing to do to stop it.")

The bureaucracy was absent from the speechwriting process. Sorensen and Kennedy worked with assistance from top officials, but drafts were not circulated for broad comment—a process that would develop in later administrations. This was not uncommon for major speeches: Kennedy and Sorensen wrote his June 1961 speech reporting on his Vienna summit with Soviet premier Nikita Khrushchev on the plane ride back to the United States, for example, with little bureaucratic input.

Sorensen was a territorial writer, believing that while consultation might be widespread, a single man must ultimately wield the pen. It was, he once explained to Schlesinger, his practice to steep himself in all available drafts but then go away and write a fresh one of his own. "The boldness and strength of a statement is in inverse proportion to the number of people who have to clear it," Sorensen later remarked. With Sorensen, the number of people who had to clear a speech was one: the president.

Sorensen, as part of his duties as JFK's chief domestic aide, was the principal speechwriter in the Kennedy White House, but Kennedy would on occasion supplement his efforts or use someone else entirely. Contributors included Myer Feldman, who in the White House continued working as Sorensen's deputy. A Philadelphia native, he had been on the law review and later faculty at the University of Pennsylvania before joining the Army Air Forces in 1942. He met Kennedy in the mid-1950s through Sorensen when Feldman was counsel to the Senate Banking and Currency Committee, and joined the senator's staff at Sorensen's invitation in 1958.

Feldman directed research in the 1960 campaign, compiling the "Nixopedia," which encompassed the Republican vice president's statements, votes, and positions from throughout his career. In the White House he handled policy on a wide swath of domestic issues—"Ted Sorensen and I kind of divided the cabinet in half," he later recalled. Sorensen took the more important cabinet departments like State and Defense, and Feldman the lesser ones, Commerce and Labor. "Whenever [cabinet department officials] wanted to see the president, they'd go through us," he said. He also handled Middle Eastern policy issues and was a secret liaison to Israel. He kept such a low profile that in 1964 *The New York Post* dubbed him "the White House's anonymous man."

Less anonymous was Richard Goodwin, who joined Kennedy's staff in 1959 fresh from investigating the "quiz show" scandals for the

House's Legislative Oversight Subcommittee. In the late 1950s, television quiz shows—*The $64,000 Question* and *Twenty-One*, in particular—achieved cult status akin to shows like *American Idol* today. Winners became nationwide celebrities, with Columbia University professor Charles Van Doren making the cover of *Time* magazine and becoming a "cultural correspondent" on NBC's *Today Show*. An eager young lawyer endowed with the power of congressional investigation, Goodwin had over several months pieced together the quiz shows' dark secret: that big winners like Van Doren were given the questions and (mostly) the answers ahead of time.*

In the midst of the investigation, in 1959, Sorensen called to ask Goodwin if he would be interested in writing speeches for Kennedy. Goodwin had met Kennedy a couple of times, when the young law student was clerking for Supreme Court Justice Felix Frankfurter, who was no fan of JFK or his father. ("I wish you a great deal of success and happiness in your own career," Frankfurter wrote upon learning that Goodwin was going to work for Kennedy, "but not in the main thing"—the presidential contest.)

Goodwin had been the latest in a string of ghosts tried out in an attempt to alleviate Sorensen's writing burdens, which the looming presidential campaign was multiplying. Nearly a dozen were tested, but only Goodwin could capture JFK's voice.

"Some, especially in those early years, found [Goodwin's] personality, in a favorite Washington word, abrasive. He was certainly driving and often impatient; those whom he overrode called him arrogant," Schlesinger wrote. "But he was a man of uncommon intelligence, perception and charm. Above all, he had immense facility, both literary and intellectual."

Goodwin, riding on the campaign bus in West Texas on September 12, 1960, had coined the name for JFK's Latin American policy. As the desolate countryside rolled by, Goodwin was searching for a slogan to encapsulate the candidate's plans for the United States' southern neighbors. Kennedy spent the campaign hammering the Republicans—never the personally popular Eisenhower—for "losing" Cuba, but he wanted

---

*The story was dramatized in the 1994 feature film *Quiz Show*.

to express a more expansive policy.* With revolution simmering across the southern continent, a Kennedy-led United States would ally itself with non-Communist leftists in favoring democratic reform and social justice. The idea was to project a sense of partnership, not paternalism.

Goodwin's eye landed on *Alianza*, a magazine published by the Tucson-based Alianza Hispano-Americano. The word clicked for Goodwin, and at the next stop he called Karl Meyer, a *Washington Post* editorial writer and friend who had Latin American expertise, to make sure *alianza* did not have any inappropriate alternative meanings (as would, for example, "liaison").

Alianza was fine, Meyer said, but it should be *for* something. Development—*desarrollo* in Spanish—was discarded as beyond the limits of the Kennedy tongue, but *progreso* was acceptable. Kennedy excised the phrase—"let's not waste this one"—because he knew it would be overshadowed by a speech he was to give later that day to Protestant ministers in Houston defusing the issue of his Catholicism.

The "Alianza para progresso" (later, at the insistence of government grammarians, "Alianza para el progresso") became one of the cornerstones of Kennedy's foreign policy, symbolizing his new approach to international affairs.

Although both Sorensen and Goodwin could write effectively for Kennedy, they were an ill-matched pair personally. "I learned a lot from Ted about the craft of politics and political speechwriting," Goodwin later wrote. "And he always appeared grateful at having found someone to share the burdens of his work, even if he seemed to look upon me as less a discovery than a creation." Given Sorensen's own disregard for or lack of interest in personal relationships, a clash was almost inevitable. "Goodwin and Sorensen did not get along," Feldman recalled. "Goodwin was always trying to substitute himself for Sorensen, which he couldn't do, but the very actions he took would irritate Sorensen."

When, just before the administration started, Sorensen tried unsuc-

---

*"Of course we never say how we would have 'saved' Cuba," the candidate said, after reading over one such draft, then laughed. "Oh what the hell, they never said how they would have saved China," he said, referring to GOP attacks against the Democrats for "losing" China after that country became Communist. (Author interview with Richard N. Goodwin.)

cessfully to have Goodwin and Feldman designated as his assistants, Goodwin decided it was time to escape his old boss's purview. He was interested neither in being a speechwriter per se nor in being in Sorensen's shadow. He sought to escape by landing a job in the State Department, a search that ended abruptly when word got back to the president. "I don't think I can work well with Ted," Goodwin told Kennedy. He was persuaded to stay in the White House and would no longer receive his assignments from Sorensen, who grew distant. It would be many years before the two became friends again.

Goodwin specialized in Latin American policy from the West Wing, angering the staid State Department with his manner and energy. He was the principal writer when JFK formally announced the Alliance for Progress in March, and would continue writing speeches on Latin American affairs. But despite Kennedy's insistence that Goodwin stay close by—"You know how we do things. I think you better stay on here for a while"—he landed in the State Department when Kennedy shook up the administration in November 1961. "I was saddened" at being sent away by Kennedy, a man whom he admired greatly, Goodwin later wrote. "Not stunned, but suffused with a milder melancholy more like that of a rejected lover."

With Goodwin's departure, Schlesinger assumed a larger role.* Though he and Kennedy had been undergrads at Harvard at the same time in the late 1930s, it was not until 1947 that they first met. "Kennedy seemed very sincere and not unintelligent, but kind of on the conservative side," Schlesinger recorded in his diary then. By 1960, Schlesinger had won a Pulitzer Prize in history; had joined Eleanor Roosevelt, Hubert Humphrey, and John Kenneth Galbraith in founding Americans for Democratic Action, a liberal lobbying group aimed at rallying the anti-Communist left; and was a veteran of both of Stevenson's presidential campaigns, among other things writing speeches. He helped JFK informally in 1960, publishing a brief book, *Kennedy or Nixon: Does It Make Any Difference?*

---

*Schlesinger and Ken Galbraith had also surreptitiously contributed to speeches during the 1960 campaign. They had had to meet with JFK in secret, the candidate explained, because "otherwise it would upset Ted too much." (Schlesinger journal, October 6, 1985.)

After the 1960 election, Robert F. Kennedy broached the possibility of Schlesinger joining the White House staff. In the administration, Schlesinger was an adviser of broad portfolio, focusing especially on Latin America but also on cultural issues, and serving as a bridge to the liberal, intellectual, and artistic communities. He was a lone voice in opposition to the Bay of Pigs invasion. (After which he had received a telegram from Cambridge, signed "Graduate Students," which said: "Nixon or Kennedy: Does it make a difference?")

"Arthur has minimal operational responsibilities," one unnamed White House staffer told *Harper's*. "He serves as a general gadfly."

Schlesinger was a political half-generation older than Sorensen and Goodwin, a difference he felt. In 1952, Stevenson had dispatched Schlesinger to New York City to pick up speech drafts from Samuel Rosenman and Robert Sherwood. Already working on his multivolume *Age of Roosevelt* series, Schlesinger was delighted for the opportunity to consult FDR's ghostwriters. Rosenman thought the speeches they submitted were as good as their Roosevelt work—a view neither Schlesinger nor Stevenson shared. "Could this team really have written the glorious FDR speeches?" he wondered.

"I learned a lesson from this experience: absence made drafts tepid and banal," Schlesinger recalled in 2007. "The response to daily crowds and politicos, the changing moods, the vital rhythms of the presidential campaign: all this atmosphere made the speeches penetrating and persuasive. Rosenman and Sherwood had not lost their talents; they had lost the atmosphere." They were also trying to write speeches from afar for a speaker with whom they were not intimate.

"I learned later a second lesson: the disillusion visited upon absent writers with a high reputation derived from previous campaigns," he added. "In 1952, John Kenneth Galbraith and Schlesinger were critical of Rosenman and Sherwood. In 1960, Ted Sorensen and Dick Goodwin were equally critical of Galbraith and Schlesinger. Could this team really have written the eloquent and witty Stevenson speeches?"

While JFK thought Schlesinger's writing was too Stevensonian, he still occasionally called upon the professor to rewrite a Sorensen draft or pen a speech of his own. Schlesinger was taken aback at the informality with which these assignments were given. "As usual, I was overwhelmed by the utter casualness of the speech-writing process," he recorded in his diary at one point.

Assignments for other writers spurred Sorensen. After a meeting about Latin American affairs on Monday, January 5, 1962, Kennedy handed Schlesinger Sorensen's draft for the State of the Union address, saying it was too long and wearisome. He asked Schlesinger to produce a new version. Schlesinger did so, staying up most of that night to produce it. Sorensen in turn spent all of Tuesday night writing a competing draft. JFK handed both to McGeorge Bundy, his national security adviser, with the Rooseveltian instruction: "Weave them together." Even in the final moments before the speech, Sorensen argued against a Schlesinger insertion, prompting Kennedy to quip to Bundy, "Ted certainly doesn't go for additions to his speeches!" When a line from the inserted material was *The New York Times'* "quotation of the day" the next day, JFK told Schlesinger, "Ted will die when he sees that."

Kennedy used the "weave" instruction again in March. He asked Schlesinger to write the speech he was going to give at the University of California at Berkley on March 23, 1962. "I am tired of the headlines," the president said. "All they describe is crisis, and they give the impression that we have our backs against the wall everywhere in the world. But this is an optical illusion." The world had changed a great deal in the previous decade, JFK added.

Schlesinger wrote a speech about the inevitable triumph of pluralism in the world. Sorensen quickly composed a competing speech, about the contrast between the "age of knowledge" and the "age of hate." "I am genuinely fond of Ted, and he has been invariably pleasant to me, but he cannot abide any one else doing important speeches for the President," Schlesinger recorded in his diary. When Kennedy told Schlesinger to "weave them together" (he liked the triumph of pluralism and the "age of reason," but neither the words nor the idea of "the age of hate"), both writers protested that they were separate speeches. JFK said he was reminded of when his father would reject memoranda proffered by subordinates. "They would ask what he wanted, and he would say, 'That's up to you,' and walk out of the room," the president told his aides. "That's what I am doing now."

"The pursuit of knowledge itself implies a world where men are free to follow out the logic of their own ideas," Kennedy told the Berkeley students. "It implies a world where nations are free to solve their own problems and to realize their own ideals. It implies, in short, a world where collaboration emerges from the voluntary decisions of nations strong in their own independence and their own self-respect. It implies, I believe, the kind of world which is emerging before our eyes—the world produced by the revolution of national independence which has today, and has been since 1945, sweeping across the face of the world."

The speech was a great success. Walter Lippmann told Bundy that it was Kennedy's best speech since the inaugural.

On Tuesday, October 16, 1962, McGeorge Bundy, the national security adviser, started Kennedy's morning with news that the Soviets had secretly set up nuclear missile bases in Cuba, a mere ninety miles from Florida.

Cuba had become an annoying theme for the administration. While JFK had hammered Nixon and the Republicans for "losing" the island nation, all he had accomplished thus far was the Bay of Pigs disaster. At the Justice Department, Robert F. Kennedy was overseeing Operation Mongoose, the CIA's largest covert program, designed to use a variety of different schemes ranging from espionage to low-grade terrorism to counterfeiting to rid Cuba of dictator Fidel Castro.

Cuba was also a public focus of both the United States and the USSR. On September 11, the Soviet government had stated that its nuclear arsenal had such reach and power that there would be no reason for arms to be based in any other countries, "for instance, Cuba." The statement had added that shipments of arms to Cuba—recently increased—were "designed exclusively for defensive purposes." In addition, Khrushchev had recently used private channels to assure JFK that his country would undertake no actions that would affect the upcoming U.S. midterm congressional elections.

For his part, Kennedy had drawn a strategic line. If Cuba were to "become an offensive military base of significant capacity for the Soviet Union," he warned at a September 13 press conference, "then this country will do whatever must be done to protect its own security and that of its allies."

All the while missiles moved onto the island. And now U.S. spy planes had discovered them, presenting Kennedy with both a problem and an opportunity. On one hand, this was a dangerous and provocative act on the part of the Soviets. While the missiles made little practical strategic difference in the global balance of power, once unveiled they would be a potent challenge to U.S. prestige.

But the Soviet secrecy gave Kennedy room to maneuver. Hours after learning of the missiles, he convened in the Cabinet Room what came to be known as the Executive Committee of the National Security Council, or simply the Ex Comm. The group consisted mainly of pre-dictable persons—in addition to Bundy, Kennedy, and Vice President Lyndon Johnson were Secretary of Defense Robert McNamara; Secretary of State Dean Rusk and their aides; Joint Chiefs of Staff Chairman Maxwell Taylor; representatives of the CIA; and the U.S. Attorney General, Robert Kennedy.

But Sorensen also was a regular and important member of the Ex Comm. Though his portfolio was domestic policies and politics, he had become increasingly involved in foreign affairs since the Bay of Pigs. His presence in the key meetings was important not simply for his role as Kennedy's top adviser on the White House staff. Whatever action Kennedy settled on, he would have to explain it to the American people and the world. It would be Sorensen to whom he would turn for that explanation. And as the week progressed, the speechcrafting itself shaped the policy decisions.

Early on, with the shock and anger of the discovery of the missile bases still fresh, the policy debate focused primarily on military means to eliminate the missiles. During the first Ex Comm meeting, JFK summarized the possibilities open to the United States: a "surgical" air strike to destroy the missile sites alone; a broader air strike, which would eliminate any Soviet ability to counterattack; a full invasion of Cuba; or a military blockade to prevent any additional Soviet forces or matériel from reaching the island.

An air attack on the missile bases is "what we're going to do *anyway*," Kennedy told his advisers. "We're going to do number one. We're going to take out these missiles." The concept of a blockade gained support, especially with the president, over the course of the week—but as quickly as a consensus seemed at hand, it would disappear. "Each of us changed his mind more than once that week on the best course of action to take—not only because new facts and arguments were adduced but because, in the president's words, 'whatever action we took had so many disadvantages to it and each . . . raised the prospect that it might escalate the Soviet Union into a nuclear war,'" Sorensen later wrote.

Try as they might, collectively or individually, a course of action with an airtight case eluded the group. To do nothing would signal weakness. An air strike could not guarantee complete destruction of the missiles, but would raise the probability of a larger confrontation with the Soviets—possibly escalating to nuclear war. An invasion would make such a conflagration even more likely.* A blockade might—might—prevent new missiles and equipment from arriving on the island, but would do nothing about those already there. And none of these options provided an answer if the Soviets compared the missiles they were trying to move into Cuba with the ones the United States had in Turkey and Italy.

"Having some pride in my own ability with words, I tried, I recall, to draft a message to Khrushchev which I thought could be as airtight as possible and require his immediate withdrawal of the missiles," Sorensen later explained. He envisioned a letter that would be delivered to Khrushchev personally by a special presidential envoy who would be instructed to wait in the Soviet premier's presence for an answer.

His draft of the letter said the United States faced an "inescapable commitment" to take military action against the missiles. "Consequently, the purpose of this note is to inform you that . . . I have no choice but to initiate appropriate military action against the island of Cuba." Only Khrushchev's personally assuring the presidential envoy then and there that he would withdraw the missiles could forestall the

---

*It was even more likely than Kennedy and company knew: nine short-range nuclear-armed rockets had been deployed to the island and the Soviet troop commander had authority to use them, retired Soviet general Anatoly Gribkov told a 1992 conference on the crisis. (Don Oberdorfer, "Cuban Missile Crisis More Volatile Than Thought," *The Washington Post*, January 14, 1992.)

attack. After such a promise was made, the letter continued, Kennedy would be willing to discuss the U.S. nuclear forces deployed in Italy and Turkey (which, by the way, "are in no way comparable in the eyes of history, international law, or world opinion").

But Sorensen was unsatisfied. "I had to admit on completion of that effort that even I could not make one that would stand the light of logic and history." Later in the week, summarizing on paper the unanswered objections to an air strike, Sorensen wrote: "Inasmuch as no one has been able to devise a satisfactory message to Khrushchev to which his reply could not outmaneuver us, an air strike means a U.S.-initiated 'Pearl Harbor' on a small nation which history could neither understand nor forget."

Debate swung back and forth. On Thursday, October 18, Sorensen wrote a draft of a speech for Kennedy to give after a military strike against the island. "This morning I reluctantly ordered the armed forces to attack and destroy the nuclear buildup in Cuba," the president's speech read. Americans should "remain calm, go about your daily business, secure in the knowledge that our freedom-loving country will not allow its security to be undermined."

That night, the Ex Comm seemed to agree on a blockade with the possibility of military action later, only to revisit the question on Friday morning—above the protests of Sorensen, who complained that they had reached decision. We're not serving the president well by reopening the debate, Sorensen told the air strike proponents. And, he added, my ulcer doesn't much like it either.

He retired to his office and tried a first draft of a naval blockade speech. But at this hour of maximum danger, his pen faltered. "Back in my office," he recalled, "the original difficulties with the blockade route stared me in the face: How should we relate it to the missiles? How would it help get them out? What would we do if they became operational? What should we say about our surveillance, about communicating with Khrushchev?"

The questions were, he said forty-four years later, the product of the "combination of my legal background and my Unitarian background—I'm a questioner and a skeptic, a dissenter."

Sorensen returned to the Ex Comm late that afternoon in the unaccustomed position of being without a speech. Rather, he brought with him the questions that had halted his hand. "As the concrete answers were provided in our discussions, the final shape of the president's policy began to take form," he noted. "It was in a sense an amalgam of the blockade-air-strike routes; and a much stronger, more satisfied consensus formed behind it." That night, he ate his first hot meal in days, sent over to the White House by a friendly Washington matron, and, using Woodrow Wilson's speech declaring the United States' entry into World War I and FDR's speech after Pearl Harbor as reference points, stayed up until three o'clock writing a draft.

All of this debate had taken place out of the public view. Kennedy had maintained his public schedule, leaving for a campaign swing on Thursday. But midmorning on Saturday, October 20, Pierre Salinger announced to the press that the president had a "slight cold" and would cut short his trip. Arriving at the White House around 1:30 pm, Kennedy read Sorensen's draft before the two went up to the Oval Room on the second floor of the presidential living quarters—selected for its location out of the eye of the press, who would notice top national security officials suddenly congregating on a Saturday afternoon in, say, the Cabinet Room—to meet with the Ex Comm.

The group debated Sorensen's draft, and also an air strike draft which Bundy had prepared and which was favored by the Joint Chiefs of Staff, the CIA, and Treasury Secretary Douglas Dillon. JFK, who always favored leaving an out for an opponent, elected the limited course of a blockade while leaving open an air strike down the road.

Even then debate over the draft continued, with Adlai Stevenson, the ambassador to the United Nations, arguing that the speech should include an offer to trade the missiles in Turkey. Kennedy conceded that such a trade would probably ultimately be necessary, but he insisted that that bargaining chip be held in abeyance rather than played in the opening gambit. (In the end, the missiles in Turkey were secretly bargained away—a fact that would not become public for decades.)

The question lingered of what to call the response: "Is this a 'nuclear quarantine' or a 'blockade' or something in between?" a talking point on the Sunday meeting agenda asked. Rusk questioned whether the word "blockade" was desirable. He argued for "quarantine." While the two words had the same meaning under international law, "quarantine" had better political connotations; it would not invite comparisons to the Soviet "blockade" of Berlin.

Other small but important changes to the speech were made over the next couple of days. A passage that acknowledged that the blockade would not stop the Soviet buildup was dropped. Also gone was a promise that the missiles in Cuba would "someday go—and no others will take their place." More important, a pair of blunt warnings about what the crisis could bring to Cuba came out. Sorensen's third draft cautioned that if the offensive buildup continued, "appropriate action will be undertaken at a time and in a manner of our own determination . . . including the targeting of these bases by our strategic forces." "Strategic forces" was a euphemism for nuclear weapons. This draft was shaking the nuclear saber not as a possible final eventuality, but as a next step. (In the final version of the speech, the U.S. armed forces were ordered to prepare for "any eventualities.")

Several pages later, Cuba was warned, "Do not become the first Latin American country to be a necessary target for massive destruction." That admonition was not in the delivered speech, but a third and similar warning—that Cuba had become "the first Latin American country to become a target for nuclear war"—was. Never in the Cold War did the United States renounce first use of nuclear weapons. But it was a measure of the seriousness with which the Kennedy administration took the crisis that they were considering such explicit, explosive, grim rhetoric.

The Ex Comm met again at 11:30 am on Monday, October 22. Secrecy had held for almost a week and Kennedy was within hours of addressing the nation. Whichever side revealed the missiles first would frame the discussion before the world. Now, as he met with the group, the president received a note. "The Russians are going to make a major announcement in two hours?" he asked. Then, turning to his advisers, he added: "They're going to announce it," referring to the presence of the missiles. A brief debate ensued: Should JFK make his announcement before the Soviets could?

From the start, Kennedy had grasped the importance of secrecy. So long as only he and his advisers knew that the United States knew about the buildup, he could maneuver and consider his options. He had directed his aides to keep the secrets and he had privately called upon *The Washington Post* and *The New York Times* to hold stories on the brewing crisis.

"From the start he knew that unless the missiles in Cuba and the American response were announced deftly, the world might be disgusted that the United States was risking nuclear war to remove missiles no more menacing than those along the Soviet border," Michael Beschloss later wrote. "Another President might not have taken such care to make sure that the missiles were not revealed by the Russians, the *New York Times* or CBS in a way that would undermine public support for his course of action."*

JFK and his advisers decided not to move up his speech—and the Russians' "major announcement" proved to be merely Foreign Minister Andrei Gromyko's routine departure statement upon leaving the country.

Five minutes before the 7 pm airtime on October 22, the president lowered himself onto the seat at his desk, a pair of pillows cushioning him. Wearing a corset to relieve his chronic bad back, Kennedy sat straight and stared into the camera as he prepared to give the most important speech of his life—and of the Cold War:

> *Good evening, my fellow citizens. This government, as promised, has maintained the closest surveillance of the Soviet military buildup on the island of Cuba. Within the past week, unmistakable evidence has established the fact that a series of offensive missile sites is now in preparation on that imprisoned island. The purpose of these bases can be none other than to provide a nuclear strike capability against the Western Hemisphere.*

Framing the issue as one of Soviet secrecy and deception, JFK quickly won the country's support. The Cuban missile crisis was the Cold War's critical moment. The lives of the world hung in large part

---

*Beschloss continued with a point worth remembering in the age of mass communications: "Kennedy's six days of quiet deliberation were a gift that no American President in a similar quandary will probably ever enjoy again." (Beschloss, *Crisis Years*, 470.)

on the decisions of fifteen men. Several factors were important in Kennedy's successful handling of the crisis—perhaps none more important than having time to consider all options. But given that time, the act of translating policy impulses and instincts into prose policy played an important role in the deliberations before Kennedy's speech. Setting policy into words had raised new questions and exposed possible weaknesses. And choosing the right words for the speech itself helped set the terms of the international debate.

This crisis was a unique situation—a literal crisis, in which the regular rules of policymaking were of necessity suspended. But Kennedy used speeches and speechwriting for policy development in other situations as well. As Truman had circumvented the bureaucracy with his State of the Union announcement of the Point Four program providing technical aid to developing countries, Kennedy used speeches to set policy outside of the departments. Soliciting first drafts from different departments was common, especially in the case of foreign policy matters, but JFK used his speechwriters to break out of the diplomatic blandness that Foggy Bottom produced. He faced a growing permanent executive branch bureaucracy that was not beholden and often unresponsive to the political administration. JFK used the president's public pronouncements as a prod for both foreign and narrowly domestic audiences.

The following spring, Kennedy used a speech to plot a broader new course on foreign policy.

Traveling in the Soviet Union in April 1963, Norman Cousins, the *Saturday Review* editor who had suggested to Eisenhower that he make a "great, sweeping" farewell address, had acted as a backchannel between Kennedy and Khrushchev. He relayed a private message from the president to the premier designed to restart nuclear test ban negotiations, begun in the Eisenhower administration, that had stalled over an apparent misunderstanding regarding the number of annual on-site inspections permitted. The Americans wanted twelve to twenty annually, while the Soviets wanted none. Kennedy was willing to go to eight to ten, but Khrushchev thought the Americans had offered three. The

Soviet leadership felt that it had been misled, circumscribing Khrushchev's options. "You can tell the president I accept his explanation of an honest misunderstanding and suggest that we get moving," the Soviet leader told Cousins. "But the next step is up to him."

Visiting the White House on Friday, April 22, Cousins reported to Kennedy that Khrushchev was willing to talk, but was feeling heat from his hard-liners and from the Chinese to denounce the United States as warmongers. Kennedy said that he wanted a test ban, but wondered how important an issue it was to American voters. Pulling out the White House's weekly mail report, he noted that such a treaty was far down the list, below questions about Caroline's pony. In addition, the mail was running fifteen to one against. He asked Cousins to keep him up to date.

Concluding the conversation, JFK got up and walked to the French doors that opened onto the Rose Garden and South Lawn. Chairs were being set up for a music students' event that he was scheduled to address in twenty minutes, at noon. "What do I tell them?" Kennedy asked Cousins. When Kennedy liked his reply—about the number of educational television stations in the country—he said, "That's great. Can you type it up?" While Cousins found a typewriter, the president went for a quick swim in the White House pool.

Over a week later, on April 30, Cousins followed up with a letter to Kennedy suggesting that he give "the most important speech of your Presidency . . . in its breathtaking proposals for genuine peace, in its tone of friendliness for the Soviet people and its understanding of their ordeal during the last war." A Soviet Central Committee meeting was scheduled for June, Cousins noted, suggesting that Kennedy "beat Mr. K. to the punch" with a peace speech. Kennedy forwarded the letter to Sorensen and they decided that the June 10 commencement at Washington, D.C.'s, American University would be an appropriate venue. It would be a sweeping address, aimed at breaking the stalemate with a serious peace offer. But the rush of events overtook Sorensen so that when Kennedy departed on Wednesday, June 5, on a trip west to inspect military facilities and meet with local officials, Sorensen had not produced a first draft of the speech.

Sorensen had been quietly consulting with Bundy, his deputy Carl

Kaysen, Schlesinger, Walt Rostow, chairman of the State Department's Policy Planning Council, and his own brother, Tom Sorensen. He also dug up material that had been cut from previous addresses—the idea of a "Pax Americana" had first appeared in early drafts of the inaugural—and dashed out seventeen typed pages of a rough draft that contained many of the elements that would make up the delivered speech. "The clamor of conflicting ideologies and political systems must not drown out the fact that we are all residents of the same planet," Sorensen's notes said in an early version of the speech's most oft-quoted line. "We are all dependent on the same national [*sic*] environment. We all look to nature's bounty for sustenance. We all have the same capacity to hope. We all feel pain and are diminished by it. And we are all mortal."

Sorensen worked late into the night on Thursday, June 6, rearranging and rewriting from his notes, producing a first draft. The next day he had "a small but select roundtable meeting," as Bundy described it, of the men he had been consulting. "We got the bugs out of it unusually quickly and with very little friction," Bundy recalled. Not in the loop were Secretary of State Dean Rusk, Secretary of Defense Robert McNamara, and General Maxwell Taylor of the Joint Chiefs of Staff, who would all be informed of the content on Saturday, the 8th. Their departments' official views had not been solicited.

As Sorensen later wrote, Kennedy "did not want [his] new policy diluted by the usual threats of destruction, boasts of nuclear stockpiles and lectures on Soviet treachery." By keeping the speech—and the policy—closely held within the White House, Kennedy and Sorensen were working around and targeting bureaucracies over which they did not feel he had control. Foggy Bottom in particular was viewed as a continuing vacuum of both original ideas and forceful language.

The recipe for a foreign policy statement from the State Department, Schlesinger wrote, "was evidently to take a handful of clichés (saying something in a fresh way might create unforeseen troubles), repeat at five-minute intervals (lest the argument become clear or interesting), stir in the dough of the passive voice (the active voice assigns responsibility and was therefore hazardous) and garnish with self-serving rhetoric (Congress would be unhappy unless we constantly proclaimed the rectitude of American motives)."

Kennedy's was not the first and would not be the last administration where the search for penetrating rhetoric and pungent phrases ran up against the bland wall of diplomatic speech. For the American University speech—and his new push for a test ban treaty—JFK's solution was to lead and let the bureaucrats catch up. "I suppose that, from the viewpoint of orderly administration, this was a bad way to prepare a major statement on foreign policy," Schlesinger reflected in his diary. "But the State Department could never in a thousand years have produced this speech. The President is fortunately ready, from time to time, to assert control over the policy of his administration, however deeply it may offend the bureaucracy."

By the time even the top political appointees of the cabinet departments had a chance to catch up, Sorensen and the speech were flying west to meet Kennedy in Hawaii, where he was giving a civil rights address on Sunday, June 9. Though the president had discussed the peace speech with Sorensen—and Sorensen certainly knew his thoughts on the issues—it was not until Kennedy was flying east again on the Sunday afternoon (well into the evening, Washington time) that he first reviewed a draft.

The president made some changes but not many and none of substance: there are strikingly few differences between Sorensen's first full draft and the speech that Kennedy gave. The biggest involved the announcement that test ban negotiations involving the United States, the United Kingdom, and the USSR would resume in Moscow—word had come from Khrushchev only on Saturday that he would be willing to restart the talks. Kennedy arrived in Washington on the morning of June 10 and after a quick stop at the White House went to American University.

He had, he told the graduating students,

chosen this time and place to discuss a topic on which ignorance too often abounds and the truth is too rarely perceived—and that is the most important topic on earth—peace. What kind of peace do I mean? What kind of peace do we seek? Not a Pax Americana enforced on the world by American weapons of war. Not the peace of the grave or the security of the slave. I am talking about genuine peace, the kind of peace that makes life on earth worth living, the kind that enables men and nations to grow and to hope and to build a better life for their children—not merely peace for Americans but peace for all men and women—not merely peace in our time but peace for all time.

The speech called upon both sides in the Cold War to reexamine their assumptions about both peace and their adversaries. The two blocs must figure out how to live and compete peacefully together, he said.

And if we cannot end now our differences, at least we can help make the world safe for diversity. For, in the final analysis, our most basic common link is that we all inhabit this small planet. We all breathe the same air. We all cherish our children's future. And we are all mortal.

Viewed from the twenty-first century, this elegant rhetoric hardly seems revolutionary, but at the time it was the kind of speech that only a proven Cold Warrior could successfully give without seeming weak in the face of the Communist threat. "Public cant about communist dangers in the fifties and sixties made it almost impossible for an American politician to make the sort of speech that Kennedy gave," Robert Dallek has written. "It was a tremendously bold address that carried substantial risks. By taking advantage of his recent success in facing down Khrushchev in Cuba, Kennedy gave voice to his own and the country's best hopes for rational exchange between adversaries that could turn the East-West competition away from the growing arms race."

Nevertheless, the speech had little initial domestic impact. Ten days later, Schlesinger was with Kennedy when the president was given a breakdown on the mail received for the previous week. Of almost 50,000 letters received at the White House, fewer than 900 had to do with the American University speech, as opposed to more than 28,000 regarding a freight rate bill. "That is why I tell people in Congress they're crazy if they take their mail seriously," Kennedy said, disgustedly.

The Western European reaction was almost uniformly positive (except in France, which was skeptical), but most important was the Soviet response, where actions let Kennedy's words speak loudly: When Voice of America broadcasted a translated version of the speech, only one paragraph in the transmission was jammed, and upon rebroadcast the Soviets let it all play.

The Moscow negotiations produced a ban on atmospheric, but not underground, testing—not the comprehensive treaty Kennedy had sought, but still a significant step forward in defusing the nuclear arms race. Schlesinger later asked Polish diplomat Marian Dobrosielski, with whom he had the occasional amiable lunch, whether the negotiation could have succeeded without the American University speech. No, came the reply, the speech was responsible for breaking the logjam.

But even as Kennedy and Sorensen had been preparing the June 10 international peace speech, the administration was monitoring a mounting situation at home. On May 21, a federal district judge had ruled that the University of Alabama must allow two black students to enter for the school's summer session, starting in June. Alabama was the last state in the Union with segregated universities, and Governor George Wallace was determined at least to make a show of trying to keep it that way.

The criticism that Schlesinger had heard in March 1961—that Kennedy had not properly used public education to sway the voters—had continued, and on no issue was it sharper than civil rights. "He has neglected his opportunities to use the forum of the Presidency as an educational institution," one writer observed in a typical criticism. But for JFK, presidential greatness lay not in rhetoric but in accomplishment. "It is clear that his measure is concrete achievement and people who educate the nation without necessarily achieving their goals, like Wilson and TR, rate below those, like Truman and Polk, who do things without bringing the nation along with them," Schlesinger noted in his diary.

The relationship between leadership and accomplishment on civil rights was particularly trying for Kennedy, and more so for his admirers. JFK wanted to maintain a position just ahead of the crest of public opinion but not too far out in front of it. A week before the federal court ruled that the University of Alabama had to admit the black students, he spent forty-five minutes with leaders from Americans for Democratic Action. That morning, the *Times*'s front page featured a picture of a Birmingham police dog lunging at a black protestor. The situation made him "sick," Kennedy told the liberals, but constitutionally he had little power to affect it. "I must confess that I have found his reaction to Birmingham disappointing," Schlesinger noted in his diary four days later. "Even if he has no power to act, he has unlimited power to express the moral sense of the people; and in not doing so, he is acting much as Eisenhower used to act when we denounced him so."

JFK was skeptical of the power of exhortation. The president's pulpit might be bully, but in order to be effective, the context in which he spoke had to be right. Dining with Schlesinger in October 1961, Kennedy had noted that a recent telecast featuring ex-President Eisenhower had scored a seven share of the viewing audience as against twenty for competing programs about cowboys and crime. "People forget this when they expect me to go on the air all the time educating the nation," he said. "The nation will listen only if it is a moment of great urgency. They will listen after a Vienna [his June 1961 summit meeting]. But they won't listen to things which bore them. That is the trouble." JFK liked to quote from Shakespeare's *Henry IV, Part I* where, in response to Owen Glendower's boast that he can "call spirits from the vasty deep," Hotspur replies: "Why, so can I, or so can any man; but will they come when you do call for them?"

Even before the Tuscaloosa confrontation reached its climax, Kennedy and his staff had debated the merits of giving a speech. The president was unsure, and his senior staff opposed. Only Robert Kennedy favored it. "We've got a draft which doesn't fit all these points, but it's something to work with, and there's some pretty good sentences and paragraphs," JFK told his senior aides on June 10, hours after giving the American University speech. "It will help us to get ready anyway, because we may want to do it tomorrow." In fact, there was no draft.

On June 11, Wallace stood in the doorway of the University of Alabama's registration building in a show of symbolic protest. Less than three hours later, the governor stood aside for Deputy Attorney General Nicholas Katzenbach, who had the commander of the just-federalized Alabama National Guard at his side. The two students were allowed to register. The crisis had been defused.

Along with the nation, Kennedy and his staff watched the confrontation on television. With no crisis at hand, Sorensen assumed there would be no speech. But Kennedy sensed that the time was finally right for presidential education of the public on civil rights, followed by new legislation. "We better give that civil rights speech tonight," he said at around 2 pm, turning in his chair toward Sorensen. (More than forty years later, Sorensen still marveled over Kennedy's use of the word "We.")

With roughly six hours until airtime at 8 pm, there was no speech. After consulting with the president on what he wanted to say, Sorensen and others, including Robert Kennedy and Assistant Attorney General Burke Marshall, worked on a draft. With an hour to go, JFK found them in the Cabinet Room still revising. "C'mon Burke, you must have some ideas," Kennedy quipped. Sorensen managed two drafts, the first incomplete.

At 7:40 pm, the Kennedy brothers retreated to the Oval Office to outline an extemporaneous speech in case Sorensen did not finish in time, with JFK taking notes on the back of an envelope and whatever scrap paper was handy. Sorensen appeared in the Oval Office less than five minutes before eight with a draft ("For the first time, I thought I was going to have to go off the cuff," JFK told Sorensen later), which the president glanced over as the minutes ticked by. Robert Kennedy suggested that he still extemporize some parts of the talk—a bold suggestion, given the gravity of the speech and the fact that it would be broadcast live to the nation. ("The speech was good," Robert Kennedy later said. "I think that probably, if he had given it [entirely] extemporaneously, it would have been as good or better.")

The country faced not a sectional or partisan issue, Kennedy told his audience. And while it had legal dimensions, it was broader than that. "We are confronted primarily with a moral issue," he said. "It is as old as the scriptures and is as clear as the American Constitution. The heart of the question is whether all Americans are to be afforded equal rights and equal opportunities, whether we are going to treat our fellow Americans as we want to be treated."

Drawing from the notes he had jotted down with Robert Kennedy, JFK extemporized a new closing on the speech.

> *This is one country. It has become one country because all of us and all the people who came here had an equal chance to develop their talents. We cannot say to ten percent of the population that you can't have the right; that your children can't have the chance to develop whatever talents they have; that the only way that they are going to get their rights is to go into the streets and demonstrate. I think we owe them and we owe ourselves a better country than that.*

The address was widely praised as one of his best, but Kennedy remained skeptical of the power of the rhetorical presidency. When Schlesinger lauded the speech to him, Kennedy replied: "Yes—and look what happened to area redevelopment the next day in the House." He was referring to the surprise defeat of a bill that would have expanded a program of loans and grants to economically depressed areas of the country. He might have summoned high ideals from the vasty deep, Kennedy was saying, but it had made little difference in the practical business of governing the country. After a pause, though, he added: "But of course I had to give that speech, and I am glad that I did."

In his diary later that week, Schlesinger noted of Kennedy, "He is deeply—excessively—skeptical about the value of speeches per se."

But the partial ad-lib also demonstrated Kennedy's facility for gathering his own thoughts and written notes or text. He had honed the skill particularly in the presidential campaign, becoming so adept at moving back and forth between his written speech and ad-libs that the press often assumed whole speeches were delivered extemporaneously when in fact they were partially written. Frustrated reporters, trying to follow along with the candidate and report his speeches, called him a "text deviate."*

---

*The pun apparently stuck in Sorensen's head. Despite rumors to the contrary, he would joke in later years, he had never collaborated with his friend, Reagan speechwriter Peggy Noonan. "I did not have textual relations with that woman, Miss Noonan."

As president, his ad-libs tended to be at small, campaign-style and other informal events. Extemporizing in a large speech was rare but not unheard of. Speaking to Congress in a special "second" State of the Union address in May 1961, JFK called for an effort to put a man on the moon by decade's end. The assembled legislators—perhaps sensing a program that would involve great sums of money directed to districts that were not theirs—responded with perfunctory applause, it seemed to Kennedy. For the only time in his short presidency, he ad-libbed before Congress. "It is a heavy burden, and there is no sense in agreeing or desiring that the United States take an affirmative position in outer space, unless we are prepared to do the work and bear the burdens to make it successful," Kennedy said. "If we are not, we should decide today and this year."

Perhaps the best-known instance of Kennedy discarding his prepared remarks came in a setting that, while campaignlike, was not in the United States. In June 1963, he made a trip through Europe, stopping in West Germany and Berlin before returning to the United States by way of his ancestral homeland of Ireland.

Berlin had been divided by the occupying powers at the end of World War II, and the Cold War had frozen that division into place. Deep inside Soviet-dominated East Germany, Berlin became the focus of early Cold War tensions. At times, for example the 1948 Soviet blockade of the Western-occupied portions of the city, it seemed on the verge of becoming the flashpoint for a third world war. And while succeeding U.S. presidents had pledged to defend Berlin, doubts about American resolve lingered. Those doubts had found voice in the hot summer of 1961.

The free sectors in Berlin were a hole in the iron curtain through which East German citizens were fleeing to a better life in the West, 2.5 million of them since 1949, mostly valuable workers and professionals. Faced with an intellectual and labor hemorrhage that was starting to impinge on production, the East German government had prevailed upon the Soviet leadership to seal the border. At midnight on Saturday, August 12, 1961, they started stringing up circles of barbed wire and posting armed guards at checkpoint crossings. Within days, the Berlin Wall cut a gash across the city.

President Kennedy was publicly silent about the Wall. He eventually sent a 1,500-strong battle group, headed by Vice President Lyndon Johnson and Berlin blockade hero General Lucius Clay, across East Germany to test that Allied access to and from the city had not been cut off. In West Berlin, 300,000 demonstrated in the Rudolph Wilde Platz, in front of the City Hall. Some brandished signs that read BETRAYED BY THE WEST or THE WEST IS DOING A SECOND MUNICH. Almost two years later, on June 26, 1963, 150,000 Berliners jammed into the same space to greet Kennedy.

Before JFK left Washington, Robert Kennedy had suggested that he say something in German to the West Berliners. As Air Force One crossed a divided Germany toward the tiny Western outpost that was the city, the president turned to Special Assistant Kenneth O'Donnell and asked: "What was the proud boast of the Romans—Civis Romanus sum? Send Bundy up here. He'll know how to say it in German." Bundy later told Michael Beschloss that Kennedy had no feeling for foreign languages. "So there we were on the goddamn airplane coming down on Berlin while he repeated the phrase over and over again . . . and it worked. God, how it worked!"

At some point Kennedy scrawled three key phrases on a piece of lined paper, spelling them phonetically to help himself remember the pronunciation: "Ish bin ein Bearl<u>ee</u>ner," he wrote, underlining the middle letters to emphasize the long "e" (with his Boston accent, it came out closer to "Beer-leener"); "Kiwis Romanus sum"; and "Lust z nach Bearlin comen." West Berlin mayor Willy Brandt coached JFK on his pronunciation before the speech.

Sorensen had written remarks outlining the city's history since the onset of the Cold War. Driving to the City Hall, Kennedy showed the speech, printed on reading cards, to General James Polke, the American commander in the city. "You think this is any good?" the president asked.

The general was blunt: "This is terrible, Mr. President."

"I think so too," Kennedy replied.

How much of the prepared remarks he intended to use is unclear. He had scribbled his three phrases on the speech cards. And he had handwritten in new lines. But after dispensing with the introductory remarks, he mostly ignored the whole thing in favor of improvisation.

"Two thousand years ago the proudest boast was 'civis Romanus sum.' Today, in the world of freedom, the proudest boast is 'Ich bin ein Berliner,'" he said, ad-libbing.

As the crowd bellowed its approval, he quipped, "I appreciate my interpreter translating my German."

> There are many people in the world who really don't understand, or say they don't, what is the great issue between the free world and the Communist world. Let them come to Berlin. There are some who say that communism is the wave of the future. Let them come to Berlin. And there are some who say in Europe and elsewhere we can work with the Communists. Let them come to Berlin. And there are even a few who say that it is true that communism is an evil system, but it permits us to make economic progress. Lass' sic nach Berlin kommen. Let them come to Berlin.

Kennedy had gotten carried away. In his speech at American University two weeks earlier, he had said, in essence, that we can work with the Communists.* Speaking later that day at the Free University of Berlin, he backtracked and spun his speech as having been about governments cooperating with local Communist parties.

Not quite ready to pick up the thread of his prepared remarks, Kennedy aimed one more improvised dart at the Soviets. "Freedom has many difficulties and democracy is not perfect, but we have never had to put a wall up to keep our people in, to prevent them from leaving us." He finally started to pick up on his prepared text, before closing with more ad-libbing, and then repeating, "Ich bin ein Berliner."

The speech was uncharacteristic of Kennedy, who avoided rhetorical excess and disliked emotionalism. Afterwards, in Brandt's office, translator Robert Lochner heard Bundy say, "I think that went a little too far." Kennedy too was disquieted. He told his military aide that "If I

---

*Two weeks later, Khrushchev commented that reading the American University speech and then the West Berlin address, one would think them given by two different presidents. (Beschloss, *Crisis Years*, 608n.)

told them to go tear down the Berlin Wall, they would do it." The crowd's passionate reaction also made Chancellor Konrad Adenauer uneasy. "Does this mean Germany can one day have another Hitler?" he asked Rusk.

Bundy later realized that he had given his boss a bad translation. Grammatically, he should have dropped the article *ein*, leaving "Ich bin Berliner" (colloquially, "ein Berliner" was a popular pastry). "Fortunately the crowd in Berlin was untroubled by my mistake," Bundy told Beschloss. "No one in the square confused JFK with a doughnut."

Flying out of East Germany that evening, Kennedy told Sorensen that he would leave a note for his successor, "to be opened at a time of some discouragement." The missive would have three words: "Go to Germany."

Around 10:45 am on November 21, 1963, Sorensen dashed across the South Lawn trying to catch the president before he boarded his helicopter. Sorensen handed up some suggestions for "Texas humor" for Kennedy's upcoming trip to the Lone Star State. The two men parted—for the last time.

Sorensen has over the decades remained a chief defender of the Kennedy memory, eloquently guarding his old boss's reputation and legacy. Part of that defense has involved explicating his own role as JFK's chief speechwriter and arguing that Kennedy had a role as well.

Because of the high level of JFK's speeches, critics have questioned the president's part in their preparation, a position expressed most crudely by Richard Nixon in 1962. The defeated pol told *Redbook* that Kennedy had been nothing more than a "puppet who echoed his speechmaker" during the presidential campaign. "It's easier for Kennedy to get up and read Sorensen's speeches, but I don't think it's responsible unless he believes it deeply himself."* Nixon's remark

---

*In April 1962, Sorensen told *Time* that when he had run into Nixon at a Junior Chamber of Commerce luncheon recently, the former vice president maintained he wished he had said some of the lines from JFK's inaugural. "That part about 'Ask not what your country can do for you . . . ?'" Sorensen asked. "No," Nixon deadpanned. "That part that starts, 'I do solemnly swear . . .'" (*Time*, April 27, 1962.)

was extreme, but it has in a milder form become common. "Along with so many others, we were thrilled by the inaugural speech, which had mostly been crafted by Ted Sorensen, helped by Ken Galbraith," the late *Washington Post* publisher Katharine Graham wrote in her memoir.

Underlying these sentiments is the notion of the president as—to use Nixon's word—a puppet, mouthing a script prepared by a speechwriter. But this is an overly simple and onesided view of the speechwriter-speechgiver relationship. It seems safe to assume that forced to operate solo, John F. Kennedy would not have produced his inaugural address—but it is as safe to conclude that the Ted Sorensen who walked into Representative John F. Kennedy's House office suite in January 1953 would also not have produced that speech. Inasmuch as he wrote the first working draft of the speech, Sorensen was operating from intense and intimate exposure to his boss's mind over eight years. Indeed, except for Samuel Rosenman and Franklin Roosevelt, Sorensen and Kennedy were a production team unique for their longevity and its attendant familiarity—and that shows through in the quality of the prose.

"Sorensen knew Kennedy's mind because he'd been with him so long," Feldman said. "Sorensen knew where Kennedy stood and he could phrase what Kennedy's ideas were better than Kennedy could do himself." They were Kennedy's ideas. And the words were ones that Kennedy worked over himself thoroughly. Indeed, to assume that Kennedy (or any other president) was a vessel for someone else's words underestimates the efforts required of Sorensen, Goodwin, Schlesinger, and others who were writing not in a vacuum but in a specific style and cadence.

"I always felt that it was more a reflection of him than me," Goodwin said in 2007. Indeed, one measure of a president's success in terms of preparing a speech is his ability to aid his writers by providing a clear tone and style and set of beliefs.

These issues occupied Sorensen in the days after he left the Johnson administration in early 1964. "A few days before he left for Cambridge, Ted called me and asked about his own original drafts of Kennedy speeches—for example, the inaugural address," Schlesinger recorded in his diary. "Should he destroy them? Might they not damage JFK's historical reputation? I said that he should destroy nothing—that his historical reputation rested on many other things besides speeches, and that in any case a President deserved credit for the writers he chose and the texts he approved."*

Sorensen has for decades fought anything that would diminish the credit Kennedy receives for speeches he gave. "I maintain with good reason that John F. Kennedy was the author—in the true sense of that word—of all of his speeches," Sorensen said in 2006. "By that I mean all the ideas, policies and decisions conveyed in every speech were his, not mine. I also mean that he was putting his name and reputation at stake. If a speech backfired or antagonized a lot of people . . . he would suffer for it—I wouldn't suffer for it. So that's why I say he's the author." He added: "If a man in a high office speaks words which convey his principles and policies and ideas and he's willing to stand behind them and take whatever blame or therefore credit go with them, it's his."

A great speech cannot simply be measured by its words. "If I was writing a speech for someone now and . . . [had them say] 'Give me liberty or give me death!' they'd laugh me off the stage," Goodwin said. "But on the other hand in Virginia in pre-Revolutionary times, that was a pretty fiery speech. So it all depends on the context at the time . . . and the person." This is especially true for presidential addresses because those words have the power of policy. If in May 1963 Ted Sorensen had announced that the time had come for the United States and Soviet Union to reconsider the Cold War, it might be a compelling and eloquent statement, but little else. When the president said it, it helped shift international relations.

There is a distinction between authorship of a speech and ownership. Ferreting out the specific author of a memorable line can be an interesting exercise (enough to write whole books about), though often a fruitless one. But of greater importance is not who first set specific

---

*Sorensen told Richard Tofel that the first draft of the inaugural address, which he quoted in *Kennedy*, no longer exists. "Finally, when asked if he destroyed the first draft of the Kennedy inaugural address, Sorensen declines to comment. Noting that some have claimed, over the years, to have the first draft of the speech, he rejoins, 'I know they don't.'" (Tofel, *Sounding*, 53.)

phrases to paper, but the care with which a president adopts them as his own, and how well those words express that president's philosophy and policies. The president must ultimately have ownership of his words—for good or ill—not only because he will be held responsible for them, but because to suggest otherwise risks the possibility that he may not.

FIVE

"Now That's What I Call a News Lead"

NOVEMBER 22, 1963

"The president is dead and the vice-president has been looking for you," Lyndon B. Johnson's chief political operative told Jack Valenti. "He wants you to come out to Love Field and get aboard the airplane." Cliff Carter and Valenti were standing in a basement stairwell of Parkland Memorial Hospital in Dallas. Valenti, Carter, Johnson aide Liz Carpenter, and a Secret Service agent commandeered a car and careered toward Love Field and Air Force One. They squeezed into the office midplane with several Texas Democratic congressmen. When Johnson came in, they rose. "Mr. President, we are ready to carry out any orders you have," Representative Albert Thomas said. Soon Valenti was on the phone to the Justice Department, making sure that they had the exact wording for the presidential oath of office.

Valenti can be seen in the photograph of Johnson taking the oath, the stricken Jackie Kennedy standing next to the forlorn LBJ. To the new president's immediate right is his wife Lady Bird, to her right Representative Thomas, Valenti hunched next to him. Standing at the back of the cabin, eyeglasses catching the camera's flash, is Johnson protégé Bill Moyers.

At 12:42 that afternoon, Moyers was with state representative Ben Barnes and University of Texas regent Frank Erwin at the toney, all-white 40-Acres Club in Austin when he was called to the telephone. Minutes later, Moyers told them: "The president has been shot and is believed dead. The governor has been shot and is critically wounded. The vice president is believed to have been wounded."

The call was from the Secret Service. Johnson had summoned Moyers. Barnes called the head of the Texas state troopers about a plane, and when he dropped Moyers at the Austin airport, a state-owned twin-engine Cessna was waiting.

At Love Field, Moyers boarded Air Force One but was barred from the presidential cabin. "I'm here if you need me," he wrote in a note to LBJ and passed it through. He was quickly ushered in, and at 2:40 pm stood quietly in the back of the cabin as Johnson took the oath.

Johnson had reached out for a pair of trusted friends and advisers. Moyers and Valenti would be key administration players, each with a critical role in shaping the rhetoric of the Johnson presidency. Once the flight was airborne, Johnson turned to Valenti, Moyers, and Carpenter, to prepare some brief remarks for him to give upon his arrival at Andrews Air Force Base outside Washington.

With Carpenter doing the writing, they put together a brief statement. "This is a sad time for every American," it read. "The nation suffers a loss that cannot be weighed. For me it is a deep personal tragedy. I know the nation, and the whole free world, shares the sorrow that Mrs. Kennedy bears. I will do my best. That is all I can do. I ask for God's help—and yours."

Johnson scrawled on it. "Every American" became "free men" and then "all people." He struck "the nation suffers" in favor of "we have suffered." He trimmed "the nation, and the whole free," leaving the more economical "I know the world shares . . ." Finally, he inverted the last sentence, finishing with the request for God's help.

At Andrews, Johnson had to raise his voice to be heard. Insecure about his speaking abilities, probably mindful of his predecessor's great skill, Johnson thought he sounded strident and harsh. Almost immediately he regretted making the statement.

Johnson had a more important statement to make five days later before a joint session of Congress. He wanted the speech to make clear, he told Walter Heller, chairman of the Council of Economic Advisers, that his administration's goal was to move past the tragedy, to promote justice, equality, and plenty, to look forward and start to move on.

Johnson asked Ted Sorensen to write the speech, and John Kenneth Galbraith to contribute. Sorensen and Johnson met on the evening of Monday, November 25. Johnson said he liked Galbraith's draft, but quickly reversed himself when Sorensen said that he did not. "I didn't think it was any ball of *fire*," Johnson said, secret recorders picking up the conversation. "I thought it was something that you could *improve* on."

When Sorensen's draft came in the next day, only a handful of Galbraith's sentences were left, including a couple in the contrapuntal style that Kennedy and Sorensen had favored: Galbraith's "The strong can be just. But the defense of justice requires strength" became the assertion that "the strong can be just in the use of strength—and the just can be strong in the defense of justice." He also kept "In this age when there are no victors in war, but when there can still be losers in peace" almost intact. This sentiment would get a small but key tweak before the final draft, becoming "In this age where there can be no losers in peace and no victors in war . . ."

Johnson took the draft back with him to his home, a French chateau–style house called The Elms in the Spring Valley neighborhood.* He fiddled over it with Valenti and his friend Abe Fortas.† Fortas told Adlai Stevenson that he had "corned it up," Arthur Schlesinger, Jr., recorded in his diary. "The corn is, so far as I am concerned, alien."

Used to having the final pen on a presidential address, Sorensen was displeased. "He is very hurt," Katharine Graham told Johnson some days later. "This is of course a new experience for him (though not, as Feldman and Dick Goodwin somewhat grimly remarked, for others in the White House who used to have to turn their manuscripts over to Ted)," Schlesinger noted in his diary. Sorensen did not see the speech again until it was set and thought it repetitious and poorly organized.

---

*"Every time somebody calls it a chateau, I lose 50,000 votes back in Texas," Johnson once sighed. ("Ormes & the Man," *Time*, November 17, 1961.)

†Fortas was an occasional but regular contributor to LBJ's speeches, a habit that continued even after Johnson put him on the Supreme Court in 1965. This later helped undo LBJ's bid to make him chief justice.

On the car ride down Pennsylvania Avenue to the Capitol to deliver the speech, LBJ turned to Kennedy aides Larry O'Brien and Pierre Salinger, who were in the car along with Sorensen. This is a fine speech, Johnson said, and it's 90 percent Sorensen, only 10 percent Johnson. Sorensen demurred: No, sir, that's not accurate, not more than 50 percent Sorensen.

Johnson replied that Sorensen's 50 percent was best. On that point, Sorensen told the president, they agreed. ("We spent the whole time [going up to deliver the speech] arguing," Johnson told Katherine Graham.)

They should have split the difference: roughly two thirds of the given speech (1,170 of 1,630 words) can be found in Sorensen's first draft, including its mournful opening: "All I have ever possessed I would have gladly given <u>not</u> to be here today." (This was changed slightly in the final speech to become the simpler, more elegant "All I have I would have given gladly <u>not</u> to be standing here today.") Sorensen's draft followed the sentence, "For the greatest leader of our time has been struck down by the foulest deed of our time," with "—and I who cannot fill his shoes must occupy his desk." This latter clause was crossed out.

Overall, the speech was true to the Kennedy-Sorensen style. "In this age when there can be no losers in peace and no victors in war, we must recognize the obligation to match national strength with national restraint. We must be prepared at one and the same time for both the confrontation of power and the limitation of power. We must be ready to defend the national interest and to negotiate the common interest. This is the path that we shall continue to pursue. Those who test our courage will find it strong, and those who seek our friendship will find it honorable. We will demonstrate anew that the strong can be just in the use of strength; and the just can be strong in the defense of justice." One of the speech's signature lines, "Let us continue," appeared in Johnson aide Horace "Buzz" Busby's November 26 draft.

Sorensen stayed on into January, and helped draft the 1964 State of the Union, but resigned to work on his Kennedy memoir. Schlesinger did much the same thing. Mike Feldman ascended to Sorensen's special counsel position, but did not assume his speechwriting responsibilities.

As Johnson started his first full year in the White House, he had to assemble a new team.

Dick Goodwin, having feuded with Sorensen all the way out of the White House in the early Kennedy days, had come to bureaucratic rest in the Peace Corps and was contemplating his next move. One afternoon in mid-March 1964, he was in the White House when he encountered the president, who drew him into the Oval Office. Soon Goodwin was writing a statement to help extricate Johnson from a diplomatic spat of his causing with Panama.

"He's got good sentence structure," Moyers, who knew Goodwin from the Peace Corps, had told Johnson days earlier, when they were contemplating bringing Goodwin in. "He'll balance it, weigh it, make it rhyme here and there. . . . Not as good as Sorensen, of course, but pretty good."

The Panama speech a success, another assignment followed, for a Democratic Party event. By the end of the month, Goodwin was reinstalled in his old West Wing office as the president's principal speechwriter. He saw an opportunity, in the tradition of Rosenman, Clifford, Hughes, and his mentor and rival Sorensen, to help influence not only how but what the president communicated. "The two roles—writer and policymaker—were symbiotic," he later wrote. "Active participation made accurate articulation likely; personal contact with the president made it far easier to ensure that his public statements reflected his thoughts and philosophy, the natural cadences of his voice, and his distinctive mannerisms of expression."

Goodwin became skilled and dogged at controlling speech drafts. He later advised one new speechwriter to wait until the last possible moment before submitting a text: that way you can make your ideas a fait accompli. There would be no time to secure an alternate draft.

Johnson admired and appreciated Goodwin's skills as both writer and ideas man, but was uneasy with him. "Almost from the outset the president had an instinctual kind of recoiling from Goodwin," Valenti recalled. "He had a feeling fixed neither in specifics nor fact that Goodwin was not the best influence and that Goodwin might at some time turn on him. He was unable to put this in more specifics, but it was that occult instinct of the president working overtime. He searched out Goodwin's character through some dimly lit passageways that I wasn't able to navigate."

Goodwin, though, was delighted to be back in the fray and to be working for Johnson, a president whose political views seemed to match his own. "Nor were any of my ambitions modest," he later wrote. "Naturally, writing this or any speech would not make me a world-historical figure. But it was a chance to help make history." And from the simple point of view of a writer, he enjoyed working with Johnson more than he had with Kennedy. "It was great working for Johnson. I didn't feel bound by any of the kind of stylistic imperatives of the Kennedy style," he said. "All [Johnson] wanted was a kind of forceful, eloquent, straightforward [speech] and a lot of that was easier to do."

Not immediately. Goodwin sifted transcripts of the speeches that the president had been giving and realized that whoever had written them was trying "to make Johnson a rhetorician, a turner of ornate phrases." Goodwin resolved to strive for something simpler.*

"There's no question about that. Johnson was always intimidated by Banquo's ghost, this specter of Kennedy, this urbane, cool, witty, marvelously elegant man," Valenti recalled. "Johnson always knew he would live under that glistening shadow and it did have some effect on him." The problem was compounded by Johnson's conflicted, contradictory personality. He admired a well-turned phrase and yearned to achieve that level of presidential eloquence. But he portrayed himself as a simple Texas farmer. "While he did not speak that way personally, he wanted his speeches to have sentences . . . march in serried ranks with movement, emotion, feeling," Valenti recalled.

The struggle to find the right balance in Johnson's rhetoric would go on for the course of his term. His insecurities and moods, skills as an

---

*Goodwin was not always successful. He was startled, one day, when Johnson draped his long arm around his shoulder and said, "No more of that Ivy League crap, huh?" (Kenneth Hechler, "These Folks Know the Funny Things at the White House," *Herald-Dispatch*, April 23, 1987.)

extemporaneous speaker and deficiencies with a text, and his inability to adapt to television had push-pull effects on the speechwriting process.

As the remains of the Kennedy legislative agenda gave way to the flood that was the Johnson program, the president was looking for a phrase to encompass the rising flow of proposals moving down Pennsylvania Avenue. Sitting for a television interview with reporters from the three major networks to mark the conclusion of his first hundred days in office, Johnson was asked if he had settled on a slogan to encapsulate his burgeoning legislative program, à la New Deal, Fair Deal, Crusade, or New Frontier. "I have had a lot of things to deal with the first 100 days and I haven't thought of any slogan, but I suppose all of us want a 'better deal,' don't we!" he replied.

Johnson had been "badgering" Goodwin to come up with something. Goodwin had consulted with Eric Goldman, a Princeton historian who had replaced Schlesinger as White House professor-in-residence. Goldman later recalled to Robert Dallek that he suggested to Goodwin the title of Walter Lippmann's book, *The Good Society* (1937).*

There was no small irony in the suggestion: Lippmann's *Good Society* was not only a broadside against Johnson's hero, FDR, but against the New Deal and activist government generally, which he equated with fascism. "Men deceive themselves when they imagine that they take charge of the social order," he wrote. "A directed society must be bellicose and poor. If it is not both bellicose and poor, it cannot be directed." Society could have "no blueprints," Lippmann noted, but should instead be guided by "the really inexorable law of modern society"—the free market. Lippmann's "good society," with

---

*Lippmann's book, in turn, appears to have been named in honor of Graham Wallas's *The Great Society* (1914). Wallas, of the London School of Economics, had been a visiting professor at Harvard when Lippmann was there. Lippmann later described him as one of the great influences on his life. Wallas dedicated the book to Lippmann. While this has led to speculation that Wallas's book was the immediate source of Goodwin's phrase, he had not heard of it. (Henry Brandon, "A Talk with Walter Lippmann, at 80, About This 'Minor Dark Age,'" *New York Times Magazine*, September 14, 1969; "Wallas's 'Great Society,'" letter to the editor by Herman Finer, *New York Times*, December 19, 1964; Safire, *Safire's New Political Dictionary*, 302.)

its emphasis on the market and disdain for activist government, bore little resemblance to the raft of legislative proposals for which Johnson was seeking a name.*

Goodwin tweaked Goldman's suggestion, and produced a draft for the March 4 presentation of the first annual Eleanor Roosevelt Award to Judge Anna Kross that included what he described as a "fragment of rhetorical stuffing"—"great society" (which had not yet achieved capitalization). The phrase immediately caught the attention of both Johnson and Valenti. "It was evident that there was meaning in this phrase far beyond just the phrase 'Great Society,'" Valenti said. "You could fit a lot of what we were trying to do within the curve of this phrase."

As had happened to another Goodwin invention four years earlier—Alliance for Progress—"great society" was held for a more important moment. In the meantime, Goodwin built a whole speech around it: a public expression of the philosophy underlying the Johnson program.

The University of Michigan's commencement address on May 22 was selected. But in the meantime, Johnson could not resist "fondling and caressing this new phrase," as Valenti put it. Starting with Rose Garden remarks to the Montana Territorial Commission on April 17, he used the phrase twenty times before the Ann Arbor speech. The press began to notice. "Johnson Pledges 'Great Society'; Will Visit 4 Needy Areas Today," *The New York Times* reported on April 24. And on May 10, the paper ran a story headlined: "President Urges 'A Great Society.'"

Goodwin pored over policy papers and proposals, consulted with Johnson, Moyers, and anyone else who might have something to contribute. His goal was not to produce a list of programs but an overarching "assertion of purpose." "The country was alive with change: ideas and anger, intellectual protest and physical rebellion," he later noted. "Without this ferment the formulation of the Great Society would not have been possible, not even conceivable." Reading over the final text in the Oval Office the morning he was to deliver it, Johnson's reaction was

---

*By the 1960s, Lippmann's political views had evolved again. He supported Johnson in 1964, writing a series of withering columns about GOP nominee Barry Goldwater. Like so many, he would break with Johnson over Vietnam.

that it was satisfactory. "It ought to do just fine, boys," he told Goodwin and Moyers. "Just what I told you."*

Standing before a crowd of 80,000 at the University of Michigan's stadium, Johnson outlined his vision for the United States:

> *Your imagination, your initiative, and your indignation will determine whether we build a society where progress is the servant of our needs, or a society where old values and new visions are buried under unbridled growth. For in your time we have the opportunity to move not only toward the rich society and the powerful society, but upward to the Great Society.*

The Great Society, he told the students, would emphasize quality of life, starting with equality and justice for all and extending to all aspects of life. "But most of all, the Great Society is not a safe harbor, a resting place, a final objective, a finished work. It is a challenge constantly renewed, beckoning us toward a destiny where the meaning of our lives matches the marvelous products of our labor."

For better or worse—with conservatives deploying the phrase as a term of derision—Johnson's Great Society endured, becoming a symbol of ambitious and well-intentioned government programs.

Weeks after the Ann Arbor address, Hugh Sidey of *Time* asked the president about Goodwin's role in drafting the address.

"I can tell you, the Ann Arbor speech came as the result of a book I read by Barbara Ward," Johnson said, referring to *The Rich Nations and the Poor Nations*. "Dick Goodwin, as far as I know, never saw it. It doesn't make any difference, but I just want to show you that somebody is trying to appear important to you, and I resent that to hell. People on the outside, on the edge, they want to appear that they know something that they don't know." To drive home his point, Johnson drew an organizational chart for the reporter. The name "Goodman"—an intentional misspelling of Goodwin—appeared at the bottom under "Miscellaneous."

• • •

*In fact, Moyers told Robert Dallek, LBJ "never really liked the term Great Society." (Dallek, *Flawed Giant*, 83.)

The torrent of new programs also increased the need for presidential words. Johnson had demanding standards for his speeches, whether they were given to a commencement audience of 80,000 or a bill-signing crowd of 80.

Douglass Cater was a soft-spoken reporter from Montgomery, Alabama, who had spent fourteen years as an editor at *The Reporter*, a weekly newsmagazine. In 1963 he was at a party at the Women's Democratic Club in Washington when Vice President Johnson pulled him aside.

"Doug, I want you to come 'thank' for me," Johnson said.

Cater replied: "What's that? Thank?"

"T-h-i-n-k!" Johnson said, perhaps regretting his offer. "Don't you know the word?"

Cater declined. The following February, he was about to have lunch with Moyers when Johnson invited them both to swim—sans bathing suits—in the White House pool and have lunch. This time Cater was receptive to Johnson's overture, and he started in the administration in May 1964. "Nothing compares with my waterlogged birthday-suit interview with the president," Cater said later. He became Johnson's top education adviser, overseeing the various initiatives in that area, and also in health. A writer with a knack for clear prose, he was involved in virtually all education speeches. He told people that he was a journalist, while speech composition was a job for playwrights.

When possible, Cater passed the work on to one of his assistants, often Ervin Duggan, a former *Washington Post* reporter who joined the staff in 1965. Duggan was particularly good at capturing Johnson's rhetorical voice "because I was from the South and had kind of a wave link—I didn't know the president, but he reminded me . . . of an uncle I had," he recalled. "And in a Method acting way, I could get inside his head. . . . There's a kind of subculture of the South that has to do with the King James Version of the Bible and all sorts of things that southerners at that time were steeped in, and Johnson started recognizing those resonances."

"Get Doo-gan," Johnson would say (mispronouncing his name, which sounds like "Dug-in") when he wanted that southern touch.

The process of helping Johnson find his style moved haphazardly into the 1964 election year. Horace Busby sent a memorandum to Johnson in September fretting about the direction of his speeches. They used to be straightforward arguments for a proposition, but "this approach has been frequently jettisoned or compromised in favor of language uses which read rhythmically but do not always come through effectively or persuasively to the ear. . . . The concept of the words in a speech must fit the man—and personalize the man.

"The people are not nearly as responsive to 'sophistication' in Presidential oratory as Washington has come to assume and believe in the last three years," he went on, and appealed to the president through his political hero. "FDR won his hold on the American people not as an old-school orator, but as a President 'explaining things simply' in his broadcasts from the White House or elsewhere. In this day of complexity, simplicity would be welcomed in this campaign."

Days later, W. J. "Bill" Jorden, a former *New York Times* reporter who had joined the State Department, sent similar advice to Cater. "Too often there is a Kennedy or pseudo-Kennedy tone in prepared remarks," he noted. "I recognize that the President undoubtedly has looked over and approved the message I refer to. This does not change my opinion that the authentic Johnson often is not coming through to the listeners and readers of his words."

Johnson occasionally reached beyond the White House for help with speeches. John Steinbeck, whose novel *The Grapes of Wrath* had won a Pulitzer Prize in 1940 and who had received a Nobel Prize for literature in 1962, had written a Johnson pamphlet for the 1964 Democratic National Convention. He was solicited for a draft of LBJ's 1965 inaugural address. Valenti passed Steinbeck's draft on to Goodwin, who was composing the address, but when he produced *his* first draft, there was no Steinbeck. "Tell Goodwin that either Steinbeck is in, or Goodwin is out," Johnson told Valenti.

"The Great Society, as I see it, is not the ordered, changeless and sterile battalion of the ants," Steinbeck had written. "It is the miracle of becoming—always becoming, trying, probing—falling, resting and trying again—but always gaining a little—not perfect but perfectible." Goodwin included that phrase.

And while this would prove the extent of Steinbeck's participation as a presidential ghost—Valenti later told a prospective speechwriter that Steinbeck "fell flat on his face"—it did not mark the limit of his relationship with the administration. He would continue to send Valenti, and by extension Johnson, a stream of policy advice on a range of subjects.

A five-page handwritten letter on April 20, 1964, for example, focused on the problem of "the drop outs, the delinquents, the unemployed and uninterested boys who are flooding the market with directionless misery, with restlessness and in many cases with destructiveness and violence." "It is far from a small problem," Steinbeck stressed. "There is a terrible unspent energy present in the destructiveness of these boys. They are bored, cynical and hopeless." Steinbeck proposed creating "Disaster Units," which would be populated by boys between the ages of sixteen and twenty-one, some voluntarily and some at the instruction of the courts and other legal authorities who deal with delinquents. These units would deal with the aftereffects of not only natural disasters but "civic difficulties having to do with civil rights, poverty, and other misfortunes." They would be "the President's Own," a sort of juvenile, disaster-oriented Praetorian Guard. "The strongest of these boys are drawn to violence," Steinbeck pointed out. "Alright, then let's give them or some of them some real violence, but creative violence, not the causing of it but the control of it."

And he was full of foreign policy suggestions. On May 19, he suggested testing Cuban antiaircraft batteries with drones or high-altitude balloons carrying a large square of aluminum. "It makes a lovely picture on the radar screen."

As for Southeast Asia, he suggested that because Red Chinese troops had aided North Korea, Taiwanese leader Chiang Kai-shek ("a rascal," but "our rascal") might deploy troops to assist in Vietnam.

Johnson's initial public communications strategy on Vietnam had essentially been to ignore it. Goodwin had drafted dozens of foreign policy speeches in the 1964 campaign but none focused on Vietnam. The 1965 State of the Union spent a total of 132 words on the issue.

On February 9, 1965, Moyers sent Johnson a memorandum suggesting that the president devote his first speech outside of Washington since the inaugural—an address at the University of Kentucky—to Vietnam. "It will be difficult—in light of all that has happened in the last few days—were you not to mention Vietnam," Moyers noted, probably referring to a Northern Vietnamese attack two days earlier that had killed seven U.S. soldiers and wounded eighty others. Moyers advocated for a "White Paper"–type speech, which would lay out the situation in detail. "Here is a chance to use the Office as an instrument of education, not just as a means of inspiration. . . . I honestly believe it would reinforce your hand, be a source of renewed energy to freedom-loving peoples around the world, and give the American people a rare glimpse into the _real_ nature of the struggle in which we are involved in Southeast Asia."

Speaking at the University of Kentucky on February 22, Johnson discussed the importance of the United States engaging with the rest of the world. He did not mention Vietnam.

Five days later, Busby weighed in. "I have some concerns about continuing public silence on Vietnam," he wrote in a memorandum. "If the people could hear you speak to the small groups at the White House, I am certain the confidence and support they would extend to you would be overwhelming—and would be effectively felt in the Congress itself. The consequences of the public not hearing you speak in this manner and spirit disturbs me."

The images charged the nation: Peaceful marchers, many in their Sunday best, trying to cross the Edmund Pettus Bridge out of Selma, Alabama, on March 7, 1965. They were confronted by vicious thugs in law enforcement garb. There was the tear gas, the frenzied swinging of clubs, and the sickening noise of wood slapping into flesh. These shattering scenes focused the nation's attention once again on the civil rights struggle.

Alabama governor George Wallace met with Johnson in the Oval

Office on Saturday, March 13, at Wallace's request, to discuss how best to maintain order in his state. Gripping his guest's arm, Johnson led him to a low-slung couch by the fireplace, taking for himself a high rocking chair. Having achieved the physical high ground, Johnson leaned in close, lowering his six-foot-four bulk over the governor. "Well, governor, you wanted to see me."

This was the "Johnson treatment," the president's full-body persuasion technique. An accomplished debater and tactician, Johnson was adept at physical persuasion as well—invading personal space, literally putting his interlocutor in uncomfortable positions—whatever it would take to keep the other person off balance. Matching the physical treatment with alternating flattery, persuasion, bullying, Johnson would wear his target down.

In intimate settings, Valenti recalled, Johnson "was like an avalanche: irresistible." Wallace received the full treatment for hours that day. "What do you want left after you when you die?" Johnson asked the governor. "Do you want a Great . . . Big . . . Marble monument that reads, 'George Wallace—He Built'? . . . Or do you want a little piece of scrawny pine board lying across that harsh, caliche soil, that reads, 'George Wallace—He Hated'?"

"Hell, if I'd stayed in there much longer, he'd have had me coming out for civil rights," Wallace would tell the press.

The upshot was that Wallace asked the federal government to intervene. Johnson had decided that the moment had come to press the attack on voting rights. He summoned congressional leaders to the Cabinet Room on Sunday, March 14, to consult with them on the timing for a voting rights bill—an exercise designed to elicit an invitation to speak before a joint session.

Dick Goodwin and his wife were at dinner at Arthur Schlesinger's Georgetown home when word arrived that the president was going to address the Congress the next day. Goodwin was apprehensive upon his return home. Would he be summoned? But no word came.

Valenti was camped outside Goodwin's second-floor West Wing office when he arrived the next morning. "He needs a speech from you . . . right away," Valenti said.

Horace Busby had been preparing a written message to accompany

the legislation up to the Hill, going through five drafts from late February into mid-March. Valenti had selected Busby to draft the statement,
but when Johnson found that out Monday morning, LBJ sat bolt upright in his bed: "The hell you did. Don't you know a liberal Jew has his
hand on the pulse of America? And you assign the most important
speech of my life to a Texas public relations man? Get Dick to do it. And
now!"

Goodwin would have to complete the speech by midafternoon to
get it onto the TelePrompTer. He locked himself in his office, telling
Valenti that he must not be disturbed. He was interrupted once, around
3 pm. Speaking softly, calmly, Johnson reminded Goodwin of his youth
teaching Mexican-American schoolchildren in Cotulla, Texas. "I
thought you might want to put in a reference to that," the president
said.

Goodwin knew that he was participating in an historical moment.
"There was, uniquely, no need to temper conviction with the reconciling realities of politics, admit to the complexities of debate and the merits of 'the other side,'" he recalled. "There was no other side. Only
justice—upheld or denied. While at the far end of the corridor whose
entrance was a floor beneath my office, there waited a man ready to
match my fervor with his own. And he was the president of the United
States."

Goodwin borrowed from Johnson's past statements and from
Busby's draft, but mostly he drew on his own knowledge of Johnson,
built up over almost a year of close collaboration. "Although I had written the speech, fully believed in what I had written, the document was
pure Johnson," Goodwin would write. "My job was not limited to
guessing what the president might say exactly as he would express it, but
to heighten and polish—illuminate, as it were—his inward beliefs and
natural idiom, to attain not a strained mimicry, but an authenticity of
expression. I would not have written the same speech in the same way
for Kennedy or any other politician, or for myself. It was by me, but it
was for and of the Lyndon Johnson I had carefully studied and come to
know."

As each sheet was torn from his typewriter, Goodwin handed it off
for presidential review. Valenti and especially Moyers gave the speech a

careful edit, as did other presidential aides, likely at Johnson's direction. When Goodwin finished the final page, he looked at his watch and saw to his astonishment that it was six o'clock. He had not made the TelePrompTer deadline. Johnson would have to read the first dozen pages from his looseleaf binder while Valenti crept across the House floor to the machine. "I almost died a thousand deaths getting it here," Valenti whispered to the TelePrompTer operator.

"I speak tonight for the dignity of man and the destiny of democracy," Johnson began. He fixed the civil rights struggle, and specifically the recent Selma confrontations, as historical turning points, like Lexington, Concord, and Appomattox. Framing the battle as neither partisan nor sectional but a moral fight that bore into the soul of the country, Johnson made a moral appeal. "This was the first nation in the history of the world to be founded with a purpose," he said. "The great phrases of that purpose still sound in every American heart, North and South: 'All men are created equal'—'government by consent of the governed'—'give me liberty or give me death.'"

These words and their underlying ideas—that all men should enjoy the benefits of liberty and democracy—had been sanctified by generations of Americans who in many cases died defending them, he reminded his audience. A failure to apply them evenly, he said, "is not only to do injustice, it is to deny America and to dishonor the dead who gave their lives for American freedom."

Passage of a voting rights bill would not be the end of the struggle. "Because it is not just Negroes, but really it is all of us, who must overcome the crippling legacy of bigotry and injustice," he said, pausing. "And we shall overcome."

There was a single clap and then a torrent as the realization washed across the room that the president of the United States had adopted the slogan of the civil rights movement (the spiritual hymn the protestors sang) as his own.

The speech's signature line arrived organically, Goodwin recalled in 2007. "It flowed naturally from the language of the preceding sentences," he said. "It's not like it was deliberately put in there, stuck in there, it just came out of the writing. . . . Did we say we're going to put in a civil rights anthem? No. But that's how it came out and of course that

160

was all on all our minds. How do you know what controls or contrives? What is deliberate or what's accidental? That was in everybody's mind."

The country was electrified. Martin Luther King, Jr., told aides that while he had never before been moved by a white man's speech, he now felt that the cause would succeed. Johnson would sign the 1965 Voting Rights Act into law on August 6.

Letters and telegrams poured in to the White House in the days following the speech. "Perhaps more than any other Negro American, I have reason to rejoice over your historic and eloquent Civil Rights message to the congress and the nation on Monday night," former Eisenhower aide Frederic Morrow, the first black presidential staffer—and speechwriter—wrote Johnson two days later. "It is hard to describe the feeling that came over me as you spoke. It was like hearing the Star Spangled Banner played, or seeing the flag raised somewhere, far away from home."

At the White House, Johnson and Valenti were making sure the spotlight remained fixed on the president. Valenti sent LBJ a memo explaining that he had told any inquiring reporters that the speech was a presidential composition. "He talked out what he wanted to say—and as drafts were prepared in response to his dictation, the President personally edited and revised."*

Valenti refused even to disclose which aides had taken notes as Johnson dictated. "I mention this to point up the interest—and to caution our people NOT to mention names of anyone who had anything to do with the speech else they will take that as evidence of someone doing the principal creative effort." The memo (presumably focused on one specific staff member) reflected Johnson's belief that the White House ghost should remain unseen and unheard by the public. "Remember those assistants of FDR who had a 'passion for anonymity,'" Johnson told speechwriter Robert Hardesty when he joined the staff. "That's what I want you to have: a passion for anonymity. Speechwriters especially."

---

*Valenti maintained for the rest of his life that "we shall overcome" was, as he put it in his memoir, a "personal touch that Johnson had inserted in the speech." (Valenti, *This Time, This Place*, 187.) Nevertheless, the phrase appears in Goodwin's first draft, which is on file at the LBJ Library in Austin.

"Send this to all staff members," LBJ scribbled on the bottom of Valenti's memo.

In the summer of 1965, the staff was starting to bleed. Horace Busby, Johnson's longtime aide whose brief included speechwriting, was preparing to leave in the fall, as was Dick Goodwin. "Most of the stuff I am now doing is trivia," Goodwin wrote in a memo to Moyers. "True, in speechwriting I make a unique contribution, but this has become mostly image-making. In foreign affairs, I have to write what Rusk, Bundy and others want to say; with little chance to reshape their views, or even be heard on them. I have much more scope on domestic affairs, but as you know, that has come almost to a standstill. . . . Essentially I am not a word man—but an idea man—and one who wants to put those ideas into action."

Johnson reacted predictably, alternately flattering and threatening, cajoling and bullying. A bigger house outside of town? Johnson could make it happen. On another night the attitude was that if Goodwin wanted to leave, that was fine, Valenti and others would easily do his work. Then it was back to threats: LBJ had checked with the Pentagon, he could draft—literally draft—Goodwin to stay.

But not even the president could sway Goodwin, a snub the president would not forget. The White House was left with several senior aides who wrote speeches, but without a principal speechwriter.

Valenti, forty-two, had been a prosperous Texas advertising executive and newspaper columnist when he first met Lyndon Johnson in 1957. Watching the senator move among young supporters, Valenti was transfixed. LBJ made an impression on him "that lay somewhere between the fascination of watching a great athlete in motion and the half-fear, half-admiration of seeing a panther on a cliffside, silken, silent, ready to spring," as he later wrote. "From that day forward, I was a Lyndon Johnson man."

He had married Johnson's attractive blond secretary, Mary Margaret Wiley, drawing him deeper into the Johnson orbit. The two couples socialized frequently and the younger man became a favored stepson to the veteran pol. Johnson had brought him on the November

1963 Texas swing as reward for helping to organize it. He would only be gone for two days, Valenti told Mary Margaret.

"Johnson chose me in Dallas to fly back with him, and any one of ten thousand guys could have done that job," Valenti later said, "except I got picked."

Like Harry Hopkins under FDR, Valenti lived in the White House for a time, becoming Johnson's everything specialist, often the first to see him in the morning and last to see him at night. "With his small, flashing eyes, metallic suits, riverboat gambler's drawl, and dogged attentiveness, Valenti . . . sometimes seems the caricature of the Presidential man Friday," *Newsweek* reported. His brief ranged from policy advice to the mundane work of tallying delivery time, the number of interruptions for applause, and the length of those interruptions for major addresses. He was editor in chief and contributor.

Valenti wrote with pep, sometimes to his colleagues' dismay. "He would seek to have the singing power of [Thomas] Macaulay and the energy of the Texas PR man," remembered Harry McPherson, who ran speechwriting during much of the latter half of the administration. "And the combination was often just awful."

Joining Valenti in the highest echelons of Johnson's White House retinue was Bill Don Moyers. At twenty-nine, the youngest member of LBJ's staff, Moyers hailed from tiny Marshall in the northeast corner of the Lone Star State. He was a true believer in every sense, having studied Greek in order to read the Bible and early Christian writings in their original texts, and having earned a bachelor of divinity degree from the Southwestern Baptist Theological Seminary in Forth Worth. He drank only a little bit, but had an affection for long, thin 25-cent Fiesta Brazil cigars, which he consumed at a clip of a half dozen per day.

As a fourteen-year-old, Moyers had seen Johnson for the first time. "I remember the sheer presence of the man," he later recalled. "And I thought, 'That's what power is.'" He interned for LBJ and later worked for him in the Senate and presidential campaign. When the Kennedy administration took office, Moyers was installed as the number two man in the Peace Corps.

At the height of the Great Society push, it was Moyers who oversaw and drove the legislative agenda. He hung a framed Thomas Jefferson quote in his White House office: "The care of human life and happiness . . . is the first and only legitimate object of good government," a phrase that he described as the administration's "charter." Moyers was a skilled bureaucratic infighter, and an inveterate practical joker. He once gave Goodwin a terrific scare by sending a fake news story to his office detailing harsh criticisms of LBJ that Goodwin had supposedly made to a reporter.

"Perhaps Moyers's most striking quality is an immense self-assurance, an aura of moral and intellectual certitude that annoys some people but awes and persuades a great many more," an admiring *New York Times Magazine* profile reported.

Joseph Califano, a thirty-four-year-old graduate of Holy Cross and Harvard Law School who hailed from Brooklyn, joined Johnson's staff from the Pentagon in mid-1965. By the end of 1966, Califano became Johnson's top domestic aide. To make sure his assistant was up on current events, Johnson had three televisions installed in Califano's office—one for each network—and ordered wire copy delivered there every half hour. When Johnson telephoned Califano and could not reach him because he was in the bathroom, the president ordered a phone installed there as well.

"It was a very activist world. We weren't waiting for someone to attack us, although many people were," Califano recalled. "We were pumping, pumping, pumping."

During his tenure in the White House, Califano—who as Jimmy Carter's secretary of Health, Education and Welfare would declare smoking tobacco "public health enemy number one"—consumed between two and four packs of cigarettes a day. By 1967 he kept regular cigarettes in one pocket and menthol in the other—that way he could keep puffing when his throat grew raw. "Califano handled the domestic program with the exuberance of a kid who finally made railroad engineer," Johnson press secretary George Christian wrote.

What these men had in common, besides an ability to write, was that it was not their sole or even main occupation. Indeed, excepting the Eisenhower era, that had been a fairly standard setup for presidents and their speechwriters for thirty years: The president's top line aides would help him with his speeches. And it helped their craft for at least two reasons. "You know what he thought," Califano recalled, and "you know where he thought the weaknesses were."

But the push toward the Great Society caused a deluge of small to medium-sized writing assignments—"Rose Garden Rubbish," as Moyers called it—that became an inconvenience for the senior staffers, who were too busy drafting the laws to also have to come up with something for the president to say when he signed them. And it was not just speeches: the Johnson White House also produced a steady stream of written messages, each requiring a surprisingly high rhetorical standard.

In 1965, Busby asked the Democratic National Committee for the fifty best political speeches of the past couple of years and their authors. Forty of the fifty, he was told, had been composed by Bob Hardesty, now thirty-three, born in St. Louis, who was ghostwriting for the U.S. Postmaster General. Valenti hired him that summer, along with Will Sparks, who had been writing for Secretary of Defense Robert McNamara.

The addition of Sparks and Hardesty marked a turning point for presidential speechwriters. It set a new level of specialization: writers in succeeding administrations would be less often in the mold of a Rosenman or a Sorensen, or even a Hughes or Larson back in the Eisenhower years. The Johnson White House was not the first to employ specialized speechcrafters, but before Sparks and Hardesty joined, it was the last not to. More than in many subsequent administrations, however, the Johnson specialists had opportunities to affect policy.

Sparks and Hardesty might roll out as many as five or six statements in a given day. "They were really running a printing press over there," Califano said. Though they shared a suite in the Old Executive Office Building, they were leery of each other, suddenly thrust into the chaos and politics of the White House. Other staffers were bad-mouthing them behind their backs.

One night at eleven o'clock, Hardesty finished his final speech of the day and wandered across to Sparks's office. Sparks had writer's block. Hardesty retrieved a bottle of Virginia Gentleman bourbon from his office and made a proposal: You and I have been eyeing each other, but writers don't compete, and we've got enough troubles anyway, so tell me what the problem is.

From then on, they worked together. One of them could get fired, they reasoned, but not both. They would write individually until they could do so no longer, at which point they would summon a secretary who would take their joint dictation.

The pressure was crushing. Waking in the middle of the night, Hardesty would realize that he had been editing a speech in his dreams. After a particularly stressful day, having caught Johnson's wrath, Califano had, he confided, taken a tall glass of whiskey just to get to sleep. Oh Christ, Hardesty replied, I've been drinking three or four martinis every night when I get home.

"Brevity was the cardinal rule," Hardesty recalled. " 'Four-letter words . . . four-word sentences . . . and four-sentence paragraphs.' Keep it simple. You've got to write it so that the charwoman who cleans the building across the street can understand it." None of the writers took Johnson literally—no one could follow those rules and come up with a serious speech. But they understood that he was exaggerating for effect, as he was prone to do, in an effort to get clarity and simplicity in his speeches.*

Johnson's insistence on the rule of four became something of a running joke in the staff. Califano and Harry McPherson, who would run speechwriting for much of the second term, produced a dummy message to Congress consisting entirely of three-word sentences.

Ben Wattenberg, a Bronx native, freelance reporter and co-author of *This U.S.A.*, a book which had used census data to analyze U.S. politics, joined the staff in 1966 and became so annoyed at the president's claims to being a Texas farmer who required simplicity in his speeches that he wrote a long memorandum. Yes, the Gettysburg Address, for example, was less than three hundred words long, but the first sentence was neither short—thirty words—nor simple. At Moyers's suggestion, he did not send the memo.

One Friday, Hardesty and Sparks realized that they were facing a rare weekend off. Sparks asked his friend how he planned to use the lux-

---

*The secret to writing speeches for Johnson, Sorensen told Schlesinger in January 1964, is "Just make every sentence a new paragraph—and the real triumph is to divide each sentence into several paragraphs." (Schlesinger journal, January 18, 1964.)

uriant free time. "I'm going to go home, drink whiskey, and do nothing for forty-eight hours but think in long, convoluted sentences," Hardesty replied.

Another Johnson rule was that speeches must make news. There were three ways to get a news lead, he told Hardesty: Announce a new program, make a prediction, set a goal. He would frequently call the speechwriter at the last minute, Cater recalled, and ask, "Can't you add something to it that will make it sexy or get us a headline?"

Johnson was obsessed with news, watching the three networks while monitoring the news wire that he had had installed in the Oval Office. When an assistant's POTUS line rang, as often as not Johnson would be asking about a news story off one of the wires.

McPherson once gave Johnson a lengthy disquisition on a particularly knotty policy problem: no matter which course of action the president chose, he explained, disaster would ensue. Finishing his presentation, the aide sat back and awaited the praise that would undoubtedly follow his nuanced analysis of the situation. Johnson stared at him silently. Finally he said: "Therefore?"

"Therefore. That's an important thing to have around Lyndon Johnson," McPherson recalled.

"In an activist administration, certainly like Johnson's in the Great Society, there's a voracious appetite for ideas and the speech becomes an action-forcing event," Duggan recalled. "If the president has to make a speech next Wednesday to a convention of teachers or professors . . . Johnson wanted to take some action and very often it would be the speechwriter who would come up with the action."

Johnson had spoken at Johns Hopkins University in April 1965 on his Vietnam policy, but the issue had still not become preeminent. The president convened key Vietnam advisers in the Cabinet Room on the morning of July 21, starting an intense series of discussions on how to proceed. Secretary of Defense Robert McNamara argued for a sharp escalation, while Under Secretary of State George Ball opposed him, alone. Subsequent gatherings focused not on whether to expand but on how to sell the decision.

Busby weighed in with a four-page memorandum. "<u>What</u> the U.S. is doing in South Viet Nam is not nearly so important as <u>why</u> it is being done," he wrote, pointing up the need for greater public explanation of the issue. "<u>But</u> the available voices within the American Government are saying little, if anything, regarding the <u>why</u>. . . . On reflection, it seems clear to me one failing of our treatment of Viet Nam has been the attempt to de-emphasize it."

The critical issue for Johnson was to prevent the growing war in Vietnam from consuming the Great Society. He "could see and almost touch [his] youthful dream of improving life for more people and in more ways than any other political leader, including FDR," he later told the historian Doris Kearns Goodwin. "I was determined to keep the war from shattering that dream, which meant I simply had no choice but to keep my foreign policy in the wings." On July 28, at an East Room press conference, Johnson announced that the United States' forces in Vietnam were being increased from 75,000 to 125,000.

Advice was coming from all quarters. "People can take almost any amount of hardship and suffering if it is active and visible," Steinbeck wrote Valenti on July 22. "What they cannot take is quiet and stalking hunger with no relief in sight. . . . Why not strike at the basic food factory, the rice paddys [sic]. I suggest that we bomb the paddys with methyline blue [a non-toxic dye] while the flooding is still on, and suggest by leaflet that it is harmless but that it will be followed on by weed killer, which, properly distributed, and it could be done from high altitude bombers, would destroy the basic food supply of the future."*

Goodwin had left in the fall, but had promised to return for the 1966 State of the Union message. It was not a chip Johnson wanted to cash: when Valenti suggested in November that Goodwin write the speech, LBJ rejected the idea. But when he was unsatisfied with Moyers's

*Steinbeck's instincts were on target: The U.S. military had been using herbicides in Vietnam since January 1962. (William F. Warren, "A Review of the Herbicide Program in South Vietnam," Scientific Advisory Group [Navy], August 1968, available online at http://stinet.dtic.mil/cgi-bin/GetTRDoc?AD=AD779797&Location=U2&doc=GetTRDoc.pdf.)

progress drafting the speech—which would come to be known as the "guns and butter" address because he argued that the nation could afford both domestic spending and a war in Southeast Asia—Goodwin was summoned in early January.

A ceaseless week of drafting drove Goodwin to his physical and mental limit in the predawn hours of January 12, the day of delivery. At the end of a thirty-six-hour jag, Goodwin could neither focus on his typewriter keys nor order his thoughts into complete sentences. Summoning the White House doctor, he begged for something to keep him going. "I only need a few more hours, otherwise there's no way I can finish," he said. The doctor produced a syringe partially filled with an unnamed red liquid and jabbed it into Goodwin's shoulder. Goodwin managed to finish the speech, sending it in at 4 am.

At 7:15 am, Johnson summoned Califano, Valenti, Moyers, and a handful of other key aides—but not Goodwin, with whom Johnson had refused to meet—to his bedroom. The speech was "getting there," the president told the group, but it would have to be reorganized and cut by a third. Valenti and Califano locked themselves away and, with staffers banging on the door, they recast it. That afternoon, Johnson edited their new draft, reviewing it in the Oval Office with Abe Fortas and former Truman speechwriter Clark Clifford, shouting his revisions to Califano and Valenti over his speakerphone. The two aides were in Valenti's office, next door, but Johnson would not invite them in.

Even so, he treated them better than he did Goodwin, who was shut out of the process entirely and made to get whatever information he could from his old colleagues. At day's end, he went back to the Mayflower Hotel and collapsed on his bed fully clothed. When the White House operator called with a presidential offer of a ride up to the Hill for the speech, Goodwin said that he would have to call back. He pondered for a moment and then told the hotel operator not to put through any more calls. He would never again speak with Lyndon Johnson. "It was just too much," Goodwin later told Califano. "I couldn't go through with it. I was exhausted and disgusted with the way I was treated."

• • •

Steinbeck's advice continued. In a four-page letter on January 7, 1966, to Valenti, he suggested deploying shotguns ("12-gauge or, if you are man enough, 10-gauge") in Vietnam, due to limited rifle accuracy in bush country: "At forty yards, one spread of [buckshot] will bring down several running men and with only casual aim."

A second idea, Steinbeck added, had been "bugging me for some time." He called it "the Steinbeck super ball." It would be a napalm grenade shaped to the exact size and weight of a baseball. Napalm, in Steinbeck's estimation, was "the most terrifying modern weapon." And "there isn't an American boy over 13 who can't peg a baseball from in-field to home with accuracy. And a grown man with sandlot experience can do much better. It is the natural weapon for Americans." It would be valuable for rooting out snipers and clearing out tunnels. "Besides," he wrote, "the kids would love it." The answer came back that the Pentagon had since 1962 been trying to introduce more shotguns into Vietnam and that the notion of a napalm grenade had been "thoroughly investigated. Unfortunately, there is not enough napalm in anything a man can throw to be as effective as the current incendiaries (white phosphorous and thermite)."

Advice from Johnson's aides focused on the question of when and how to talk about Vietnam. "We have to, simply, logically and honestly, tell the people why we fight, and how enormous are the stakes in their future," Valenti wrote to the president that January. "One reason for some unpopularity of the war is the queasy notion that we ought not be there since our vital interests are not really involved."

Valenti pressed Johnson on the importance of using the presidency to educate the public on the stakes in Southeast Asia. He encouraged LBJ to do a series of ten-minute television appearances—one every six weeks or so—laying out why the United States was in Vietnam, what were the objectives, what kind of progress was being made. Johnson never declined to do it, but never agreed. "I must confess I was never certain why he was so fearful (perhaps that is not the word) or uncertain about television," Valenti admitted.

Decades after the end of the Johnson presidency and the Vietnam War, some of his top aides could not explain LBJ's failure to lead the public with greater care on the issue. "He never felt comfortable with

Vietnam," Valenti said in 2006. "I don't think he ever felt comfortable talking about Vietnam. The answer is, I don't know. I don't think anybody knows."

"Why didn't Johnson do a better job? One of the hard things, one of the real answers to that, painfully, might be that it was almost impossible to make the case," McPherson commented.

The guns-and-butter balance made the whole exercise trickier. Johnson could not push too hard selling the war lest it drown out his domestic priorities. "What he was trying to bring off in the American public is something like a semi-satisfactory sexual experience," McPherson argued in January 1969. "It's like necking, a hard neck, you know, but not going to bed. He knew that if he really did stomp them up and say, 'Kill the little slanty-eyed bastards over there, let's go get them,' that the demand for really winning the war would be overpowering."

Bob Hardesty was dining at home on a March night in 1966 when he received a call from the White House around 9 pm. Johnson was the next day to receive the prestigious Robert A. Goddard Trophy for his work on the space program. He had initially planned on accepting with a perfunctory thank-you, but had decided at the last minute to make a speech—and Hardesty would draft it. Hardesty drove to his office, wrote some remarks, and sent them in to Johnson's night reading. The speech was sitting on his desk the next morning when he arrived at the office, with a presidential note attached: There's not a news lead within five miles of this.

Johnson was to speak at shortly past noon, so Hardesty had a few hours to fix the remarks. He called around to NASA and the National Aeronautics and Space Council, checking the status of the Apollo program. Where do we stand? Will we beat the Soviets to the moon? Hardesty had included standard language reaffirming President Kennedy's promise to put a man on the moon by the end of the decade, but he and the other writers had always been careful not to promise to do it first—the Soviets had, after all, beaten the United States into space, and had achieved the first unmanned soft lunar landing in February. The previous week, NASA administrator James Webb had said,

"There is more chance than I thought a year ago that Russia will be [on the moon] before 1969."

Now Hardesty was being told—unofficially, off the record—that winning the moon race was feasible if the country were willing to spend the money. It was a big if. The initial luster of the moon project had worn off, its worth was increasingly questioned, and Congress had underfunded the program. "We intend to land the first man on the surface of the moon and we intend to do it in this decade of the sixties," Hardesty wrote into Johnson's speech. The president would see the pledge and excise it, he reasoned, but at least he could no longer complain about not having a news lead.

Shortly before he was to speak, Johnson interrupted a meeting with Secretary of State Dean Rusk, former Secretary of State Dean Acheson, and Ambassador "Chip" Bohlen to watch on television as the Gemini VIII rocket launched in Florida. Perhaps it inspired him.

The hairs stood up on the back of Hardesty's neck when, listening to the one o'clock news on his desk radio, he heard the newscaster talk about "a dramatic announcement at the White House." Johnson must not have read the speech through before giving it, he thought. His phone started ringing. Ed Welsh, the executive secretary of the National Aeronautics and Space Council, wanted to know what the hell Hardesty thought he was doing. Do you know you've thrown the entire U.S. space program into chaos? ("I'll bet that's not half what I've thrown the Soviet space program into," Hardesty thought.)

At day's end he got a summons from Valenti and made what he assumed was his parting walk across to the West Wing. But Valenti merely talked about the upcoming speech schedule. Leaving Valenti's office, Hardesty fancied himself home free—until he saw a tall figure silhouetted in the door to the Oval Office. "Robert, aren't you even going to stop long enough to shake hands with your president?" Johnson asked. Enveloping his aide's hand in his own, Johnson smiled. "That speech you wrote for me this morning," the president said, "now that's what I call a news lead."

In a front-page story the next day, *The New York Times* reported that "because of budget cuts, space officials have recently expressed concern over the chances of meeting the deadline," but Johnson's speech "seemed today to be telling the National Aeronautics and Space Administration to get on with the lunar landing job regardless of the difficulties." Far from having forgotten to take out the pledge to win the moon race, the president put his prestige behind the program, laying a challenge to both NASA and the Congress. (That very night, the country was reminded of the program's dangers: After docking with an Agena satellite—the first outer-space docking in history—the Gemini VIII capsule and satellite started a dangerous tumble, which continued after the astronauts detached their ship from the Agena. They returned home safely, but the incident shook a public that had started to view space missions as routine.)

Not everyone approved of such attempts to generate news. "You damned speechwriters spend more money than all the rest of the Executive Branch put together," Charles Schultze, Johnson's director of the Bureau of the Budget, once told Hardesty.

But the speechwriters were not the only offenders. Swearing in Robert Bennett as commissioner of Indian Affairs on April 27, 1966, Johnson communed with the predominately Indian audience and went on an ad-lib tear. "Commissioner Bennett, your President thinks the time has come to put the first Americans first on our agenda," Johnson said. "I want you to put on your hat and go back over there to that Bureau and begin work today on the most comprehensive program for the advancement of the Indians that the government of the United States has ever considered." The audience hollered their approval. An aide on the Council of Economic Advisers spied Sparks and Hardesty standing at the back of the room. "Holy God," the aide said. "Someone run over to the Budget Bureau and get Charlie Schultze. He's giving the country back to the Indians!"

Here was the rub. These programs were not free. "The real menace to a balanced budget around here isn't the departments, it's the speechwriters," Schultze complained to Sparks. This, Sparks wrote in 1971, was shortly after he and Hardesty "had solved a speechwriting problem at two o'clock in the morning by creating a new 'program' with a sexy title which could be used in a Presidential bill-signing ceremony the following morning in the East Room. The last time I looked at that 'program' it carried a price tag of $140,000,000. It was and is a good program for which I make no apologies. . . . But how many chances does a writer get to commit that kind of money to a worthy cause with three paragraphs on a single sheet of paper?"*

Looking for a news lead for a May 1966 Johnson speech at a Democratic Party dinner in Chicago, Hardesty stumbled on the neglected issue of occupational health. "If we can reduce sick leave in this country by only one day per worker every year, we can add $3 billion to our gross national product," Johnson said in the speech. Develop that idea, he told Hardesty. He did, and six days later, speaking to the International Labor Press Association, Johnson directed the Secretary of Health, Education and Welfare to conduct an "intensified study" of all occupational health. The results of that study led to the introduction of the Occupational Safety and Health Act—and the creation of the Occupational Safety and Health Administration or OSHA.

Valenti left the White House on May 15, taking the job as head of the Motion Picture Association of America.† Johnson had not been pleased with the idea ("I choose not to accurately recount what he said because even at this distance I still shudder," Valenti later wrote. "I will say that the nicest thing he called me was 'Benedict Arnold'"), but Valenti was more skilled at handling the president than Goodwin. When he left the staff, it was with LBJ's blessing. "I guess I just didn't want to admit that a man should need another man quite so much," Johnson wrote him.

The speechwriting operation also needed Valenti. The level of controlled chaos that Johnson nourished in his White House grew in the scramble to fill Valenti's duties. In theory, speechwriting would be run by Robert Kintner, an ex-reporter and a former president of NBC News who had joined the administration at the end of March. He had known Johnson since the 1930s; at fifty-eight, he was the oldest of

---

*A speechwriting joke: The origin of "Great Society" was that at three in the morning Goodwin could not come up with the subject for a speech, so he invented a phrase . . . and it ended up costing the country $600 billion.

†Over a year earlier, Johnson had been pushing Sorensen for the same job. (Beschloss, *Taking Charge*, 183.)

Johnson's aides, but he could not cope with the president's mood shifts. "When the president blew up and said, 'I don't like this!' . . . Valenti would just say, 'Oh, it'll pass,'" Hardesty recalled. "But Kintner . . . was terrified of the president. Absolutely terrified."

At the same time, Moyers moved to bring the writing operation under his control. "Looking at the fact instead of the theory, the writing operation continued as it had under Valenti, only without Valenti it continued unhappily," Charles Maguire, a Valenti deputy who continued in the same position under Kintner, said later. "Kintner and I continued to assign speeches, receive the writers' work, send it to the President, talk with the President about speeches, plan speeches in advance—but Bill Moyers seemed to be running the writing operation. It was all very confusing."

Moyers would get hold of the speech drafts and with the help of a new deputy, Ben Wattenberg, would edit, rewrite, or replace them. The addresses that Hardesty and Sparks produced "were really dreadful," Wattenberg thought. "Stuff came out that was just inane, didn't say anything, empty-headed, wooden kind of prose."

"The material that is being developed for [the president's] consideration is not adequate, fresh enough or sufficiently significant," Kintner wrote in a confidential memo to the senior staff on May 17. "This is because Messrs. Sparks and Hardesty have had to dream up the ideas with some help from the departments, but not much."

Kintner tried to lessen the pressure on Hardesty (who shortly left speechwriting for congressional relations) and Sparks by beefing up the staff. He hired news veterans, political operatives, and professional speechwriters. Jack McNulty, William Schoen, and Walter Coyne served in the speechwriting staff at various times. In February 1967, he hired an editor from *Newsweek* named Peter Benchley. Harry Middleton, who later became the director of the Johnson Library, also joined in this period.

But Johnson—ever aware of JFK's "glistening shadow," as Valenti called it—complained about the speeches. "As you know the President has been anxious to improve the quality of his speech material," Kintner wrote to Hardesty and Sparks in July 1966. "The President wants simple sentences; easily understood prose and relatively short addresses."

Kintner later said that Johnson was "always angry" about the drafts he was getting. "He always felt they were inferior to Kennedy's," he said. "I've never known him to be satisfied with a speech, either before, after, or at any point."

The third and most important change in the speechwriting operation in the summer of 1966 was the entry of Harry McPherson into the process. A Hill veteran who had joined the administration in 1965, McPherson had ascended to the special counsel job in 1966. McPherson was a lawyer, though rather by accident. Upon graduating the University of the South in 1949, he went to Columbia University to get his master's. He aspired to become a teacher and a poet but exams showed he did not have the aptitude. After serving in the military during the Korean War, he got his law degree at the University of Texas Law School.

McPherson would ultimately run speechwriting in the last years of the Johnson administration. "McPherson is one of the few lawyers . . . who does not write as if he were riding bareback on a tractor," Valenti noted. A burnt-out Moyers left at the end of 1966, telling the press that "after you've worked with LBJ, you can work with the Devil." Kintner left in the summer of 1967 for health reasons.

The lower-echelon writers, who were the principal target of Johnson's ire, started a complaint that would become common among speechwriters in future administrations: lack of exposure to the president, and for that matter to his top advisers. How could they write for their boss if they were cut off from him and cut out of the policy development process? The writers were doing their job blind, without guidance even from the assistants to the president, Sparks complained to McPherson in a March 1967 writers' meeting. Things would improve immeasurably with more guidance, he added. "That's the ideal world," McPherson shot back. The writers should "try a little adventurism," he said; something "quirky, angular, conscientious."

"There shouldn't be quite the proximity" that a writer would like, Peter Benchley later conceded. But "there should be a great deal more than there is [because it is] difficult to get to know the boss if you don't know whether you're writing to what he wants."

Sometimes the writers took their complaints to the president. They thought in one meeting that they had scored a victory. "All right, damn it," LBJ exclaimed. "I want you to come to every meeting I go to, I want you to talk to everybody I meet, I want you to just see me." The writers were ecstatic at the prospect. The idea was never mentioned again.

Benchley, a former *Newsweek* editor, was a particularly problematic speechwriter. Handsome—"movie star handsome," recalled Middleton, with whom he shared an office—and young, Benchley seemed to operate on his own wavelength. He was "a sort of a different cat," Middleton remembered. "I don't know how to describe Peter but he was a sort of a golden boy." "I was the least competent, most incompetent, least capable person imaginable for that job," Benchley said years later. "He is somewhat [shy], diffident, and young but I believe he could be developed well," Kintner wrote Johnson in February 1967.

He could be funny: along with Wattenberg, Benchley was one of a half dozen or so White House aides whom Liz Carpenter would gather in her office every week or so. They would sip scotch and try to come up with jokes for Johnson's upcoming speeches. Carpenter called it "the White House humor group."

And Benchley could be unintentionally funny: Writing a toast for Johnson to welcome King Mahendra of Nepal for a state dinner on November 1, 1967, he phoneticized all of the foreign names—except that of the country. Johnson, as Benchley recounted it, welcomed the king of the great kingdom of "Nipple."

"I was convinced that Peter was the worst writer I had ever read," McPherson recalled. Tired of rewriting Benchley's "Rose Garden Rubbish," McPherson repeatedly tried to have Benchley fired, but Kintner would always intervene.

One night in 1968, Middleton recalled, Benchley was tracked down by the White House switchboard at a party in Georgetown with an emergency assignment from Califano. But Benchley did not think it a crisis and said he would deal with it in the morning. The next day, Califano summoned Benchley and suggested that he would be happier working for Betty Furness, Johnson's special assistant for consumer affairs.

Are you trying to fire me? Benchley asked.

I wouldn't put it that way, but yes, Califano responded.

Joe, you didn't hire me, Benchley said. He added: If the president wants to fire me, he can do it.

Benchley returned to his office. Califano, according to Middleton, relayed the situation to LBJ. The president summoned McPherson. Every time I pick up *The Washington Post*, Johnson said, I read about how Joe Califano is the second most powerful person in Washington, but he can't fire a writer. You're in charge of the writers, Johnson told McPherson, you take care of it.

McPherson had the same conversation with Benchley. "So Peter came back to the office and the upshot of it was that for the rest of the administration . . . he got no more assignments," Middleton recalled. "He got guitar lessons and he would come back and practice his guitar."

Califano disputes Middleton's account, though he acknowledges that Benchley did linger in his office for a few months: "He didn't get paid," Califano recalled. "The thing about security in those days—we didn't take the badge away from him. . . . He stayed around for a couple of months."*

McPherson laughs and adds: "I don't remember that very much. I think [Middleton] may be exaggerating that a little. . . . I did try to get [Benchley] fired because I just thought he was a bad writer, but I never could do it because of Kintner."

In 1974, Benchley wrote a book about a great white shark that terrorized a New England resort community. It was called *Jaws*. One of the shark's first victims was named Kintner.

Perhaps the writers' biggest problem was that they could not write to LBJ's speaking strengths. He was most effective in relatively small settings, speaking extemporaneously. Lady Bird would say that he was the

---

*In future years Califano would make Benchley the main character in another speechwriting joke: A long-suffering speechwriter promised one last address for his ungrateful boss. The first page of the speech says: "Some say we can't save the cities, improve the military and balance the budget—I say we can, and I'm going to tell you how right now. Some say you can't have environmental protection and economic growth—I say we can and I'm going to tell you how right now." The politician flips to the second page of the speech, which simply says: "OK, now you're on your own." (Author interview with Joseph Califano.)

last of the courthouse square politicians—meaning a crowd that could fit into a small-town courthouse square was the ideal size for Johnson.

"He is one of the last spellbinders," said Charles Maguire, the Valenti assistant who would himself help run the speechwriting operation by the end of the LBJ's tenure. "He has within himself a forty foot shelf of anthologies, thesauruses, dictionaries, histories, lexicons, all of which he can draw up by the virtue of his magnificent memory and deliver with great effectiveness." He generally made ad-libs, almost always more effective than his prepared remarks, on smaller and mid-sized speeches rather than big ones.

"I always considered myself successful when Johnson liked what he was saying so much that he'd start ad-libbing," Hardesty said. If Johnson simply read it through, it was a sign that the speech had not engaged him. "When he started ad-libbing he could just be wonderful and really himself."

Johnson once was explaining to a roomful of aides the kind of emotional connection he wanted to make with an audience, Ervin Duggan recalled. "I want to get my hand up their dresses," he said, mildly shocking his audience. Johnson paused for a moment. "Now somebody is probably going to eventually leak to the press that I said this and there'll be a story about the barnyard humor or LBJ's crude way of expressing himself. But I'll tell you one thing: None of you will ever forget it."

Johnson's problems speaking from a text were compounded by the fact that television had become the dominant medium. He had been one of the first television station owners in the country, but he was never able to adjust himself to the camera's unblinking lens. Johnson rarely allowed himself to flash his witty, gregarious private side. Harry Truman faced a similar situation: he had succeeded a popular and eloquent president from whom he had to find a way to distinguish his rhetorical style. And like LBJ, Truman was less effective when tethered to a written text than when he ad-libbed and showed his winning, informal side. But whereas Truman allowed his speechwriters to help him develop that strength, Johnson was unwilling or unable to do so.

Kintner sent Johnson a steady stream of memoranda suggesting ways to improve his television performance, but they did little good. After virtually every appearance LBJ would get feedback from other friends in network television. "No matter how much he was told or how much television was explained to him, he could never acclimate himself to the new media," Kintner recalled. "He treated it like an old time southern orator, rather than Jack Kennedy's conversational treatment."

Johnson broke through once. His 114th press conference, on the morning of November 17, 1967, started normally, with the president taking questions from behind a podium in the East Room. But eight minutes in, when a reporter asked about his having completed four years in office, LBJ took off his glasses and stepped out from behind the podium. A military aide quietly plugged in the small portable microphone Johnson wore under his jacket. Johnson prowled the stage, displaying the relaxed, engaged, folksy side familiar to aides and small groups. "He waved his arms, chopped the air, drew imaginary lines with his fingers, clutched his glasses, scowled, laughed and ran his voice through a range of sound from high-volume anger to quiet, self-deprecating gentleness," *The New York Times* reported the next day. The courthouse steps had finally been brought to life for the cameras.

His staff was ecstatic after the performance and told him so, justifying their own conclusions with telegrams and phone calls from a public amazed by this new, unfamiliar president. One anonymous Republican congressman told the *Times* that LBJ was "pretty darned effective." Representative Richard Bolling, a Missouri Democrat, told the paper, "he can't be Ronald Reagan. The only way is to be himself. And he was himself today."

Kintner told him that he had to do it more often. Goddammit, Johnson said, unimpressed, I'm not in show business. He never used the lavaliere microphone again, saying that it was insufficiently "presidential."

A number of factors were likely at work: one was Johnson's sense of how a president should act when the nation was watching, especially in measuring himself against his predecessor. Also at work may have been LBJ's sense of himself. On November 17, Johnson the courthouse pol strutted around the stage in his glory. But repeat performances could have brought out the petulant, angry, or self-pitying Johnson. Not all of his ad-libs were effective—it was when departing from the text that LBJ started denouncing "nervous nellies" and "cussers and doubters."

"I think he was especially good that day because he was in a certain kind of balance within himself," McPherson recalled. "He was at ease with himself. There are times when I frankly would not like to see Lyndon Johnson being Lyndon Johnson. I can imagine him a week later, having had this great success, doing it again, and I can imagine him spending the entire thirty minutes berating the press and the Eastern Establishment and all the rest of it, and all the worms would come out just as all the attractive qualities came out in that particular session."

"And so, my friends of many years, my colleagues, my fellow countrymen in your homes tonight," Johnson said, "I have come before you to announce that in this year of nineteen and sixty-eight, I will not, under any circumstances, be a candidate for reelection as President of the United States."

In his mind's eye, Johnson was speaking to a packed House chamber and nationwide television audience, offering a surprise ending to his 1968 State of the Union address. In reality he was in his pajamas, lying in his memorandum- and newspaper-covered bed on a damp, dreary January Sunday, performing for an audience of one: Horace "Buzz" Busby.

It was January 14, three days before he was to give the State of the Union address, and, dissatisfied with the progress made thus far under McPherson's careful hand, Johnson had characteristically called in a raft of other advisers and draftsmen to throw their perspectives into the rhetorical stew. "This goddamn draft they've given me wouldn't make chickens cackle if you waved it at 'em in the dark," Johnson had told Busby on the phone earlier in the day. "It's too long, too dull, too flat, too bureaucratic—every little two-bit bureau in the government has managed to get at least one line in on their pet project.

"I get the best minds in Washington together, and what do they come up with? Vomit," he said, angrily spitting out the words. "Fifty pages of vomit."*

*McPherson, who had produced this "vomit," later described the experience as "the worst" he had ever endured. "Every State of the Union speech has been a trauma for President Johnson," he recalled. "He gets into an incredible mood, horrible mood, and things start flying out. Other people get brought in, everybody but the cook get brought in to make it more personal or human or whatever. I gave up in the last two days, I just couldn't bear it any more." (McPherson OH, LBJ Library, 8.)

LBJ had summoned Busby, among others, to try to get "a little Churchill in this thing." But when Buzz arrived, LBJ revealed his real reason for summoning his old aide: "I have made up my mind," he declared with surprising force. "I can't get peace in Vietnam and be president too."

As Busby tried to absorb what he had just heard, Johnson went on. The Vietnamese, he said, "won't let me have both," while the Congress "doesn't want me to have either."

So he envisioned for Busby the scene on the coming Tuesday when he would read through his report to Congress, and as the final applause thundered on, he would pull two extra pages out of his jacket and drop his political bombshell.

"That ought to surprise the living hell out of them."

Busby's job was to compose this fare-thee-well. He was a logical choice for the assignment—and not just because, as Johnson said, as a *former* White House aide he could be relied upon to keep it a secret.

Buzz had first joined Lyndon Johnson's staff in 1948, finding his new desk in room 504 of the Old House Office Building (today the Cannon House Office Building) surrounded by stack upon stack of books—dozens of them—all by or about Winston Churchill. His first brief for Representative Johnson was to learn to write as Churchill spoke. More broad, he was "to read, think, and come up with new ideas." He would spend much of his seventeen years working for and around Johnson in similar capacities.

Square-faced and quiet, Busby was a graduate of the University of Texas and had worked as a reporter for a year before joining Johnson's staff. A heavy smoker, he sometimes held his cigarette in his mouth at such an angle that, lost in concentration, he would singe his eyeglasses. Middleton, who not only went on to run the Johnson Library but also worked with the president on his memoirs, described Buzz as the writer to whom Johnson felt closest over the years. "You feel each other," Hugh Sidey had once asked Busby. "Yes," he replied, "especially in the silences."

"Ultimately I had fitted into his life in such a way that I sometimes knew more what he wanted to say than he did," Busby told an interviewer in 1981. "Now that's not a grandiose statement. I think that's true in any good relationship between a public figure and a person who writes speeches. . . . You are close enough to the individual that you are really in their mind and in their life, and you know more what they want to say than they do because they don't have time to stop and think about what they want to say."

It was not the first time that LBJ had entertained thoughts of leaving the White House. One morning in June 1964, he told Valenti that he had dictated a withdrawal statement and felt better for it. He would be able to pursue his agenda without accusations of politics. In October 1967, Johnson had summoned White House press secretary George Christian to the ranch and sounded him out about a withdrawal. When Christian was supportive (surprising himself), Johnson dispatched him to confer with Texas governor John Connally, a longtime friend who also supported withdrawal. The two men composed a statement on which Mrs. Johnson signed off.

Like those two statements, the one Busby drew up for the 1968 State of the Union address went unused. Explaining to Christian afterwards why he did not make the dramatic announcement, LBJ told a story likely more humorous than truthful: Hours before the State of the Union, he showed Busby's draft statement to Lady Bird, who approved. Standing in the House chamber, reaching the end of the speech, he told Christian, he had felt his pockets for the statement. "This is a hell of a note," he thought to himself. "The President of the United States can't quit because his wife's got the papers in her purse."

The other explanation he proffered seems more plausible: "It just didn't fit," Johnson had said. "I couldn't go in there and lay out a big program and then say, 'Okay, here's all this work to do, and by the way, so long. I'm leaving.'"

The problem, of course, was the tension between an elusive victory in Vietnam and the big program he continued to push at home. In the 1966 State of the Union Johnson had declared, in effect, that it was not necessary to choose between guns and butter, that the country could have both. Now he was faced with the reality that he had been wrong. As a member of the U.S. Senate, Johnson had watched a conflict in Asia consume and destroy Harry Truman's presidency. Korea and accusations of losing China killed Truman and the Fair Deal, Califano recalled Johnson saying. "We're not going to let that happen to the Great Society," he would add.

McPherson's early drafts of the State of the Union address had contained a long section on Vietnam that Johnson removed. He preferred to focus on that in a separate speech, he said. With so much opposition to the war in the House, he did not want to dwell on it there. He instructed McPherson to start drafting a stand-alone address.

At the end of January, the North Vietnamese army and the Vietcong launched a coordinated, nationwide surprise attack that coincided with the Tet holiday. Though militarily a failure, it was a devastating propaganda blow to the United States, whose forces had been caught off guard.

As McPherson consulted and wrote through February and March—to what extent should the speech defend the status quo? should it include an announcement of a pause in the bombing?—Johnson dwelled on his retirement. He brought up the subject at Sunday lunches in the residence with his family, though they would not take him seriously.

On March 12, Minnesota Democratic senator Eugene McCarthy, who had been trailing Johnson badly in polls, took 42 percent in the New Hampshire primary. Like Tet, it was a victory in name only for Johnson. He told McPherson and Califano at a mid-March lunch that he was considering withdrawal. When McPherson tried to argue that Johnson was the only one who could get anything done, Johnson told him that he had it backwards: any of the leading presidential candidates—former Vice President Richard Nixon, McCarthy, or Senator Robert Kennedy—could get their programs through Congress because they would be fresh faces and get honeymoons. "Congress and I are like an old man and woman who've lived together for a hundred years," he said. "We know each other's faults and what little good there is in us. We're tired of each other."

Through February and most of March, the developing speech had essentially been a status quo document—defending the war and rallying support for it. But at a meeting of McPherson and top foreign policy and national security officials in Rusk's office on Thursday, March 28,

Clifford, named Secretary of Defense on March 1, argued that the address would be out of step with the country. McPherson was charged with preparing an alternate draft that instead of attempting once again to rally support for the war, sought negotiations with North Vietnam. He sent two drafts in to Johnson: the original, and the alternative, marked "1A."

When LBJ called McPherson the next morning, he started straight in on edits: "Now, I don't want to say that on page three . . ." McPherson glanced through both drafts—Johnson was referring to the alternative. He had elected to change course on Vietnam. McPherson did not know just how much Johnson was shifting course, though he soon got a hint. Johnson and his senior staff spent Saturday, March 30, poring over the speech, discussing the bombing halt, replacement troops, and the like. At the end of the session LBJ asked McPherson where was the peroration? McPherson had pulled it because it had been a remnant of the more truculent original drafts and no longer fit the tone. He promised to draft a new, short one quickly.

"That's OK," Johnson said with a smile. "Make it as long as you want. I may even add one of my own." McPherson turned to Clifford after the president had left. "Jesus, is he going to say sayonara?" Clifford, on the job only four weeks, looked at McPherson as though exhaustion had sapped the White House aide of sense.

But Johnson had already called Busby and asked him to "write out for me what you and I were talking about in January." Busby was summoned to the White House on Sunday, March 31, to keep reworking and revising the statement. "You and I are the only two people who will ever believe that I won't know whether I'm going to do this or not until I get to the last line of my speech on the TelePrompTer," Johnson told his old aide.

Johnson hid him in the residence, away from the prying eyes of the regular White House staff. When LBJ left him to go back to West Wing, Busby retained the draft peroration. "You'd better keep this," he said. "I'm going over to the West Wing for a while and it might fall out of my pocket. I don't want this falling into the hands of the enemy."

Even in the residence, Busby was not safe. "If this happens, I'll never have a chance to vote for Daddy," Luci Nugent, the president's youngest daughter, just of voting age, plaintively told assembled family and friends, including Buzz.

Even without its bombshell ending, the speech was a shock: "Tonight, I have ordered our aircraft and our naval vessels to make no attacks on North Vietnam, except in the area north of the demilitarized zone where the continuing enemy buildup directly threatens allied forward positions and where the movements of their troops and supplies are clearly related to that threat," Johnson began.

But this was just prelude.

> With America's sons in the fields far away, with America's future under challenge right here at home, with our hopes and the world's hopes for peace in the balance every day, I do not believe that I should devote an hour or a day of my time to any personal partisan causes or to any duties other than the awesome duties of this office—the Presidency of your country. Accordingly, I shall not seek, and I will not accept, the nomination of my party for another term as your president.

Even as Johnson was still on the air (his dramatic announcement came at around 9:38 pm), White House staffers were calling key political figures and close friends to spread the news. Democratic National Committee chairman Larry O'Brien, reached at 9:11 pm by White House staffer Larry Temple, reacted matter-of-factly. "Okie doke," he said quickly. "Thanks for calling."

Former Defense Secretary McNamara, reached at 9:17 pm by staffer Marvin Watson, said that it was nice of the president to have him called with the news. Orville Freeman, the Secretary of Agriculture, was "obviously distraught," according Temple. "Good Lord!" Freeman said, reached at 9:18 pm. "I'm astounded. Thank you for giving me this advance call."

Chicago mayor Richard J. Daley was also not calm: "He will not," Daley said, reached at 9:21 pm by Watson. "By God. Oh oh. OK. Thank you."

Johnson had stopped in to see Vice President Hubert H. Humphrey on his way home from church that morning. According to Humphrey's autobiography, Johnson had shown his vice president both possible endings to the speech, saying that he had not decided which to use. Reached by Watson at 9:22 pm, Humphrey reacted somewhat oddly: "I thought this is what he tried to talk to me about this morning," Watson's memo has Humphrey saying. "Tell him I am 100 percent for him whatever he does."

Attorney General Ramsey Clark, reached by Temple at 9:29 pm, was practically struck dumb, pausing for a long moment before answering almost inaudibly, "OK. Thank you for calling me." Speaker of the House John McCormack "appeared stunned" and "speechless," White House aide Barefoot Sanders recorded. Other top Democrats in the Congress were also astonished. An unhappy Senator Richard Russell, who had mentored Johnson but sharply disagreed with him on civil rights, thought the move was "a helluva mistake," according to Sanders's memo. "Great mass of American people are for him. All this hurrahing comes from a small minority," Sanders recorded.

Senator Mike Mansfield, the Democratic leader, said that excepting the last two minutes, he thought it Johnson's finest speech. Several Democratic politicians wanted to know who would carry the standard in Johnson's place. "Will Humphrey be the man?" Senator Russell Long of Louisiana asked, as did Senator Robert Byrd of West Virginia.

Newspaper publisher Eugene Pulliam, a Republican who had supported Johnson in 1964, offered to organize a draft of the president at the Democratic Convention. Representative Cornelius Gallagher, a New Jersey Democrat, agreed. "We have the delegates," he said. "We have the votes." Illinois Democrat Roman Pucinski flatly guaranteed a draft. "He is whistling Dixie in the grave yard," Pucinski said. "He will be drafted. He will be nominated. He will be elected. He will serve."

At the White House, they knew better. "Afterwards, there were bottles pulled out and some rather masochistic drinking done in the lower depths of the White House," Maguire recalled. The revelry was halted temporarily when Cater realized that he still had to finish a speech for the next day. Much laughter was had about the problem of getting a news lead out of it.

SIX

"Concern for Image Must Rank with Concern for Substance"

JANUARY 18, 1969

Richard Nixon and Raymond Price finished working on the inaugural address at around midnight on Saturday, January 18, in Nixon's Pierre Hotel suite in New York City. Nixon split a bottle of Heineken with his speechwriter and put his feet up on the desk. "Only the short ones are remembered," he had told Price. "Lincoln's second was a great one—Theodore Roosevelt's was damn good, even though it came in the middle of his presidency. Wilson's was very good, and FDR's first. Kennedy's basically stands up because it has some good phrases, and because it caught the mood and it caught himself."

Ray Price had spent two years running the editorial page of the liberal Republican *New York Herald Tribune* before it folded in late 1966. He had written the *Tribune*'s editorial endorsing Lyndon Johnson in 1964. Nixon had called him in February 1967, and despite Price's initial skepticism, he had signed on. He went for lofty, philosophical rhetoric.

Nixon had drawn ideas from sources that ranged from the previous inaugurals to top aides such as Henry Kissinger, who would serve as national security adviser, and domestic policy aide Daniel Patrick Moynihan to friends including the Reverend Billy Graham and *Laugh-In* scriptwriter Paul Keyes.* Kissinger contributed a couple of sentences that had been negotiated with Soviet representatives as a public affirmation that the new administration would seek more relaxed relations.† Price had made a key contribution in an early draft, suggesting that the country should "lower our voices." The speech had taken form in the final week before the inauguration. Price joined Nixon in Key Biscayne, Florida, for the final push, and they flew to New York City a few days before the swearing-in, where they finished the speech on the 18th.

January 20 was cold, raw, and overcast, with dark clouds threatening. "Greatness comes in simple trappings," Nixon told the country.

> *The simple things are the ones most needed today if we are to surmount what divides us, and cement what unites us. To lower our voices would be a simple thing. In these difficult years, America has suffered from a fever of words; from inflated rhetoric that promises more than it can deliver; from angry rhetoric that fans discontents into hatreds; from bombastic rhetoric that postures instead of persuading. We cannot learn from one another until we stop shouting at one another—until we speak quietly enough so that our words can be heard as well as our voices.*

In many ways, Nixon's eloquent address echoed his old rival John F. Kennedy's: lofty talk of summonses, contrapuntal phrasing ("We find ourselves rich in goods but ragged in spirit; reaching with magnificent precision for the moon, but falling into raucous discord on earth"), and at least one instance of borrowed language (Kennedy: "Finally, to those

---

*Nixon had made a cameo on *Laugh-In* on September 16, 1968, delivering the show's signature line in the form of a surprised question—"Sock it to *me*?" The producers tried to get Democratic nominee Hubert Humphrey to make a similar appearance—saying, "I'll sock it to you, Dick!"—but he declined. Humphrey later said that not doing the show might have cost him the election. (Elizabeth Kolbert, "Stooping to Conquer," *The New Yorker*, April 19, 2004.)

†Kissinger submitted: "To those who, for most of the postwar period, I have opposed and, occasionally, threatened us, I repeat what I have already said: let the coming years be a time of negotiation rather than confrontation. During this administration the lines of communication will always be open," which became "After a period of confrontation, we are entering an era of negotiation. Let all nations know that during this administration our lines of communication will be open." (Price, *With Nixon*, 43–44.)

nations who would make themselves our adversary . . ." Nixon: "Those who would be our adversaries . . ."). But where Kennedy spoke of bearing "the burden of a long twilight struggle, year in and year out," Nixon promised that he did not "call for a life of grim sacrifice."

A little over a month into his White House tenure, Nixon made his first trip abroad as president, a weeklong European swing that took him through Belgium, Great Britain, Germany, Italy, France, and the Vatican. He read the remarks prepared for the various stages of the trip on the seven-hour flight across the Atlantic.

Nixon was welcomed by King Baudouin I in Brussels on a cool February 23 evening. "It was exactly half a century ago this year, in 1919, that one of America's greatest presidents made an historic postwar visit to what was then a devastated Belgium," the president said. "That was the last occasion on which an American President set foot on Belgian soil." Watching with the rest of the staff, speechwriter William Safire paled. Nixon had pulled those remarks from a folder marked "Statements: Brussels." They were the departure remarks. As the president spoke, Safire feared that Nixon would thank the Belgians for their hospitality and wish them a fond farewell. He did not: He had not liked the arrival remarks, so he had substituted the departure ones and ad-libbed a conclusion.

Bill Safire, public relations expert, had worked with Nixon since the 1950s, and on the 1960 presidential campaign. He had also aided a number of other New York State politicians, including Governor Nelson Rockefeller in his 1964 presidential bid and his 1966 gubernatorial reelection. Safire viewed himself as an ideological centrist or, as he called it, an "opportunist. I would go one way and then the other, depending on the circumstances."

Safire had a playful, clever style, quick with a quip or witticism, both in speeches and in person.* Thirty-nine years old when the administration started, he served as a mentor to younger staffers. "I would like to

---

*Safire once got a lengthy speech draft back from Nixon, with each page crossed out. "Now I know what he doesn't want to say," he quipped. (Author interview with John Andrews.)

have been what Presidentologists call an "intimate adviser," but [White House chief of staff H. R.] Haldeman explained once that Nixon considered me too 'brittle'—that was the President's word for someone who would not hang tough over the long haul—and too much a loner," he later wrote. "No complaints: I am better off in print than in court or in jail."

Nixon next flew on to London, where again he joined his statement to an ad-lib. The following night he was the guest of honor at a small stag dinner at 10 Downing Street. There was tension at the gathering. Expecting Lyndon Johnson to be reelected, Prime Minister Harold Wilson had appointed John Freeman, editor of the left-leaning *New Statesman*, as the new British ambassador to Washington. Freeman had been a Nixon critic for more than a decade and his position in Washington figured to be uncomfortable.

"You could feel the strain in the room, especially from our side, and poor John was perspiring and trying to look at ease," one British diplomat told Safire. Safire had prepared a brief toast for Nixon, who recited it without notes. "They say there's a new Nixon. And they wonder if there's a new Freeman," he said. "Let me set aside all possibility of embarrassment because our roles have changed. He's the new diplomat and I'm the 'new statesman.'" The room broke up.

Safire had written it as a light wordplay, but Nixon delivered it with gravity. "That was one of the kindest and most generous acts I have known in a quarter century in politics," Wilson wrote on the back of his dinner menu. "Just proves a point. You can't guarantee being born a Lord. It is possible—you've shown it—to be born a gentleman. H."

Later, on Air Force One, Nixon told Safire of the note. "That was your crack," he said. "It went over very well."

In West Berlin on February 27, Safire noticed a sign: HO-HA-HAY, NIXON IS OK—from a German soccer chant, "Ho-ha-hay"—and the president quoted it in his speech at a Siemens factory, eliciting a roar from the crowd. It was as close as he dared come to speaking in German: when he quoted Goethe—"Without haste, but without rest"—he did so in English because trying to say it in German would have sounded too much like Kennedy's "Ich bin ein Berliner."

Flying from Berlin to Italy, Nixon summoned Rose Mary Woods, his longtime secretary, and Safire to his private cabin. Kennedy got the Berliners all excited, then let them down, he said. "He is constantly competing with Kennedy—not with Johnson," Safire noted in his diary. "In my London arrival statement, I referred to his accompanying the Queen in 1958 to the dedication of the American Chapel in St. Paul's and recalled the 'unforgettable' playing of the Battle Hymn of the Republic. He killed the paragraph, telling Kissinger: 'That's a Kennedy song'—a reference to the spontaneous singing of the Hymn at the Robert Kennedy funeral train."

Nixon's statements for the trip were originally drafted by the State Department, then rewritten by the National Security Council staff under Kissinger's supervision, and redrafted by the writers, with Kissinger's final approval. Nixon had read all the drafts. Incredible, the stuff the State Department produces, Nixon told Safire. No heart at all or feeling in it. It was always safe, he said, always empty. But while he was pleased with the trip, Nixon was thinking about shaking up the speechwriting process for foreign policy speeches. With Bob Haldeman he discussed adding a speechwriter to the National Security Council who would focus solely on foreign policy.

On March 19, at Safire's invitation, Samuel Rosenman dined in the White House mess with Safire, Price, speechwriter Patrick Buchanan, research and writing staff head James Keogh, and domestic adviser John Ehrlichman. Rosenman said that he was impressed that Nixon had "found his own medium—the televised press conference—so early in his administration, and it comes over so well because those guys [the press] are vultures." Nixon of course had firsthand experience with the power of television: In 1952, he had saved his vice-presidential spot on the GOP ticket when he responded to allegations of a secret slush campaign fund with a speech acknowledging receiving some gifts but refused to give back at least one of them—his little dog, Checkers. In 1960, television viewers thought that Kennedy had won their debates, while radio listeners believed the opposite.

Rosenman compared Nixon's facility for ad-libbing with those of his former bosses. "President Roosevelt could never read, retain and ad-lib the way Nixon does, nor could Truman," Rosenman told his hosts. "President Nixon has a legal mind that is trained for that. And there's no doubt that showing that you know your subject, without notes, instills confidence."*

It was a perceptive comment. Nixon preferred to speak without notes. When he could, he studied his subject as much as possible, outlined his thoughts on yellow legal pads, committed to memory the salient facts and the gist of what he wanted to say, and then spoke. He reminded Buchanan of a "workaholic student" hoping to get high honors on his oral exams. "If you're talking about a disciplinarian, a student, a guy who really worked very, very, very hard on his speeches and his press conferences and really felt the importance of them, that this was a real performance and that he had to get it down just what he wanted to say and precisely, that was Nixon," Buchanan recalled. "You could trust his ad-libbing because he thought about it beforehand," Safire said. "It was as if he had a tape recorder in his head that warned him before he said something that would be a mistake." Raymond Price, who would stay in the administration for the duration and headed the writing staff for two years, estimated that only one in twenty talks that Nixon gave were from a written text. "He was more comfortable without a text than with one," he said. "We had what was called a 'writing and research staff,' not a speechwriting staff," Price noted. "This was deliberate and partly because our writing was not all speeches and Nixon's speeches were not all written."

On most occasions, what Nixon wanted from his writers were "suggested remarks," two to three typed, double-spaced pages with statistics, historical references, juicy quotations, puns, jokes ("My staff was a little concerned today when I told them that tonight we were going to 'turn on' at the White House," went one suggested joke for a ceremony unveiling a new exterior lighting system for the White House in November, 1970). One writer, Lee Huebner, who had a particular talent for them, described "suggested remarks" as "ornaments he would hang

---

*Given that Truman's greatest oratorical strength was his off-the-cuff, extemporaneous style, Rosenman's comment is surprising. He may have meant that Nixon had a sharp grasp of the nuances of policy, whereas Truman's strength was stylistic, not substantive.

on the tree of his outline," akin to a Chinese menu of items Nixon would choose from.

"Whenever he was able to get the time to get to work on his remarks, he invariably used the staff suggestions largely to fuel his own thoughts, and he wound up developing a great deal of material from personal recollections and experience," Keogh recalled.

Of particular importance in the suggested remarks, Nixon thought, were anecdotes that he could weave into a speech. "Anecdotal material is the most important part of the speech," he told Haldeman.

An April 14 meeting of the writing and research staff turned into a discussion of the administration's philosophical thrust. Buchanan said that it was a conservative White House, not a moderately progressive one. Price, Keogh, Safire, and another writer, Jamie Humes, disagreed: moderately progressive sounded about right to them. Price tried to bridge the divide. There is an old Chinese proverb, he said: He who wears two faces sees the entire horizon. It was an apt proverb for Nixon and his writers, and illustrates the ideologically and tonally diverse staff he had assembled. Nixon knew his writers' philosophical predilections and he used them as needed. "Nixon was a reflective man, but he reflected those he wanted to reflect, when he wanted to reflect them," Safire noted.

If Price was the staff liberal and Safire the centrist, Buchanan was the conservative. He had been a twenty-eight-year-old editorial page writer at the *St. Louis Globe-Democrat* when he joined Nixon's staff in early 1966. "It was merely Rose Mary Woods and me," Buchanan recalled. He handled all of Nixon's writing in the 1966 campaign. "My own relationship was very, very close with him," Buchanan said. He would affectionately refer to Nixon as "the Old Man." The word most often used to describe Buchanan was "pugnacious," but he was quick with a hearty laugh. He kept the administration's lines open to the conservative movement, and was wary of influences that he thought pushed the president toward liberalism. He had a sharp, confrontational sense of how to handle the media, prepared Nixon's briefing book for press conferences, and was in charge of the daily news summary. His writing style was "to try to bring it to the concrete rather than these Latinate, abstract words and phrases," Buchanan said. "I was called in when Nixon wanted a strong, tough, direct, pointed statement or speech."

Price, Safire, and Buchanan were Nixon's big three, but the staff had several junior writers. Jamie Humes specialized in historical anecdotes. Lee Huebner had met Nixon in 1963, when he was with the Ripon Society, a liberal GOP group he had helped found. He worked for and traveled with Nixon during the 1964 campaign season. "Lee was our best guy on substance, bar none," Price said. "The most complex [assignment] you could give to Lee, you knew it would be done right. A very first-rate mind, a very thoughtful guy, a very serious guy." Perhaps the speechwriter with the most unusual background was William Gavin, who had been a high school teacher in Philadelphia in 1967 when he wrote a letter to Nixon encouraging him to run for president. It led to a lunch with Nixon's friend Leonard Garment, and eventually to a writing spot on the staff. If Price, Buchanan, and Safire were, in Peggy Noonan's formulation, "Murderer's Row," Gavin said, "I was the utility infielder."

In charge of the writing staff was James Keogh, a former *Time* reporter who had written a biography of Nixon in 1956. His arrival on the campaign after the 1968 Republican Convention marked a shift in the writers' relationship with the candidate. They had had unfettered access to their principal, but once Nixon was officially the GOP nominee, Keogh was interposed as an executive editor. He had a good sense of how to handle the writers, though, Safire recalled, and rarely wrote himself.

By June, Nixon felt that he needed to give a speech reaffirming his conservative credentials. His inaugural had been conciliatory and he had pursued a surprisingly progressive agenda both domestically, where tax reform had benefited low-income workers, and on the foreign front, where he was starting to withdraw troops from Vietnam (he had given a speech on May 14 laying out a number of peace proposals). Aside from a push for an anti-ballistic missile system, he had had surprisingly few run-ins with the progressives. "Richard Nixon realized he was in mortal danger of being perceived as a liberal," Safire wrote. "Worse, he felt this false perception could lead to a weakening of America's national will."

The president was concerned that a leftward drift would spur the peace movement at home and a feeling abroad that America's resolve was weakening. He decided to use his June 4 commencement address at the Air Force Academy in Colorado Springs to dispel the notion that he had softened. He would send a shot across the bows of liberals and adversaries at home and abroad. On May 24, he dispatched Kissinger to brief Buchanan on what should go into the speech.

This was fairly standard procedure. Sometimes Nixon would outline a speech with his writers, but as often he would have one of his inner circle, a Kissinger or Haldeman, give the writer guidance. "Sometimes he would have a firm idea of what he wanted to say," Safire recalled. " 'Don't deviate from this line, Safire. Don't soften this.' And we would give him back what he wanted. Other times he would . . . give a general theme. And then he would be able to get back to campaign speeches from years before—saying, 'Remember when I talked about this? Get some of that feeling into it.' So he would assign the general mood of the speech—'Let's be tough about this one,' or 'Let's take them to the mountaintop.' And then on specifics he would direct you to 'Go see John Connally on this.' "

By choosing Buchanan for the Air Force Academy speech, Nixon signaled that he wanted a blunt piece that would appeal to a conservative base that might be concerned that he was straying. Buchanan delivered. "It is open season on the armed forces," he wrote in his first draft, dated May 25. "The military profession is derided in some of the 'best' circles. Patriotism is considered by some to be a backward practice of the uneducated and unsophisticated men."

Not wholly satisfied with Buchanan's first draft, Nixon assigned the redraft (after a round of Kissinger editing) to Safire, a writer with a more gentle tone. Safire scrapped much of Buchanan's draft, including the patriotism line, and shifted the pitch from a straight attack on supposed anti-military sentiment among the country's elites to a broader indictment of what Safire styled the "new isolationists."

Safire sent Nixon a memo covering his third draft of the address giving his view of the speech. "The time is ripe for your own rhetorical

MIRV*—a speech that explodes at several separate but close targets," Safire wrote, citing seven purposes for the address, from rallying the air force cadets, to showing "the Kennedy crowd" that the Nixon administration could conjure its own villains, to demonstrating for the Russians that the United States would maintain a firm line on national security.

Safire was summoned to Kissinger's home to discuss the speech on Sunday, June 1. The national security adviser tried to dictate a rewrite. Safire refused. Negotiations ensued. "That may seem odd or improper," Safire later wrote. "A speechwriter, one might think, is no policy setter, only an articulation aide whose highest duty is to reflect the desires of the President and his expert adviser. Not so. Nixon knew the predilections and biases of his writers, as well as their respective styles, and if he moved from right to center in writers, he knew what he was doing."

Nixon resurrected much of Buchanan's original text, including the defense of patriotism, which he sharpened by substituting "fetish": "Patriotism is considered by some to be a backward fetish of the uneducated and the unsophisticated," he said in the final address. This was typical Nixon. "He did indeed weigh words. He was a pleasure to work with as a writer," Safire recalled. "He was a real collaborator when it came to a speech and made you feel like a collaborator. So the speechwriters for Nixon were generally happy men. And, I should say, none of us went to jail."

Nixon was an aggressive and intelligent editor. "He would use that as a means of refining ideas and also on challenging policy things and so forth too," Price later recalled. "He said, 'If things don't work on paper, they probably don't work.'" Nixon's edits would spill out from text and curl around the page. "The other writers knew I was reading Nixon's comments because I was turning the page around clockwise," Safire wrote.

The Air Force Academy speech met with the predictable and sought reaction: The old, abrasive Nixon had reared his head. Here was "Nixon

---

*Multiple Independently targetable Reentry Vehicle, an intercontinental ballistic missile that carries multiple warheads capable of hitting separate targets. The question of whether to build MIRVs was under debate at the time.

at his familiar but recently obscured worst," *The New Republic*'s John Osborne wrote. "Here, too, was Nixon precisely as he intended to present himself." The *Detroit Free Press* noted that while "the cries of outrage from the left will increase in the days to come," it was reasonable to think that "Mr. Nixon knew that before he went to Colorado Springs."

"The accurate term to describe the reception to the President's speech is <u>controversial</u>—not hostile," Buchanan wrote in a memo to Nixon on June 6. "While [NBC news anchor Chet] Huntley was beside himself, [ABC News anchor] Howard K. Smith thought the President had done a national service."

At 11 am the next morning, Thursday, June 5, Nixon met at the Newporter Inn near his San Clemente, California, home with the big three writers, as well as Keogh, Haldeman, Ehrlichman, counsel Leonard Garment, and international trade adviser Peter Flanigan. He held forth on his reasons for taking such a belligerent tone in Colorado. "Put yourself in the Russians' position," he said. "All they hear in the U.S. is 'no' to the ABM and MIRV; 'cut the defense budget by fifteen billion'; 'pull out of Vietnam'; 'the arrogance of power.' That's what they read in the papers and see on the television. Now, if all they were to hear from this administration is comments from me about how we really want peace, then they'd be likely to interpret it as weakness. We can't let that happen."

He covered a breadth of topics. Senate Foreign Relations Committee Chairman William J. Fulbright, a sharp Vietnam War critic, was "a fanatic—we don't brief him fully," Nixon said,* whereas Democratic leader Mike Mansfield "is different, we can brief him."

He scolded the writers for being too focused on the written press at the expense of television. He had announced his nomination of Warren Burger for Chief Justice of the Supreme Court in prime time on May 21. In the past, he said, that kind of announcement would have been made at eleven o'clock in the morning so that it would be in both the morning

---

*The Air Force Academy speech "has produced only a few really outraged reactions," including from Fulbright, Buchanan noted to Nixon in his June 6 memo analyzing the reaction. (Pat Buchanan memorandum for the President, June 6, 1969, private papers of Patrick Buchanan.)

and evening papers. "The hell with it," he said. "This way, for eight minutes, forty million people saw it. Eighty percent of people make their minds up on TV." He added: "On remarks—think of TV. Two minutes, something that will get 'em. And the writing press—forget 'em!"

Later, in his memoirs, Nixon wrote that "Since the advent of television as our primary means of communication and source of information modern Presidents must have specialized talents at once more superficial and more complicated than those of their predecessors. They must try to master the art of manipulating the media not only to win in politics but in order to further the programs and causes they believe in; at the same time they must avoid at all costs the charge of trying to manipulate the media. In the modern presidency, concern for image must rank with concern for substance—there is no guarantee that good programs will automatically triumph."

"The President is very much concerned about the level of writing ability," Bob Haldeman noted in talking points for himself dated September 2 for a meeting with Keogh. Nixon wanted to add a new, young writer, "who is not beaten down with eastern cynicism. He's thinking of someone of the type of approach of Billy Graham or Norman Vincent Peale. He feels that the present writers are all now good on facts but not on heart."

Nixon also felt that the writers were not getting enough anecdotal material into his speeches. "What he is looking for is anecdotes, color, etc., perhaps a choice of options that the President can utilize in selecting some memorable phrases for each speech or remarks that he makes," Haldeman's notes stressed. "He is concerned that we turn out excellent intellectual prose, but that it's dull. The point here is that you will agree, I'm sure, that no one remembers much of what's said in a speech except the one or two colorful phrases that become quoted and repeated."

Nixon rarely issued these criticisms directly to his writers. "It was natural for him to be dissatisfied with a lot of things and especially—he had his own style because again he had been a champion debater from high school days on and he hardly ever used texts and so forth," Price recalled. "He didn't complain that way to us. He might have to Bob [Haldeman] but he would be more gentle, I think, in trying to coax and get us a little more in his style.

"He would look at things differently on Tuesday than he would on Wednesday," Price added. "He was a person of changing moods. Which he usually didn't display very much, he kept them pretty much to himself but a lot of changing moods and satisfaction and dissatisfaction and so on. That was simply a fact of life."

Three days later, at a September 12 writing staff meeting, Keogh passed the word. "The President says he likes the substance, the language and all that, but he wants more parables, stories, anecdotes and similes," he told the writers, spurring some wisecracking. "He needs the speechwriting team of Jesus and Aesop," said Gavin, the former teacher. "With Matthew, Mark, Luke and John as staff assistants," Keogh joked.

In the 1968 presidential campaign, Nixon had campaigned on a promise to end the war in Vietnam, what came to be called his "secret" plan for peace. During nine months in office he had sent mixed signals, giving a peace-focused speech on Vietnam in May, and the strongly worded speech in Colorado in June. All the while critics of the war voiced their opposition. A pair of non-violent, nationwide demonstrations—"Moratorium" days—were scheduled for October 15 and November 15. Nixon planned a speech to the nation on November 3, between the two protests, to show he would not be cowed.

The president made sure that word leaked to the press that on the evening of October 15, as protestors circled the White House with candles, he was watching a football game—a display of what he called "cool contempt," the message being that he had better things to do than pay attention to the marchers.* In fact, they were very much on his mind. "Don't get rattled—don't waver—don't react," he wrote across the top of the page that night as he started preparing the address.

---

*It was a neat trick: October 15, 1969, was a Wednesday—not typically a football evening.

More than any modern president, Nixon carved time into his schedule for working on speeches, often spending long hours alone with his thoughts, scribbling on yellow legal pads. "For perhaps three or four days before a major speech, like the Inaugural or the State of the Union or a major foreign policy speech, I try to get totally away from the subject and to put it in the perspective of history—in terms of this country, its place in the world, what we mean," he once told his top aides. For the November 3 speech, Nixon shunned his speechwriters entirely. In the early morning hours of October 22, he wrote in his notes: "They can't defeat us militarily in Vietnam. They can't break South Vietnam. Include a paragraph on *why* we are there. They cannot break us."

As Nixon worked in solitude, speculation built on what he would say. News reports talked about massive withdrawals and bombing reductions. Senate Republican leader Hugh Scott called for a unilateral cease-fire, and House GOP leader Gerald Ford said that all U.S. troops could be out of Vietnam by July. "The 30-minute address to be carried nationwide via television and radio might be used to announce U.S. troop withdrawals beyond the 60,000-man reduction already ordered," *The Washington Post* reported.

"Big problem building, as liberals have (very cleverly) shifted ground away from blasting [Nixon] to saying they're with him," Haldeman wrote in his diary. "The main result is a massive buildup of hopes for major breakthrough in November 3 speech. Problem is there won't be one, and the letdown will be tremendous. Obvious they are intentionally building him up for the biggest possible fall. . . . Under the present situation, a massive adverse reaction could conceivably be developed the next day, and built up over ten days into the November 13–15 demonstrations with horrible results. No real way to stem this now."

On October 24, Nixon retreated to Camp David and worked twelve- to fourteen-hour days, redrafting different portions of the speech. Haldeman cleared most of Nixon's schedule for the following week as he continued to refine it in Washington. He returned to Camp David on Halloween and again worked through the night. Around 4 am, he wrote a sentence asking that "the great silent majority of Americans" support him.

In the 1968 campaign Nixon had talked about "quiet Americans," the "quiet majority," and "the silent center, the millions of people in the middle of the American political spectrum who do not demonstrate, who do not picket or protest loudly." Vice President Spiro Agnew had in May argued that it was "time for America's silent majority to stand up for its rights" and that "America's silent majority is bewildered by irrational protest."* But neither Nixon nor anyone else in the administration yet grasped that the phrase would endure. He later told Safire that if he had thought "silent majority" would be picked up, he would have capitalized it. When Safire first saw the line, it did not grab him either—no catch phrase, he thought, but no harm done.

Nixon called Haldeman at eight o'clock on the morning of November 1 to tell him that the speech was finished. "The baby's just been born!"

Safire received a copy of the final text at 8:30 pm, a half hour before Nixon was scheduled to go on the air. He noticed a minor factual error in the peroration. "Fifty years ago in this very room and at this very desk, President Woodrow Wilson wrote words which caught the imagination of a war-weary world during World War One. He said: 'This is the war to end wars.'" Safire, an expert on political etymology, knew that the phrase came from a book by H. G. Wells with that title, and that Wilson had probably never written it. Safire flagged the mistake for Haldeman, who told him that Nixon is "right down the hall from you, you go ahead in" and let him know. "Better hurry."

Nixon was in a cozy hideaway office he kept in the Executive Office Building, where he did a great deal of his work. Fifteen minutes before the most important speech of his presidency, Nixon must have been startled to hear that Woodrow Wilson's big slogan was not his. "Not many people are as close a student of Wilson as you are," Nixon said. "Leave it in. Let somebody prove he never wrote it." Nevertheless, five minutes before the broadcast, Nixon called Safire to say that he would

---

*Safire notes that John F. Kennedy wrote in *Profiles in Courage*: "They were not all right or all conservatives or all liberals. Some of them may have been representing the actual sentiments of the silent majority of their constituents in opposition to the screams of a vocal minority, but most of them were not." (Safire, *Before the Fall*, 708.)

finesse the issue by crediting Wilson with having said the words rather than having written them.*

Contrary to expectations, Nixon did not unveil conciliatory moves in his speech. He expounded what he called the "Nixon doctrine": that the United States would keep its treaty commitments, provide allies a shield of its nuclear weapons, and that while it would provide economic and military assistance to countries whose freedom was threatened, those nations would primarily have to defend themselves. After laying out the history of the Vietnam conflict, and pointedly noting that he had been warned not to make the war his own, he argued that the United States needed to hang tough in Vietnam. That if he could not withdraw on his terms, there would be no withdrawal.

> *And so tonight—to you, the great silent majority of my fellow Americans—I ask for your support. I pledged in my campaign for the Presidency to end the war in a way that we could win the peace. I have initiated a plan of action which will enable me to keep that pledge. The more support I can have from the American people, the sooner that pledge can be redeemed; for the more divided we are at home, the less likely the enemy is to negotiate at Paris.*

It was, Safire later wrote, "detailed, building a case a lawyer would." This was a hallmark of the Nixon rhetorical style—"He was a logical student of persuasion. Painstakingly prepared," Huebner recalled. Gavin added: " 'Let me make one thing perfectly clear' was of course the famous thing. There was a reason he said that, because he liked clarity. He liked to lay the thing out." Haldeman, in one of his "Talking Papers" on Nixon's rhetorical style, wrote that "The most significant characteristic of the President's speech style in his view is that he builds his speech like a building—a complete organization so that it marches.

---

*At least one viewer noticed the mistake. "Like the reviewer for *Field & Stream* who concentrated on the gamekeeping passages in *Lady Chatterley's Lover*, I read the President's Vietnam speech from my own nutty viewpoint," Richard Hauser of Larchmont, New York, wrote, making the same correction that Safire had. Subsequent research also disclosed that the desk from which Nixon spoke—the Wilson desk—was named not for Woodrow Wilson but for former Vice President Henry Wilson.

He builds one point on the other and they are all related." When she put a Nixon speech into a reading copy, Rose Mary Woods would write them out in outline form, with different sections of paragraphs indented and numbered.

On November 3, the television analysts, expecting a dramatic peace overture, were not persuaded. "Nothing of a substantial nature or a dramatic nature that is new," CBS's Eric Sevareid told viewers. "There wasn't a thing new in this speech," ABC's Bill Lawrence said. "In his campaign he said he had a plan that would end the war and win the peace. He said that again tonight. I still don't know where it is."

At the White House, Nixon dined alone in the Lincoln Sitting Room, and did not watch the television commentary. His daughter Tricia told him it was hostile. "They talked as if they had been listening to a different speech than the one you made," she said. But better news was coming in: Haldeman reported that White House aides, in unsolicited reactions and calls to contacts, were getting positive initial results. Nixon was keyed up and directed the administration's reaction: find out what editors are saying around the country; make sure in the morning to get out the story of wires and letters sent to the White House; criticize the networks for biased news coverage. "Then a plea," Haldeman recorded in his diary: "if only do one thing get 100 vicious dirty calls to *New York Times* and *Washington Post* about their editorials (even though no idea what they'll be)."

The public reaction exceeded Nixon's expectations. The more than 50,000 telegrams and 30,000 letters set new records. An instant Gallup poll showed 77 percent approval. "Very few speeches actually influence the course of history," Nixon wrote in his memoirs. "The November 3 speech was one of them. Its impact came as a surprise to me; it was one thing to make a rhetorical appeal to the Silent Majority—it was another actually to hear from them." The speech became a touchstone for Nixon. He would refer his writers to the November 3 speech as an example of the style he liked.

The call-and-response between president and nation also served as an ideological pivot for Nixon and his administration. "Nixon always had a feeling that 'folks' were with him and were the majority, but he always felt the necessity of winning over the swing voter, the sophisticated folks or folksily sophisticated," Safire noted. "The realization that the old Nixon 'enemies' and the new, all lumped together, did not pose a great threat to Nixon's majority, but might even help solidify it, caused a sea change in the Nixon mood, from an analytical how-do-we-run-against-them to a satisfied run-'em-out-of-town."

It was neither a conscious nor an immediate change, but it was marked. The new mood, Safire wrote, was "superpartisan," building a majority by harping on the unpopularity of the minority. " 'Bring us together,'* never the Nixon watchword, was used to bring 'us' together—the like-minded, the forgotten Americans, the 'good, decent, taxpaying, law-abiding people'—and the best way to do that was to frequently point to the difference between the quiet movers and the noisy 'movement.' "

Nixon called Safire on November 4 to talk about the "Silent Majority" speech. I hope you don't plan to write all of your speeches yourself, Safire told his boss. "No, thanks," the president replied with a chuckle. "I did write this one all by myself, you know, but that's the last one I'm going to do alone for a long time." But it was a grudging admission, not one of deep satisfaction with his speechwriters.

"We have got to discuss the speech writing problem again and see if we can't work a way out," Haldeman wrote in a "personal and confidential" memo to Keogh on November 7. An August speech on welfare, which "had strong input from Safire, who does have considerable ability for a good phrase or cheer line," had worked well. And several speeches on which Nixon had been able to work closely with Price had worked well too, but in those cases Nixon had translated them into "his own method of speaking. The problem is that even Ray does not seem to develop the knack of putting those same directions into his own original product so that the President doesn't have to spend time with him," Haldeman noted, adding, "He feels this need very strongly."

---

*During one of the campaign rallies in 1968 a teenager had held aloft a banner saying: BRING US TOGETHER. Nixon used that sign and sentiment as the focus of his victory remarks the morning after the election.

In particular, Haldeman noted, a September 18 speech to the UN General Assembly and one on Latin America (likely his address to the Inter American Press Association on October 31) "were fine from the standpoint of content, but both were deadly from the standpoint of having to deliver them."

Keogh replied three days later: The United Nations and Latin American speeches were dull because "they were produced under the heavy hand of Henry Kissinger," he told Haldeman. "In the case of the Latin America speech, Henry put Ray through so many drafts with short deadlines and with such insistence on his own organization and language that Ray said later, 'I'm sick of being Henry's stenographer—if we can't change this pattern he'll have to get a new one.'* If this office is to have responsibility for these speeches then we should have control of them." Keogh added: "We continue to work almost entirely in the dark as to what the President wants in specific cases—which makes personalizing difficult."

Nixon thought the writers were talented but not precisely in tune with what he wanted: they were oriented more toward the written than the spoken word, as he had pointed out to them. And there were also in Nixon's attitude hints that he suspected the writers of being—as writers—too much a part of the elites, more interested in egghead arguments over gut appeals that would reach regular folk but that his writers might think lowbrow. "Feels our people are all too intellectual and are ashamed of using the devices and approaches that move people," Haldeman noted in his diary. "Need is to reach folks, not intelligentsia."

"I know how you and Ray hate those letters from folks, but the polls show that's what the people remember," the president told Safire once, explaining why he was inserting into a speech quotes from letters to the White House.

---

*Winston Lord, a National Security Council staffer under Kissinger, sometimes wrote drafts of foreign policy speeches before they were sent over to the main writers. Kissinger repeatedly rejected drafts of one speech, asking each time if it was the best Lord could do. Finally, exasperated, Lord said that yes, it actually was the best he could do. "In that case, now I'll read it," Kissinger said. (CNN interview with Ambassador Winston Lord; transcript on National Security Archive Web site at www.gwu.edu/~nsarchiv/coldwar/interviews/episode-15/lord1.html.)

Nixon told Haldeman that Safire "is too damn smart to want to, to want to just put out a little emotional schmaltz." He said of Price that "it repels him to put in something that is going to grab people."

"The President has the feeling that we still have a major problem regarding the need for a writer in Kissinger's shop to help on speeches," Haldeman's "Talking Paper" for December 15 noted. "The result we get out of Kissinger now is too turgid." Nixon wanted a full-time speechwriter in the shop.

Preparation for the 1970 State of the Union address had begun at what Keogh called a "bull session" in mid-August in San Clemente. Nixon wanted a thematic speech rather than a "laundry list," he told his speechwriters. Discussion picked up again in mid-November when Nixon met with them in the Executive Office Building. He repeated his desire for a thematic State of the Union. "Why do we have to have all that dull stuff about agriculture and cesspools?" he said. "I want an idea speech rather than a pragmatic one. Let's get the dull subjects out of the way in a paragraph toward the beginning." He leaned back and put his feet up on a desk. "Good God," he said with a frown. "Agriculture in a State of the Union isn't worth a damn."

Raymond Price was given the assignment to write the speech, which Nixon said should focus on environment, inflation, and crime. The speech was scheduled for January 22, and Price handed in his first draft on Friday, January 9. Nixon reviewed the speech and told Haldeman that it was an eloquent disaster—no substance, no applause lines, no organization. "Led to a new harangue for a speechwriter who can write a Nixon speech," Haldeman wrote in his diary. "Tough. Hard for Ray to hit it right when he has no direct contact with [Nixon] and no real guidance."

Price had another excuse. Powered by White House doctor–prescribed amphetamines—"greenies"—he had pulled two consecutive all-nighters. "I'd get more done sometimes working through the night," he recalled. Working for a third day without sleep, Price saw that his desk was simultaneously in front of him and against a far wall. It was "complete spatial disorientation." The desk was "in front of me but

I also saw it over there. And this was a little disorienting." A young aide, Richard Blumenthal, got Price home, where he caught up on sleep. Nevertheless, the hallucinations "took several days to settle down," Price remembered. "I would still walk the corridors and see corridors on right angles where there were not. It was sort of unsettling." Even months later he got occasional echoes of the experience.*

Starting Monday, January 12, Haldeman limited Nixon's schedule so that he could work on the speech. Nixon holed up again. The solitude did not induce productivity: he spent Monday and Tuesday engaging in what Haldeman characterized as "forced procrastination." "All this hemming and hawing about getting to work on a major speech is pure Nixon," Haldeman said. "I tried to develop a basic plan for handling it more efficiently but found it was usually best just to clear the decks and let the process run its course. There did not seem to be any way to change Nixon's personal modus operandi."

By Wednesday, Nixon was at Camp David, and after puttering through the morning he finally focused, asking for Price to produce a new section on the environment, Safire one on inflation, and Buchanan one on crime. He wrote notes to himself: "Lift spirit of people . . . Pithy, memorable phrases. Need for a name—Square Deal, Fair Deal, New Deal, New Frontier, Great Society." He stayed at Camp David until Saturday, sleeping late and then working deep into the evenings.

Nixon returned to the White House that night, January 17, and continued to work on the speech. He lit a fire in the Lincoln Sitting Room fireplace—which was blocked up. The resulting alarm caused a scramble of activity, but when everything was cleared, Nixon stayed up working until two thirty. "I love the smell," he said of the lingering smoke.

He finished his work on the speech on Wednesday, January 21, the day before he was to deliver it. "We can be the best clothed, best fed, best housed people in the world, enjoying clean air, clean water, beautiful parks, but we could still be the unhappiest people in the world without

---

*"I don't think it was common," Price added of speechwriters using amphetamines. "I did a lot. It was legal then." (Author interview with Ray Price.)

an indefinable spirit—the lift of a driving dream which has made America, from its beginning, the hope of the world," he told the Congress.

On April 20, 1970, Nixon surprised the nation in a speech broadcast from San Clemente by announcing that he planned to withdraw 150,000 of the 434,000 troops remaining in Vietnam. It was a public relations triumph because he had arranged for leaks to both *The New York Times* and *The Washington Post* saying that the next withdrawal would be in the 40,000 to 50,000 range.

But the seeds were already planted for his next major speech, ten days later, which would have the opposite effect. In Hawaii on April 19, after meeting with the astronauts who had safely returned from the troubled Apollo 13 mission, Nixon had had breakfast with Admiral John McCain, Jr., the head of U.S. military forces in the Pacific, whose son, a navy pilot, was a prisoner of war in Hanoi. Admiral McCain spent an hour and forty minutes discussing Vietnam and Cambodia. The Cambodian government was in danger of falling to the North Vietnamese, he said. If Cambodia fell, it would threaten Vietnamization, the South Vietnamese government—the entire war effort.

The arguments were not new to Nixon, and he found them persuasive. Over the next week and a half, Nixon and Kissinger plotted a joint United States–South Vietnam strike across the border, assaulting North Vietnamese pockets that the U.S. military had been secretly bombing for thirteen months. It was a week in which Nixon's darker, weirder side was on display as the enormity of the decision bore down on him: jags of isolation, multiple viewings of *Patton*, late-night phone calls to Kissinger and other aides. "Our peerless leader has flipped out," the national security adviser told his staff on the evening of Friday, April 24.

The move would require a speech. "This was not the time, the President was sure, for Ray Price's uplift or my tightrope walking," Safire later recalled. Pat Buchanan was the man to provide the proper slant for the speech.

Kissinger had prepared a draft, but Nixon did not like it. He dictated ten or twelve pages to Buchanan, "and said marry this, get this portion of what Kissinger says here, get this in," Buchanan recalled. It was typical Nixon. "Anybody that worked with him on a major speech would find that you're going through draft after draft after draft and it's essentially being turned and twisted and moved around and in the end it's far more him than it is a speechwriter," Buchanan recalled. They went through eight drafts, with Nixon working alone on the speech until after midnight in the Lincoln Sitting Room—more calls to Kissinger—and then to bed. After an hour's sleep, he was up and working again, returning to bed at 5:30 am.

Kissinger briefed the staff on the talking points the evening of the speech. Safire, who asked a number of pointed questions during the session, piped up: "Doesn't this fly in the face of the Nixon Doctrine?" Should the Cambodians not be defending themselves? "We wrote the goddamn Doctrine and we can change it!" Kissinger shot back, probably half kidding. "We never said U.S. troops would never be used."

"The speech gave it to the people 'with the bark on,' as Nixon liked to say—patriotic, angry, stick-with-me-or-else, alternately pious and strident—and he would soon be criticized for heightening and harshening the crisis with his pitch," Safire said.

"If, when the chips are down, the world's most powerful nation, the United States of America, acts like a pitiful helpless giant, the forces of totalitarianism and anarchy will threaten free nations and free institutions throughout the world," Nixon told the nation on April 30, in the speech's best-remembered line. If the November 3 speech had drained "the venom from the protest," Price later wrote, Nixon "did the opposite with his speech announcing the incursion into Cambodia." Campus reaction was swift and vociferous, including at Kent State University in Ohio, where four days later national guardsmen clashed with demonstrators, leaving four students dead.

Foreign policy speechwriting remained an issue throughout 1970. The National Security Council had tried to recruit Lawrence Eagleburger, a former Kissinger aide who had the previous fall joined the U.S. mission to NATO. They had also sought Philip Quigg, an editor with *Foreign Affairs*. Staffers like Winston Lord and—until his resignation over Cambodia—Anthony Lake helped prepare initial drafts; but Nixon wanted someone who could handle the process through the final draft.

"My monthly question," Haldeman wrote to Kissinger aide Al Haig on May 5: "What's happened regarding a foreign policy writer?" On September 14 he wrote, "It is getting kind of ridiculous now, we still have to get a foreign policy writer." And on October 1, "I hate to keep riding on the same subject, but it keeps coming up. We still have to get a foreign policy writer on your staff."

Nixon's speech to be given to the UN General Assembly on October 23 was twice as long as the president had asked for. "The first draft was worse than nothing at all. It was the usual laundry list," Haldeman's "Talking Paper" for a meeting with Haig said. "Apparently there is no way to get State or the NSC to understand the value of a short speech. There is apparently a lack of understanding of the fact that we are in a powerful position and we should act that way."

Haldeman's repeated queries came to nothing. The NSC never hired a speechwriter, and instead stuck with the part-time work of staffers such as Lord. On November 15, Nixon made notes to himself. The third point on his list was that "My speech & idea group is inadequate—but part of the problem is that I have spent too little time with them." By December, Nixon got the idea of having a writer attend all of his meetings with an eye toward, as an aide wrote, "'the little things'—the witticisms and catch-phrases, the expressions, the poignant moments . . . all of which when occurring in the Presidential environment reveal in a variety of ways the warm and generous and human side of the man who serves as President." The anecdotalist would then make sure that the vignettes were placed in the media. Enlisted were Dick Moore—an aide who during the campaign had specialized in gathering local color, and in the White House occasionally wrote or contributed to speeches—and Safire. The rest of the writing staff was soon recruited.

After Keogh left at the end of 1970, Nixon selected Price to take his place as top man in the writing department. Price hired several new writers. One was John Andrews, a young navy veteran who had been working for White House press secretary Ron Ziegler. Andrews was a

Christian Scientist. "He would come reliably along about October with the sniffles, which would lead into full-blown walking pneumonia and keep it until some time in May," speechwriter Noel Koch, who started around the same time, recalled. "But John was a superb writer, he was very, very good and a real clean desk guy."

Andrews was conversant with the Bible, and brought some of the emotional "lift" Nixon sought. He recalled that Kissinger said of him that when Nixon was in a patriotic or flag-waving mood, Andrews was the right ghost, but that if Nixon had to go against his own grain, then Andrews was the wrong choice because his instincts jibed with Nixon's.

"Which wasn't particularly a compliment to Nixon or to me, but I didn't take it amiss," he said. "I was pretty dazzled by rubbing elbows with Henry Kissinger." He quickly became a Nixon favorite. "He's got a sense of contemporary, up-to-date, sharp quick wit," the president told Haldeman in February.

The new year brought another State of the Union and another round of Nixon grousing. On January 12 he called Ehrlichman. "Tell everyone there's to be no contact with the president for the next two days," Nixon said. He wanted time to work alone. "I've read every inaugural speech ever given. And I've read many of the State of the Union speeches. None of them that were over three thousand words were any good."

For the meat of the speech, Nixon was to unveil his plan for a new federalism and reorganization of the government. He planned to reduce the cabinet agencies from twelve to eight, which he viewed as the maximum number of secretaries that a president could have reporting to him. He wanted to reduce the number of social aid programs, too, replacing them with block grants of money. "We've been searching for a slogan," Nixon told Price. "What I've decided on—it's going to shock the people like yourself, the purists, the intellectuals—it's the 'New American Revolution.'"

"The intellectuals." Again, Nixon was suggesting that some of his writers were too highbrow to appreciate the phrase, which the president thought would appeal to his silent majority. Nixon had awakened at 3:30 am with the idea. (Unlike "silent majority," "New American Revolution" was initially capitalized—but did not last nearly as long.)

On January 19, three days before the speech, Haldeman aide Larry Higby sent Safire and others a memo asking for "a list of superlatives" for spinners. The missive had HIGH-PRIORITY stamped in red capitals. Safire thought this a bit heavy-handed. "Somebody is using your name to circulate a supposedly high-priority memo that is an hilarious satire on our public relations efforts," Safire wrote back. "It is a clever put-on—calling for a 'list of superlatives'—but I think you will want to track down and burn any copies in case some historian a century from now sees it and does not realize it was intended to be tongue-in-cheek." Nevertheless, Safire sent Higby nine different superlative descriptions of the speech on the following day.

At 9 pm on Friday, January 22, 1971, Nixon extemporized a quick tribute and moment of silence for Senator Richard Russell, the Georgia Democrat who had died the previous day. Then he congratulated the winners and commiserated with the losers of a recent set of competitive congressional leadership elections. "I know how both of you feel," he said to general laughter. He went on to lay out "six great goals" on his legislative agenda, encompassing his "New American Revolution." "If we act boldly—if we seize this moment and achieve these goals—we can close the gap between promise and performance in American government," he said. "We can bring together the resources of this nation and the spirit of the American people."

Two days later, on Sunday, January 24, Nixon called Safire at home at 6:40 pm to chew over the speech. "How'd you feel about only twelve cheer lines in the State of the Union?" he asked. "Three of them were yours, five were mine and four were Ray's—he doesn't like them you know."

Talk turned to Rosenman's comment that Nixon had made television his medium. "FDR only averaged three or four fireside chats a year, you know," the president said. "But he's right. It's okay to try and deal with the press people, but you have to go directly to the people. That's the way I played the State of the Union—I didn't work to the Congress, I went after the TV audience."

•   •   •

Discussion in mid-November 1971 focused on whether Nixon should speak at the AFL-CIO's annual convention in Bal Harbour, Florida. AFL-CIO chief George Meany had been harshly critical of Nixon and the president did not want to offer him a presidential appearance. On the other hand, Nixon thought that he could appeal to the blue-collar union members or, failing that, put on a "Daniel into the Lions' Den" show for the rest of the country: the solitary president bravely facing his enemies in their lair.

Noel Koch wrote a "barn-burner" of a speech that eschewed the usual litany of administration pro-labor accomplishments in favor of a discussion of where Nixon and the labor movement had differences and where they agreed. Word came back that the president wanted the speech rewritten—he wanted a laundry list speech detailing the administration's labor record.

On Wednesday, November 17, Nixon decided to go to Florida and the trip was slotted in for Friday morning. Meany made sure there was no band in the hall to play "Hail to the Chief" when the president entered. In fact, there was no announcement of his arrival. The president sat in the second row of seats on the stage.

Nixon started by announcing that while he had a prepared text, he was not going to read it. "You like it straight from the shoulder," he told the crowd. "I am going to talk to you about our differences, and I am also going to talk to you about some areas where we agree, and there are several of both, as you know."

Nixon's talent for planned-libbing offers an insight into his appreciation of the twin audiences of his presidential appearances. On the one hand were "folk," or "Joe six-pack," as he liked call them, the silent majority who wanted it "straight from the shoulder." On the other hand were the elites—the media, the politicos, the eggheads. "In one breath, Nixon would dismiss a politician with 'He's not "folks," he'll never understand,' but in the next breath, he could be one of them, telling a speechwriter who was getting too verbose, 'we sophisticates can listen to a speech for a half-an-hour, but after ten minutes the average guy wants a beer,'" Safire later noted.

• • •

1

FDR used a variety of key policy advisers to help write speeches, including Raymond Moley, pictured here with the president-elect going over Roosevelt's first inaugural address.

2

Clark Clifford (above, right) first gained Harry Truman's attention by, among other things, helping organize his regular poker games. Later, Clifford, who became Truman's top aide and ran his speechwriting in the first term, and his assistant, George Elsey (below), were invited to join the games.

3

4

Bryce Harlow (above, left) captured Dwight Eisenhower's plainspoken style, but Ike bridled against his partisanship. Malcolm Moos (below, left), a former political science professor and journalist, had an important role in shaping Ike's famous farewell address.

5

6

Ted Sorensen credited months spent traveling and campaigning with JFK during the late 1950s for his ability to capture the president's rhetorical style. Sorensen and Kennedy had as close and fruitful a collaboration as any president and speechwriter.

7

JFK would occasionally call on others for speech drafts, including historian and White House aide Arthur M. Schlesinger, Jr.

8

LBJ initially mixed in his own top aides, such as Jack Valenti (above, second from right) and Bill Moyers (above, second from left), with JFK holdovers like Ted Sorensen (above, middle; also pictured is Press Secretary Pierre Salinger, above, left). While LBJ was the first president since Eisenhower who had full-time speechwriters, most of his major speeches were written by top policy aides such as (below, from left) Moyers, Valenti, and Horace "Buzz" Busby (also pictured, at right, is aide Marvin Watson).

9

10

Johnson brought former JFK aide Richard Goodwin (above, left) back into the White House, with the support of Moyers (above, middle). LBJ's aides burned out quickly. Goodwin, shown below (left) working on the 1966 State of the Union speech with Valenti (middle) and Joseph Califano (right), was so disgusted with his treatment during the drafting of that address that he never again spoke to Johnson.

11

Richard Nixon, who privately grumbled about his talented group of writers, spent more time than any modern president working on his speeches. He is shown meeting in the Oval Office with his writing staff (left to right): Ray Price, Lee Huebner, Pat Buchanan, Bill Gavin, Jim Keogh, and William Safire. White House Chief of Staff H. R. Haldeman is seated in the background on the couch.

13

Gerald Ford tapped the irascible Robert Hartmann, his longtime aide, to run speechwriting. Hartmann, shown above with Ford shortly before Ford announced his pardon of Richard Nixon, fought a running battle against what he viewed as a "Praetorian Guard" of Nixon holdovers. Ford and Hartmann hired television gag-writer Robert Orben (with Ford in the Oval Office, below), who had enough skill writing speeches that he eventually became the top speechwriter.

14

15

Jimmy Carter had never worked with a speechwriter before the 1976 presidential campaign. He never grew comfortable with speechwriting, and his first chief speechwriter, James Fallows (above, standing next to Carter), quit after growing frustrated with his lack of influence in the White House. Fallows later wrote a devastating critique of the administration. Hendrik Hertzberg was Carter's last chief speechwriter and collaborated on his key speeches during the second half of his term. Perhaps the most notable was the July 1979 speech on the nation's spiritual crisis, which Hertzberg (below) worked on with Carter at Camp David, along with speechwriter Gordon Stewart (below right).

16

17

Ronald Reagan's speechwriters viewed themselves as "Musketeers" protecting the president's conservative rhetoric despite the objections of his more moderate senior staff. Above, Reagan meets with speechwriters (from left to right, on the couch facing the camera, Tony Dolan, Peter Robinson, and Dana Rohrabacher; and from left to right, facing away from the camera, Communications Director Tom Griscom and speechwriters Clark Judge and Josh Gilder) in the Oval Office. Below, Reagan meets with speechwriter Peggy Noonan (second from right) and Communications Director Mari Maseng, herself a former Reagan speechwriter, to discuss his farewell address.

18

19

President George H. W. Bush was never comfortable speaking rhetoric supplied by others. He had good relations with the writers themselves, however: the night before the U.S. invasion of Panama, as the operation was already secretly under way, Bush invited his speechwriters (above, from left, Curt Smith, Dan McGroarty, and Chriss Winston) for a drink in the residence. By the Bush administration, presidential speechwriting had become a sprawling group effort (below).

20

21

Like Carter, Bill Clinton had never worked with speechwriters before his presidential run. Clinton often extemporized from his prepared remarks, but he learned over the course of his two terms to work with the writers. While Clinton preferred plain language, he occasionally indulged in rhetorical lift, as with his 1994 speech memorializing the D-Day invasion, which he discussed (above) on Air Force One with his wife Hillary, Counselor David Gergen, speechwriter Jeremy Rosner, and Chief Speechwriter Don Baer. Below, he worked on the 1997 State of the Union with Baer, Michael Waldman, NSC speechwriter Tony Blinken, and Clinton college roommate Tommy Caplan.

23

Clinton edited his speeches straight through rehearsal, as with the 2000 State of the Union rehearsal with (above, right to left) speechwriters Josh Gottheimer, chief Terry Edmonds, and Jeff Shesol, who worked to enter Clinton's changes as he made them. Below, Clinton works with aides George Stephanopoulos, Jonathan Prince, and Baer.

24

President George W. Bush called his top speechwriters—Michael Gerson, John McConnell, and Matthew Scully—the "Troika" for their habit of writing and editing everything collaboratively. Above, he meets with the Troika and senior aide Karen Hughes (from left, McConnell, Hughes, Bush, Gerson, Scully). Below, he works with Gerson and Hughes hours before delivering his 2002 State of the Union address, in which he described Iraq, Iran, and North Korea as an "axis of evil."

At the start of December, Nixon was on about the speechwriting staff again. "It's not simply writing for the ear," he told Haldeman in a December 2 telephone conversation. "Also they still are not going back and reading how I speak, how you build up a line or something like that. They don't get in tune with the people enough." "Writing for the ear" rather than for the eye was a concept he continued to stress. After saying in one speech that he would not be "cooped up in the White House," he told Safire, "that's the kind of word-picture my mother would have used back in Indiana. You can just feel the chicken coop, with the wires pressing down on the chickens all jammed together in the pen."

Perhaps recognizing the success of the "silent majority" speech, Nixon toyed with the idea of making that process the norm. "I may decide to go very, very hard the other way here now, as to frankly leave the Price group in there to make up statements and the rest and I'll have to do the speech stuff myself," he said. "The speeches they send over to me, there's no fire in the belly. . . . I think that I may have spoiled them myself by taking their remarks over and over again" and using bits and pieces of them.

The State of the Union process had set Nixon off. "He's really concerned about the speech writing problem because Ray blew the fourth draft of the State of the Union, and he thinks we really have trouble on that score," Haldeman wrote in his diary.

A second major speech was also in the works, though it was a secret—or was supposed to be. On January 16, 1972, Safire was enjoying warm sunshine at Tulane Stadium in New Orleans, watching the Dallas Cowboys dismantle the Miami Dolphins in the Super Bowl, when the stadium's public address system paged him to call his office. When he phoned the White House, Larry Higby told him, "This has to be absolutely top secret, but get back here fast." When Safire questioned how secret something could be when announced at the Super Bowl, Higby said that the announcement had been picked up on television for 60 million home viewers. They agreed that no one would suspect a summons for a secret assignment to be so ineptly relayed.

Safire returned to find a memo from Nixon ("Top Secret/Sensitive/Exclusive Eyes Only"):* The president wanted to talk about the peace offers that the United States had made over the years. Kissinger had been making secret trips to Paris to conduct negotiations with the Vietnamese but had met with no progress. In his memo, Nixon explained that Kissinger's staff had produced a draft which was fine on substance, but had "too much turgid prose and too much complex discussion." Nixon told Safire to fill out an outline. He wanted to speak on January 25, five days after the State of the Union.

The problems with the "turgid prose" included too many repetitions of the phrase "I asked Dr. Kissinger"—which Nixon replaced with "I directed." "All the way through, it said 'Dr. Kissinger did this,' 'Dr. Kissinger did that.' I mean it was every third sentence!" Nixon told Haldeman on January 17 in the Oval Office.

Nixon called Haldeman on January 18 to say he was pleased with Safire's effort: the writer had improved on his outline and had gotten the speech in on time. Meanwhile he was holding the draft of the State of the Union closely—so much so that some of the speechwriters asked Haldeman when they would get to see the latest version. "I dunno," the chief of staff said, slumping in his chair and running a pencil through his crew cut. "This may be the first extemporaneous State of the Union in American history."

Nixon had thought of another innovation. He carried two texts with him to the lectern in the House of Representatives at 12:30 pm on Thursday, January 20. The first was the speech, which weighed in at slightly under 4,000 words. The second was a 17,000-word written message with the detailed programmatic list. He hoped to use the system to get the best out of the State of the Union: a briefer, thematic—and television-friendly—speech, but also a document that laid out his agenda and could serve as a map and a discipline for the bureaucracy.

Meanwhile, the January 25 speech had become not only a tale of se-

---

*Safire learned his lesson about classification when working on an October 1970 Vietnam-related speech. Feeling somewhat pompous at handling classified information, he wrote: "Top Secret/Eyes Only, NoForn" (no distribution to foreigners) across the top. When for three days he did not see the draft with the president's edits, he asked Haldeman about it. I'm very sorry, Haldeman said, you're not cleared for Top Secret/Eyes Only material—I can't show it to you. (Author interview with William Safire.)

cret diplomacy but the subject of hidden maneuvering within the White House. Kissinger and Secretary of State William Rogers had a long-running feud as to who should be Nixon's top foreign policy adviser, a squabble that often manifested itself in the creation, editing, and polishing of speech drafts. Kissinger would cut Rogers out of the process, so in this case, Nixon made sure that all drafts were typed by Rose Mary Woods. That way he could oversee distribution of the drafts and make sure that Rogers was not out of the loop.

He instructed Safire, who was consulting with both sides in the drafting, not to take sides. "We were [Nixon's] personal extensions in expressing himself, and could weave in and out as neutrals in his behalf between other, more important appointees," Safire recalled. Safire's neutrality was rendered moot the day before the speech. After a private meeting, Nixon gave Kissinger free rein on the flow. Kissinger called Safire and told him that no more drafts would be forthcoming to either the speechwriter or the Secretary of State. "Isn't that for the president to decide?" Safire asked. "I'm telling you what the president said," Kissinger replied. In this domestic battle over foreign policy, he had won out.

A mid-April speech to the Canadian Parliament precipitated another Nixon blowup. The president was scheduled to address the Parliament on April 14, and two days earlier had gone "into quite a blast" to Haldeman and John Ehrlichman about the speechwriters and having to rewrite the Canadian speech in its sixth draft. "It was the usual tirade," Haldeman noted in his diary. Lee Huebner had rewritten some NSC-supplied passages that Nixon did not want touched.

As usual, the president was more temperate with the writer. He called Huebner and said that because of those stickler foreign policy specialists it would have to be changed back. "The littler you were, the more courteous he would be . . . he was always overly solicitous; you felt badly," Huebner remembered. Nixon invited Huebner up to Camp David for the evening—the only such trip Huebner made—so that he would be on hand if any further changes were required. Of all the speeches that Huebner had worked on, Nixon was the least engaged in this one—surprising for a speech to a foreign legislature.

After dinner that night with the senior staff, Alex Butterfield, Nixon's appointments secretary, suggested that he and Huebner walk the latest draft over to the president's lodge, Nixon having dined alone. They entered the cabin and found the president sitting by himself in the dark, staring out a picture window at the far end of the living room. The scene struck Huebner as spooky. Then Nixon came alive and started trying to make small talk. Are you having a good time at Camp David? he asked. Would you like to go bowling, skeet shooting? No, he added, it was nighttime—skeet shooting would not work. Perhaps a movie?

It was a bizarre and oddly endearing performance. What Huebner did not find out until later was that while he was putting the fine points on the Canada speech, Nixon was overseeing a renewed buildup of air and naval power off the coast of Vietnam, and also pondering a stepped-up bombing campaign, along with the mining of Haiphong Harbor in North Vietnam. And all of this was occurring within weeks of the president's scheduled trip to the Soviet Union for a May 1972 summit. The section Huebner had tried to rewrite, regarding the responsibilities of great powers to act with restraint, had been designed, he later thought, as a message to the Soviets not to let Nixon's new strategy interfere with the trip.

Nixon did not always hide his profane side from his writers. John Andrews, the young Christian Scientist who had been hired in early 1971, was called in to help Nixon and Kissinger draft the address to the nation on May 8 announcing the mining of the North Vietnamese ports. Mindful that the trip to the Soviet Union was now less than two weeks away—Nixon would leave on May 20—Andrews said that he supposed the president would want to send a careful signal to the Soviets that this was a measured response and not meant to upset the summit. Nixon startled him with his response. "I don't give a shit what the Soviets think," he said.

It was not the first time Andrews had heard such language from Nixon. He helped draft the eulogy for J. Edgar Hoover, who died on May 2. The liberals are out there pissing on Hoover's grave, Nixon told him. We're going to go against the grain and tell everyone what a great American he was. "That popped my eyes," Andrews recalled.

The first time that David Gergen, a young naval veteran who had joined the staff as Price's assistant in 1971, heard Nixon cursing, he asked press secretary Ron Ziegler what in the world was going on. "Don't worry," Ziegler replied. "He can get like that. That's a signal that he trusts you when he starts talking like that in front of you."

June brought more writing reinforcements for the gear-up to the re-election campaign. A handful of junior writers were brought in, including a former reporter named Vera Hirschberg, who was the first female presidential speechwriter. Also joining was Aram Bakshian, a self-taught expert—he had not graduated from college—in military and European history who had been writing speeches for Republican National Committee chairman Bob Dole. Bakshian smoked cigars constantly, and played classical music while writing. As one colleague in a later administration described him, he was "brilliant, eccentric—knew everything about history. [He was] born in the wrong place in the wrong century—he really deserved to have been a London gentleman."

On November 7, 1972, Richard Nixon won one of the most lopsided victories in presidential history. He garnered more than 60 percent of the vote, winning forty-nine out of fifty states.

The second term brought the dissolution of the big three speechwriters. Buchanan had remained involved in communications and strategy, but his speechwriting had eased after the Cambodia speech. Price took on a free-floating "house philosopher" role. He tapped David Gergen as his successor, with Huebner as Gergen's deputy. Possessing a great, boisterous laugh, Gergen had a facility for making the office run and was something of a perfectionist. "Gergen was a very smooth broker of projects or viewpoints, self-assured and penetrating, and turned out to be a very good writer himself," Andrews recalled. "He was an excellent editor; he could take a piece of copy and bring it to the next level of polish or succinctness in just a few minutes."

A week after the inaugural, *The New York Times* announced it had hired William Safire as a conservative columnist for its op-ed page. "H

& Buchanan—Safire a conservative? Be sure to inform *Human Events*!" Nixon scrawled on that day's news summary. Safire's last day in the White House was March 21. He shook hands with a Secret Service agent stationed outside the closed door to the Oval Office. "You want to say goodbye to the Old Man?" the agent asked. "He's inside there with his lawyer." Safire paused. Nixon was not happy about his new job, and he was not much for small talk. And he was probably busy. To hell with it, Safire thought, and walked out to his car.

The lawyer Nixon was sequestered with was his White House counsel, John Dean. "We have a cancer—within, close to the Presidency, that's growing," Dean told Nixon that morning. "It's growing daily. It's compounding, it grows geometrically now because it compounds itself." A great deal of money had already been paid to E. Howard Hunt and the Watergate burglars, and now they were asking for more. Their continued silence would require a million dollars over the following two years. "We could get that," Nixon told Dean.

"Had I gone in, Nixon would probably have told me to listen to the lawyer's worrisome story," Safire later reflected. "He might well have asked me, a former PR man, to make some suggestions about how to handle it, and perhaps to draft a statement in his style, which was my specialty. The fateful Nixon-Dean meeting, of course, was secretly taped, and whatever I would have said would have ultimately made me a grand jury witness, possibly a target of hot-eyed prosecution. . . . But I walked on past that dark confabulation and out into the sunshine of a spring day. That was some break for me."

Two days later, Judge John Sirica read in open court a letter from Watergate burglar James McCord alleging that he and the other burglars had been subjected to "political pressure" to cop a guilty plea and remain silent. There had been perjury, McCord said, and a broader conspiracy. "We are now forced to some sort of a position on Watergate," Nixon, in Key Biscayne, wrote in his diary.

Price reluctantly sent an "eyes-only" memo to Haldeman urging his resignation. It was a wrenching memo to write—he liked Haldeman and thought that he had done a good job. But Watergate was growing and Price thought the only way to stem it was for someone high up to fall on his sword. Whether Haldeman was involved in any wrongdoing was beside the point, Price argued; they needed to "divide the presidency in order to save it." Haldeman should assume responsibility for whatever had gone wrong. Haldeman did not respond to the suggestion.

Buchanan weighed in with Nixon directly. "Anyone who is not guilty should not be put overboard," he wrote. "However, presidential aides who cannot maintain their viability should step forward voluntarily. . . . There is a *Titanic* mentality around the White House staff these days. We've got to put out the life rafts and hope to pull the presidency through."

By the middle of April, Haldeman and John Ehrlichman's viability was ebbing. On April 15, Nixon broached the idea of their taking leaves of absence, but they resisted. Nixon would give his first Watergate speech on Monday, April 30. He would announce that the two aides had resigned, along with John Dean and Attorney General Richard Kleindienst. He brought Price back into speechwriting for the talk. Price would remain Nixon's main writer for Watergate speeches and statements.

Nixon passed the speechwriting marching orders through Ron Ziegler. He was worried that Price might try to write too accommodating a speech. "Look, if we went in sackcloth and ashes and fired the whole White House staff, Price must realize that isn't going to satisfy these Goddamn cannibals," the president told Ziegler on April 27. "They'd still be after us. Who are they after? Hell, they're not after Haldeman or Ehrlichman or Dean; *they're after me*, the President. They hate my guts.

"Tell him make it *strong*, not cross, not apologetic," Nixon went on. "Just say this is the fact. I assume the responsibility. Be a president and not a peon. You tell him that. Goddammit, Price does not usually understand this. He normally—you know, sometime he doesn't, but he thinks that you've got to be in sackcloth and ashes."

Price and Ziegler went to Camp David on Saturday morning and spent the day hammering out a draft for the president. They debated over coffee or double scotches—depending upon the time of day—the necessity of the resignations. They collaborated with the president in an indirect and isolated way: they would send speech drafts over to his cabin and he sent them back, marked up.

"Oh, hell, as far as sackcloth, I would be willing to go a lot further," Nixon said to Price on the phone on the morning of April 30. "I always had this weak[ness], I'm one of the few men in Washington that never blames the secretary when the poor damned secretary misspelled a word. I mean sometime the boss is always to blame, so the boss did it, hell, I appointed [John] Mitchell [U.S. Attorney General during the first term and head of the Committee to Re-Elect the President] and I appointed Haldeman. I appointed Ehrlichman. I appointed Dean. Christ, these are all my people. [Charles] Colson [White House special counsel in the first term]. If they did things, they did them because they thought—they thought that's what we wanted. And so I'm responsible. . . . If you go too far in terms of saying, well, I take all the blame, and I don't blame these poor fellows and all that, then you think well, Christ, this poor damn, dumb President why didn't he resign? Which might not be a bad idea." Price had to chuckle as Nixon added that the problem with resignation would be President Spiro Agnew. "You want Agnew?"

Talk of resignation was more serious when they met face-to-face that afternoon. Price had never seen Nixon so unmoored. The president was listless and had trouble concentrating. At one point he dropped some pages and they lay on the floor, apparently without Nixon noticing that they had fallen. His mind wandered, as did his gaze, and he spoke in a flat, defeated tone. "Maybe I should resign," Nixon told Price. "Do you think so? You've always been the voice of my conscience. If you think I should resign just write it into the next draft, and I'll do it."

Price turned around the president's morning joke about Agnew. You cannot resign, he said. Agnew is not equipped to do the job. Your foreign policy work is too important to entrust to Agnew. When Nixon twice more pressed later in the day, Price deflected him with the same response. If anything would snap Nixon out of his funk, it would be matters of world policy. The more Price talked about that, the more Nixon seemed to come back to life. He decided to go for a swim. Price accompanied him, fearful that in his unraveled state, the president might trip or hit his head and drown.

Price was relieved when he watched the speech in his office that night to see that the president got through in a calm, authoritative manner, not betraying the emotional turmoil and self-doubt he had revealed earlier.

"In any organization, the man at the top must bear the responsibility," Nixon said.

> *That responsibility, therefore, belongs here, in this office. I accept it. And I pledge to you tonight, from this office, that I will do everything in my power to ensure that the guilty are brought to justice and that such abuses are purged from our political processes in the years to come, long after I have left this office.*

The first Senate Watergate Hearings were gaveled into session on May 18, 1974. A steady and damning flow of revelations hit the front pages of the newspapers: Dean alleged that the president knew of the cover-up. Watergate investigators found a memo addressed to Ehrlichman detailing plans to break into the offices of a psychiatrist whom Daniel Ellsberg, the defendant in the Pentagon Papers case, had seen. The crisis reached a new level on July 13 when former White House aide Alexander Butterfield publicly revealed the existence of the White House taping system. Ten days later, Nixon refused to turn the tapes over to the Senate committee or to Archibald Cox, the special prosecutor who had been appointed to investigate.

Nixon scheduled another speech on Watergate for mid-August and John Andrews was tapped to help write it. The president was increasingly isolated, even in the White House, so Andrews was sent to Kissinger and Ziegler for guidance. Kissinger told Andrews that the key idea was contrition. Citing John F. Kennedy after the Bay of Pigs, Kissinger said that the American people wanted to think well of their president and believe him. This will work again, Kissinger said.

"Contrition is bullshit," Ziegler told him. "This president has nothing to apologize for. This president will not grovel to the American people." The scandal was a cooked-up plot by Nixon's enemies.

Andrews was reminded of FDR's famous "weave them together" dictum. He consulted with Price. "The answer is you couldn't make a coherent speech out of it," Andrews recalled. He ended up sending in a draft that leaned too far toward Kissinger's contrition.

On July 12, Safire had sent Nixon a memo on how to regain the initiative. He advised against "constant contrition" ("you could never humiliate yourself enough for your critics, and a steady stream of apologies would only dissipate the faith of the people who believe in you"), a "counterattack" ("It would mean three years of trench warfare, interminable investigations, and probably a black eye in the light of history") or hunkering down and trying to ignore the whole affair.

Instead, Safire argued for a tone of personal redemption: that Nixon, having learned the lessons from Watergate, should become a reformed sinner who can save the rest of the country. "The great lesson of Watergate," Safire wrote his old boss, "is what happens when a nation is driven by a philosophy of 'us against them'—when partisanship leads to the fear of excessive counter-partisanship and when men in both camps think they see a higher law than the written law." Watergate and the unrest of the 1960s were of a piece, Safire suggested that Nixon say. Nixon should position himself as wiser for having been caught up in the "us-against-them" fever, and willing to lead the country back to a level of respectful discourse. He said that the president should pledge the remainder of his term to "creative controversy"—respectful debate about big issues.

In his speech on August 15, Nixon again took "full responsibility" for the Watergate abuses, claiming that he had no prior knowledge of the crimes or the cover-up, and said that he wanted full disclosure, though he could not give up the tapes for reasons of protecting presidential executive privilege.

As we look at Watergate in a longer perspective, we can see that its abuses resulted from the assumption by those involved that their cause placed them beyond the reach of those rules that apply to other persons and that hold a free society together. The notion that the end justifies the means proved contagious. Thus, it is not surprising, even though it is deplorable, that some persons in 1972 adopted the morality that they themselves had rightly condemned and committed acts that have no place in our political system. . . .
But ultimately, the answer does not lie merely in the jailing of a few overzealous persons who mistakenly thought their cause justified their violations of the law. Rather . . . it requires that we learn once again to work

together, if not united in all of our purposes, then at least united in respect for the system by which our conflicts are peacefully resolved and our liberties maintained.

Five days later, Safire praised the speech in his *Times* column, calling it a "thoughtful speech" and critiquing his own paper for using "irrelevant but effective" arguments to attack Nixon. "Take it from a President who, tempered in the fires of excessive partisanship, has become far more temperate," Safire wrote. "He has found that the future of creative controversy 'lies in a commitment by all of us to show a renewed respect for the mutual restraints that are the mark of a free and a civilized society.'"

He did not mention his July memo to Nixon.*

Watergate moved on through its grim and shocking—to those within White House as well as those without—revelations. October brought the "Saturday Night Massacre." Nixon fired Archibald Cox, the special prosecutor, and abolished his office, which led to the resignations of Attorney General Elliott Richardson and his deputy, William Ruckelshaus. "People have got to know whether or not their President is a crook," Nixon said in a question-and-answer session with Associated Press editors in November. "Well, I am not a crook."† In December, an eighteen-and-a-half-minute gap was discovered in one of the subpoenaed tapes.

Huebner was acquainted with *Washington Post* journalist Carl Bern-

---

*In retrospect, Safire said in 2007, he should have noted in his column that Nixon had picked up on a theme that he suggested. "I had on the occasion of my memo forgotten that I had crossed the street from insider to outsider. This mistake was driven home to me afterward by A. M. Rosenthal, then executive editor of the *Times*, when I showed him a copy of my memo to Nixon. 'The next time you give advice to a politician,' he said, 'be sure you write it in the *Times*.' I took Abe's admonition to heart for the subsequent thirty years." (Author interview with William Safire.)

†Buchanan had prepared the briefing book for the appearance before the Associated Press editors. When he got it back, Nixon had made a notation on the front: "I am not a crook." "It was obviously spontaneous, but he had prepared to say it," Buchanan said. (Author interview with Pat Buchanan.)

stein and Gergen knew Bob Woodward, the other half of the reporting team that had stayed on the Watergate story when other reporters let it go. Huebner and Gergen would run into each other in the hallway and say, guess what question I was asked today? "Journalists are always saying, 'Who's your source at the White House?'" Huebner recalled. "In this case it was, 'Who's your source in the press?'" By the time of the Saturday Night Massacre, Huebner was starting to suspect how high the scandal reached. When he was offered a job in New York that week, he leaped at the opportunity. He left the White House staff in January 1974. He would go on to be the publisher for fourteen years of the Paris-based *International Herald Tribune*.

Andrews had resigned in December 1973, disgusted with events, and feeling "soiled" to have been a party to them. "I was not effective anymore," he recalled. "I increasingly seemed unable to earn my pay every day. I couldn't get up for the intense intellectual and emotional involvement that it takes to effectively put words in the mouth of the president of the United States. It got to be where I didn't want to be part of it anymore." In 1998, he was elected to the Colorado state senate, where he served two terms.

Spring and summer brought the shocking tape transcripts, setbacks in the Supreme Court, and the wheels of impeachment. "Emotions ran high during the final days, as each week brought a new round of mortar shells into the White House compound, and we lived on adrenaline, counterattacking an increasingly expanding field of attackers," recalled John Coyne, who had joined the writing staff in October after his previous position as an Agnew speechwriter disappeared with the vice president. "But the context was very different. It was no longer a matter of real or imaginary revolutionary threats. The context now was the survival of one man, and few of us, no matter how rabid, could quite believe Dan Rather was a Weatherman."

A few minutes before 6:30 pm on Thursday, August 1, 1974, Raymond Price arrived at the office of Al Haig, Haldeman's successor as White House chief of staff. It was a strategy meeting on how to handle the impending articles of impeachment. Others drifted in, including Buchanan, Gergen, and writer Ken Khachigian, who had joined the staff as Buchanan's assistant in 1971 and had become a speechwriter in

1973. Haig arrived fifteen minutes late and announced that the meeting was to organize for a "total mobilization" against impeachment. He unveiled organizational charts detailing how the different White House staffers would be deployed: strategy, rapid reaction, task forces addressing each article of impeachment—Price would lead the task force combating Article I, pertaining to Watergate and the cover-up.

After about three quarters of an hour, the meeting broke up. Price was outside Haig's office chatting when the chief of staff's secretary, Muriel Hartley, quietly told him that Haig wanted him back inside. "We need a resignation speech," Haig told Price. The previous hour had been a facade. Nixon had decided that the release of a tape from June 23, 1972—the "smoking gun" tape on which he ordered that the CIA be brought into the cover-up—would make his position untenable. He would announce his resignation on Monday, August 5. He had dictated notes to Haig to pass on to Price: He would concede that he no longer had the political support necessary to govern, and acknowledge a mistake, but did not, as Nixon later recalled it, "want Price to write a groveling mea culpa."

Price started working on the speech on Friday in secret: no Nixon decision was final until he had announced it, and this one required the utmost discretion while there was still doubt. In late July, he had hired a new assistant, a young lawyer named Ben Stein, the son of Council of Economic Advisers Chairman Herbert Stein, and a devoted Nixon loyalist. Not knowing Stein well enough to trust him with such a secret, Price created make-work assignments for him, at one point telling him to write up a draft of a speech for the president announcing that he would *not* resign.

As he wrote, Price started to have doubts: Maybe the June 23 tape was not as damaging as advertised. Buchanan had not yet seen a transcript of the tape either, so the two writers convened in Haig's office late that afternoon with Haig aide George Joulwan and White House Watergate counsel Fred Buzhardt. Price and Buchanan passed the pages of the transcript between them. Price shook his head quietly. Buchanan banged his clenched fist on the conference table, yelling: "Jesus Christ."

Saturday brought word that Nixon would not resign. He would release the transcripts to the public and address the country on Monday, but would hold off on resignation until he saw how things went. The president was now determined to see the constitutional process through to the end. He wanted the speech to include a pledge that he would testify at his impeachment trial, answering any questions the senators put to him. Price was distraught. Their congressional liaison and allies on the Hill had already told them that the votes were not there for Nixon to survive. Better to end it quickly, Price thought.

Haig called Price as the writer tried to switch gears to draft a steadfast speech. The president wanted him at Camp David the next day. Then Haig asked: Did he want anyone else along? Buchanan, Price replied. Nixon had viewed Buchanan and Price as the heart and soul, respectively, of the administration. Now Price was hoping that they could sway their boss.

The two men met on Sunday morning at Buchanan's office and Price found that his old ideological rival had shifted positions: Yes, the Old Man would have to go eventually, but there was no reason not to play it out. That way there would be no nagging questions later for Nixon as to whether it was avoidable. But with no resignation, they wondered about the need for a speech. The president agreed. At Camp David, Haig told the assembled aides that Nixon was holding open the possibility of resignation, but would see how the Monday release played.

The transcripts exploded on Monday, closing off Nixon's options. Sitting in his Executive Office Building hideaway with a yellow legal pad on Tuesday, August 6, he wrote: "Resignation Speech" across a fresh sheet. It would be on Thursday night.

"We'll need a thousand words," Haig told Price.

"As I believe you know, I think this has been a sad but necessary decision in the circumstances," Price told Nixon in a cover memo on the first draft of the speech on Wednesday. "But I do hope you'll leave office as proud of your accomplishments here as I am proud to have been associated with you, and to have been and remain a friend. God bless you; and He will."

They worked down the hall from each other that day, with Nixon in his hideaway office. Things had come full circle from their collaboration on his inaugural to their working together on his departure. The president contributed key lines—"I have never been a quitter. To leave office is abhorrent to every instinct in my body." He included a favorite Teddy Roosevelt quote about the man in the arena "who at the best knows in the end the triumphs of high achievements and who at the worst, if he fails, at least fails while daring greatly." Price persuaded him to trim the opening—"It is not the critic who counts; not the man who points out how the strong man stumbles, or where the doer of deeds could have done them better"—lest Nixon be accused, again, of belligerence in defeat.

Elsewhere in the building, the writers milled about in a daze. "We wander from office to office drinking, watching the blanket coverage on television," Coyne wrote. "The EOB has filled up with wandering people. Ben Stein, not a drinker, walks by carrying an open bottle of scotch. It's the first time we can remember seeing a Nixon staffer walking through the White House compound with an open bottle." Safire wandered through both as commiserating former colleague and as columnist seeking details "for history."

The writing staff had been pumping out speeches for friendly members of Congress to give on the House floor. Minutes before Nixon was supposed to go on the air, Coyne heard a solitary typewriter click-clacking down the hall. Finding someone still writing, Coyne put his hand on their shoulder. "Look," he said, "it's over."

Nixon's staff assembled on the morning of August 9, many in tears. He rambled a farewell to the White House staff in which he talked about his mother ("she will have no books written about her, but she was a saint"), his father ("they would have called him sort of a, sort of a little man, common man"), his own inadequacies ("I'm not educated, but I do read books"), and the ups and downs of life ("only if you have been in the deepest valley can you ever know how magnificent it is to be on the highest mountain"). Appropriately, the speech was extemporaneous. It was pure Nixon.

SEVEN

"Go Back and Give Me *One* Speech, Not *Two* Speeches"

AUGUST 5, 1974

As the Nixon administration was collapsing, one man was tucked into the Executive Office Building trying to generate a few laughs. Robert Orben had occasionally helped out Vice President Gerald Ford with "upfront," as he called it, or jokes to kick off speeches. And Ford was scheduled to take a twelve-day trip through California and the West.

On the afternoon of August 5, Orben was in the office of Robert Hartmann, Ford's gruff chief of staff and head speechwriter. He spent two hours as Hartmann was intermittently summoned by phone call or a knock on the door. When Hartmann would return, he kept alluding to "If we go across the street . . ."

"Which street are you talking about, Bob?" Orben finally asked. "West Executive Avenue, or Seventeenth Street?"

West Executive Avenue was the narrow road that separated the Executive Office Building from the White House, while 17th Street ran along the building's opposite side. What Orben was jokingly asking was whether the Ford crew was on the verge of ascending to power, or getting swept out with the current crowd.

Implied was that Orben would be part of the "we" going across the street. He was a novel choice. Tall and balding, with a crew cut and a quick laugh, Orben had spent most of his life in show business, principally in comedy. But he had a sharp sense of what worked in speeches, especially for Gerald Ford. Orben had first encountered Ford in 1968, when the then-Republican House leader was scheduled to speak at the Gridiron Club Dinner, the regular black-tie spring fête where the Beltway's political and media elites drink and dine and laugh. There were skits performed, and a main speaker from each party was expected to amuse the diners.

That year, Ford was scheduled opposite Vice President Hubert Humphrey, who was running hard for the presidency. Facing the prospect of being overshadowed by the witty and garrulous Humphrey, Ford sent Hartmann to Hollywood for aid bearing two names. One was George Murphy, a Republican senator who had been a Hollywood actor, and would know where to look for a humorist with GOP sympathies. Murphy sent Hartmann to comedian Red Skelton, who passed him on to a producer, who passed him on to gag writer Bob Orben. The other name on Hartmann's list was a former Barry Goldwater speechwriter: Bob Orben.

Ford was the surprise hit of the 1968 Gridiron Club Dinner. "Let me assure the distinguished Vice President of the United States that I have absolutely no designs on his job," Ford said, to great laughter. "I'm not at all interested in the vice presidency. I love the House of Representatives despite the long, irregular hours. Sometimes, though, when it's late and I'm tired and hungry on that long drive home to Alexandria, as I go past 1600 Pennsylvania Avenue, I do seem to hear a little voice say, 'If you lived here, you'd be home now.'"

Now, six years later, the joke seemed prophetic. Before he flew back to New York City that night, Orben was approached by a network news correspondent. What's going on, Bob? Why are you here? Orben responded: I'm just a writer, what do I know?

Watching the news that night, Orben got a chuckle when the reporter announced on the news that something must be afoot, as Ford had brought a writer down from New York. What does he know? Orben said, nudging his wife. He could not imagine Richard Nixon leaving the White House voluntarily. The president would go down fighting.

The situation was evolving quickly. During a break in meetings the next day, Tuesday, August 6, Ford told Hartmann to start thinking about what he should say at a swearing-in—nothing fancy, that was not his style.

"How much time do we have?" Hartmann asked.

"Two or three days—maybe less," Ford said. "It will probably all be over in seventy-two hours."

Ford knew that he could count on Hartmann, one of his closest aides, to produce words appropriate to the occasion. A native of Rapid City, South Dakota, Hartmann had gotten his bachelor's degree at Stanford and then stayed in California. He reported for the *Los Angeles Times* for twenty-five years, excepting a World War II navy stint, before leaving in 1964. Never abashed about his politics, or anything else, Hartmann had become a staffer to the House Republican Conference in 1966, growing close to Ford, the House GOP leader. When Ford accepted Nixon's 1973 vice-presidential appointment, he brought Hartmann along as chief of staff.

That appointment, Ford came to conclude, was ill-advised: Hartmann was a capable manager of neither men nor an office. He was, to put it mildly, gruff. Ford called him "brusque." Short, ruddy, somewhat pudgy, with a raspy, growly voice and matching temperament, Hartmann gave the appearance of an old-school newspaper editor. He smoked a pipe and had a penchant for bourbon. He proudly kept on his desk as a paperweight a piece of carborundum used to abrade steel. He saw himself as serving a similar purpose for the vice president.

"Bob liked to give . . . the impression that he was tougher and harder to get along with" than he was, remembered Jack Marsh, a conservative former Democratic member of Congress who, like Hartmann, Ford would name as counselor. "Beneath that was a very interesting and a very talented, able person. But he used the brusque approach at times in order to get attention or to let people know, I think, who was boss." Marsh was one of the few people who saw through Hartmann's crust.

"Bob Hartmann may have more enemies than any other man in Washington," *The Washington Post*'s Sally Quinn later wrote in a lengthy Sunday *Style* section profile. "It's hard to find anybody who, once safely 'on background,' won't have something nasty to say about him." The nickname Hartmann cultivated for himself was SOB—"Sweet Ol' Bob."

Ford described his aide as "suspicious of everyone." In August 1974, his suspicions were directed against the die-hard Nixonites, or as he referred to them, "the Praetorians." To Hartmann, they were trying to hold onto power and push the Nixon agenda or their own sinister designs. Every slight was the calculated work of the Praetorians. He made his views plain to the incoming president. "You don't suspect ill motives of anyone until you're kicked in the balls three times," Hartmann told his boss. "As a human being, that's a virtue. As a president, it's a weakness."

Hartmann might have seemed an unlikely match for the open, easygoing, friendly Gerald Ford but, Ford later recalled, he had "an uncanny ability to craft a sentence or phrase so that it expressed my sentiments." At three o'clock in the morning on Wednesday, August 7, Hartmann's alarm clock went off. With his wife Roberta asleep, he set a pot of coffee to boil and started concentrating on the task at hand. He jotted words and phrases on a scratch pad: "take charge," meaning that Ford would immediately have to convey the authority of his new office; "legitimacy," a recognition of the fact that Ford—appointed under the terms of the Twenty-Fifth Amendment to replace Vice President Spiro Agnew in 1973—had never been on a national ballot. Finally he wrote: "Truth is the glue," a phrase denoting the polestar by which the new president would steer the ship of state.

Hartmann slipped a sheet of paper into his typewriter and started with one of Ford's favorite biblical passages. "The Bible upon which my hand just rested was opened to Proverbs, third chapter, the fifth and sixth verses," Hartmann typed. "I learned these verses many years ago, and have often said them as a prayer, as I do now: Trust in the Lord, etc."

False start. Hartmann tried again. "The oath I have just taken is the same oath that was taken by George Washington and by every President under the Constitution . . ."

Now he was rolling.

"It is difficult to express, but I still am haunted by the feeling that some unseen hand was guiding mine that morning," Hartmann later wrote. "Is there such a thing as inspiration? Can a ghost have a ghost? I don't know."

The following day, Ford picked out the lynchpin phrase of the speech. Hartmann had imagined the sigh of millions of his fellow countrymen at the knowledge that the ordeal of Watergate was finally ended. The key phrase "didn't struggle to be born," he later remembered. "It just flowed naturally." Ford was not so sure: "Isn't that a little hard on Dick?" he asked. Hartmann was sure of himself. "Junk all the rest of the speech if you want to, but not that," he implored. Ford acceded.

Standing in the East Room at shortly past noon on Friday, August 9, Gerald R. Ford gave his first address as president of the United States, "just a little straight talk among friends," as he called it. Acknowledging that he had not won a national election, he also said that he did not achieve office through any "secret promises." As he had "not subscribed to any partisan platform, I am indebted to no man." This a declaration that he had not made any deals with Richard Nixon.

"I believe that truth is the glue that holds government together, not only our government but civilization itself," he said. "That bond, though strained, is unbroken at home and abroad."

Ford promised openness in his administration and then delivered the key line, the one Hartmann had begged him to preserve:

My fellow Americans, our long national nightmare is over.

More than any other utterance in his public life, Gerald Ford would be remembered for these nine words. His address struck the proper note of soothing normalcy after almost eight hundred days of Watergate, and more than a decade of national turmoil that included assassinations, protests, riots, Vietnam, Watts, Chicago, and Watergate.

Hartmann moved quickly to purge the Nixon holdovers. Arriving late at a farewell lunch for another Nixon staffer at Trader Vic's, chief speechwriter David Gergen told his colleagues that he had just learned that he was being replaced—and that he learned that from a wire service report. Newly minted White House press secretary Jerald terHorst announced the departures of speechwriters Pat Buchanan and John McLaughlin (a Jesuit priest who had unsuccessfully run for Senate in 1970 and joined the writing staff in 1971) before either had been informed that he was leaving.*

Hartmann brought in Orben full time, mainly to add levity to the president's speeches. The Washington press corps and Ford opponents were delighted, suddenly presented with the target of a gag writer on the presidential speechwriting staff. Orben would ask if it might not be a good idea for him to leave, but Ford ignored the criticisms—he wanted Orben.

Another new speechwriter who had a history with Ford was Milton Friedman, a former Washington bureau chief for the Jewish Telegraph Agency who had written speeches for House Republican leader Bob Michel, among others. Friedman, who spent his life being confused with the economist of the same name, specialized in foreign policy speeches. He was, Nixon holdover John Coyne wrote, "an older man, amiable, a gangling sort of fellow with an odd, loose gait."

To replace Gergen as head of speechwriting, Hartmann brought in Paul Theis (pronounced "Tice"), a World War II bomber pilot who had worked at *Newsweek* before taking a job in 1960 running public relations for the Republican Congressional Campaign Committee. Soft-spoken, he was also a soft touch: At Christmastime he sent notes to various White House clerical workers—the telephone operators, for example—thanking them for their work.

Later in the year, two more writers were added. Like most of the Ford writers, they did not specialize in specific policy areas. Jack Casserly was a veteran journalist—he had covered the Korean and Algerian wars as well as the Middle East—who had written speeches at the Ford Motor Company and then worked at the U.S. Census Bureau. Working for ABC News in 1968, he had had to call Representative

---

*McLaughlin refused to leave, despite repeated announcements of his imminent departure. In fact, when terHorst resigned early in September, McLaughlin was still on the White House staff. He did not leave until terHorst's successor Ron Nessen forced him out in early October.

Ford at 5:30 am for an early morning deadline. Ford groggily answered his question and then told him politely never to call at that hour again. Casserly was struck by his gentle kindness. Years later, he would recall how, when the speechwriters met with Ford, the president would jauntily call out: "Hiya fellas!"

The other new scribe was Frances "Kaye" Pullen, who had been the first female field reporter at two different television stations in Memphis, Tennessee, and was also the first woman editorial writer at the *Commercial Appeal* newspaper. She had joined the press department of the Republican Congressional Campaign Committee in the late summer, working for Theis. A week later, he moved down Pennsylvania Avenue and asked her to join him. As the campaign committee had paid for her to move to Washington and was clearly facing a November disaster, she decided she owed it to the party to stick around through November 5. Shortly thereafter, she moved over to the White House.

Two Nixon writers were retained: John Coyne (despite having the distinction of being both a Nixon and Agnew vet) and Aram Bakshian. Bakshian, Hartmann wrote in a December memorandum to Ford, "is the best of the old speechwriters (Atlantic City) and is cooperative, not very costly, but somewhat set in the old mold and more leisurely in his work habits than our new crew."

There was irony in this commendation. The Atlantic City reference was to a full-throated defense of Nixon that Ford had given in mid-January, tearing into administration opponents as "a few extreme partisans . . . bent on stretching out the ordeal of Watergate for their own purposes." The speech had bombed, particularly when it became known that it had been drafted in Nixon's speechwriting shop. But Hartmann and Ford had apparently appreciated its craftwork.

Bakshian liked the fact that the writers had more access to Ford than they had to Nixon. Years later he said that this was a reflection of Hartmann's power struggles—by getting presidential access for his staff, he confirmed and augmented his own standing.

The first order of business for the new speechwriting staff was to learn Ford's style. The word that is most often used to describe Ford's rhetorical voice was "midwestern"—unpretentious, straightforward, simple, lacking great elegance or linguistic flights. "Ford was not oratorical," Marsh later explained. "He was more pragmatic." "His approach to a speech was that of a legislator," Hartmann wrote. "It required something on paper to spark its further development. You start with some kind of draft bill and then amend, delete, revise, substitute, and perfect it into a considerably different, and more palatable, final product."

Friedman tried to bring the new recruits up to speed. "Ford, he told us very seriously, suffered something he called 'swimmer's breath,' the result of which affliction, apparently, being the inability to make it all the way through a long sentence without drawing a shuddering gasp somewhere in the middle," Coyne recalled.

As counselor to the president, Hartmann was a senior adviser with a portfolio virtually as broad as he wanted it to be. But the speechwriting shop itself was separated from the administration's policy development operations, a division that produced occasional disconnects. Meeting with Hartmann in the Oval Office shortly after assuming office to discuss an upcoming speech at Ohio State University, Ford waxed philosophical about education. "Kids in college today keep complaining their education is irrelevant," he said. "Of course they love that word and use it for everything they don't like. But when you really try to get to the bottom of their gripes they mean that what they're required to master on the campus has little or nothing to do with getting a job afterwards, or getting ahead in life."

Ford and Hartmann decided that the speech would announce a federal program to bring work and education into closer alignment. They checked legislation pending in Congress and touched base with the Departments of Labor and Health, Education and Welfare. The speechwriters cranked out a text. But no one thought to run the speech by the Office of Management and Budget (OMB), which evaluates and signs off on any new programs that cost money.

"The Department of Labor will shortly announce a pilot program to improve occupational information for graduates and others in making career choices," Ford told Ohio State's summer graduating class on

August 30. "There will be grants for state and local initiatives to provide data on occupations available and to help channel the potential employees into positions which are not only personally satisfying but financially rewarding."

The press called the OMB, looking for details. Deputy director Paul O'Neill, the resident specialist in such programs, was pestered with queries he could not answer. He charged around the Executive Office Building trying to find the roots of the new program. His search finally brought him to the speechwriters.

In the end the idea died a bureaucratic death—another sign, to Hartmann, of enemy activity. "The Praetorian pattern was a thing of beauty," he wrote. "What they could not prevent they could delay. What they could no longer delay they could cause to fail. What they could not make fail they could alter."

Ford held his first presidential press conference on August 28, 1974, and was apparently shocked when the questions focused on Nixon: Did he think Nixon had immunity from prosecution as a former president? Would Ford pardon him? The experience focused Ford on the issue. He consulted with a handful of aides, including Hartmann.

Hartmann counseled against a pardon. "Mr. President, you'll have to expect a lot of flak [after a pardon]. No one can predict just how deep the resentment will go, but there will be strong editorial condemnation, for sure," Hartmann said. "There will be all hell to pay with the news media, and the White House press corps will go up the wall."

Ford was not impressed. A Nixon prosecution would take years, he believed, and would overshadow everything. And he doubted that the public relished the notion of a former president in a prison cell. He announced his decision—a pardon—to his senior aides on Thursday, September 5, and declared that he wanted to announce it publicly no later than the following Sunday. In the Oval Office on Saturday, Ford dictated the outlines of his statement, which Hartmann was to refine into a final address.

"Can I ask you just one question?" Hartmann said, pausing at the doorway to the Oval Office.

"Sure," Ford said, grinning. "So long as you don't try to talk me out of it."

"What's the rush?" Hartmann asked. A Nixon trial would likely drag on for years, so why hurry? Left unsaid was the fact that in just under two months the party of which Ford was suddenly the head would face the voters and a pardon could only hurt the GOP.

"Well someone—one of the news people—might ask me about it again," Ford responded.

"But all you'd have to do is say you haven't decided," Hartmann said.

"But I *have* decided," Ford said, ending the discussion. He *had* decided, and to say otherwise would be to lie (truth, after all was the glue . . .). Ford's character proved his undoing. His decision, and his determination to quickly make it public, ended his political honeymoon. He could have made a concerted effort to prepare the public for the decision, softening the blow. As it was, that decision was probably the single biggest reason why Ford was denied a full term in office on his own. (It immediately cost him his press secretary: Jerry terHorst resigned in protest shortly before Ford announced the pardon.)

Ford went to St. John's Episcopal Church, across Lafayette Square from the White House, at eight o'clock on Sunday morning. He returned to the Oval Office, and read Hartmann's draft twice. Using a felt-tip pen, he wrote in a line about Nixon's health and telephoned key members of Congress to let them know of his decision. Shortly after 11 am Ford addressed the nation. The Nixons, he said, were part of "an American tragedy in which we all have played a part. It could go on and on and on, or someone must write the end to it. I have concluded that only I can do that, and if I can, I must.

"My conscience tells me clearly and certainly that I cannot prolong the bad dreams that continue to reopen a chapter that is closed. My conscience tells me that only I, as president, have the constitutional power to firmly shut and seal this book. My conscience tells me it is my duty, not merely to proclaim domestic tranquility but to use every means that I have to insure it."

In New York City, Orben was awakened by his telephone's ringing.

It was a Broadway actor friend. Do you know what that sonofabitch you're working for has done? he asked.

Still bleary, Orben thought: He knows I don't work for Red Skelton anymore. What's he talking about?

Public reaction was predictable. " 'Surprise', 'stunning' pardon of RN by GF dominated Sun. w/all nets having specials and wires full of comments from Hill," the White House Weekend News Review read. "Liberal GOPs joined all Dems commenting save [one] along w/most TV commentators in sharp criticism or in questioning the timing."

Ford decided that he wanted to retain Al Haig as his chief of staff on a permanent basis. Haig agreed on one condition: that he have the power to hire and fire White House staffers as he saw fit. "You have at least one fellow who doesn't belong here," Haig said. That fellow's identity was no mystery. Hartmann viewed Haig as a power-hungry Praetorian—an "asshole." Bridling when Haig continued to run White House staff meetings in the days following Nixon's resignation, Hartmann had boycotted them. It was a move that might have satisfied a visceral need of Hartmann's to display his independence, but—since the meetings went on anyway—it was self-defeating.

Haig thought Hartmann was in over his head and good for no more than four hours a day. Anti-Haig items started appearing in the press. Ford thought Hartmann was responsible for them and he told him to cut it out—but the squabbling only got worse.

Ford had been a star football player in college, from which he had learned the importance of teamwork. "I guess this goes back to experiences I have had in athletics," he once told John Hersey. "A feuding team never got anyplace. A feuding staff in the White House is never going to get anyplace." As a leader in the House of Representatives— where he had been first among equals—he tried to balance desires and avoid offending people. As a result, although he understood how destructive infighting was, he was ill-equipped to end it. "Throughout my political career, nothing upset me more than bickering among members of my staff," Ford wrote in his memoirs. "It was time-consuming, terribly distracting and unnecessary. I had told my aides I wouldn't tolerate it. But it continued, even accelerated, when I entered the White House and—given the ambitions and personalities of the people involved—there didn't seem to be any way to put an immediate stop to it."

Ford pondered Haig's condition and rejected it. "You'll have to let me deal with Hartmann myself," the president said. On Sunday, September 15, Ford announced that he was appointing Haig commanding officer of NATO. Hartmann had scored an apparent victory, but he soon had a new rival to reckon with.

At the end of September, Ford tapped Donald Rumsfeld, the U.S. ambassador to NATO and a former U.S. House member from Illinois, as "staff coordinator." Rumsfeld had been a member of the "Young Turks," Republican members who had engineered Ford's initial foray into the House GOP leadership in 1965. He left the House in 1969 and played a succession of roles in the Nixon administration, escaping Watergate by being abroad.

Initial results of the Rumsfeld-Hartmann matching looked promising: Hartmann showed up for Rumsfeld's first senior staff meeting, the first such gathering that he attended since early August. He would, *New Republic* White House reporter John Osborne wrote, attend enough meetings "that nobody could say he refused to attend, and not enough to acknowledge that he had to be there."

Ford addressed the Congress at 4 pm on Tuesday, October 8, his second appearance there since taking office. On August 12, he had told the legislators that he did not want a "honeymoon with you. I want a good marriage." Now he was going to focus on the economy. He wore on his lapel a red pin with WIN—"whip inflation now"—in white letters. The program was a voluntary call for Americans to do their part to kill inflation, which—up over 12 percent—had become a serious drag on the U.S. economy. "My conclusions are very simply stated," Ford said. "There is only one point on which all advisers have agreed: We must whip inflation right now."

The idea had sprung from the speechwriters. The program had its roots in a month-old idea that Hartmann's deputy, Paul Theis, suggested for a voluntary anti-inflation program. Businesses and labor unions were to pledge to hold down costs, and would be called "Infla-tion Fighters," or IF—hardly a stirring acronym, and one made worse when Hartmann and Theis presented the idea to Ford. Why not make it "Inflation Fighters and Energy Savers," the president had asked. The idea lay dormant until Ford convened a national summit conference on inflation on September 27, at which the financial writer Sylvia Porter made a speech calling for a nationwide campaign of recycling and vol-untary energy conservation measures.

At Ford's urging, Porter agreed to lead a joint effort of inflation fighters and energy savers, and he unveiled the plan, WIN, on October 8. Ford and his advisers hoped that WIN could become a visible symbol like the New Deal–era NRA's "Blue Eagle." It would become an endur-ing symbol of the Ford administration, but not in the way they hoped. The buttons became a symbol of administration ineptitude.

There were substantive problems in the speech, which Friedman had written. Ford proposed to reduce dependence on foreign oil by converting the nation's oil-fired power plants to coal by 1980—a goal that was completely impractical. The speechwriting shop had mangled a more modest and feasible proposal, unnamed White House officials complained to the press. Part of the problem was that Hartmann had closed the speechwriting process, cutting out policy officials who could have caught programmatic mistakes. He got the speech for final editing on Monday afternoon and had not let anyone else see it—including Roy Ash, the head of the OMB, and Treasury Secretary William Simon. Last-minute policy changes did not make it into the draft.

Rumsfeld determined to make speechwriting more transparent, opening up Hartmann's inner sanctum. "One area in which our present staffing system is seriously out of kilter is the staffing of Presidential speeches and remarks," he wrote in a five-page memo to Ford on Octo-ber 15. "Because of inadequate staffing several errors of facts and con-flicts with previous Presidential statements have recently crept into speeches. None have been disastrous, but some embarrassment has been caused."

Rumsfeld proposed an elaborate new clearance system by which suc-ceeding drafts would be circulated to all interested parties. The practical effect was to cement the speechwriters' new role as wordsmithing functionaries, and not incidentally to diminish Hartmann's power by circumscribing his ability to work directly with the president, without interference from other staffers. It also locked in a system of group editing that would drive a generation of speechwriters to distraction.

On November 5, the GOP reaped the rewards of Watergate and the Nixon pardon: a forty-seat loss in the House and four-seat setback in the Senate. It was a generation-defining election, and it left Ford in a perilous political position. As 1975 opened, he decided to try a double-barreled approach to revive his agenda, and his administration. He would preview the January 15 State of the Union address with a January 13 "fireside chat" to be televised nationwide.

The stakes, thought press secretary Ron Nessen, who had joined the White House staff from NBC News in September, were tremendous. If Ford failed to score with the speeches, the press secretary wrote in a note to himself, "the Ford presidency is never going to get off the ground and he is going to be President for two and a half years and that is all."

Ford's television adviser, Bob Mead, scouted locations around the White House for the fireside address, seeking the perfect locale to strike a cozy, relaxed note. He suggested three possible sites: the ground floor Lincoln Library; the grand hall on the second floor of the White House residence; or—Mead's preference—the main family room in the residence. "This is the most ideal location for such an informal chat, the President's own living room," he wrote Nessen on January 7. "However, much family disruption would occur during set-up, and TV lines would have to be dropped from the balcony area on the South Portico." The Lincoln Library it would be.

Hartmann's draft prompted the Praetorian machinations he feared. Nessen thought it was too long, too flowery, too full of clichés and flaccidly written. He edited it a little bit while putting it onto the TelePrompTer. Hartmann, following along as Ford rehearsed, muttered: "Those are not my words. I wonder whose words those are." Nessen took his concerns to Rumsfeld. "Do you think it can be salvaged?" the chief of staff asked. It could, Nessen replied, with very heavy editing. Rumsfeld told him to write his own version of the speech. He also commissioned drafts from Council of Economic Advisers Chairman Alan Greenspan and Robert Goldwin, the White House's liaison with the academic community.

Ford meanwhile had been streamlining the copy with Hartmann, making it more direct and occasionally putting in more substantive detail. "Tonight, if I might, let me give you a preview of my plan" became "Tonight let me preview this plan for you." Likewise, "Higher energy costs compound both the inflationary problem and the recessionary problem" became "Higher energy costs compound both inflation and recession."

Nessen and Rumsfeld saw their chance on Sunday, January 12, the day before the speech was to be given. Hartmann sent Orben to deal with any last-minute edits. After Ford read through the speech and watched his performance on videotape, Rumsfeld suggested he read it once more so that they could mark the TelePrompter copy for emphasis and pauses. As Ford went though it, Rumsfeld and his allies started suggesting changes—inserting a word here, deleting one there. Soon whole sections were eliminated, including a laundry list of Ford's proposals.

Ford did another read-through on Monday afternoon, performing flawlessly for the videocameras. "If I drop dead before tonight, you can still use the tape," he quipped.

That evening the president, the television crew, Rumsfeld, and Nessen crowded into the small Lincoln Library, which is lined on three walls with floor-to-ceiling bookshelves. The fireplace that evening had special logs that, because they were made of compressed sawdust, burnt quietly—no crackling to interfere with the president's speech. While much of the furniture had been removed for the broadcast, a small desk remained, at which Ford sat, though, as practiced, partway through the speech he got up to lean on it—the better to reinforce the informal mood.*

"Good evening," Ford started. "Without wasting words, I want to

---

*This was a pale echo of Bob Mead's more elaborate vision, which contemplated Ford starting at one end of the room, perusing (and possibly quoting from) a book, and then moving to the desk which he sat at, leaned on, or stood next to—the very definition of forced informality. (Memo from Bob Mead to Ron Nessen, January 7, 1975, Subject File Speeches, Box 1, 10/1/74–2/28/75 folder, Gerald R. Ford Library.)

talk with you tonight about putting our domestic house in order. We must turn America in a new direction. We must reverse the current recession, reduce unemployment, and create more jobs." He made several proposals in his address, including increased fuel taxes to discourage consumption, new special cash payments from the federal government to individuals, businesses, state and local governments, $16 billion in tax rebates, and a moratorium on new federal spending programs outside of energy projects.

When the camera's red light flicked off, Nessen grabbed Rumsfeld's arm and shouted: "We did it! We did it!"

The euphoria did not last long—the State of the Union was scheduled for 1 pm on January 15, two days later. Once again Rumsfeld, Nessen, and their colleagues disliked Hartmann's effort. Ford's assessment was that the speech was "short on specifics and long on rhetoric; worse it didn't have a clear and central theme."

On January 10, Nessen had written Theis a brief memo saying that while he had not had time to read the State of the Union draft thoroughly, "it seems to me that the initial portions of the speech and message in which the President sets the mood are somewhat repetitive and uninspiring. Then, the detailed portion of the proposals seems somewhat jumbled and unorganized."

Domestic council director Ken Cole was as blunt: "There is no vision of what the President wants for America—there is no statement of what he wants—and there is no rationale for why what he proposes will get us to where he thinks we ought to go," he wrote on the same day. "In short, it fails to indicate any leadership."

Now, with twenty-four hours left, Rumsfeld, his deputy Dick Cheney, Greenspan, Nessen, and others sat at a conference table in Rumsfeld's office, writing, rewriting, cutting and pasting (scissors and glue in the pre-computer age). They worked for eight hours, fueled by cookies, peanuts, steak sandwiches, and beer.

Their version of the address arrived at Ford's desk at the same time as Hartmann's, roughly 9 pm. Rumsfeld's rump group, Hartmann, and Ford, gathered in the Oval Office. Ford, wearing a blazer and gray shirt, issued a presidential diktat: "Go back and give me *one* speech, not *two* speeches."

But his staff could not agree on which paragraphs and sections would remain in. Ford had to sort it out personally, sitting with the two versions of the State of the Union on his desk—Hartmann's on the left, the redraft on the right, the two warring camps sitting in front of it. He went through them page by page and arbitrated the squabble.

It was an embarrassing and enraging process for Ford and it was almost four in the morning before the speech was final. "It was a long, disagreeable night and a waste of time, but it did teach me a lesson," Ford later wrote. "In the future, I told Hartmann, important speeches had to be submitted to me well in advance of the scheduled delivery date. I simply couldn't tolerate any more performances like that."

It was the wrong lesson. Rather than expecting his aides to get along simply because he told them to, or because it was good for the team, Ford needed to settle the situation. This was not creative tension. The president could not control his top advisers. The problem would linger through the remainder of his administration.

Operating on less than three hours sleep, Ford did a credible job delivering the speech. He opened by recalling that as a freshman member of the House in 1949, he had heard Harry Truman pronounce the state of the Union to be good. "Today, that freshman member from Michigan stands where Mr. Truman stood, and I must say to you that the state of the Union is not good," he said. Telling the truth went against the conventions of the occasion.

He added, in another line he had inserted: "Now, I want to speak very bluntly. I've got bad news, and I don't expect much, if any, applause."

He got little.

"The President's main problem as concerns public speaking is the somewhat flat tone of his speaking voice," Orben wrote in a memo to Hartmann reviewing the week's speeches. "There is an absence of highs and lows and gradations of tonal qualities. All of these lend interest to what is being said. The President is aware of this and is making substantial improvement in these areas."

Orben's solution was for Ford to get the speeches further in advance. Using the show business parlance to which he was accustomed, and taking an apparent shot at Rumsfeld and his group, Orben argued that the president should rehearse on a " 'closed set'—with as few people as possible in the room. . . . Distractions as to speech content and even unnecessary audience keeps the performer from concentrating on his primary responsibility—to deliver it well." And in a mild shot at his own boss, who had been quoted in a *Washington Post* story on January 14 talking about the preparations for Ford's setup speech, Orben added that "it is also axiomatic in show business that technique is what doesn't show."

Ford allowed John Hersey to shadow him for a week, starting Monday, March 10, 1975, and to write about it for *The New York Times Magazine*. (Hersey had done something similar on President Truman in 1950.) Hersey was present at 3:48 pm on March 10, when Hartmann, Theis, Friedman, and Orben descended upon the Oval Office to discuss Ford's upcoming appearance at the White House Radio and Television Correspondents Dinner, and at a March 17 St. Patrick's Day speech at the University of Notre Dame. After Ford read a draft of his Correspondents' Dinner remarks, a brainstorming session commenced for the Notre Dame speech. The discussion meandered. Perhaps the speech should focus on foreign policy (though not Vietnam or Cambodia), or maybe on the relationship between education and the private sector, or perhaps it should announce a quasi-governmental agency where students could buy tuition bonds? None of these topics excited Ford. But touching on the fact that some Notre Dame students were eating only rice so as to help feed the world's hungry, he finally settled on a theme of staying globally engaged.

"I am still profoundly disturbed by what seemed to me the aimlessness of the speechwriting session," Hersey reflected at day's end. "I keep thinking . . . of a speechwriting session of Harry Truman's, at which most of his principal advisers, including Dean Acheson, were present, and during which policy was really and carefully shaped through its articulation."

Hartmann for one wished that Ford would take a more active part in the drafting process. "He rarely took the time to put his thoughts on paper in more than a note or outline form," he wrote. "It was flattering that he obviously felt I knew him well enough to divine what he wanted to say. But it was frustrating that he was so unconsciously intolerant of the communications process. Presidents do have more important things to think about. But except for a few memorable exceptions, Ford rarely faced up to the fact that making a major address *is one of the most important things a President does*."

This was the life cycle for a major speech: discussion with Ford—usually with the speechwriters bringing a couple of suggested topics—then one of them producing a draft that Theis and Hartmann would edit. Lesser speeches often did not merit a presidential audience, in which case guidance was sparse.

Then speeches would be subjected to the staffing process, which the speechwriters had grown to despise. Clearing a speech now involved more than a dozen senior officials signing off—and in many cases trying to insert their own language. The opportunity to contribute to presidential prose with rhetoric or bureaucratic blandness often proved irresistible. "I feel like a man watching an old tree being cut down," Jack Casserly had noted in his journal at the end of February after watching one speech get picked apart by bureaucrats. "However weatherbeaten and battered, it seems to me that it has more integrity than the two men axing it down."

And the department had other problems that spring. Casserly and David Gergen, who was now writing speeches for Treasury Secretary William Simon, separately heard about one speechwriter who had developed an odd sartorial writing habit: He would come to work each day in a suit, change into old pants—his "writing pants"—and work the morning. He would change into his suit again before lunch, back into the trousers afterward, and into the suit before leaving for the day. His bizarre practice became an issue when a cleaning lady walked in on him changing a couple of times and complained.

Orben, who thought working in Hollywood made him an expert on stress, had gained about thirty pounds since joining the staff. And he was having crushing headaches, bad enough that he went to see doctors. Waiting in a specialist's office, he recognized several other White House staffers. The specialist gave him a clean bill of health, ascribing the headaches to stress. Orben noticed a couple of weeks later that, talking on the phone, he was pressing the receiver into the side of his head. He spent a few weeks using the speakerphone instead of the handset and his headaches disappeared.

Pat Butler, a Capitol Hill veteran who had been working at the Appalachian Regional Commission, joined the writing staff in mid-April 1975. A son of a minister, Butler had worked as a press secretary for Representative Wilmer "Vinegar Bend" Mizell (R–NC), a former major league pitcher, and had observed Ford when he was minority leader. "On the House floor, we were not swept away by his rhetoric," Butler later remembered. "What he had going for him was his sincerity and he was solid in his principles. He was never a demagogue."

Butler, twenty-five, had watched a Ford speech the previous October that he concluded was the worst presidential address he had ever heard. He wrote Hartmann a letter and enclosed a draft of a speech that Ford could have given during his first appearance to a joint session of Congress, back in August. Once he joined the administration, he was struck that the speechwriting staff had a kind of "pick-up team quality" to it. There had been no election campaign to forge the group, so it was Ford vets Hartmann and Friedman and whoever else was added along the way. Other writers had been detailed over from other departments or hired on temporary bases only to leave or be let go after a few months.

Butler spent his first few months handling "Rose Garden Rubbish" and the like, before getting his first bigger speech on a Ford trip to Ohio in early July. He assumed that his first road speech would bring a briefing or guidance on what was expected, where they were going, what were the objectives and themes of the speech, and so on. "What I got was: 'We're going to be in Cleveland next Tuesday,'" he recalled. "So you would find yourself with actually quite a lot of flexibility and freedom that I didn't know we would have."

Butler learned that he had a political flair. As the 1976 presidential election campaign heated up, he would increasingly be the man called upon when the president needed red meat for sympathetic audiences. "What we really need in this country, in this decade, and the rest of this century, is not a New Deal," Ford told the 1,300 faithful GOPers on the evening of July 3, "but a fresh start."

The speech played well and Butler was pleased, until he saw the front page of the next day's *Washington Post*. "The President's speech was viewed by his supporters and strategists as a rehearsal of the themes he will attempt to develop in his campaign for his first full term," the story read. The implication was that "a fresh start" and the rest of the speech were the product of a long-simmering, carefully thought out political strategy developed at the highest levels. Butler, who knew better, was irate and then bemused.

Aram Bakshian left at the end of August 1975, severing the writing shop's last link with the Nixon White House. Coyne had left in February. Hartmann's ongoing quarrels with Cheney and Rumsfeld were causing him to lose influence, and "I had the feeling that as Hartmann's last fiefdom, the speechwriting department was losing connection with the senior level," Bakshian said. "Some of the people that were coming in might have been called 'old hacks.' Before, you always felt you were part of, I won't say 'the best and the brightest,' but there was some unit pride. There was a little less of that. There was very little reason to want to just hang on and stay there for the duration."

The speech team's mood was eroding as fall arrived—ground down by the Hartmann-Praetorian feud. "We've got a morale problem here in the Editorial/Speech Office," Theis wrote to Hartmann on September 18. "It has been developing for nearly a year now." At issue were the perks that many White House staffers took for granted: the right to dine in the White House mess and to park close to the Executive Office Building. Neither veteran speechwriters Jack Casserly and Kaye Pullen nor Patrick Butler had been granted mess privileges, while other more recent additions to other portions of the White House staff (presumably Rumsfeld allies) had gotten such privileges immediately.

"I understand that Bob Haldeman used to employ White House Mess and parking privileges to reward some staff members and punish others," Theis concluded. "Obviously, this isn't the case today, I'm sure." Even if Theis was sincere in giving Rumsfeld the benefit of the doubt, not everyone was as forgiving. "The speechwriting staff is not anti-Rumsfeld, but we are aware it is his fine hand that blocks accreditation to the White House Mess for some, better parking for others," Casserly had recorded in his journal on September 9. "He is a person of detail but, it strikes us, a petty individual."

"Mess privileges were invaluable," Butler recalled, because they helped the speechwriters stay informed about what was going on in the administration.

Ford's October 6 speech to the nation on tax policy darkened the mood among members of the writing staff. They had not written it. Rumsfeld and Cheney had summoned David Gergen to the White House late on Friday night, October 3. Gergen met with Ford and then spent the weekend working closely with Rumsfeld and economic advisers. When Hartmann learned about the speech on Sunday night (it was not publicly announced until Monday morning), he prepared a draft, but Ford mainly used Gergen's. The rest of the speechwriting staff found out about the speech along with the public on the day it was delivered.

Insult compounded injury a week later when a front-page story in the *Chicago Tribune* described the speechwriters' embarrassment. "The president himself is bored by the speeches, so why shouldn't his listeners be?" an anonymous White House official complained. An unnamed speechwriter said that the administration was gaining a reputation for having "no social conscience." Hartmann set Theis out to discover the source of the leak.

Rumsfeld and Cheney brought in Gergen for alternative drafts. When New York City officials pleaded for a financial bailout—the city was on the brink of bankruptcy—Ford decided to give a speech explaining why he opposed it, and what his alternative was. Gergen's draft included some rough paragraphs that he assumed would be tempered before going to the president, so he was taken aback when they ended up, unedited, in the final presidential text of what turned out to be a very tough speech. The following day's *New York Daily News* headline read: "Ford to City: Drop Dead."

•   •   •

On October 25, a Saturday, Ford summoned Rumsfeld and Henry Kissinger, who held both the positions of Secretary of State and national security adviser, to the Oval Office and told them of sweeping changes he planned for the administration: James Schlesinger would be fired as Secretary of Defense, to be replaced by Rumsfeld; William Colby would resign as head of the CIA, to be replaced by former House member George H. W. Bush; and Kissinger would give up the National Security Council, with his deputy, Brent Scowcroft, succeeding him. In the White House, Rumsfeld's deputy, Cheney, would fill the chief of staff position.

Three days later, at a private lunch, Ford told Vice President Nelson Rockefeller, whom he had appointed in 1974, that he was a drag on the ticket among GOP conservatives. Former California governor Ronald Reagan, a favorite of the right wing, was contemplating a primary challenge. Ford had declared for reelection in July, but his aides had pointedly noted that the president was seeking a return to the White House on his own, not as part of a team with the former New York governor. Rockefeller had tried to become more palatable to the conservatives, but he only ended up offending his liberal GOP constituents. By the summer of 1975, polling showed that one in four Republicans would not support a ticket with Rockefeller on it. "I came here to help the President, not to complicate his life," Rockefeller said on November 6, three days after officially withdrawing from the ticket.

The decisions were uncharacteristic of Ford in their decisiveness and sweep. For once he was not satisfied to try to balance people's feelings and acted aggressively.

The next morning, November 4, Hartmann told the president that the moves inspired him to shake up the speechwriting staff, cutting out poor performers and taking a greater hand in the writing. Hartmann and Cheney had a congenial lunch. The wildcat speechwriting will end, Cheney assured Hartmann. There would be no more circumventing the process or the speechwriting shop for presidential addresses. In December, Cheney asked Hartmann if he would object to Gergen coming in to handle television-oriented communications. "I have nothing at all personally against Gergen, I hardly know the guy," Hartmann responded. Cheney was soothing: "Well, the president told me I'd have to check with you," he said. "But I assure you Gergen will have absolutely nothing to do with speeches. . . . We won't interfere with your speech-writing business at all—I'll see to it."

As 1975 closed, Hartmann executed the promised staff shake-up. Theis left for the Department of Agriculture. Pullen moved to Betty Ford's staff at the end of January 1976. Casserly took a job at the Department of the Interior. Orben, to his surprise, was promoted to Theis's position as head speechwriter. Orben's job had evolved. Brought on to provide jokes, he had become the one who punched up other writers' speeches. And he had become Ford's informal performance coach, sending memos to Hartmann rating the president on delivery and timing. Eventually he was writing whole speeches, which he found easier than writing jokes. "People will clap at the end of a speech, but if they don't like a joke they won't laugh," he said.

Butler became Orben's number two. Friedman also survived the purge, but as the speechwriting staff entered the election year it was still short-handed. Orben's first order of business was to try to bulk it up. He approached the Praetorians without success. President Ford had mandated that White House staff be cut, and Orben was told that there were no more slots available to augment the speechwriting staff. My God, Orben said, Can't we let a gardener go?

Hartmann had begun to work on the bicentennial year's State of the Union in the final months of 1975. In early October, the president started sending Hartmann handwritten notes—lists, outlines, suggestions—on yellow lined paper. "An image of an 'embattled President fighting against the 'evil forces' in Washington," Ford suggested in one such note. "Again, a crack at [former California governor Reagan's] buddy allegations. This is difficult, but a thought."* Hartmann, meanwhile, traveled with the president on foreign trips—one to Europe and one to China—and he used the time to think about what approach and themes might be developed for 1976.

---

*Reagan, challenging Ford for the GOP presidential nomination, had used the phrase "buddy system" to describe Washington's insider culture.

"Mr. President," he said in a memo written in Beijing, "There is nothing more certain in my own mind than that we are going to lose the 1976 election unless you make a dramatic breakthrough in the perception of your qualities of leadership and do so very soon." He noted that Ford's biggest mistake "has been your retention of and reliance on Nixon Administration figures from a past you are trying to put behind you."

When Hartmann returned at the beginning of January from his holiday vacation to St. Croix, a handwritten note was waiting: "In case you get back before I do on Monday you might start right away on the most important project of 1976—SOTU [State of the Union]," the president wrote. "I want you to concentrate 100% on that + can call on any resources immediately. Isolation at Camp David with a group is a possibility."

Hartmann was enthusiastic about the idea of a Camp David retreat to kick off the writing, and he was determined to retain control of the speechwriting process. "I have heard that there are a number of people working on their own State of the Union drafts," he wrote to Ford on January 6. He wanted the president to make clear to the staff that he, Hartmann, was in charge.

When Ford called a staff meeting on January 7, he handled the situation in classic fashion. He said that Hartmann was in charge of the process, but did not say that any attempts to bypass him or cut him out would be dealt with harshly.

Camp David was occupied, so Hartmann decided that Colonial Williamsburg would be the place to capture the spirit for Ford's address. He led a group that included assistant to the president for public liaison William Baroody, domestic policy adviser James Cannon, and the OMB's Paul O'Neill, among others, down to Williamsburg's historic Lightfoot House. They arrived on Thursday, January 9, ten days before the State of the Union.

With a fire crackling in the hearth, they gathered in a room where Patrick Henry and other revolutionaries had plotted treason against their king. Hartmann saw contemporary plots. "It soon became clear that new sedition was brewing," he wrote. "Half the participants made it obvious they were not there to draft a good speech but to prevent mine from being drafted." The group broke apart on Friday, and Hartmann and Friedman stayed until Saturday working up a first draft, which they showed Ford and others early the following week. Hartmann's draft included the assertion that Americans were losing confidence in their government because "it is too big and bumbling." Perhaps feeling the sting of comedian Chevy Chase's *Saturday Night Live* portrayal of him as an inept klutz, Ford crossed out bumbling and substituted "impersonal."

Hartmann worked all of Wednesday night, taking an hour's nap while waiting for his typewriter, whose keys had started to stick, to be replaced. He gave Ford a final first draft—its theme "common sense," reprising the revolutionary pamphleteer Thomas Paine—on Thursday, January 15, twenty-two minutes before his noon deadline.

Cheney had dismissed Hartmann's initial draft as a laundry list of stale legislative proposals; he asked Gergen and Greenspan to write up a more thematic address, with an emphasis on an overarching vision for the nation for the remainder of the decade. The Gergen-Greenspan speech—which Hartmann and his crew dubbed "Roman Numeral Two"—arrived on Ford's desk at roughly the same time as Hartmann's. It focused on the idea that the relationship between the government and the private sector had gotten out of balance and that a new balance had to be established in American life.

The president was not expecting, yet again, to have competing drafts, but if he was upset, he did not show it. He took the two speeches and, after dinner and a swim on Thursday evening, dictated a new mishmash version to his secretary, Dorothy Downton. "Go through theirs once more and see if I missed anything good that can be incorporated into ours," Ford told Hartmann. "But I'm satisfied this is about ninety-nine percent done, and I don't want a lot more changes."

Ford "was unwilling to come down hard on those who had tried to undercut the established procedure," Hartmann recalled. "So he sat down with his secretary and he plucked little morsels from all these different texts and put them together like a string of beads. He thought that was pretty dandy. Nobody was willing to tell him how terrible it was. He gave it to me and I went home and virtually rewrote it. I threw enough of the other people's words in there to make them happy and so [Ford] wouldn't balk."

The showdown came on the afternoon of Saturday, January 17, in the Cabinet Room. Except for the timing, it could have been 1975 all over again, with the two camps squabbling over the message. Three hours into a second consecutive year of petty infighting among his top advisers late in the process—and determined not again to find himself mediating his staff until hours before he was to speak—Ford finally lost his temper.

"Damn it," he said, slamming his hand down on the table so hard that it shook. "We've got to stop this bickering over these little details. I want a final draft by noon tomorrow."

Hartmann took charge, and after three and a half hours of haggling, the group broke up, leaving Hartmann, Friedman, and Orben to produce a near-final draft, which they did around midnight. In the end, the majority of the speech was drawn from the Hartmann version, with a couple of sections from Gergen-Greenspan. The rest was anticlimax, and the speech, like most State of the Union addresses, was forgettable.

There were enduring repercussions. Cheney, who had promised that Gergen would have nothing more to do with speeches, was now firmly entrenched on Hartmann's enemies' list. This bothered neither Cheney nor Gergen, who would perform as a shadow speechwriting department for the rest of Ford's term.

Hartmann and Orben brought on a new writer in February 1976. David Boorstin, twenty-five, the son of Librarian of Congress Daniel Boorstin, had been writing for *Editorial Research Reports*, one of the galaxy of Washington niche publications that cover every gear in the federal machine. Boorstin had spent three years working in theater in London, and he found that that background with the spoken word, combined with his journalistic experience of having to master new subjects quickly, helped him learn speechwriting.

But Boorstin also had to learn politics. "Insofar as I was anything at that age, I was a liberal Democrat coming out of the radical college days," he recalled. "I said to them, 'I'm not a Republican . . . I don't even know what the party line is, much less that I would hew to it.'" By his own admission, he was "not a political person." "It never remotely occurred to me I would ever be working in the White House, much less for a Republican." He was told not to worry about it, that he would not have to write anything he was not comfortable with.

Boorstin was another odd choice for a speechwriter—especially for a president facing a stiff primary challenge from his party's burgeoning conservative wing. Ronald Reagan was indeed challenging Ford in the primaries, rallying conservatives against the president by painting him as part of the Washington establishment. And while Ford publicly predicted that former Vice President Hubert Humphrey would bear the Democratic standard in the fall, one-term Georgia governor Jimmy Carter had emerged as a dark horse for the nomination in a field of a dozen serious candidates.

Other would-be writers were less lucky. Orben hired Al Parsons of Tallahassee, Florida, as a speechwriter, but when Parsons showed up for his first day of work in March, he was not allowed into the building. Journalist Michael Johnson of Galesburg, Illinois, quit his job and rushed to D.C. to take a ninety-day trial job as editor of Ford's written messages, but he encountered a similar problem. Cabinet Secretary James Connor, a Cheney ally, had sat on their paperwork, apparently as part of the ongoing internecine squabbling. And a pay increase promised to Orben for becoming chief speechwriter had not yet materialized.

How long Ford would be in the White House remained an open question, but things started out looking bright: He won a narrow victory in the New Hampshire primary over Reagan on February 24—the first election he had ever won outside of Michigan's 5th congressional district. On March 9, he won the Florida primary with 53 percent of the vote. A week later, Ford bested Reagan in the Illinois primary with 59 percent of the vote. The tide turned on March 23, when Reagan beat Ford in North Carolina with 52 percent of the primary vote. It was only the third time in U.S. history that a challenger had defeated an incumbent president in a primary, and the previous two incumbent losers had ended up withdrawing from their nomination races.*

---

*Harry S. Truman lost to Tennessee senator Estes Kefauver in 1952; Lyndon B. Johnson lost the Wisconsin primary to Minnesota senator Eugene McCarthy in 1968, after Johnson had already withdrawn from the race.

Three days later, Orben sent an SOS to Hartmann: "If we consider our goal to be effective and accurate speeches prepared on time, it is unlikely that this goal will be achieved unless substantial changes are made in our present method of operation. The speechwriting staff is apparently limited to a fixed number of people. The number we now have is too small to cope effectively with the volume of work required. If the volume increases, as it will, the Speech Department will just break down. . . . Because we have so few experienced writers, I am forced to give brand new writers fairly major speeches and hope for the best—or frantically rewrite them at the last minute. This is not the stuff that campaign winning speeches are made of."

"In show business you can wrangle with yourself, but you're not going to do anything to hurt the client," he later reflected. "And in politics that ain't necessarily so."

Reagan skipped the New York and Wisconsin primaries on April 6 and the Pennsylvania primary three weeks later. Ford hoped to finish off the conservative challenger in Texas on May 1, but Reagan scored a victory there.

Two days later, Ford was campaigning through Indiana and Alabama, two states that, along with Georgia, held their primaries on May 4. A late-afternoon speech was scheduled for Wilson Park in Birmingham. Pat Butler, who would become chief campaign speechwriter before the year was through, realized that Ford's prepared speech would not work in the relaxed setting—it was too long and too detailed. They needed a brief, patriot-stirring crowd-pleaser, and he banged one out in about fifteen minutes.

"In two hundred years we have forged from a struggling group of colonies to the greatest nation in the history of the world," Ford told the crowd. "Our progress in every field has been unprecedented, and much of that progress has always been due to the strength and to the character of young Americans."

Butler had not checked with Hartmann before rewriting the speech and Hartmann exploded—How can you take things on yourself like this?—and then told Butler he was fired. Hartmann never spoke of it to Butler again, did not apologize, but Butler was not fired.

Reagan swept all three primaries. Through the remainder of May and into early June, Reagan and Ford battled to a standstill. They split two dozen primaries where they squared off head-to-head. As the primary season closed on June 8, Ford held a plurality of delegates, but not a majority. He would have to spend June and July personally wooing delegates in the eleven states that used party conventions to pick delegates.

One event where Ford might shine came in early July, as the country celebrated its two hundredth birthday. The president was scheduled to speak at celebratory events in the first five days of July—the opening of the Smithsonian Air and Space Museum and at the National Archives in Washington; at Valley Forge; and at Monticello. "Very, very important," Ford jotted in a note to Hartmann on June 1. "What about asking several outstanding historical writers like Dan Boorstin (Dave's Dad), [Neoconservative] Irving Kristol + maybe others to help plan and write the outline suggestion."

A week later, Hartmann submitted a selection of speech themes, and another volley in his ongoing bureaucratic struggle: "It will be possible to develop four or five outstanding speeches of very high quality with a consistent tone and theme, IF I can obtain the full cooperation of everyone concerned and the motivation, concentration and creativity required are not destroyed by conspiratorial game playing, secret double and triple tracking and last minute power and policy contests which have been disrupting our efforts to attain orderly development of superior speech drafts all this year," he wrote the president. "Competition has degenerated into clandestine contests which waste your time. Their sole object is neither producing a superior product nor serving your interest best, but the unworthy end of showing who's 'king of the mountain.'"

He added a plea: "To this end I must remind you that since the first of April, I have been permitted only 5 personal meetings with you, and would hope that we can work together on this project as much as is necessary to make the speeches truly your own."

As far as some on the staff were concerned, five audiences with the president were too many.

"What I'm going to say next . . . epitomizes the root cause of many of your problems," David Hume Kennerly wrote to Ford in a memo on June 10. Although Kennerly was the White House photographer, Ford liked his brash, irreverent manner, his willingness to be blunt with the president of the United States, and had come to rely on his judgment. "Your speeches are usually long, boring, and filled with rhetoric that turns people off," Kennerly said. "I've seen advancemen literally cry when after ten or fifteen minutes after you started speaking the people would start leaving. . . . Your speech-writing department has driven mediocrity to new heights. If this were my opinion alone, I'd say perhaps I could be wrong. It's not. It's universal."

One critic who had a chance to do something was Craig Smith, thirty-two, a University of Virginia professor who specialized in the theory of rhetoric. He had listened to a Ford speech before the North Carolina primary and had been appalled, not just by the substance but by technical aspects such as unclear transitions and poor organization. He wrote Ford a letter critiquing the speech. The note ended up in the speech-writing office; after a couple of interviews, he was offered a job.

Smith's first assignment was to read and analyze everything Ford had uttered since he had been nominated as vice president three years earlier. Hartmann asked Smith what he thought of the president's style. The problem is, he doesn't have one, Smith responded. He has several styles, and it depends on who's doing the writing—and that's not a good thing because you're not conveying a consistent persona when you're doing that. "I had paragraphs from one speech and paragraphs from another speech and I said, 'This isn't the same man,'" Smith recalled. "The language is too different—and too disparate."

Smith's first assignment was a June 15 address to the Southern Baptist Convention in Norfolk. Smith thought of it as something of a test for him, a Catholic, to write a speech for Ford, an Episcopalian, to be given before a group of Southern Baptists. He had several sessions with Ford. The president gave him specific instructions: Please don't use phrases like "I have been saved," Ford told him, I'm not that kind of religious person. I don't want to talk about Jesus as my personal saviour or any of that kind of thing.

This would set him apart from Jimmy Carter, now the presumptive Democratic nominee, who had spoken in the primaries about his religious convictions. "Jimmy Carter's open espousal of his Christian beliefs in the 1976 Presidential campaign has raised the issue of religion's place in politics more arrestingly that it has been raised in any Presidential race since John F. Kennedy's in 1960," *The New York Times* had reported in April.

Keep it pretty high-minded, Ford told Smith.* They also discussed Ford's style. I want to speak the language of the common man, Ford told him. Smith pointed out that FDR had used simple language. Roosevelt used repetition, he said, he used rhythm, but it was all small words.

Ford was impressed. And the results were good. *The Washington Star*, not a presidential booster, gave Ford's Baptist Convention speech a good review in a story headlined: "Righteous Ford Talks Like Carter, Wows Baptists."

Hartmann had received many drafts and suggestions from a variety of sources for the bicentennial addresses. They included submissions not only from the senior Boorstin and Kristol, but from Gergen, Baroody, White House counselor Jack Marsh, academics such as Notre Dame president Theodore Hesbergh, Dr. Martin Diamond of Northern Illinois University, Dr. Herbert Storing of the University of Chicago, and a host of others—and of course from the speechwriting staff. On June 8, Hartmann sent Ford a memo with the various suggestions so the president could choose the ones he preferred. "Excellent," Ford wrote, sending it back. "It worked well."

---

*Smith was also told by other speechwriters to avoid certain words with which Ford would have trouble: "Judgment," for example, which Ford tended to pronounce judge-a-ment. Other such words included "guarantee" (garn-tee), and "monorail" (mona-rail). (Author interviews with Pat Butler, Robert Orben, and Craig Smith.)

The half-dozen bicentennial speeches that Ford gave at the start of July were a high point of his rhetoric and statesmanship.

"They came here in the snows of winter over a trail marked with the blood of their rag-bound feet," Ford said at Valley Forge on the morning of July 4, 1976, in a speech drafted by Smith.

> *The iron forge that gave this place its name had been destroyed by the British when General Washington and his ragged Continental Army encamped here—exhausted, outnumbered, and short of everything except faith. We gather here today, the 200th anniversary of our independence, to commemorate their sacrifices even before we celebrate the glorious Declaration. Americans will remember the name of Valley Forge as long as the spirit of sacrifice lives within their hearts.*

The Republican National Convention was scheduled to convene on August 16, in Kansas City, Missouri. The nomination was still up for grabs between the president and the challenger, but Ford turned his attention to the acceptance speech he hoped to give. He told Hartmann that he liked the process used for the bicentennial and wanted to do it again. Hartmann saw this as a sort of Kabuki ritual: Ford wanted him to go through the exercise of gathering opinions before they worked on it exclusively. "To me it was a lot of bother," he wrote. "To him it was the essence of politics."

The lesson from the bicentennial experience, Hartmann thought, was that a good speech should focus on a single theme. He suggested three options: Heal and charge up the party; use the moment as a showcase for his own character; or go after the Democrats. Ford responded predictably: "Why don't we do all three? Well, let's see what everybody recommends."

On July 13, Hartmann followed up: "The lesson of the Bicentennial speeches seems to have been that to be effective a speech should have only one main purpose or point to get across. . . . It may be argued that the speech can and should accomplish all three of these objectives. My view is that it is perhaps possible to combine [any two] but not all three."

He attached a list of thirty-two people from whom he might solicit suggestions, the fewer the better. Ford checked every name on the list, excepting Attorney General Edward Levi, who was supposed to remain non-political. "Go home and write it," he told Hartmann. He had one key instruction: "Since 1956 no candidate for Pres. could accept nomination + say U.S. not at war," Ford scribbled on a piece of White House notepaper on August 9.

What the speech needed, Hartmann thought, was a news hook— something to grab the voters' imagination. He solicited ideas. A variety came in: David Boorstin suggested a new Marshall Plan "to reassert America's leadership position in the free world, or to establish such a position with the Third World." Charles McCall, head of the speech-writing department's research division, suggested announcing that Reagan would either be put in charge of the Panama Canal negotiations or appointed ambassador to the United Nations (Reagan had been highly critical of Ford's foreign policy during the primary campaign, especially the possibility of handing over the canal to Panama). Smith suggested that Ford "take the unprecedented step of pledging to give no more than five campaign speeches in the fall. Such a strategy would gain national attention from both the media and the audience. It would allow each speech to be fully developed and crafted. It would enhance the Presidential image by insuring [*sic*] that campaigning would not interfere with Presidential duties." Hartmann thought this last suggestion inane.

Ford had already come up with an idea of his own, but he was keeping it secret.

Shortly after midnight, on the morning of Thursday, August 19, Ford won the Republican nomination. That evening, he would have to give a speech to rouse the nation and rally his campaign against the large lead Democratic nominee Carter had built in the polls.

Ford had rehearsed the speech all week. Don Penny, a former television writer and stand-up comedian who had joined the staff as a speech coach, produced a videocamera and tape player so the president could judge his own performance. Ford's gestures were too exagger-

263

ated. He had a tendency to shift side to side on his feet. He did not smile enough when on TV, Betty Ford pointed out. Sometimes Ford would stand in his hotel suite practicing for pace, timing, and emphasis. Jack Marsh would listen in an adjoining room, within earshot but out of sight, because Ford would feel self-conscious speaking to a visible audience of one.

At 5:30 pm on the day of the speech, Ford summoned Cheney and Marsh to his hotel suite to spring the surprise he had already shared with Hartmann. He showed them a paragraph he had written on a yellow legal pad: "And I will tell you one more thing. This year the issues are on our side. I am ready, I am eager to go before the American people and debate the real issues face to face with Jimmy Carter. The American people have a right to know firsthand exactly where both of us stand."

The promise energized the campaign. These would be the first presidential debates since Kennedy and Nixon in 1960. The speech was a huge success, and the speechwriters identified the lesson to be drawn: sufficient time for preparation, do not step on the message. They argued that repeating the success would require time and focus—a few great speeches as opposed to a campaign crammed with hastily produced ones.

Butler argued in an August 24 memo to Hartmann that "fine craftsmanship is always sacrificed when quantity is a more important consideration than quality. That is why Rolls-Royces are better cars than Chevrolets, and why the President's acceptance speech was better than his campaign speeches in Texas." He added: "Making speeches 'by the gross' will inevitably debase the currency of the Presidential address."

Butler was not alone in this advice. The speechwriters were pondering an idea that Hartmann had thought idiotic. On the same day that Butler sent in his memo, David Boorstin suggested that Ford confine himself to "a limited number of important speeches." George Denison, a Michigan native and lawyer who had written for *Reader's Digest* before joining the speechwriting staff in April, suggested—on the same day—that Ford be limited to two major policy speeches per week. And that same day, Orben sent Hartmann a memo advocating "one major speech a week. This would allow for sufficient lead time for a well thought-out and constructed speech to be written, learned and rehearsed."

Thirty years later, neither Butler nor Orben recollected any coordination in the flurry of like-minded memoranda. "As I recall, it wasn't a coordinated response but rather a common belief that the president had been speaking publicly so often—without saying much new—that his currency was being devalued and people were simply tuning him out," Butler said. What they were grasping for was a technique that would become common political practice within a decade.

"A few years later, President Reagan and Mike Deaver perfected 'the message of the day' approach to presidential communication wherein the president would make at most one major statement so as to preserve the impact of presidential speeches and avoid confusing the public (and journalists) about what was important to focus on," Butler recalled. "That's what we were all trying to get at in 1976. Our specific recommendation was just a tad too extreme."

A typical campaign day in late October started in San Diego with the release of a radio address on inflation. At 8:32 am, Ford announced the creation of a regional economic development zone. Then it was on to Seattle, Washington, where he made remarks at the airport about noise pollution at 10:45 am, and downtown at 12:46 pm on national defense, taxes and spending, economic growth and national pride. An hour later Ford appeared at a Veterans Administration hospital to speak about the importance of keeping the peace and providing health care for veterans. From there it was back to the airport and south to Portland, Oregon, where he spoke about the greatness of America before a crowd at the airport at 3:21 pm. At 4:24 pm at the Sheraton-Portland Hotel, Ford participated in a question-and-answer with the National Association of Broadcasters. At 5:20 pm he took questions from reporters one more time before boarding the plane for a cross-country flight to Pittsburgh.

There were advantages to such a pace. Perpetually on the move, the campaign speechwriters did not have to circulate their drafts to the usual litany of staffers, so there were fewer people trying to dull down or, ineptly, punch up the talk. "Ford was in real control of his subject matter and he became quite comfortable on the stump," Butler recalled. "The secret of our success was that we went through fewer editors in the relative isolation of the campaign plane." But that did not put the speechwriters out of reach of the Hartmann-Praetorian battles.

Ford was scheduled to speak at the Pittsburgh Economic Club the next morning, October 26, and David Boorstin had written a speech focused on the economy for the occasion. Butler edited it and was taking it up to Hartmann in the VIP cabin on Air Force One when Cheney intercepted him and asked where he was going.

When Butler said that he had the president's speech for the Pittsburgh Economic Club, Cheney responded that in fact *he* had it, a Gergen-written foreign policy speech. Butler wanted no part of the staff warfare: he said he would give the Boorstin version to Hartmann and the two senior aides could work it out.

No dice. Cheney insisted, and as Butler was handing over his draft, Hartmann appeared. What are you doing? he growled.

I'm giving the president's speech to the chief of staff, Butler explained.

Who do you think you work for? Hartmann asked.

I work for you, Bob, Butler said.

"The hell you do!" Hartmann sputtered. This was the third time Hartmann fired Butler. A screaming match erupted between Cheney and Hartmann. The young aide slunk back to his seat. He was 40,000 feet in the air, flying east on Air Force One, and now unemployed. It was his twenty-seventh birthday. When the yelling up front quieted, Cheney came back, sat next to him, and patted him on the knee. "I think he's serious this time," Cheney said.

"That's the impression I got," Butler replied.

It's okay, Cheney said: "If he's fired you I've hired you and I'm giving you a raise." As with the two previous "firings," however, Hartmann did not mention it again.

The next day, appearing before the Pittsburgh Economic Club, Ford discussed U.S. foreign policy.

On November 2, 1976, Jimmy Carter achieved a narrow victory over Ford, less than 2 million votes. Ford had closed a late July 33-point gap and almost pulled off the most remarkable comeback since Harry S. Truman in 1948.

A number of factors contributed to Ford's loss, the most important his pardon of Nixon. He also stalled his own momentum when in the second televised debate with Carter he made one of the great historical gaffes, declaring that "There is no Soviet domination of Eastern Europe and there never will be under a Ford administration." Ford had been trying to make a statement about the spirit of the Eastern Europeans, but it was widely played as a huge foreign policy blunder.

The arc of Ford's administration can be traced in his speechwriting and speechgiving. In many ways, Ford understood the importance of presidential communications. He was willing to endure ridicule over hiring a gag writer because he thought that Orben would make solid contributions. When Ford was able to make the process work properly and work well with his writers—the bicentennial speeches, the convention acceptance speech, the 1976 campaign—he benefited from it. But the internal staff warring that Ford allowed to linger crippled the speechwriting process. As counselor to the president, Hartmann was in a position to play a role akin to Clifford or Sorensen, but his effectiveness was undercut by the sniping between him and the Rumsfeld-Cheney camps, and by Ford's unwillingness or inability to end it. The main speechwriting shop suffered the collateral damage from these fights, whether in terms of staffing, perks, or being cut out of the speechwriting process. Given chaos and civil war, it is not surprising that the process only worked in fits and starts.

In early January 1977, Orben met with James Fallows, Carter's incoming chief speechwriter. After Orben had run him through the pointers of the job, from the washrooms to the staffing process, Fallows inquired if there were anything else Orben could tell him. Orben paused. Could he properly explain the stress? Should he tell Fallows about how his gallbladder was removed the week after the election?

"You're on such a treadmill," he recalled years later. "The last year I would say I got an average of four hours sleep at night. I would still have a gallbladder if it weren't for two and a half years at the White House."

"There's a lot of tension," Orben told Fallows.

EIGHT

"Don't Give Any Explanation. Just Say I Cancelled the Damn Speech"

JANUARY 1977

Jimmy Carter labored alone.

Patrick Anderson, his campaign speechwriter, had supplied Carter with a first draft of an inaugural address, but the former Georgia governor wrote at least three more drafts himself, his precise, right-slanted handwriting filling every other line of a legal pad. As he sometimes did with important speeches, Carter had written a numbered outline of the points that he wanted to cover (forty-one in all). Each one consisted of two- or three-word summaries—"4. 3rd cent—consider—Δ"—that corresponded to brief sections of his speech.* Those sections, each on its own piece of paper, were spread in front of him on the large desk in his ranch-style home in Plains, Georgia. He was rearranging them, an engineer looking for the proper structure for his first presidential speech.

"Carter thinks in lists, not arguments," speechwriter James Fallows

---

*The Δ is the scientific symbol for change, so this point, number 4, was: "As we begin our third century it is well to consider what we have been and what we ought to be. We have provided both governmental continuity and a framework for constant and dramatic political change." (Handwritten inaugural draft, undated, "[Inaugural Speech Drafts—Notes and Suggestions] [1]" folder, Office of Staff Secretary, Jimmy Carter Library.)

later wrote. Indeed, during his first year in the White House, Carter would instruct Fallows that in preparing speeches he should first "prepare simple <u>list</u> of points to be made in speech, arranged in proper order."

The final product was largely unfamiliar to Anderson, with "only a few sentences here and there" from his original draft. Anderson, a writer whose works included a novel called *The President's Mistress*, had decided not to accompany Carter to the White House. Carter had never worked with a speechwriter before the campaign, and the early results were not good: his first speechwriter, Democratic political consultant Robert Shrum, quit in a billow of acrimony. Now Carter was preparing to enter the White House with Anderson's deputy, Fallows, a twenty-seven-year-old former reporter, in the top speechwriting spot.

Carter had studied his predecessors' inaugurals, admiring John Kennedy's, and especially Woodrow Wilson's 1913 speech, which touched him "most of all." Like Wilson, Carter thought, he was taking office at a time when the country "desired a return to first principles by their government." He had discussed the themes with his wife, Rosalynn, who had read the drafts "over and over," she said. He solicited ideas from friends, aides, and allies. "In simplistic terms, you could say that right now we suffer from a spiritual malaise . . . a crisis of the spirit," Gerald Rafshoon, Carter's television ad guru, advised in a January 4 memo. Carter opted for a more positive focus on a renewal of spirit.

The president-elect sent a draft of the speech to Fallows, who suggested a new opening. So, on a cold and clear January 20, Carter, wearing a three-piece business suit that he had purchased the previous week in Americus, Georgia, for $175, began his inaugural address with a word of gentle praise: "For myself and for our nation, I want to thank my predecessor for all he has done to heal our land."

The rest of the speech was understated—some said underwhelming. (Carter had been warned to speak slowly so as to minimize distortion from the loudspeakers, but he felt that he spoke too slowly.) He focused on the theme of a "new spirit" in the country, quoting from his high school teacher and from the biblical prophet Micah.* He spoke of limits and fallibility: "I have no new dream to set forth today, but rather urge a fresh faith in the old dream," he said, adding: "Your strength can compensate for my weakness, and your wisdom can help to minimize my mistakes."

"With his sense of the moment, this first President from the Deep South in more than a century has chosen modest beginnings and has forsaken the traditional boldness of inaugural rhetoric that contributed to the now fallen mystique of the Presidency," *The New York Times* reported in a front-page analysis.

"The more familiar I am with the arguments and assumptions that lie behind your decisions, the more successful I will be in helping present them," Fallows wrote Carter in a memo on January 21. "For that reason, I would ask that, without getting seriously underfoot, I be routinely included in as many staff meetings, Cabinet meetings, and other gatherings of the sort as possible. During the campaign, I found the ambience of the plane, and the frequent opportunities to talk with [Carter's top aides] . . . were [a] great help in providing me that background."

A Philadelphia native who had grown up in Redlands, California, Fallows had worked a summer for the consumer advocate Ralph Nader and two years for the liberal *Washington Monthly*. Before joining the Carter campaign after the Democratic Convention, he had been freelancing in Texas, where his wife was getting her graduate degree. He took the White House gig because "it was clear to me this was the best job I could get in the administration," he explained. "Speeches were not something I was especially fond of, but there was no area of policy where I had enough credentials to get an equivalently substantial job."

The word most often used to describe Fallows was "boyish," as in "tall, slim, boyish-looking," (*Newsday*) and "boyish-faced" (*New York Times*). "Fallows is bright and younger than most [upper-level staffers],

---

*Carter ordinarily shunned quotes. "He would not quote things unless they were a part of his own experience," Achsah Nesmith recalled. "If he hadn't read a book, he wouldn't quote it, essentially. He felt as if he hadn't experienced it. . . . If you put in three quotations he normally would take out two just as a matter of course." (Carter speechwriters OH, Jimmy Carter Library, 110.)

a mere 27 years old, which is approximately 10 years older than he looks," a *Washington Post* article reported.

He headed a small staff. Jerry Doolittle had worked for the United States Information Agency in Laos and then covered the Vietnam War as a freelance reporter. Upon deciding that he wanted to join the Carter campaign, he drove from Connecticut to Georgia, and randomly met Carter's spokesman, Jody Powell, in the men's room at campaign head-quarters. He ended up giving Powell and his wife a ride to the airport. He's given as references all the people he's lied to in Southeast Asia, Doolittle recalled Powell saying to his wife, so he's got to be pretty good; we'll hire him.

Griffin Smith was a Rice University graduate who had dabbled in both politics and journalism. He had been the first full-time reporter for *Texas Monthly*.

Hendrik "Rick" Hertzberg was a New Yorker who had worked, ap-propriately, at *The New Yorker*. Like Fallows, Rick was a Harvard grad-uate, and the two men knew each other through the informal network of *Crimson* former staffers. He had done some speechwriting in 1976 for New York governor Hugh Carey.

The only member of the speechwriting staff who had known Carter before the campaign was a former journalist named Achsah Nesmith. The first woman hired in the newsroom of the *Atlanta Journal-Constitution*, Nesmith covered Carter's 1966 gubernatorial run. Often she was the sole reporter on the trail, and sometimes the traveling party consisted only of Carter, Nesmith, and the campaign plane pilot. She noticed that when speaking to crowds, Carter would look above the heads of his audience. She assumed that it was a trick to help him not lock onto a single pair of eyes, but it gave the impres-sion that he was searching for an exit. One day Carter asked her what she thought of his stump speech. She told him about his search for a door. "He looked hurt and I rather regretted it," she recalled. But she never saw his eyes dart around the room again.

Nesmith was also the only southerner on the speechwriting staff. And she was active in her Presbyterian church, making her the only speechwriter who was particularly religious. The speechwriters "were—for the most part, except for Achsah—a little band of secular humanist northern exotic lefties in the midst of this bunch of good old boys," Hertzberg recalled, referring to Carter's closest aides, who had come to Washington with the president and were also known as the "Georgia mafia."*

One of the first speeches the writers had to work on was a joke—literally. On January 26, Carter was scheduled to speak at the Washington Press Club Dinner, where he was expected to be funny. Humor has a special role in Washington—a politician can generate great goodwill with a witty performance—and it was the Carters' first "social appearance" as first couple. The mantle of making Jimmy Carter funny fell to Jerry Doolittle.

At the dinner, Carter started by recounting how after his inauguration he had walked down Pennsylvania Avenue. He "could hear the vast crowd saying, 'Look, look, look,'" he remarked, "and I was feeling very good until they said, 'There goes Billy's brother.'"† Doolittle had studiously avoided jokes about the first brother in the material that he had drafted for Carter. "Oh shit," he thought. Then Carter rattled off a slew of other unfamiliar jokes. Doolittle was so down afterward that he missed the motorcade back to the White House.

"In an evening where tradition demands that seriousness never stands in the way of a good joke, [Carter] held his own," *The Washington Post* reported the next day. Doolittle received plaudits from his fellow White House staffers, none of whom believed that Carter had written his own material. For the rest of his tenure at the White House, Doolittle was called upon when Carter had to be funny and it earned him, to his irritation, a reputation as Carter's gag writer. A couple of days after

---

*"We used to joke that it was no accident that the man's initials were J.C.," Hertzberg wrote. "It seemed like one of those odd coincidences that make you think maybe there is a God after all and that He has a pretty good sense of humor." (Hertzberg, *Politics*, 54.)

† Carter's younger brother, Billy, had become a punch line with a reputation as a beer-swilling (and endorsing) redneck. "Yes, I'm a real southern boy," he told reporters during the campaign. "I got a red neck, white socks, and Blue Ribbon beer." (www.pbs.org/wgbh/amex/carter/peopleevents/p__bcarter.html.)

the speech, though, Fallows got back the memo of the Doolittle jokes he had originally passed on to Carter. Carter had written a note on it: "Jim, Very poor—Next time do more work on it & don't blame Doolittle. At last minute I had to write my own."

Fallows had been working on Carter's first post-inaugural address to the nation—a fireside chat on the president's legislative program. He included in an early draft of the speech the word "cynical," which Carter excised with a stern lecture: average people, the president told his speechwriter, would not understand the word. Carter's test of language was whether a man at a certain gas station in Georgia would understand a word. He replaced "cynical" with "callous." "Working people understand calluses," the president said. "They see their hands get hard." While Fallows endorsed clarity of language, he thought Carter could take it too far, noting later that "When simplifying words Carter too often simplified ideas."

Carter was a precise editor in other ways, bracketing phrases for deletion and tightening wordy prose—for example, dropping the "it" in "Tomorrow it will be two weeks since I became president." A small edit of his fireside chat proved an inadvertent omen to problems that would mar his administration. Discussing his upcoming energy plan, in a passage saying that he would "ask the Congress for its advice and help in enacting responsible legislation," Carter bracketed and crossed out the "advice and."

The president was wearing a beige wool cardigan sweater as he dined with his family on February 2, the evening of the fireside chat. He kept it on when he went to the White House Library for the final rehearsal and asked image man Rafshoon and TV adviser Barry Jagoda what they thought of it. They told him to look at himself in the television monitor and he decided it worked. Later, when Carter's presidency was faltering, the cardigan would become a symbol of nagging ineptitude, but with the president still enjoying a honeymoon, it was hailed as a sign of Carter's mastery of modern presidential communications. *Time* called it "the most memorable symbol of an Administration that promises to make steady use of symbolism."

The speech was a pastiche. Carter covered everything from energy to federal government reorganization to his plans to host a live call-in radio show from the Oval Office. The address was modeled on FDR's old fireside chats, but it lacked Roosevelt's optimistic confidence ("I am sure to make many mistakes"), and Carter on television could not match the relaxed, informal combination of FDR and radio.

The president was scheduled to give his first major foreign policy speech at the University of Notre Dame on May 22. As statements of administration policy, such speeches would become a focus of clashes between the hawkish, traditional Cold Warrior Zbigniew Brzezinski, the president's national security adviser, and the more moderate Secretary of State, Cyrus Vance. The national security adviser would often cut the Secretary of State out of the editing and approval process. "Brzezinski tended to be more devious in his dealings with Vance than Vance was with Brzezinski," Hertzberg recalled.

Brzezinski had supervised the drafting of the Notre Dame speech, which would focus on the shortcomings of the United States' position in the world. *The New York Times* was shown a copy of the speech, presumably by Brzezinski,* for a preview story running the day Carter was supposed to speak. "President Carter has concluded that the system of Western alliances established after World War II under American leadership no longer suffices to meet the challenge of international conditions," the *Times* noted. "He intends to propose a broader international system." In fact, Carter would give a different speech.

Doolittle, the speechwriter who had worked as both spokesman and reporter in Southeast Asia, thought the Brzezinski draft reflected a harder-line Cold War view than the president—who had campaigned on withdrawing U.S. troops from the Korean peninsula and taken steps toward normalizing relations with Cuba†—espoused. "Carter seemed

---

*"The address, as outlined, carried many marks of the thinking of Zbigniew Brzezinski, the President's national security adviser," the paper reported. (David Binder, "President to Ask Broader System of U.S. Alliances," *New York Times*, May 22, 1977.)

†On March 15, Carter had issued a secret presidential directive ordering that "we should attempt to achieve normalization of our relations with Cuba," and mandating direct, confidential talks with the Castro government regarding reestablishing diplomatic relations. (National Security Archive, www.gwu.edu/~nsarchiv/news/20020515/cartercuba.pdf.)

to me to have a more rational approach," he recalled. "If you grew up as I did in the McCarthy era . . . you lived in this weird world where you expected at any moment to be bombed into oblivion and yet you could look at the empty shelves in the [Soviet] stores, you could look at the failure of the agriculture, you could look at everything they did except for the big show stuff like Sputnik. And you could feel like you're living in two parallel worlds and one of them is completely blacked out. I thought—and Carter saw this too—and realized you were dealing with a very large and clumsy failed state that could only do nothing." Doolittle wrote a memo to Fallows arguing that the Notre Dame draft failed to distinguish Carter's foreign policy from that of his immediate predecessors. Where the Nixon-Kissinger foreign policy focused on the pessimistic need to accommodate a strong Soviet Union, Carter proceeded from an optimistic view of a triumphant democracy, Doolittle said. "In the past, our foreign policy was based on the implicit assumption that communism is superior to democracy. So powerful are they that if we give them an inch, they will take the globe. But the truth is that if we give them an inch, they are very likely to choke on it."

The speech should explicate what was different about Carter's approach, Doolittle stressed. "When you are confident of democracy's future, you are free of that inordinate fear of communism which once led us to embrace any dictator who joined us in our fear."

Fallows passed the memo on to Carter, who used it to overhaul the speech. Hertzberg got the impression that the hawkish Brzezinski—who saw nothing misplaced about fearing the Soviets—did not get to see the revised copy of the speech before it was distributed to the press. This did not stop the national security adviser from backgrounding it to reporters a few minutes later, presenting the "inordinate fear" formulation "as the end result of long cogitation and subtly suggesting it was a victory over Vance," Hertzberg said. "And actually it had been the joke writer's passionate memo to Carter and Carter keeping control of his own speech."

"Being confident of our own future, we are now free of that inordinate fear of communism which once led us to embrace any dictator who joined us in that fear. I'm glad that that's being changed," Carter told the Notre Dame graduates. "For too many years, we've been willing to adopt the flawed and erroneous principles and tactics of our adversaries, sometimes abandoning our own values for theirs. We've fought fire with fire, never thinking that fire is better quenched with water. This approach failed, with Vietnam the best example of its intellectual and moral poverty."

The president spoke with "obvious intensity and feeling," *Time* reported, adding that one listener said afterward, "This is either a very important speech or a prayer."

The "inordinate fear" line became one of Carter's best remembered,* though the sudden switch of speeches caught some White House insiders by surprise. "President Carter has left many of his administration's own officials wondering how literally to take the soaring rhetoric of his foreign policy speech at Notre Dame University," *The Washington Post* reported. "It clearly was the President's intention to have the address serve as a major guidepost for the future, associates say. However, even enthusiasts cannot foretell precisely what the speech foreshadows in specific policies, for it was cast, as one admirer noted, in 'rather Delphic terms.'"

Critics had no problem forecasting the problems to which the speech would lead. Former California Republican governor Ronald Reagan warned that the Soviet Union was too dangerous for the United States to start criticizing allies. New York Democratic senator Daniel Patrick Moynihan warned against being distracted from "the reality of the military and ideological competition with the Soviet Union which continues and, if anything, escalates." Henry Kissinger, who had re-

---

*The phrase and underlying reasoning had historical ripples. "We neocons were a small group of political thinkers who broke with fellow liberals during the war in Vietnam," Joshua Muravchik wrote in *The Washington Post* in 2006. "Most liberals came to believe that the United States had gotten into Vietnam out of what President Jimmy Carter later called an 'inordinate fear of communism.' By contrast, neocons held to the conviction that communism was a monstrous evil and a potent danger. For our obstinacy, we were drummed out of the liberal camp and dubbed 'neoconservatives'—a malicious gibe to which we eventually acquiesced." As John Patrick Diggins noted in 2003, "Particularly upsetting to the neoconservatives was Carter's commencement speech at Notre Dame University in May 1977." (Muravchik, "Can the Neocons Get Their Groove Back?" *The Washington Post*, November 19, 2006; Arthur M. Melzer, Jerry Weinberger, and M. Richard Zinman, eds., *The Public Intellectual: Between Philosophy and Politics* [Lanham, MD: Rowman & Littlefield, 2003], 105.)

ceived withering criticism from candidate Carter, warned that the president was underestimating Communist forces in Western Europe.

The speechwriters sometimes used less conventional ways to get their thoughts to Carter.

He had been invited to address the Urban League's national convention on July 25, and had declined. When Nesmith joined his staff, Carter had told her to let him know if he was doing something wrong. She wrote him a six-page memorandum arguing in favor of League appearance. "All the recent policy statements have dealt with bombs and bombers, policy, reorganization, budget-balancing, energy—all things that either seem far away from the lives of the poor and minorities and the problems of cities or which, if they reach them at all, seem to vaguely threaten jobs and other opportunities," Nesmith wrote.

When, even with Fallows's support, staff secretary Rick Hutcheson dismissed Nesmith's concerns as a "scheduling complaint," she took matters into her own hands. "You can arrange to be in the basement corridor when he was going to be passing through, there were ways a lot of times that you could have a minute or two with him," she recalled. She passed Carter a note saying that he should address the Urban League and that her message to him had not been allowed to get through. He made the speech.

But often the speechwriters were frustrated by the remoteness of their boss. "He had not gotten used to using speechwriters, didn't much like the idea of using them, ever," Nesmith recalled. "He saw it as a kind of necessary evil." Hertzberg added: "He did not particularly value or see the importance of [speechwriters]. . . . He essentially had become the president without a speechwriter. So how important could a speechwriter be—and the speeches that had made him president were this heartfelt, off-the-cuff stuff."

Especially in the first year, Carter often eschewed prepared remarks, believing that he could speak off the cuff just as successfully. "The President believes it is much more effective to appear unprepared than to seem to be well-prepared," an anonymous longtime aide told *The New York Times*. In October, Carter took a six-state swing to promote his energy program, which was stalled in Congress. But his ad-libbed remarks were so diffuse that the message failed to punch through. "Carter Campaigns in Iowa," the *Des Moines Register* reported. "Carter, on Six-State Trip, Defends Policies, But Avoids the Jobs Bill," read *The New York Times* headline.

Fallows took the issue directly to the president. "As you know, I share your belief that you should speak extemporaneously whenever you can," Fallows wrote to Carter. "But the results of last weekend's trip suggest to me that sometimes we must choose a different approach. Specifically, I think that when we are trying to sell a substantive program—the energy plan, the Canal,* tax reform, SALT [ongoing negotiations for a second Strategic Arms Limitation Treaty]—we have to prepare texts, release them in advance to the press, and have you use them."

Without proper emphasis and guidance, Fallows argued, the media was unlikely to pick up the specific story line that the administration wanted. "One phrase from your Notre Dame speech—about outgrowing our 'inordinate fear of communism'—has turned up all over the place in columns and editorials about your foreign policy," he wrote. "If you had given the speech extemporaneously, you and your audience might have felt more elated about your delivery, but it is far less likely that journalists would have dug up the recorded transcripts of the speech to find phrases to quote."

He added: "I am not talking about anything illicit, underhanded, corrupting, or unfair. This is not a matter of trying to trick the press into doing our work for us. The only weapon we need in these matters is our ideas, and I think we must do a better job of giving our ideas a chance to speak for themselves."

Doolittle sent in a memo along the same lines, arguing that though Carter might be more comfortable extemporizing, it did not work on all occasions. "While Arthur Ashe would no doubt feel more comfortable on the golf course with a racket in his hand, he would do better with a nine-iron," he pointed out.

---

*Carter had signed a pair of treaties to give control of the Panama Canal to the Panamanian government.

The ineffective energy trip revealed another communications problem: Carter had given a pair of major speeches in April unveiling his energy plan, one broadcast nationwide in which he declared, in a passage he wrote himself, that the country's effort to combat the looming energy crisis must be the "moral equivalent of war,"* and then an address to a joint session of Congress two days later. And then his administration had moved on to other things. "There's a real aversion to planning for effect," one of the speechwriters anonymously told a reporter. "There's no news management. No follow through. Look at energy—there's an example. We put out an energy program and then there's no follow through for months."

In mid-October, the presidential focus moved back onto energy and a speech was set for November 8, as the House and Senate prepared to try to merge into a single bill the energy legislation that each had passed. Richard Goodwin, the Kennedy and Johnson speechwriter, was brought in for a week to work with Fallows. Not pleased with the results, Carter wrote his own version of the speech in a single day.

It was a disaster. "In the unwritten book of presidential records, many entries are clustered under the heading 'Worst Speech Ever Given,'" *Time*'s Hugh Sidey wrote. "So it is inevitable that Jimmy Carter will make a run at the record. He probably did not break it in his televised energy talk last week, but it was a commendable warmup. . . . He said nothing new. He smiled as he described an energyless catastrophe. He issued this clarion call: 'All of us in government need your help.' And he explained further. 'These are serious problems, and this has been a serious talk.'"

Syndicated columnist Nicholas von Hoffman was even tougher. "The talk around town is that President Carter is going to be a one term president, but the question is when is he going to start serving it," von Hoffman wrote. "His energy speech of the other evening was so poor it had to have been made by someone who hopes to be president some

---

*Carter did not originate the phrase "moral equivalent of war," which dates to the philosopher William James in 1910. It was Carter's use, however, that prompted *New York Times* columnist Russell Baker to observe, devastatingly, that the phrase's acronym is "MEOW." (Stefan Kanfer, "Moral Equivalents and Other Bugle Calls," *Time*, May 2, 1977; William Safire, *Safire's New Political Dictionary*, 461.)

day, not by one who is. . . . Either the people who hand Carter these texts should send away to the Great Writers' School, or, heaven forefend, the president is writing his own stuff."

The speech marked a turning point, as Carter began to accept that he could not do everything himself. "There is a silver lining in this abysmal speech," Fallows wrote to his staff. Carter had sent a caustic note to Fallows and press secretary Jody Powell, saying that since his workload on the speech had been "tripled" by having to write it himself, he wanted ideas on how to revamp the system. "I figure this is our opportunity to suggest such novel ideas as him letting us know what he wants before we write the speech," Fallows added.

Fallows spent the rest of the month devising and getting Carter to okay a new, formal system of approval, which would involve getting the necessary sign-offs from senior staff, bringing Carter into the process earlier to shape the speech, and getting him a finished product in plenty of time to put his own finishing touches on it. It would be the first of several such procedural reorganizations. "From time to time the president would be dissatisfied with something done at the last minute and he'd get Jim and Jim would come back with yet another plan of how we were going to do it and the next time a major speech came up we would follow the plan and it would get shot down in flames," Doolittle recalled. "It never worked in any explainable fashion, it just sort of grew."

"Morale in this department isn't exactly low, it's just sort of sluggish," Hertzberg wrote in his journal on December 2.

That same day, Fallows sent a three-page, five-point memorandum to his immediate boss, Jody Powell, summarizing the problems plaguing the president and his speeches. Carter was stuck in campaign mode, he said. Before the election and during the initial months of the term, the challenge had been to sell the president as a person; but now "the President will be judged as a leader, not a candidate, and the function of his public appearances is to educate the people and explain his policies." The White House staff arranged campaign-style events that had no larger purpose—or when they did have a specific policy to unveil or message to push, it would get drowned out by the other Carter events.

"We can always round up a crowd to listen to the President at short no-tice, but we can't afford to have him appear too often with little to say," Fallows urged.

Finally, he implored: "No speechwriter can do a decent job if he or she doesn't know what his employer thinks. The earlier the President can let us know his wishes, and the more we're allowed at least to ob-serve the first stages of policy making, the better job we can do explain-ing the policy that's finally decided."

It was good advice, and reads like basic communications planning, but it went largely unheeded.

Part of the problem the speechwriters faced was illustrated when *Newsday* reporter Martin Schram wrote in December about visiting the speechwriters' office. He noticed that the writers kept referring to the senior administration staff as "they." "That is part of the difficulty," he wrote. "The Carter speechwriters are outsiders within. They were never part of the inner circle of the Carter campaign and they are not advisers who are consulted with respect by the President or his handful of policy and image makers." Schram mentioned to the speechwriters that he had just met with Hamilton Jordan, Carter's top aide,* with whom he discussed the Panama Canal—a subject for which the speech-writers had prepared several drafts without any indication as to when a speech would be given. "You actually spoke to him?" one writer asked. A second writer: "Then you know more than we do." And a third: "What's going to happen?"

Carter was scheduled to take a trip around the world to close out 1977, stopping in Poland, spending New Year's Eve in Tehran, and on to India before heading back west through Saudi Arabia, France, and Belgium. Hertzberg, who had developed a specialty in foreign affairs, was assigned to write Carter's address to the Indian Parliament. He drafted it in consultation with a National Security Council staffer, but accidentally discovered that Brzezinski deputy David Aaron had heavily

---

*Of Jordan, one administration staffer told *Time*: "He is everywhere because of his access to the President. He is nowhere because he has no line of responsibility and can put himself in or take himself out as he—and the President—want." ("The President's Boys," *Time*, June 6, 1977.)

rewritten the speech—not simply policy-related changes, but also stylistic ones. When the irate Hertzberg went to Brzezinksi's office to complain personally about the situation, he found the national security adviser and his team sipping champagne and some Russian vodka that had been a gift from Soviet foreign minister Andrei Gromyko.

Hertzberg knocked back a shot of the vodka in the spirit of collegiality, but talk quickly turned to the speech and Hertzberg vented: The speechwriters were supposed to be the experts on stylistic matters and should be consulted when changes were made to their work. Brzezinksi affected the attitude that such disagreements were easily ironed out. Hertzberg left feeling somewhat mollified. "The idea of me sitting around arguing with people like Brzezinski about what the President should say is so absurd, and yet it happens," Hertzberg marveled in his diary. "What a quirk. Playing with the big boys." Nevertheless, he remained skeptical of Brzezinski, whom he said could be "bland, disingenuous and a double-dealer."

The next day, December 22, Brzezinski urged Carter to abolish the speechwriting staff and instead create a foreign policy speechwriting spot in the National Security Council and move the other speechwriters into the domestic affairs office. The idea went nowhere. Ostensibly, the incident ended well all around: Hertzberg eventually conceded that the modifications by the NSC staff worked, while Brzezinski sent him a cable the day after the speech reading, "Your speech the highpoint of the trip so far. Congratulations."

But the run-in was one in a series of skirmishes between the speechwriters and Brzezinski. "We were kind of allied with Vance because Zbig wanted to control when Vance would see it and how long he'd have to look at it and he wanted it to be as messy and irritating as possible," Hertzberg said. The speechwriters eventually developed a backchannel to Vance to make sure that his views were incorporated into speeches.

Two days after Hertzberg's run-in with Brzezinski, on December 23, Fallows and he were in a meeting with Stuart Eizenstat, who was another member of the "Georgia mafia" and Carter's domestic policy adviser, plotting out the 1978 State of the Union address. The Carter program needed a catch phrase, Hertzberg argued, a slogan akin to "New Deal" or "New Frontier." The administration, he said, was almost as innovative as Roosevelt's and might be more so than JFK's. A successful slogan would not only serve public relations purposes but could also act as a guide for bureaucrats and others within the administration and galvanize them.* Carter would strongly resist something like this, Eizenstat warned—an assertion with which Hertzberg could not disagree, but he thought it worth trying.

Hertzberg hit upon a phrase within two weeks. A friend told him that the civil rights activist John Lewis talked about building a "beloved community," and Hertzberg was immediately taken with the phrase: It nicely summed up everything Carter was trying to achieve. "I worry that the picture people are getting of the Administration is getting to be a very cold one," Hertzberg noted in his diary. "Carter was elected on warmth and love, and now he's looking cold."

Hertzberg sent a nine-page, single-spaced memorandum to Fallows on January 5, 1978, pitching both the general need for a slogan and specifically Jimmy Carter's "Beloved Community" ("I'm beginning to think of it in capital letters," he noted two days later). "Every reforming President of this century has adopted a brief, evocative phrase summarizing his program and approach," Hertzberg wrote. "Three of these phrases were adopted after the Administration identified with it had been in office for some time. . . . There must be a vocabulary of common feeling between leader and led—a vocabulary based to some degree on what people are thinking. But it must go far beyond merely telling people what they want to hear. It must embody the people's inchoate yearnings and combine them with the President's own vision of where he wants to take the country."

The phrase was worked into the opening and peroration of drafts of

---

*Observing from afar, Arthur Schlesinger, Jr.—no Carter fan—also noted the absence. "It is, I think, more than a public relations point," he wrote in his journal. "It reflects the evident facts that (a) he is not an innovator and (b) he has no vision to project, no underlying pattern or unifying purpose behind his random proposals. I do not suggest, of course, that if Pat Caddell or Jerry Rafshoon could come up with a label, this would solve Carter's problem." (Schlesinger journal, November 12, 1977.)

the State of the Union. On January 10, Carter sent a handwritten note to Fallows admonishing him that the latest draft of the speech "needs a lot of work. . . . Your draft has a real need for a) memorable lines b) applause lines." Fallows had put in thematic material at the start of the speech, where Carter would compare himself with Andrew Jackson, Theodore Roosevelt, Woodrow Wilson, and Harry Truman as presidents who made great reforms without acute crises menacing the country. The president kept taking most of this thematic material out.

"Whenever he edited a speech, he did so to cut out the explanatory portions and add 'meat' in the form of a list of topics," Fallows recounted. Like Eisenhower before him, Carter avoided flashy rhetoric. "If you sent a speech to Carter and it had some sort of grandiloquent, lofty piece to it and if it wasn't substantive, he would cross that out, then there would be a quote or some poetry and he would cross that out," said Bernie Aronson, who would succeed Fallows as top speechwriter. "And [after] you'd crossed all that out, you'd have an engineer's treatise."

Nesmith suspected that Carter's aversion to such oratorical style was rooted in his southern background. "He distrusted rhetoric in a way because southern politicians had used rhetoric so much to bring out the worst in people," she said.

Over the next nine days, "Beloved Community" was in and out of the speech, as was Eizenstat's favorite—and the inaugural theme— "New Spirit" ("yes, he capitalized," Hertzberg noted in his diary). At one point Eizenstat quipped that he would accept "New Spirit of the Beloved Community." When Carter delivered the speech on January 19, "new spirit" was mentioned twice, and "beloved community" once. Neither won much notice.

Carter was scheduled to give a nationwide address at the start of February 1978, pushing for ratification of the Panama Canal treaties that had capped fourteen years of international negotiations. Rioting in Panama in 1959 and 1964 had cost three American soldiers and twenty-one Panamanians their lives, and after the latter incident President Johnson had started work on a new treaty governing the canal. By the time

Carter entered the White House, the negotiation was a hot political topic—coming so soon after Vietnam, the fate of the canal was in some quarters a point of national pride and strength. Ronald Reagan had battered Gerald Ford in the 1976 GOP primary by painting the potential treaty as a threat to national security interests. "We bought it. We paid for it. We built it. And we are going to keep it," Reagan repeatedly said on the campaign trail.

The August 1977 agreement with the Panamanian government only sharpened the criticisms. Two treaties had been signed: one covered U.S. administration of the canal for the balance of the twentieth century, and the other transferred control over the canal to Panama in 2000 while stipulating U.S. rights of access. Ford and all living former secretaries of state endorsed the treaty, and it enjoyed majority backing in public opinion polls. But the Republican National Committee voted in 1977 to oppose it, and conservatives saw it variably as a sign of U.S. weakness, a threat to national security, or a massive giveaway.

The speechwriters had produced drafts for a fireside chat on the treaties as early as August 1977, but Carter had not given a speech on the subject. With the Senate set to begin debating the treaties in February 1978, he decided to speak on February 1 to frame the issue and push for ratification. In late January, Doolittle and Fallows produced several drafts of a speech that set up and then knocked down the objections to the treaty, dismissing them as the product of misinformation. Carter's guidance to Fallows had been to keep the speech simple and to make it tough. "He asked me to make it 'mean,'" Fallows told Rosalynn Carter.

Carter hated the speech. "Having made 20 or so speeches/statements on Panama, I was aggravated this weekend to have your draft of completely different emphasis & language," he wrote Fallows sternly on January 30. He attached a nineteen-page handwritten draft and told Fallows to use it. He also attached his previous statements and a handful of other materials to compose a new version.

The Carterized version—assembled as instructed from his notes and especially from his previous ad-libbed remarks on the subject—was choppier and less forceful. Where the early Doolittle/Fallows drafts addressed critics head-on, the new version was like a one-man Q&A, with the president asking and answering "common questions" about the treaties. It was a small change, but one that drew some of the conflict and tension from the speech.

Nevertheless, the Senate ratified the two treaties in March and April, marking a pair of high-point victories for the Carter presidency.

When the president was invited to address the Los Angeles County Bar Association in early May 1978, Fallows pitched the event as an opportunity to reprise the themes of a speech Carter had given four years earlier as governor of Georgia. Given off the cuff and on short notice—Nesmith, the Georgian speechwriter, thought it was the reason Carter had so much confidence in his ability to speak extemporaneously—the 1974 address was considered a landmark Carter speech.* He had spoken about the need to find solutions for racial and income-related inequities in the justice system: "In every age or every year, we have a tendency to believe that we've come so far now, that there's no way to improve the present system. I'm sure when the Wright Brothers flew at Kitty Hawk, they felt that was the ultimate in transportation. Well, we haven't reached the ultimate. But who's going to search the heart and soul of an organization like yours or a law school or state or nation and say, 'What can we still do to restore equality and justice or to preserve it or to enhance it in this society?'" Carter liked the idea of making a similar speech now and signed off on an outline. The most important thing about the speech, he told his speechwriter, is that no lawyers work on it ("That made me almost uniquely qualified among the whole staff here," Fallows observed).

Fallows sent successive drafts to Carter. Finally, the day before the speech was to be given, the president told him that it was too shrill and did not reflect the judgment that had been put into it. "He hated it," Fallows recalled. Nevertheless, Carter gave the speech almost exactly as Fallows had written it. "A child of privilege frequently receives the benefit of the doubt; a child of poverty seldom does," he told the Los Ange-

---

*Hunter S. Thompson witnessed the speech and was so impressed that he got a tape recording of it that he would listen to at all hours of night. ("Jimmy Carter's Big Breakthrough," *Time*, May 10, 1976.)

les County Bar audience. "We have the heaviest concentration of lawyers on Earth—one for every five hundred Americans. . . . We have more litigation, but I am not sure that we have more justice. No resources of talent and training in our own society, even including the medical care, is more wastefully or unfairly distributed than legal skills. Ninety percent of our lawyers serve ten percent of our people. We are over-lawyered and under-represented."

The president decided that he wanted the speechwriting process revamped: For major addresses in the future, the speechwriters should canvass authorities on the topic in advance and send their ideas to him. He would select the ones to go into the speech. Hertzberg viewed the change as a potential bureaucratic victory for the beleaguered speechwriters. "One of our biggest problems has been a simple lack of clout," he wrote in his journal. "Carter simply doesn't take us as seriously as he takes Stu [Eizenstat] or Hamilton or Jody or the rest. We aren't in a position to ride roughshod over them or even to get their attention until the last minute. We can send in ideas, but they are, after all, our ideas, and can therefore be ignored. But if the ideas we send in have the names of Famous Authorities on them, they will be treated seriously."

Another major change came in the middle of May when Carter asked Jerry Rafshoon, the consultant who had produced his television commercials during the campaign and had remained an informal adviser, to join the White House staff. Rafshoon later recounted that Carter had told him that 90 percent of his advice was good, and that since the other 10 percent did not work because he did not know what was going on in the White House, he should officially join the administration. As part of his new role—which he described to *The New York Times* as "developing the themes of the presidency and getting them out"—Rafshoon would be in charge of speechwriting.

The new consult-the-experts scheme got its trial run in Carter's June 7 commencement speech at the U.S. Naval Academy in Annapolis, from which Carter had graduated in 1946. The speechwriters solicited ideas from a list that included former diplomats (Averell Harriman, George Kennan, Dean Rusk), retired military (CIA director

Stansfield Turner—a Naval Academy classmate of Carter's—and retired Admiral Elmo Zumwalt), and a novelist (Alex Haley of *Roots*), among others.

On Thursday, June 1, Carter summoned Doolittle (Fallows was out of town) to the Oval Office and took him into the small adjoining study. He thanked Doolittle for the excellent material that the speechwriters had collected, said that it was exactly what he was looking for—but that he was changing the speech. There was a misperception, he told Doolittle, that his foreign policy was in disarray or that there was disharmony between Brzezinski and Vance, when in fact there was none. The speech was going to make clear that everyone in the administration was in perfect agreement. (In his memoirs, Carter noted that the purpose of the speech was to "spell out more clearly the overall relationship between" the United States and the Soviet Union.)

In fact, the Vance-Brzezinski feud was well known both inside and outside the administration. Reporters would often label Carter pronouncements or policies as having the mark of Brzezinski or Vance. More broad, after giving the conciliatory Notre Dame speech in May 1977, Carter had given a strongly anti-Soviet address at Wake Forest in March 1978. The thrust of his foreign policy was unclear and, to some, confusing.

Carter gave Doolittle a ten-page, single-spaced typewritten letter from Vance to the president—marked "Top Secret/Nodis [No Distribution]"—recommending a thoughtful speech about U.S.-Soviet relations, aimed at ending the swings between gloom and euphoria. Without naming him, it took several slaps at Brzezinski. Carter told Doolittle that he could borrow the letter and show it to Hertzberg, who would work with Carter on the address, but that while they could take notes, they could not make copies. (He had written: "No copies—return to me," on it.) Carter said that he would use the Vance letter and opinions that he had solicited from Brzezinski and Turner, and would write a draft over the weekend (the first weekend of June) at Camp David. When Brzezinski's contribution came in, Doolittle thought it was typical Cold Warrior boilerplate—the opposite of the Vance approach.

Carter spent the weekend composing in longhand. He again numbered and wrote out the points he wanted to make, determined the proper order in which to arrange them, and then wrote out the speech, which, with some additional rearranging, was substantially the talk he ended up delivering.

On Wednesday, June 7, Carter strolled the grounds of his alma mater, showed his wife the room in which he had lived as a plebe. He then delivered a speech to the class of new naval officers that he thought would clarify his foreign policy.

The first part was straight from the Vance letter:

We must avoid excessive swings in the public mood in our country—from euphoria when things are going well, to despair when they are not; from an exaggerated sense of compatibility with the Soviet Union, to open expressions of hostility. Detente between our two countries is central to world peace. It's important for the world, for the American public, and for you as future leaders of the Navy to understand the complex and sensitive nature.

The president talked about his desire for a peaceful world, and about the need to show the Soviets that cooperation was preferable to conflict. "I'm convinced that the people of the Soviet Union want peace," he said. "I cannot believe that they could possibly want war." He talked about how the prospects for a SALT II treaty were good. "Beyond this major effort, improved trade and technological and cultural exchange are among the immediate benefits of cooperation between our two countries," he said. "However, these efforts to cooperate do not erase the significant differences between us. What are these differences?"

Fallows was watching with the reporters, who had been given advance copies. At this point, one of the newspapermen who had read ahead said, "And now—war!"

With the next line, the mood swung:

To the Soviet Union, detente seems to mean a continuing aggressive struggle for political advantage and increased influence in a variety of ways. The Soviet Union apparently sees military power and military assistance as the best means of expanding their influence abroad. Obviously, areas of insta-

bility in the world provide a tempting target for this effort, and all too often they seem ready to exploit any such opportunity.

Carter had essentially taken the Vance letter and the Brzezinski memo and poured them side by side into the same speech. "It had an obvious break in the middle, like the splice in a film," Fallows recalled.

No one missed the seam. "Mr. Carter's speech had aspects that often seemed contradictory," reported *The New York Times*, which quoted a pair of unnamed State Department officials, one of whom was "pleasantly surprised" that the speech was not a "Brzezinski-like blast," the other who was stunned by its "jingoism." The headline of *The Washington Post*'s news analysis read: "Two Different Speeches." Another *Post* story cited unnamed White House, State Department, and Pentagon officials as saying that since Carter had written the speech himself, it "should not be subjected to rigorous diplomatic analysis" because it "contained ambiguities, 'oversimplifications' or 'mistakes' in precise phrasing that might be misinterpreted by the Soviets."

"It is precisely because our problems have been so constant, not to say repetitive, that we feel some outside force—such as you—is necessary to put things in order," Fallows wrote to Rafshoon in a five-page memo on June 8, the day after the Annapolis speech. To demonstrate the point, he attached other memos he had written along the same lines over the nearly year and a half the administration had been in office.

Fallows listed a half-dozen problems with speechwriting, starting with lack of guidance from the president. "In all but the most unusual cases, we end up working in the dark, without any clear instructions about what <u>he</u> wants his speech to say," he noted, adding that even when Carter gave guidance, he tended to be unsatisfied with the drafts that came back. "Fundamentally, the problem is that the President has not taken—and perhaps never will—the step of looking on us as his extensions, his tools, for saying what he wants to say."

That problem was compounded by the fact that the speechwriters' lack of a relationship with Carter was well known throughout the administration. "The policy staff have a bias toward encyclopedic thoroughness (to avoid leaving anything out), toward hedged and cautious statements (to avoid offending anyone)," Fallows explained. "They also have a bias toward mushy-mouthed language, since that is the way they think and write." And unless the speechwriters were empowered, these tendencies would continue to muddle the speeches.

This was more than a catalogue of complaints; it was also a handoff. Fallows sent Carter a letter on June 21 explaining that he wanted to return to journalism and would resign after the fall elections. He would take a job at *The Atlantic Monthly*. He had joined the administration hoping that his role would allow him to influence the formation of policy—"I had always been interested in one way or another working my will upon the world," he told an interviewer—but never had the opportunity. He had spent his first few months firing off memoranda on various subjects, from tax policy to smoking to the volunteer army—not to mention things specifically in his purview like speech staff operations—but got virtually no response and eventually gave up. "The mistake was in failing to see that this was a bureaucratic organization, in the sense Max Weber defined: interchangeable people performing strictly limited tasks," he later noted. "Everyone was safe within the confines of his organization box; few were welcomed outside."

"It is precisely because I want to have more influence over public events that I am leaving; to stay here any longer would be to choose the appearance of influence over the reality," Fallows wrote to *Washington Post* columnist Colman McCarthy. "I have seen that those who write from the outside . . . can have a far greater impact than those who, on the inside, are supposed to confine themselves to their organizational niche."

He did not, Fallows told friends and colleagues, intend to write about his administration experiences.

Fallows made his first trip to Camp David on Saturday, September 16, 1978. Carter had been sequestered there for eleven days with Egyptian president Anwar Sadat and Israeli prime minister Menachem Begin, trying to forge a peace accord. In November 1977, Sadat had visited Jerusalem and addressed the Knesset, marking the first break in implacable Arab hostility to the Jewish state. But little progress toward a formal agreement had been made since.

Hoping the quiet of the Maryland woods—not to mention his own ministrations—could spur a breakthrough, Carter had invited the two leaders to his presidential retreat. He was risking his political prestige on an historically intractable problem. Little news had been forthcoming from the summit, and when Fallows arrived he found the mood grim and the outlook bleak. He spent most of the day preparing closing statements for a failed meeting.

Then, as Fallows later put it to Hertzberg, "Carter broke Begin." An agreement was reached.

It was the high point of the Carter presidency—and an opportunity to turn around his faltering political standing. "If Jimmy Carter looks out over the White House fence these next few days through those weary eyes of his, he may find out that America just loves it when a President succeeds, no matter what party he is from or how his brother behaves in public," *Time*'s Hugh Sidey wrote. "A successful summit in the Maryland mountains is not a cure for Carter's leadership problem. But surely it is a kind of achievement at the critical time needed to bring people a little closer to their President, to silence for the moment a lot of petty grievances that grew bigger than they should have because of Carter's fumbling."

Carter addressed the Congress on Monday, September 18. "Finally, let me say that for many years the Middle East has been a textbook for pessimism, a demonstration that diplomatic ingenuity was no match for intractable human conflicts," he said. "Today we are privileged to see the chance for one of the sometimes rare, bright moments in human history—a chance that may offer the way to peace. We have a chance for peace, because these two brave leaders found within themselves the willingness to work together to seek these lasting prospects for peace, which we all want so badly. And for that, I hope that you will share my prayer of thanks and my hope that the promise of this moment shall be fully realized."

Vice President Walter Mondale, in charge of producing the speech, had convened a speech meeting with Fallows and the principal foreign policy advisers. "Jim wrote a very good speech for Carter to give at a joint session of Congress Monday night," Hertzberg noted in his diary. "It was good for a reason. Instead of being written in the usual way, it was written in a sensible way."

The first planning meeting for the 1979 State of the Union address took place in Fallows's office (he was still ten days from his departure) on November 14. He had just come from playing tennis and was still in his whites. Hertzberg, speechwriter Robert Rackleff, Labor Department officials Walter Shapiro and Paul Jensen (Jensen also in tennis whites having just played with Fallows), and Fallows brainstormed about the big upcoming speech.

Carter had been interviewed on PBS the night before by Bill Moyers, the Lyndon Johnson aide turned reporter. Moyers had pointed out that Carter's administration lacked a theme or vision and asked if the president hoped to mold one during the balance of his term. "Well, I think it was also Kierkegaard who said that every man is an exception," Carter said. "And the multiplicity of responsibilities that a president has, the same issues that our nation has to face, I think, causes some lack of a central focus quite often."

The writers assembled in Fallows's office were persuaded that the State of the Union would be the logical place for Carter to unveil a theme. It would need two words, they decided, the first word almost certainly being "New," à la "New Deal" or "New Frontier." (They toyed briefly with "Improved" but quickly returned to "New.") "New Groundwork?" "New Building Blocks?" Hertzberg—who had pressed hard for a slogan in the 1978 State of the Union address—played around a bit with a Jensen idea and suggested "New Foundation." The group liked it, though Shapiro, who would do a stint as a Carter speechwriter for several months in 1979, wondered, "Can't we do better?"

Fallows was leaving, however, and as Rafshoon did not like the idea of a theme—he thought it would be artificial—no one mentioned it to him and it disappeared.

Fallows's departure also portended a larger shake-up for the speechwriters. Bernie Aronson, a former official with the United Mine Workers union who had spent the first half of the term as Mondale's speechwriter, was named as Fallows's replacement in November, though in a circumscribed capacity: Rafshoon and his deputy, Greg Schneiders, would keep a tighter rein over the writing staff, with Schneiders handling speech assignments.

Fallows was not the only one on the way out. Doolittle was shown the door, as was another writer, Caryl Conner. Doolittle, who would go on to become a mystery writer, had an irreverent sense of humor and it rankled some of the senior Georgians. He had, the *Boston Globe* reported, "a reputation for making wisecracks about Carter himself. This is considered improper conduct by members of Carter's inner circle." Rafshoon denied that it was a purge, but he and Schneiders were indeed remaking the staff. As early as the previous summer, Rafshoon had told the press, "We need to get some people out of the speechwriting business and some people in."

Schneiders in particular had little patience for the speechwriters. "I've had it with these people," he wrote to Rafshoon in November in a note marked "Confidential." "They may be the 'fine arts' division of our operation here, but I think their sensitivities have already been indulged too long."

On December 12, Pat Caddell, Carter's pollster, sent him a memo about the upcoming State of the Union address. The electorate was becoming "volatile . . . hostile, suspicious, and in many cases, bitter," he warned. "We must candidly address the damage of past events [such as Watergate and other upheavals from the previous decade and a half]. The country, just like an individual, needs that catharsis. In addition, we need to address the present condition of psychological drift, estrangement from the political process and disbelief in personal efficiency."

Carter read the first draft of the State of the Union at Camp David during Christmas week, and did not like it. He summoned Mondale, Eizenstat, Jordan, Rafshoon, Schneiders, and Aronson to an Oval Office meeting on January 2, 1979, to discuss the speech. They met for thirty-seven minutes, from 2:53 pm to 3:30 pm. Talk kept returning to the complex, intractable nature of the problems the country faced—inflation, energy, government inefficiency—and how, because the solutions were all long term, there were no political dividends in addressing them. Afterward, Rafshoon, Aronson, Schneiders, and Hertzberg huddled in Rafshoon's office, where they resurrected "New Foundation."

"The New Foundation does actually sum up Carter's methodical approach, his tropism for 'comprehensiveness,' his fussing over procedural and process reforms like civil service reform and reorganization," Hertzberg wrote in his diary. "The New Foundation also suggests that nobody should expect a building, because we're just putting in cinder blocks for some hypothetical future. Cynical but true. Also, on an emotional level, it addresses itself to the fact that people have a sense that the basis of things is crumbling—the family, the community, etc. Everybody's watching TV, and there's nothing good on."

He added: "Nobody liked the New Foundation idea when I first talked it up, but now it's filling a vacuum."

The theme stayed in the speech. When Carter addressed Congress and the nation on the evening of January 23, he mentioned "foundation" thirteen times. "The problems that we face today are different from those that confronted earlier generations of Americans," Carter said. "They are more subtle, more complex, and more interrelated. . . . The challenge to us is to build a new and firmer foundation for the future—for a sound economy, for a more effective government, for more political trust, and for a stable peace—so that the America our children inherit will be even stronger and even better than it is today."

Hertzberg had lunched the day before the speech with William Safire, the Nixon speechwriter, now a *New York Times* columnist, and explained the "New Foundation" concept to him, even drawing him a diagram. "The idea of a 'new foundation' is fitting for this President, since the metaphor helps get across the idea of a return to fundamentals, and also helps explain why so few achievements are apparent after two years," Safire wrote in his column two days after the speech. "The building metaphor helped pull the speech together."*

---

*Not everyone was impressed. Senator Daniel Patrick Moynihan wrote to *The Washington Post* to point out that "new foundation" appeared in the first stanza of the Communist *Internationale*—the Soviet Union's national anthem until 1943. ("An Old Refrain," letter to the editor, *Washington Post*, January 28, 1979.)

Rafshoon geared up the administration for a big "new foundation" publicity push; the slogan was gaining cultural traction: the political comic strip *Doonesbury* even devoted a week to ridiculing it. Then Carter brought it to an abrupt halt. At a press conference on the afternoon of January 26, a reporter noted that for two years Carter had avoided an administration slogan. Did he think this one would stick? "I doubt if it will survive," Carter said. "We are not trying to establish this as a permanent slogan. It was the theme that we established because of extreme logic . . . for one State of the Union speech."

Carter's discomfort with slogans foisted upon him reflects his larger issues with speechwriting. Once, in an attempt to illustrate the sheer volume of federal regulations that Carter had eliminated, Rafshoon arranged for Carter to have a huge stack of paper sitting on the table during a June 30, 1978, Cabinet Room session with editors and news directors. He was supposed to dump all of the paper into the trash can—providing the evening news with a nice visual. Instead, he carefully explained that the stack of paper, which he described as a "prop," "happens to be blank" but represented regulations. The evening news led with something else that night. "He regarded the whole process of a cooked-up impression prepared ahead of time with suspicion," Hertzberg said. "If there was anything that sort of smacked of that kind of calculation he was suspicious of it." And that suspicion extended to the speechwriters themselves. "My personal guess is that he always felt that what I did was wrong in some way ideally and he was probably wrong for having somebody like me there doing it, that this was somehow a deception being practiced on the American people," said Gordon Stewart, who joined the speechwriting staff later that spring.

The drafting of the 1979 State of the Union was also a turning point for Bernie Aronson. Rafshoon and Schneiders could not make up their mind what they wanted from the top speechwriter. In the midst of writing the State of the Union, they told Hertzberg, who had also vied for the spot, to prepare a separate draft. That set up the tragicomic scene of two speechwriters, sitting in their offices across the hallway from one another, each drafting a State of the Union address. "It was a bad scene from a human point of view," Hertzberg recalled. "It was an unpleasant period." With little fanfare Rafshoon increasingly favored Hertzberg, who ended up assuming the duties and eventually the title of chief speechwriter. Aronson eventually became a deputy to London Butler, Jordan's assistant who handled labor relations.

In mid-April, Fallows published an article, "The Passionless Presidency," in *The Atlantic*—the first installment of a two-part indictment of Carter and his staff. He criticized the president for running a flat, bureaucratic administration without vision. "For certain aspects of his job—the analyst and manager parts—Carter's method serve [*sic*] him well," Fallows wrote. "He makes decisions about solar power installations and the B-1 [bomber] on the basis of output, payload, facts, not abstract considerations. But for the part of his job that involves leadership, Carter's style of thought cripples him. He thinks he 'leads' by choosing the correct policy; but he fails to project a vision larger than the problem he is tackling at the moment."

Fallows was not malicious: he was trying to jolt the administration out of bland lethargy before it was too late. But his choice of a public forum backfired. "It was very, very accurate," Hertzberg recalled. "It was a very, very, good piece. . . . We were glad that he wrote that piece, but not that he published it."

In early April, Hertzberg espied an early copy of the article in Powell's office on which Carter had written a note: "We all have to make a living."

"Do not begin so many sentences with 'I think,' 'And,' or 'But.'" In a nine-point, handwritten note dated May 3, Carter was giving his speechwriters basic drafting tips. "Do not overuse 'decade.'" Much of it was remedial grammar: avoid split infinitives, avoid ending sentences with prepositions. "It is <u>not</u> 'with Jerry and I.' Minimize the use of commas." It was emblematic of Carter: down in the weeds, focused on process. Gordon Stewart, who started that spring, stopped using commas entirely, just to see if Carter would notice. A couple of days later he got a terse note back saying it was okay to use them.

Rafshoon had larger issues on his mind, such as how to salvage the

Carter presidency. By mid-May 1979, the president's approval ratings had dipped into the low thirties. He trailed Senator Edward M. Kennedy in a potential Democratic primary match-up for the presidential nod. Inflation was at 13 percent annually—a four-year high. In January, Shah Mohammed Reza Pahlevi—with whom Carter spent the 1977–78 New Year's Eve—had fled from Iran into exile, allowing Ayatollah Ruholla Khomeini to return to the country from France and seize control, eventually establishing a theocracy. The revolution had caused a spike in gas prices and lines of cars were starting to stretch out from gas stations.

"In politics—or at least 1980 presidential politics—style is everything," Rafshoon wrote Carter in a memo that summer. The problem, Rafshoon argued, was not that Carter had failed to provide leadership, but rather that "you don't <u>look</u> like you're providing leadership. . . . <u>You're going to have to start looking, talking and acting like more of a leader if you're to be successful—even if it's artificial</u>. Look at it this way: changing your position on issues to get votes is wrong; changing your style (like the part in your hair)* in order to be effective is just smart and, in the long run, morally good. I know you think it's phony and that you're fine the way you are but that pride is, by far, your greatest political danger."

Specifically, Rafshoon argued, Carter needed to improve his speaking style. "Your ability (or lack of it) to move an audience and a nation by your words is no longer a minor matter of personal concern to you. It is the single greatest reason (under our control) why your Presidency has not been more successful than it has."

By the time Carter departed for a seven-nation economic summit in Japan on June 23, the domestic situation was melting down. Gas lines were growing longer and tempers shorter, independent truckers were on strike, and inflation remained stifling. It was Carter's second foreign trip in less than a week: He had returned on June 18 from a four-day summit

---

*Carter had shifted the part in his hair from right to left. ("'He Can Catch Fire,'" *Time*, May 7, 1979.)

in Vienna with Soviet president Leonid Brezhnev that had produced another SALT Treaty. His senior advisers had discussed a fireside chat between trips, but no one could come up with a compelling message.

Stuart Eizenstat, Carter's chief domestic adviser, was not sure that Carter and the others with him in Tokyo understood the gravity of the situation. When he and Vice President Mondale briefed members of Congress on the Japanese summit for two hours on June 27, all the legislators wanted to discuss were domestic issues. They spent the whole time talking about gasoline-related problems and how much they feared—"members are literally afraid," Eizenstat told Carter—going back to their districts to face their irate constituents.

"Back home everything is going down the drain," Hertzberg wrote in his diary in Japan on June 27. "We are out of touch with the country to a frightening degree. How else is it possible that we left on this trip without doing something, anything, any appearance of anything, about the gas lines?"

On June 28, Eizenstat sent Carter a memo on energy. "Since you left for Japan, the domestic energy problem has continued to worsen," he wrote. Gas lines were spreading from the East to the Midwest, causing tempers to flare and instances of violence to crop up; gas station operators were threatening to strike and the price of gas had risen 55 percent since the start of the year. "I do not need to detail for you the political damage we are suffering from all of this," Eizenstat added. "It is perhaps sufficient to say that nothing which has occurred in the administration to date . . . [has] added so much water to our ship. Nothing else has so frustrated, confused, angered the American people—or so targeted their distress at you personally."

That day, Carter canceled a planned three-day stay in Hawaii on the return trip. Instead, he would fly directly back to Washington to consult with aides on the gasoline crisis. On June 29, the speechwriters who remained in the White House sent Rafshoon and Hertzberg a four-page "eyes-only" memorandum on the situation. "The mood in the country is grim," they wrote. "People are mad—fighting mad. The situation has deteriorated alarmingly since the President left for Japan." The public does not understand what is happening or what the administration is doing about it, the speechwriters said. "We strongly advise against another televised energy speech—unless the President has a bold, new, and ambitious policy to announce. People want action on energy. They do not want Presidential preaching or the administration piously saying, 'We told you so, but you didn't listen to us.'"

Carter returned to Washington on Monday, July 2, and plunged into a series of meetings on the crisis, including a 2:30 pm gathering in the Roosevelt Room that was so crowded Hertzberg sat on the floor and had to be alert not to get hit in the head when the door opened. Rafshoon, Jordan, Powell, Eizenstat, cabinet secretary Jack Watson, and Hertzberg met with Carter in the Oval Office for an hour at 4:15 pm, sitting in a semicircle around the president's desk. They were exhausted. Carter mentioned that he had had trouble staying awake during some of the day's meetings. The group debated back and forth whether he should give a speech. Carter was not inclined to.

Though Eizenstat was opposed, he was so intent on being an honest broker that he made too strong a case in favor. Powell and Rafshoon chimed in that Carter should go on television just to show the people that he was doing something. Carter said he did not like the idea of conning the voters. But no one made a strong case against a speech, and Carter agreed to speak on Thursday, July 5. He would spend a day resting at Camp David, he said, and then wanted to see a draft. It would be his fifth speech to the nation on energy, and he was aware that each succeeding speech had drawn a smaller and smaller audience.

Hertzberg and Rafshoon then went to Eizenstat's office to discuss the speech. In a moment of bravado, Rafshoon picked up the telephone and asked for the television network press pool. "The president will address the nation at 9 pm on Thursday night," he said, adding after a pause, "He wants to talk about nationalizing the TV networks." Then after another pause: "Energy of course." Hanging up, he explained that the person on the other end of the phone had said, "I was wondering when you were going to call." They had the airtime—but there was no speech yet, and in their exhausted state Hertzberg doubted one of any quality could be produced. Gordon Stewart, who actually wrote the draft, agreed—"I was just feeling worse and worse about it," he later said. "I never felt worse about anything, and I knew it was not going to fly."

Two days later, at Camp David, the speech draft in hand, Carter shifted course. In a fifteen-minute conference call with Vice President Mondale, Rafshoon, deputy press secretary Rex Granum (filling in for Powell), and Jordan (with Hertzberg, having dismantled the mouthpiece on the extra phone in Rafshoon's office, listening in), Carter said that he was not going to give the speech. He said he did not want to "bullshit the American people."

Granum asked if he could tell reporters that Carter had not liked the draft he was given, and the president said no, that the speech was fine—it was just more of the same. "Don't give any explanation," he said. "Just say I cancelled the damn speech." Mondale, Carter recalled, "almost lost control of himself" about the decision. "I felt a remarkable sense of relief and renewed confidence after I canceled the speech, and began to shape the thoughts that I would put into next week's work," Carter wrote in his diary.

His confidence was not widely shared. "President Carter has reached the low point not only of his Administration but perhaps of the postwar Presidency," *The New York Times*'s Tom Wicker wrote. "Mr. Carter's celebrated cancellation of his energy speech may well have been the worst public relations blunder since Richard Nixon's 'Saturday Night Massacre.'"

The president remained at Camp David, with no word forthcoming on why he had cancelled the speech or what he planned to do. Over the next ten days, he brought more than one hundred people from all walks of life—members of Congress, religious leaders, labor leaders, governors, mayors, county supervisors, and ordinary Americans—to the mountain retreat. The country wondered what was going on in the Maryland mountains, with most of the news coming from reports by returning guests. Though the crisis was energy-related, Carter was discussing a broader, more diffuse set of problems. "He said he had a lot of time to think, during his recent travels," said Clark Clifford, the former Truman speechwriter and Johnson Defense Secretary, now a Washington wise man. "He had the feeling that the country was in a mood of widespread national malaise."

Hertzberg and Gordon Stewart were summoned to Camp David on Monday, July 9, to start preparing a speech. "We were off in some cabin in a sweatshop," Hertzberg recalled. "Every once in a while you would look out the window and see some *Time* magazine cover subject wandering around."

The administration was split as to what kind of speech the president should give. "For the last several days, I have been compiling speech suggestions from everyone connected with this problem—from the extreme optimism of the Vice President to Stu's [Eizenstat's] desire to have a very substantive speech to Pat's [Caddell's] apocalyptic first draft," Rafshoon wrote to the president on July 10. "People don't want to hear you talk about their problems and they certainly don't want to hear you whine about them. They don't want to hear you talk about hope and confidence. They don't want to hear you talk about leadership. They want to perceive you beginning to solve the problems, inspire confidence by your actions, and lead. You inspire confidence by being confident. Leadership begins with a sense of knowing where you're going."

All sides gathered in the main lodge at Camp David for what Eizenstat described as the most acrimonious debate of the entire administration. Caddell, who had produced a 107-page memorandum about the country's spiritual problem, favored a broader speech on that topic, an idea that Eizenstat, Rafshoon, and Mondale opposed. Rumors were spreading that Carter had had a mental breakdown, and they feared that if he went on television to talk about something ephemeral like a crisis of confidence it would play into that notion. Eizenstat argued that the president needed to give an energy speech that had a detailed plan for dealing with the gasoline problem. A spiritual crisis was a non sequitur, he said. People do not care about spirit, Mondale said. But Caddell was in tune with Carter, who had been ruminating about the broader question.

Hertzberg worried that it would be Annapolis all over again: two speeches visibly jammed into one text. All the while Carter watched the debate unfold, keeping his own counsel.

The meeting continued. Stewart kept baiting Eizenstat on the energy program—It's not compelling, Stu—until Eizenstat exploded, rattling off an impassioned summation of the energy program that became the basis of that section of the speech. After that, Hertzberg and Stewart pulled most of the speech together in less than an hour; Carter supplied the rest with a self-critical opening. The disparate ideas in the speech would be fused: Carter could argue that there was a spiritual crisis in the country, and that it was so broad and pervasive that it could not be addressed all at once. Then it would pivot on energy: if the country could solve the energy crisis, it would help restore the people's confidence and start rolling back the sense of despair. The solution "made it possible to pass this thing off as an actual, coherent speech, when it was actually a hodgepodge of different sensibilities," Stewart recalled.

Carter had a final meeting with his aides at Camp David. Concluding the meeting, he told the group to leave him alone in the room so that he could practice on the TelePrompTer in front of the camera. Stewart was working on the speech that Carter would give in Kansas City the day after the national address, so he was allowed to stay.

Before joining the speechwriting staff, Gordon Stewart had split his time between politics and the theatre. A native of Chicago's South Side, he graduated Phi Beta Kappa from Oberlin College, and had a master's degree in European history from the University of Chicago, a certificate in theatre and music from the University of Vienna, and a master's in fine arts from the Yale University Drama School. Hertzberg and he had met in New York in 1976 when Rick was writing for Hugh Carey and Stewart was working for Mayor John Lindsay. He had been directing *The Elephant Man* on Broadway when a collapsed lung forced him to withdraw from the production. Hertzberg recruited him to the White House, and the two lived in neighboring apartments in D.C.

Listening to Carter rehearse his speech, Stewart's directorial instincts took over. He muttered to himself, interrupting the president. Carter glared over at him. I'm sorry, Stewart said, I didn't hear that. Carter started over, speaking louder. Stewart chatted out loud to an imaginary person sitting next to him: I don't know what this guy is talking about, he said, something about a sickness. Carter was becoming noticeably angry.

Mr. President, Stewart said, what I'm trying to suggest is that you are just not *telling* me to hear you. I am going to get up and start walking out the door, the speechwriter-cum-director told his boss, and I would like to see if you can stop me.

Carter started reading again. Stewart sat and listened and then got up and wandered around the room, prompting Carter to raise his voice. Then, when Stewart headed toward the door, Carter put more authority into his delivery. Stewart turned—Now you've got it. He told the president: I don't have to listen to you just because you're the president; if I'm in a bar, I can and will change the channel. You have to care whether I listen to you.

It was a basic director's trick, the kind of thing employed in beginner's acting class, and it worked.

On the evening of July 15, Carter started his speech with a mea culpa, which he had written himself, a confession of presidential ineptitude that involved reading from the notes he had taken during his meetings at Camp David: "Mr. President, you are not leading this nation—you're just managing the government." Or: "Don't talk to us about politics or the mechanics of government, but about an understanding of our common good."

Then he turned to the underlying problems the nation faced:

> The threat is nearly invisible in ordinary ways. It is a crisis of confidence. It is a crisis that strikes at the very heart and soul and spirit of our national will. We can see this crisis in the growing doubt about the meaning of our own lives and in the loss of a unity of purpose for our nation. The erosion of our confidence in the future is threatening to destroy the social and the political fabric of America.

After stressing the country's historic but faltering confidence, he made the pivot:

> Energy will be the immediate test of our ability to unite this nation, and it can also be the standard around which we rally. On the battlefield of energy we can win for our nation a new confidence, and we can seize control again of our common destiny.

He delivered the speech with force and passion. "The rhythm of his speech—the emphases and the pauses—made you think that in his mind's eye Carter was not seeing the camera and TelePromptTer, but the faces of those early audiences [from the 1976 campaign]—waiting for the nod of the heads that told him they had understood and agreed with his last point," *The Washington Post*'s David Broder wrote. "As a result, in this most critical speech of his presidency, he delivered his text more effectively than he has ever done before. He avoided the sing-song rhythm, the misplaced stresses, and the falsetto squeaks that have marred past performances. His voice was strong throughout, and, on occasions, ringing."

The voters responded: The White House received a record volume of mail, most of it positive, and Carter's poll ratings shot up by 11 points overnight. Carter thought it his best speech ever.

Two days later, however, he asked for the resignations of every member of his cabinet, saying that he would decide which ones to accept. He let five cabinet members go, including the Treasury and Energy secretaries and Attorney General Griffin Bell. He hoped this would mark a new beginning for his presidency, with fresh ideas and new faces recharging the government. But the move came across as weakness and sent the administration back into the polling darkness. "On an individual basis, each of the dismissals was not surprising; a few had been long expected," *Time* reported. "But the sum total of them, and Carter's wholesale slaughter approach, damaged the brave new leader image he is trying so hard to create."

Though Carter never uttered the word in the July speech, to this day it is known as the "malaise" speech. The word was in the air— Carter had used it in his meetings at Camp David, and then Caddell used it in a background briefing with reporters—and as the speech became a symbol of Carter's futility, it stuck.

Rafshoon left the administration in the fall of 1979. The speechwriters would again have a new boss. While it might have made sense to simply make Hertzberg senior staff and have him report directly to the president, the speechwriters ended up under Alonzo McDonald. McDonald was the White House staff secretary, which meant that he controlled the paper flow around the West Wing. "Of all the problems of the presidency, speechwriting is absolutely the worst," Carter told him. "It's a plague of this office."

The John F. Kennedy Presidential Library was dedicated in Boston on October 20, and Carter was on hand to speak. It was a moment fraught with meaning: A president damned for his lack of eloquence paying tribute to one immortalized by his words. (When Hertzberg suggested in a memo that Carter's message should be that he was carrying out Kennedy's legacy, the president wrote in the margin, "Rather, He & I both carry out legacy of America. I'm not carrying out his legacy.") Carter sat on the dais a seat apart from Senator Edward M. Kennedy, brother of the fallen president, presumptive challenger to the falling one.

It was a speech that Carter prepared in a manner more like JFK's than was his norm: he got involved in the process early and worked extensively on it. He told Hertzberg, I know that I approach this like an engineer and I often edit out good rhetoric, and you just have to fight me on that.

Carter opened the speech with the right humorous touch. "In a press conference in March 1962, when the ravages of being president were beginning to show on his face, [JFK] was asked this two-part question: 'Mr. President, your brother Ted said recently on television that after seeing the cares of office on you, he wasn't sure he would ever be interested in being President,'" Carter said, to general laughter. "And the questioner continued, 'I wonder if you could tell us whether, first, if you had it to do over again, you would work for the Presidency and, second, whether you can recommend this job to others?' The President replied, 'Well, the answer to the first question is yes, and the second is no. I do not recommend it to others—at least for a while.'" There was more laughter and the Carter gave the kicker, which he had written himself: "As you can well see, President Kennedy's wit and also his wisdom is certainly as relevant today as it was then."

Carter spoke eloquently about Kennedy's presidency—his role as "not only a maker of history but a writer of history" (another Carter addition), his accomplishments, and the "things he set in motion," both at home and abroad. Then he took an atypically personal turn:

On that November day, almost sixteen years ago, a terrible moment was frozen in the lives of many of us here. I remember that I climbed down from the seat of a tractor, unhooked a farm trailer, and walked into my ware-house to weigh a load of grain. I was told by a group of farmers that the President had been shot. I went outside, knelt on the steps, and began to pray. In a few minutes, I learned that he had not lived. It was a grievous personal loss—my president. I wept openly for the first time in more than ten years—for the first time since the day my own father died.

Hertzberg did not include in the speech the rest of Carter's recollection: Going to a Georgia Tech football game in the days after the assassination, and being sickened when some of the spectators booed during a moment of silence for the late president. "I wish I'd put that in the speech and drawn the lesson that now it's a golden glow and we look back in the past and everybody claims kinship with Kennedy and how much they all loved Kennedy—but they hated Kennedy, and they hated him for what he stood for," Hertzberg said in 2006. "I wish we'd put that in."

The Iranian situation worsened. Mohammed Reza Pahlevi, the deposed shah, had been admitted to the United States for medical treatment on October 22. Slightly less than two weeks later, on Sunday, November 4, thousands of Iranian students stormed the U.S. Embassy in Teheran and seized as hostages the U.S. citizens there, plunging the Carter White House into an administration-defining crisis.

Domestically the Kennedy challenge proved more potent in theory than in fact. Carter had stumbled out of the gate: When CBS journalist Roger Mudd asked Ted Kennedy why he wanted to be president, the senator's answer was rambling and incoherent. Carter used a "Rose Garden strategy" to great effect, appearing on the job while declining to meet Kennedy in any debates. Americans were being held hostage in Iran and the Soviets had invaded Afghanistan—the kind of international crises that rallied voters to the president. Carter won a string of early victories, in the Iowa, Maine, and Minnesota caucuses.

Achsah Nesmith went to New Hampshire to campaign for Carter. Canvassing door to door gave her a bad feeling: Carter had pro-gun voters on his side. He had anti-Kennedy voters, and disaffected voters. But she did not find a lot of pro-Carter voters. On February 26, 1980, Carter won 49 percent of the Democratic vote to Ted Kennedy's 38 percent, but it was a hollow victory. "We won with the wrong people," Nesmith recalled.

Kennedy hardly contested Florida, Georgia, and South Carolina, hoping that he could break through in Illinois on March 18, but the president drubbed him there. "As the first major testing ground in the industrial Middle West, Illinois was an important, perhaps decisive, prize for both President Carter and Ronald Reagan yesterday, putting the two front-runners well on the path toward a head-to-head race in the fall," *The New York Times* reported in a front-page news analysis on March 19. While Kennedy ran off a string of primary victories after Illinois, Carter won enough delegates to sew up the nomination.

Hertzberg was jarred awake around 1:45 am on the morning of Friday, April 25, by his ringing telephone. It was Caddell, calling from California. "What do you know? What's going on?" the pollster asked. Hertzberg was groggy: About what? "Are you kidding?" Caddell was shouting now. An attempt to rescue the hostages had ended in fiery disaster in the Iranian desert when a C-130 tanker collided with a helicopter, killing eight. Caddell held the telephone up to his television so that Hertzberg could hear ABC News's Ted Koppel discussing the tragedy.

Carter is going to address the nation at seven am, Caddell said. You had better get into the office. Hertzberg lay in the dark in his bedroom, he later recorded in his diary, "thinking of the scene in the desert, in the pitch blackness, in the middle of nowhere, when the helicopter and the C-130 crashed—the flames, the screams, the terror, the sick disappointment and dread."

At the White House Jody Powell was a center of controlled calm amid shell-shocked staffers, many with tear stains on their faces. He told Hertzberg to revise the speech draft with Al Friendly, the associate press secretary for the National Security Council. "The ending of the thing was too despairing—it was just a bleak appeal for help from God," Hertzberg wrote in his diary. He composed a new last paragraph and strengthened the emphasis on diplomatic ways to resolve the crisis.

"We have been disappointed before," Carter told the nation. "We will not give up in our efforts. Throughout this extraordinarily difficult period, we have pursued and will continue to pursue every possible avenue to secure the release of the hostages. In these efforts, the support of the American people and of our friends throughout the world has been a most crucial element. That support of other nations is even more important now."

"Paradoxically—despite the fact that this is on one level a metaphor for three years of Carter Administration fuckups—it has made me feel better about the Administration," Hertzberg wrote in his diary the following day. "This was a rational, intelligent thing to have tried. It would have been a solution to the problem. There is all the difference in the world between this and blockade/mining. I just wish it had worked. I just wish it had worked."

When the Democratic Party met for its nominating convention in New York City in August, Kennedy gave a stirring address in defeat. Hertzberg was the nominal writer for Carter's acceptance speech. "In reality there were many authors, and my main role was to do the suturing, like an emergency-room trauma surgeon after a gas-main explosion," he recalled. A poor speech was helped neither when the TelePrompTer malfunctioned nor when Carter, partially ad-libbing, made a tribute to "a great man who should have been president, who would have been one of the greatest presidents in history—Hubert Horatio Hornblower! Er, Humphrey."*

As Carter entered the fall election against Ronald Reagan, the speech-writers typically got little direction. "All the political dinners and all the road shows we did, we had to come up with them [from] nothing," recalled Chris Matthews, who had joined the speechwriting staff in the late fall of 1979.

A Philadelphia native and former Peace Corps volunteer, Matthews had worked on the Hill, and for consumer advocate Ralph Nader, and had made an unsuccessful primary challenge against a Democratic member of Congress in 1974. He had worked on government reorgan-

---

*In 1976, the Carter campaign staff had scornfully nicknamed their rival for the nomination after the hero of C. S. Forester's tales of naval adventure. (Hertzberg, *Politics*, 138.)

ization, including civil service reform, on the White House staff, and had helped out on some previous speechwriting, including the 1979 State of the Union address. "Chris is no Sorensen, but he is a fast, solid writer and a hard worker," Hertzberg wrote in October, pushing to hire Matthews. "He is politically <u>very</u> savvy, he has a firm grasp of the Carter program and record, and he is very good at working with people."

The speechwriters had sat down with Caddell a couple of times to talk about the campaign's general themes. They would send someone to the campaign's eight o'clock morning meeting at the K Street headquarters, but mostly they winged it. As late as the start of October, they were not getting the White House's "Daily Political Report." "<u>We write the words the President speaks,</u>" Hertzberg wrote to Jordan. "<u>It makes no sense at all for us to have to do without information that would help us do our job better</u>."

The opinion polls stayed close into the first days of November. The final *New York Times*/CBS Poll had Reagan winning 44 to 43, with 8 percent going to independent John Anderson, while the final Gallup Poll had Reagan ahead 46 to 43, with 7 percent to Anderson. But on November 4, Reagan won a crushing victory, tallying more than 50 percent of the vote to Carter's 41 percent.

Work on a farewell address began in November. For the final speech, Hertzberg and Stewart bypassed the regular clearance process: They did not circulate the speech to anyone else or send it through the bureaucracy for approval. "There was no longer anything to fight over," Hertzberg recalled. "You could sit in the building and feel the power draining out." They worked directly with Carter.

On January 14, 1981, Carter spoke for the last time to the nation, about the atomization of society, the dangers of splitting into a country of special interest groups. He went on to discuss the dangers of nuclear war, the need to protect the environment, and the importance of human rights. It was, Stewart recalled, the only time that Carter accepted metaphor and vivid language from his writers:

> *Nuclear weapons are an expression of one side of our human character. But there's another side. The same rocket technology that delivers nuclear warheads has also taken us peacefully into space. From that perspective, we see*

our Earth as it really is—a small and fragile and beautiful blue globe, the only home we have. We see no barriers of race or religion or country. We see the essential unity of our species and our planet. And with faith and common sense, that bright vision will ultimately prevail.

We know that democracy is always an unfinished creation. Each generation must renew its foundations. Each generation must rediscover the meaning of this hallowed vision in the light of its own modern challenges. For this generation, ours, life is nuclear survival; liberty is human rights; the pursuit of happiness is a planet whose resources are devoted to the physical and spiritual nourishment of its inhabitants.

Carter inscribed a copy of the speech for Hertzberg: "Rick—not bad for a 10th draft. Maybe we should have been more careful on earlier speeches, & saved this one 4 more years. Jimmy Carter."

NINE

The Musketeers

JANUARY 1981

As was his long custom, Ronald Reagan had had his speech printed out on nineteen index cards, and now, as the time to speak approached, he made final edits, marking up the speech for ease of reading. He drew lines separating each sentence, giving him easy reference points for pausing and finding his place. When a sentence ran from one card onto the next, he would complete it in block letters on the first card. And though he and others had been working on the speech for months, he made at least thirty-three last-minute changes to the cards. It was a long-ingrained process, and the fact that this was his inaugural address was no reason to do anything differently.

Work on the speech had commenced shortly after Reagan's victory over Jimmy Carter. He collaborated with Ken Khachigian, who had written speeches during the campaign. Khachigian had learned the trade in the Nixon White House, where he worked his way up from being Pat Buchanan's assistant. Now he was poised to join the White House staff for what he said would be a brief stint as Reagan's chief speechwriter.

Reagan had handed Khachigian a six-inch-high stack of four-by-six index cards from his speeches over the years. In a sense, though, he had given one speech over his entire career. During the 1950s,

Reagan hosted the weekly *General Electric Theater* on television and spoke at GE plants around the country. There he had developed what came to be known as "The Speech"—his standard statement of a philosophy that favored country and business and opposed government and communism. He had debuted it to a national stage in October 1964 on behalf of GOP presidential nominee Barry Goldwater. The Speech would be standard reading among his White House speechwriters.

Khachigian had sent Reagan a batch of memos with suggestions for the inaugural, but the president-elect had hardly glanced at them. He wanted themes from The Speech and from his 1967 inaugural address as governor of California, a speech he had written by hand and in which he had declared "We the people" to be the most meaningful words in the Constitution.

"This ceremony itself is evidence that government belongs to the people," Khachigian wrote in notes from an inaugural meeting. "Want optimism and hope, but not 'goody-goody.' . . . There's no reason *not* to believe that we have the answer to things that are wrong." And Reagan had a Hollywood thought: There was a World War II movie about Bataan, he told Khachigian and image adviser Michael Deaver, in which an actor named Frank McHugh said something like, "We're Americans. What's happening to us?" Khachigian spun this thought into a line in his first draft—"We have great deeds to do. . . . But do them we will. We are after all Americans"—which in turn evolved into the delivered speech's closing, in which Reagan said that the country had to believe that it could overcome the crises it faced. "And after all, why shouldn't we believe that? We are Americans."

Khachigian gave Reagan a first draft of the inaugural on January 4, 1981, and the president-elect started to seriously edit it four days later flying from Washington back to California. He thought it too flowery. "As God watches over us and guides us in our time of renewal, I shall pray to him for the sustenance given by this moment and this panorama," Khachigian had written, referring to the view upon which Reagan would gaze while speaking. Reagan had decided to break with tradition and be sworn in on the Capitol's west front steps—facing the Washington Monument, with the Lincoln and Jefferson memorials arrayed beyond it, and in the distance Arlington National Cemetery—rather than the east front.

Reagan did want to mention the monuments and particularly the cemetery, but in a way that personalized them to a greater degree. Scrapping his attempt at editing, he pulled out a yellow legal pad and started his own draft, incorporating elements of Khachigian's text. For the peroration, he took his listeners to Arlington Cemetery, and to the grave of a World War I soldier named Martin Treptow. Reagan had read Treptow's story in a letter from a friend: That he had been killed in action and that found on the flyleaf of his diary were "My Pledge," and "America must win this war. Therefore I will work, I will save, I will sacrifice, I will endure, I will fight cheerfully and do my utmost, as if the issue of the whole struggle depended on me alone."

When Khachigian asked for a copy of the letter so as to check the tale of Treptow, Reagan flashed a pained look. Khachigian—with the aid of Nixon and Ford speechwriter Noel Koch, then working at the Pentagon—discovered that Treptow had indeed been killed in action in France but was buried in his hometown of Bloomer, Wisconsin. Reagan told Khachigian to leave the story in the speech.

In his final edits on his speaking cards, Reagan cut out extraneous words, wrote in additions in careful block letters, rearranged words with tangles of arrows—changing "of, by and for the people," for example, to "for, by and of the people."* His edits tightened thoughts and smoothed transitions. And it was a process he continued as he spoke, making changes during the delivery. One was substantive: Reagan thanked Carter for the smooth transferral of power, which, he said, helped maintain "the continuity which is the bulwark of our Republic." His speech card had that continuity as the "hallmark of the Republic."

"In this present crisis, government is not the solution to our problem," Reagan said. "Government is the problem." (This was a rewrite on speech card number five, which read, "In this present crisis, government is not the solution; it is the problem.")

The president closed with Martin Treptow. He talked about the rows of markers in Arlington National Cemetery, which "add up to

---

*"Of, by and for" is the order Lincoln used at Gettysburg.

only a tiny fraction of the price that has been paid for our freedom." Introducing Treptow, Reagan described him as lying "under one such marker"—though he was careful not to explicitly place him in Arlington. "Ronald Reagan has a sense of theater that propels him to tell stories in their most theatrically imposing manner," Khachigian told Reagan's biographer Lou Cannon. "He knew it would break up the story to say that Treptow was buried in Wisconsin."

Reagan closed as he always did: "God bless you, and thank you." Then he slipped the cards into his Bible—where they would remain undisturbed for four years until the next time he was sworn in.

On Friday, February 13, 1981, the Reagans went to Camp David. It was a working weekend for the president, who, after sleeping in on Saturday, spent the afternoon working at his desk, including on the speech pitching his economic plan that he would deliver to a joint session of Congress the following Wednesday. He did not finish it that day, and that night he and his wife, Nancy, celebrated Valentine's Day—they managed to surprise each other with secretly purchased Valentines—and watched the movie *Nine to Five* with the White House physician and others.*

The president spent Sunday working on the speech, finishing by bedtime. Writing in his rounded, cramped script on Camp David stationery, he produced a twenty-one-page draft that consisted of seventeen Reagan-written pages and four Reagan-edited pages from a Khachigian draft. Especially for major addresses at the start of his presidency, such heavy speech drafting on his part was standard. Working with a speechwriter's first drafts, he had already produced handwritten drafts of his inaugural and a February 5 Oval Office address.

Reagan's Camp David draft was substantially the speech that he gave on Wednesday night, February 18, though it still had some spaces

---

*Reagan wrote in his diary that *Nine to Five* was "Funny—but one scene made me mad. A truly funny scene if the 3 gals had played getting drunk but no they had to get stoned on pot. It was an endorsement of Pot smoking for any younger person who sees the picture." (*Reagan Diaries*, 4.)

to be filled in with the proper numbers. "We will fill in the blanks with figures, won't we?" Reagan wrote on the top of a February 17 draft. "This was the big night—the speech to Cong. on our ec. plan," he wrote in his diary on the evening of the 18th. "I've seen Presidents over the years enter the House chamber without ever thinking I would one day be doing it. The reception was more than anticipated—most of it of course from one side of the aisle. Still it was a thrill and something I'll long remember."

Reagan laid out his program that night: slowing the growth of both wasteful spending and taxes, and increases in military spending that he said would be partially offset by savings from ferreting out Pentagon fraud and abuse. "I'm here tonight to . . . ask that we share in restoring the promise that is offered to every citizen by this, the last, best hope of man on Earth," he said, the last phrase borrowed from Lincoln and used in The Speech.

In the senior staff meeting the next morning, Khachigian jotted down the early returns on the speech: 961 calls—three times the normal volume for a first such speech—95 percent favorable. The following day, a *Washington Post*/ABC News Poll showed that two thirds of the country supported Reagan's plan.

The president spoke on March 30 to the AFL-CIO's Building Construction Trades Department at the Washington Hilton, a little over a mile from the White House. Speechwriter Mari Maseng, who had drafted the talk and who, at twenty-eight, was the youngest writer on the new staff, walked out a little bit ahead of the president as he left the building's side entrance. She later realized that she had walked past the spot where John Hinckley, Jr., waited with a handgun. She was getting into her car in the motorcade, perhaps twenty-five feet ahead of Reagan, when she heard a popping noise. "I can still see it all," she said twenty-five years later. "It was such a traumatic event: the popping, the race to the hospital. . . . It still upsets me even when I think about it. It was the first time I'd seen any violence."

Less than a month after being shot, Reagan made his first public appearance, before a joint session of Congress on April 28. He received a hero's welcome. Two days later, White House staffers held a farewell soirée in the Roosevelt Room for Ken Khachigian, who was making good on his promise not to stay long into the administration. He had planned on leaving earlier but had delayed his departure when the president was shot. "It's time for Ken to go away," the invitation for the party read. "Let's get together so we all can say—goodbye, good luck—come back in May!"

In mid-June, under a general White House staff reorganization, former Nixon speechwriter and Ford shadow speechwriter David Gergen assumed the newly created position of communication director. Gergen had helped with the preparation for the Carter-Reagan debates and had conceived Reagan's devastating question: "Are you better off today than you were four years ago?" One of Gergen's first tasks was to find a replacement for Khachigian.

Running the speechwriters on an interim basis was a former reporter, Anthony Dolan, the only one of the staff who would stay through all eight years. The child of Democrats who had concluded that their party was insufficiently tough on communism—Tony was raised on *National Review*—Dolan had been a "Reagan-bopper" since age thirteen when, volunteering at the Citizens Anti-Communist Committee of Connecticut, he came across a handout called "Losing Freedom on the Installment Plan," featuring The Speech. A graduate of Yale and a disciple of conservative luminary William F. Buckley, Jr., Dolan had won a Pulitzer Prize in 1978 for a *Stamford Advocate* series exposing mafia corruption in the municipal government in Stamford, Connecticut. He had worked for William Casey, the campaign manager, but had not done any speechwriting until he drafted Reagan's election eve remarks.

Directly upon leaving college, Dolan had spent time as a conservative folk singer, performing compositions like "Join the SDS." A proud Irishman, he now clomped around the Executive Office Building in cowboy boots and smoked seven or eight Partagas No. 10 cigars daily, which created what one colleague called an "industrial cigar-haze" in his office. "It was like going into a bat cave, because it was dark and there was smoke in the air, cigar smoke, and Tony's this kind of mysterious person with this anti-Communist view and papers piled up, and so it was like this mysterious world when you went into Tony's office, and his mind was working [in] the same Machiavellian way," speechwriter, Landon Parvin, recalled.

Dolan was a fan of Whittaker Chambers, the former Soviet spy who had a religious conversion and renounced communism. Like Reagan, Dolan had devoured *Witness*, Chambers's book detailing his disillusionment with communism. Dolan was a movement conservative, who viewed communism in the same deeply moralistic, philosophical terms that Reagan employed. "Tony was able to flesh out the moral dynamics of the battle with totalitarianism, with Communism, in a way that nobody else could," recalled second-term colleague Josh Gilder. "Tony had a deep understanding also of the spiritual dynamics of evil."

This proved a double-edged sword in the Reagan White House. After besting more moderate adversaries such as former CIA director and former Republican National Committee chairman George H. W. Bush in the primaries, Reagan had quickly moved to bring Bush (as vice-presidential nominee) and his aide James Baker III into his campaign, helping to unite the party and bringing an added element of political savvy to his team. In the White House, many of Reagan's senior aides were ideologically in the Baker mold, including Gergen. This set up a dynamic of internal discord between the "pragmatists" and the "true believers," with each side certain that it was carrying out Reagan's wishes.

Nowhere was that tension more pronounced than in the relations between the senior staff and the speechwriters. "We considered ourselves like the Musketeers who were guarding the royal jewels," said speechwriter Dana Rohrabacher, who matched Dolan's conservatism. "The senior staff was constantly trying to basically browbeat us into putting things in the speeches that would moderate the President's stand on this or that or move him in a direction other than that which he had stated publicly.

"You know they called them pragmatists—the pragmatists versus the ideologues—as if we didn't think that what we were doing could work, we were just someone who was interested in some ideology that was not attached to reality," added Rohrabacher.

The senior staff viewed the conservative speechwriters as a necessary nuisance. "We took periodic heat from fellow centrists for harboring so many red hots as speechwriters," Gergen wrote. "Their drafts were often scorching, and flares would then go up around the administration. The National Security Council staff and the State Department were particularly apoplectic at the prospect of Reagan saying some of the things these writers drafted. But Baker and I and [staff secretary Richard] Darman thought it important that Reagan have writers who were in sync with his views. We could fight out policy choices and take disputes to the President, but if he were going to govern in bold colors, as he said, his writers shouldn't be composed in plaid."

But the pragmatists were leery of leaving a hard-charging true believer in charge of the speechwriters. "Sometimes, I wondered if even Reagan thought he [Dolan] could be a pain in the ass," Gergen noted.

The situation lingered into the fall, with Dolan running the speechwriting shop and the pragmatists trying to figure out what to do. One White House official described Dolan to a reporter as "the wild-eyed, mean dog you use when you don't want them wondering what you said." A solution crystallized during the preparation for Reagan's first major foreign and defense policy speech, which he was scheduled to deliver at the National Press Club on November 18.

Although Dolan took a special interest in foreign policy speeches, the senior staff often tried to keep them out of his hands for fear of what he might produce.* But Nixon veterans such as Gergen knew that there was another capable speechwriter in the White House. Aram Bakshian, who had written for Nixon and then been one of the few holdovers in the Ford administration, was working in the Reagan administration Office of Public Liaison doing outreach to the arts and humanities community.

The State and Defense departments had each produced drafts, and the National Security Council had tried to knit together a compromise text. The address was going to present an arms control proposal to the

---

*"The reason I've done international speeches . . . is because I'm not as hard-core," Landon Parvin, who was more of a political moderate, told an interviewer on leaving the White House in late 1983. "They were reluctant to give such speeches to Tony Dolan and Dana Rohrabacher because of their rhetoric." (Parvin, OH exit interview, Ronald Reagan Library.)

Soviets a dozen days before negotiations were set to resume in Geneva. Soviet deployments of intermediate-range missiles throughout Eastern Europe had prompted the Carter administration to promise to deploy U.S. intermediate-range missiles in Western Europe while also pursuing negotiations to limit the weapons. Reagan had committed to the same course and would unveil his proposal in the Press Club speech.

The State Department and Defense Department could not agree on the terms of a proposal. And while Reagan would ultimately have to resolve the substantive issue—settling on a "zero option" proposal for the Soviets to withdraw their intermediate-range missiles in exchange for the United States not deploying its missiles*—the senior staff in October asked Bakshian to translate the competing drafts from the ponderous language of foreign and defense policy bureaucrats into a single, Reaganesque speech.

Reagan reworked Bakshian's draft, creating a new opening that excerpted from a letter to Soviet president Leonid Brezhnev, which he had written while recovering in the hospital from his gunshot wound. The president now crossed out whole paragraphs, rewrote or tightened sentences, and merged it into four pages of his own creation, two of them handwritten and two typed from his letter.

"There is no reason why people in any part of the world should have to live in permanent fear of war or its specter," Reagan said. "I believe the time has come for all nations to act in a responsible spirit that doesn't threaten other states. I believe the time is right to move forward on arms control and the resolution of critical regional disputes at the conference table. Nothing will have a higher priority for me and for the American people over the coming months and years."

"Today was the big day—the speech to the world at the Nat. press club," Reagan wrote in his diary. "Funny—I was talking peace but wearing a bullet proof vest. It seems Kadaffi put a contract on me & some

---

*The "zero option" was a Defense Department proposal that had been designed by Defense Secretary Caspar Weinberger and Assistant Secretary of Defense Richard Perle to be unacceptable to the Soviets (though Reagan's interest in disarmament was sincere). Nevertheless, it eventually led to the 1987 Intermediate Nuclear Forces Treaty, which eliminated ground-based ballistic and cruise missiles whose range was between 500 and 5,500 kilometers. (Cannon, 302–03.)

person named Jack was going to try for me at the speech. Security was very tight." "West Europeans Are Enthusiastic; Soviet Accuses President of 'Ploy,'" *The New York Times* reported the next day.

On November 17, the day before Reagan's speech at the Press Club, the White House press office put out two press releases, one announcing that Bakshian had been appointed director of the speechwriting office and the other saying that Anthony Dolan had been made chief speechwriter. The latter was a title without authority, designed to mollify Dolan and his friends in the conservative movement. Bakshian assigned writers and edited speeches. Years later Dolan explained the setup at a meeting of the Judson Welliver Society of former presidential speechwriters: "In the Reagan administration we have an enlightened view," he quipped. "When we have staff conflicts we don't fight them out, we institutionalize them."

In addition to Dolan, the toughest of the firebrands—and one of the biggest characters in the shop—was Dana Rohrabacher. A Californian, he had been a student volunteer on Reagan's 1966 gubernatorial campaign and had worked as a press aide in the 1976 presidential bid. He would walk around the speechwriters' offices in cutoff jeans and flip-flops, a suit and tie hanging on the back of his office door in case of an Oval Office summons. On one such occasion, he realized that he had not brought dress shoes into the office, and scrambled around the Executive Office Building looking for appropriate footwear. He showed up at the Oval Office, much to his colleagues' amusement, wearing wing-tipped shoes that were several sizes too big. Another time he brought his guitar onto Air Force One—the buttoned-down senior staff took a dim view of that. He was, Dolan recalled, "very much a flower child manqué."

Rohrabacher was a skilled and florid writer, though an inept speller. "He once merged destiny and Greek cheese when he referred to something being a 'feta accompli,' by which he meant *fait accompli*," Bakshian recounted. "There were other instances—oh, the Hollywood Bowel, which must have been part of the UCLA medical school."

Rohrabacher befriended an amazing array of anti-Communist

fighters from places like Afghanistan and Nicaragua, whom he would take to the White House mess for lunch. "The amusing thing was watching these guys get cleared into the building because they'd have two knives down this sock and [bandoliers] and a gun," said Peter Robinson, who joined the speechwriting staff later in the first term. "Then we'd go off to the White House mess and try to make polite conversation. You'd say something like, 'How are things going?' He'd say: 'Very well: Last week I personally killed twelve Soviets.' 'Oh. And would you like the tuna salad?'"

Rohrabacher would be elected to the U.S. Congress in 1988. Another conservative on the speechwriting staff was a former television writer and producer for CBS named Bentley Elliott. "He was central casting's idea of the typical English professor: tweed coat, thinning blond hair, debonair, equally capable of the bon mot and caustic remark, an insouciant surface that covered a pleasant vulnerability and genuine concern for his colleagues," wrote William Muir, a speechwriter for Vice President George Bush. Elliott described himself as a "bleeding heart conservative." Pat Buchanan, who would be White House communications director in the second term, described Elliott as a "Green Beret in the Reagan Revolution." An ardent proponent of supply-side economics, he could translate complicated economic concepts into easily understood prose.

Mari Maseng had been a reporter at the *Evening Post* in Charleston, South Carolina, when, in 1978, she joined Senator Strom Thurmond's reelection campaign as press secretary. She moved to Washington the following year, working for Senator Robert Dole's presidential campaign, and then joined the Reagan campaign as a media strategist. Upon receiving back a particularly bland rewrite of a speech from a State Department functionary, she once said with glee: "You know what I think? I think we can do without State's edits. I think we can stick with our draft!"

Rounding out the speechwriting team—and giving it an element of ideological balance—was Landon Parvin, who had done some volunteer speechwriting for the campaign while working in public relations. He had a background in comedy, having written for Rich Little in 1976 and 1977. He did most of the writing when Reagan had to deliver humorous remarks at events like the Gridiron Dinner. Parvin also did some writing for Nancy Reagan and developed a friendship with her. He was orderly and precise—he liked to be in to work by eight in the morning so that he could leave by five thirty and get out to a friend's farm to go horseback riding. The word that was most frequently used to describe him was "facile."

Like Parvin, Bakshian was not a movement conservative. He had his idiosyncrasies: while the rest of the speechwriters were learning to use word processors, Bakshian refused to give up his typewriter. He "spiced his words with wit, virtually everything he ate with Tabasco sauce, and wrote à la Mozart, fluidly and effortlessly, sentence to sentence, paragraph to paragraph with nary a pause of hesitation," Elliot recalled. Perhaps most important, Bakshian had good relations with the senior staff, and was able to act as an intermediary between them and the Reaganites on the speechwriting staff.

And Bakshian was favorably impressed with Reagan. "That was a pleasant discovery in comparison to the two other presidents I worked with—Nixon and Ford—in a speechwriting capacity: that he's quite a craftsman in this field and heavily involved in the process, especially the important speeches," he said.

A dense blizzard, the worst in two years, engulfed Washington on January 13, 1982, leaving up to six inches of snow on the city. In his office in the Old Executive Office Building, Aram Bakshian was contemplating Dolan's draft of the State of the Union address, which Reagan was scheduled to give in thirteen days, when he saw a disaster unfolding on television. An Air Florida 737 taking off from National Airport failed to get enough altitude because of the icy conditions and clipped the 14th Street Bridge, causing a thirty-five-foot gash in the railing, before slamming onto the ice-covered Potomac and slowly sinking.

Reaction was swift, but hampered by the weather. As Bakshian watched, a bystander dove into the frosty river, fishing out a woman who had lost her grip on a rescue rope. His name was Lenny Skutnik, and his moment of heroism gave Bakshian an idea. "It just made sense," he recalled. "It so fitted what Reagan believed and what was in character for him to say. Plus, he had been a life guard. He would clearly understand and appreciate it, and it would come out well." "It" was a peroration for the address that Reagan employed to great effect.

"We don't have to turn to our history books for heroes. They're all around us," Reagan said on January 26, gesturing to Skutnik, who was sitting with Nancy Reagan in the House spectator's gallery. "Just two weeks ago, in the midst of a terrible tragedy on the Potomac, we saw again the spirit of American heroism at its finest—the heroism of dedicated rescue workers saving crash victims from icy waters. And we saw the heroism of one of our young government employees, Lenny Skutnik, who, when he saw a woman lose her grip on the helicopter line, dived into the water and dragged her to safety."

Reagan and Bakshian had created a tradition: the guests in the first lady's box during the State of the Union. Years later, someone asked Bakshian what innovations as a White House speechwriter he was most and least proud of. "The best thing I think was Lenny Skutnik, in and of itself," Bakshian said. "The worst thing was that gimmick—which wasn't a gimmick doing it once. . . . [But it] got so milked to death and then diluted too."

Reagan was pleased with the speech. "I wonder if I'll ever get used to addressing the joint sessions of Cong?" he wrote in his diary before heading over to the Capitol. "I've made a mil. speeches in every kind of place to every kind of audience. Somehow there's a thing about entering that chamber—goose bumps & a quiver." Afterward he added: "But it turned out fine—I was well received & I think the speech was a 4 base hit."

In early June, Reagan would become the first U.S. president to address a joint session of the British Parliament. By mid-May, National Security Council staffers had written a draft that Bakshian "tried to return . . . to the mother tongue," as he told Reagan in a May 14 memo. He succeeded in translating the bureaucratese into English, but not into the Reagan idiom—the president was unhappy with the speech.

Dolan's ongoing feuds with the pragmatists had left him off the speechwriting schedule for several months, so he had used the spare time to work up his own version of the address. He wrote a twenty-three-page draft that had a rich sense of history and philosophy and a heavier emphasis on themes of individual liberty versus statism and, ultimately, good versus evil than were in the other drafts. Historians looking back from the future would find "in the councils of those who preached the supremacy of the state, who declared its omnipotence over individual man, who predicted its eventual domination of all peoples of the earth, surely historians will see there . . . the focus of evil," he wrote. (Reagan edited this down to read that historians would "find in the councils of those who preached the supremacy of the state the focus of evil.") Dolan's draft also included a reference to the Soviet Union as "a militaristic empire whose ideology justifies any wrongdoing or use of violence if done in the name of the state" and "a sad, bizarre, dreadfully evil episode in history, but an episode that is dying."

William Clark, the national security adviser, mentioned Dolan's draft to Reagan, who asked for it. This was what the president had been looking for. "The reason Reagan had warmed to my draft was it was all the stuff he'd been saying for thirty years," Dolan recollected. He viewed the job of speechwriters as plagiarizing the president's old speeches and giving them back to him.

Reagan did his usual editing job: tightening, crossing out whole paragraphs, inserting pages in his own hand. He eliminated the references to the Soviet Union as a militaristic empire and an evil episode in history. His moderate advisers toned down some of the speech's other hot rhetoric. Reagan had retained the assertion that in the supremacy of the state lay the "focus of evil" in the world—a paraphrase of Whittaker Chambers in *Witness* that "I see in communism the focus of concentrated evil of our time"—but it was expunged before the president addressed the gathered legislators at Westminster.

The NSC staffers were appalled by the tone of his draft. They pleaded with Dolan to change the speech: Do what we want, one NSC staffer told him, and then we'll really leave the Soviets on the "ash heap of history." Oh, replied Dolan, what an interesting phrase. Can you say that again? He inserted into the next draft of the speech a line about democracy leaving Marxism-Leninism "on the ash heap of history." He described it as an NSC contribution.

Others contributed as well. The conservative columnist George Will, who years later would marry speechwriter Mari Maseng, provided the opening about Westminster being one of "democracy's shrines," as well as a line that "regimes planted by bayonets do not take root."

Reagan's speech marked a rhetorical and philosophical high point for the president. He asked whether civilization must "perish in a hail of fiery atoms? Must freedom wither in a quiet, deadening accommodation with totalitarian evil?" Citing former Prime Minister Winston Churchill, he said war was not inevitable. "In an ironic sense, Karl Marx was right," Reagan said. "We are witnessing today a great revolutionary crisis, a crisis where the demands of the economic system are conflicting directly with those of the political order. But the crisis is happening not in the free, non-Marxist West, but in the home of Marxist-Leninism, the Soviet Union. It is the Soviet Union that runs against the tide of history by denying human freedom and human dignity to its citizens."

His Westminster speech and its analysis of the Communist system were prescient. He said that the Eastern bloc was in "decay," as evidenced not only by the abject economic failure of the Soviet Union but by the resistance of Poland's Solidarity labor movement and that country's "being magnificently unreconciled to oppression." He called upon other democratic nations to join the United States in fostering "the infrastructure of democracy, the system of free press, unions, political parties, universities, which allow a people to choose their own way to develop their own culture, to reconcile their own differences through peaceful means."

He described his proposal as "a plan and a hope for the long term—the march of freedom and democracy which will leave Marxism-Leninism on the ash heap of history as it has left other tyrannies which stifle the freedom and muzzle the self-expression of the people."

"Soviet Says Crusade by Reagan May Risk Global Catastrophe," *The New York Times* reported in a "news analysis." "It was a bad week for relations between Moscow and Washington," *Time* added. Reading the "indignant cables from Moscow" a few days after the speech, Dolan recalled, "I can assure you we were giggling like schoolboys."

• • •

By March 1983, Reagan and his aides were increasingly concerned that the nuclear freeze movement—which advocated halting production of nuclear weapons and freezing stockpiles at their current levels—was gaining support among religious activists. Various protestant denominations and organizations, including the National Council of Churches, had endorsed it, while the Synagogue Council of America had declared the United States "morally bound" to reduce the danger of nuclear war. The National Conference of Catholic Bishops was scheduled to vote in May on a pastoral letter that was expected to endorse a nuclear freeze.

Reagan's scheduled speech to the National Association of Evangelicals, meeting in Orlando, Florida, seemed a logical place to tackle the issue. It was a routine speech venue—"on the B-list," Bakshian recalled—that did not merit nationally televised coverage, but it would reach the targeted audience.

Dolan and Rohrabacher went to a steakhouse near the White House with officials of the religious group. "The freezeniks" were making inroads into the evangelical heartland, Richard Cizik, one of the officials, told the speechwriters.

It was the kind of speech that Tony Dolan relished: an opportunity to discuss issues in the sort of black and white moral language that Reagan had long employed and that drove the moderates crazy. Dolan's belief in the importance of speaking the truth about wickedness had been reinforced by his days reporting on the mafia in Connecticut. "The human conscience is such that evil acts bother people, and I've found that if you let the bad guys talk, they'll get preoccupied with trying to rebut [accusations of wrongdoing], and in the end they concede it," he said. "That's why they have coined phrases like Wars of National Liberation and the People's Republics."

Dolan borrowed from the early drafts of the Westminster speech. Back came the Soviet Union as the "focus of evil in the modern world"; back came a lengthy quotation from C. S. Lewis's *Screwtape Letters* that the greatest evil in the world is done by cold, quiet bureaucrats who never have to raise their voices; back came the reference to communism as "sad" and "bizarre," a "chapter in human history whose last pages even now are being written"; and, most important, back came the "empire" concept, couched this time in terms that were more arch: the nuclear freeze movement, the speech said, incorrectly labeled both sides in the Cold War equally at fault, ignoring "the fact of history and the aggressive impulses of an evil empire."

The Orlando speech was not considered a foreign policy speech, however, and mostly focused on domestic issues: the anti-Soviet language came in the final third, after sections on prayer in school, abortion, and family values. Dolan's draft included several barbs at liberals and secular humanists whose alleged depredations threatened the country.

When Bakshian read the speech, he understood the reaction it was likely to elicit: "the State Department would have conniption fits," he said. "So I made a point of not flagging it." He called Sven Kraemer, a National Security Council staffer who was frequently responsible for clearing speech drafts. Obviously there are going to be some people who don't like this, Bakshian said, but we both know that what it says is true and it's not going to lead to World War III, so I don't see any reason to start screaming from the rooftops about it. If anyone wants to bitch about it, he added, let them find it—let's let it through to the president. He called it the "stealth speech." Because it was a routine domestic policy speech and not flagged by the NSC, the text was not widely circulated or noticed in the Defense and State departments.

One senior staffer who did notice it was David Gergen, who worried that it was too strident. It was true that this was Reaganesque rhetoric, but in the practical world the president was also trying to negotiate nuclear arms reductions with the Soviets, and such harsh language could spoil the efforts. He pulled Robert "Bud" McFarlane, the deputy national security adviser, out of a meeting. "Bud, we've got to go over this," he said. The speech kept coming back to Dolan, he recalled, with the entire "evil empire" section crossed out in green ink, "on orders of the West Wing," where the pragmatists were housed.

The speech, tough language mostly intact, eventually got through to Reagan. The pragmatists figured that it was a minor speech, not likely to garner much attention, so there would be little harm in rallying the faithful. The president inserted two pages of handwritten material in the domestic section, eliminated a reference to "abortion on demand" as "a great moral evil," and added a statement that "Unless & until it can be proven that the unborn child is not a living entity, then it's [*sic*] right to life, liberty & the pursuit of happiness must be protected." He also toned down some of the gibes at the "liberal secularists" and elite "glitter set." He eliminated a section decrying the mafia, writing a note to Dolan on the first page saying that if the speech came in too short, they could put it back in. (They did not.)

In the foreign policy section, Reagan wrote in and then scratched out a line about continuing to pray that the Communists would one day learn "the joy there is in knowing & serving ~~God~~ Him." The strong anti-Communist language remained untouched.

The speech, delivered on March 8, 1983, drew numerous cheering interruptions. And it quickly garnered national attention, with *The New York Times* giving it front-page coverage under the headline, "Reagan Denounces Ideology of Soviet as 'Focus of Evil.'" This was not mere good luck: Dolan had called *Times* reporter Francis X. Clines the previous evening, tipping him off as to what was coming and giving him a sense of the key points. Dolan knew that the *Times* set the news agenda, so that the speech and its assertions of an "evil empire" would get widespread discussion.

It drew swift and broad denunciations. "What is the world to think when the greatest of powers is led by a man who applies to the most difficult human problem a simplistic theology—one in fact rejected by most theologians?" asked the liberal *New York Times* columnist Anthony Lewis. "The president has every right to oppose a nuclear freeze, but he has no right to stigmatize those who disagree with his brand of 'civil religion,'" Rabbi Walter S. Wurzburger told *The Washington Post*. Rick Hertzberg, now writing for *The New Republic*, said the speech was "not presidential, it's not something a president should say. . . . If the Russians are infinitely evil and we are infinitely good, then the logical first step is a nuclear first strike. Words like that frighten the American public and antagonize the Soviets. What good is that?"

Gergen, who had questioned the speech, had to defend it in public. "The President knows what he is doing with his speeches," he told *The Washington Post*. "He knew when he gave the speech it would draw fire from the left and some sophisticated observers. The president feels it's very important from time to time for him to talk in terms of fundamentals and base, core beliefs so that everyone can understand reality as it is seen by the White House."

"I hate to admit it, but it's true: history has shown that Tony Dolan was right and I was wrong," Gergen later wrote. "That phrase, the Evil Empire, allowed Reagan to speak truth to totalitarianism. . . . In retrospect, I'm glad Tony won. The conservatives knew their boss and served him well."

The president's next national address was scheduled for March 23, when he would pitch his national defense program and try to shoot down budgetary assaults on it as the federal deficit rocketed out of sight. But he had a surprise ending for the speech that only a few of his closest aides knew about.

Reagan had had a long lunch with the Joint Chiefs of Staff on February 11, their regular quarterly meeting to report to the commander in chief. "Out of it came a super idea," Reagan wrote in his diary that night. "So far the only policy worldwide on nuclear weapons is to have a deterrent. What if we tell the world we want to protect our people, not avenge them; that we're going to embark on a program of research to come up with a defensive weapon that could make nuclear weapons obsolete? I would call upon the scientific community to volunteer in bringing such a thing about." It was the Strategic Defense Initiative, also called SDI, or, as it would come to be popularly called, "Star Wars," after the 1977 science fiction film.*

Reagan had long dreamed of a world no longer threatened by the "hail of fiery atoms" he had mentioned at Westminster. Some friends dated the wish to a role he had played—that of Brass Bancroft—in the 1940 science fiction film *Murder in the Air*, which had featured a device that could shoot rockets and airplanes out of the sky. More recent, McFarlane, the deputy national security adviser, had conceived of the

---

*"Star Wars" tropes were popular: The "evil empire" speech was also sometimes referred to as the "Darth Vader" speech. Together, the two addresses prompted *The Washington Post* to headline one story: "Writers of Speeches for President Claim Force Is with Him."

idea of a national missile defense shield as a useful bargaining chip against the Soviets: handled properly, the United States could trade the mere notion of such a program for actual arms concessions from the Soviets. He called the idea "The Sting." McFarlane had arranged for the Chief of Naval Operations to broach the subject of missile defense at the Joint Chiefs' February luncheon with the president, and Reagan had run with it, taking an unusually proactive approach to the issue. He wanted to announce the program as soon as possible. When national security adviser William Clark told him that the White House had arranged for television time on March 23, Reagan replied: "Let's do it."

On March 19, McFarlane drafted "MX Plus," the surprise ending to the speech.* Secretary of State George Shultz only found out about the plan on the morning of March 21, and thought it "lunacy." Vice President Bush found out when his chief of staff, Admiral Daniel Murphy, burst into his office and said, "We've got to take this out! If we go off half-cocked on this idea, we're going to bring on the biggest arms race that the world has ever seen!" Bush thought Murphy was correct, but did not do anything. Secretary of Defense Caspar Weinberger was at a NATO conference in Portugal when he found out about the plan, and tried to get the address delayed for twenty-four hours so that he could brief the European allies, but was told no on the grounds that television network time had already been scheduled.

Reagan edited the main body of the speech on March 22. "Much of it was to change bureaucratic into people talk," he wrote in his diary that night. "What if free people could live secure in the knowledge that their security did not rest upon the threat of instant U.S. retaliation to deter a Soviet attack, that we could intercept and destroy strategic ballistic missiles before they reached our own soil or that of our allies?"

Reagan told the nation:

I know this is a formidable, technical task, one that may not be accomplished before the end of this century. Yet, current technology has attained a level of sophistication where it's reasonable for us to begin this effort. It will

---

*The MX missile was a controversial intercontinental ballistic missile that the Reagan administration favored.

take years, probably decades of effort on many fronts. There will be failures and setbacks, just as there will be successes and breakthroughs. And as we proceed, we must remain constant in preserving the nuclear deterrent and maintaining a solid capability for flexible response. But isn't it worth every investment necessary to free the world from the threat of nuclear war? We know it is.

"I guess it was O.K.," Reagan wrote in his diary after the speech. He had hosted for dinner a group that included the Joint Chiefs, several former secretaries of state, and distinguished nuclear scientists. "They all praised to the sky & seemed to think it would be a source of debate for some time to come. I did the bulk of the speech on why our arms build up was necessary & then finished with a call to the Science community to join me in research starting now to develop a defensive weapon that would render nuclear missiles obsolete. I made no optimistic forecasts—said it might take 20 yrs. or more but we had to do it. I felt good."

Mari Maseng was up most of the night of August 2, 1983, writing. That afternoon, a group from the Annual Convention of the National Federation of Business and Professional Women's Clubs had been turned away from a tour of the White House because of a scheduling mix-up. It was the kind of publicity that the Reagan administration—which had a reputation for being insensitive toward women—did not need. An incensed Reagan arranged to appear before the convention on August 3 to apologize.

"The Reagan White House was a little sexist," Maseng said later. "It was a lot sexist. It was back in the eighties, times were different. . . . There weren't any women there to speak of." It got better as the administration went on, she recalled, but at the start, the director of the Office of Public Liaison was the "woman's slot." Elizabeth Dole was the first to fill that position, "and she did not have a necessarily happy time with the West Wing boys," Maseng said. She later filled the public liaison slot herself and recalled her own problems. "Just getting access to meetings sometimes was hard. Sort of beating down the doors, so it was a different time and some dinosaurs from an earlier generation . . . still roamed the earth."

Maseng never felt that Reagan was sexist. He would always greet her with a big smile. Once, toward the end of his tenure in the White House, when she was communications director, she and another female staffer, the director of public liaison, were running to Air Force One—running because Reagan was already aboard. As it was later told to Maseng, the president looked out the window and with obvious delight said, "There's going to be girls on board!" But, she added, "the fact that the two of us would change the mix on the airplane tells you a lot."

On the morning of August 3, Reagan was "just so sorry that this had happened," Maseng recalled, "and wanted them to know that he didn't hate women." He ignored the speech Maseng had prepared and spoke extemporaneously. Usually when he spoke on the topic of women and his administration, the president cited statistics about his appointments, tax law changes that helped women, and discrimination lawsuits that the Justice Department was pursuing. But this time he skipped the list. "I believe that it's not enough just to say, 'I'm sorry,' so I intend to do penance," he told the crowd. "And we have been doing a number of things here with regard to the thing of great interest to you, and that is the recognition of women's place. I want you to know I've always recognized it, because I happen to be one who believes if it wasn't for women, us men would still be walking around in skin suits carrying clubs."

The joke drew some moans from the crowd, while on stage, standing off to the side, Maseng reminded herself not to change her expression or otherwise react. Reagan was a master of delivering a text that he had absorbed, but speaking off the cuff could be problematic.

The national president of the association told reporters that she thought Reagan's quip was "very degrading . . . inappropriate, and I was offended." In his diary that night, Reagan noted that he thought the businesswomen were "wonderful. I was warmly received & left to quite an ovation. . . . The TV evenings news played up the episode of my apology but refused to show the applause I received & played it as a great embarrassment for me." The next day he added, "The morning papers were worse than the TV news. I reached the boiling point." He was mollified, however, by a telegram from the woman who had introduced him, apologizing for the national president's comments.

By the end of August 1983, Aram Bakshian was leaving. He did not want to be on the staff through the grind of a reelection campaign, so when he was offered a regular newspaper column he took the job, leaving at the start of September. It was a time of turnover for speechwriting: Maseng left around the same time to work for Elizabeth Dole at the Department of Transportation, while Parvin would leave at the end of November to become executive assistant for the new U.S. ambassador to Great Britain. Gergen would leave at the end of the year as well, his duties supervising the speechwriters taken up by Richard Darman, another pragmatist.

A successor to Bakshian was chosen quickly: Ben Elliott, the committed supply-sider and former CBS newsman, took the director spot, with Dolan remaining the chief writer. Elliott was no less of a true believer than Dolan, and probably more of one than Bakshian, but he understood the necessity for compromise in getting a speech completed. "There were many tussles on the margin, and sometimes we went to the mat, but I'm not as willing to condemn them as some. I think we worked well together," Elliott said later. "We were more fervent than they, but we believed that we managed to provide the president a consistent and compelling product."

"When Aram Bakshian left, we stopped having the Friday meetings of the speechwriters with the President," Gergen wrote in an October 18 memo to Mike Deaver and Jim Baker. "Now that Ben Elliott has taken charge of that shop, I would like to request that we reinstitute them on as many Fridays as possible. They made a good deal of difference in the quality of the writing (not to mention the morale of the shop) and the President seemed to enjoy them."

The regular meetings would not return, though the speechwriters were not shut out entirely during the first term: They saw the president but not as much as they would like—they often complained that their lack of access made their jobs harder, partly because seeing him helped them understand his thinking and also get the sound of his voice.* Access was also important for more ephemeral reasons. "Everyone in the White House counts who gets to go through the door, and the fact that we got to go through the door made us at least on the sheet of who was a player," Maseng recalled. "It was important for that and it was important for our psyche because we got a lot of charge out of being with the president and felt the personal bond. I'm not sure the president got a lot out of those meetings."

Despite being increasingly remote from the president, the speechwriters felt that they could still effectively capture his speaking style. Over his decades in the public eye, Reagan had left a long trail of speeches, remarks, and articles, which the writers plundered. They were also aided by a backchannel they had to Anne Higgins, who handled Reagan's personal correspondence. She would send over copies of letters that he wrote to people around the country explaining how he felt about different issues. The speechwriters could see the language and arguments he used.

Peggy Noonan was at work at CBS Radio in early 1984 when she picked up the pink message slip that said a Ben Elliott had called from the White House. He probably runs speechwriting, Noonan thought, and he's probably going to offer me a job; my life is about to change. A partisan stuck in a journalist's job, Noonan admired Reagan and yearned to write for him, but doubted her chances of making it happen. She had no political connections and few friends who shared her ideology. She had told everyone who might help that she wanted to write for Reagan, and then one day she got the pink message slip. She would keep it for years as a memento.

"I guess everyone gets a president, one president in their adult life who's the one who moved them," she told Elliott in her job interview. "For me, it's Reagan." Her next interview was with Darman. "I'm sure

---

*This was not a universally held complaint: though the weekly meetings were never restarted, Elliott gives Jim Baker credit: "He allowed us to see the president. He opened the avenues of access so that we could speak to the man and present what we thought he wanted, and he had the opportunity to say yea or nay." (Author interview with Bentley Elliott.)

you've heard all about this White House," he told her. "That there's a great deal of infighting, and we're split into separate warring groups which leak unpleasant things about each other to the amusement and delight of the media, which are not slow in passing it on." She nodded. It was terrible that the media traded in such scurrilous rumors. "It's all true of course," he said.

Bush speechwriter William Muir described Noonan as "tall and blonde, a reincarnated Carole Lombard, with a tart wit that could protect her even in the most captious of literary circles." A Brooklyn native, she had grown up on Long Island and in New Jersey and lived in New York before joining the administration. She stood out: She dressed with more flair than the others and, recalled Maseng, whom Noonan replaced, she had "a personality that's larger than life sometimes."

On February 23, Elliott sent Reagan a memo letting him know that he was interviewing Noonan for a speechwriting job. "The rub is that she is Dan Rather's radio writer," Elliott explained. "I've read through his scripts and can assure you that the radio Dan Rather bears little resemblance to his left-wing TV twin. I've also talked to Peggy twice for a total of 4 hours and am convinced she yearns deeply to defect, and to write for you with all the dedication and Irish spirit she can muster." The president sent the memo back with the notation: "OK. RR" Noonan got the formal offer that month while covering the Democratic presidential primary in Manchester, New Hampshire.

Nevertheless, there were some lingering questions among the White House staff about the hire. "I wasn't sure why you requested Peggy Noonan's resume," Elliott wrote to Michael Deaver on March 16, "but I want you to know she is the most distinguished writer among a very large number of candidates. . . . Peggy is well-known—and sometimes ridiculed—for being the in-house conservative at CBS." Deaver had a good relationship with Nancy Reagan, often serving as the staff conduit to her, and she had opposed Noonan's hiring.

Noonan started at the White House on April 2. She would roll into work around 9:30 or 9:45 am—wildly tardy by the standards of the workaholic White House, but she was sleepy and muddle-headed at eight in the morning, she figured, so why get in then? She worked better at night and stayed late anyway. Writing made her nervous. She would sometimes need to down a couple of cups of coffee and get a pack of smokes and force herself to plunge in. Or she would pretend that she was not writing a speech at all, but a letter to someone. "Dear Peggy . . ." she would write.

Reagan left Washington on June 1, 1984, for a ten-day European trip that included a visit to Ireland, the commemoration of the fortieth anniversary of D-Day in Normandy, and an economic summit in London. After a Deaver-produced pilgrimage to Ballyporeen in County Tipperary, the small town from which Reagan's great-grandfather had emigrated, the president addressed Ireland's national legislature. Dolan had drafted the speech, with the usual resistance from senior staff: It started with a conciliatory review of various U.S. peace initiatives during Reagan's term and ended on a tough note about the march of freedom around the world.

Dolan was delighted at the notion of the Soviets fulminating about the back-end tough talk while the world media focused on the peace side of it. "It was a wonderful paradox," he said. But he was worried that once he was no longer around to protect the speech, the moderates would water down the hard-hitting section. So he booked a flight to Ireland on his own dime. He huddled with Ben Elliott and Darman in Ashford Castle, where the traveling party was staying, and made final revisions to the speech. Dolan had a White House staff pin which allowed him access to the castle without a problem. Deaver was incredulous when he saw Dolan. "After that, Deaver revoked all the staff pins," Dolan recalled.

Two days later, on June 6, the Reagans alighted from Marine One at Pointe du Hoc, a desolate cliff overlooking the French coastline that Allied forces had seized on D-Day. Forty years earlier, as Allied troops waded ashore on neighboring beaches, a group of Army Rangers had scaled the sheer walls of the cliffs and taken the German gun emplacements at their top. Of 225 who made the assault, 90 were still able to fight the next day. "We're here to mark that day in history when the Allied armies joined in battle to reclaim this continent to liberty," the president said.

Noonan had been delighted and surprised when Elliott tapped her to write the D-Day speech. "I hired you to write this speech," he told her. It was a daunting mission. She had been at the White House just long enough to know that such an address was sure to attract critics, especially since she was still an unknown quantity. She was "a little paralyzed" by the task—a condition not helped by bits of advice and exhortation that floated in over the transom: Make it like the Gettysburg Address—make people cry. Or: Deaver planned to use clips from the speech at the Republican National Convention in August.

She paced. She tried writing on weekends, at odd hours. She tried doing it as a letter to an aunt. She hoped the speech would just come. It took fifteen drafts before she had something that she could share. She gave it to Elliott, who made minimal changes and sent it out for "staffing." The staffing process had grown since its bureaucratic formalization in the Ford administration. By Noonan's estimate an insignificant speech would go to twenty people for approval, a major one to fifty. Suggested changes—how much "suggested" as opposed to "mandatory" depended upon the identity of the sender—would come back, and Darman had final say on what got in and what did not.

This process was "like sending a beautiful newborn fawn out into the jagged wilderness where the grosser animals would pierce its tender flesh and render mortal wounds," Noonan wrote in her speechwriting memoir, *What I Saw at the Revolution*. "But perhaps I understate." She was still figuring out which changes she could ignore and which she could not. "It was really awful for me because rhetoric is a form of communication between a leader and his people," she said. "Anything that is art or part art is delicate. And anything that is delicate can't survive the tinkering hands and mauling of twenty-five people."

The problems were compounded by the facts of the speech. "It was controversial," she recalled. "One reason was that a woman wrote it. I have to tell you I have learned about the military and how they think over in Defense. . . . And the idea that a woman wrote the speech and that I have never seen combat upset them beyond belief. Cliques tried to tear it apart, and I saw that what they were doing was without the intention of being helpful."

Even the editorial comments that were intended to be helpful were only partly so. The "boom" of the cannon became the more graceful "roar." But other suggestions were inelegant—coming either from wonks too busy with the trees of policy to think about the forest of form, or nonwriters trying to be poets. The NSC wanted a paragraph paying tribute to the Russian loss of life in the war. "I have <u>not</u> incorporated this suggestion because it is irrelevant (the subject here is Normandy, and the Russians weren't at that party), unneeded (brings up the whole new topic of what losses each nation suffered in the war when we don't talk about the millions of French, British, German and American dead), and . . . it has that egregious sort of special pleading ring that stops the <u>flow</u>," she wrote to Elliott in a memo on May 30. "It sounds like we stopped the speech dead to throw a fish to the bear."

She and Bud McFarlene, now the national security adviser, had a tug-of-war over changing words in the last sentence of the speech from "borne by their memory" to "sustained by their sacrifice." He would change it and she would reject the change. "I prefer 'borne . . .' because it is more personal, more lyrical and more positive," she wrote Elliott. "Better to be borne than sustained, I always say." In the end, the sop to the Russian dead stayed in, but she was sustained by the survival of "borne . . ."

The crucial creative moment came when Noonan was talking to the head of the White House advance team, who was complaining that the speech still did not elicit tears. "But they'll be there," he kept telling her. It took her a few moments to realize that he meant the Rangers—the vets who had taken the cliffs would be in the audience, not scattered among the other guests but sitting as a group directly in front of the president.

On June 6, Reagan told their tale of heroism, of how they scaled and seized the cliffs of Pointe du Hoc. "Behind me is a memorial that symbolizes the Ranger daggers that were thrust into the top of these cliffs," he said. "And before me are the men who put them there. These are the boys of Pointe du Hoc.* These are the men who took the cliffs. These

---

*Noonan had just finished reading Roger Kahn's *The Boys of Summer*, about the Brooklyn Dodgers. "O happy steal," she thought. (Noonan, *What I Saw at the Revolution*, 87.)

are the champions who helped free a continent. These are the heroes who helped end a war."

Noonan watched the speech on television at 7:20 am East Coast time. There had been a fight with the French over timing: The French had scheduled a formal welcoming ceremony for Reagan at 4 pm French time, 10 am on the east coast. Deaver wanted Reagan to speak earlier so that he would be broadcast live on the morning shows back home. (An intended side effect of the timing was that it supplanted coverage of the California Democratic primary.) Sitting in her New York apartment, Noonan was disappointed with the speech: it was the twentieth draft and she knew that the eleventh was the best.

She met Ronald Reagan for the first time almost six weeks later, when the speechwriters had one of their meetings with him. It lasted half an hour. As they were leaving, he took her hand. "You know, a while ago I wanted to call you about something, but . . ." He could not remember what it was. Elliott stepped in: "Peggy wrote the Pointe du Hoc speech, Mr. President." That was it. "That was wonderful," he said, "it was like 'Flanders Fields.'"

Later that month, Reagan was scheduled to address the U.S. Olympic team competing at the Games, which were to be held in Los Angeles that year. It was fluff: a patriotic pep talk to get the athletes and—not incidentally in an election year—the country jazzed. Rohrabacher got the assignment and wrote a talk ending with Reagan exhorting the athletes to "do it for the Gipper."* It was a perfect Reagan line: a bit hokey, a bit inspiring, a bit humorous. The kind of thing that he would deliver flawlessly. But Rohrabacher had to fight for it. Word came back that it was too schmaltzy and ran the risk of reminding people of Reagan's film career. "The senior staff, people who worked around Reagan, the ones who were not his Reaganites, were always embarrassed that they worked for a former movie star," Rohrabacher said.

---

*In 1940, Reagan had played Notre Dame running back George Gipp in the movie *Knute Rockne—All American*. Gipp, known affectionately as "the Gipper," had died during his senior year in 1920. According to school legend, on his deathbed he had told his coach, Knute Rockne, that when the team needed inspiration during a big game, he should tell them to "Win just one for the Gipper." Rockne did so eight years later, the story goes, and the team won.

"They shuddered at any mention of it. That was Ronald Reagan—and there was nothing to be embarrassed about." Rohrabacher won that fight, and Reagan delivered the line perfectly.

Writing another set of remarks for the Games, Noonan wanted Reagan to refer to the "gaiety" of the event. She got a phone call. "You have him use the word gaiety," an advance man admonished. "I think you better strike that." Why? "It sounds like he's calling them gay."

"Listen," an exasperated Noonan responded. "I want to tell you something from deep in my heart: *No it doesn't.* No one will think, *no one would ever think*, that the president of the United States would hail our Olympic heroes by accusing them of being homosexual. I promise you this." The advance man conceded the point, and then excised the word.

Reagan won a landslide reelection, carrying forty-nine states, the District of Columbia, and nearly 60 percent of the vote against the hapless Walter Mondale. The victory brought sweeping changes to the administration. During the first term, the White House had been run under the "troika" of chief of staff James Baker; Michael Deaver, who was ostensibly Baker's deputy; and counselor Ed Meese. Baker traded places with Treasury Secretary Donald Regan, and Meese became U.S. Attorney General.

On January 14, 1985, Tony Dolan sent Donald Regan a four-page memo with suggestions on how to handle his new job and what to expect from the conservative camp. "The single greatest mistake made by the current White House leadership—and the single greatest burden they have carried—is their inadequate understanding of the power of conservatism," Dolan wrote. The memo was not only an invitation to Regan but a warning. "When some White House staffers began to encounter heavy flak on the right, most of the time they thought the fire was being orchestrated by personal enemies in their own camp. In fact, their own instincts had made them stumble into hostile territory and they didn't know it. They had no idea they were bucking the tides of history; tides that were in large part the political creation of their own president." If the moderates on the staff were attacked, in other words, it was their own fault for trying to stand athwart history as embodied by Reagan.

"The Conservatives didn't expect to win every battle; but they grew concerned when they met White House aides who did not seem to understand that any final success in changing the ways of the past could only be won by going over the heads of the [encrusted] Washington oligarchy and appealing to the conservative instincts of the people," Dolan noted in what could well have been a cri de coeur. "Instead, they found aides (some of whom had good motives) with a private agenda: to move—through slow calibration or fine-tuning—the President (who ultimately was not moved at all) into the old snares and traps of Washington politics."

In the second term, the dynamics of the tensions between the speechwriters and the senior staff changed. The writers were, as a group, more uniformly Reaganite conservative. Not that Bakshian and Parvin would be considered liberals, but their roots did not lie in the Reagan revolution. By the start of the second term, true believers such as Dolan, Elliott, and Rohrabacher had been joined by Noonan, Peter Robinson, and later in 1985 Josh Gilder.

Robinson, an upstate New York native, had graduated Dartmouth and then spent two years studying at Oxford and a third trying to write a novel there. He gave up the book and looked for a job back in the United States, ending up as Vice President Bush's speechwriter. A year and a half later, in 1983, Robinson joined Reagan's staff. Gilder had succeeded Robinson on Bush's staff. He was an unlikely Reaganaut: His grandfather had been blacklisted as a Communist in the 1950s and his mother, also a Communist, had raised him as one. He brought what he described as "a convert's zeal" to his conservatism. "When you're writing, don't you feel as though you're working on your soul?" he had once asked of Robinson. Gilder's first assignment was a March 1985 challenge to would-be tax raisers in Congress. He borrowed from Clint Eastwood for Reagan: "Go ahead, make my day."

Some tensions and problems the writers encountered were not ideological. Each dealt differently with the perils of the staffing system. "You pretty quickly understood there that writing the speech was a small part of your job," Gilder said. Navigating a draft through the rounds of edits required political skills, negotiations, and compromises. "If you treated it as if these were your magnificent creations, you weren't effective and I didn't feel that you were doing your job," he said. Dolan added, "Speeches could be yanked away from writers if they'd get [too] contentious because there was too much at stake."

As important were the changes outside of the speechwriting staff. Elliott had developed a modus vivendi with Baker and Darman. But with Regan, the senior staff dynamic changed; he was shorter-tempered and more controlling than Baker had been. Access to the president was almost completely closed off. Pushback or end runs that might have been excusable in the first term were no longer so. Surrounding Regan were four aides unflatteringly dubbed "the Mice": Dennis Thomas, Al Kingon, David Chew, and Thomas Dawson. They were loyal to Regan, dismissive of virtually everyone else, brusquely officious, and widely disliked. And they were editing speech drafts.

When Reagan took a ten-day trip to Europe at the start of May 1985, Noonan and Elliott saw an opportunity for him to give a frank, sweeping, philosophical address. In a trip that became known for Reagan's widely criticized visit to Bitburg Cemetery, whose permanent residents included late members of the Nazi SS, Noonan and Elliott wanted his speech to the 434-member European Parliament in Strasbourg, France, to be memorable. The opportunity seemed ripe: The event would mark the fortieth anniversary of V-E Day, May 8, and Reagan would be the first U.S. president to address the assembly.

Noonan, in particular, wanted him to say "serious and thoughtful" things to the people of Europe. Though she had been hired for her skills as an impressionist writer, she was interested in substantive speeches that made serious arguments. "One of the things that has disturbed me about writing for the president in the modern White House is that in a way everyone wants a jazzy speech, and that mostly means they want sloganeering, they want a peppy line," Noonan told an interviewer when she left the White House in 1986. "But they never want to be thoughtful about this stuff. This is true of the pragmatists, but the ideologues too. I'm not interested in lines like 'Evil Empire.'"*

The State Department had sent over a version that discussed Europe in soothing beiges and dull grays, but Noonan wrote a draft in bright colors. "One odd thing about foreign policy professionals is that for all their sophistication, they tend to think the way to communicate with allies and potential allies is to compliment and soothe, compliment and soothe," she noted in her memoir. "But that isn't polite, it's patronizing, and to patronize is to insult. Candor is a compliment, it implies equality, it's how true friends talk."

"I speak as a friend and admirer of the people of Europe, but I am disturbed by what is reported to me about trends in Europe that I have also seen in America," Noonan's draft said. It lauded the powers of the free market system. It condemned those who described the Cold War in terms that implied moral parity between the two sides. "We speak of 'East-West' tensions as if the West and the East were equally responsible for the threat to world peace today." It identified the Soviet Union as the main destabilizing force in the world: "History has taught us a lesson we must never forget: Totalitarians do not stop—they must be stopped."

"It was all unauthorized," Noonan recalled. "But it was administration policy in that it was what the president thought. Having followed his statements and career for years, having seen him in speeches and give-and-take . . . I was clear about what he thought. Send it out this way; it will get changed, but the essential character may remain."

There was a lesson here that she and the other speechwriters had learned: As Noonan told Lesley Stahl of CBS, "There were times when I would write a whole speech with 'red meat,' but I'd really layer it thick in the fourth paragraph. I would know that in staffing they would fixate on that and leave the rest." Gilder recalled that the speechwriters wrote mentions of abortion into every speech, knowing that it and other hot-button issues would be taken out in the staffing process—mostly.

---

*It was an ironic comment given that the March 1983 speech to the evangelists from which "evil empire" came was the kind of broader philosophical exposition of which Noonan was speaking. Her friend Lesley Stahl, the CBS reporter, dubbed Noonan's first draft of the Strasbourg speech "Evil Empire Revisited." (Stahl, *Reporting Live*, 231.)

"Within a speech you knew that ten of these lines were going to come out, so you put in eleven and that's just how you did it," he said.

In the first term, Darman had excised the hottest bits of "red meat" before passing a speech through to the staffing process. But he had joined Baker at the Treasury Department, and Regan had hired Pat Buchanan, the Nixon firebrand, as the communications director. Where Nixon was like an anxious honors student, Buchanan found that Reagan was much more relaxed and would make jokes before press conferences. Depending on Reagan's level of interest he might read speeches as given to him, or "send down long things and a lot of material he wanted in the speech. He was very big on getting facts and figures in there." Buchanan—who did not know that the red meat was often toned down and was sympathetic to the point of view expressed in the speech anyway—passed Noonan's draft through largely unchanged.

Then the alarms started going off. Secretary of State George Shultz told Reagan that the speechwriters were trying to make policy—again—and had to be reined in. Biting memoranda shot around the White House complex: "The draft which has been circulated of the president's speech in Strasbourg will be an unmitigated disaster in Europe if it is delivered in this form," one NSC aide said.

After several rounds of rewrites, a frustrated Noonan sent a caustic missive of her own, writing that under her bureaucratic foes' tender mercies, JFK's "Ich bin ein Berliner" would have be rewritten as, "We in the United States feel our bilateral relations with West Germany reflect a unity that allows us to declare at this time that further concessions to the Soviet Union are inappropriate." She went on: "You would not have been serving your President well with this edit. But you would have made it because a) 'Ich bin . . .' was an inherently dramatic statement, and dramatic personal declarations serve as red flags to Committees (sorry I said 'red,' that must be the 11th communist reference in this memo); b) the Official Worrier on the Committee would have pointed out, 'A statement that strong really paints us in a corner when it comes to negotiations down the road. The press'll pick up on it and use it against us in the trade talks'; and c) the Literal Mind on your Committee would have pointed out, 'The President isn't from Berlin and everyone knows it.'"

The fight spilled over to the daily morning senior staff meeting, where Bud McFarlane exploded at Buchanan, who was befuddled by the whole quarrel. "Speech writers aren't supposed to make policy," McFarlane snapped. Staffers allied with McFarlane leaked the whole story to *The Washington Post*, explaining that he wanted a "thoughtful and reflective speech" on U.S.-Soviet relations. And, as a final irony, the unnamed officials held up Reagan's 1982 speech at Westminster—in which he had said that freedom and democracy would leave the Soviet system on the "ash heap of history"—as the model of "presidential-type" non-confrontation.

In the end, McFarlane rewrote the speech, replacing the bulk of Noonan's text with one of his own that was couched in mild diplomatic language. "The United States does not seek to undermine or change the Soviet system," Reagan told the Parliament in what must have been news to anyone who had ever heard him denounce that system as "evil." As witty, and justified, as her ripostes may have been, Noonan had lost control of the draft. Reagan ended up giving a speech that was more noticed for his TelePrompTer malfunctioning than for its content.

Buchanan sensed a "potentially serious problem" in Reagan's speeches, he wrote to Regan in a December 9 memo marked "Administratively Confidential." Reagan's speech on November 14, 1985, before leaving for the Geneva summit with Soviet leader Mikhail Gorbachev, had elicited 150 phone calls and 42 telegrams, "an astonishing expression of public nonchalance about a Reagan address to the nation just prior to the most important summit of his presidency," Buchanan wrote. A talk Reagan gave at Fallston High School in Maryland had not been interrupted for applause once.

"Stated simply, both speeches were crashing bores," Buchanan wrote. He cited two problems. While Reagan and McFarlane had settled on a theme of "optimism, tempered by realism, hope modified by caution," he wrote, "the 'realism,' the 'caution,' have been consistently carved out to such an extent that not only is the President puzzling his audiences . . . but he is also beginning to elicit a measure of ridicule."

The problem lay in the speeches having been hijacked not only by

NSC interference on substance and tone, but by stylistic tinkering by the Mice. The pre-summit speech had been originally drafted as a tough, traditional Reagan, anti-Communist address. Regan's aides had rewritten it in a lower key, with the president talking about cultural exchanges, envisioning "Soviet children watching 'Sesame Street'"—an image that prompted the conservative *Washington Times* to describe it as being full of "infantile hopes."

"Now, admittedly a couple of fairly competent house painters can tell you why Michelangelo's work is cracked and peeling," Buchanan wrote. "Still, you don't want a pair of house painters re-doing the Sistine Chapel." In the future, he suggested, all of the usual suspects should be consulted, but they should "<u>leave the word-smithing to folks who do that for a living</u>."

Buchanan's memo made little impact, as staff conflicts built to a crescendo in the run-up to the 1986 State of the Union address, which the president was scheduled to deliver on January 28. Elliott and Gilder submitted a first draft on January 15. The Mice thought the speech was disjointed and overly ideological. "It didn't meet the specs," Regan complained. After two days, they sent out a "Draft Revised." Long sections of the original on the march of freedom, the importance of free markets, the evils of communism, and praise of family values were diluted, reduced, or eliminated. An early applause line in the original draft, "America is ready," was changed to "America is back!"—which Reagan had used in the 1984 State of the Union. Banality or gibberish was inserted: "We cannot perpetuate these problems no longer," the revised draft read. "I believe the President is being badly served by such high-handedness," Elliott wrote in a note. Buchanan called Regan at home, furious.

"This speech doesn't read like a Ronald Reagan speech," domestic policy aide Jack Svahn wrote in a memo to Elliott, mistakenly thinking that the speechwriters had produced the revised draft. "There isn't that quick, sharp, crisp approach. It looks almost as if it gets started in some places and then mushes down or loses a few sentences. . . . Clearly I'm not a great speechwriter and you are, but this just doesn't sound like a Reagan speech, it doesn't hang together and flow the way it should." Elliott passed the memo on to Regan's aides with a note written in the corner saying that the authors of the redraft deserved Svahn's "kudos. You have done a great disservice to the President."

Buchanan, Elliott, and Gilder rewrote the speech, but the row over the drafting spilled into the media. The two sides "have resorted to name-calling," *The New York Times* reported, "with aides to Mr. Buchanan suggesting that the Regan associates lack political courage, while Mr. Regan's aides call Mr. Buchanan's speechwriters politically naïve hard-liners." *Newsweek* said that "the very tone of the Reagan message" was at stake. Would it be "conservative evangelism or board-room bromides?"* One "insider" told the magazine that the Mice "don't trust the speechwriters. They say everything they write is about abortion and right-wing stuff. And the speechwriters think Regan's men are philistines."

The president was typically removed from the fray. He lightly edited the "Draft Revised,"—changing "American is back!" to "America is moving!"—and subsequent drafts. Ever the movie buff, he inserted a line quoting from the current popular *Back to the Future* that "where we're going we won't need roads."

Reagan was in the Oval Office with spokesman Larry Speakes on the morning of January 28, preparing for his scheduled lunch with the network anchors—a routine on the day of the annual address, to spin them for their coverage—when Vice President Bush rushed in, followed by Buchanan and new national security adviser John Poindexter. "Sir, the *Challenger* just blew up!" Buchanan said, interrupting the vice president. Reagan, standing by the fireplace, looked at his aide and asked, isn't that the one the teacher is on? Christa McAuliffe, the first civilian astronaut, was indeed a passenger on the flight. The men moved into the small office off the Oval and watched on TV as debris fell from billowy smoke into the ocean off the Florida coast.

Noonan was on the phone when Elliott's assistant rushed in and

---

*The *Newsweek* story was written by Walter Shapiro, the former Carter speechwriter. "For five years the White House speechwriters have loyally labored in obscurity," he wrote with some sympathy. "Their words have been the glue that helps bind Ronald Reagan with the American people. That's why the flap over the State of the Union Message cannot be dismissed as much ado about adverbs." (Shapiro, with Margaret Garrard Warner and Thomas DeFrank, "Of Mice and Metaphors," *Newsweek*, February 3, 1986.)

gave her the news. Elliott's seven-year-old daughter was also in the office and asked if the teacher was all right. Noonan, reporter training taking over—"handle the horror by writing the show"—started typing. NSC spokeswoman Karna Small had been with Reagan when he got the news and had taken notes on his reaction. She sent them over to Noonan. "What can you say? It's a horrible thing. I can't rid myself of the thought of the sacrifice of the families of the people on board," Reagan said. Asked what he wanted to say to the children, he said: "Pioneers have always given their lives on the frontier. The problem is that it's more of a shock to all as we see it happening, not just hear something miles away—but we must make it clear that life goes on."

Noonan worked quickly and was soon with Buchanan, the Mice, Speakes, and Regan in the chief of staff's office. No one except Buchanan liked the speech. "Did you see how he held it?" Buchanan later said of one of the Mice. "Like a dog had relieved himself on it!" Noonan was depressed, but on the up side there was also no time for a full round of staffing. She had concluded the remarks by quoting from John Gillespie Magee's poem, "High Flight," saying that the astronauts had " 'slipped the surly bonds of earth' to 'touch the face of God.'" One pudgy young NSC staffer, apparently inspired by the old telephone jingle, tried to rework the line to read that the astronauts had slipped the surly bonds to "reach out and touch someone—touch the face of God." Noonan thought that it was the worst edit she encountered at the White House.

"The crew of the space shuttle Challenger honored us by the manner in which they lived their lives," Reagan said, closing his brief televised remarks to the nation that evening. "We will never forget them, nor the last time we saw them, this morning, as they prepared for their journey and waved goodbye and 'slipped the surly bonds of earth' to 'touch the face of God.'"

Reagan gave his State of the Union address on February 4. Not too long afterward the speechwriters met with Regan in his office. Pollster Richard Wirthlin briefed them on which words and phrases had tested well, and then talk turned to the editing process: Some of the speeches were being rewritten after the president had signed off on them, the writers complained. The integrity of the process was being compromised, one said. Regan was on his feet—and screaming: You're questioning my integrity! "It was a non sequitur," Rohrabacher recalled. "I was shocked that someone who held so much responsibility was acting in an irrational, arrogant, egotistical way. But that reflected his whole approach to people." Noonan thought it was all an act—"his voice was hot but his face was cool."

Act or uncontrolled outburst, it signaled Regan's boiling point ire with the writers. In March, he instructed Buchanan to fire Elliott, whom he viewed as a troublemaker. Buchanan liked Elliott and delayed until Regan told him again in early April. The specific cause was a mystery to the speechwriters, who mostly came to believe that Elliott had slipped one draft too many past Regan and into the Oval Office. Talking to a *New York Times* reporter, Elliott pointed to the long string of speech conflicts that, the paper reported, "had surfaced on almost all of Mr. Reagan's major policy statements." Administration officials denied to the paper that Elliott had been sacked, though one of Regan's aides told *The Washington Post*'s Lou Cannon that Elliott had been fired because he was troublesome.

"Every time Ben fought the bureaucracy to get the right draft to Reagan—to get the president's own conservative views to him—Ben made an enemy," Noonan wrote years later. "He faced a million swords, and without bureaucratic protection. In politics, friends come and go but enemies accumulate. By the time the bad guys got him, Ben looked like a human pincushion." She seethed at his callous dismissal and laid the blame not only outside the writing shop but inside, blasting colleagues she viewed as disloyal and incompetent. "There's no doubt about it, the speechwriting shop, our shop, always had its own problems inside it and tensions there," Buchanan recalled. He pushed Noonan to replace Elliott, but Regan vetoed it. She departed the staff shortly thereafter as well. Elliott's departure left the staff chastened: For all of the squabbles they had been in, none of their number had been fired, and some thought that as keepers of the ideological flame they had been protected.

Most suspected that the president did not know about Elliott's dismissal. When Elliott had his farewell photograph with Reagan in May, he resolved to tell him. "Mr. President, it's a great honor to work for you, I'm not leaving of my own accord," Elliott said.* He told Noonan that the president replied, "Oh," and recoiled as if Elliott were brandishing a weapon. Elliott later told Lou Cannon that Reagan had responded, "I didn't know that."

Writing in his diary, Reagan betrayed no knowledge of the firing. "A photo with the speechwriters & staff," he wrote on May 22. "They're a great bunch. Ben Elliott—head man is leaving. We're thinking of giving the job to Jim Brady [severely wounded during the 1981 assassination attempt] whose Dr. says it would be good for him to have more to do." In early 2006, Nancy Reagan telephoned Landon Parvin and asked whether he had known about Elliott's dismissal. When he said yes, she replied that she and Ronnie had had no idea, and asked Parvin to relay the message to Elliott.

"The Groundhog saw his shadow!" Reagan wrote in his diary on February 2, 1987. "Pat [Buchanan] is leaving us and I've told Don R. to see if we can augment the speech writers by bringing back Landon Parvin." Two days later, Reagan personally called Parvin to discuss the idea.

Parvin did not rejoin the White House speechwriting staff, but he would return for specific speeches. He got another phone call around February 26, when the Tower Commission report examining the Iran-Contra affair was released to the public. The president wanted Parvin to come back and work on the speech he would give to the nation on March 4 explaining his role in the scheme that had sold arms to a hostile country, Iran, in the hopes of springing hostages in Lebanon, and had then used profits from the sales to illegally fund the Contra revolutionaries in Nicaragua.

Parvin thought that perhaps Nancy Reagan, for whom he had written some speeches and with whom he had a good relationship, was re-

---

*Peggy Noonan quotes him as being more blunt: "Mr. President, I hope you know I was fired." (Noonan, *What I Saw*, 293.)

sponsible for his summons.* He thought that she wanted someone she could trust from outside the White House because "There were shades of Watergate [in terms of] who knew what on the White House staff and when," he recalled. Parvin telephoned her and asked who he could trust. She told him David Abshire, the former U.S. ambassador to NATO who had recently been appointed as White House counselor coordinating the response to the Iran-Contra scandal. At some point, he told the first lady, he would need to talk to the president.

Parvin started consulting with people inside or close to the administration and with those whose judgment he respected: White House spokesman Marlin Fitzwater (who had replaced Speakes); Treasury Secretary Baker; pollster Wirthlin; deputy national security adviser Colin Powell; and even Richard Cheney, the former chief of staff to Gerald Ford, who was now a member of Congress. At day's end on Friday, February 27, Parvin went to the White House to meet with the president.

Parvin and Stuart Spencer, Reagan's longtime political adviser, rode up the elevator together to the White House residence. John Tower himself was awaiting them when the elevator doors opened—he had been snuck into the White House because he was more knowledgeable than anyone else about the contents of his commission's report. The three men would have to convince the president of the gravity of his situation—and Parvin would have to figure out what Reagan should say in the speech. The three huddled with the president in the residence sitting room. Mrs. Reagan floated in and out.

"At one point Tower was just very straight with him about the problem he was facing and advised him to get counsel because it could have been impeachment," Parvin recalled. Reagan said that it was not until he started reading the footnotes of the report that he realized how much was going on without his knowledge. When the president started to thank Tower for his work on the report, Tower began to weep.

Parvin's biggest problem, however, was that Reagan could not accept the fact that his administration had traded arms for hostages.

---

*On other occasions, most notably Reagan's May 31, 1987, speech on AIDS, Parvin was brought back for ideological reasons. "It was the first time the president ever spoke about AIDS," Parvin recalled. "Mrs. Reagan was worried that it might go too far right [if written in the speechwriting office], so I was brought back to do that." (Author interview with Landon Parvin.)

Parvin struck upon a formulation that matched both the facts as Reagan saw them, and as everyone else did: "A few months ago I told the American people I did not trade arms for hostages," Reagan said on March 4. "My heart and my best intentions still tell me that's true, but the facts and the evidence tell me it is not."

Reagan edited the speech lightly, making small deletions or insertions. Over the course of his two terms, the amount of his own writing inserted into speeches and the level of editing that he did had diminished. There were exceptions—he substantially wrote his speech upon returning from the October 1986 Reykjavik summit—but the scope of speeches that inspired Reagan to his previous level of engagement was narrowing.

There are a number of explanations. Rohrabacher argued that the speechwriters had learned to write in Reagan's style and that "If the President had to add in a lot of stuff or had to correct things and put it in another style, we felt that we were failures." And Bakshian argued that it was a function of having moved through much of his agenda. "That's just the natural progression of a presidency," he said. "That is, setting the tone and articulating your basic thoughts and goals happens at the outset for the most part, especially with a man who had chosen some fairly basic objectives that were coherent and were fairly easily articulated if you were articulate.... Part of it is getting disengaged, but part of it is getting sucked into the daily routine of a presidency." The extent to which his age and health played a role in this process is unknowable.

"Our wedding anniversary," Reagan noted in his diary on March 4. "Nancy says my speech tonite is her present from me." After the speech, he recorded that there were more phone calls than for any other speech and that they had run 93 percent positive. "Even the TV bone pickers who follow the speech with their commentaries said nice things about it," he commented.

The United States and Soviet Union had made lurching progress toward détente in the mid-1980s. Reagan met Mikhail Gorbachev at the Vienna summit in late 1985, which was viewed as a success. The summit at Reykjavik in 1986, however, was seen as a failure after Reagan broke off talks over his cherished anti-missile system. But negotiations were moving forward over an Intermediate Nuclear Forces treaty;* and, more broad, Gorbachev was starting to push reforms of the Soviet system.

In late April, Peter Robinson traveled to West Berlin. Reagan would be going there as part of an early June European trip, and Robinson had gotten the assignment of writing the remarks he would give in front of the Brandenburg Gate and Berlin Wall. He went over with the advance team to get a feel of the setting. Robinson's first stop was a meeting with John Kornblum, the ranking U.S. diplomat in the city. He struck Robinson as being anxious over the prospect of Reagan visiting Berlin. He gave the speechwriter a list of things the president should *not* say. There should be no chest-thumping or truculent language. And don't say anything about the Wall, Kornblum warned, the locals were long accustomed to it.

That night, Robinson dined at the home of a local couple, Dieter and Ingeborg Elz, a pair of German retirees. Dieter had worked at the World Bank in Washington. They had invited other Berliners over so that Robinson could get a sense of local sentiments. Discussion covered an array of topics, according to Robinson's notes, including the economy (unemployment was a problem, one guest said, adding that the United States should try to make the city more attractive for American companies), attitudes toward the United States ("Anti-Americanism in universities is long gone"), and the East-West atmosphere ("Lack of enthusiasm, compared to J.F.K., shows, in a way, normalcy, success," he wrote in his notes. "Difference between J.F.K. and now: No <u>immediate</u> danger. This gone compared to ultimatum of Khrushchev"). A guest named Strauch said of the division of the city: "750 years [the age of Berlin] a long time in German history. 45 years of separation is almost nothing. The division is one we do not recognize."

Robinson asked about the Wall directly, he later wrote, and brought the conversation to a stop. "Then one man raised an arm and pointed. 'My sister lives twenty miles in that direction,' he said. 'I haven't seen her in more than two decades. Do you think I can get used to that?'" Others chimed in. Each morning on his way to work, another guest related that he passed the same soldier atop the Wall. "That soldier and I speak the same language," the guest said. "We share the same history. But one of us

---

*The treaty would be signed in December at a summit meeting in Washington, D.C.

is a zookeeper and the other is an animal, and I am never certain which is which." Finally the hostess, Ingeborg Elz, red-faced, pounded her fist into her open palm. "If this man Gorbachev is serious with his talk of *glasnost* and *perestroika*," she said, "he can prove it. He can get rid of this wall."

Jotting swiftly, Robinson noted: "If the Russians are willing to open up, then the wall must go. Open the Brandenburg Gate." He wrote so fast that he mistakenly attributed the comment to Strauch. The idea of getting rid of the Wall "represented a sudden illumination, almost a detonation," he later said.

Robinson had the core of Reagan's speech: Get rid of the Wall. Returning to Washington, he started writing and rewriting. He had trouble getting the phrasing precisely right. Over the weeks leading up to the speech, he tried different variations of the key sentence. One draft had: "Herr Gorbachev, bring down this wall." Another: "Herr Gorbachev, machen Sie diesses Tor auf,"* which translated to "Mr. Gorbachev, open this gate." The next: "Come here, to this gate. Herr Gorbachev, reissen Sie diese Mauer neider," which translated to "Mr. Gorbachev, tear down this wall." Another draft combined the German exhortation to open the gate with the English one to tear down the Wall. That survived until a week before the speech was to be delivered.

Dolan, director of speechwriting since Elliott's departure, realized that while talking about tearing down the Wall might appeal to Reagan, it would cause a furor with the foreign policy establishment and White House staff. Robinson and he both knew that if they were not careful, the president might never see the line—it would be taken out by staffers before it reached the president. Dolan held a war council of the speechwriting staff: This is going to be the toughest fight we've ever had, he told them. They alerted all of their allies inside and outside the administration who had any influence. "We knew that there would be volcanic explosions" among the moderates when they saw the language, Rohrabacher recalled.

---

*There was internal administration discussion about whether to include German in the speech—Reagan might mispronounce and it would require a great deal of rehearsal, communications director Tom Griscom recalled. The final speech did contain some German. (Author interview with Tom Griscom.)

The Berlin stop was one on a nine-day trip. The speechwriters all worked to get their drafts done at the same time, but Dolan waited until late on Friday, May 15, before sending them out for the president's weekend reading material. The speechwriters reasoned that the senior staff would not be able to read through the whole pile of speeches before Reagan left for the weekend. The other speeches were in effect a convoy for the Berlin Wall speech.

The following Monday, the writers met with the president in the Oval Office to discuss the speeches. The great hope at each such meeting was that Reagan would engage on a topic and give the writer something he could drop into a speech. Josh Gilder had been tapped to write the speech at the Vatican, and he asked the president what role he thought religion might play in reforming Eastern Europe. Reagan engaged, and Gilder used his remarks almost verbatim as a couple of paragraphs in the speech.* Robinson told the president that the broadcast of his Berlin speech would reach into East Germany and the Soviet Union, possibly as far as Moscow, and wondered if there was anything the president would like to say. Reagan cocked his head and thought. "Well, there's that passage about tearing down the wall," he said. "That wall has to come down. That's what I'd like to say to them."†

---

*When Gilder's speech was staffed out, it came back from the State Department with the section entirely crossed out. Upon asking why, he was told that it was inappropriate to use so much language about God. "So much language about God?" the incredulous speechwriter replied. "The President will be talking to the *Pope*." Told that the verbiage had come straight from the president, the State bureaucrat relented, but added that he wanted State to be "on the record" as objecting to the speech. (Author interview with Josh Gilder.)

†Dolan and Tom Griscom have slightly differing memories of the origin of "Tear down this wall." Dolan recalls that he, Griscom, Robinson, and Colin Powell met with Reagan in the Oval Office in April, before Robinson had written any drafts, possibly before Robinson had gone to Germany. Before Robinson could suggest the Wall coming down, Reagan, asked what he wanted in the speech, said, "Well, tear down this wall." The Reagan Library has a Dolan memo to Reagan dated June 15 where he writes: "We're grateful for your kind words about the Berlin draft which I've passed along to Peter Robinson. In view of all you told us about what you wanted in Berlin—including the outline and the killer lines you gave us—it was particularly generous of you." However, neither Robinson nor Griscom remembers Reagan originating the line. "There was prompting," Griscom said. His recollection of the May 18 meeting was that Reagan had not yet seen a draft of the speech, that at most there was an outline, but probably it was all verbal. (Author interviews with Dolan, Robinson, and Griscom.)

Robinson was crushed. He wanted a new pearl, not a rehash of what was already in the speech. He did not immediately realize that Reagan had given him a key tool: with the presidential imprimatur, he could withstand pressure to excise the phrase. And there was pressure: as the speech came back from successive rounds of staffing, the section would be scratched out by the NSC or State. Or it would be changed: Kornblum, the Berlin diplomat, suggested: "One day, this ugly wall will disappear." What did that mean, Robinson wondered, "That the wall would just get up and slink off of its own accord?"

On June 1, the National Security Council's Colin Powell sent a memorandum to White House communications director Tom Griscom about the speech. "We still believe that some important thematic passages (e.g., pp. 6–7 [which contained the key line]) are wrong," he wrote. Powell and the others worried that it would be an affront to Gorbachev and ruin the budding good relations with the Soviets. They asked: Would we like it if Gorbachev came to the United States and told us what to do?* On several occasions, Griscom took the question back to the president—he told Reagan that there were many objections to the line and asked whether he was sure that he wanted it in. At one point he brought the president the murkier State Department language, causing Reagan to roll his eyes.

Griscom was summoned to the office of White House chief of staff Howard Baker—who had replaced Regan in February 1987, and thought the line "unpresidential"—where Secretary of State George Shultz was waiting. Progress has been made with the Soviets, Shultz said, and this could reverse it or end it entirely. Griscom stood his ground: He had heard Reagan read the line out loud, he said, and knew the president wanted it. It will work, he said.

There were further attempts to remove the line even after the president had left Washington for his European trip, but Reagan remained

---

*Concern about Soviet sensitivities could reach absurd levels. Josh Gilder recalled that descriptions of the Soviets as "Communist" were often edited out of speeches. "That was always a struggle, even to say 'Communist'—even in the Reagan administration. But in the culture at large it was just something that wasn't done—needlessly provocative. And of course they called themselves Communists and knew pretty exactly what they were about." (Author interview with Gilder.)

steadfast. "The boys at State are going to kill me," he told deputy chief of staff Ken Duberstein, "but it's the right thing to do."

Reagan could hear anger in his own voice as he spoke the key lines. His ire was not directed at Gorbachev but rather at the East German police. Just before he spoke, they had forced people on their side of the Wall away from the loudspeakers so that they could not hear him.

"There is one sign the Soviets can make that would be unmistakable, that would advance dramatically the cause of freedom and peace," Reagan said, stumbling over "dramatically."

> *General Secretary Gorbachev, if you seek peace, if you seek prosperity for the Soviet Union and Eastern Europe, if you seek liberalization: Come here to this gate. Mr. Gorbachev, open this gate [he paused while twenty-five seconds of the crowd's cheers spent themselves]. Mr. Gorbachev, tear down this wall!*

When Josh Gilder went to Moscow in 1988, it elicited little reaction from the Washington bureaucrats, but he did have a run-in with the Soviet variety. Gilder was writing the speech Reagan would give at Moscow State University on his May trip for a summit there. Reagan and Gorbachev had signed the Intermediate Nuclear Forces Treaty in December in Washington, and now the president was preparing for a victory lap in Moscow. The speech at the university would be the showcase of the trip.

The Moscow University building struck Gilder as being out of a "science fiction nightmare"—grim, scary, totalitarian architecture. A school official showed him the auditorium, which was dominated by a mural celebrating the October Revolution; in front was a huge bust of Lenin. You're going to have to move the bust and cover the mural, Gilder told the school official. Ronald Reagan giving a speech in front of a bust of Lenin—was the guy joking? The school official looked distraught. He excused himself to check, leaving Gilder alone with his thoughts. The more he pondered, the more he thought that it actually would be pretty amazing for Ronald Reagan to stand in front of those icons and deliver a speech about freedom. The functionary was overjoyed when Gilder told him to leave the mural and Lenin where they were.

"Standing here before a mural of your revolution, I want to talk about a very different revolution that is taking place right now, quietly sweeping the globe without bloodshed or conflict," Reagan told the students at Moscow State University on May 31, 1988.

Its effects are peaceful, but they will fundamentally alter our world, shatter old assumptions, and reshape our lives. It's easy to underestimate because it's not accompanied by banners or fanfare. It's been called the technological or information revolution, and as its emblem, one might take the tiny silicon chip, no bigger than a fingerprint. One of these chips has more computing power than a roomful of old-style computers.

"Dear Mr. President, these are my thoughts."

At the end of 1988 Reagan was preparing to leave the White House, handing over the government to President-elect George H. W. Bush. Peggy Noonan had been given one last chance to work with her hero, much to the irritation of others still in the administration who wanted to write the final speech. Reagan had asked for her help with his hail and farewell, and she had written him a letter to start him thinking. He should find new ways to say old things, she told him, and he should think of the speech as a "tone poem aimed at subtly reminding people what a giant you are." For the first time since JFK, the American people were losing a president that they could love.

"They love you, Mr. President, but you're still a mystery man to them in some respects," she wrote. "We're going to reveal more of you than they've seen in the past, mostly by talking about big things in a personal and anecdotal way."

"They" were the American people, but "they" were also Peggy Noonan. For eight years, Ronald Reagan's speechwriters had had diminishing access to a president who was remote from even his closest aides. He had presented a clear ideology and style so they had gotten his voice even though they might go months without seeing him. They knew him and in many cases they loved him. But he remained a mystery.

Noonan met with Reagan five times in December 1988 and January 1989. He had sat amiably as she laid out her vision of the speech—

"a sort of Jim Cagney kind of view," Mari Maseng, back as the communications director, recalled—but did not like it. They worked out a theme and Noonan wrote. She spent a week working on a couple of poetic endings to the speech, one about the magic of the White House and one about the city on the hill. "But at the end I admitted to myself: both endings had more to do with me than RR," she wrote to Maseng on January 1.

Next to this part of the note, she had written in the margin, "I got to know him," but then scratched it out. In her memoir, she noted: "The attempt to elicit some kernel of unknown information yielded little. I would never know him, but now I thought I knew why. He did not need to be known. He did not need to ease his loneliness, if that is what he had."

On January 11, 1989, Noonan sat in the Oval Office. For the first time, she was going to watch Reagan deliver a speech in person there. As technicians bustled around, he started reading his speech out loud: even the great ones have to practice. Then, just before airtime, he nodded his head down and closed his eyes. "What is he doing?" Noonan asked Maseng. "He's praying," the communications director responded. He opened his eyes, lifted his head, and with a wink toward the two women, began:

> I've spoken of the shining city all my political life, but I don't know if I ever quite communicated what I saw when I said it. But in my mind it was a tall, proud city built on rocks stronger than oceans, windswept, God-blessed, and teeming with people of all kinds living in harmony and peace; a city with free ports that hummed with commerce and creativity. And if there had to be city walls, the walls had doors and the doors were open to anyone with the will and the heart to get here. That's how I saw it, and see it still.

Noonan got her city on the hill after all.

Ronald Reagan was known as the "Great Communicator," and had a deep appreciation of the power of words. Especially at the start of his tenure in the White House, he spent a great deal of time carefully selecting and honing those words. But there was often conflict in the process that produced those words—a surprising amount for an administration so well known for its powerful rhetoric and clear style.

The running tension between the ideologue speechwriters and the pragmatic senior staffers—whether in its constructive period in the first term under Baker and Darman or during its destructive phase under Regan and the Mice—remains a fascinating aspect of his administration. Each side was sure that it was right: The conservative speechwriters were simply trying to give back to Reagan what he had been saying for thirty years. The moderates composed most of Reagan's inner circle and spent hours with him daily. "Reagan at the time shared the political realism of his aides," Lou Cannon wrote. "He placed a high premium on success throughout his various careers, and he often complained that some of his erstwhile conservative supporters wanted to go 'off the cliff with all flags flying.'"

Several speechwriters came to see Reagan's hidden hand at work in the setup. "When I look back now I see the tensions of those times as the consequence of critical but competing priorities that Reagan himself set in motion and allowed to persist," Ben Elliott said. "The priorities of the Baker/Darman group were to govern successfully. The speechwriters were mindful of the responsibility but sought to rally the country and the world around the president's larger vision of the boundless possibilities of freedom, free ideas and free people."

Clark Judge, a Harvard Business School graduate who joined the staff in 1986 after writing for Vice President Bush—following the path trod by Peter Robinson and Josh Gilder before him—surmised that Reagan was using a technique he picked up from his days as president of the Screen Actors Guild. Reagan had taken the Guild on strike and had learned the art of negotiation with the union. The true believers "help Reagan stake out his positions," Judge argued. "And where do the pragmatists come in? They help Reagan cut his deals. . . . It's not that we're right and they're wrong or that they're right and we're wrong. Reagan is very deliberately using us both."

"I'm Not Going to Dance on the Berlin Wall"

SUMMER 1988

"Know where I want to go—have the experience to get there—jobs, peace, education," Vice President George H. W. Bush wrote to his campaign speechwriter, Peggy Noonan. And: "My background is one thing . . . I've worked, I've fought for my country, I've served, I've built—I want to lead." In the summer of 1988, trying to capture the White House himself, Bush sent Noonan a stream of notes and thoughts to prepare for his speech accepting his party's presidential nomination. "Others may speak better, look better, be smoother, more creative but I must be myself. I want you to know my heartbeat—this is where I'd lead."

He sent a list of words that had special meaning for him. It included "kindness," "caring," "decency," and "heart"—words that inspired Noonan to write a sentence into a draft of the speech that read: "I wanted a kinder nation." Bush scribbled "gentler" in next to it.

Bush's desire for a "kinder, gentler" America was one of three lines in his convention address that lingered in the public memory longer than almost anything he said as president. Senior campaign officials resisted "kinder, gentler" and the comparison of the groups that make up America to "a thousand points of light in a broad and peaceful sky,"* thinking the lines sounded soft. Not Richard Darman, the former Reagan administration official who would become Bush's budget director—"Make sure that is always in," he said of the points of light.

Darman had his own reasons: He hoped Noonan might reciprocate by helping remove the "Read my lips: No new taxes" line. Echoing Clint Eastwood, it would make Bush look tough. But Darman thought a president should not lock himself into such a position, and he argued that the line would sound inauthentic coming from Bush. "From the perspective of the campaign, however—down by ten points—I was indulging in the fantasy of governing without attending to the prior imperative of winning," he later wrote. The line stayed in.

Charges that the Democratic nominee, Massachusetts governor Michael Dukakis, was soft on crime, insufficiently patriotic, and a tax-raising liberal combined with Ronald Reagan's enduring popularity and, of course, "Read my lips . . ." to carry Bush to 53 percent of the vote and 426 electoral votes on November 8, 1988.

He met with his speechwriters in the Roosevelt Room early in his term and spoke about what he expected in speeches, what he liked, what he did not like. He gave the writers three rules. The first was that he did not like the word "I." "He didn't want to say, 'I want a crime bill that's going to stop crime,' because he thought that was disrespectful to the police who actually had to put their lives on the line," recalled Mary Kate Grant, whose job was writing magazine articles under the president's byline. The second rule was that they should not write speeches that were too emotional. "If you give me a ten, I'm going to send it back and say, 'Give me an eight,'" Grant recalled Bush saying. "And you'll be lucky if I deliver like a six." Bush's third rule was that the writers should use a lot of Yogi Berra quotes. I would rather quote Yogi Berra than Thomas Jefferson, he said.

---

*"Why a thousand?" Noonan wrote. "I don't know. A thousand clowns, a thousand days—a hundred wasn't enough and a million is too many." (Noonan, *What I Saw at the Revolution*, 312.)

One of the writers asked him who else he liked to quote. Eisenhower, he said, and Mark Twain. Bush said that he wanted them to write his speeches imagining that they were addressing an audience in Lubbock, Texas—a typical middle-America town. He wanted things written in a clear, direct manner. "The president detested anything that smacked of the florid or the smarmily insincere," speechwriter Mark Davis recalled. Bush specifically said that he did not like the way Lyndon Johnson had used "my fellow Americans."

Bush told them a story about Ronald Reagan. Vice President Bush had been going with Reagan to an event and as they were getting into the limousine an aide handed Reagan his speech cards, apologizing for their lateness. "No problem," Reagan said, and read through the cards, marking them for pauses and emphasis. Bush asked if this was the first time he had seen the remarks. "Yes," Reagan replied, "but it will be okay, don't worry about it." At the event Reagan knocked the speech out of the ballpark.

"I am not President Reagan," Bush told his speechwriters. I couldn't be if I wanted to. Reagan was acknowledged as a master of speechmaking—he was the "Great Communicator." And his administration had revolutionized the art of presidential stagecraft—consciously arranging events to showcase a specific sound bite or image. Bush and his top advisers did not attach the same value to speechmaking that Reagan had. In the Bush administration, image would flow from substance—no special crafting would be required.* "He felt that he would be judged—and should be judged—on actions and on decisions and on policies," recalled David Demarest, Bush's communications director. "This kind of atmosphere of you're going to be a successful or not successful president depends on how [good] of an orator you are—he just didn't buy into that. It wasn't in his DNA."

Neither was practicing speeches. Davis asked Bush once whether he

---

*Bush admired and respected his predecessor, as did his senior advisers, but as this substance-over-style attitude filtered out from the inner circle, it became in some cases a "condescension that was stunningly unattractive," speechwriter Curt Smith said. He would sometimes get speech drafts back in which a few sentences would be crossed out by a midlevel staffer with the notation "sounds like Reagan," or "Too much like Reagan. Take it out." (Author interview with Curt Smith.)

read speeches out loud before delivering them, and Bush said no. Davis asked if the president thought about how he wanted a speech to sound when he delivered it, and again Bush said no, that that would take too long.

The composition of the speechwriting team was also an intentional departure from its Reagan counterpart. As a public affairs official at the Department of Labor during the Reagan administration, Demarest had concluded that Reagan's speechwriters were out of control: leaking to the press, having too high a profile, and worst of all trying to drive their own policy agenda. For Bush, he had put together a group of writers that would not run amok or push their own agendas.

The staff was headed by Chriss Winston, with whom Demarest had worked at Labor. Winston had held a variety of political communications jobs, including on Representative James Leach of Iowa's staff and during the Reagan administration at the Occupational Safety and Health Administration, before joining Labor. She did little writing but assigned speeches and edited drafts. She was the first woman to head a presidential speechwriting office.

Mark Davis, a former reporter, had written speeches for Republican National Committee chairman Frank Fahrenkopf. Davis quickly figured out that Bush would engage more on foreign policy because he found it more interesting than domestic matters. A foreign policy speech would often begin with a meeting with the president, but domestic policy speeches almost invariably began with a meeting with a policy aide. Davis resolved to focus on foreign policy addresses. Davis's turn of mind tended to run toward conspiracies, and as a writer he was fastidious: he would sweat over each word, at times wandering the halls with the text until Winston corralled him and forced him to give it up.

Curt Smith had written for Richard Schweiker at the Department of Health and Human Services and "Silent" Samuel Pierce at the Department of Housing and Urban Development. He was the most conservative member of the writing staff, envisioning an America of the *Saturday Evening Post* (where he had been an editor), baseball (about which he had written several books), and "Mayberry, USA," which he would refer to in speeches, until Winston edited them out—"I'm not going to have the president of the United States quote Barney Fife on my watch!" she would say.* Smith specialized in speeches that appealed to the conservative base of the GOP—rallying-type addresses that touched on values issues and conservative philosophy.

Dan McGroarty, who in the Reagan years had written speeches for Secretaries of Defense Caspar Weinberger and Frank Carlucci, had previously worked at Voice of America. The Defense background helped him write many of the Persian Gulf War speeches. And he was a natural leader: He was, recalled speechwriter Ken Askew, who joined the staff in 1992, "the guy you want to be captain of the baseball team. Brainy—he'd be the catcher."

Also at the meeting with Bush on January 21 was Mary Kate Grant, who wrote magazine articles for Bush. She had studied foreign affairs at the University of Virginia and had expected to pursue a State Department career, but in between passing the Foreign Service exam and actually getting a diplomatic job, she ended up working for the Bush presidential campaign. She had joined when he trailed in the polls and thought that she could resume her career track once the election was over. Instead, she ended up in the White House. By the start of March, she would be writing speeches as well and eventually joined the staff officially.

Two men who were not at that first meeting joined the staff within a few weeks. Ed McNally had worked on Bush's presidential primary campaign in 1980. Eight years later, he was a federal prosecutor in New York when he contacted Winston about writing speeches. "He had a real writing gift for writing unlike a lawyer," Demarest recalled. "He was somebody that I think really saw it as a wonderful craft. And he had a very strong ego to go with it. He'd really argue for his approach in language—very effectively." And he was the staff bon vivant: he had the Irish blarney, would roller-skate to work and through the halls of the Executive Office Building, and wore sunglasses around the office.

Like Bush, McNally was a Yale graduate, and had been a member of the school's mysterious Skull and Bones Society. Members are required

---

*Mayberry was the fictitious, idyllic small town that was the setting for *The Andy Griffith Show*; the dedication to Smith's book on presidential libraries, *Windows on the White House*, reads: "To the America that is Mayberry."

to leave the room at the mention of the group's name, so Davis enjoyed occasionally mentioning it just to drive McNally out of the room. Later in the administration he would return to practicing law, becoming the chief federal prosecutor in Alaska, and eventually the general counsel to the White House's Office of Homeland Security in the George W. Bush administration.

Another recruit, Mark Lange, had written for Ann McLaughlin and Elizabeth Dole, both secretaries of Transportation under Reagan. Lange had voted for independent candidate John Anderson in 1980 and had written speeches for Colorado governor Richard Lamm, a Democrat. He was hired to focus on business and economic addresses, but like Davis he quickly discovered that foreign policy speeches were more appealing. He rode a motorcycle to work every day.

The speechwriters were made acutely aware that they were not on a par with the Reagan speechwriting staff. Fairly or not, word quickly spread around the White House and around Washington that they did not have the clout of their Reagan predecessors. Some of the gossip was overblown (Demarest called "a bunch of bullshit" the idea that the speechwriters' pay had been cut—it was adjusted down to entry levels after eight years of salary creep, he said), but some was not. They did not have mess privileges, which were not only a high-profile perk, but as Mari Maseng had said, "very important because that's where we'd sit and do our lobbying and get our ideas and become part of the team."* Similarly, Bush's writers' access to the West Wing was curtailed. They had to share the passes that would allow them to walk through there without escort—whether to hear the president deliver their speeches or to meet with him to discuss them. "There never seems to be enough of these passes at the right time and [it] is continually causing delays," Demarest wrote in an April 11 memorandum.

"It was a signal to the rest of the staff that we're in this box and that

---

*Mess privileges for speechwriters had been an issue since the Ford administration. Rick Hertzberg left a message for his successor on the word processor in his office: "Get your mess privileges right away." Ken Khachigian, Reagan's first head speechwriter and a veteran of the Nixon administration, knew the importance—symbolic and practical—of mess privileges and quickly moved to secure them. (Carter speechwriters OH interview, Jimmy Carter Library, 118; author interview with Mari Maseng-Will.)

we're not to be taken seriously," Davis recalled. The treatment of the Bush speechwriters was the visible demonstration that the Bush administration did not care as much as its predecessor about public communications. "Are they important in terms of the political pecking order?" Peggy Noonan was quoted as saying in *The New York Times*. "They're just above the people who clean up after Millie [the Bush family dog]."

The USS *Iowa* was doing combat exercises roughly three hundred miles northeast of Puerto Rico on April 19 when an explosion tore through its number two gun turret. The *Iowa*, a battleship, had the largest guns mounted on any ship in the world. The explosion killed forty-seven men.

Five days later, Bush addressed three thousand mourners, including a thousand from the battleship, in the largest hangar at the Norfolk naval station. "They all were, in the words of a poet, the men behind the guns," Bush said. "They came from Hidalgo, Texas; Cleveland, Ohio; Tampa, Florida; Costa Mesa, California. They came to the Navy as strangers, served the Navy as shipmates and friends, and left the Navy as brothers in eternity. In the finest Navy tradition, they served proudly on a great battleship, USS *Iowa*."

The line was from the poem "The Men behind the Guns," by John Jerome Rooney. Davis, who wrote the speech, used the phrase as a refrain. The emotional pinnacle of his initial drafts came with the president talking about his own naval experiences—he had been a U.S. Navy pilot in World War II, earning the Distinguished Flying Cross—and how he knew what it was like to return from a mission to find the neighboring bunk empty. But Bush kept editing that section out of the speech: I can't say this, he told his speechwriter; if I say this, I'll just break down in front of everybody. "We underestimated how visceral this was for him and how hard it was for him to do it," Davis recalled.

Chriss Winston watched the speech broadcast on CNN in her office in the Executive Office Building. As Bush spoke, she realized that he was starting to choke up—she was not sure he was going to get through the speech. "Your men are under a different command now, one that knows no rank, only love, knows no danger, only peace," Bush said in Norfolk, his eyes filled with tears. "May God bless them all." He swallowed hard and abruptly turned, leaving the speech unfinished.

"I kept rehearsing and reading my speech aloud," he wrote in his diary. "I did pray for strength, because I cry too easily, so I read it over and over again. I tried not to personalize it when I gave it. I tried not to focus on a grieving parent or a grieving spouse; I tried to comfort individually in the speech; but then I got to the end, I choked and had to stop."

Less than a week later, Bush was addressing the U.S. Chamber of Commerce, speaking at the DAR Constitution Hall a few blocks from the White House. He was discussing the budget deal his administration had reached with congressional Democratic leaders on April 13. "One word more about the budget agreement for 1990," the president said. "We've agreed to $5.3 billion in new revenues as part of the deal. And let me say a word about that $5.3 billion. I mean to live by what I've said: no new taxes."

Neither *The New York Times* nor *The Washington Post* mentioned that Bush had repeated his campaign pledge. There was no reason to: it was the tenth time the president had publicly reiterated or referred to the pledge—it was a standard part of his speeches, and, with the budget settled for the year, it was not newsworthy. But inside the administration, it was an issue. Winston started getting drafts back from the Office of Management and Budget with "no new taxes" scratched out.

Finally, after the fourth or fifth time this happened, Winston got a call from a superior in the West Wing. Stop putting it into speeches, she was told. She was dumbfounded. Are you telling me we're going to renege on this pledge? she asked. Surely they could not be so stupid. It had been the heart of the campaign. It would be political suicide. The reply was: I'm not saying that. Just don't put it in anymore.

"No new taxes" disappeared from Bush's speeches.

Events were moving quickly in Eastern Europe as the Cold War neared its abrupt conclusion. The Polish government agreed in April 1989 to hold free elections in June. In May, Hungary started dismantling the fence along its Austrian border. Bush made a pair of trips to Europe that spring and summer trying to foster the liberalization without angering the hard-liners behind the disintegrating iron curtain.

The president was scheduled to speak in Mainz, Germany, on May 31, to discuss the United States' unfolding Eastern European strategy. Davis worked on the speech for two weeks and fine-tuned it on the trip. He and Demarest went through a line-by-line edit of it with White House chief of staff John Sununu and national security adviser Brent Scowcroft. As Davis was putting the final polish on it the day before Bush was to speak, his foot bumped the power supply button for the computer and the screen blinked off. The speech disappeared: there was no trace of it on the computer. All of the hard copies had gone into burn bags. The president asked to see the speech so that he could read it through. As Demarest, deputy chief of staff James Cicconi, and deputy national security adviser Robert Gates looked on, Davis had to explain to Bush that his speech had been accidentally erased. Fine, Bush told them, unfazed, I'll look at it in the morning.

Demarest had a plan: They would all go out to dinner, have a few bottles of wine to relax, and then return to the hotel and reconstruct the speech from scratch—which is what they did. "The Cold War began with the division of Europe," Bush said the next day at the Rheingold-halle in Mainz. "It can only end when Europe is whole. Today it is this very concept of a divided Europe that is under siege. And that's why our hopes run especially high, because the division of Europe is under siege not by armies but by the spread of ideas."

Bush was scheduled to visit Poland and Hungary in July to spur the Cold War thaw and to encourage cracks appearing in the Soviet bloc. At Gdansk, the Polish shipyard, Bush would make remarks and partici-pate in a wreath-laying at the monument for workers from Solidarity, the anti-Communist labor union movement that had been critical to ending totalitarian rule in the country.

On June 26, a researcher named Bob Simon sent a four-page memo to McNally, who had been assigned the speech. "The President is speaking at a place and at a time that could be one of the turning points in world history, assuming the Polish move toward democracy flour-ishes," Simon wrote. "By giving a good speech, I think we can make that moment even more dramatic. My greatest hope is that the press and the public will look back on this speech in two or three years and say George Bush helped inspire the people of Europe without provoking a Soviet backlash—something that just a few months ago most people thought was impossible."

But the drama was provided by the setting and the crowd. Solidarity leader Lech Walesa seemed overwhelmed by the quarter million people who jammed into the square on July 11. "Oh my God, oh my God," he kept muttering, speaking in English, as he and Bush drove through.

The crowd waved American flags and hand-painted placards and flashed the "V" sign. "Your time has come," Bush told the throng. "It is Poland's time of possibilities; its time of responsibilities. It is Poland's time of destiny, a time when dreams can live again." His speech was interrupted first by chants of "Lech Walesa," and then by chants of "President Bush!"

"Just before I left a few days ago, I was asked in my beautiful Oval Office in the White House by one of your journalists if I would leave Poland and go to America, were I a young Pole," Bush recounted. "And I answered that in this time of bright promise, of historic transition, of unique opportunity, I would want to stay in Poland and be a part of it, help make the dream come true for all the Polish people." The crowd started a chant in Polish that neither Winston nor NSC staffer Condoleezza Rice, with whom she was standing, could understand. So Rice walked over to one of the local State Department officers and asked what it meant. "Stay with us!" was the reply. "Stay with us!"

Bush and his party flew on to Budapest, but were delayed by a summer thunderstorm. Thousands gathered in Kossuth Square in the city center, waiting in the rain for the American leader. When Bush arrived, Hungarian president Bruno Straub plodded through his full, fifteen-minute introduction as the rain fell. Bush finally approached the microphone, and, holding his text over his head, said: "I'm going to take this speech, and I'm going to tear it up. You've been out here too long."

Curt Smith had written the remarks. At that moment he was sitting in his office in Washington listening to Bush with researcher Stephanie Blessey, who had helped him prepare the speech. He tried to hide his surprise. Her head hit the table in shock. Later, Bush sent him a picture of the scene with the inscription: "It's raining in Budapest. I'll wing it."

By the fall, Bush had still not yet given a nationwide Oval Office address. There was concern among his senior aides that he had not achieved presidential stature in the public mind, which a prime-time address from the White House could remedy. Drugs had been on the public's mind that summer. A *Washington Post*–ABC News poll in late May found that 36 percent of respondents identified drugs, crime, and violence as their primary concern—more than double the response for any other issue.

The speechwriters and Demarest were brainstorming when Winston asked if anyone had ever actually *seen* crack cocaine. She doubted whether most Americans had, and she had heard that it looked like innocent rock candy. If they could get some crack from an arrest that had occurred somewhere in Washington—the closer to the White House the better—it could make a powerful visual for the speech. The key, everyone agreed, was that the cocaine would have to come from existing evidence; they specifically did not want a bust arranged for the speech. If that happened and something went wrong, it would be a disaster.

The drug prop first appeared in the speech's fifth draft—by Davis—dated August 17, as having been "seized . . . just ten blocks from where I'm sitting now." That formulation stayed in for the rest of the month. The request had meanwhile reached James Milford, executive assistant to the head of the Drug Enforcement Administration (DEA). On August 25, Milford called William McMullen, the number two man in the DEA's Washington office. "Do you have anything going on around the White House?" Milford asked. McMullen replied no. With a permanent police and Secret Service presence, the neighborhood of the White House was not a smart place for drug dealers to ply their trade.

McMullen said, though, that his agents were arranging a drug buy four or five blocks from there. "Any possibility of you moving it down to the White House?" Millford asked. "Evidently, the president wants to show it could be bought anywhere." When DEA agents asked eighteen-year-old drug dealer Keith Jackson if they could make the deal near the White House, his tape-recorded reply was, "Where the [expletive] is the White House?" Nevertheless, they were able to lure him into Lafayette Park, across Pennsylvania Avenue from the White House, and at about 11:30 am on September 1, he sold them three ounces of crack cocaine for $2,400.

That same day, Davis produced two new drafts of the drug speech, numbers 10 and 10A. The prop was dropped from the former, but the drugs were still said to have been purchased ten blocks away from the White House in 10A—until someone crossed out "just ten blocks" and wrote in "just across the street."

On the evening of September 5, the president, speaking from the Oval Office, held up a plastic bag. "This is crack cocaine seized a few days ago by Drug Enforcement agents in a park just across the street from the White House," he said. "It could easily have been heroin or PCP. It's as innocent-looking as candy, but it's turning our cities into battle zones, and it's murdering our children. Let there be no mistake: This stuff is poison. Some used to call drugs harmless recreation; they're not. Drugs are a real and terribly dangerous threat to our neighborhoods, our friends, and our families."

The next day, James Cicconi sent Bush a memo detailing the public reaction: 339 calls, 280 of which were positive.* "Jim: Isn't this a small response compared to other such speeches by RR etc etc.??" Bush scribbled on the memo. Cicconi responded the next day that the "bottom line is that it is probably consistent, especially when you consider that people stayed on the line longer due to the nature of this speech (thus allowing fewer total calls). Also, your speech began later (9 pm) than most of Reagan's."

The Washington Post ran a front-page story on September 22 detail-

---

*There were also a number of telegrams. "What a great speech Tuesday night," one said. "I'm a recovering addict with six years sobriety. What can I do to help with your war on drugs?" It concluded: "Your friend, Johnny Cash." "We've got to get you involved," Bush wrote back. (Johnny Cash telegram to the president and reply, September 8, 1989, "9/5/89 Address to the Nation on Drugs, 1st by Pres. Bush, Case No. 070721 to Case No. 071574" folder, WHORM files: SP-589, George Bush Library.)

ing the acquisition of the cocaine. "White House speech-writers thought it was the perfect visual for President Bush's first prime-time address to the nation—a dramatic prop that would show how the drug trade had spread to the president's own neighborhood," *Post* reporter Michael Isikoff wrote. "But obtaining the crack was no easy feat. To match the words crafted by the speech-writers, Drug Enforcement Administration agents lured a suspected District drug dealer to Lafayette Park four days before the speech so they could make what appears to have been the agency's first undercover crack buy in a park better known for its location across Pennsylvania Avenue from the White House than for illegal drug activity, according to officials familiar with the case."

Confronted by reporters that day, Bush grew testy, finally asking them: "Has somebody got some advocates here for this drug guy?"

"I keep hearing the critics saying we're not doing enough on Eastern Europe," Bush wrote in his diary on November 8. "Here the changes are dramatically coming our way and, if any one event—Poland, Hungary or East Germany—had taken place, people would say, 'This is great.' But it's all moving fast—moving our way—and you've got a bunch of critics jumping around saying we ought to be doing more."

He was at his desk in the Oval Office the next afternoon when national security adviser Brent Scowcroft came in with news: There were reports that the Berlin Wall had been opened.* The two men went into the small office off the Oval, where Bush turned on the television and they watched the euphoric crowds swell around the symbol of oppression that was suddenly an artifact. Press secretary Marlin Fitzwater rushed in with a handful of wire service reports. He recommended that

---

*This historic event was, according to Bush and Scowcroft, the result of a clerical error: "On November 9, East Germany announced it was relaxing its border-control policy on all its frontiers with West Germany," they wrote. "The announcement, through a bureaucratic oversight, did not exclude Berlin—which was usually given a special status. Crowds began to build along the infamous Wall dividing the city, demanding that the border guards open the checkpoints to West Berlin. After some hesitation on the grounds that they had no instructions, the guards gave in to the press of people and allowed free passage. In that brief moment, the Wall fell." (Bush and Scowcroft, *A World Transformed*, 148.)

Bush make a statement to the press about the developments. "Why?" Bush asked. He had other audiences in mind than the domestic one. "Listen, Marlin," he said. "I'm not going to dance on the Berlin Wall. The last thing I want to do is brag about winning the Cold War, or bringing the wall down. It won't help us in Eastern Europe to be bragging about this."

They settled on an informal press briefing in the Oval Office. Bush was cautious. "I don't think any single event is the end of what you might call the Iron Curtain, but clearly this is a long way from the harshest Iron Curtain days—a long way from that," he said. When CBS correspondent Lesley Stahl said that he did not seem "elated" about the news, he replied: "I am not an emotional kind of guy."

Across the street in the Old Executive Office Building, the speechwriters had other ideas. The next day, Friday, November 10, McNally sent Demarest a four-page memo suggesting a full presidential publicity blitz. "Set forth below is a five-point plan for you to become the architect of the most popular presidency in modern history," McNally wrote. Bush should fly to Berlin the next day and go to the Wall. " 'Historic opportunity' has been overused, and cheapened," McNally wrote. "But this is different. This is the real thing. History has offered the President a chance to place his stamp on an era—not at the end of an era, after it's proven itself out—but at the beginning, at the turning point. The hostage situation became a 'CRISIS' in part because Carter declared it one. What's happening at the wall probably <u>is</u> a turning point for the Cold War. And if we declare that it is, we may help the prophecy become self-fulfilling." Lech Walesa was to be awarded the Medal of Freedom in Washington, D.C., on Monday, November 13, and McNally suggested that the ceremony be moved to prime time and that Bush "declare Monday night that <u>the Cold War is over</u>."

Such theatrics would have given Bush an indelible Berlin Wall moment. But it would not have been Bush—not merely because he was trying to find a prudent path that would not spark a hard-line backlash, but also because placing his stamp on an historic moment was not the style of a president who disliked the word "I."

The speechwriters would keep on urging that Bush capitalize on the moment by making a decisive statement. But by the time Bush did lay claim to the end of the Cold War, the opportunity to link himself with it in the public mind had passed.

At 3:29 pm on November 8, Bush spoke on the phone with West German chancellor Helmut Kohl, who had just returned from Berlin, which, he said, "has the atmosphere of a festival." He told Bush, "Without the U.S. this day would not have been possible. Tell your people that." But the president remained cautious, asking Kohl whether it would be okay if he told the U.S. press about their talk.

Days passed with little presidential comment, and pundits and pols started criticizing Bush for not seizing the moment. House Democratic leader Richard Gephardt and Senate Democratic leader George Mitchell suggested that Bush show his emotions and dance on top of the Wall.

Bush and Kohl spoke again on November 17. "In spite of the Congressional posturing, the U.S. will stay calm," Bush told Kohl. "The euphoric excitement in the U.S. runs the risk of forcing unforseen action in the U.S.S.R. or [East Germany] that would be very bad. We will not be making exhortations about unification or setting timetables. We will not exacerbate the problem by having the President of the United States posturing on the Berlin Wall."

Five days later, on Thanksgiving eve, Bush finally addressed the nation, his first full public response since the Wall had come down nearly two weeks earlier. "On other Thanksgivings, the world was haunted by the images of watchtowers, guard dogs, and machine-guns," he said. "In fact, many of you had not even been born when the Berlin Wall was erected in 1961. But now the world has a new image, reflecting a new reality: that of Germans, East and West, pulling each other to the top of the wall, a human bridge between nations; entire peoples all across Eastern Europe bravely taking to the streets, demanding liberty, pursuing democracy. This is not the end of the book of history, but it's a joyful end to one of history's saddest chapters." To "those who question our prudent pace," he said, "they must understand that a time of historic change is no time for reckless-ness. The peace and the confidence and the security of our friends in Europe—it's just too important."

Davis had drafted the speech and was particularly proud of the peroration, which touched on Bush's early December summit meeting with President Gorbachev off the Mediterranean island of Malta.

And when we meet, we will be on ships at anchor in a Mediterranean bay that has served as a sea-lane of commerce and conflict for more than 2,000 years. This ancient port has been conquered by Ceasar and sultan, crusader and king. Its forts and watchtowers survey a sea that entombs the scuttled ships of empires lost—slave galleys, galleons, dreadnoughts, destroyers. These ships, once meant to guard lasting empires, now litter the ocean floor and guard nothing more than reefs of coral. So, if the millennia offers [sic] us a lesson, perhaps it's this: True security does not come from empire and domination. True security can only be found in the growing trust of free peoples.

Davis watched the speech with his family and afterward awaited their approbation. Their reaction was flat. He talked to other people, and "they didn't buy it for a minute: It didn't sound like [Bush], it just wasn't right for him," Davis recalled. "That's when I realized I'd done a terrible disservice by trying to make him somebody he wasn't."

Bush was scheduled to address the crew of the aircraft carrier USS *Forrestal* off Malta when he arrived in the area on December 1. Curt Smith, the conservative Mayberry-loving speechwriter, had the assignment. He sent his fifth draft to Bush on November 29, and Bush returned it edited with a covering note that the president had typed himself. Bush was a prolific note writer, sending forth a steady stream of "self-typed" notes, as he called them, small sheets of paper banged out on a typewriter in his office.* "Please re-do," Bush wrote, typing poorly. "i don't understand some of the humor. I'd prefer to leave out most of the references to my own Naval experience."

"An old Indian proverb says: 'No one can really know a man until he's walked in his moccasins,'" Smith had written. "Well, I was your age when Malta was under assault [in World War II]. I'm an old Navy man.

---

*The notes were often unsigned. No one warned speechwriter Mark Davis to expect them. This is horseshit, he thought of the mysterious notes, and threw them out—until someone explained where they were coming from. (Author interview with Davis.)

Flew a plane—a torpedo bomber called the Avenger. One of 34 planes assigned to an aircraft carrier. I've **walked** in your moccasins. I know what the Navy means to you. And even more, **what you mean to the United States of America**." In the margin next to this paragraph, Bush had written: "Too ego."

The speechwriters were scheduled to join the rest of the communications staff as well as reporters at a White House holiday party on December 19. Winston got a call in the middle of the afternoon: Might the speechwriters join the president for a drink before the party? Sure, she said. In the Oval Office? No, came the reply, in the residence. He does know that we're coming to the Christmas party tonight, right? a befuddled Winston asked.

The speechwriters and Bush sipped coffee, Heineken, or a buttery chardonnay, and chatted. He showed them around the residence, grandchildren running about, their toys scattered underfoot. Millie, his English springer spaniel, panted around, hoping, it seemed to Curt Smith, for some beer. She licked his hand but did not get one. Bush showed them the Lincoln Bedroom, noting that it was where Lincoln had signed the Emancipation Proclamation. He pointed out a painting of Lincoln and his generals—called *The Peacemakers*—on the wall. He drew deep inspiration from knowing what Lincoln had done there, Bush told his guests.

They made small talk for an hour. A couple of times Brent Scowcroft, the national security adviser, summoned the president to the doorway, where they talked quietly. Bush seemed at ease, even jovial. At the end of the hour, they all rose and Smith heard the president mutter under his breath, "I feel a thousand years old." They were all headed to a reporter-filled party—that would be enough to age any GOP president, Smith thought.

Unable to sleep that night—too much coffee—Smith turned on his television at around two in the morning and saw White House press secretary Marlin Fitzwater: The United States had invaded Panama, deposing dictator Manuel Noriega. Days earlier, Noriega had declared war on the United States and Panamanian soldiers had killed an unarmed U.S. marine. Bush ordered the invasion to restore Panamanian democracy and bring Noriega to justice on drug-related charges. Smith thought Bush must be the coolest customer in the world. The whole time that he had been entertaining the speechwriters, he had known that the troops were on their way in.

Budget negotiations between the White House and congressional leaders continued through the spring and into the summer of 1990. On the morning of June 26, Bush, budget director Richard Darman, chief of staff John Sununu, and Treasury Secretary Nicholas Brady met in the residence with the Democratic leaders—House speaker Tom Foley, House majority leader Richard Gephardt, and Senate majority leader George Mitchell. The meeting was intended to reestablish trust in order to move forward the broader negotiations, which included other members of Congress from both parties. Foley made Bush an offer: They should agree that a bipartisan solution was required that would include entitlement reform, defense and domestic discretionary spending cuts, budget reform, and—yes—tax increases. "Okay," Bush replied, "if I can say you agreed."

As quickly as that, "Read my lips: no new taxes" was finished. Darman wrote a two-sentence statement which Sununu edited, changing "tax increases" to "tax revenue increases" in the hope that they could argue the deal did not violate Bush's pledge. Fitzwater was given the statement and told to simply post it on a bulletin board—no spinning, explaining, or contextualizing. Demarest was in the West Wing when business community liaison Bobbie Kilberg approached him, frantic. Sununu who was formerly governor of New Hampshire, happened by. Governor, the business groups are going crazy, Kilberg said, what am I supposed to tell them? Sununu huffed: Don't tell them anything. He turned and walked away.

"I wish I had never said, 'Read my lips, no new taxes,'" Bush told an interviewer years later, "because had I not made it so pronounced, people would say, 'Well, you know, he has to do this.' President Reagan raised taxes several times, but he just kept saying, 'I'm against a tax increase.' And he was very convincing about it, and for some reason, the right wing of our party that still criticizes me for a tax increase has nothing to say about the Reagan tax increase, which is good. I'm not trying to undermine his legacy. I just wish I'd been that good."

It was a case of not giving a speech that damned Bush. Reagan used communications—speeches especially—to set a context in which it was clear that any tax increases must have been enacted over his objections. "I was appalled that no one thought about how to bring the public along, to position us in a way," Demarest said. "Ronald Reagan raised taxes a bunch of times—nobody thought he was the great tax raiser. Well, he positioned himself properly. Dragged, kicking and screaming, you know. We did none of it. We posted it on a bulletin board. It was horrible."

As if to underscore his continuing lack of understanding about presidential communications, at a press conference on July 17, Bush said: "I'll make you a slight confession. I still am trying to find the appropriate way to discuss, using the bully pulpit of the White House, these matters you talk about—talking about religious values, family values or whatever. . . ."

Bush hit a bucket of golf balls during the day on Wednesday, August 1, leaving his shoulders sore—enough so that at eight twenty that evening he was wearing a T-shirt, sitting on the edge of an examination table in the White House Medical Office getting deep heat treatment. Scowcroft and NSC Middle East expert Richard Haass appeared with disquieting news. "Mr. President, it looks very bad," Scowcroft said. "Iraq may be about to invade Kuwait."

Bush and his team reacted quickly, condemning the invasion and gathering worldwide support for action to roll the Iraqis back. Some time after 8 pm on the evening of August 7, Mark Lange, the motorcycle-riding speechwriter, got a call summoning him to Demarest's office in the West Wing. The rest of the night he shuttled between there, a conference room, and his own office, furiously pounding at his word processor.

"In the life of a nation, we're called upon to define who we are and what we believe," Bush said at 9 am on August 8. "Sometimes these choices are not easy. But today as President, I ask for your support in a decision I've made to stand up for what's right and condemn what's wrong, all in the cause of peace. At my direction, elements of the 82nd Airborne Division as well as key units of the United States Air Force are arriving today to take up defensive positions in Saudi Arabia." Operation Desert Shield had begun.

Bush continued to speak about the situation throughout August, with his rhetoric heating up. The speechwriters wanted to compare Saddam Hussein to Hitler, but the National Security Council excised the language—and then Bush ad-libbed it himself. Even then, the NSC refused to let the speechwriters put it in a speech. We don't want to compound it, they told Winston. Bush kept on ad-libbing it.

A speech to a joint session of Congress was scheduled for September 11. Richard Darman, the budget director who had run the Reagan speechwriting operation for a couple of years, wrote a detailed eight-page outline, sending it to Bush at the end of August. The "guidance for speechwriter" was that the "speech should be about <u>25 minutes</u> long excluding applause. It should be designed to produce at least 25 interruptions for applause—i.e., an average of <u>one applause line per minute</u>."

Bush edited the outline before it was passed on to Mark Davis, the speechwriter. To the objectives listed, he added: "A new world order under which the world can no longer be blackmailed by Saddam H by threatened use of chemical weapons, nuclear weapons." Bush had first used the phrase "new world order" in February, at a political fund-raiser in San Francisco, referring to the collapse of the Soviet Union. He used it again at a press conference: "As I look at the countries that are chipping in here now, I think we do have a chance at a new world order, and I'd like to think that out of this dreary performance by Saddam Hussein there could be now an opportunity for peace all through the Middle East." The day before, he had received the outline and written the insert.

William Safire traces the origin of the phrase to Alfred Lord Tennyson's poem *Morte d'Arthur*, where the dying King Arthur says: "The old order changeth, yielding place to new." FDR used the phrase once (an unflattering reference to Nazi dreams of world conquest), as did each of Bush's predecessors since Nixon, but only with Bush did it gain lasting fame. Whether he had Tennyson or any of his predecessors in mind is unclear. The phrase was "kicking around at the time," Davis later recalled. The NSC, for example, was "bandying it about in memos." He added: "I think it is one of those phrases whose true father is the zeitgeist."

Davis wrote the speech. Bush was "very focused," he recalled, and sent many of his little typed notes.* Davis was still stung by having failed to write properly for Bush at Malta. "If he's not Winston Churchill or Ronald Reagan or JFK, who is he?" the speechwriter wondered. "What's the best George Bush out there? And the best I could think of was Gary Cooper. . . . You know: short, clipped declarative sentences, plain-speak, kind of humble but in a menacing way."

Bush's edits on the speech demonstrate a dry wit and a sense of propriety. The third draft said, "Saddam will fail." He circled the name and wrote in the margin: "1st name??" In the final speech he said, "Saddam Hussein." The same page had the sentence: "We cannot permit a resource [oil] so vital to be dominated by so ruthless and unprincipled a power." Bush wrote "dictator" over power and underlined the "so" before "ruthless" three times, querying in the margin whether a lesser dictator could be permitted to dominate the resource. He conceded on that point as the final text read: "We cannot permit a resource so vital to be dominated by one so ruthless."

Further down, the draft contained a transition from foreign to domestic topics. "I also want to use this occasion to say some things to the American people," it stated. Bush wrote in the margin: "What's rest of speech been doing?"

"We stand today at a unique and extraordinary moment," Bush told the Congress on September 11, 1990. "The crisis in the Persian Gulf, as grave as it is, also offers a rare opportunity to move toward an historic period of cooperation. Out of these troubled times . . . a new world order—can emerge: a new era—freer from the threat of terror, stronger in the pursuit of justice, and more secure in the quest for peace."

---

*Curt Smith, who worked on Bush's August 20 speech to the Veterans of Foreign Wars and the "Just War" speech he gave on January 28, 1991, recalled that through his notes Bush was very involved with the composition of the war addresses. "I would come into the office day after day after day to find page after page after page of self-typed text from the president," he said. Smith estimated that about half, "the important fifty [percent], was him." (Author interview with Curt Smith.)

Watching Bush deliver the speech, Davis thought that he had reached a personal high point—it could not get any better. The next day, he gave in his resignation.

The president was scheduled to address the UN General Assembly at the start of October, and McNally made one last appeal for officially ending the "Cold War." "The U.N. speech also marks our <u>last</u> opportunity—and our <u>best</u> opportunity—to say that 'the cold war is over'—a predictable 'headline' likely to resonate on into [election year] 1992," he wrote Bush in a September 28 memo covering the seventh draft of the speech. He argued that such a declaration would match Bush's vision for a new world order, and that it would be "the <u>last</u> opportunity because most observers will mark German reunification on Oct. 3 as the formal end of the cold war era. And it's the <u>best</u> opportunity because it's before not only 'a' world forum, but <u>the</u> world forum."

Bush agreed. "We are hopeful that the machinery of the United Nations will no longer be frozen by the divisions that plagued us during the cold war, that at last—long last—we can build new bridges and tear down old walls, that at long last we will be able to build a new world based on an event for which we have all hoped: an end to the cold war," he told the UN General Assembly.

> *Two days from now, the world will be watching when the cold war is formally buried in Berlin. And in this time of testing, a fundamental question must be asked, a question not for any one nation but for the United Nations. And the question is this: Can we work together in a new partnership of nations? Can the collective strength of the world community, expressed by the United Nations, unite to deter and defeat aggression? Because the cold war's battle of ideas is not the last epic battle of this century.*

But with all attention focused on the crisis in the Persian Gulf, the moment had passed. The president's declaration that the Cold War was over was little noticed in the press or by the public.

The agreement to flip on "no new taxes" and the subsequent budget agreement—which sent GOP conservatives into fits—were the subject of debate within the White House through the summer and into the fall of 1990. Someone came up with the analogy that the budget deal was like a dead cat you found on your front steps: No one liked it but something had to be done about it. Some argued that Bush should say that the budget deal was an unhappy necessity. Others argued that Bush should make a mea culpa speech and renounce the deal. Any speech dealing with the budget agreement became known as the "dead cat" speech.

Bush was getting hammered by both Democrats and conservatives, the latter under the leadership of House Republican whip Newt Gingrich. A budget agreement was announced on September 30, but with Gingrich rallying the opposition, conservatives and progressives joined to vote it down in the House on October 5. "There's a story in one of the papers saying that I am more comfortable with foreign affairs, and that is absolutely true," Bush wrote in his diary on October 6. "Because I don't like the deficiencies of the domestic, political scene. I hate the posturing on both sides."

The month of October careered toward the 1990 midterm elections with budget negotiations and preparations for war. Consequently, Bush's stump speech had him explaining that he had only reluctantly accepted the budget deal (dead cat) and deplored the Democrats' taxing and spending ways, but then invoking the late GOP senator Arthur Vandenberg's remark that politics stops at the water's edge,* and praising the cooperation he had gotten from leaders of both parties. "We had a total mixed message," Demarest recalled.

Toward the end of October, the anti-budget agreement forces appeared to have the upper hand: Bush was going to make a campaign trip starting November 1 and would use it to rid himself of the "dead cat." He would come out swinging and declare the agreement a mistake. The speechwriters wrote a half-dozen speeches for him, decrying the agreement.

On Halloween, Chriss Winston was about to leave work to take her two-year-old son, Ian, dressed in a mouse costume, trick-or-treating,

---

*According to William Safire, Vandenberg in 1950 defined "bipartisan foreign policy" as "a mutual effort under our indispensable two-party system to unite our official voice at the water's edge. . . ." (Safire, *Safire's New Political Dictionary*, 860.)

when her phone rang. There had been a meeting that morning and the budget deal was going to be defended, not renounced. No one had bothered to tell the speechwriters. Winston rewrote all half-dozen iterations of the "dead cat" address as her son, the mouse, nodded off on her couch. She finished well past midnight and decided then that the job was not worth the hassle. Though she stayed on through the war, her decision to quit was made that night.

Bush spent Thanksgiving Day with the U.S. troops stationed in Saudi Arabia. F-15 Eagle fighter jets escorted Air Force One. With the day's remarks drafted ahead of time, mostly by McNally, who was not on the trip, Demarest felt home free. He was proud of the speeches: the writers had worked in quotes from soldiers' letters from home and other devices to tug the heartstrings. On the flight he showed them to General Norman Schwarzkopf, the head of U.S. Central Command. The remarks brought tears to the general's eyes.

A steward told Demarest that the president wanted to see him. The commander in chief looked up at him as he entered the cabin. "Dave, what are you trying to do to me?" Bush asked. "These speeches . . ." Demarest was startled and did not understand. "Sir?" he asked. Bush repeated himself. "You'd like me to tone them down a bit?" Demarest queried. "Has Schwarzkopf seen these?" Bush asked. "Yes, he got teary," Demarest replied. Bush flashed him a look that said: You see what I mean? "I'll take care of it," Demarest said, hurrying from the cabin. The speeches had succeeded too well—the president was worried that he would not be able to keep his own emotions in check.

Demarest rushed back to his seat to cut out chunks and try to tone the speeches down. Even after he had done his job, Bush kept cutting. The first stop was in Saudi Arabia, at Military Airlift Command at Dhahran International Airport, where he met with air force personnel. "This is a real world situation, and we're not walking away until our mission is done, until the invader is out of Kuwait," Bush told the cheering crowd. On his reading card, he had bracketed the next section, which he skipped: "I think of Lt. Mary Danko, a flight nurse who volunteered for Saudi Arabia. Her husband, a C-130 navigator, was already flying in support of Desert Shield. When asked if leaving their baby with relatives was a hard thing to do, Mary said: 'It's the <u>right</u> thing to do. We're needed.' When asked: 'But what about the <u>kid</u>?' Mary explained: 'We're doing it <u>for</u> the kid.'"

From Dhahran, Bush flew by helicopter to an army base in the desert. Once again, he cut more from his remarks than Demarest had already taken out. From there, he flew to the USS *Nassau*, to participate in a Thanksgiving Day service with the sailors. "What is so remarkable about the first Thanksgiving is that those hearty souls were giving thanks in an age of extreme adversity, recognizing the Lord's bounty during extraordinary hardship, understanding that his bounty is not in things material but more importantly in things spiritual," Bush said. He had scratched out the next two paragraphs on his speech cards, reflecting his dislike for talking about himself: "You all bring back thoughts of a Thanksgiving I spent 46 years ago on a carrier, the *San Jacinto*, off the coast of the Philippines during WWII," the speech would have had the president say. "I found that the Lord provides many blessings to men and women who face adversity in the name of a noble purpose. They are the blessings of faith and friendship. Strength and determination. Courage and camaraderie. Dedication to duty. I found that the Lord allows the human spirit the inner resolve to find optimism and hope amidst the most challenging and difficult times."

The final stop of the day was at a Marine base in the desert. Bush significantly shortened his speech there, too. "It started to dawn on me that he understood this situation a whole lot better than I did," Demarest recalled. "The power of him being with the troops really was the message, and that the words that he used were less important because the emotion was all there." The Marines crowded around Bush. It seemed to Demarest that they just wanted to touch him—one would reach over the shoulder of another. "It was something out of ancient Rome that if you touched the emperor you're going to be safe in battle," he said.

"The debate has become simplified," Bush wrote in his diary on Sunday, January 13, 1991. "You are for war, or you are against. Who is for War? I am against it." January 15 was the United Nations–set deadline for Hussein to withdraw his troops from Kuwait. "It is my decision—my decision to send these kids into battle, my decision that may affect the lives of innocence [*sic*]," he wrote. "It is my decision to step back and let the sanctions work. Or to move forward. And in my view, help establish the New World Order. . . . And yet I know what I have to do this Sunday night. This man is evil, and let him win and we rise again to fight tomorrow. . . ."

"There is no way to describe the pressure," Bush wrote on January 15 as the deadline ticked closer. He did not sleep well that night and the next day his lower gut hurt—"nothing like when I had the bleeding ulcer"—so he took a couple of Mylantas. The bombing would commence at 7 pm Washington time and Bush would address the nation two hours later. He wanted to do this speech himself. Dan McGroarty had written drafts on January 14 and January 15. Bush appears to have had McGroarty's draft at hand when he wrote his final text himself. And he had McGroarty sitting in the outer office by the Oval Office, on hand in case he needed help with a line or to check a fact.*

The president retained bits and pieces of McGroarty's draft, most notably a refrain answering: "Why act now?" "While the world waited, Saddam Hussein systematically raped, pillaged, and plundered a tiny nation, no threat to his own. . . . While the world waited, Saddam sought to add to the chemical weapons arsenal he now possesses, an infinitely more dangerous weapon of mass destruction—a nuclear weapon," Bush said. "And while the world waited, while the world talked peace and withdrawal, Saddam Hussein dug in and moved massive forces into Kuwait."

Typically, Bush did not use one line McGroarty suggested: "As a young man—like millions of Americans—I was there: I've seen the face of battle—I know what it's like to lose a friend, to see a comrade fall."

"Five months ago, Saddam Hussein started this cruel war against Kuwait," Bush said. "Tonight, the battle has been joined."

---

*Demarest was jealous—he wanted to be the one helping the president write for history. Late in the day, he got a summons from Bush to the small study off the Oval Office. The president asked him about an inconsequential line in the speech. As Demarest glanced at it, the White House photographer walked in, took his picture, and left. Demarest realized that Bush had understood he would want to be part of the moment. (Doro Bush Koch, *My Father My President*, 349.)

Bush wrote in his diary again at 10:45 pm: "I am about to go to bed. I did my speech to the nation at 9 o'clock. I didn't feel nervous about it at all. I wrote it myself. I knew what I wanted to say, and I said it. And I hope it resonates."

The press took note of a new, sharper tone to Bush's domestic speeches when he gave the University of Michigan's commencement address on May 4. The Gulf War was over—Bush had addressed the nation on February 27 to announce that the United States and its allies would "suspend" combat operations. His approval ratings had topped 90 percent in March and were still comfortably north of 70 percent.

A conquering hero abroad, Bush still needed to communicate— some would argue formulate—a domestic agenda. Commencement speeches had long been a good venue for such major announcements: It was at the same University of Michigan twenty-seven years earlier that Lyndon Johnson had formally unveiled and defined his "Great Society."

The University of Michigan had been one of more than a hundred schools across the country that had enacted speech codes to try to eliminate hateful language from college life, though its rules had been struck down as an unconstitutional infringement upon freedom of expression. "Ironically, on the 200th anniversary of our Bill of Rights, we find free speech under assault throughout the United States, including on some college campuses," Bush told the crowd. "The notion of political correctness has ignited controversy across the land. . . . What began as a crusade for civility has soured into a cause of conflict and even censorship. Disputants treat sheer force—getting their foes punished or expelled, for instance—as a substitute for the power of ideas."

The speech drew front-page play in *The New York Times*. "The speech to Michigan graduates reflected the influence of the President's new head speech writer, Anthony Snow . . . who was hired to bring a harder edge and ideological spirit to Mr. Bush's speeches as he moves toward the 1992 election," Neil A. Lewis reported.

"People were concerned about the PC bit" in the speech, Snow told Washington's *City Paper*, an alternative weekly. It was kept in because he had told the president about the Michigan speech codes and gotten his early buy-in on the thrust. It was an early, and ultimately rare, victory for the new head speechwriter.

Snow, thirty-five, had been the editorial page editor of *The Washington Times*, the city's conservative broadsheet, since 1987. The paper's editorials had not always been kind to Bush. "George Bush and his people came to Washington untarnished by dreaminess," one had said. "They skipped the idealistic phase and jumped directly into an Imperial Presidency. There, gatekeepers control access to the leader of the Free World. They seal off leaks and fresh air. And in the president's case, they have created sort of a yuppie regency, complete with a vigorous, intelligent, decent and utterly removed head of state."

Chief of staff John Sununu had brought in Snow as Winston's replacement without consulting David Demarest, which created some tensions. Snow brought energy and good cheer to the writing department, trying to lift its chronically low morale. He instituted regular seminar-style meetings with conservative thinkers. And he mandated that the president's speeches must consist of complete sentences—putting an end to a practice of trying to write in the fragmentary bursts that were Bush's natural style. "It went too far," Snow told *The Washington Post*. "If he wants to end up talking in fragments, that's fine. But we're going to give him complete sentences."

"Prodded by a new chief speech writer, Tony Snow . . . Bush has also begun road-testing more hard-edged speeches," Kenneth Walsh and David Gergen of *U.S. News & World Report* observed in June.

There were ominous signs for Snow, however. In August, he would run afoul of Scowcroft when a line of his in a speech delivered in the Ukraine about "suicidal nationalisms" was interpreted by the press as a discouragement to the newly independent former Soviet states not to stray too far from Moscow's orbit. (William Safire dubbed this the "Chicken Kiev" speech, to Bush's enduring irritation.) And having his name appear in the *Times* did not help him.

More worrying for Bush and his administration was the coverage that *The Washington Post* gave to the Michigan speech. The paper devoted a 262-word sidebar to his attack on political correctness. It ran next to a 746-word story headlined: "Bush Hails 'Power of Free Enterprise.'" "President Bush today hailed the free enterprise system in a commencement speech to thousands of graduating University of Michigan students who are embarking into the worst job market in a decade," the story said.

The speechwriters lunched with Bush at noon on November 20, 1991. Chicken salad and tuna salad were on the menu, along with cottage cheese on lettuce surrounded by fruit. Cappuccino frozen yogurt with cream and shaved cinnamon on top rounded out the meal (Bush took off the cream and ate only the yogurt). The president, wearing a blue shirt and presidential tie tack, put Tabasco sauce on his tuna and mixed both sweetener and thyroid medicine into his coffee.

Bush started out by telling the writers that while they may not real-ize how much he appreciated them, they were doing a great job. They talked about the campaign: Congress would be a major theme, he said. "We need a formulation for placing the blame without losing support," read the notes of one researcher from the speechwriting shop. "In the next few weeks, POTUS wants to let the people know he is concerned, he cares, and is in touch with the American people." The economy was sagging badly and Bush was being charged with spending too much time on foreign affairs.

"JFK got away with a lot of intellectual stuff; POTUS doesn' [sic] feel comfortable doing that," the notetaker added. Bush emphasized strongly that speeches should be short and have more jokes. He told the group that he didn't like "high-flying" rhetoric, that he did not think it natural.* "You can't undermine who you are and what you believe," he said.

Bush told them not to overdo religious and biblical references in his speeches. While he believed in the Bible, he said, he viewed religious beliefs as personal, not something he wanted to wear on his sleeve. In particular, he said that he was not comfortable discussing abortion. "We made our view clear, and we stand with that decision," he said. Al-

---

*All of the speechwriters feared seeing "too much rhetoric" scribbled in the margin of a draft. (Chriss Winston, "State of the Union Stew," *Christian Science Monitor*, January 28, 2002.)

though he had campaigned in favor of abortion rights in 1980, by 1988 he had embraced an anti-abortion rights position.*

Bush talked about how much he admired Reagan's speaking abilities. He knew that he could not match Reagan—he blamed it on his "genes"—though he had tried to learn from the master. He cited Reagan's D-Day speech—"These are the boys of Pointe du Hoc"—as something that he could not have pulled off. Unlike Reagan, he said, he could not "separate the words from his heart." He talked about his personal interests: he genuinely liked country music, naming his favorite artists—Reba and Crystal—by their first names. And he played golf to get away from reporters: "It's the only thing I can do to relax," he told the writers.

Finally, the talk turned to the growing political problem presented by the primary challenge he was facing from conservative commentator and former Nixon speechwriter Patrick Buchanan. His speeches should be nice to Buchanan, Bush told them, so that he would come back into the fold once the primaries were concluded. "He's out there on a weird platform," Bush said.

The next day, November 21, the Gallup organization would start a three-day poll that pegged Bush's approval rating at just over 51 percent. It marked the last time he had majority approval in the poll until January 1993, when he was leaving office.

A week after Bush had lunched with his writers, Snow sent a memo to the group that underscored something the president had mentioned: the importance of getting across the message that he cared about people's problems. "I know many of you have been wondering just how we ought to handle upcoming speeches on the economy," Snow wrote.

---

*Bush did not avoid religious references altogether. In a "self-typed" note for a January 1990 speech introducing a lecture on Abraham Lincoln and the presidency, he instructed Curt Smith to "work in" that "I have President for less than a year, but I am now ["personally" written by hand] more cionvinced than ever that one cannot be President of this country without believing in God, without a belief in prayer. . . . Lincoln talked about spending timeso n one's knees. Though not tested as lincoln was tested, I know nwo how true those words were." (Bush note to Curt Smith, undated, private papers of Curt Smith.)

"We generally have three goals: First, to reassure people that the President knows what's happening; Second, that he cares; third, that he has a plan for getting changes enacted; and fourth, in the interim he will do whatever he can unilaterally to prod the economy."

December 7 would mark the fiftieth anniversary of the Japanese surprise attack at Pearl Harbor. Curt Smith and Mary Kate Grant wrote the speeches. Smith was assigned the address that Bush would give standing on the white, crescent-shaped monument to the USS *Arizona* officially commemorating the event, while Grant wrote the speech he would give in Honolulu to World War II veterans and their families.

Bush gave both speechwriters similar admonishments. "Now, look, I have to be careful," he told Smith. "I don't want to break down." Smith did not tell him what he was thinking: Mr. President, I do want you to break down. "Because that's the Bush that we knew [and that] I wanted more Americans to know," Smith recalled. "In fact, I think one mistake we made was not showcasing Bush and showing America more of the human behavior that we were privileged to know . . . in the White House."

When Grant and Demarest met with Bush in the Oval Office to discuss the Honolulu speech, he was in a lighter mood. As he talked, he tossed pieces of popcorn into the air and caught them in his mouth. Grant asked where he had been when he heard about Pearl Harbor. On the quad at Philips Academy in Andover, he said, a seventeen-year-old. He had decided to sign up as soon as he turned eighteen. He told her of being on the deck of an aircraft carrier when the person standing next to him inadvertently backed into a plane's propeller. His leg landed in front of Bush. Do you want to talk about that in the speech? she asked. Oh my God, no, he replied.

Grant asked if he knew people who had died in the war, and did he want to mention them? Bush told her that he would not be able to do it without crying. "I remember seeing the look on his face and you could just see the wheels turning of him remembering these people and how difficult it still was for him," Grant recalled. "It's still very real to him, even after all these years."

Flying on Air Force One to Hawaii, Bush summoned Grant to his cabin. He had been reading her draft, he said, and noticed that it said that over two thousand men had died in a matter of minutes during the attack. Didn't any women die? he asked. She was back within ten minutes to report that in fact all of the Pearl Harbor dead on board the ships were male, but she was impressed that he had thought to ask the question.

Demarest meanwhile was lining up allies to make sure that Bush did not try to tone down the Pearl Harbor speeches as he had the Thanksgiving speeches in Saudi Arabia. He asked Scowcroft for help. He's going to say it's too over the top, Demarest told the national security adviser. When they went over the speeches with the president, Bush did hesitate over the *Arizona* address, and Scowcroft spoke up: This is a good speech, he said, you should give it the way it is. Bush agreed.

Bush spoke at 8:10 am on a morning much like the infamous one a half century earlier: bright sun in a mostly clear sky, a slight breeze. The water gleamed. And he spoke with unusual eloquence:

> *Think of how it was for these heroes of the harbor, men who were also husbands, fathers, brothers, sons. Imagine the chaos of guns and smoke, flaming water, and ghastly carnage. Two thousand, four hundred and three Americans gave their lives. But in this haunting place, they live forever in our memory, reminding us gently, selflessly, like chimes in the distant night. Every fifteen seconds a drop of oil still rises from the* Arizona *and drifts to the surface. As it spreads across the water, we recall the ancient poet: "In our sleep, pain that cannot forget falls drop by drop upon the heart, and in our own despair against our will comes wisdom through the awful grace of God." With each drop, it is as though God Himself were crying. He cries, as we do, for the living and the dead.*

Bush did not cry during his remarks, but his voice cracked three times.

Sununu resigned as White House chief of staff in mid-December 1991 and was replaced by Transportation Secretary Samuel Skinner, in what was just the start of a year of churning that proved to be, as speechwriter Andrew Ferguson put it, "chaos."

Skinner brought in a management consultant named Eugene Croisant (quickly dubbed "French Breakfast Roll Man"), who suggested that Demarest get axed. Early in January 1992, Skinner told *The Washington Post* that one of the administration's "obvious" problems was a failure to communicate "a significant number of things the president has done" on the domestic policy front. (The story ran the same day that Bush vomited into the lap of the Japanese prime minister, with the photo running in all the newspapers.) Indeed, after three years of neglect, the speechwriters suddenly were being told that they were the key to the presidential reelection. Starting with the State of the Union address, campaign chairman Bob Teeter declared every major address Bush gave to be the one that would turn the campaign around.

Almost a year after ordering troops into combat in the sands of the Middle East, Bush made a foray into the snows of New Hampshire to try to rescue his faltering political fortunes. A mid-January Gallup poll showed for the first time that those disapproving of his presidency exceeded the number approving. The reason was, as the strategists for Democratic candidate Bill Clinton would put it, "The economy, stupid." The nation was in the grip of the longest recession since the Great Depression, entering its eighteenth month with the New Year, sapping more than 1.2 million jobs, as well as the nation's confidence. "In one of history's most painful paradoxes, U.S. consumers seem suddenly disillusioned with the American Dream of rising prosperity even as capitalism and democracy have consigned the Soviet Union to history's trash heap," *Time* reported.

The speechwriters prepared remarks for the stops on the president's January 15 campaign swing, tailoring each to the locale where he would be speaking. But Bush decided he would ad-lib. He told community leaders in Portsmouth that while he did not want to sound like "Mrs. Rose Scenario," he thought the economy would soon recover. In a town hall–style meeting in Exeter, he told the crowd what he had been telling his staff for months, "Message: I care." Speaking to voters in Dover, he said they should not feel bad for him—"Don't cry for me, Argentina."

The State of the Union address was the closely held product of Snow, Skinner, Darman, Teeter, and Bush. It was going to be brief and thematic, avoiding the standard laundry list approach. Unfortunately, when Snow produced it five days before the January 28 delivery date, Bush rejected it. Peggy Noonan was summoned from New York on Friday, January 24, and worked all weekend with Teeter, Darman, and Skinner, but to little avail.

"Rarely had a speech raised so many advance expectations," *The Washington Post* reported the day afterward. "Virtually all of Bush's political aides, watching in horror and gloom, acknowledge now that the strategy of the past 10 weeks of waiting until last night to offer a program to combat the recession was a mistake. 'There's no place to go but up from here,' said one before the speech, referring to Bush's poll ratings, which have skidded to the lowest of his presidency and put him in a category with the hapless Jimmy Carter."

Noonan was among those Skinner had sought out to replace Demarest, but she had passed, as had Reagan vet Tom Griscom, and Jim Lake, a veteran of the successful Reagan and Bush presidential campaigns. Skinner eventually convinced press secretary Marlin Fitzwater to take the communications director title, with Demarest becoming head speechwriter and Snow head of media affairs.

Bush's speaking style, his unwillingness to practice and habit of ad-libbing continued to dog him. He gave a typical performance at the American Legislative Exchange Council on February 21. "He ad-libbed significantly—embracing some lines verbatim, but mostly opening his arms to his own words," staffer Michele Nix reported to the speechwriters and researchers in a memo that day. "When he did look down to the lines on the cards, it sounded like bumper car met bumper car; lines ran head on into other lines, paragraphs into paragraphs. Transitions in almost every case were lost."

A week and a half later, Dan McGroarty, who had become deputy director of speechwriting the previous year, sent the writers and researchers some notes about recent addresses. "The President, Mrs. Bush and senior staff continue to measure the success of a speech by the number of applause lines," he wrote. "The President interprets long stretches of silence as a failure on his part to connect. From the podium, nodding heads may be nodding off. Let's face it, applause lines are a kind of currency. . . . POTUS performs better when the next speech picks up the best lines from the last speech. If we keep feeding him New! Improved! language—we only out-smart ourselves."

The creeping chaos of the White House was illustrated in an April speech to which Andrew Ferguson was assigned. Ferguson had been a reporter with Scripps-Howard when Snow hired him in early 1992. As the commentator and—for a few months in 1988, Reagan speechwriter—John Podhoretz put it, Ferguson had "a comically hangdog expression," accentuated by his droopy mustache and bow ties. Ken Askew, a speechwriter who joined the staff in 1992, described Ferguson as "very studious, very methodical, a fierce thinker. He was very comfortable in the realm of ideas."

Ferguson was told that Bush would be speaking before the Detroit Chamber of Commerce, but when a researcher called there to get more background information on the event, an official had no idea the president was due. In fact, the speech was to be given at an industrial automation plant in the Detroit suburbs. Next came the guidance problems: What should the speech be about? Depending upon whom Ferguson listened to, it was a speech on either government reform or job training.

Ferguson wrote a speech on reform at the instruction of Demarest and deputy chief of staff Henson Moore. It went through the staffing process and was ready for the president when Roger Porter of the Domestic Policy Council called Ferguson, saying how excited he was about the job training speech. Ferguson went to Porter's office to try to explain that there was no job training speech, that the speech was about reform and was about to hit the president's desk. More discussion resulted in a job training section getting shoehorned into the reform speech, leaving it a muddle that received scant attention.

On April 29, an all-white jury returned a verdict of not guilty in the case of four white Los Angeles police officers who had savagely beaten black motorist Rodney King. The decision sparked riots that lasted for nearly a week. On the third day of rioting, May 1, King himself asked: "Can we all get along? I mean, we're all stuck here for a while. Let's try to work it out."

Demarest was driving in to work that morning when he was paged to go see the president in the Oval Office. Bush wanted to go on the air that night to talk about the situation in California. He had made brief statements, but this would be a full-blown address. The key question was tone: Would this be a law and order speech or a speech focusing on the need for better race relations and racial justice?

"He clearly wanted to make the point that there can be no civil justice when there is the kind of lawlessness, the kind of chaos that was clearly occurring in Los Angeles," Demarest recalled. "So in short it was going to be a law and order speech."

Demarest consulted with members of the senior staff and then started writing. He was circulating a first draft by one o'clock in the afternoon. Snow came to see him: He had written a draft on his own, what one staffer later described to *The New York Times* as "a deep-think piece on racial problems in the United States." It acknowledged that racism existed and exhorted the nation to come together to end it. He showed it to Demarest, Skinner, Moore, and Fitzwater, among others. It was the approach that Fitzwater favored, and after the midafternoon meeting of the communications group, Demarest got a call from the press secretary: We're going with Snow's speech, he said. Has the President seen it? Demarest asked. He had not.

Demarest went to Skinner, who told him to soften the tone of his speech slightly. The chief of staff then walked both drafts in to the Oval Office. He emerged quickly, handed Demarest his draft of the speech. The president wants to go with your draft, he said. Demarest was gratified but still amazed at how chaotic the process was.

"What we saw last night and the night before in Los Angeles is not about civil rights," Bush said from the Oval Office that evening. "It's not about the great cause of equality that all Americans must uphold. It's not a message of protest. It's been the brutality of a mob, pure and simple. And let me assure you: I will use whatever force is necessary to restore order. What is going on in L.A. must and will stop. As your President I guarantee you this violence will end."

• • •

Bob Teeter, the campaign chairman, met with the speechwriters in the third week of June. He passed around an elaborate chart he had produced on his computer, laying out a structure that he wanted the speechwriters to follow in drafting speeches on such topics as education, values, jobs, and crime. The different topics each had a box in the chart, but one was empty. It read: "Theme/Slogan/Name"—"What I want from you, is to help fill this empty box," he told the speechwriters.

On July 8, Skinner announced to a stunned White House staff that he had finally found a new communications director, a thirty-two-year-old spokesman for Kentucky Fried Chicken named Steve Provost. He had previously written speeches for former New Jersey governor Thomas Kean, but he had never worked in the White House or in a presidential campaign. "This is absolutely ludicrous," one anonymous official told *The Washington Post*. "I am sure the guy is fine, maybe great in what he does, but this is a presidential campaign. This is a crisis. You don't go out and get a guy who's never laid eyes on the president or tried to maneuver through this horrible White House bureaucracy to be your chief speechwriter and communications director. It is totally ridiculous." The *Post* article ran with a picture of Provost standing next to a statue of Colonel Sanders, the founder of the fast food chain.

"This seals it," a Bush political adviser told the *Post*. "This is the end of Skinner. I predict right here and now James Baker will be back and he'll bring a team of professionals with him."

A friend faxed Provost the *Post* article and it gave him pause as to the wisdom of taking the job. He called his wife and said he did not think he could go to Washington, but she talked him out of quitting before he had even begun. "Provost came from a totally different point of view of slogans and jingles and applause lines, and really, really understood speeches in a way that I didn't," Andrew Ferguson recalled. "Bush really liked that very pithy, idiomatic, PR language—slogans, as opposed to sentences and paragraphs and arguments."

In some instances, Provost's lack of experience in the ways of the White House proved a boon. Faced with a process for staffing speeches out and waiting—often too long—for comments from a couple of dozen people, Provost occasionally told his staff to bang out a dummy speech to feed to the bureaucracy while they worked on the actual address. But other times his political ignorance showed. In August, he shook up the staff, canning about half, while keeping on vets Smith, Ferguson, and McGroarty (the other original members of the staff were all long gone). It was standard procedure in the corporate world: A new boss comes in, evaluates the staff, and shakes it up, but Provost was surprised by the stir it caused in Washington.

Provost had been on the job a little over a month when the next political temblor hit the White House. On August 13, James Baker, who had been Bush's Secretary of State, did indeed make a reluctant return to the position of White House chief of staff, bringing with him aides Margaret Tutwiler and Robert Zoellick, who took charge of the communications operation, bumping Provost from communications director to chief speechwriter.

All the while Bush wallowed in the polls, never able to gain traction in the general election's three-way race against Arkansas governor Bill Clinton and independent billionaire H. Ross Perot. The campaign concluded in Houston on November 3 at the Houstonian Hotel. Provost was tapped to write both a victory speech and a concession speech. "When you're in the bubble . . . you feel momentum and the crowds are lively and you know in the outside world you're behind, but in the inside world you're thinking, 'This is going to be 1948 all over again,'" he recalled. He passed in his drafts in the morning and waited. Late in the afternoon he ran into speechwriter Christina Martin, who had started four years earlier as a researcher in the speech shop. She was in tears. He asked what was wrong—no official word had come in. She told him to look around—"They had replaced the Secret Service detail, and the first detail was flying south to Arkansas so that they could guard [the new president-elect], and the sinking feeling of 'Oh my gosh, we blew it,' just sunk in at that time," he later remembered.*

The draft of the concession speech came back from Bush, more

---

*Although the election of a new president does not mean a diminution in the size of the incumbent's Secret Service detail, some senior elements will shift from the current to the incoming president after the election. This typically does not happen on Election Day, so whether that is what Provost and Martin saw is unclear.

heavily edited than anything Provost had seen before from the president—much shorter, and much more to the point. Bush said that he wanted to make clear that any mistakes made were his, that he wanted the transition to be smooth and, he said, if it's okay with you, Steve, I don't want to speak very long. "We got in the motorcade," Provost recalled, "we went in and he gave it that night and—ah—it hurts just even talking about it."

In 2000, while moderating a panel on leadership at his presidential library, ex-President Bush summarized the problems he had had with speechwriters:

> *My problem, very frankly, was that I wasn't articulate. I didn't feel comfortable with some of the speechwriters' phrases, so I would cross them out. . . . And I think it was maybe a mistake—because part of being seen as a visionary is being able to have flowing rhetoric and . . . you know, coming out of the clouds and being quoted all the time. My vision was for a kinder and gentler nation, my vision was for more freedom, more democracy around the world. My vision, as it turned out in the war—stand up against aggression and let some able people do the job. So I feel comfortable with what I felt was a vision.*

Bush felt comfortable with it, but he never learned to properly communicate it, or to use his speech staff properly. They had had other problems. In the best of times they were ignored and in the worst of times they were alternately blamed for the administration's political collapse or ordered to reverse it. But they had gotten steady exposure to him and were genuinely fond of their boss.

After Bush left office, several of the speechwriters realized that he would have to go on giving speeches. Curt Smith organized a volunteer effort, and he, McNally, Lange, Grant, and another former speechwriter named Beth Hinchliffe offered their services as an ongoing speechwriting staff, gratis. Demarest and McGroarty had already done so.

"The answer, before you change your minds: I accept your offer!!!"

Bush wrote Smith and the others on June 14, 1993. He invited those on the east coast up to Maine "to get things moving. Inasmuch as Ed [McNally] and Mark [Lange] are out West maybe you and Les Girls, make that politically correct—'Les Women,' could come up here first," he wrote. "If that makes sense let me know and the plane tickets will be in the mail."

ELEVEN

"No, No, No, This Is a Speech—I Just Want to Talk to People"

JANUARY 20, 1993

Vice President–elect Al Gore's head drooped down and then bobbed back up. Down and up—he was fighting a losing battle with sleep. The ceremony that would make Bill Clinton the forty-second president of the United States was hours away, but, amid friends and aides, Clinton was still editing and rewriting his inaugural address.

Work on the speech had begun in Little Rock weeks before with communications aide George Stephanopoulos filling a three-ring binder with drafts, memos, and suggestions from staff and luminaries, including JFK speechwriters Ted Sorensen, Richard Goodwin, and Arthur Schlesinger, Jr. Clinton had selected two aides to write the address: Michael Waldman, a dark-haired, deep-voiced policy staffer, had worked as a public interest lawyer and lobbyist before joining the campaign. He suggested focusing the speech on renewing American democracy. Clinton paired him with campaign speechwriter David Kusnet. Kusnet, the incoming White House chief speechwriter, was "shy and gentle, with studious glasses," Waldman said. He was a veteran of the Walter Mondale and Michael Dukakis presidential campaigns, and had written a book in 1992, *Speaking American*, about how liberals could communicate with ordinary Americans. "Our job was to capture [Clinton's] thoughts, feed him ideas, try to wrestle it into some sense of structure and organization," Waldman later wrote. They produced at least twenty drafts of the speech, by Kusnet's estimate.

Kusnet, adapting a slogan that Clinton had used on the campaign trail—"Every problem in America has been solved somewhere . . ."— conceived the signature line: "There is nothing wrong with America that cannot be cured by what is right with America." From the late Father Timothy Healy, a past president of Georgetown University, Clinton's alma mater, they drew the idea of "forcing the spring," or speeding the cycle of renewal. Healy died before sending his notes to Clinton, and they were found on his computer.

Clinton dictated a call for political reform: "This capital, like every capital since the dawn of civilization, has been a place of intrigue and calculation," the draft said. "Powerful and wealthy people come here and maneuver with an obsessive concern about who is in and who is out, who is up and who is down, often forgetting about the people to whom it belongs." (Final version: "This beautiful capital, like every capital since the dawn of civilization, is often a place of intrigue and calculation. Powerful people maneuver for position and worry endlessly about who is in and who is out, who is up and who is down, forgetting those people whose toil and sweat sends us here and pays our way.")

Clinton and his staff had decamped from Little Rock to Washington, arriving four days before the inauguration. Work on the speech continued, with a growing pool of contributors that included Clinton's college roommate, Tommy Caplan, and Taylor Branch, the Pulitzer Prize–winning biographer of Martin Luther King, Jr. Branch brought a King quote that inspired the peroration, Clinton's exhortation to Americans to "begin anew with energy and hope, with faith and discipline. And let us work until our work is done." But work on the speech was not done. "He's never met a sentence he couldn't fool with," Hillary Rodham Clinton later observed. After a gala inaugural eve celebration, the president-elect had a final rehearsal at Blair House, the governmental guest quarters across Pennsylvania Avenue from the White House. Rehearsal meant more revisions. "Clinton never knew exactly what he wanted to say until he heard himself say the words," Stephanopoulos later wrote in his White House memoir.

Acutely conscious of his reputation for long-windedness, Clinton cut words, lines, paragraphs, even whole pages. He was finally satisfied around 4:30 am, and the group broke up in the early morning to grab a bit of sleep.

The speech was well received. "Bill Clinton was equal to the occasion," *Time* reported. William Safire gave the address a "B+". *The New York Times*'s R. W. Apple, Jr., portended some administration problems, however. "Even at their moment of triumph, many of the Clinton people seem acutely aware that their margin for error, never great, has been reduced by the conflict, the disorganization and the resultant tardiness that marred the transition," Apple wrote the day after the inauguration. "When a reporter complained this week to George Stephanopoulos, the White House communications director, that his answers to her questions were flat and unilluminating, he replied, 'I can't afford to be colorful.'"

It was the economy, stupid. Clinton's presidential victory had been fueled by the perception that he was in tune with the suffering of working-class voters. Where George H. W. Bush had declared, "Message: I care," Clinton had bit his lip and expressed empathy. He promised that as president he would "focus like a laser beam on the economy." So Clinton's first major speeches would unveil his economic plan. He would do it in two stages: a February 15 Oval Office address previewing the unpalatable portions of the program—tax increases—and then a State of the Union address two days later revealing the rest of the plan.* The hope was that the initial backlash against raising taxes would spend itself in time to give the rest of the program a fair public hearing.

The speechwriters, armed with what Waldman called "ambitious, wide-ranging and indiscriminate" instructions from Clinton, prepared the talks while the president and his economic team hashed out the ac-

---

*February 17 was chosen for the official unveiling of his plan because it would allow Clinton partisans to argue that his administration had produced his economic plan faster than had Ronald Reagan, who explained the details of his plan on February 18, 1981. (John Harris, *Survivor*, 19.)

tual plans in the Roosevelt Room. Only occasionally did the two efforts intersect.

Clinton's advisers were split. Deficit hawks, such as economic adviser Robert Rubin and budget director Leon Panetta, argued that impressing Wall Street with fiscal discipline was of paramount concern because it could lead to lower interest rates and increased economic growth. Aides such as Labor Secretary Robert Reich, Stephanopoulos, and Rubin deputy Gene Sperling favored increasing spending to stimulate the economy. Clinton split the difference with a strong tilt toward deficit reduction, with two dollars of cutting for every one of new spending. The middle-class tax cut upon which he had campaign was dispensed with.

The debate was emblematic of the early days of the administration. Clinton had run for office as a "New Democrat." He was a former chairman of the centrist Democratic Leadership Council and portrayed himself as a southern governor who was willing to break with his party's liberal orthodoxy. But he was a philosophical dabbler. His advisers reflected both this impulse and the fact that much of the Democratic establishment was still "old Democrat." Much of the first term was spent working out the tensions between the two wings of the party.

Campaign consultant Paul Begala and deputy communications director David Dreyer, both veterans of House Democratic leader Richard Gephardt's office, composed the first Oval Office address, while Kusnet and Waldman wrote the second speech, to Congress. Only Kusnet was technically on the speechwriting staff. None of them had a background in economics, and none knew where the deliberations by the president and his team were heading. "Was the budget to be sold as investment or deficit reduction?" Waldman was wondering. "How strongly should the arguments about fairness be made? Were we still putting people first?" ("Putting people first" had been a Clinton campaign theme.)

Like Jimmy Carter, Clinton had never worked with speechwriters before his presidential campaign. "You know, I never had a speechwriter before I was president," he would tell his writers. "Gave three speeches a day when I was governor, never needed a speechwriter." He would say that, recalled second-term writer Jeff Shesol, "as if he was just making small talk—with someone who had a thing against speechwriters." "No one looked to the Carter experience as a successful presidential experience, so to find a winning Democratic team you would have to go back to the Kennedy-Johnson people," Kusnet said.

Clinton spent most of Monday, February 15, working on the Oval Office speech. He scrawled all over the pages with a black felt-tip marker. One speechwriter described his handwriting as looking like a "string of cursive 'u's." The deadline for getting an advance copy to the media came and went. The final draft was loaded onto the TelePrompTer at 8:48 pm, leaving Clinton time for one read-through.

Clinton attacked a dozen years of Reaganomics and bragged about his tenure as governor of Arkansas. "Those who profited from the status quo will oppose the changes we seek," he said. "Every step of the way they'll oppose it. Many have already lined the corridors of power with high-priced lobbyists. They are the defenders of decline. And we must be the architects of the future."

Clinton, Stephanopoulos, and the senior staff were pleased with the speech. Later that evening, Stephanopoulos was disabused when he was the surprise guest at a meeting of the Judson Welliver Society, the association of former presidential speechwriters. Gathering in the basement of ringleader William Safire's home, former ghosts from the Truman administration onward had eaten dinner and watched the speech. The reviews were not good. Ted Sorensen had said that he did not like to talk about Democratic speeches that he could not praise. Stephanopoulos's appearance brought an uncomfortable silence, which was broken when Sorensen rose: Mr. Stephanopoulos, he said, I thought the speech was wonderful!* The room cracked up.

The laughter loosened the group. They told Stephanopoulos the speech was strident and the delivery rushed. Safire asked Stephanopoulos to describe the speech-drafting process and jaws dropped as he recounted it. "You mean," Patrick Buchanan asked, "he didn't practice for the first time until ten minutes before *nine*?" Tony Snow of the Bush administration exclaimed: "George, you guys are bungee jumping without a rope." "What's bungee jumping?" Arthur Schlesinger, Jr., asked

---

*Waldman had been at the dinner, but was so nervous that he had left early, listened to speech in his car, and then driven away. (Author interview with Michael Waldman.)

Tony Dolan. When Dolan explained that it involved people tying a rope around themselves and jumping off a cliff, Schlesinger stared at him for a time and then made a "harrumph" noise.

The speechwriters' assessment was on target. *Time* described the address as "one of the worst speeches" of Clinton's life. The stock market fell nearly 83 points the following day. White House chief of staff Thomas "Mack" McLarty worried to Waldman that businesspeople and legislators had heard too much class warfare. But there was little strategic guidance regarding the next speech two days later to Congress.

The speechwriters did get some detail help from Sperling, though he was feverish and groggy with the flu. As Waldman, Dreyer, Begala, and others worked through Tuesday night on the State of the Union in Dreyer's office, Sperling sat propped in a chair, covered in blankets and coats, half-conscious. "Hey Gene, how much does a surcharge on millionaires pick up?" Dreyer would shout. His eyes never opening, Sperling would mumble the answer after a few seconds and then slip back into his stupor.

On Wednesday morning, the speech was still pitching economic stimulus, even though the plan now was emphasizing reduction. Domestic policy adviser Bruce Reed and National Security Council speechwriter Jeremy Rosner wrote a new centrist opening to the address, which Clinton liked. A furious Hillary Clinton convened an editing session in the Roosevelt Room where the speech was revised paragraph by paragraph. The final text had to be to the printer by noon to get advance copies up to the Hill, another deadline that blew right by.

When Clinton arrived at the family theatre in the West Wing at 6:30 pm, he had time for one rehearsal, and he revised as he went. "We never received anything but a finished draft from Bush," one Army Signal Corps TelePromptTer operator told Taylor Branch. "We put it in, and he read it."

The speech was still in disarray when Clinton ascended to the rostrum in the House of Representatives that evening. As he spoke, he saw "lawmakers stir and respond to points and fall silent for others, [and] he began to feed off their response," Waldman wrote. "He began to riff— to ad-lib, to revise entire paragraphs." Clinton improvised roughly a quarter of the speech. Jammed in the well of the House, Waldman and Sperling high-fived each other. "He's ad-libbing the State of the Union!"

They should not have been surprised. Clinton speeches were often a dialogue: he could read a crowd and adjust accordingly, seamlessly departing and returning to the prepared text. The analogy most Clinton speechwriters use is a jazz musician. "The job of the speechwriters, especially on the domestic side, but also on the foreign policy side, was to try to establish what the main theme was and give him then the freedom to riff," National Security Council speechwriter Tony Blinken said.*

And Jazz does not mean chaos or randomness, argued Don Baer, a Clinton chief speechwriter. Jazz is a "very structured, disciplined form. . . . But it is the very structure and discipline that actually allows it to have the appearance of spontaneity and to open the door for the emotional component to sort of breathe through where otherwise you might not feel it," he said. "Riffing is not just free and easy—there's a purpose and a direction to it. . . . It's controlled in such a way that you lose sight of the controls."†

Waldman and Sperling cheered during the 1993 State of the Union, but the president's speechwriters were often exasperated when he discarded a text that they had toiled over. Clinton knew it was frustrating too, once telling Terry Edmonds, his last chief speechwriter, that it was just his style and that he did it with his own writing. "It's when he gets up there, he sees people he knows, stories come to his mind, connections are being made from past experiences," Edmonds said. "So then

---

*Speechwriters Jonathan Prince and Jordan Tamagni once discussed what was the optimal balance in a Clinton speech between how much came from the prepared text versus how much was improvised. "It's clearly fifty-fifty," Tamagni said. "Because if he only just reads yours that means he's bored and he's droning and if he doesn't read anything of yours that means he's rambling and he hated what you wrote . . . but if he does fifty-fifty then you know that he's engaged and you feel that you've done a good job." That's not it at all, Prince replied, the optimal ratio is 150 percent—the speech you provided and another 50 percent of Clinton riffing. (Author interview with Jordan Tamagni.)

†Reagan speechwriter Clark Judge extends the musical analogy. Not only did Clinton's style resemble jazz, he says; Reagan was "symphonic: every element of emotion, nuance, he could convey"; George H. W. Bush "was like rock'n'roll: simple, driving beats"; and George W. Bush "like country music . . . very strong structure, a kind of a moral message underpinning and a note of evangelical lyricism." (Author interview with Clark Judge.)

he's off, he's off doing his own thing. He uses the speech, of course he knows the policy nugget that's in there, he studies it, and makes sure he gets it out. But he'll do it in his own style."

Clinton's speechwriters would eventually learn to **boldface** the crucial talking points in a speech so that the president would include them. Mostly he did, though if he thought a sentence too rhetorical or too banal he might skip or rephrase it. Speechwriter Jordan Tamagni called this the "that's the way the cookie falls apart syndrome," for how he would interpolate a hoary phrase like "that's the way the cookie crumbles."

Returning to the White House on the evening of February 17, after the State of the Union, Clinton told Begala to bring "the kids," as he called the younger staffers, to the solarium in the residence for a celebration. Carrot cake with cream cheese frosting was served, and then cherry pie. At evening's end, Bill and Hillary turned on a C-SPAN rerun of the speech.

National security adviser Anthony Lake and his deputy, Sandy Berger, fought to get a foreign policy speech onto the schedule. Each had speechwriting backgrounds, and they placed great stock in the importance of presidential communication. Lake had written drafts for the NSC under Nixon before he resigned in protest over the 1970 invasion of Cambodia. They had recruited Jeremy Rosner as an NSC speechwriter. Rosner had worked for Gary Hart, and at the Democratic Leadership Council. He had helped with national security speeches during the campaign, and was "a tremendous writer with force and punch," Don Baer said. Speeches are written by the White House speechwriting shop, Rosner pointed out to Lake. Not anymore, Lake replied. He told Rosner to tell Kusnet that the NSC would be handling national security speeches.

Rosner and Kusnet had worked closely on the 1984 Mondale campaign. When Rosner told Kusnet that national security speeches would be written in the National Security Council, Kusnet just looked at him, and said, okay. "And that was it," Rosner recalled. "It was the biggest turf grab in White House history. It was huge."

NSC staffers had long produced initial drafts for presidential speechwriters, and this writer-expert relationship had always been strained. Henry Kissinger with Nixon and Zbigniew Brzezinski with Carter had both suggested bringing foreign policy speeches entirely inside the NSC. Now Lake had done it. "The reason for doing this was simply efficiency," Lake recalled. It made sense to have the speeches drafted "in the NSC by a speechwriter who knows the substance of foreign policy so that you're not then getting behind and trying to fight over nuances."

Lake and Berger finally got a foreign policy speech scheduled for February 26, when Clinton was to speak on globalization and economics, leading up to the push to pass the North American Free Trade Agreement (NAFTA), at American University's centennial celebration. Rosner sent several drafts to Clinton and got little response. That morning, Rosner, Lake, and Berger joined a scrum in the Oval Office to go over the speech. Things were running late. Clinton was not working from the most recent draft, so Rosner gave the president pages from the current version. The two versions got jumbled. Rosner was panicking. During the campaign, he had never dealt with Clinton in person. Then an aide told Clinton that it was time to leave for American University. Come on Jeremy, Clinton said, get in the car.

The motorcade wound along the Rock Creek Parkway. Pages from the two drafts, covered with Clinton's scribble, were everywhere. The president, eyeglasses down on his nose, edited. What was that line we wanted to add? We should move this section over here. Which of these pages is from the new draft? Rosner answered while holding Clinton's coffee cup as the car traveled a well-worn February road. Oh my God, he thought, the speech is screwed up, we're about to hit a pothole, and I'm going to spill coffee on the president and lose my job. It occurred to him that it was his son's third birthday. Even if he avoided scalding the president, he was sure the speech was doomed: Clinton had not focused on the substance, which was still all over the place.

Rosner did not spill the coffee but watched with trepidation as Clinton took the jumble of papers to the podium and told the crowd an anecdote about his Georgetown University days and dating a girl from American University. Then he launched into the speech. "It was perfect," Rosner recalled. "He ad-libbed some sections, he found the key paragraphs. And it was this gorgeous speech . . . much better than anything we wrote."

Evoking memories of JFK's peace speech at the same school thirty years earlier, in which he appealed for peace on the grounds that "We all breathe the same air. We all cherish our children's futures. And we are all mortal," Clinton said that managing globalization was the major challenge of the age and that the United States could not withdraw from a post–Cold War world. "Washington can no longer remain caught in the death grip of gridlock, governed by an outmoded ideology that says change is to be resisted, the status quo is to be preserved," he said. "Will we repeat the mistakes of the 1920s or the 1930s by turning inward, or will we repeat the successes of the 1940s and the 1950s by reaching outward and improving ourselves as well? I say that if we set a new direction at home, we can set a new direction for the world as well."

Rosner felt calmer about the whole process on April 1, when the same last-minute scene unfolded. Clinton was scheduled to lunch with midshipmen at the Naval Academy in Annapolis, Maryland, and then speak to the American Society of Newspaper Editors on his plans for dealing with Russia in a post–Cold War world. Again the NSC had sent drafts in to the president and had got little response. Once again Rosner ended up in the presidential limousine, this time with Lake as well, trying to put the final touches on the speech. Clinton held his own coffee cup, clutching it in his teeth as he rewrote.

Then the car hit a bump and the coffee spilled down the front of Clinton's shirt. Oh man! Clinton yelled. What am I going to do? This is my first visit to a military academy and my shirt is ruined! He instructed the Secret Service to divert the motorcade into Annapolis to stop at a department store, and was informed that this sort of security nightmare was impossible. Lake offered Clinton the shirt off his own back, but the president declined—his national security adviser was too small. The Secret Service agents radioed up and down the motorcade until an agent whose shirt size matched Clinton's was found. At a hastily arranged stop, the president donned the agent's shirt in the back of his limousine.

• • •

411

Rosner was drawn into domestic speeches as well, as when the president was to speak to a joint session of Congress on September 22, 1993, to unveil the health care plan that Hillary Clinton had spent months crafting behind closed doors. The official domestic speechwriters were led by Kusnet, but the president dismissed their draft of the speech as "pedestrian." David Gergen, who had joined the administration in May, called Rosner at around 11 am on Tuesday, September 21. The Clintons do not like the draft of the health care speech, Gergen told him; they want you to rewrite it.

Rosner said that it would be unfair to his domestic speechwriting colleagues. What he did not say was that he was overburdened, drafting a major speech for Lake as well as Clinton's September 27 address to the UN General Assembly. He agreed on the condition that David Dreyer, the deputy communications director, be enlisted.

Rosner and Dreyer were close friends from working for Gary Hart in the mid-1980s. Rosner was Dreyer's best man. With his ponytail, earring, and colorful ties, Dreyer was the kind of young Clinton staffer who sent conservatives into fits. They were an intense team. They asked Hillary Clinton what she wanted in the speech and locked themselves in Rosner's office, unplugged the phone, and said they were not to be disturbed. They had what Rosner told *Washington Post* journalists Haynes Johnson and David Broder was a typical session: "He'll suggest something and I'll yell at him, and then he'll suggest something and I'll yell at him again, and we'll yell at each other for about ten minutes and then come up with a great sentence," Rosner said. "We've got great creative tension."

The Clintons spent Tuesday night reworking the Rosner-Dreyer draft. When the president's senior aides assembled in the family dining room of the residence on Wednesday morning, the president was scribbling on the text with his left hand while chewing on his right thumb. His wife stood behind him, rubbing his shoulders. Clinton wrote all over it in shorthand notes: "—Δ—Dislocation—uncertainty—Future w/Fear—in trust gov't." Rosner and Dreyer had written that the American story started more than 350 years ago, which Clinton changed to "Our forebears enshrined the American Dream: life, liberty, the pursuit of happiness. Every generation of Americans has worked to strengthen that legacy. . . ."

Rosner and Dreyer had detailed the benefits of a part of the plan, before acknowledging that there would be some drawbacks. "And [Clinton] said, 'No,'" Rosner recalled. "He said, 'Start with the bad news. If you lead with all the gumdrops people are going to get, everyone's going to say bullshit. But if you start at the very start with here are the things you've got to accept are going to be true, people go, Jeez, this guy's being blunt with us. And then they'll be more receptive to the good news later.' At one level, that's a nice little rhetorical trick—but that's a big rhetorical trick."

Rosner and Dreyer left to incorporate the edits and were soon joined by, it seemed, everyone else: senior aides, political consultants, forming what Rosner called a "little frenetic knot of people that was following the speech." One White House staffer told Johnson and Broder that when the group—"the pack"—assembles, "everyone becomes the speechwriter, everyone has an opinion, everyone has an equal say." As the pack worked, pages of Clinton suggestions or comments were faxed over and incorporated.

Rehearsal extended past 8 pm. One group of aides listened as Clinton rehearsed and rewrote, while another entered changes. Corrected pages were run from one group to the other. Dreyer made the last edits and dashed for the motorcade. On the ride down Pennsylvania Avenue, Clinton was editing.

At the rostrum in the House Chamber, Clinton surveyed the legislators, cabinet members, and aides. Then he looked at the TelePrompTer screens. His February economic speech was loaded. He had a hard copy of the health care address, but it was not in the large-type format and he did not have his glasses. As the applause continued, Clinton turned back to Al Gore, sitting as president of the Senate, and told him to get Stephanopoulos to fix the problem. Stephanopoulos scrambled to get the proper text loaded as Clinton, as he later put it, "just sort of whipped back and did it." "I knew what I wanted to say anyway, so I wasn't too worried, though it was a bit distracting to see all those irrelevant words scrolling by on the TelePrompTer," he wrote in his memoirs.

My fellow Americans, tonight we come together to write a new chapter in the American story. Our forebears enshrined the American dream: life, liberty, the pursuit of happiness. Every generation of Americans has worked to strengthen that legacy, to make our country a place of freedom and opportunity, a place where people who work hard can rise to their full potential, a place where their children can have a better future. . . . If Americans are to have the courage to change in a difficult time, we must first be secure in our most basic needs. Tonight I want to talk to you about the most critical thing we can do to build that security. This health care system of ours is badly broken, and it is time to fix it.

After the longest seven minutes in Stephanopoulos's life, the correct text flashed onto the TelePrompTer screens.

The theatrical high point came when Clinton held up a blue card emblazoned with the United States seal and "Health Security Card" written on it. "Under our plan, every American would receive a health care security card that will guarantee a comprehensive package of benefits over the course of an entire lifetime, roughly comparable to the benefit package offered by most Fortune 500 companies," Clinton said. "This health care security card will offer this package of benefits in a way that can never be taken away."

The speech was generally positively received. Clinton's approval rating moved up 10 points in the Gallup Poll. "He gave a thoroughly grown-up, sometimes stern, sometimes passionate and sometimes even angry speech about health care, with a direct and forceful demeanor and few contrivances," *The New York Times* reported. But a second *Times* piece portended the problems the plan would encounter: "Members of Congress registered strong support tonight for the outlines of President Clinton's plan to recast the nation's health care system, but many lawmakers immediately began to pick fights with details relating to expected increases in taxes and costs."

Hillary Clinton had produced legislation that totaled 1,342 pages. The plan consisted of interlocking proposals that aimed to use the best aspects of regulation and the free market to guarantee universal health care. But such a sweeping and complicated plan had several political flaws. It was hard for proponents to describe simply, but easy for critics to skewer as being too complicated. And even potential allies could find some flaws in a plan so sweeping, making it hard to hold together a coalition broad enough to support it.

The plan's political and substantive problems were exposed, exploited, and compounded by a massive lobbying effort with different special interests spending around $100 million to lobby the Congress. In addition, tens of millions of dollars was spent on television advertising, including the devastating series sponsored by the health insurers' association in which a fictional couple—"Harry and Louise"—sat at their kitchen table and fretted at how complicated the plan was.

In his 1994 State of the Union address, Clinton vowed to veto any health care bill Congress passed without universal health care coverage. It seemed a political master stroke at the time, but it only closed off avenues of compromise. The underlying assumption—that Congress would pass some health care bill—seemed reasonable when he made the declaration; but by the time he and Hillary Clinton were willing to cut a deal, in the summer, the GOP leadership had concluded that there was no reason to throw Clinton a lifeline. When the health care effort died, a scant five weeks before the 1994 midterm election, it had become a symbol of liberal overreach and political ineptitude.

In November 1993, Clinton's pursuit of passage of the North American Free Trade Agreement was at full steam. On Saturday, November 13, he flew to Memphis, Tennessee, to give a pair of talks, one of them at the Church of God in Christ—sacred ground both literally and as the house of worship where Martin Luther King, Jr., gave his last sermon.

Carolyn Curiel, the first Latina presidential speechwriter, suspected Clinton would not closely follow a text for the church speech, so she gave him three pages of talking points and a *Washington Post* article about an eleven-year-old girl who was so afraid of gang violence that she planned her own funeral. Clinton jotted his own notes: "MLK didn't die $\rightarrow$ 13 yr old the freedom to get semi auto shoot 9 yr old . . . $\rightarrow$ teenage girls freedom to have children & watch father of their child walk away . . . $\rightarrow$ young freedom destroy lives w/drugs or bld pers. fortunes destroying lives of others."

At the church, Clinton spoke briefly about the importance of trade, but quickly moved on to what he called "the great crisis of the spirit that is gripping America today." His notes had helped him order his thoughts, but now he discarded them. He imagined what King would say were he before them. He would praise them for making progress in expanding political power for minorities and for creating a black middle class. But he would scold them as well: "I did not live and die to see the American family destroyed," he would say. "I did not live and die to see thirteen-year-old boys get automatic weapons and gun down nine-year-olds just for the kick of it. I did not live and die to see young people destroy their own lives with drugs and then build fortunes destroying the lives of others."

Clinton told tales of violence and sadness, including that of the eleven-year-old girl. "How would we explain it to Martin Luther King if he showed up today and said, yes, we won the Cold War," he said. "Yes, the biggest threat that all of us grew up under, communism and nuclear war, communism gone, nuclear war receding. Yes, we developed all these miraculous technologies. . . . How would we explain to him all these kids getting killed and killing each other? How would we justify the things that we permit that no other country in the world would permit? How could we explain that we gave people the freedom to succeed, and we created conditions in which millions abuse that freedom to destroy the things that make life worth living and life itself? We cannot."

He concluded:

So in this pulpit, on this day, let me ask all of you in your heart to say: We will honor the life and the work of Martin Luther King. We will honor the meaning of our church. We will, somehow, by God's grace, we will turn this around. We will give these children a future. We will take away their guns and give them books. We will take away their despair and give them hope. We will rebuild the families and the neighborhoods and the communities. We won't make all the work that has gone on here benefit just a few. We will do it together by the grace of God.

"The Memphis speech was a hymn of praise to a public philosophy rooted in my personal religious values," Clinton wrote in his memoirs of his most eloquent speech. "Too many things were falling apart; I was trying to put them together."

I understand that you're not altogether happy with the speechwriters and the speeches, Don Baer told Clinton in the winter of 1994. I don't know, Clinton said; up until a year and a half ago, I didn't have a speechwriter and I did all my own things.

The administration's ongoing attempts to master presidential communications had brought Baer to the verge of becoming Clinton's speechwriting director. He had grown up a "nice Jewish boy in Fayetteville, North Carolina," had a law degree from the University of Virginia and a master's in international relations from the London School of Economics. He'd had, in his word, an "eclectic" career: The summer after his third year of law school he had worked at a New York City law firm where a young litigation partner recently out of the Ford Justice Department, Rudolph Giuliani, was a mentor. (Even as Baer was negotiating with Clinton administration officials about joining the White House staff, he was declining a job offer with Giuliani, who had been elected major of New York City in 1993.) Baer had also worked on North Carolina governor James Hunt's 1984 senatorial bid against conservative Jesse Helms. He had settled on journalism, working for *American Lawyer* magazine and then for *U.S. News & World Report*. In 1991, he assigned himself a story on the two up-and-coming southern Democrats who might run for president: Arkansas governor Bill Clinton and Tennessee senator Albert Gore, Jr. He interviewed Clinton on a long flight from Washington to Memphis as the weather caused the plane to circle for an hour. David Gergen had first approached Baer in the summer of 1993 about joining the administration.

"I don't think [Clinton] liked the idea that someone else thought they were going to put words in his mouth, basically," Baer recalled. The president would be more willing to accept speech advice from pollsters, Baer said, because they could back up their arguments with data. "That's got something that has a faux-scientific bent to it," he said. "Speechwriters—typically it's just a choice of style, and I think he felt like he had a better grasp on his style than others."

Part of the problem also lay in Clinton's speechwriters' political bent. In addition to Kusnet, the speechwriting staff in the first year included Curiel, who had come from a journalism background that included *The Washington Post*, *The New York Times*, and ABC News, and Alan Stone, a veteran congressional staffer who had joined the Clinton campaign from the failed bid of liberal Senator Tom Harkin of Iowa. They were later joined by Carter Wilkie, a former aide to Boston mayor Thomas Menino. They did not, as a group, share Clinton's centrist views.

Kusnet saw Clinton with some frequency but it was rarely if ever one-on-one. Neither Kusnet nor his colleagues got the time to learn Clinton's style. Their efforts tended to be more liberal substantively and more rhetorical stylistically than Clinton favored. They saw him in speech-editing scrums. Reagan's writers had succeeded with limited access to their boss because he had a clear, simple message that never varied.

Clinton's pace also wore down his writers. "If you were running against an incumbent president in a campaign, that's the way you'd campaign," Kusnet remarked. "Pretty much the same people who had run the campaign were running the White House in the first year, and so that was sort of a campaign-type schedule. . . . There's always a sense of 'let's do one more event.'" Campaigns ran on adrenaline continously for a few months, while a presidential administration, though high energy, had to maintain a pace that could last four years. "Many of us were being asked to work on a campaign schedule, while many others weren't and it didn't quite mesh all the time," Kusnet said. The cumulative result was an unhappy speechwriting staff that was burning out.

When he joined the staff in March 1994, Baer looked at the number of speeches the president had given during the year's first quarter and extrapolated for the coming year. Clinton was on pace to deliver 496 speeches—more than one per day.* "It was meatball surgery," Baer said. And there was little thought given that they were crowding the schedule and that the president was drowning out his own message. "There

---

*Michael Waldman, who succeeded Baer as director of speechwriting in 1995, did his own count: "In a typical year, Clinton spoke in public 550 times. In a similar year, Ronald Reagan spoke 320 times; Harry Truman, 88 times." (Waldman, *POTUS Speaks*, 16.)

are few voices that can drown out a president's voice—but his own voice can," Kusnet said. "Instead of having an echo chamber that would last that same day, he was competing with the echoes of his own voice."

"We are the children of your sacrifice." The line had come to Baer while he reflected on the generational themes of the Passover celebration. He was thinking about Clinton's upcoming European trip to commemorate D-Day's fiftieth anniversary and the fact that the president would stand atop the same cliff at Pointe du Hoc upon which Reagan had so eloquently spoken a decade before. Baer saw the Normandy events—Clinton was to give four sets of remarks on June 6, 1994—as a great opportunity.

Baer knew that Clinton needed a short line. He had gone back and counted the number of words in Reagan's "These are the boys of Pointe du Hoc" and had been thinking about an equivalent. "We are the children of your sacrifice" had some poetry. His headline-writing instincts taking over, Baer weighed the elements of the phrase: "children" was problematic—it might imply that the world's leaders were too young. "Sacrifice," though, struck the right chord. Around such a phrase one could build an elegant speech. And it could pivot that address, he thought, turning it from an elegy for a great generation to a challenge for a new one.

Now Baer had to sell it to the NSC. He started with Rosner, who was preparing to leave the White House. He liked it, and with the approval of Lake and Berger, brought Baer into the process. It helped form a bridge between the operations—from then on, Baer too weighed in on major foreign policy speeches. Baer and Rosner worked with deputy NSC speechwriter Eric Liu, a former Senate staffer whose parents were Chinese immigrants and who had joined the NSC the previous fall. Rosner and Liu had learned to speak in a shorthand, finishing each other's thoughts.

The three writers had an extended session with the president, who spoke about his father, who had died in a car accident months before Clinton was born, and about an uncle who had served in the war. He remembered the stories he had heard from veterans. He talked of being the first baby boomer president—not only the first to be born after World War II but the first to take office after the Cold War. It was a chance not only to pay homage to the G.I. Generation but to articulate a vision for twenty-first-century Europe.

The president hosted a dinner at the White House for World War II historians and veterans, including members of Congress who had fought in the war, some who had taken part in the D-Day invasion. Stephen Ambrose, whose *D-Day* was just being published, delivered an impassioned speech about the boys who had gone ashore that day. Those young men saved the world, the historian said, looking at the president. The sessions were helpful, Baer thought, because they focused Clinton on the idea of saluting "the great devotion and personal sacrifices" of the people who had stood for basic principles of freedom and liberty and were now "beginning their passage from the stage."

Baer, Rosner, and Liu spent days working on the speeches. They were ghosts wrestling with ghosts, trying to honor the spirits of the World War II generation, trying to overcome the challenge of Reagan and Peggy Noonan. Work continued on the speeches on the flight across the Atlantic and into the night of June 5 on the USS *George Washington* in the English Channel. The next morning, Clinton spoke briefly on the deck of the ship. He and his entourage were scheduled to fly by helicopters to Pointe du Hoc. A thick fog enveloped the Channel and the decision was made that one helicopter would go. The three speechwriters squeezed in with the Clintons, skimmed across the water and up the cliff face, landing by Pointe du Hoc.

"We look at this terrain and we marvel at your fight," Clinton said to the veteran Rangers and their families assembled before him.

> *Here are the generations for whom you won a war. We are the children of your sacrifice. We are the sons and daughters you saved from tyranny's reach. We grew up behind the shield of the strong alliances you forged in blood upon these beaches, on the shores of the Pacific, and in the skies above. We flourished in the nation you came home to build.*

D-Day presented a rare opportunity for the speechwriters: along with the King speech, it was one of the few times Clinton allowed his speeches to soar. "He both liked rhetoric and also distrusted it," said Tom Malinowski, who headed the NSC speechwriters in the second term. "He wanted to inspire people, he wanted to get that reaction from the audience. He saw a good line, he said, 'I like that.' At the same time, he sometimes just said, 'Man, this is just rhetoric. I just don't want to go out there blowing smoke about this stuff. Sometimes can't we just make a serious argument?'" He could be more blunt, scribbling "WORDS, WORDS, WORDS" in the margin next to a particularly high-flying paragraph.

Speaking at the cemetery at Colleville-sur-Mer, Clinton talked about the thousands of G.I.s who did not return home. "They were the fathers we never knew, the uncles we never met, the friends who never returned, the heroes we can never repay," the president said. "They gave us our world. And those simple sounds of freedom we hear today are their voices speaking to us across the years." It was a line that Rosner had written, and which had special meaning for him: His uncle had died when his bomber was downed, by friendly fire, over Germany.

It was a powerful generational moment for Clinton as well. The baby boomers, many of whom had struggled with the moral ambiguities of the Vietnam War, had an opportunity to honor their parents.

"You're going to lose the Senate and House," consultant Dick Morris told the president four days before the 1994 midterm elections.

"Not the House, no way," Clinton replied. Democrats had controlled the House for forty years.

"*And the House,*" Morris said. "And by significant margins."

"No way, no way," Clinton said. "Not the House. Not the House. You're wrong. You really think so? You're wrong."

Morris and Clinton went back to Arkansas in the 1970s. A New York native, Morris was a practitioner of negative advertising. He helped get Clinton elected governor in 1978. Clinton fired Morris after the campaign, but brought him back in the last days of his failing 1980 reelection campaign. Though it had been too late to win that race, Morris worked for Clinton for the remainder of the decade, starting with his 1982 victory, and he moved away from negative advertising, developing an issue-focused style. The two men's relationship was tense, each drawn to the other's political acumen but disdainful of their personality. By 1994, his clientele was almost exclusively GOP and included Senate Republican whip Trent Lott of Mississippi.

Morris had spoken to Clinton from time to time since his inauguration, and more frequently with the first lady. "You can say things that you don't propose to Congress," Morris recalled telling Clinton. "You don't have to have a legislative program behind every speech—you're president. . . . You're acting too much like a majority leader or a prime minister, whose speaking is only to carry a legislative program, as opposed to a president, who can talk about anything." Morris was struck by the fact that there was no separate focus on speechmaking and communication—it was all a subset of legislating.

In his first two years, Clinton had worked closely with congressional Democrats. But they were more liberal than he was, pulling him to the left. "When he spoke, too often it was as a legislative leader, worrying about subcommittee votes and the details of bills," Waldman wrote. "He would need to learn how to speak as president—both as head of state, for the whole nation, and as sole chief of the executive branch."

The president and his aides were also the source of self-inflicted wounds, from a two-hundred-dollar haircut Clinton had at Los Angeles International Airport to such blunders as the health care fiasco. The economic plan had passed by a single vote, and now hung around the necks of Clinton and vulnerable Democrats. So did the assault weapons ban, which had been the centerpiece of an anti-crime bill that Congress passed in September. The electorate saw Clinton as in over his head. They were in no mood for the government to take their money or their guns.

Leading the charge was Newt Gingrich, the House Republican whip. Gingrich, from Georgia, had been elected to Congress in 1978 after a failed bid in 1974. He had long plotted a GOP ascension, developing an attacking style that was feistier than was the norm for his party, which he thought had grown complacent in the minority. The GOP was running on a ten-point platform, Gingrich's "Contract With America," that promised, among other things, a balanced budget, a tougher crime bill, tax cuts, term limits, a general scaling back and reform of the federal government. Republicans were promising all would be voted on within their first hundred days.

By the time Clinton reached out to Morris in mid-September 1994, his approval rating was hovering in the high 30s and low 40s. They spoke a lot in private in the weeks preceding the election. Morris offered polling data. Stephanopoulos picked up "an unfamiliar frequency in Clinton's monologues," but did not know its source. And Clinton still could not bring himself to believe the magnitude of what was coming. "Just in case what you're sure won't happen happens, I'll fax you the statement I think you should give when the returns come in," Morris told him. Clinton grunted and hung up.

November 8 produced a fifty-four-seat GOP gain in the House and eight more seats in the Senate. Every Republican seeking reelection won. And on the state level, the GOP picked up hundreds of local legislative seats and seized a majority of governorships, including the Texas statehouse with George W. Bush's victory. Clinton maintained an air of near detachment on election night, dispassionately analyzing the results for stunned staffers. Walking with Baer close to midnight, he smiled and said, "This could be liberating." Morris's phone rang early on November 9. "You saw I gave your statement," Clinton said. "What should I do?"

Clinton and Morris started meeting, secretly, away from the White House staff. The "Republican Revolution" was dominating Washington. Some Democrats thought Clinton's White House tenure had effectively ended, that he would serve out his term ineffectually. "Party leaders wonder whether Clinton can or should seek a second term," *Time* reported. Calm on election night, Clinton now retreated in gloom, emotionally and physically checking out. He worked more often now in the residence, away from his staff, as he and Morris grappled with how to deal with the setback.

Clinton could neither parrot the congressional Democrats, flatly opposing whatever the Republicans favored, Morris argued in early December, nor could he accept the Contract With America and a GOP agenda of dismantling the federal government, from environmental regulations to whole cabinet departments, like Education. "Triangulate," Morris said. To illustrate, Morris used his hands to form a triangle. Clinton would be the apex, between and above the political parties. "Identify a new course that accommodates the needs the Republicans address but does it in a way that is uniquely yours."

Morris faxed suggestions, sometimes at a clip of a half dozen per day, and talked with Clinton deep into the night. That December, he started meeting with the Clintons in the residence on Wednesday nights. But he remained in the shadows. To the extent White House staffers knew about him, it was under his pseudonym: "Charlie."

Speechwriting became, as one writer put it, Morris's "beachhead. That's where he invaded Normandy." The assault started in mid-December, when Clinton gave his first address to the nation since the election, aimed at appeasing an angry electorate and politically reasserting himself.

Morris suggested that they work as they had in Arkansas: Clinton would tell him what he was thinking of proposing, Morris would poll-test it, and then send him a speech draft. Clinton was not the flip-flopper or poll slave that some charged him to be. Rather, Morris compared him to a sailboat moving toward a fixed destination through a series of tacks. "He asks the pollster to help him determine which current he should try to harness to move him closer to his destination," Morris later wrote. These tacks should not be confused with "the zigzag of a flip-flop. These zigs and zags bring you ever closer to the place you want to be." At the time, Morris was in Paris on a scheduled trip, so he faxed drafts back and forth with Clinton through the president's personal secretary, Nancy Hernreich. Morris's wife conceived of the idea that became the focus of the speech, a "Middle-Class Bill of Rights," playing off the post–World War II G.I. Bill of Rights.

"Who came up with this language on the middle-class bill of rights?" Stephanopoulos asked the Clintons. The president ignored him. Hillary wore a Cheshire cat grin so he assumed it was she. Baer, who with Bruce Reed had been the ostensible speechwriter on the speech, did not know about "Charlie." He first saw the Clinton-Morris draft of the speech on the morning of December 15. He called it the "Immaculate Conception" because it had apparently come from nowhere.

Morris advocated cutting taxes—the discarded middle-class tax cut—and spending. "I know some people just want to cut the government blindly, and I know that's popular now," Clinton told the country. "But I won't do it. I want a leaner, not a meaner government, that's back on the side of hardworking Americans, a new government for the new economy—creative, flexible, high quality, low cost, service oriented—just like our most innovative private companies."

The address was seen as a sop to the GOP. "Just about everybody in Washington jumped on the tax-cut bandwagon last week," *Time* reported. "But Bill Clinton was the only one who had to do a backflip while eating his words. Such are the contortions of political reincarnation." *New York Times* columnist Anthony Lewis noted: "A democracy also needs leadership—leadership that speaks to citizens in terms of reality, not popularity. On that score Mr. Clinton's speech was a disaster, for the country and for him."

The speech contained the essence of the strategy that would bring the president back to the center ideologically and politically: addressing issues the GOP had raised, but doing it with a Democratic slant. If it was an indication of Clinton's final course, however, it was not a turning point. It was the first signal that the Clinton administration's ideological battle was resuming, with the president reestablishing a centrist path.

Clinton was to give his State of the Union address on January 24, 1995, and the question was should it be a partisan attack or a humble note of conciliation? A competing national vision? The quandary occupied the speechwriters, senior aides, and consultants. Clinton's December address had signaled a possible new tone for his speeches, but Morris remained behind the scenes, and there was no strategic guidance from the president or anyone else. Clinton "did not regard the people who worked for him as reliable instruments of his will," John F. Harris writes in his history of Clinton's presidency. "It was as if his staff was simply one more constituency with which to be reckoned." The speeches in early 1995 were episodic struggles for control of the administration's direction.

Preparing for the State of the Union, Clinton riffed, trying to imagine what the voters who elected a GOP Congress must be feeling. "These white guys thought they were working harder for less money, sleeping less, couldn't even afford a vacation and now the damn guy— he didn't give me a tax cut and now he's coming after my gun," he said.* He needed to acknowledge the electorate's anger, he told his aides, but make people see that the GOP plan "would be law of the jungle"— everyone fending for themselves. "So maybe you'd have sixty percent of the people that would be happy as clams, but they'd be living behind fences," he said. He wanted to illustrate that the "law of the jungle" was contrary the nation's values by featuring in the first lady's box ordinary citizens who did public service around the country.† And, he told his aides, he wanted a short speech. "My gut is, we ought to try to do this in half an hour—no more than half an hour."

A first draft came to Clinton on Thursday, January 19. The writers heard nothing. They did not know that Clinton was huddling with Morris. The president had commissioned "the mother of all polls," as Morris termed it, a 259-question marathon that tested the GOP offensive. The Republicans, especially in the House, had mistaken the anti-Clinton mood for a blanket endorsement of their anti-government philosophy. Morris's poll gave Clinton a road map on where to compromise and where to hit back: he spent five hours briefing the president on Thursday.

White House ushers found a typewriter, a "green monster" of an IBM, dusted it off, and put it in the Treaty Room on the second floor of the residence. With Clinton occasionally standing over his shoulder, Morris wrote a draft of the State of the Union. He was using the typewriter because a White House computer document would have appeared on the inhouse network. The president, sitting in his yellow

---

*"Large numbers of men abandoned Democratic candidates in Tuesday's elections, a trend that gave Republicans an edge in races around the nation and one that Democratic leaders fear might be hard to reverse," *The New York Times* reported after the election. According to exit polls, 62 percent of white men voted Republican. (Richard L. Berke, "Defections Among Men to G.O.P. Helped Insure Rout of Democrats," *New York Times*, November 11, 1994.)

†Mrs. Clinton's six guests at the 1995 State of the Union were the most since the 1990 State of the Union, when Barbara Bush's four guests included Arkansas governor Bill Clinton.

dressing room off his bedroom, chewing on an unlit cigar, copied the pages, writing the new lines onto the speechwriters' draft. As FDR had done six decades before, he wrote out the speech to conceal a helper from prying eyes.*

Baer got a call early Sunday afternoon: Clinton wanted him to come to the residence, alone, to work on the speech. Using his usual felt-tipped pen, Clinton had struck out sections and written in new ones. "Here, listen to this," he said, and read them to Baer, who approved of most. Some language seemed overblown, unlike Clinton's. "In November, we not only heard America singing, we heard America screaming," said one (it would be softened to "We didn't hear America singing, we heard America shouting"). Baer was unaware of Morris, but he sensed something. It was like astronomers discovering celestial objects through their effects on other bodies. "You couldn't see the planets, but there were these other gravitational forces," Baer said.

Baer's role the next day, Monday, was shuttle diplomat. Morris was hidden in the residence. Baer would bring pages, which he assumed were Clinton's, to the West Wing, where he entered the changes and circulated the new draft. Suggestions he got from the writers and senior staff were taken back to Clinton.

Stephanopoulos joined him on one trip to the residence. A line about "tax cuts for the wealthy"—a classic of Democratic talking points—had been dropped, and Stephanopoulos questioned that. Hillary Clinton cast him an irritated look. "It's your speech, Bill, you should say what you want," she told the president. That's weird, Stephanopoulos thought, she usually likes a good pop on the Republicans.

The speechwriting "pack"—writers, staffers, consultants—were hunkered in the pizza box–littered Roosevelt Room. "It was coming down to the president's new draft versus the one we had written under staff and consultant direction," Baer said. "Don't you understand?" one of the consultants told Baer. "We like your draft better than this." Baer's recollection is that the disputes focused mainly on the speech's opening.

---

*Without realizing it, Clinton was also imitating his hero, JFK, who had hand-copied portions of his inaugural address to hide Ted Sorensen's role in it.

Morris remembers more substance to the disagreement: "Theirs was the standard Democratic rebuttal to the Contract With America, focusing on the cuts and not indicating any desire to work with the Republicans," Morris said later. "Ours was our first effort to articulate the options for the third way."

That night, Clinton sent a copy of the speech to Al From, the head of the Democratic Leadership Council. From was another participant in Clinton's effort to reemphasize his "New Democrat" roots. From collaborated with domestic policy adviser Bruce Reed, to suggest more New Democrat–style language to Clinton.

On Tuesday, January 24, the pack assembled in the family theatre for the president's rehearsal. He never came down. He was in the residence, rewriting. Al Gore left.

> *Tonight we must forge a new social compact to meet the challenges of this time. As we enter a new era, we need a new set of understandings, not just with government but, even more important, with one another as Americans. . . . I call it the New Covenant. But it's grounded in a very, very old idea, that all Americans have not just a right but a solemn responsibility to rise as far as their God-given talents and determination can take them and to give something back to their communities and their country in return. Opportunity and responsibility: They go hand in hand. We can't have one without the other. And our national community can't hold together without both.*

The "New Covenant" went back to the campaign, and it signaled a return to the "New Democrat" ideas he had run on. Clinton laid out areas where he was willing to cooperate with the Republicans and drew lines as to how far he would go. The speech was "by turns conciliatory and studded with pointed delineations of difference," *The New York Times* reported. "We all agree that we have to change the way the government works," Clinton said. "Let's make it smaller, less costly, and smarter; leaner, not meaner."

Clinton's thirty-minute limit went by the boards. At 5,800 words, the final draft would have run just under an hour if he had spoken at his regular clip of 100 words per minute and no one applauded. But with nearly 100 interruptions for applause, the speech—9,200 words after ad-libs—ran a record eighty-one minutes. It was, in effect, two speeches. There was Morris and Clinton's prepared text, which tried to sap the GOP momentum by agreeing to their most popular agenda items while putting Clinton's spin on it—make government "leaner, not meaner." And then there was the president extemporizing. "In those final thirty minutes, the public saw Clinton at his best, without artifice or pretense, genuinely enjoying his chat with them," Morris wrote. "The informal language, the familiar style, his obvious enjoyment at having a chance to speak with them was deeply comforting to the American people, no matter how tedious it seemed to me."

And Morris was not alone in sensing tedium: For those "who hoped for signs of a new political acuity and a new personal discipline in the White House, it must have constituted a disappointment—almost an hour and a half long and a reminder of Mr. Clinton's seemingly endless nominating speech at the 1988 Democratic convention," *The New York Times*'s R. W. Apple, Jr., wrote the next day.* But if the diagnosis was on the mark, the prognosis was not. Baer was at the White House post-speech reception, when deputy chief of staff Harold Ickes brought news from the White House pollsters: the reaction was off-the-charts positive.

The State of the Union gave Clinton a bump in the polls, but overall he continued to founder. Gingrich was running the House with drilled effectiveness, passing the items of the Contract With America in fewer than the promised one hundred days. Problems were starting to emerge as the Speaker grappled with his newfound celebrity, as well as with members of the new class of Republican legislators who felt more obligated to their conservative principles than to their party leadership. The Senate, under the leadership of crusty veteran Bob Dole, a front-running potential presidential candidate, was moving at a more leisurely pace.

---

*In 1988, Clinton had delivered the keynote convention address. The speech was so long-winded and rambling that the loudest applause came when he said, "In conclusion . . ."

The White House remained a picture of inefficiency. Clinton might have thought that the State of the Union would set a new ideological tone, but there had been no follow-up. Morris remained a secret to most of the staff and the president was still withdrawn.

Clinton had changed playbooks but had not informed the team. Many of the regular staff favored a Trumanesque confrontation with Congress. Morris continued to advise a careful selection of battles. Part of the problem was practical: the White House staff had still not learned the lessons of how to plan a message strategically. "Every presidential event, each radio address, had become a battleground," Stephanopoulos wrote. "One draft would be prepared by the staff, a second would whir through the president's private fax."*

Clinton was frustrated by the staff texts, which drew on the congressional Democrats' oppose-the-Republicans playbook. "I get up there, and all I have in front of me is liberal, populist, partisan stuff," Clinton complained to Morris. "I need more balance back in those speeches." Why are we doing this? he would yell at Baer. "As Newt Gingrich was orchestrating House passage of the Contract with America, we were responding with a symphony of mixed signals," Stephanopoulos recalled.

In January 1995, Hillary Clinton had stopped attending the Wednesday strategy meetings and other senior staff members had joined. By March, the attendees included Vice President Gore and his chief of staff, Jack Quinn; pollster Doug Schoen; Leon Panetta, who had been appointed chief of staff the previous July and who disliked Morris; deputy chief of staff Erskine Bowles; and deputy chief of staff Harold Ickes, who knew Morris from New York politics and *really* despised him.

Morris's polling had shown a bump from the State of the Union, but with no follow-through the numbers sank through February. By March, the GOP Congress was heading south as well. Their roll-back-the-government agenda was frightening the public. "Our ratings and Dole's and Gingrich's are joined at the hip," Morris wrote in a meeting agenda

---

*The practice of alternative drafts continued even after Morris emerged. Writing Saturday radio addresses, Jonathan Prince would sometimes submit three versions, one based on Dick Morris's direction, one on chief of staff Leon Panetta's, and a hybrid. (Author interview with Jonathan Prince.)

for a March 16, 1995, weekly strategy session. "We go up or down together." Legislative gridlock would encourage an anti-incumbent mood, Morris argued, endangering Clinton's prospects for 1996.

Morris proposed a "Pile of Vetoes Speech," to be given "with drama and flair to mark [an] important point" of new cooperation. Clinton would list the Contract With America items on which deals could be made and those on which they could not. The key line would be: "I was not elected . . . to produce a pile of vetoes or a stack of issues for the next election." And a tougher passage: "Ideological purity is for dictatorships, compromise . . . and negotiation are the substance of democracy." (When Clinton finally gave the speech this became "Ideological purity is for partisan extremists. Practical solution, based on real experience, hard evidence, and common sense, that's what this country needs.")

"Be sure all White House staff is on board for new line." This was a problem. Liberals like Ickes and Stephanopoulos opposed searching out areas of agreement with the GOP. Centrists Baer and Reed were natural Morris allies before they even knew of his existence. In the middle was Panetta, who had tried to instill order on the chaotic Clinton White House. He had not approved of Stephanopoulos and Begala's free rein in the first half of the term and was as unhappy with the notion of Morris operating without constraint now. And while he was no liberal, Panetta came from Congress and was disinclined to triangulate away from his old colleagues.

The opponents of a "Pile of Vetoes Speech," led by Panetta, argued that the unified Democratic opposition to the GOP was working; this was no time for Clinton to break with the congressional wing of the party. The argument played out inconclusively over several weeks. Clinton was scheduled to address the American Society of Newspaper Editors on Friday, April 7—the end of the GOP's first one hundred days. Clinton's top staffers achieved rare unanimity, agreeing that he should speak on education. He would challenge the GOP Congress not to cut federal education funding. He would kick off an administrationwide week of education-related events. David Shipley, a former editor at *The New Republic* who had recently joined the speechwriters, wrote the address, which was finished and had gone through the staffing process by Wednesday night, April 5.

Harold Ickes called Baer at home early the next morning and told him to come into the office. At 7:15 am, Ickes told Baer that the speech was now not on education. Baer should head to the office of Democratic consultant Bob Squier. Someone named Dick Morris would explain. Baer should tell no one. The only people on the White House staff who knew about Morris were the senior staff who attended the weekly strategy sessions.

At Squier's office, Morris pulled out his draft of the address with a flourish. It was the "Pile of Vetoes Speech"—listing the areas of the Contract With America where deals could be cut—that had been secretly debated in the Wednesday night meetings for weeks. Baer liked it: "It had bite, it made a point, it wasn't some sprawling policy thing, which was what we were doing," he recalled. Morris wanted Clinton to "try to use the moment to turn the tables on these guys and I was all for it." But Morris had not learned how to write for a president. He wrote in short, rapid-fire sentences and the speech had too snipey and combative a tone. The line about America "screaming" instead of singing had returned.

Baer made the speech more presidential and took it to Clinton. What do you think? Clinton asked. It's pretty good, Baer said. His colleagues were calling: What does the president think of the speech, the education speech? they asked. When will we see him? Baer tap-danced. "I was having to mislead my colleagues about what was really going on," he said. He started to feel as if there were two White Houses: The one he went to work in every day and another where the decisions were really being made.

Morris had one more idea: Clinton should extemporize from talking points. I can do that, he replied.

The next day, as Waldman was giving his college roommates a West Wing tour, he caught bits of the speech on TVs in staff offices. "That's odd," he told them. "I don't remember that."

"In the first 100 days, it fell to the House of Representatives to propose," Clinton was telling the newspaper editors. "In the next 100 days and beyond, the President has to lead the quiet, reasoned forces of both parties in both Houses to sift through the rhetoric and decide what is really best for America."

Clinton had already signed two elements of the contract into law: one applying to Congress the safety and workplace laws that it passed for businesses; the other limiting the government's ability to impose unfunded mandates on states. He threatened to veto six of the remaining seven items that had passed unless they were changed to his specifications.*

"We stand at a crossroads," Clinton said. "In one direction lies confrontation and gridlock; in the other lies achievement and progress. I was not elected president to pile up a stack of vetoes. I was elected president to change the direction of America. That's what I have spent the last two years doing and that's what I want to spend the next 100 days and beyond doing. Whether we can do that depends upon what all of us in Washington do from here on out."

Stephanopoulos walked by Waldman. "How's the speech?" he asked.

"I don't think it's an education speech," Waldman said. "He's about halfway through the Contract With America, saying what he'll sign and what he'll veto. Right now he's up to tort reform." Stephanopoulos ran down the hallway as if, Waldman recalled, he had been told his office was on fire.

"Um, it's not always like this," Waldman told his startled friends.

"Mr. Clinton for the first time in months put Speaker Newt Gingrich on the defensive by delivering his speech hours before the House Republican leader was to give a televised address summing up his party's first 100 days," *The New York Times* reported.

April 12, 1995, the fiftieth anniversary of FDR's death, would be commemorated at the cabin in Warm Springs, Georgia, where he had died. Baer had argued unsuccessfully that it was a natural event for Clinton: Gingrich and the Republican revolutionaries were rolling back the government that Roosevelt had helped build. It was a chance for the president to wrap himself in Roosevelt's aura. Morris agreed, and it got on Clinton's schedule.

---

*A term limits provision had failed, but the other nine elements of the Congress had passed the House.

433

Air Force One flew into Fort Benning and Baer rode in the press bus forty miles to Warm Springs. Shooting the breeze, Chris Matthews, the Carter speechwriter turned political commentator, threw out an idea about what Clinton's message ought to be. FDR's coffin was placed on a train that traveled from Georgia to Washington, he said. At every crossroads, poor people, white and black, waited in tears. That was FDR's contract with America and that's the contract with America we ought to be honoring.

When the presidential party arrived at Warm Springs, Baer caught up with Clinton and Harold Ickes, whose father had been in FDR's cabinet, as they toured the Little White House. Baer leaned in to Ickes's good left ear and whispered that he had a line from Matthews and that it was good. Ickes agreed and told him to run it by Clinton, who told Baer to write it down.

"And just remember this: President Roosevelt died here, and they took his body on the train out and America began to grieve," Clinton said.

> *Imagine what the people looked like by the sides of the railroad track. Imagine the voices that were singing in the churches. They were all ages, men and women, rich and poor, black, white, Hispanic, and whoever else was living here then. And they were all doing it because they thought he cared about them and that their future mattered in common. They were Americans first. They were Americans first. That was his contract with America. Let it be ours.**

Six days later, on April 18, Clinton held his first prime-time press conference since the midterm election. One reporter noted that the Republican-controlled Congress had dominated the political debate.

---

*Arthur Schlesinger, Jr., a historian of FDR, was in the audience and unimpressed. "Clinton seems by temperament an accommodator," he told *The Washington Post*. "Accommodation has its uses but it can easily become appeasement." Clinton blew up when he saw the quotes. He wrote Schlesinger a letter disputing the idea that he did not relish a fight. Then he invited Schlesinger and other prominent liberals, including Ted Sorensen and Joe Califano, for lunch at the White House to win them over. (Harris, *Survivor*, 177.)

"Do you worry about making sure that your voice is heard in the coming months?" he asked. Clinton made his voice heard in a way that made his staff squirm. "The Constitution gives me relevance," he said. "The power of our ideas gives me relevance. . . . The President is relevant here, especially an activist President." Politicians are trained to answer not the question asked but the question they would have preferred be asked. But in this case Clinton answered a question he had not been asked and gave the wrong answer: A president who has to assert his relevance undermines it.

The next day, Baer was talking with speechwriter Jonathan Prince when news flashed on television—a bomb had destroyed part of a federal office building in Oklahoma City.

Prince was one of Baer's additions to the speechwriting staff. During the first year of the administration, he had worked on communications strategy for the economic plan, the crime bill, and the assault weapons ban, and had periodically helped with speechwriting. He joined the writing staff after the 1994 elections. Resembling John Cusack, Prince had, as his colleague Jordan Tamagni put it, "style in the absence of all style." He wore three-button suits—Waldman called them "zoot suits"—and stylish shoes. He was cocky, but smart—he got a law degree while working at the White House—a fast writer who could perform under pressure.

With Baer standing over his shoulder, Prince wrote. Soon they were running over to the Situation Room in the basement of the West Wing. No one had called—no one on the senior staff had thought to alert the speechwriters. The administration was in its third year but communications was still a secondary concern.

Prince's first clear memory of the day is standing in the Situation Room, a warren of office and cubicles in the White House basement. The statement was short—he was ready to argue if anyone said it was too short. But Clinton approved: This is good, he said. "He was very serious," Prince recalled. "We were fast-paced but not frenzied."

Clinton stepped into an office and made a quick phone call, Baer thought it was to Hillary, to run the remarks by her. Then he addressed the press. "The bombing in Oklahoma City was an attack on innocent children and defenseless citizens," Clinton said. "It was an act of cowardice, and it was evil. The United States will not tolerate it. And I will not allow the people of this country to be intimidated by evil cowards."

Prince had written the last line to read that the country would not be "intimidated by cowards"—Clinton had added the "evil."

The memorial service in Oklahoma City was set for four days later, Sunday, April 23. Curiel produced a first draft, and on Saturday Baer gave it to Prince to work on. He punched it up and integrated some other material, including a suggestion from Clinton's speech coach, Michael Sheehan, which became "You have lost too much, but you have not lost everything. And you have certainly not lost America, for we will stand with you for as many tomorrows as it takes." Prince specialized in Old Testament material and recalled a line from Proverbs about inheriting the wind. Clinton added an opening to the sentence about teaching children: "Let us teach our children that the God of comfort is also the God of righteousness," he said. "Those who trouble their own house will inherit the wind. Justice will prevail."

Typically, Clinton had edited until delivery, scratching and scribbling on his reading copy. He scratched out "deed" from a promise to "bring to justice those who did this evil deed." At the conclusion, he scribbled in the margin, at an angle from the text, "Belong to God/Until we are with them/Let our lives be their legacy." In the speech he said, "Those who are lost now belong to God. Some day we will be with them. But until that happens, their legacy must be our lives."

"It was the first time that he was able to articulate national emotion and give it focus and give it vent and he was able to be healing balm, and I think it was very effective and very important," Morris said. "I learned from it, because I didn't really appreciate that that's what he could do."*

Oklahoma City was a key moment in Clinton's, and his administration's, grasping the power of the communications tools available to a

---

*Morris had wanted the speech to contain specific policy proposals, many of which were later incorporated into the USA Patriot Act after the September 11, 2001, terrorist attacks. "I felt that by offering just fluff, as I thought he did, and sympathy, that he was really squandering an opportunity to stake out an important program," Morris said. (Author interview with Dick Morris.)

president. "It changed dramatically," Prince said. "In Oklahoma City he really was able to give voice to what the country was feeling. And I think that helped him. You know, he grew, he changed. Oklahoma City completely changed him. . . . It was just as if the weight of the office kind of descended on him like chain mail and he grew large enough to support it."

Baer was named White House communications director in August. Waldman, the policy aide who had been dragooned into writing numerous speeches, succeeded him as director of speechwriting. A lawyer, Waldman had been special assistant to the president for policy coordination. His speechwriting staff affectionately called him "Marshall Tito," in the sense that he was the first among equals, and because of his ability to keep potentially conflicting personalities at peace. When new speechwriters joined, Waldman carefully instructed them in the wiles of the staffing process.

The Clinton administration was a throwback to LBJ's. There was more crossover between the speechwriters and policy aides than in any presidency since. Waldman had a policy background. Domestic policy adviser Bruce Reed—who had preceded Kusnet as 1992 campaign speechwriter—and Gene Sperling often co-wrote major speeches.

Clinton preferred to work on speeches with aides who could answer substantive questions about policy. After leaving speechwriting in 1997, Prince became senior policy adviser at the Domestic Policy Council. The NSC's Liu was deputy domestic policy adviser in the administration's last two years; NSC speechwriting chief Tony Blinken eventually became the top man in the council's European directorate; Daniel Benjamin became director of transnational security threats after three years as an NSC speechwriter.

"Often the speeches were written by writers working with the president and policy people who were also integrally involved with it," Baer said. "Certainly when he could find a writer who understood that stuff better, I think he found that [to be] more of a one-stop shop."

The staff that Waldman took over in 1995 had almost completely turned over. Kusnet, Wilkie, and Stone were gone. Curiel, Shipley—

the former reporter whose first speech was supplanted by the "Pile of Vetoes Speech"—and Prince were still on the staff. They had been joined by Terry Edmonds, an African-American who had grown up in the inner city of Baltimore. He had written speeches for Secretary of Health and Human Services Donna Shalala and he was an aspiring poet. Clinton once told him, "Every time you write something for me, it makes me want to sing." Jordan Tamagni, a lawyer from New York whom Morris had recruited, would also join the staff, first as a kind of office manager but working her way into speechwriting within a few months.

Waldman's first big speech was the 1996 State of the Union. It was especially important because it would kick off the election year, and because the likely GOP nominee, Kansas senator Bob Dole, would give the Republican response. Morris polled everything: Should the speech be long, like the detail-packed 1995 State of the Union, or a brief "tone poem," as White House press secretary Mike McCurry suggested? Morris's surveys, conducted by New York–based pollster Mark Penn, showed that people liked substance, even if it took time. Lines, themes, and ideas were thrown into the polling machine to see what stuck. Bruce Reed thought all of the programs in the speech smacked of pandering. "America was built on challenges, not promises," he told Waldman, recalling a line he had written for Clinton years earlier that echoed JFK. "Challenges, not promises" went into the poll and came back a big winner.

Americans were concerned "that their values were under threat—not by the forces of 'secular humanism,' as the religious right would have it, but by an increasingly coarse and commercialized culture," Waldman recalled. "If we could answer this concern, then we could win the suburban vote." Issues such as school uniforms, tobacco, TV violence, and medical leave were introduced under this banner. Policy development, Morris said, started with a poll-tested sound bite. Then the cabinet departments would be checked to see if any policies were percolating to fit the sound bite. Once everything was vetted, an event would be put on the calendar. "I would write the sound bite and go to the speechwriters and say, 'Your job is to make the rest of the speech so boring that it is not covered, and heaven help you if there is a line in the speech that is so quotable that it overshadows the sound bite,'" he recalled.

Waldman and company stuffed the State of the Union, but Morris wanted still more. Three days before Clinton was due to speak, Morris faxed over a rewritten version that Waldman thought was tighter, more "tabloidy"—and brilliant. "In contrast to the stately pace of my prose, Morris' was staccato, condensed," Waldman recalled. It was "urgent, clipped, [with] ellipses instead of transitions. No idea was carried more than a sentence or two." One change particularly stuck out. Waldman had written that "the past thirty years has taught us that big government is not the answer, and the past twelve months has taught us that no government is not the answer." Morris condensed this to read: "The era of big government is over. But the era of every man for himself must never begin."

It would be a startling announcement for a Democratic president. It could easily be interpreted as a renunciation of the faith in government that had been the party's hallmark since the New Deal. And it would come at a time when the debate about the size and reach of the federal government had led to a pair of shutdowns of the government, one in November 1995 and the second in December into January 1996, because of budgetary wrangling between the White House and the Republican Congress.

The end of "the era of big government" may not have been merely a speechwriter's interpolation. Addressing a National Italian-American Foundation dinner on October 21, 1995, Clinton had called "the era of big government" a "myth," saying that the size of the federal government as a percentage of the civilian workforce was smaller than at any time since FDR. Nine days later, in a morning address to the White House Conference on Travel and Tourism, he made the same observation, concluding, "The era of big government is done. The era of smart government is here." Three days later, speaking to the National Jewish Democratic Council on the evening of November 2, Clinton said, "The era of big government is over, but the era of good government and strong government cannot be over."

The "era of big government" being "over" was a developing thought buried in three minor speeches, two of which had been given after reporters' deadlines.* It received no press attention. Baer, Waldman, and Morris don't even recall Clinton using the lines, and Baer is certain that "era of big government" was not in the prepared text of any of those speeches. It was not uncommon for Clinton to use speeches to develop arguments or refine phrases. In the summer of 1996, Waldman would originate the campaign theme of building a bridge to the future after listening to Clinton riff on the image through the spring. Morris said Clinton's use of the phrase in the months before the State of the Union was a "coincidence." It may be; or the writers may have picked up on their boss's evolving thinking.

The speechwriters expected that the president declaring an end of the "era of big government" would trigger a philosophical debate within the administration. But what they got was a complaint from campaign spokeswoman Ann Lewis that "era of every man for himself" was sexist. The men thought this was political correctness run amok: the balance and contrast of repetition might have made the whole line memorable, but a weak second sentence would be forgotten. Every person for himself would violate Clinton's strict grammar, so they would have to find something else. It was "the death of liberalism at its own hands," Waldman commented to Stephanopoulos.

"The era of big government is over," Clinton told the Congress on January 23, 1996. Republicans, sensing the surrender they had waited for since they took control of Congress, leaped to their feet and applauded. Clinton waved them quiet. "But we cannot go back to the time when our citizens were left to fend for themselves." The end of the "era of big government" made headlines the next day. The rest of the thought was ignored.

"Clinton Embraces GOP Themes in Setting Agenda; 'Era of Big Government Is Over,' Clinton Tells Nation," was the headline in the January 24 *Washington Post*. "House Republicans are muttering that Clinton hijacked their agenda," *Time* reported. "But to paraphrase T. S.

---

*"Reporters soon learned that the best way to know what Clinton thought was to listen, not just to his words during the workday, but especially to the ones that came after deadlines, when he spoke at night without prepared remarks to political supporters," John F. Harris has noted. (*Survivor*, 208.)

Eliot's line about poets, good politicians borrow, great politicians steal. Now Republicans are finally learning what Bill Clinton means by common ground: your land is my land."

Not everyone was pleased. It proved "that we had won some battles but lost the larger war, that we were the prisoners of conservative rhetoric," Stephanopoulos later wrote. "Even if the phrase reflected reality . . . the triumphalist tone of the declaration felt dishonest and vaguely dishonorable, as if we were condemning Democrats from Franklin Roosevelt to Lyndon Johnson to the trash heap of history for the sake of a sound bite."

The State of the Union gave Clinton a 53–36 lead over Dole in Morris's polls, which held for nine months until the contest tightened slightly in November. "The reason lies in the president's unveiling of a 'values' agenda in the State of the Union speech," Morris noted in his White House memoir. "His elaboration on that theme in speeches and [television] ads throughout 1996 and the emphasis on it in his speech at the convention increased his lead and enabled him to do it."

Clinton often spoke extemporaneously on the stump. Tom Freedman, Morris's right-hand man, traveled with Clinton, and whenever the president riffed something new off his standard speech, Freedman sent it to Morris for polling. The next morning, Morris would send a memo to Clinton telling him what worked and what did not. On August 8, Clinton was in Salinas, California, talking about the community's efforts to crack down on gang violence. "You think about it; we all want to belong to a gang," Clinton told the crowd. "We just want to be in good gangs. . . . Every church, every synagogue, that's a good gang. If you like your school, it's a good gang. People have a need." Comparing churches and synagogues to gangs did not test well—"we polled it and it blew up," Morris said—he made sure Clinton did not say it again.

After his speeches, Clinton would linger with the crowd, shaking hands and enjoying brief snatches of conversation as Secret Service agents watched intensely. Afterward, backstage, he would tell his staff the stories he had heard: people who had benefited from family and medical leave, or more police on the streets, or had served in Ameri-

Corps, a domestic community service organization. The aides would slip out and make sure the details were correct—they knew that Clinton would weave them into his stump speeches.

Late in the evening of November 4, 1996, at the last campaign stop before his last election, Clinton addressed a crowd at Sioux Falls, South Dakota. He opened the folder that Jonathan Prince, the speechwriter traveling with the campaign, had given him with his speech for the stop. His text had the standard heading: "President William J. Clinton, Sioux Falls, South Dakota, November 4, 1996." Then the entirety of the speech: "DITTO."

"There is no person living in this country today who has been given more gifts, who feels more humble on this night than I do," Clinton said. "Fifty years ago, when I was born in a summer storm to a widowed mother in a little town in Arkansas, it was unthinkable that I might have ever become president. . . . We just need to run our country the way we want to run our lives. That is what I have learned in twenty-three years, and that is what I ask you to vote for tomorrow as we build our bridge to the 21st century."

"I loved your speech," Clinton told Prince afterward.

The next day, he won 49.2 percent of the popular vote—8.5 percent more than Dole—and 379 electoral votes.

For the Clinton administration, 1997 was a relatively quiet year. New White House chief of staff Erskine Bowles kept things running smoothly on an essentially centrist course. The president continued to try to use his pulpit, with mixed success, on a number of fronts, most notably his "race initiative," an effort to explore and heal the country's lingering legacy of racial discord. On May 28, the U.S. Supreme Court had ruled that sitting presidents can be sued for actions outside the scope of their official duties—meaning that a civil lawsuit brought against the president by former Arkansas State employee Paula Jones, who alleged that Governor Clinton had propositioned her, would go forward.

The Clintons and his administration had been dogged by allegations and scandals of varying degrees throughout his term in office, from circumstances surrounding the Whitewater land deal when Clinton was still a governor to the firing of the White House Travel Office staff to bizarre allegations regarding the suicide of White House aide Vince Foster. Some of the scandals were fueled by conservative activists and publications like *The American Spectator*, which later prompted Hillary Clinton to blame a "vast right-wing conspiracy" for the claims against her husband.*

A December 1993 *Spectator* story would prove the greatest threat to Clinton's presidency. The article quoted former state troopers from Clinton's Arkansas security detail saying that they had arranged trysts for the governor, including with a woman named Paula. She turned out to be Paula Jones, who then filed a sexual harassment suit against Clinton. She said that when she was working at a state jobs fair he had arranged for her to be brought to his hotel suite, where he had propositioned her. Clinton's lawyers had argued that presidents were immune to civil suits while in office, else the legal system become a venue for tying up a president's time with nuisance suits. Now the Supreme Court had said no, that the suit could go forward.

Perhaps the biggest news of the year was economic. The economy grew at 8.2 percent in 1997, and the budget deficit was only $22 billion.† When Clinton's senior team met in the Cabinet Room on December 1, 1997, to discuss the agenda for 1998, the economic news had gotten even better: budget surpluses as far as the eye could see.

Waldman and domestic advisers Bruce Reed and Gene Sperling worked out the contours of the 1998 State of the Union speech over the

---

*The phrase "vast right-wing conspiracy," which Hillary Clinton coined during an appearance on NBC's *Today Show* several days after the Lewinsky scandal broke, quickly entered the political lexicon. It became a rallying point and conceptual frame, not unfounded, for Clinton's defenders and a gleeful badge of honor for his critics. Mrs. Clinton had for several days been discussing with White House aide Sidney Blumenthal the efforts arrayed against her husband. Blumenthal prepared talking points for her and they spoke about ten minutes before she went on the air. But she ad-libbed "vast right-wing conspiracy." "The phrase was hers, on the spot," Blumenthal recalled. (Blumenthal, *The Clinton Wars*, 373–74; author interview with Sidney Blumenthal.)

†President Bush's last budget had projected a budget shortfall of $292 billion in 1994 and a $305 billion deficit in 1997. (Robert Pear, "Clinton Backs Off His Pledge to Cut the Deficit in Half," *New York Times*, January 7, 1993.)

next few weeks. The three had become, Waldman wrote, "like a basketball team: I could throw the ball to a precise spot down the court, without even looking, and know that one of them would be there to catch it." Gone were the days when policy and speeches were developed on separate tracks. A major speech would start with Baer or Waldman writing an outline and then sitting around the computer with Sperling and Reed filling in the details.

With the Treasury suddenly flush, Clinton would propose a number of initiatives in the 1998 State of the Union more expensive than anything he had proposed in the previous two years. It "would be a far-reaching attempt to persuade the public that government could do big things again," Waldman recalled.

January 1998 was also Paula Jones month. Jones's lawyers would depose the president on January 17, ten days before the State of the Union. Waldman would have to finish the first draft early so Clinton would see it before he was distracted. Also on the Jones's lawyers' witness list was Monica Lewinsky, a former White House intern and then staffer who had secretly had several sexual encounters with the president over a span of months starting during the first government shutdown.

On January 21, Jeff Shesol was at his gym when he opened *The Washington Post*. "This looks bad," he thought. He was a former Rhodes Scholar and cartoonist—his *Thatch* ran daily in more than 150 newspapers. The previous September, Shesol had published *Mutual Contempt*, a history of the Lyndon Johnson–Robert F. Kennedy feud. Clinton had sent him a congratulatory note about it, and the next thing Shesol knew, Waldman was interviewing him for a speechwriting position. A mid-January meeting with Clinton lasted five minutes; they did not even sit down. A job offer seemed imminent. Now there was this, spread across the *Post*'s front page: CLINTON ACCUSED OF URGING AIDE TO LIE; STARR PROBES WHETHER PRESIDENT TOLD WOMAN TO DENY ALLEGED AFFAIR TO JONES'S LAWYERS.

Kenneth Starr was the independent counsel who had been appointed in August 1994 to investigate the Whitewater land development deals in Arkansas. The woman was Lewinsky, the former White House intern. A Lewinsky confidante had tape-recorded the young woman talking about her trysts with Clinton and the president coaching her on her testimony in the Jones case. Informed of the relationship, Jones's lawyers had repeatedly asked Clinton about Lewinsky. He denied having sexual relations with her. Starr's lawyers were informed of the tapes and Clinton's testimony, and Starr expanded his investigation to include whether Clinton had lied or told Lewinsky to lie in the Jones civil suit.

An hour after Shesol got home, the phone rang and Waldman was calling with the job offer. It would have been a normal call on any other day. They had been talking about the job for two months, so it would have been absurd—*more* absurd—to back down now, Shesol thought. They set a starting date a few weeks hence.

Shesol needed advice. The next day, he called Arthur Schlesinger, Jr. Pundits were speculating that Clinton's term was numbered in weeks or days. "It's an exciting time to be there," Schlesinger said. "You'll either see a White House fighting for its life or a White House in a state of dissolution, both of which would be very interesting." Schlesinger was "surprisingly sanguine" about Clinton's survival, Shesol wrote in notes to himself.* "Have you ever written political speeches before?" Schlesinger asked. "It's a particularly low form of rhetoric."

The atmosphere inside the White House was surreal. "Now the speech has to be *really* poetic," Waldman quipped in a senior staff meeting. "Yeah," shot back deputy chief of staff John Podesta. "Now it's going to have to be in iambic pentameter." There were serious issues: Nixon had mentioned Watergate in his 1974 State of the Union; Reagan had touched on Iran-Contra in his 1987 speech. Should Clinton mention Lewinsky? "If I have anything to do with it, he won't say a word," promised Rahm Emanuel. With Clinton since the campaign, Emanuel had become one of the president's senior advisers. Known for his blunt, aggressive style, he was one of the key aides in deciding a speech's direction, dispensing instructions that were politically apt and occasionally sadistic: When Jordan Tamagni consulted with him on a speech on Clinton's "millennium program," Emanuel gave her one instruction: Don't use the word "millennium."

---

*Schlesinger later testified before the House Judiciary against impeaching Clinton, arguing that gentlemen always lie about their sex lives.

Clinton was rehearsing the State of the Union on Saturday, January 24, doing his usual close editing as he rehearsed. He reached the section on how to deal with the budget surplus. "What should we do with the surplus? Social Security first," he said, and then stopped, scribbled on his draft, and looked at his aides. "What should we do with our surplus? I have a simple four-word answer," he said. "*Save* Social Security first!" He grinned and opened his arms. "See? I haven't totally lost it."

But the stress was telling on the president. As he worked through the speech, he made bitter allusions to members of Congress who were after his head. "The notion that President Clinton had this . . . superhuman compartmentalization ability and he just put it away in a little box and didn't think about it—totally not true, I'm sorry," said speechwriter Lowell Weiss later. "It was just clear how much stress he was under."

The rehearsals went on for several days as Clinton edited from the lectern. In the spectator seats, the senior staffers scoured the text not for awkward phrases, but for double entendres or lines that could be interpreted as referring to his problem. "Quiet crisis" out. Experiencing "more change more suddenly than ever before," no.*

"What is usually a gladiator's arena was instead a soothing cocoon," *The New York Times* reported after the speech. "With thundering applause rolling over him from both sides of the aisle, the President took command with a steady smile and smooth diction, and the suspense quickly ebbed. For a little more than an hour, Bill Clinton escaped from the noise, humiliation and danger that has surrounded him ever since the Monica S. Lewinsky scandal erupted."

The Clintons hosted the customary post-speech party in the East Room. Waldman was standing with Tony Blinken, the NSC's chief speechwriter. Clinton brought over the Reverend Jesse Jackson and made the introductions: These are the guys who took down my speech, he said. It was a favorite Clinton joke. A year earlier he had introduced Waldman and Prince the same way at the same event.

• • •

*The need to excise potential double entendres did not end with the State of the Union; some speechwriters kept a running list of deleted lines that became "very, very long."

Starr's investigation consumed the country as 1998 wore on. The special counsel was focused on proving that Clinton had indeed had sexual relations with Lewinsky and that he had committed perjury in his deposition and had encouraged the former intern to lie. Congressional Republicans had raised the possibility of impeachment almost as soon as the sex scandal had broken. But Starr's efforts were slowed by the fact that Lewinsky had refused to cooperate with the investigation.

For Shesol, 1998 had a sense of unreality. The investigation was like "white noise" in the background. "The White House was one of the few places you could be in the United States and not be that focused on the latest allegations or the latest leaks from the Starr Report," he recalled.

Clinton's advisers decided early that he would not talk about the scandal, so the closest the speechwriters came to dealing with it was some drafted remarks for friendly members of Congress. Rather, they helped in as much as his defense was that he was busy, as the mantra went, doing the business of the American people. And Clinton demonstrated that with a procession of speeches and policy pronouncements. The twenty-four-hour news networks were suddenly covering every Rose Garden appearance in the hopes that Clinton might, as Waldman put it, "slip up mid-paragraph and start free-associating about the scandal." The writers laughed about the new blanket coverage: the news channels were covering substantive policy speeches in spite of themselves.

Paul Glastris, a reporter with *U.S. News & World Report*, who was interviewed for a speechwriting job that summer, asked to be assured that it would not simply be Lewinsky- and impeachment-related work. It was a great time to work in the administration, he was told, because the news networks would break into their programming virtually any time Clinton made a public appearance. "Part of the strategy to surviving Monica was to portray the president doing his job," Glastris said.

"I was wrong. I have to apologize to the American people," Clinton said. "But this is outrageous what Starr has done. If I don't say that, no one else will. I can't just let this go."

It was early evening on Monday, August 17, 1998, and Clinton was in the White House solarium with his senior staffers, defense lawyers, and consultants. In late July, Monica Lewinsky's lawyers had reached an immunity agreement with Starr's team and she had testified before the grand jury on August 6. She had handed over a blue dress with what she said were semen stains on it, physical evidence of the relationship. The developments had prompted Clinton to testify before the special counsel. The president had spent most of the afternoon sparring with Starr and his aides over whether he had perjured himself in his Jones testimony when he denied having sexual relations with Lewinsky. He maintained that, within the narrow definitions operative during his January deposition, he had not lied. "It depends on what the meaning of the word *is* is," Clinton told them.

Like many Clinton friends and staffers, Paul Begala, who had returned to the White House staff in 1997, was furious that the president had lied to them about the scandal for much of the year. But he had put aside his ire and written remarks for Clinton to make to the nation that evening. A draft solicited from veteran Democratic consultant Bob Shrum had been too contrite: "I have fallen short of what you should expect from a president. I have failed my own religious faith and values. I have let too many people down." Begala wrote a less groveling speech.

But Clinton had written his own, and while it contained an apology, it brimmed with righteous anger. People had to understand that Starr's investigation was an outrageous, politically motivated invasion, he argued. Clinton's political advisers warned him that it was too strident and that it missed the point. "People don't care about you or your problems, they only care about what you are doing for their problems," Emanuel told Clinton as they all sat in the solarium. But he and the other political pros were fighting a losing battle.

Hillary Clinton had watched the debate quietly, looking tired and dour. When she weighed in, she seemed almost to be taunting her husband. "It's your speech, Bill," she said sharply. "Say whatever you want." She had said the same thing to him before the 1995 State of the Union, encouraging him then to give a speech that had set the course for his political resurrection. Now her advice proved less constructive.

"As you know, in a deposition in January I was asked questions about my relationship with Monica Lewinsky," Clinton told the nation that night. "While my answers were legally accurate, I did not volunteer information. Indeed, I did have a relationship with Ms. Lewinsky that was not appropriate. In fact, it was wrong." The second half of the speech laid blame.

> *I had real and serious concerns about an Independent Counsel investigation that began with private business dealings twenty years ago, dealings, I might add, about which an independent federal agency found no evidence of any wrongdoing by me or my wife over two years ago. The Independent Counsel investigation moved on to my staff and friends, then into my private life. And now the investigation itself is under investigation. This has gone on too long, cost too much, and hurt too many innocent people.*

It was three and a half weeks before Clinton corrected his mistake, reading a text that he had written by hand that had a dramatically different tone. "I have been on quite a journey these last few weeks to get to the end of this, to the rock bottom truth of where I am and where we all are. I agree with those who have said that in my first statement after I testified I was not contrite enough," he told religious leaders at a prayer breakfast on September 11. "I don't think there is a fancy way to say that I have sinned."

Later that afternoon, Starr released his 445-page report. It recited in detail alternately pornographic and clinical the Clinton-Lewinsky encounters. Starr hoped to so appall the public that Clinton would leave office either in response to public outrage or after an impeachment conviction for perjury. Republicans driving toward the midterm elections focused on the scandal, insisting that they were fixated on dishonesty, not sex, and opened impeachment hearings. The entire exercise—the report, the impeachment inquiry—backfired spectacularly, and voters gave Democrats a five-seat increase in the House in November, an unheard-of result for a presidential party in a midterm election.

On December 19, the Republican House voted to impeach the president, meaning that he would be giving his 1999 State of the Union address in the middle of his trial, addressing a Congress that included his jurors, the U.S. Senate. Would Congress even allow the president to come to the Capitol to give the speech? White House staffers briefly looked into other settings in which he could give the address, including the National Archives.*

One thing was certain: Clinton would not mention Lewinsky or impeachment. As the 1999 State of the Union speech arrived at the point of rehearsal, he would spend a couple of hours with his lawyers, and then walk down the hall to the family theatre to spend a couple of hours practicing and editing. Always aware that he was considered too long-winded, he would start each session by announcing how many words he had cut from the latest draft, and then would dictate additions over the course of the rehearsal.

On January 19, 1999—the day his impeachment defense opened—Clinton presented to the Congress and the nation an unbowed president doing the people's business. "Without once uttering the word 'impeachment' or making any obvious reference to the deeds that had put him on trial, Mr. Clinton tonight made a forceful argument against conviction with a virtuoso 77-minute performance," *The New York Times* reported the next day.

The mood was exuberant in the senior staff van riding back to the White House. I won't be surprised if they call off the impeachment, one of the president's aides said. The trial ran its course and the Senate acquitted him on February 12.

The Balkans had been a lingering source of foreign policy problems for Clinton for much of his first term. The end of the Cold War let old ethnic tensions flare up in places like the former Yugoslavia, which had rapidly disintegrated, with Bosnia becoming an independent state in 1992. The Serb-dominated Yugoslav army attacked the new country and as it occupied territory it expelled Bosnians in a policy called "eth-

---

*According to the Constitution, the president "shall from time to time give to the Congress Information of the State of the Union, and recommend to their Consideration such Measures as he shall judge necessary and expedient." There is no requirement that the State of the Union be delivered in the form of a speech or that if the president does give a speech it has to be in the House chamber.

nic cleansing." Candidate Clinton had made this a campaign issue, vowing he would do "whatever it takes to stop the slaughter of civilians." This moral approach contrasted with the Bush administration's realist view that had led Secretary of State James Baker to say that the United States didn't "have a dog in that fight."

But President Clinton had discovered that his options were narrow. He lacked the desire and—with JCS Chairman Colin Powell skeptical of military intervention—the clout to use the armed forces to stop the killing. Yet sitting still was not a viable option, either. The administration had adopted a policy that one Pentagon official aptly called "muddling through": condemning the ethnic cleansing, urging a cease-fire, talking to European allies about other steps. This continued into the summer of 1995, when Bosnian Serbs captured Srebrenica, an enclave that the United Nations had designated a "safe area." Women and children, 23,000 of them, were expelled from the city; an additional 8,000 men and boys were put to death and interred in mass graves. The atrocity spurred the administration to action, instituting a new policy of punishing aggression with air strikes and starting a new round of negotiations. By year's end, a peace agreement was reached.

Now, in the spring of 1999, the former Yugoslavia was smoldering again. Kosovo was a small province of Serbia that had enjoyed semi-autonomy, but the country's Serbian majority had a history of ethnic strife with the Kosovar Albanians and yearned for control of the territory. The situation had worsened throughout 1998, with Serb attacks into the province and a limited response—economic sanctions and negotiations to prevent further violence—from the Clinton administration. The problems accelerated in early 1999, when the Serbs broke the cease-fire and massed forces on the province's borders. They attacked on March 20, triggering NATO strikes on March 24. Clinton would have to go on television that evening and explain why U.S. military forces were going into harm's way.

The chief NSC speechwriter was Tom Malinowski, who had joined the staff the previous year after a stint writing speeches for the Secretary of State. He had a talent for the rhetoric of argument and a deep knowledge of foreign affairs: he would amuse himself by naming all of the foreign capitals around the world.

In foreign affairs, Malinowski knew, the maxim is that you can start a war with the wrong punctuation mark. The difference between "serious" and "grave" can mean pulling an ambassador out versus dropping bombs. "If you think about the tools of foreign policy, one percent of the time it's bombs, two percent of the time it's dollars, ninety-seven percent of the time it's words," he said. "And it means you have to be very careful because every time you speak out on China, there's somebody in the Chinese Foreign Ministry in Beijing who's going to read and parse every single word, phrase, and intonation to discern what the United States means and what it intends to do."

The key question in the Kosovo speech was whether the United States was willing to commit ground forces. It was a sensitive issue. Many in the Congress, particularly Republicans, were opposed to "nation-building," and questioned the decision to use force. On the other side, Clinton had been criticized, as in Bosnia, for moving too slowly. One draft of the speech had the president saying "I will not" commit ground troops, but Sandy Berger, who had succeeded Tony Lake as national security adviser in 1997, rewrote the line. "If NATO is invited to do so, our troops should take part in that mission to keep the peace," Clinton would say that night. "But I do not intend to put our troops in Kosovo to fight a war." They hoped that the "do not intend" formulation would be sufficiently ambiguous to mollify Republicans, while leaving open the threat of committing ground troops.

Editing continued until the last minute, with Malinowski typing changes into the TelePrompTer until the president went on the air. David Halperin, another NSC speechwriter, was printing the backup hard copy that Clinton would have in front of him, but he was only able to get it half done. "If the TelePrompTer had failed in the latter half of his speech, I don't know what would have happened," Halperin said.

Clinton told the nation that the mission was "clear: to demonstrate the seriousness of NATO's purpose so that the Serbian leaders understand the imperative of reversing course . . . if President Milosevic will not make peace, we will limit his ability to make war." If Milosevic did not stop, in other words, he would be hit hard. But Malinowski saw a hole in the threat. "The implication of that was that if he resisted and did not make peace, didn't give in to our demands, we wouldn't . . . compel him to leave Kosovo," Malinowski recalled. "The most we would do is just make him bleed a little bit."

"In his televised speech tonight, Mr. Clinton left no easy way out for Mr. Milosevic, insisting that he would have to agree to allied terms to end the bombing," R.W. Apple, Jr., wrote in a *New York Times* "news analysis." "On the other hand, the President let the Serbian leader know that he need not fear an American invasion. 'I do not intend to put our troops in Kosovo to fight a war,' Mr. Clinton said, apparently seeking to reassure the American public but at the same time giving Mr. Milosevic an incentive to hang on."

The underlying assumption was that like most bullies, Milosevic would retreat if pushed back. Wrong: The Serbs stepped up their campaign and area refugee camps filled at an alarming rate. Malinowski, among others, did not think victory could ultimately be attained if Milosevic still controlled an ethnically cleansed Kosovo.

Clinton was going to reiterate the war aims and praise the U.S. military for its performance in the air assaults on Kosovo in his weekly radio address on March 27. Malinowski inserted a line saying that no resolution could be imagined that did not involve the refugees returning home. Berger was soon on the phone: What are you trying to do? The line would mark a fundamental shift of allied aims for the war, from merely stopping Milosevic to rolling him back. I agree with you, Berger told Malinowski, but we cannot just slip it into a Saturday radio address—we have to get the president's approval and consult with the rest of the NATO allies.

Speaking to reporters on April 5, Clinton added the new aim, saying that Milosevic could end the conflict by, among other things, "making it possible for all refugees to return." "Mr. Clinton's aides said that his remarks today—some of his sharpest words yet—were meant to warn Mr. Milosevic that a return of the refugees had become a precondition of any end to NATO's assault," *The New York Times* reported the next day in the eighteenth paragraph of its story on the war. A new condition had been added to ending the war, and it scarcely raised an eyebrow.

"I'm not saying that this whole thing was triggered by me putting that line in, people were already thinking along these lines, but it probably clarified the choice," Malinowski recalled. "I've always been amazed by this: It was not noted as a major change in policy even though it was. It was a huge change in policy."

By early June, with air strikes having limited effectiveness, Clinton was preparing to take the next step. Berger recommended that the president immediately deploy 100,000 U.S. troops to the Balkans. Then it was suddenly over: Milosevic announced that he would accede to the allied demands and withdraw from Kosovo. NATO had won.

Terry Edmonds, the speechwriter who also wrote poetry, returned to the White House in August 1999, succeeding Waldman as director of speechwriting and becoming the first African-American to hold that position. He and Paul Glastris, who had joined the administration from *U.S. News & World Report* during the summer of Lewinsky, did the initial draft of Clinton's speech for the Democratic Party Convention speech in August. Clinton half dictated and half scribbled a new draft, and Jeff Shesol and speechwriter Josh Gottheimer pulled it together.

It was originally conceived as one third retrospective, looking back at Clinton's two terms; one third about where the country stood in the year 2000; and one third painting Vice President Al Gore as the man of the future and where he would take the nation as president. Gore's senior advisers vetoed the outline—because of the scandals they did not want Clinton talking up their candidate. The move raised eyebrows among the Clinton staff, who questioned the wisdom of Gore trying to distance himself. And it required a significant reorientation of the speech.*

The speech became a full-throated celebration of Clinton's administration, going through what Shesol called "the litany," the burgeoning list of its accomplishments. Clinton labored furiously on it. "No, no, no," he said, "this is a speech—I just want to talk to people." He kept asking for more detail, down to inane levels of the mundane. At four o'clock one bleary morning, Shesol decided that he could not be party to a president uttering the word "salmonella" at a major party convention. He removed a section on food safety.

---

*Ironically, Clinton was criticized for focusing too much on himself during the address.

"What happened to salmonella?" Clinton asked later that day. Gene Sperling, the national economic adviser, stepped in: "Mr. President, that one's just a little too much detail." Clinton looked crestfallen and shook his head. "I loved that salmonella," he said.

Edmonds was in his office in December with Glastris and John Pollack, a former Hill staffer, pun champion,* and the last speechwriter hired, when word came that the U.S. Supreme Court had halted the recount of presidential election ballots in Florida, ensuring that Texas governor George W. Bush would be the next president. The writers each drafted a statement, melded their work, and faxed it to Clinton, who was at prime minister Tony Blair's country residence in England, on his final trip abroad as president.

The draft was faxed back to them a few hours later. It was black with Clinton's edits. They pored over the pages and slowly realized how much he had rewritten. Three words remained from their original draft: "Vice," "President," and "Gore."

"I want to say I am profoundly grateful to Vice President Gore for eight extraordinary years of partnership," Clinton said on December 14. "Without his leadership, we could not have made the progress or reached the prosperity we now enjoy and pass on to the next administration."

---

*Sent Pollack's résumé with the decision memo on his hiring, Clinton circled the pun champion notation and wrote: "Great!" (Author interview with John Pollack.)

TWELVE

"The Troika"

"Did you see that?" Vice President Dick Cheney asked his speechwriter, John McConnell. The two men were in the vice president's West Wing office, discussing an upcoming speech. Cheney had ABC News on, and they had been staring at the TV in silence as smoke and flames poured from the North Tower of the World Trade Center when the second plane hit. Cheney's office quickly filled up: national security adviser Condoleezza Rice; White House deputy chief of staff Josh Bolten; I. Lewis "Scooter" Libby, Cheney's chief of staff; and Richard Clarke, the National Security Council's counterterrorism coordinator. Cheney was on the phone, trying to reach President Bush, who was in Florida. McConnell slipped out. No one had questioned his presence, they all knew him, but he figured that it was better to leave than be told to leave. And anyway, he wanted to call his mother.

Matthew Scully was in his office in the Old Executive Office Building, placing the last pages on a stack in front of him. He was a presidential speechwriter, but this manuscript was his passion and the fruit of more than two years' work: *Dominion*, a book on the moral and theological case for animal rights. He had come in as usual around five that morning, carving out time to work on his book. His phone rang. It was Pete Wehner, the deputy director of speechwriting. Turn on your TV,

Wehner said, a plane just crashed into the World Trade Center. "A commercial airliner?" Scully asked. Scully's grandfather, a New York City politician named Robert Moran, had been in the Empire State Building on a July 1945 Saturday morning when a B-25 bomber slammed into it. On television he heard that the White House was being evacuated. Then he heard someone walking through the halls giving the same order: Everyone out. He stuffed his manuscript in a bag and joined the flow out of the building.

Michael Gerson, the director of speechwriting for President George W. Bush, was working at his Alexandria, Virginia, home that morning when Wehner called. Gerson got into his car and headed to the White House. At around 9:37 am he was driving on Interstate 395 near the Pentagon when he saw a commercial airliner flying by too fast and too low. He could see the windows on the plane. An overpass prevented him from seeing it hit but he saw smoke start to rise. Traffic ground to a halt. Police on the highway turned Gerson around and he headed home, but not before he had written on his notepad: We are at war.

David Frum, another presidential speechwriter, had been late arriving to work and got the news from his wife, writer Danielle Crittenden Frum, just as he reached his desk. He was scheduled to lunch at the Pentagon with a friend that day, so he called to cancel. "They're evacuating this building," the friend's assistant said. "I cannot talk. We must leave." The television news was now reporting the Pentagon strike, along with unconfirmed reports of a car bomb at the State Department and fires on the National Mall. Frum's wife called again: "The White House will be next! You have to get out of there—don't wait, please hurry!"

"No!" he said angrily. His ears felt hot. "*No!* I am not leaving!" He clicked off his cell phone. That was when the Secret Service agent stuck his head through the doorway. "*You!* Out—now! *Now!*" Frum joined the White House staffers flowing out into the clear, beautiful morning.

On the far side of Lafayette Park, Frum ran into McConnell. "We're just a couple of blocks from the American Enterprise Institute," Frum said, referring to the conservative think tank. "They'll have land lines and television sets. And maybe we'll be able to think of something useful to do." Frum and McConnell finally reached Gerson at his home. He told them that the White House staff was gathering at DaimlerChrysler headquarters (a White House staffer was married to a DaimlerChrysler employee) eight blocks away. They set out again. "There are going to be thousands and thousands of funerals in this country over the next week," McConnell said to Frum. "Everybody is going to know someone among the dead."

Scully had wandered north from the White House. He saw Tony Snow, a speechwriter from the first Bush administration and now a Fox News anchor, standing outside the Mayflower Hotel talking on his cell phone. The two had worked together years earlier at *The Washington Times*. They waved hello. Scully finally heard from his wife, Emmanuelle, who told him that the White House staff was gathering at *The Weekly Standard*, the conservative weekly opinion journal.* There he learned that everyone had already moved on to DaimlerChrysler. It was only when he arrived at the auto company's office that he found out that the World Trade Center towers had collapsed.

The Bush speechwriters started working on a statement for the president, who was making a circuitous journey by air back to the capital. Scully, McConnell, and Frum, with Gerson on the telephone, tried to write. Frum, Scully recalled, "was trying to crack the whip and get us focused," with limited success. On speakerphone, Gerson tried to explain to Scully a concept that Rice wanted included in the remarks, but there was too much going on. Scully picked up the receiver so he could hear him. Rice wants to include the idea that the United States would deal with terrorists and the nations that aided them in the same manner, Gerson said. Scully produced the line: We will make no distinction between the terrorist groups and the nations that aid them.

They sent their text to Gerson for a quick edit, and he passed it on to Karen Hughes, Bush's close adviser and White House communications director, who was assembling the brief address. She used practically nothing from the speechwriters' draft. At Bush's instruction, she took out a passage that read: "This is not just an act of terrorism. This is an act of war." Speaking to her by phone during the day, the president ex-

---

The Weekly Standard and the American Enterprise Institute are located in the same building.

plained, "Our mission is reassurance." There would be time later for war talk.

Hughes's pastor had e-mailed her a message of support that mentioned the Twenty-third Psalm—"The Lord Is My Shepherd"—and she decided to include a passage from it in the remarks. She was waiting on the patio outside the Oval Office at 6:54 pm when Marine One, the president's helicopter, touched down on the South Lawn.

Standing between the White House and the Old Executive Office Building, on the other side of the West Wing, McConnell could hear the *whup-whup-whup* of the helicopter blades as the president arrived. Just for a moment he had a lump in his throat as he considered the possibility that the terrorists' plan had included destroying the White House and the president with it, but that both still stood. Scully, Frum, and he had slowly made their way back to the White House, impeded by ever tighter layers of security. Despite having their White House badges, they had had to wait half an hour outside the Northwest Gate. "There were men with long guns on the lawn," McConnell recalled. Once inside, they went to the White House mess and got hamburgers. McConnell was not sure if the mess stewards had ever left.

At some point, Hughes, Gerson, and Dan Bartlett, a communications aide whose Bush service went back to Texas, had decided to ask the president to revisit including "This is an act of war." None wanted to broach it with Bush, who disliked late changes to speeches, and Bartlett had finally gotten the duty. Edits are over, the president said. Now, as airtime approached, Bush and Hughes gave the remarks one last look. The translation of Psalm Twenty-three was unfamiliar and Bush did not like it. "You need to get a good translation," he said. And he tweaked the phrase Scully had produced about not making a distinction between terrorists and the countries that helped them—the only line from the speechwriters' draft that made it into the final speech. Bush inserted the word "harbor."

"We will make no distinction between the terrorists who committed these acts and those who harbor them," he told the nation that evening.

Tonight I ask for your prayers for all those who grieve, for the children whose worlds have been shattered, for all whose sense of safety and security has been threatened. And I pray they will be comforted by a power greater than any of us, spoken through the ages in Psalm 23: "Even though I walk through the valley of the shadow of death, I fear no evil, for You are with me."

Gerson thought the speech was "unequal to the moment—too much sentiment, not enough resolve, too much forced word play." Bush looked "stiff and small." Frum, listening with Scully and McConnell, was not impressed either. Bush looked weak and tentative, he thought. "At the center of the speech, where Bush ought to have explained who the enemy was—and then pledged to destroy him utterly—the public was offered instead a doughy pudding of stale metaphors," he wrote. Someone on the White House staff would nickname the speech "the Awful Oval Address." It was not a strong start.

Gerson drove in before dawn the next morning. Passing the Pentagon, he could smell the building burn through his open car window. He, McConnell, and Scully gathered in McConnell's office. The president would be speaking at the National Cathedral in two days at a day of prayer and remembrance. Working from an outline prepared by Gerson, they set to writing. At a time when the world around them had changed, the three men were returning to a familiar routine.

Bush called them "the troika," "the lads," "the team," or sometimes "the A-team." Almost every prepared speech Bush had given since the start of his campaign for the presidency bore the fingerprints of Gerson, Scully, and McConnell. If they had not composed the speech, then they had likely sat around McConnell's computer editing a text written by one of the other speechwriters. It would start with an outline from Gerson—"the Scribe," as Bush sometimes called him. Gerson had neatly combed hair that exposed a high forehead and circular glasses that gave him, as one reporter put it, an "owlish" appearance. He would scribble on a yellow legal pad in his wild handwriting.* "One of his

---

*Presidential adviser Karl Rove once showed one of Gerson's pads to a reporter and said, "You know, when these go into the archives, future generations will be amazed that we let a crazy person this close to the President of the United States." Another former colleague compared Gerson's handwriting to the elaborate elvish script that J. R. R. Tolkien created for his "Middle Earth" stories. (David Frum, *Right Man*, 25.)

great talents is the ability to put together an intellectual construct for a speech," McConnell said. "He would think about these things for great lengths of time and go off and read and think and pick people's brains and very often he would come in with a speech outline."

Gerson was born in Belmont, New Jersey, but his family moved to St. Louis when he was ten. His father was a Nixon Republican and his mother a Kennedy Democrat. At age twelve, Gerson was a Jimmy Carter supporter, debating for him in school and handing out literature. He thought that Carter "represented a contrast to the moral bankruptcy of the Nixon era," and he also liked the former Georgia governor's openness about his religious beliefs. Gerson, an Episcopalian evangelist, split with the Democratic Party over abortion, which he viewed as a social justice issue.

Gerson studied briefly at Georgetown University's School of Foreign Service, but left when he had "sort of a crisis determining what I really believed," he later said. He transferred to Wheaton College, outside Chicago, where he studied theology. He was planning to enter the Fuller Theological Seminary in Pasadena, California, when a friend introduced him to Charles Colson, the former Nixon counsel who had started a prison ministry after spending time in jail for Watergate-related crimes. Colson asked Gerson to put off Fuller and come work for him as a researcher. Gerson never made it to the seminary.

After Colson, Gerson worked for various political figures, writing speeches for Indiana senator Dan Coats and then for Senator Robert Dole, on whose 1996 presidential campaign he first met Scully and McConnell. He went on to work as a senior editor at *U.S. News & World Report*, where he covered the Clinton impeachment trial. One day in 1999 he got a call from Texas governor George W. Bush's office—the governor was going to be in Washington and wanted to meet.

Gerson was reportedly so nervous before the meeting that he was spotted in the hallway of the J. W. Marriott Hotel in Washington hyperventilating. He later said he had no recollection of the panic attack. "I've read your stuff," Gerson recalled Bush saying. "This isn't an interview. I want you to write my announcement speech, my convention speech and my inaugural." There was, Gerson thought, "an infectious confidence there." Bush talked about how he wanted to transform the

GOP's domestic agenda by promoting education and welfare overhauls and faith-based initiatives. Within weeks Gerson had moved to Austin to work on the campaign.

Gerson developed what one staffer called "a mind meld" with Bush. "When you bring the West Texas approach to the heavy debates of the world, there has to be a translator," explained Dan Bartlett. "Mike is the translator." In the White House, Gerson had a reputation for intensity. It was not unusual for him to ignore staffers he passed in the hallway, lost in thought. He might chew on a pen until it exploded in his mouth (it was, Frum said, a box-a-week habit). He won plaudits for the eloquence of many of Bush's speeches. He also assumed policy-related duties beyond speechwriting, dealing with promotion of democracy, international development, and disease prevention, focusing especially on AIDS and Africa. He had a cramped office in the West Wing, but would often retreat to a Starbucks coffee shop to work on his outlines.

In Austin, in April 1999, Gerson had invited Matt Scully to join the Bush staff. Scully had just started writing his book and figured that he could use the income while working on it in his spare time. And his parents lived in Houston. Anyway, he had always enjoyed Gerson's company, so he accepted the job.

Born in Casper, Wyoming, Scully had never graduated from college, but had built a successful career on his graceful writing. McConnell described him as "the best writer in the English language that I know of." He had been a literary editor of *The National Review* and had worked at *The Washington Times*. He had written speeches for Vice President Dan Quayle during the first Bush administration, where he met McConnell.

Scully kept a Ziploc bag of peanuts in his office which he fed the squirrels on the White House lawn. Thoughtful and soft-spoken, he gained attention when his book was published not only for making a conservative case for animal welfare, but for being a strict vegetarian in an administration of carnivorous Texans. He "is the most interesting conservative you have never heard of," columnist George Will noted. "He speaks barely above a whisper and must be the mildest disturber of the peace. But he is among the most disturbing."

In Austin, Scully and Gerson had at first written pieces of speeches and sewn them together. Within a few weeks, the two men had started writing the speeches jointly. In January 2000, John McConnell joined, completing the trio.

A Yale-educated lawyer, McConnell had written speeches for Quayle and eventually took the same job with Vice President Cheney. A native of Bayfield, Wisconsin, McConnell had a square jaw and an unreconstructed earnestness that was not influenced by years in Washington. "I love the history of the [White House], and always have, all my life," McConnell said in 2006. "I feel so grateful to be a part of it. It's never lost the thrill for me. I've got a better view than the President— he doesn't get to look at the White House!" It was the kind of comment that would be written off as affected schmaltz coming from almost anyone else, but from John McConnell it was just true. "Imagine a typical all-American good guy circa 1950," fellow speechwriter Joe Shattan said. "That's McConnell."

"In his hands moral and religious ideas . . . had a more solid feel," Scully wrote of McConnell. "As a general rule in Bush speeches, if the writing is graceful, judicious and understated, and makes you think about the subject at hand instead of anyone's particular craftsmanship or religiosity—there's a better-than-even chance that it is by John McConnell."

McConnell had a capacity for producing original phrases, but he often risked losing them by trying to improve on them. This happened on September 12, 2001, when the three men were trying to come up with an opening for Bush's National Cathedral speech. They knew they needed something with lift and ring. McConnell suggested that Bush say the country was in the "middle hour of our grief." Gerson and Scully looked at each other, thrilled with the eloquence. Then McConnell started second-guessing himself until one or both told him to stop.

"Usually when you're a speechwriter, even for a president of the United States, the words don't make that much difference," Gerson said years later, in a startling admission. "It's important to have a high standard. It's important to have some knowledge of the tradition. But there are a few moments, historical moments, where the words really matter and count. And I lived through a couple of them. And if we had not done a good job [for the Cathedral speech] it would have hurt the country."

"We are here in the middle hour of our grief," Bush told an audience that included four former presidents and most of the capital's political, military, law enforcement, and intelligence leadership—and the nation. "So many have suffered so great a loss, and today we express our nation's sorrow." He talked about those who had lost their lives just going through their regular day and those "who defied their murderers" to save other lives.

The president made one apparent slip. "Our responsibility to history is already clear: To answer these attacks and rid the world of evil," he said. Scully is "reasonably certain" that the final draft of the speech had the word "this," as in "rid the world of this evil"—an enormous difference in describing the scope of the challenge. "It is no small goal," R. W. Apple, Jr., wrote in *The New York Times*, "reminiscent in a way of Woodrow Wilson's promise that World War I would make the world safe for democracy." Some diplomats, reported Dana Milbank and Dan Balz in *The Washington Post*, viewed the statement as a vow of "final victory over terrorism that is not realistic."

Scully doubts that Bush intentionally dropped the "this." "I'm sure that the man didn't stand up there promising to rid the world of evil," he said.

Gerson, who usually made it a practice not to watch Bush's speeches in person, was at the National Cathedral. He described it as a "profoundly emotional experience" that reached a peak when the audience sang "The Battle Hymn of the Republic." He teared up. It hit him again that the country was at war. "I hadn't expected that," he said. "I had come as a domestic policy person. You could see that life was going to change, that everything was going to be different."

For the speech to the nation on September 11, and for virtually all foreign policy speeches, the troika had help from John Gibson, the NSC's speechwriter. He was unique in speechwriting history, a holdover from a previous administration of another party. Gibson had started at the NSC as a Clinton speechwriter in 2000. During the transition, a standard e-mail was sent to all NSC staff—political appointees and civil servants, though as a practical matter it traditionally was meant only for the latter—instructing people how to request to stay on in the new ad-ministration. Gibson had previously worked at a law firm with Stephen Hadley, the incoming deputy national security adviser, so he sent in his name. When Hadley called him with a job offer, Gibson figured that he could stay on for a short time while thinking about what he wanted to do. And anyway, the differences between the incoming Bush adminis-tration and the outgoing Clinton administration on foreign policy did not seem sharp. He thought writing for the president and helping the country was a high honor.

Going to work on January 20, 2001, was "an extremely odd experi-ence," Gibson said. "I felt like somebody who had been left on the roof of the Saigon embassy and all my friends had gotten on the last helicop-ter." He expected some level of suspicion given his background, but was treated as if he had been on the team from the start. "Except for the ide-ological vertigo, it was great," he quipped.

But there were differences between the administrations. The Bush crowd ran things more efficiently and seemed to have less internal poli-ticking. They also took themselves more seriously. The Clinton crowd had a greater sense of fun. More immediate, where Gibson had been one of several NSC speechwriters reporting to the national security adviser under Clinton, he was the only one in the new administration. He reported to Gerson and as well to Rice. He was well liked by his col-leagues, most of whom assumed that he was a civil servant rather than a former Democratic political appointee. Bush called him "the Clintonite," with good humor and warmth. When in 2003 Bush learned that Gibson was finally leaving the administration, he remarked, "Good soul."

Bush spent the weekend after 9/11 at Camp David.* He returned to the White House on Sunday afternoon and met with Hughes and other communications staffers in the residence to talk about what he would

---

*Present at Camp David that weekend were Cheney, Rice, Hadley, Secretary of State Colin Powell, Deputy Secretary of State Richard Armitage, Secretary of Defense Donald Rums-feld, Attorney General John Ashcroft, FBI director Robert Mueller, CIA director George Tenet, Deputy Secretary of Defense Paul Wolfowitz, and CIA counterterror chief Cofer Black. (*9/11 Commission Report*, 332.)

like to say in a speech to the nation. The date had not yet been set. Hughes took notes: "America is united and strong. . . . Praise Congress. . . . By uniting in capital, we've helped unite nation. . . . Single out, we're Americans now, not Republicans or Democrats. . . . Here's what we need to do. . . . The world has rallied. . . . Call to action, we will rout them out . . . Define mission . . . War is not against one person or one group, it's against terrorism." She suggested that the speech should evoke examples of the everyday heroism that had been displayed since the attacks. ("We have seen the State of our Union in the endurance of rescuers, working past exhaustion," Bush would say in his speech to Congress. "We have seen the unfurling of flags, the lighting of candles, the giving of blood, the saying of prayers in English, Hebrew, and Arabic. We have seen the decency of a loving and giving people who have made the grief of strangers their own.")

Hughes saw Bush again the next morning, Monday, September 17. Military action could come at any time. "If we've done something, discuss what we have done," Bush instructed for the speech. "If not, tell people to get ready." ("And tonight, a few miles from the damaged Pentagon, I have a message for our military: Be ready," he would say.) He wanted a draft that evening, Bush told her. That would be impossible, Hughes said. "I want it by 7," he said. When she told Gerson, he said, difficult, if not impossible. "I already tried that," Hughes told him. McConnell said the same thing when Gerson passed that on. We can't do that. I already tried that with Karen, and she tried it with the president, Gerson replied.

The three men sat down around the computer set up in McConnell's office—they almost always wrote in McConnell's office. They had a few shorthand notes on the screen from their conversations with Bush the previous Thursday, and with Rice, political aide Karl Rove, and others: "Darkness. Light . . . harm/evil . . . challenge . . . enemy . . . defeat and destroy. Eyes open . . . alerted. We've been a continent shielded by oceans. Carnage known only in Civil War. Foe: Political ideology, not a religion. Our view of the world—challenge we did not ask for in a world we did not make.' People turn to America. Much grief but many questions. Who is the enemy?"

Little of this made it directly into the final address. "The only way to defeat terrorism as a threat to our way of life is to stop it, eliminate it, and destroy it where it grows," Bush would say in his speech. And, "Americans have many questions tonight. Americans are asking, who attacked our country?"

They worked quickly, falling into one of their grooves. "Tonight we are a country awakened to danger . . ." That worked. "Freedom is at war with fear." No, better: "Freedom and fear are at war." (Later they would add, "and we know that God is not neutral between them.") Gibson had sent over a memo answering questions about the nature of al Qaeda and the Taliban. Scully: "We're not deceived by their pretenses to piety." Gerson: "They're the heirs of all the murderous ideologies of the 20th century. By sacrificing human life to serve their radical vision, by abandoning every value except the will to power, they follow in the path of Fascism and Nazism and Imperial Communism." ("Totalitarianism" would be substituted for "Imperial Communism" lest the Russians be offended.) Scully again: "And they will follow that path all the way to where it ends." A lull now, as they contemplated where exactly it *did* end. Then McConnell: "You know, history's unmarked grave." Almost. They played with it. "It will end in discarded lies," McConnell added. Here it was: "And they will follow that path all the way, to where it ends, in history's unmarked grave of discarded lies."

At some point that week, the three men received a contribution they were unaware came from a former White House ghost. Like most Americans in the wake of the attacks, Tom Malinowski, the former chief NSC writer under Clinton, wanted to help the president. "We were all Americans after 9/11," he said. "And our president was not doing so well—which people tend to forget—rhetorically." After a hesitant performance on September 11 itself, Bush had lurched tonally. He referred to the terrorists as "folks" and then called for a "crusade"—a heretical word in the Muslim world—and said that al Qaeda leader Usama bin Laden was "wanted, dead or alive." "Bush Negotiates a Rhetorical Minefield" was the headline of one *Washington Post* story. The president's father told him to rein in his tone.

Malinowski tried to help the way he knew best: He wrote up a page and a third of suggested lines for the speech and sent them to John Gibson, his old NSC colleague. "One tough line: 'We will bring them to justice, or we will bring justice to them. But there will be justice.' [A bit loftier than 'dead or alive,' but it means the same thing!]" Malinowski had written at the top of the first page.

"Now for the squishy, but vital part," he added, continuing with more suggested sound bites. Gibson passed on the "justice" line—but did not say where he had gotten it. The fact of its origin might have disqualified it. "There's nothing wrong about it: one of your jobs as a White House speechwriter is to solicit ideas," Malinowski said. "The president is entitled to the best stuff." The troika liked the "justice" line and included it. The draft they submitted to Bush on Monday night was rough, but it was serviceable, and it was in by 8 pm, if not by seven.

The speechwriters and Hughes met with the president the next morning in the Oval Office. He was not satisfied with the speech, particularly the peroration. The writers suggested including a Franklin Roosevelt quote—"We defend and we build a way of life, not for America alone, but for all mankind"—but Bush was not interested. "I don't want to quote anyone!" he said. "I want to lead! I want to be the guy they quote!" He did not want to close on a note of introspection but of leadership. "This is what my presidency is about," he said more than once.

Rice walked in with an ultimatum that Secretary of State Colin Powell was going to issue to the Taliban, the fundamentalist Muslims who controlled Afghanistan and were allied with al Qaeda. They must hand over any al Qaeda leaders and shut down any terrorist camps there, Powell planned to say. Bush liked those demands. He decided to announce them himself in his speech.

As Gerson pulled into his driveway that night at around 9:30 pm, his cell phone rang. It was the president, with more changes. They were heading in the right direction, he said. They spent about thirty minutes line-editing the speech, as Gerson sat in his car.

"You all have smiles on your faces, that's good," Bush said the next day, when Hughes and the speechwriters met with him at 1 pm. He was feeling loose, feet up on his desk. When he read through the latest draft of the speech, he even parodied a couple of lines that did not work. A

Hughes line that analogized al Qaeda to the Mafia—al Qaeda is to Arabs what the Mafia is to Italians—gave him pause ("Isn't that kind of a slight ethnic insult?"), but he kept it. He was, overall, pleased. "Let's call the Congress," he said—he would address the joint session the next evening, Thursday, September 20.

There had been some discussion about the setting for the speech: Congress? A war college? Some aides had favored another Oval Office speech, but Bush generally preferred speaking on his feet—he was uncomfortable at a desk. Rove had argued for the Congress. Bush fed off crowds and it would help build national unity. The president's key political adviser, Rove had come from Texas with him and had been dubbed "Bush's Brain." His direction carried a great deal of weight on speech matters. He would notice if some policy pronouncement differed from Bush's previous statements going back years. And on major speeches he would send in long handwritten memos explaining his edits. "Karl is a very serious thinker, and not just a political strategist but as a policy theorist," Gerson later said.

Bush ambled into the family theatre that night at 6:30 pm, wearing a blue tracksuit and a baseball cap for his first podium rehearsal of the speech. The atmosphere was informal. Spot, his dog, ran around the room. He again made fun of lines that were overwrought. (Mocking overwritten speech language was standard for Bush in rehearsal. On another occasion when the speechwriters gave him baroque lines about spreading freedom around the globe, he paused, looked up, and said, "What is this stuff? I sound like Spartacus or someone.") He cut others that did not fit—it was not the time for something like "This crisis found us making progress on many fronts, from education to energy policy." "Take it out," he ordered. He complained to Hughes that she was allowing too many inserts without his knowledge. "I probably rejected a hundred suggestions for every one we took," she protested. "Well, you took too many," he replied. He inserted "After all" into the start of a sentence about the United States being the largest source of humanitarian aid to Afghanistan—a pause there would allow him to take a breath. He came to the end of the speech, where he would hold up the police badge of New York City Police Officer George Howard. "And I will carry this," Bush said, picking up a bottle of Dasani water.

"It is the police shield of a man named George Howard, who died at the World Trade Center trying to save others."

The president met with his war cabinet at 7 pm. Secretary of Defense Donald Rumsfeld was concerned that singling out bin Laden would elevate the terrorist in stature. Rice said that the decision had been made—he would be named once. (Al Qaeda "and its leader, a person named Usama bin Laden, are linked to many other organizations in different countries," Bush would say, warning that there were "thousands of these terrorists in more than sixty countries.")

Bush had a second practice session at 11:10 am on Wednesday, September 20. He was wearing a suit, and was a bit more grave. At the third and final rehearsal, that afternoon, there was a different air in the family theatre, it seemed to Scully, and a new man reading the speech. For the first time, Bush brought the speech to life. This time, when he came to the "And I will carry this" line, he pulled out the actual badge. Logan Walters, Bush's personal aide, asked him if he wanted to read it through once more. "No," the president said. "I'm ready."

That night, the president made a rare appearance before a joint session of Congress without the vice president sitting behind him. To underscore security, Cheney was kept away from the Capitol,* as was House majority leader Richard Armey—though there were likely few places in the country that night more secure than that building. Fighter jets and military helicopters circled overhead. Barriers of concrete and wire blocked the approaches. Police and soldiers massed outside while bomb-sniffing dogs checked the galleries around the House chamber. A fleet of ambulances, fire trucks, and unmarked SWAT vans awaited any contingency. "The Capitol looked as if it had suddenly been moved to Beirut, or Mogadishu," *The Washington Post* reported.

As Laura Bush walked to her seat in the gallery, accompanied by

---

*Cheney's being in a "secure, undisclosed location" became something of a national running joke after 9/11. It was later disclosed that the phrase was just a generic description but that most often he was at Camp David. (Stephen F. Hayes, *Cheney: The Untold Story of America's Most Powerful and Controversial Vice President* [New York: HarperCollins, 2007], 349.)

New York mayor Rudolph Giuliani and New York governor George Pataki, the assembled legislators burst into thunderous applause, with shouts of "Bravo!" The two New York leaders seemed taken aback by the welcome. Bush was greeted as a conquering hero, with bipartisan whoops and unceasing applause.

"In the normal course of events, Presidents come to this Chamber to report on the state of the Union. Tonight, no such report is needed. It has already been delivered by the American people," he began. "Tonight we are a country awakened to danger and called to defend freedom. Our grief has turned to anger and anger to resolution." (This was an example of the speechwriters giving Bush back a polished version of what he had been telling them, as was the sentence, "We will not tire, we will not falter, and we will not fail.")

"Whether we bring our enemies to justice or bring justice to our enemies, justice will be done," he said in one of the signature lines. When Malinowski heard it, he felt "kind of funny, kind of queasy." He had not known that Gibson had included any of his suggestions in the speech. ("This is the great irony of my speechwriting career," Malinowski said. "I worked for Clinton for seven years. I'm a Democrat. I think I had a lot of success, a lot of speeches that were influential that were quoted all over the world, plenty of ego gratification and all that. But as it turned out, the line that I wrote that I think will probably be remembered and quoted more than any other was uttered by not Clinton but Bush.")

"Al Qaeda is to terror what the Mafia is to crime," Bush said. "But its goal is not making money. Its goal is remaking the world and imposing its radical beliefs on people everywhere." Secretary of State Colin Powell had objected to this line on the grounds that it might unnecessarily offend "the anti-Soprano crowd," presumably a reference to the protests against the popular HBO television series *The Sopranos* as being anti-Italian. Bush had kept it in after tweaking its original form.

"Americans are asking, what is expected of us? I ask you to live your lives and hug your children," Bush said, using another Hughes line, and following with one of Rove's. "I know many citizens have fears tonight, and I ask you to be calm and resolute, even in the face of a continuing threat." The line about the children had met resistance in the White House. Scully, for example, thought it was "a little bit of a Hallmark touch." "We have suffered great loss," Bush said. "And in our grief and anger, we have found our mission and our moment." The "mission" line had its roots in Scully's observation about Bush in the days after the attacks.

Gerson watched the speech at home. Bush called him from the limousine. "I have never felt more comfortable in my life," the president told his speechwriter softly. "Mr. President, this is why God wants you here," Gerson said. Bush replied, "No, this is why God wants us here."*

Although Bush was known and derided for verbal fumbles and errors, he understood the importance of presidential communications. He put a great deal of time and energy into speech preparation and faith in his speechwriters. Bush and top aides such as Karen Hughes and Karl Rove "understood the importance of speechwriting," Scully said later. "Whereas his father—and they clearly drew this lesson—his father really didn't. . . . There's no doubt in my mind that . . . Governor Bush and a few others who observed that, saw that this was not the way to run a presidential speechwriting department and that this was obviously a great resource that wasn't being used."

"The President wants in his speaking action and directness," Gerson said. "That said, the President also demands an element of elevation in his speeches that shows some continuity with the great traditions of American political rhetoric."

"He would often say that each speech is a chance to educate," said Noam Neusner, who became a Bush economic speechwriter for two years starting in late 2002. And he would stress the virtues of repetition. Bush "would always say, 'You may get tired of writing it, but this has to be explained. And I like to explain things and you have to make an argu-

---

*Gerson relayed the story at a dinner of the Judson Welliver Society of former White House speechwriters. The anecdote brought a moment of uncomfortable silence that was deflated when a Clinton speechwriter audibly whispered, "God must really hate Al Gore." Rick Hertzberg then rose to respond. I'm sure we're all gratified to hear that your man was put in office by the almighty, he said; the rest of us had to make do with a plurality of the vote. (Jeffrey Goldberg, "The Believer," *The New Yorker*, February 13 and 20, 2006; author interview with David Boorstin.)

ment, and lay it out, and you have to do it again and again and again,'" Scully recalled. It might be standard to the speechwriters, but it was often new to the audiences.

When a writer's speech had been submitted to Bush, he was expected to be at his desk by 7 am, because that was when the president would call with questions. "He'll say, 'Yeah, the speech? A couple of little things—page five, this paragraph, what is this? Why are we saying this?'" McConnell recalled. "Or, 'We need to move a few things around, we need to make some edits.' It could be anything—a question, a comment, a change. It's never just chitchat. . . . It is a specific, action-oriented call."

Bush stressed organization in his speeches, logical order. He disliked sloppy transitions. "It's just words, isn't it?" he might say. "Take it out." He had the ability, McConnell said, to read a speech through once and grasp its structure and be able to point out which paragraphs were out of place. "He'll spot it and he'll say, 'The paragraph at the bottom of five belongs in the middle of three,'" McConnell said. "In one reading he'll do this. . . . The logical marching thing is something that he really grabs onto quickly and he'll catch the little flaws."

Bush's tips could get minute: Do not start sentences with the word "it." Or they could be broad. "He was very clear," Noam Neusner recalled. "He said, 'I like my speeches to be very clearly structured. I think what we need to do always at the beginning of a speech is articulate what the problem is we're trying to solve and make sure that we're clearly defining that problem. Then we should talk about the principles that we bring to bear when we address the problem. What do we believe? . . . Then the next part is the policy: What are we proposing? What addresses the challenge that reflects the principles in the policy? And do it in that order every time."*

Bush could also catch what he called "cram-ins," his expression for clunky phrases and extraneous points that bureaucrats or senior aides

---

*Scully would tease Gerson that on "compassionate conservative" related speeches, he too had a predictable structure. "We begin with great and inexorable 'callings' of history, then move on to hard moral 'duties' and 'nonnegotiable demands' of conscience, proceeding through the bramble patch of 'temptations'—not to be merely avoided but *actively confronted*—arriving in due course at the solution, and with that the 'confident hope' of a better day," he wrote. (Matthew Scully, "Present at the Creation.")

would stuff into the draft. Often the speechwriters would dismiss the new language; but if they could not, if it came from too senior an aide or if they were feeling mean, they would leave it in for the president to take out. "Who put this in?" he would ask, and guess at which nonspeech-writer was the offender.

When delivering a speech, he once told Scully, he would focus on two or three people in the audience and keep going back to them. He liked to get their reaction as a gauge for the audience and tried to feel as if he was talking to just those people.

Meeting with the writers in late 2001 to discuss his upcoming State of the Union address, Bush thought aloud about making the spread of democracy and promotion of women's rights in the Muslim world its focus. The spread of democracy was a theme to which he would repeatedly return, but it caused enough disquiet in the foreign policy bureaucracy—too radical a shift in relations with the Muslim countries—that he let the idea go for the time being. But it prompted him to examine more closely the U.S. role in the region. "Bush decided that the United States was no longer a status-quo power in the Middle East," Frum wrote. "He wanted to see plans for overthrowing Saddam, and he wanted a speech that explained to the world why Iraq's dictator must go."

Iraq was not a new preoccupation for Bush. During the 2000 campaign, he had criticized the Clinton administration as insufficiently tough on Iraq, and had vowed to be more aggressive in dealing with Hussein. "No one envisioned him still standing," Bush told a BBC interviewer in 1999, referring to the Gulf War, when his father had stopped short of removing Hussein from power. "It's time to finish the task." As early as February 2001, the administration had ratcheted up pressure against Iraq by approving new funds for insurgent groups inside the country and by stepping up air strikes, hitting targets outside of the no-fly zones for the first time since late 1999.

When, in mid-February 2001, Bush met with the speechwriters for a get-acquainted session, one of the priorities he discussed was, as Frum put it, "his determination to dig Saddam Hussein out of power in Iraq."

In the initial hours and days after the September 11 attacks, the question of attacking Iraq as part of the response had been debated but put aside. The United States had started bombing targets in Afghanistan on October 7 and within two months the Taliban regime had crumbled. Now the administration was turning its sights once more to Iraq.

"Here's an assignment," Gerson told Frum one day in late December 2001. "Can you sum up in a sentence or two our best case for going after Iraq?"

Frum was an odd choice for the assignment. He had, in fact, considered himself an unlikely choice to be a speechwriter at all. He was a Canadian, had neither government experience nor Bush connections, and had publicly doubted whether Bush was up to the job of being president. And the fact of a president and administration that proudly proclaimed their religious faith "was disconcerting to a non-Christian like me." As a contributing editor to the conservative *Weekly Standard*, columnist with the Canadian *National Post*, and former senior editor at *Forbes* and assistant editor on *The Wall Street Journal*'s editorial page, he did have the right credentials for a speechwriting job. A well-known political commentator, he was, Scully said, "a highly conscientious person, a gentleman, and . . . the most accomplished author on our staff."

Gerson had persuaded Frum to sign on as an economic speechwriter, but now he was giving him an important foreign policy assignment. Frum pondered it. The case could not merely be Hussein's past transgressions. That would raise the question of timing—why take him out now? He reread Roosevelt's speech to Congress after the attack on Pearl Harbor. The Axis powers in World War II—Germany, Japan, and Italy—had been a menace, he thought, because of their "recklessness." Iraq was like the old Axis powers. And as Pearl Harbor had served as a warning about the dangers of Germany, so too September 11 could highlight the dangers of Iraq, especially since it was presumed to have chemical and biological weapons.

The more Frum thought about it, the more the "terror organizations and the terror states"—al Qaeda, Hezbollah, Iran and Iraq—"resembled the Tokyo–Rome–Berlin Axis." Sure, Iran and Iraq had fought a bloody war in the 1980s, and al Qaeda had denounced Iraq's secular

Baathist regime and hated the Shiites who dominated Iran; but the various groups had had moments of cooperation, or at least of truce. Iraq had flown half its air force to Iran in advance of the 1991 Gulf War (the planes were never returned), and some al Qaeda leaders had fled to Iran after the fall of Afghanistan (the Iranian government claimed to have arrested them). And anyway, Frum thought, the original Axis had been a tenuous alliance: Had they won the war, they would have fallen on each other.

The terror groups and terror states did have commonalities, Frum reasoned. They hated freedom, democracy, rationality, Jews, and the West. They celebrated death. Though they may not realize it, they were united in their hatreds. "So there was our link—and our explanation of why we must act: Together the terror states and the terror organizations formed an axis of hatred against the United States," he wrote. "The United States could not wait for these dangerous regimes to get deadly weapons and attack us; the United States must strike first and protect the world from them."

Frum put his conclusion into a memo to Gerson and sent it in, not expecting to hear any more about it.

In early January, Bush huddled with the speechwriters in the Oval Office to discuss the agenda for 2002. The writers proposed various domestic or quasi-domestic issues—health care, trade, and so forth—and he batted them away. He was going to devote minimal time and energy to domestic issues.

The troika gathered to prepare the State of the Union. For eight, nine, ten days running, the routine would be the same: The three sequestered themselves in McConnell's office and word-by-word, line-by-line, wrote the speech. After several days McConnell's office resembled, as he put it, the "back room of a cheap restaurant"—coffee-stained papers piled up, bits of food, half-full coffee cups and water bottles lying around. McConnell, who kept a supply of Wet Ones towelettes on hand, endured the chaos with good humor.

They called these efforts "death marches," but the fact was that the three men enjoyed themselves. For one thing, having two other people there relieved the pressure of the job. "There was this unspoken sense of relief that there wasn't one man alone in the room who was going to . . . have to generate something really good," McConnell said. "We knew that we could do this together." Throughout their collaboration, amidst trying to write speeches in tones of "high seriousness," the three would crack each other up with humorous digressions, coming up with absurd, inappropriate, or rude things Bush might say in whatever speech they were working on. For all of his seriousness, Scully said, Gerson was "hilarious company," while McConnell could do impressions of everyone from Harry S. Truman to crude *Saturday Night Live* characters. Other staffers would poke their head into McConnell's office to find out what all the howls were about. "Education speeches in particular—with their endlessly complicated programs and slightly puffed-up theories, none of which we could ever explain quite to the satisfaction of our policy people—were always good for a laugh," Scully later wrote. "As John observed in late 2003, around draft twenty in the typically chaotic revising of an education speech, 'We've taken the country to war with less hassle than this.'"

Gerson summed up the feeling of happy companionship toward the end of the 2002 death march when he said that it was a rare thing in life when one is cooped up with two other people for nine days running and still look forward to going in to work on the tenth morning. There was nevertheless trouble brewing: media accounts of the speechwriting process and profiles of Gerson mostly portrayed him as working alone, a solitary artist crafting the president's speeches. And it was not clear to Scully whether even their White House colleagues knew precisely how the speeches were produced.

To Frum's surprise, his Iraq argument was incorporated into the State of the Union. The topic of weapons of mass destruction and terrorists had first been raised in preparations for the September 20 speech, but Bush had put it off—it might be too frightening an idea so soon after 9/11. Now might be the time. And while Frum's "axis of hatred" focused on Iraq and terrorist groups, national security adviser Condoleezza Rice worried that singling the country out might tip the administration's hand concerning the war planning that was already secretly under way. She and her deputy, Stephen Hadley, suggested adding Iran and North Korea.

"Axis of hatred" was slightly revised. "I hate *hatred*," Scully said when Gerson brought up the phrase. It reminded him of "forces of hatred," a formulation that Clinton used. Scully suggested that "evil" be substituted—it fit with the "evil-doers" that Bush had mentioned in the months since 9/11. The three discussed it and agreed on "evil."* "For a time, I congratulated myself on at least preventing the even more melodramatic 'axis of hatred' from marching into history—though, looking back, I suppose 'axis of evil' was a case of how the very intensity of these speeches could sometimes give events a false momentum and fill the air with needless drama," Scully wrote.

"North Korea is a regime arming with missiles and weapons of mass destruction, while starving its citizens," Bush charged in his State of the Union address on the evening of January 29, 2002. "Iran aggressively pursues these weapons and exports terror, while an unelected few repress the Iranian people's hope for freedom. Iraq continues to flaunt its hostility toward America and to support terror. . . . States like these and their terrorist allies constitute an axis of evil, arming to threaten the peace of the world."

"Axis of evil" ignited a firestorm. Not surprising, the three countries denounced Bush, but friendly nations also found it disquieting. Bush did little to settle matters two days later when he followed up on the nations "on our watch list." "People say, 'What does that mean?' It means they better get their house in order, is what it means," Bush said in Atlanta on January 31. "It means they better respect the rule of law. It means they better not try to terrorize America and our friends and allies, or the justice of this nation will be served on them, as well." "The testosterone talk from the White House may be grist to the mill of President Bush's domestic popularity, but it's getting U.S. allies abroad a little nervous," *Time* reported.

Conservatives hailed the speech. "He is using his war popularity to

---

*Gerson was asked in a C-SPAN interview broadcast in January 2007 who it was that wanted the word "evil." "I did," he said. "I think it's a better-sounding phrase." (Gerson on *Q&A*.)

seek support for more war—far wider, larger and more risky," columnist Charles Krauthammer wrote. "Bush's three bad guys—North
Korea, Iran and Iraq—are ideologically well chosen." He said that the
speech only just stopped short of declaring war against Iraq.
Afghanistan would merely be "prologue," the first step in a gambit
whose final stage would be Saddam Hussein's overthrow.

Frum resigned on February 25. He had decided that an economic
speechwriter did not have much to do in a wartime White House. He
was replaced by Joseph Shattan, who, like McConnell and Scully, had
worked for former Vice President Dan Quayle. As Frum was packing
up his office, a colleague told him to turn on CNN because Robert
Novak had just reported that Bush had fired him. The crux of the controversy, such as it was, was that Frum's wife had e-mailed some family
and friends bragging that Frum had conceived of "axis of evil." Her
e-mail had been forwarded to a reporter with the Internet opinion magazine *Slate*, who published it.

That Frum would be fired for even directly leaking authorship of a
phrase in a speech seems unlikely. A *New York Times* reporter had been
encamped with the speechwriters when the September 11 attacks took
place, producing an insider blow-by-blow of the writing of the speech
to the joint session of Congress. Hughes and Gerson had given similar
inside accounts to other reporters. Gerson was the subject of flattering
profiles. The Bush White House was not shy about publicity for its
speechwriters.

Speculation about war with Iraq increased from spring through summer of 2002, stoked by Bush's speech on June 1 at West Point unveiling
the "Bush doctrine." The United States would strike preventively
against perceived dangers before they blossomed into actual threats.
Bush was scheduled to speak at the United Nations on September 12.
Gerson brought Bush an outline for a speech focusing on "the non-
negotiable demands of human dignity." "No," Bush told him. "We're
gonna talk about Iraq."

It was an important speech. It would be his best chance to make the
case to the international community that a move against Iraq was neces-

sary. Domestically, it kicked off a coordinated administration publicity blitz that included strategic leaks to the press and administration officials arguing the case on television talk shows, all meant to prove that Iraq was a threat. Scully, who had taken a leave of absence in July to promote his book, briefly returned to work on the speech, temporarily reassembling the troika. Gibson, the Clinton holdover on the NSC staff, also contributed. "I'm not totally there yet," he told Gerson, referring to the case for war against Iraq. "Then you're probably the perfect person to write the speech," Gerson replied. "If you can convince yourself, you can convince the country."

On September 11, Gibson was at the Waldorf-Astoria Hotel in New York City—Bush was marking the one-year anniversary of the attacks with a brief speech at Ellis Island—finalizing the UN speech. Gerson called to say that there was a new piece of intelligence that might fit into the speech. Gibson should get on a secure phone and call Robert Joseph, the NSC's proliferation expert who had, reporters Michael Isikoff and David Corn later wrote, "a reputation for pushing evidence related to Iraq as far as it could possibly go." The information that Joseph had for Gibson would become one of the best known and most controversial elements of the case against Iraq: Hussein's regime, Joseph said, had been trying to acquire a substantial amount of yellowcake uranium—a key ingredient in the enrichment process used to make fuel for an atomic weapon—in Africa.

Joseph faxed Gibson three sentences to insert laying out the allegation and its significance. The CIA had cleared the language, and Gibson and Joseph talked about how best to insert it. But then word came from the CIA that it was backing off the claim. Based on a single foreign source of information, it was too tenuous to put into a presidential address.

The common security of all nations, Bush told the diplomats on Thursday, September 12, was threatened by a confluence of factors, including terrorism, weapons of mass destruction, and rogue states. "In one place—in one regime—we find all these dangers in their most lethal and aggressive forms, exactly the kind of aggressive threat the United Nations was born to confront," Bush said. He ticked off a litany of Iraq's misdeeds, which did not include the yellowcake claim. "In 1991, the Iraqi regime agreed to destroy and stop developing all weapons of mass destruction and long-range missiles and to prove to the world it has done so by complying with rigorous inspections," he said. "Iraq has broken every aspect of this fundamental pledge."

There had been intense debate within the administration about whether the president should request a new resolution from the UN Security Council demanding that Iraq submit once again to weapons inspections. Powell favored a new resolution and Cheney opposed one, arguing that it was not necessary. Powell had apparently won the fight. The line was in the speech, but when Bush reached it, he skipped it. Sitting in the General Assembly chamber, Powell gasped. But it was an unintentional omission, and after a sentence, Bush ad-libbed: "We will work with the U.N. Security Council for the necessary resolutions." Powell exhaled. But Bush had said "resolutions." Rice and her deputy, Stephen Hadley, wondered if they should clarify that he meant only one, but decided not to, hoping it would go unnoticed.

Bush issued a challenge: Iraq must abide by the UN resolutions and the terms of the 1991 peace agreement—in other words, it must give up its stores of weapons of mass destruction. "The purposes of the United States should not be doubted," Bush said. "The Security Council resolutions will be enforced, the just demands of peace and security will be met, or action will be unavoidable. And a regime that has lost its legitimacy will also lose its power."

The administration's anti-Iraq push continued through the fall, with efforts focusing on gaining congressional approval to take action against Hussein. Speaking in Cincinnati on October 7, Bush was to give a nationally televised address on Iraq and its growing stockpile of lethal weapons. On October 4, the NSC sent the sixth draft of the speech to the CIA for clearance. It contained the assertion that "the regime has been caught attempting to purchase up to 500 metric tons of uranium oxide from Africa—an essential ingredient in the enrichment process." Gibson had worked on this speech as well, using the National Intelligence Estimate on Iraqi weapons of mass destruction programs issued by the CIA on October 1 for guidance. The assertion was in the intelligence estimate, so Gibson reasoned that it must be usable now.

The following day, the CIA sent a three-and-a-half-page, single-spaced, twenty-two-point reply to Gerson, deputy national security ad-

viser Stephen Hadley, and others, pointing out places where the assertions against Iraq could be made tougher. The draft stated that Iraq had
admitted to having twenty-five liters of anthrax and other biological
weapons, when the figure should be thirty. The CIA memo also pointed
to instances where the speech needed to be toned down. Regarding the
uranium assertion, the memo said: "Remove the sentence because the
amount is in dispute and it is debatable whether it can be acquired from
the source. We told Congress that the Brits have exaggerated this issue.
Finally, the Iraqis already have 550 metric tons of uranium oxide in
their inventory."

When the CIA received draft seven on Sunday, October 6, the line
had been modified but not removed: ". . . and the regime has been
caught attempting to purchase substantial amounts of uranium oxide
from sources in Africa." At this point the CIA officials dealing with the
draft brought Director George Tenet into the discussion. He telephoned Hadley and told him that Bush "should not be a fact witness on
this issue" because the "reporting was weak." More bluntly he added,
"You need to take this fucking sentence out because we don't believe it."

After Tenet's call, CIA officials dealing with the speech sent another
memo to Hadley and Rice underscoring their concerns with the uranium story. It said: ". . . More on why we recommend removing the
sentence about procuring uranium oxide from Africa: Three points (1)
The evidence is weak. One of the two mines cited by the source as the
location of the uranium oxide is flooded. The other mine cited by the
source is under the control of the French authorities. (2) The procure-
ment is not particularly significant to Iraq's nuclear ambitions because
the Iraqis already have a large stock of uranium oxide in their inventory.
And (3) we have shared points one and two with Congress, telling them
that the Africa story is overblown and telling them this is one of the two
issues where we differed with the British."

The sentence came out of the speech. It was not the only one the
CIA excised. Gerson and Gibson wanted to include a line to the effect
that a single canister of one of Hussein's chemical weapons could wipe
out New York or some other major city. It was a compelling image, but
the CIA would not sign off on it.

The October 7 address was plenty tough and startling even without the specific uranium allegation.* "Some citizens wonder, after eleven years of living with this problem, why do we need to confront it now?" Bush said. "And there's a reason. We've experienced the horror of September the 11th. . . . Knowing these realities, America must not ignore the threat gathering against us. Facing clear evidence of peril, we cannot wait for the final proof, the smoking gun, that could come in the form of a mushroom cloud."

The mushroom cloud image had first appeared publicly when an anonymous administration aide was quoted in a September 8 *New York Times* story. It was a Gerson creation. He had brought it up at a meeting of the White House Iraq Group, or WHIG, a collection of senior staffers that included Rice, Hadley, Scooter Libby, Karl Rove, and Gerson. The WHIG had coordinated the fall rollout of the anti-Iraq publicity campaign. One of its members had used the "mushroom cloud" line when speaking to the *Times* reporter. Rice had echoed it later, on September 8, and now almost a month later Bush finally got to use it.

Three days later, on October 10, 2002, the House of Representatives passed a resolution authorizing Bush to employ military force against Iraq. The Senate passed the same resolution hours later.

As Gerson, McConnell, and Scully—who had returned from promoting his book—geared up for another "death march" to produce the 2003 State of the Union, making the case for war against Iraq remained a priority. Sitting around McConnell's computer, with the National Intelligence Estimate before them, they sought to build the strongest case against Saddam Hussein that they could muster. "These findings seemed very credible and compelling and there was a certain drama and almost a chill in the air when we got to certain passages," Scully recalled. He cited one line: "Imagine those nineteen hijackers with other weapons and other plans, this time armed by Saddam Hussein," Bush would say. "It would take one vial, one canister, one crate slipped into

---

*Nonetheless, Bush later described the Cincinnati address as "the speech that nobody listened to" except a few conservative commentators and "my mother." (Draper, *Dead Certain*, 185.)

this country to bring a day of horror like none we have ever known." They wrote that passage very fast, Scully remembered, it came quickly. "We certainly believed that this was a very grave moment and that we were drawing attention to a very serious danger," he said.

An Iraqi nuclear threat remained a potent argument. And the claim about attempts to purchase yellowcake was still in the National Intelligence Estimate. The speechwriters often pushed the evidence to the limit. Their reasoning, Scully said, was, "this will be checked. . . . We're not competent to judge in every case what intelligence is sound, what intelligence is useful, what claims should or should not be made. That's for others. . . . We felt a certain freedom in that because what typically happened was others would pull us back." And pulled back they were. "We had stuff taken out of speeches all the time," McConnell said. "I know that we often did overstate the case and it would fall to someone like Steve Hadley, a very capable man, or Condi or Colin Powell to sort of pull us back a little bit and tone it down," Scully agreed.

To deal with the allegation that Iraq had tried to purchase uranium, now specifically in the African country of Niger, the speechwriters settled on the specific phrasing that "The British Government has learned . . ." in an effort to make the claim as specific as possible. They felt that "it was more cautious and guarded and of course more defensible to state it as a fact that British intelligence has determined some of this," Scully said. That was strengthened by Karen Hughes, who had left the administration but came back to help on big speeches. The section of the speech listing Iraq's transgressions had been written as a litany of factual statements, each starting with "We know," including, "We also know that [Saddam] has recently sought to buy uranium in Africa." Say where the evidence comes from, Hughes told them. Hence, "The British Government has learned . . ."*

---

*Robert Joseph, the NSC proliferation expert, told the Senate Intelligence Committee that the speechwriters had come up with the formulation citing the British government as the source of the information. However, Alan Foley, the director of the CIA's Weapons Intelligence Non-Proliferation and Arms Control Center, told the same committee that Joseph "came up with the idea to source the uranium information to the British during their conversation when he was attempting to come up with an unclassified way to use the uranium reporting." (*Senate Intelligence Committee Report*, 65–66.)

Intelligence was not the only place where the speechwriters stepped beyond their bounds. Secretary of State Colin Powell, reviewing a draft of the speech, was surprised to read that he had just been "directed" to go abroad on a mission. Bush had given no such order—the speechwriters had written themselves into a corner and solved their problem by dispatching the Secretary of State. The line was removed.

Although intelligence regarding yellowcake and Niger had twice been removed from previous presidential speeches, it remained in the State of the Union. Hadley and Gerson both later said that they had forgotten about the previous warnings. Tenet was given a hard copy of the speech the day before Bush was to deliver it, but did not read it. He handed it off to an assistant to take to the deputy director for intelligence, who handled the CIA clearance for such speeches. It is not clear whether it was delivered, or to whom. Asked about it by the Senate Intelligence Committee, no officials from that office could remember receiving the speech for coordination. And while the head of the agency's Weapons Intelligence Non-Proliferation and Arms Control Center did speak to a National Security Council official about the assertion, he was worried about revealing intelligence sources and methods—not about the credibility of the intelligence.

When the facts underlying the Niger claims came to light—that it had been repeatedly removed from previous speeches, and that the CIA did not think the claim was credible—it became a prime citation of the theory that the administration had knowingly used bad intelligence to take the nation to war in Iraq. The speechwriters bristle over the assertion.

McConnell points out that the British never withdrew their original allegation that Iraq had sought to buy uranium in Africa. "The final conclusion was, that's not the evidentiary standard we would ordinarily want in a State of the Union," he said. "And that's fine, as a standard you want to adopt. If the standard is, we will not accept something that is maintained by British intelligence if it is not also specifically adhered to by American intelligence, that's a coherent standard. It doesn't make the sentence a lie. The sentence is true as he said it. And so I am personally bothered . . . when something like that is cited as a lie by the president of the United States, it's really a so deeply unfair interpretation."

On Saturday, February 1, McConnell was in bed in his apartment at a little before 9 am, contemplating the first day since Christmas that he had nothing to do. The phone rang. The space shuttle *Columbia* had blown up during reentry, he was told, and all aboard were lost.

McConnell rushed into the office and started writing with Gerson and Scully. Somebody suggested that they look at Reagan's remarks from the *Challenger* disaster. "Our instant reaction was: We're not going to look at what Reagan said!" McConnell recalled. "We didn't look at it. It's not our job to say what did the other guys do. Our job is to serve our president now. And we just kind of bristled at that."

Karen Hughes was at home in Austin when she got the call. She started browsing through her Bible, looking for a suitable verse. She turned first to the Twenty-third Psalm, but remembered that Bush had used it on September 11. Psalm Nineteen looked promising, mentioning "The heavens," which "declare the glory of God." But its tone was too upbeat. Her Bible had a footnote that referred to Isaiah. She read through that book and finally settled on Isaiah 40:26–29. She e-mailed the verses to Gerson.

Bush spoke from the Cabinet Room shortly after 2 pm. "The cause in which they died will continue," he said.

Mankind is led into the darkness beyond our world by the inspiration of discovery and the longing to understand. Our journey into space will go on. In the skies today we saw destruction and tragedy. Yet farther than we can see, there is comfort and hope. In the words of the prophet Isaiah, "Lift your eyes and look to the heavens. Who created all these? He who brings out the starry hosts one by one and calls them each by name. Because of His great power and mighty strength, not one of them is missing." The same Creator who names the stars also knows the names of the seven souls we mourn today. The crew of the shuttle Columbia did not return safely to Earth. Yet we can pray that all are safely home.

• • •

The first bombs dropped on Iraq on March 19, 2003. That was sooner than the United States and its allies had planned to strike,* but the CIA had reports indicating that Hussein was at a complex in southwest Baghdad called Dora Farms, and they hoped a quick, decapitating strike could end the war before it began. In fact, he had not been to Dora Farms since 1995, the military later learned. According to the advocacy group Human Rights Watch, a civilian was killed in the attack. Hours later, the ground assault began. U.S. and allied forces moved steadily toward Baghdad, turning up no chemical or biological or nuclear weapons along the way. Within three weeks, the first U.S. units entered Baghdad, making quick strike "thunder runs" into the city at first, but then remaining. The conventional battle for Iraq was essentially over.

The president was going to speak on May 1 to declare success in Iraq. The staging would have made the Reagan team proud: Bush would pilot a plane that would land on the aircraft carrier USS *Abraham Lincoln* and walk before the cameras in a flight suit before giving his speech. *The New York Times* called it "one of the most audacious moments of presidential theater in American history."

Gerson came in with a copy of General Douglas MacArthur's "the guns are silent" speech in one hand and a muffin in the other.† He had an outline and an opening. "The sirens of Baghdad are quiet," he had written. "The desert has returned to silence. The Battle of Iraq is over, and the United States and our allies have prevailed."

"These are beautiful sentences," Karen Hughes wrote on the third draft when the writers sent it out for review, "but may overstate the case—there is still shooting going on." Secretary of Defense Donald

---

*By March 27, 2003, forty-eight countries had signed on to support Bush's coalition to remove Hussein from power. Twenty-one countries contributed military forces to the invasion and occupation of Iraq, but only Great Britain, Australia, and Poland sent significant numbers of troops.

†"My fellow countrymen, today the guns are silent," MacArthur said, speaking on the deck of the battleship *Missouri* in Tokyo Bay after the official surrender ceremonies that ended World War II. "A great tragedy has ended. A great victory has been won. The skies no longer rain death—the seas bear only commerce—men everywhere walk upright in the sunlight. The entire world is quietly at peace."

Rumsfeld also objected, saying that it was a serious overstatement of the facts. They took out the passages about the sirens of Baghdad being quiet.

Bush spoke on the *Lincoln* before a huge banner proclaiming "Mission Accomplished." As Iraq festered in the months after the speech, the banner became a symbol of administration overreach and arrogance. Rumsfeld told Bob Woodward that he had personally removed the phrase "mission accomplished" from a draft of the speech Bush gave on the *Lincoln*. But according to Scully, the phrase was never included in any draft of the speech. He added that "mission accomplished" did appear in "our jumble of notes that we sometimes had on the screen when we wrote." They had spoken on the telephone with Scott Sforza, a former ABC News producer who worked at the White House arranging the televisual backdrops of Bush's speeches. Sforza spent several days on the carrier preparing the event. "Scott was simply reporting to us, describing what the television audience would see," Scully recalled.

On Sunday, December 14, McConnell was again trying to sleep a bit later, so he had some trepidation when his visiting mother woke him to say that Scully was on the phone, and that he said it was important. Oh no, McConnell thought, bad news. Have you been watching? Scully asked. We got Saddam Hussein! "That was the first time that I'd ever been called in to work [suddenly] for good news," McConnell recalled.

For Scully, that morning was the only time that working at the White House seemed in real life as it often did in the movies: Driving through the White House gate and heading directly for the Oval Office to confer with the president. Bush had gotten a tentative heads-up the day before from Rumsfeld. "Mr. President, the first reports are not always accurate," the Defense Secretary had started before Bush interrupted him. "This sounds like it's going to be good news," the president said.

Bush called in the troika to prepare brief remarks for a speech to the nation. He took a telephone call from his father, who had years earlier been targeted for assassination by Hussein. The mood among the president and his aides that Sunday was businesslike, Scully recalled. "There was no false confidence even then," he said. "They knew it was a good day for the cause in Iraq, but there was no sense that this was going to turn everything around and this was the decisive moment. There was no kind of personal vindictiveness, none of that, no undue relishing of the moment. President Bush—I can truly say that he was always above that."

"The capture of Saddam Hussein does not mean the end of violence in Iraq," Bush said, speaking to the nation from the Cabinet Room. "We still face terrorists who would rather go on killing the innocent than accept the rise of liberty in the heart of the Middle East. Such men are a direct threat to the American people, and they will be defeated."

After the speech, everyone reassembled briefly in the Oval Office. Bush put on a white cowboy hat—Scully had never seen it before—and went on his way.

Bush won reelection on November 2, 2004, defeating Democratic senator John F. Kerry of Massachusetts. The president collected over 50 percent of the popular vote and 286 electoral votes, 16 more than needed. Two days later, he held a cabinet meeting to discuss plans for the second term. Afterward, he pulled Gerson aside to chat briefly about his second inaugural address. "I want this to be the freedom speech," Bush said. Almost a month later, on the morning of December 3, Bush called Gerson in to discuss the speech further. "The future of America and the security of America depends on the spread of liberty," the president told his aide.

It would be an ambitious address, and Gerson was excited. Bush and he shared "a belief in the power and importance of idealism, to set out historic goals and ideals. He is an ambitious person," he recalled. "He is disdainful of what he calls 'small ball.' He likes big goals and to set out leadership ideals. You saw that for example in the process of the second inaugural where he wanted to set out in stone this new foreign policy approach that was quite controversial, but it fit his approach."

Gerson rose early—usually at 4:30 or 5 am—and powered himself through the day with a steady stream of coffee. On the morning of December 17, downstairs in his home, he felt numbness in his hands, a cold sweat and then was on the floor and could not get up. He called out for his wife and was able to wake her up. Within ninety minutes he was in surgery at Alexandria Hospital—it had been a heart attack. "In a certain way it was not a disastrous heart attack, not a whole lot of serious, long-term damage," he said. But it was a grim warning for Gerson, then thirty-nine, whose father had died of a heart attack before he was sixty and whose grandfather had died from one younger than fifty. "A lot of this is just genetic," he told an interviewer, an air of resignation in his voice.

Gerson managed to keep a sense of humor. He had been arguing the day before with OMB director Joshua Bolten about the upcoming budget. Gerson e-mailed him from the intensive care unit: "I told you that budget was too extreme and shocking," he wrote. "I couldn't take it." Bush started calling. "I'm not calling to see if the inaugural speech is OK," he said. "I'm calling to see if the guy writing the inaugural speech is OK." But, Gerson said, "he was really asking about the speech."

Gerson knew that his work habits would have to change. Nevertheless, within a week and a half he was back at work on the inaugural. He and McConnell wrote the speech over three days.

On the morning of January 20, 2005, the president told Gerson, "I can't wait to give this speech." Unlike four years earlier, Gerson watched the speech in person, among those on the inaugural platform. "No longer running for anything other than history's judgment, George W. Bush delivered his second Inaugural Address under a cold sky to a sea of hats—fur and knit and 10 gallon," *Time* reported.

"There is only one force of history that can break the reign of hatred and resentment and expose the pretensions of tyrants and reward the hopes of the decent and tolerant, and that is the force of human freedom," Bush said after taking the presidential oath of office. "We are led, by events and common sense, to one conclusion: The survival of liberty in our land increasingly depends on the success of liberty in other lands. The best hope for peace in our world is the expansion of freedom in all the world." He declared that the tension which had long existed in American foreign policy—between the demands of idealism and the requirements of practical, real-world considerations—was no longer operative.

So it is the policy of the United States to seek and support the growth of democratic movements and institutions in every nation and culture, with the ultimate goal of ending tyranny in our world. This is not primarily the task of arms, though we will defend ourselves and our friends by force of arms when necessary.

The speech echoed both Harry S. Truman—"I believe that it must be the policy of the United States to support free people . . ."—and John F. Kennedy—"Now the trumpet summons us again—not as a call to bear arms, though arms we need . . ."

It met with mixed reviews. William Safire placed it "among the top five of a score of second-inaugurals in our history." Peggy Noonan, who had written for both Bush's father and his presidential model, Ronald Reagan, blasted it. "The inaugural address itself was startling. It left me with a bad feeling, and reluctant dislike," she wrote. "Rhetorically, it veered from high-class boilerplate to strong and simple sentences, but it was not pedestrian. George W. Bush's second inaugural will no doubt prove historic because it carried a punch, asserting an agenda so sweeping that an observer quipped that by the end he would not have been surprised if the president had announced we were going to colonize Mars."

"It is for historians to judge how well Mr. Bush's actions have fit, or may yet fulfill, his words," a *New York Times* news analysis reported. "There remains a wide gulf between his eloquent aspirations and the realities on the ground, from Capitol Hill to the Middle East. Executing his ideas will not be easy, at home or abroad." Even Bush's own aides undercut his message by stressing pragmatism over soaring rhetoric. "Bush Speech Not a Sign of Policy Shift, Officials Say," was the headline of a front-page *Washington Post* story two days after Bush was sworn in. "White House officials said yesterday that President Bush's soaring inaugural address, in which he declared the goal of ending tyranny around the world, represents no significant shift in U.S. foreign policy but instead was meant as a crystallization and clarification of policies he is pursuing in Iraq, Afghanistan, the Middle East and elsewhere," the *Post* reported. "Nor, they say, will it lead to any quick shift in strategy for dealing with . . . allies in the fight against terrorism whose records on human rights and democracy fall well short of the values Bush said would become the basis of relations with all countries."

Whether Bush wanted it to or not, the tension between declared ideals and practical realities still held sway. "Two and a half years after Bush pledged in his second inaugural address to spread democracy around the world, the grand project has bogged down in a bureaucratic and geopolitical morass, in the view of many activists, officials and even White House aides," Peter Baker of *The Washington Post* reported in August 2007. "Many in his administration never bought into the idea, and some undermined it, including his own vice president. The Iraq war has distracted Bush and, in some quarters, discredited his aspirations. And while he focuses his ire on bureaucracy, Bush at times has compromised the idealism of that speech in the muddy reality of guarding other U.S. interests."

Bush remained frustrated that his declarations had far outpaced his ability to move government and nation. He told an Egyptian resistance leader in June 2007 that he too was struggling against an oppressive government regime. "You're not the only dissident," Bush said. "I too am a dissident in Washington."

The troika had broken up before the end of the first term. Scully left the White House for good in the summer of 2004, moving to California with his family, though he would occasionally return to help out on major speeches. After his heart attack, Gerson was told by his doctor that he needed to cut back on his work. "I'm a worrier," Gerson said. "I put a lot of pressure on myself. I know people think it's funny, but these aren't charming eccentricities."

So, at the start of 2005, Gerson dropped his official speechwriting duties and became a presidential assistant for policy and strategic planning. He would work on major addresses, but divested himself of the day-to-day pressures of producing speeches. McConnell turned down an opportunity to succeed Gerson, so William McGurn, a former editorial page editor of *The Wall Street Journal* whom Gerson had twice before recruited to join the speechwriting staff, succeeded him as chief speechwriter. McConnell continued writing for Cheney and, as McGurn assembled his own team, wrote less frequently for Bush.

Michael Gerson's departure from the White House in the summer of 2006 prompted another wave of adulatory profiles and articles. "The man whose words helped steady the nation after the 'deliberate and massive cruelty' of Sept. 11, 2001, is no longer at George W. Bush's side," a *USA Today* article gushed.

The profiles of Gerson—both in print and on television—continued to paint him, either explicitly or by inference, as a solitary writer laboring in communion with his president. He was typically credited as "author of nearly all of [Bush's] most famous public words during the past seven years," as one 2006 *Washington Post* story put it. After innumerable "death marches" and countless days huddled in John McConnell's office with Gerson sharing laughs, stress, and writing, Scully decided a year later to set the record straight.

In a scathing piece in *The Atlantic* for September 2007—the same journal that James Fallows had used to score Jimmy Carter nearly thirty years earlier—Scully lambasted his former colleague. "He allowed false assumptions, and also encouraged them," Scully wrote of Gerson. "Among chummy reporters, he created a fictionalized . . . version of presidential speechwriting, casting himself in a grand and solitary role." Typical was a December 2002 appearance on ABC News's *Nightline*. Asked "physically" how he writes a speech, Gerson talked about how he liked to do the initial work at Starbucks because "it breaks the solitude of writing to be around the buzz of people." Eventually, he said, he does "go to a computer screen."

Scully accused his former colleague of self-absorption ("I think they look at my writing as the fine china, to be taken out on special occasions," Scully recounted Gerson telling his two colleagues) and manipulation. Gerson, Scully wrote, had led the press and other White House staffers to believe the solo speechwriter story line. "The artful shaping of narrative and editing out of inconvenient detail was never confined to the speechwriting," he wrote. "(The phrase *pulling a Gerson*, as I recently heard it used around the West Wing, does not refer to graceful writing.)"

Gerson told *The Washington Post* that he was shocked by Scully's portrayal. "I wasn't out there looking for attention all the time," he said, his voice filled with emotion. "They're the president's words, and I was the chief speechwriter."

Scully's article set Washington abuzz. It illustrates clearly how the role of speechwriters has evolved in the early twenty-first century. "For me, the poignancy of Scully's story is that speechwriting is supposed to be the opposite of what Gerson stands accused of doing," Bruce Reed, the Clinton domestic adviser who had helped craft numerous speeches, wrote in *Slate*. "By definition, it's a profession based on self-denial, not self-promotion. Far from taking credit for the work of others, a speech-writer's job is to write words that others can stand to claim as their own. Most speechwriters soon learn the basic pleasure-pain principle of the craft: Satisfaction comes from finding words the boss can use, but taking credit for those words can only embarrass the very person you're supposed to be helping."

Yet, as the Scully-Gerson contretemps—and the press attention Gerson received over the course of the Bush campaign and presidency—demonstrates, that was an old-fashioned view of the White House speechwriter. For better or worse, the White House ghosts had come fully into view.

Notes

NOTE ON SOURCES: The author interviewed more than ninety current and former White House speechwriters and other aides over a two-year period. The interviews were performed in person, on the telephone, and via e-mail, and in several cases some combination thereof. For simplicity's sake, they are referred to below as author interviews.

Except where noted, quotations from presidential speeches and other public utterances come from the public papers of the presidents, as put online at the American Presidency Project, John Woolley and Gerhard Peters, *The American Presidency Project* [online]. Santa Barbara, CA: University of www.presidency.ucsb.edu/ws/.

INTRODUCTION

1 *When George Washington considered*: Matthew Spalding and Patrick J. Garrity, *A Sacred Union of Citizens: George Washington's Farewell Address and the American Character* (Lanham, MD: Rowman & Littlefield, 1998), 45–54.

1 *Stooped, nearsighted*: Arthur M. Schlesinger, Jr., *The Age of Jackson* (Boston: Little, Brown, 1945), 70.

2 *One Jackson critic*: Robert V. Friedenberg, *Communications Consultants in Political Campaigns: Ballot Box Warriors* (Westport, CT: Praeger/Greenwood, 1997), 14.

2 *The historian George Bancroft*: Henry Franklin Graff, *The Presidents: A Reference History* (New York: Simon & Schuster, 2002), xxviii.

2 *As Abraham Lincoln*: William Safire, *Safire's New Political Dictionary* (New York: Random House, 1993), xxvi–xxvii.

2 *"literary clerk"*: Ibid., 738.

2 *A snub-nosed, soft-spoken*: "Encyclopaedia," *Time*, April 8, 1929.

2 *Welliver had been*: Hendrik Hertzberg, *Politics: Observations & Arguments, 1966–2004* (New York: Penguin Books, 2005), 114.

3 *"a journalist of the highest"*: H. L. Mencken, *On Politics: A Carnival of Buncombe* (Baltimore: Johns Hopkins University Press, 1996), 132.

3 *"writes the worst"*: Ibid., 42.

3 *Welliver was not only*: John W. Dean, *Warren G. Harding* (New York: Times Books, 2004), 73.

3 *When Harding was elected*: Russell D. Buhite and David W. Levy, eds., *FDR's Fireside Chats* (New York: Penguin Books, 1993), xiii.

3 *The 1924 Republican and*: "The First Convention Broadcast: Radio at the 1924 Conventions," PoynterOnline, September 2, 2004 (updated Dec. 22, 2004).

4 *In his only term*: Lyn Ragsdale, *Vital Statistics on the Presidency* (Washington, DC: Congressional Quarterly Press, 1998), 183, quoted by the American Presidency Project, Santa Barbara, CA.

4 *Speechwriters, Clifford would say*: Author interview with William Safire.

1. "GRACE, TAKE A LAW"

5 *In Chicago*: Arthur M. Schlesinger, Jr., *The Crisis of the Old Order* (Boston: Houghton Mifflin, 1957), 305.

5 *He had passed*: Samuel I. Rosenman, *Working with Roosevelt* (New York: Harper & Bros., 1952), 70–71.

5 *Franklin Roosevelt and Rosenman*: Ibid., 13–14.

6 *Clean-shaven*: Author interview with David Ginsburg.

6 *For the last two years*: Samuel Rosenman oral history, Columbia University, 1960 (cited hereafter as OH), FDR Library, 51–52.

6 *Rosenman had in March*: Rosenman, *Working*, 56–57.

6 *Now, Rosenman was determined*: Ibid., 71.

6 *In 1933, FDR*: Typed-up copy of Cyril Clemens letter to the editor in *The Washington Post*, June 16, 1952, "Working with Truman—Rosenman, Samuel" folder, Papers of Kenneth Hechler, Harry S. Truman Library (HSTL).

6 *Rosenman would dismiss*: Rosenman, *Working*, 71.

6 *Raymond Moley, who*: Raymond Moley, *After Seven Years* (New York: Harper & Bros., 1939), 23n.

7 *A Columbia University professor*: Schlesinger, *Crisis*, 399–400; Jonathan Alter, *The Defining Moment: FDR's Hundred Days and the Triumph of Hope* (New York: Simon & Schuster, 2006), 95.

7 *He had first met*: Raymond Moley, *The First New Deal* (New York: Harcourt, Brace & World, 1966), 11–12.

7 *After Roosevelt was elected*: Ibid., 12.

8 *Also awaiting the candidate*: Schlesinger, *Crisis*, 340; Alter, *Defining Moment*, 36.

8 *"very devious"*: Rosenman, OH, 112–13.

8 *"patently on the smug side"*: "Roosevelt Sets His Cap," *Saturday Evening Post*, June 24, 1939.

8 *When during the convention*: Moley, *After Seven*, 29.

8 *The professor fought*: From the plane landing in Chicago, the account comes from Rosenman, *Working with Roosevelt*, 76–77.

10 *Moley always bristled*: Moley, *The First*, 96.

10 *"My job"*: Moley, *After Seven*, 55.

10 *The topic of the inaugural speech*: Except where noted, the account from the train ride through Moley burning his draft comes from Moley, *The First New Deal*, 99–114.

11 *"the Inaugural Address"*: Handwritten draft of inaugural address with March 25, 1933, cover note, "March 4, 1933 [Inaugural Address]" folder, FDR Speech Files, FDR Library.

11 *"a keen sense"*: Moley, *The First*, 114.

11 *the absence of any extant copy*: For his 2006 book on FDR's Hundred Days, Jonathan Alter

conducted a thorough study of Moley's papers, concluding, "When he threw his draft into the fire at Hyde Park, [Moley] apparently immolated any proof of his authorship of the speech" (372).

12 *He edited it himself*: Moley, *The First*, 115.

12 *Like the phrase "new deal"*: Alter, *Defining Moment*, 211.

12 *A 1931 edition*: "Business to Make Stabilization Study," *New York Times*, February 9, 1931.

12 *but that advertisement has disappeared*: Jonathan Alter and his research assistants conducted "an exhaustive search of newspapers in New York and Washington that Howe might have read—and searched several databases and department store archives—but failed to find any such advertisement containing the 'fear itself' line or anything approximating it." (372).

13 *Howe, appointed as Roosevelt's*: Rosenman, *Working*, 94; Moley, *After Seven*, 18; Rosenman OH, 113–14.

14 *Moley took a nominal position*: Moley, *After Seven*, 275–80.

14 *"in this instance"*: Moley, *The First*, 515–16.

14 *"I was no"*: Ibid., 96.

14 *Five days later*: "Roosevelt a Topic in Moley's Weekly," *New York Times*, October 25, 1933.

14 *his notes from his initial*: Moley, *The First*, 104–05.

14 *Quiet invitations*: Moley, *After Seven*, 283–84.

15 *In December 1933*: Ibid., 284–85.

15 *was brash and blustery*: Rosenman, *Working*, 115.

15 *He played piano*: Stanley High, *Roosevelt—And Then?* (New York: Harper & Bros., 1937), 47–48.

15 *"I'd be called in"*: Moley, *After Seven*, 284.

16 *"For every time"*: Moley, *The First*, 516–17.

16 *Moley was openly*: Arthur M. Schlesinger, Jr., *The Politics of Upheaval* (Boston: Houghton Mifflin, 1960), 576–77.

16 *"the extent to which"*: Moley, *After Seven*, 332.

16 *For five more months*: The account of the drafting of the 1936 State of the Union message through Moley hoping Roosevelt will be more business-friendly comes from Moley, ibid., 332–33.

16 *His attitude became*: Ibid., 343.

16 *he invited the Rosenmans*: Rosenman, *Working*, 98–99.

16 *A Chicago native*: "Democrats' St. Paul," *Time*, Monday, June 1, 1936.

17 *Moley allowed FDR*: Moley, *After Seven*, 344.

17 *"this generation of Americans"*: Schlesinger, *Politics*, 584.

17 *What Moley did not know*: Rosenman, *Working*, 104.

17 *Three days before the speech*: Ibid., 105.

17 *Moley downplayed the exchange*: Moley, *After Seven*, 346.

17 *Moley produced a draft*: Ibid., 345.

18 *As he had four years earlier*: Moley, *After Seven*, 347.

18 *Roosevelt and Moley went through*: Ibid., 349.

18 *Years later he told*: Schlesinger, *Politics*, 579.

18 *Roosevelt marked up*: Except where noted, the account of the drafting of the second inaugural address comes from Rosenman, *Working*, 142–44.

19 *He sometimes prefaced . . . "you boys can fix it up"*: Robert E. Sherwood, *Roosevelt and Hopkins* (New York: Harper & Bros., 1948), 213.

19 *Sometimes his inserts*: Ibid., 266.

19 *"They won't let me"*: Ibid., 218.

19 *"I'll just ad-lib it"*: Rosenman, *Working*, 484.

19 *When a final text*: Ibid., 144; reading copy of the second inaugural address, "FDR Inaugural Address—Capitol—January 20, 1933" folder, FDR Speech Files, FDR Library.

19 *The president's phone*: Grace Tully, *F.D.R. My Boss* (Chicago: People's Book Club, 1949), 234–35.

20 *" 'Stay out of war' "*: George Gallup, "What We, the People, Think About Europe: A Cross-Section of Opinion on Our World Role," *New York Times*, April 30, 1939.

21 *Roosevelt had himself added*: Rosenman, *Working*, 189; undated second draft of September 3, 1939, fireside address, "FDR—Radio Address—White House—Sept. 3, 1939—War in Europe (Fireside No. 14)" folder, FDR Speech Files, FDR Library.

21 *From 1939 onward*: Rosenman, *Working*, 181.

21 *When Roosevelt gave*: Ibid., 198.

21 *High was expelled*: Charles Michelson, *The Ghost Talks* (New York: G. P. Putnam's Sons, 1944), 192–93.

21 *"Nearly all the Democratic"*: Rosenman, *Working*, 227.

21 *Bullitt contributed briefly*: Ibid.

21 *Librarian of Congress Archibald MacLeish*: Ibid., 269.

22 *Like Howe, Hopkins*: Rosenman OH, 170–71.

22 *Winston Churchill once told*: Sherwood, *Roosevelt and Hopkins*, 5.

22 *Hopkins's greatest strength*: Rosenman, *Working*, 228.

22 *the advent of the 1940 campaign*: Rosenman OH, 180.

22 *Their first choice*: Rosenman, *Working*, 128; Rosenman OH, 180.

22 *They finally lit upon*: Rosenman OH, 181.

22 *"Those of us"*: Robert E. Sherwood letter to Roosevelt, May 16, 1933, "Sherwood, Robert E." folder, President's Personal File 7356, FDR Library.

22 *"I saw Harry Hopkins"*: Robert E. Sherwood letter to Roosevelt, January 25, 1940, "Sherwood, Robert E." folder, President's Personal File 7356, FDR Library.

23 *Hopkins ran into Sherwood*: Sherwood, *Roosevelt and Hopkins*, 49–50.

23 *Sherwood would get his chance*: Rosenman, *Working*, 232–33; Sherwood, *Roosevelt and Hopkins*, 184.

24 *Work on the speeches generally*: The description of the cocktail and dinner-hour speechwriting process comes from Sherwood, *Roosevelt and Hopkins*, 213; Rosenman, *Working*, 19; and author interview with Ginsburg.

24 *Rosenman drank Coca-Cola*: Rosenman, *Working*, 5.

25 *in a phrase coined*: Quoted in ibid., 260–61.

25 *The 1941 message*: Except where noted, the account of preparing the 1941 State of the Union address comes from Rosenman, ibid., 262–65.

25 *his secretary Dorothy Brady*: Ibid., 297.

25 *"The first is freedom"*: Undated handwritten peroration for 1941 State of the Union message, "FDR message to Congress delivered in person—January 6, 1941" folder, FDR Speech Files, FDR Library.

26 *Sixty years later*: Michael Waldman, *My Fellow Americans: The Most Important Speeches of America's Presidents, From George Washington to George W. Bush* (Naperville, IL: sourcebooks mediaFusion, 2003), 110.

26 *Shortly before 5 pm*: This account comes from Tully, *FDR*, 256, and from the original draft of FDR's December 8 speech to Congress, on file at the FDR Library. Tully's recollection of the wording of the first draft is incorrect—she uses the as-delivered remarks—but we can assume her other details are correct.

27 *Rosenman continued commuting*: John Hopkins interview of Samuel Rosenman, June 3, 1969, 8, "Rosenman, Samuel—Oral History Interview" folder, Papers of John Hopkins, HSTL.

28 *Roosevelt had at first suggested*: Clark Clifford, *Counsel to the President* (New York: Random House, 1991), 54.
28 *"Next week Biddle"*: Rosenman OH, 198–99.
28 *In the spring of 1945*: Sherwood, *Roosevelt and Hopkins*, 877.
28 *Returning in late March*: Ibid., 877–80.
28 *"Because we know"*: Ibid., 880.
29 *"It was really best"*: Rosenman OH, 182.
29 *Taken into the Cabinet Room*: William Safire, *Before the Fall* (New York: Doubleday & Co., 1975), 15–16.

2. "MISSOURI ENGLISH"

31 *If the activity*: Samuel Rosenman oral history, Columbia University, 1960, FDR Library, 215; Samuel Rosenman oral history, October 15, 1968, HSTL, 49–50; John Hopkins oral history interview with Samuel Rosenman, June 3, 1969, 12, "Rosenman, Samuel— Oral History Interview" folder, Papers of John Hopkins, HSTL.
31 *Rosenman had not spoken*: Rosenman Columbia OH, 210.
32 *no more than twenty people*: Richard Neustadt, "Notes on the White House Staff Under President Truman," June 1953, " 'Notes on the White House Staff Under Truman' by R. E. Neustadt" folder, Papers of Richard Neustadt, HSTL, 5. Neustadt places the figure at seventeen people late in 1944; it is reasonable to assume that he did not have a sudden influx of new hires in early 1945.
32 *which would have paid*: Rosenman Columbia OH, 212.
32 *Stay until V-E Day*: Ibid.
32 *FDR was always pleasant*: Ibid., 222–23.
32 *On April 18*: Description of the Map Room from George M. Elsey, *An Unplanned Life* (Columbia: University of Missouri Press, 2005), 19–20; Hugh Sidey, "How a Secret Room Got Its Start in WWII," *Time*, September 29, 2002.
32 *Lanky and good-looking*: David McCullough, *Truman* (New York: Simon & Schuster, 1992), 448; author interview with Kenneth Hechler,
33 *He had been a graduate*: Elsey, *An Unplanned Life*, 70.
33 *On that first visit*: Author interview with George M. Elsey,
33 *Stay until V-J Day*: Rosenman Columbia OH, 212.
33 *"one of the ablest"*: Robert H. Ferrell, ed., *Off the Record: The Private Papers of Harry S. Truman* (New York: Harper & Row, 1980), 46.
33 *He and press secretary Charlie Ross*: Rosenman HSTL OH, 50.
33 *it was the first speech*: Rosenman Hopkins OH, 11.
33 *"It's very easy"*: Ibid., 2.
33 *Early that month*: Clark Clifford, *Counsel to the President* (New York: Random House, 1991), 50.
34 *"He was like a Greek god"*: Author interview with Hechler.
34 *"I handled fourteen"*: Richard Holbrooke interview of Clark Clifford, December 28, 1987, "December 28, 1987 [2 of 3]" folder, Papers of Richard C. Holbrooke, HSTL, 21.
34 *Looking back*: John Hopkins oral history interview with Clark Clifford, "Clark M.—Oral History Interview folder," Papers of John Hopkins, HSTL, 2–3.
34 *"He was energetic"*: Elsey, *An Unplanned Life*, 133.
34 *Clifford quickly discovered*: Clifford, *Counsel*, 53–56.
34 *He again asked Truman*: Rosenman Hopkins OH, 9.
34 *By this time*: The account of the drafting of the September 1946 message to Congress comes from Rosenman HSTL OH, 50, 58–63.

35 *Rosenman later estimated*: Rosenman Columbia OH, 216.

35 *When Rosenman ran into*: Ibid., 222.

36 *Clifford too had noticed*: Clifford, *Counsel*, 74.

36 *He would lean so far*: Clifford Hopkins OH, 5.

36 *He would look up*: Author interview with Elsey.

36 *He sped through*: Clifford, *Counsel*, 199.

36 *He would read the speech*: Leonard Reinsch oral history interview, March 13, 1967, HSTL, 40–41.

36 *His secretary, Rose*: James Sundquist, oral history interview, July 15, 1963, HSTL, 26; Kenneth Hechler, *Working with Truman* (New York: G. P. Putnam's Sons, 1982), 224–25.

36 *And because she put*: Reinsch OH, 10–11; John Hopkins oral history interview with Charles Murphy, May 16, 1969, "Murphy Charles—Oral History Interview" folder, Papers of John Hopkins, Murphy, HSTL, 19.

36 *During the 1944 campaign*: Reinsch OH, 7–8.

36 *Rosenman approached Truman*: Rosenman Hopkins OH, 9.

37 *Truman appealed to him*: Clifford, *Counsel*, 66.

37 *"Comes the deluge"*: Elsey, *An Unplanned Life*, 134.

37 *In the mid-1940s*: Clifford, *Counsel*, 87.

37 *When the rail workers*: McCullough, *Truman*, 498–99.

38 *Truman handwrote his remarks*: Handwritten Truman draft of railworkers speech to nation, "May 24, Railroad Speech—President Truman's Notes for" folder, Papers of Clark Clifford, 1946, HSTL.

38 *"perilously out of control"*: Clifford, *Counsel*, 89.

38 *"It was as though"*: McCullough, *Truman*, 500.

38 *Truman likely never meant*: Ibid., 480; Clifford, *Counsel*, 89–90.

39 *For Clifford, it was a decisive*: Clifford, *Counsel*, 69–71.

39 *a six-page draft*: May 24, 1946, draft of Truman speech to the nation, with Truman markings, "1946, May 24, Railroad Speech [re strike]" folder, Papers of Clark Clifford, HSTL.

39 *Clifford later confessed*: Holbrooke Clifford interview, December 28, 1987, 27.

39 *Clifford and company missed*: Clifford Hopkins OH, 3.

40 *An hour before the speech*: McCullough, *Truman*, 504.

40 *Shortly after 4 pm*: "The Decision," *Time*, June 3, 1946.

40 *The moment was so dramatic*: Clifford, *Counsel*, 91.

41 *"There is no policy-making body"*: Elsey, *An Unplanned Life*, 134.

41 *"We used to call"*: Stephen J. Spingarn oral history interview, March 24, 1967, HSTL, 832.

41 *"He did not do"*: Murphy Hopkins OH, 13; "An Investigation of the Speech and Statement Preparation Process During the Presidential Administration of Harry S. Truman, 1945–1953," Unpublished dissertation by John Hopkins, on file at HSTL.

41 *"Clark Clifford is an excellent"*: Spingarn OH, 832.

41 *"President Truman's speeches"*: Richard Neustadt, "Notes on the White House Staff Under President Truman," "Notes on the White House Staff Under Truman' by R. E. Neustadt" folder, Papers of Richard Neustadt, June 1953, HSTL, 18.

42 *"Three years in the Map Room"*: Author interview with Elsey.

42 *"I wrote slowly"*: Clifford, *Counsel*, 74.

42 *"Read my annual message"*: Quoted in Elsey, *An Unplanned Life*, 148.

42 *Republican senator Arthur Vandenberg*: Joseph Marion Jones, *The Fifteen Weeks* (New York: Harcourt, Brace & World, 1955), 142.

42 *He was willing*: Clifford, *Counsel*, 132.

43 *He accompanied Truman on weekends*: Elsey, *An Unplanned Life*, 138.

43 *a devastating eighty-one-page case*: Once locked away, the report can now be found in its entirety on the HSTL Web site at www.trumanlibrary.org/whistlestop/studycollections/coldwar/documents/index.php?documentdate=1946-09-24&documentid=41&study collectionid=&pagenumber=1.

43 *Truman called him*: Clifford, *Counsel*, 123–24.

44 *A heavy-flaked . . . sent to Clifford*: Jones, *Fifteen Weeks*, 153–54.

44 *That day Elsey had sent*: George Elsey letter to Clark Clifford, March 7, 1947, "1947, March 12, Speech to Congress on Greece [re aid to Greece and Turkey]" folder, Papers of Clark Clifford, HSTL.

44 *"This speech must be"*: Clifford, *Counsel*, 133.

44 *Truman thought the State draft*: Ibid., 134.

44 *Truman believed that*: Francis H. Heller, *The Truman White House* (Lawrence, KS: Regents Press of Kansas, 1980), 74.

44 *"Subjunctives, passives, polysyllabic"*: Hechler, *Working*, 224.

45 *Once the writers*: Clifford, *Counsel*, 74–75.

45 *"What impressed me"*: Milton P. Kayle oral history interview, November 9, 1982, HSTL, 91.

45 *speaking from his own experience*: Jones, *Fifteen Weeks*, 153–54.

45 *"Totalitarian regimes are born"*: Clark Clifford handwritten "Notes on Greek-Turkish speech," undated, "1947, March 12, Speech to Congress on Greece [re aid to Greece and Turkey]" folder, Papers of Clark Clifford, HSTL.

45 *"It is a grim job"*: Ibid.

46 *The revised State draft*: Clifford, *Counsel*, 135.

46 *"I was worried"*: Elsey, *An Unplanned Life*, 149.

46 *"I believe it must be the policy"*: Hand-marked, "Suggested Draft (Revised March 9, 1947)," "1947, March 12, Speech to Congress on Greece [re aid to Greece and Turkey]" folder, Papers of Clark Clifford, HSTL.

46 *Elsey sensed*: Author interview with Elsey.

47 *Clifford received*: Clifford, *Counsel*, 190–91. The original Rowe memorandum can be found at www.trumanlibrary.org/whistlestop/study_collections/1948campaign/large/docs/documents/index.php?documentdate=1947-09-18&documentid=17&studycollectionid=Election&pagenumber=1; the revised Clifford version at www.trumanlibrary.org/whistletop/study_collections/1948campaign/large/docs/documents/index.php?documentdate=1947-11-19&documentid=10&studycollectionid=Election&pagenumber=1.

47 *It "must be controversial"*: Elsey, *An Unplanned Life*, 158.

48 *"looks and acts"*: Spingarn OH, 73.

48 *"It was the kind of work"*: Hechler, *Working*, 50.

48 *"Congress meets"*: Ferrell, ed., *Off the Record*, 122.

48 *"the Bible for the Democratic Party"*: "Something for the Boys," *Time*, January 19, 1948.

48 *But Truman was so pleased*: Elsey, *An Unplanned Life*, 159.

49 *Clifford had tried to have*: Clifford, *Counsel*, 109.

49 *"He was suddenly"*: Quoted in Hechler, *Working*, 66–67.

49 *The result*: Harry S. Truman, *Years of Trial and Hope* (Garden City, NY. Doubleday & Co., 1956), 179.

49 *"The audience gave me"*: Ferrell, ed., *Off the Record*, 134.

49 *"Returns from the radio"*: Ibid.

50 *There were kinks*: McCullough, *Truman*, 626–27.

51 *"We got the wrong rigs"*: Meyer Berger, "Democrats Match Quaker Sabbath," *New York Times*, July 12, 1947.

51 *The passage of an historic*: Robert Donovan, *Conflict and Crisis: The Presidency of Harry S Truman*, 1945–1948 (New York: W. W. Norton, 1977), 406.

51 *In Washington, confusion*: Charles Murphy, "Some Aspects of the Preparation of President Truman's Speeches for the 1948 Campaign," December 6, 1948, "Speech Preparation memo, 1948 Presidential campaign" folder, Papers of Charles M. Murphy, HSTL, 7.

52 *Four hours later—at 1:42 am*: McCullough, *Truman*, 641.

52 *Rayburn was introducing*: "Emma & the Birds," *Time*, July 26, 1948.

53 *Of 2,622 words Truman spoke*: Acceptance speech word count with underscores, undated, "1948, July 15, Acceptance Speech [before the Democratic National Convention, Philadelphia] folder," Papers of Clark Clifford, HSTL.

53 *"Entire speech was superb"*: William Batt telegram to Clark Clifford, July 15, 1948, in ibid.

53 *As Truman departed*: Clifford, *Counsel*, 226; *sore throat*: Ferrell, ed., *Off the Record*, 149.

53 *"I remember it"*: Clifford, *Counsel*, 187.

53 *"I cannot remember"*: Richard Holbrooke interview of Clark Clifford, April 21, 1988, "April 21, 1988 [1 of 2]" folder, Papers of Richard C. Holbrooke, HSTL.

53 *First built as one of a series*: Description of *Ferdinand Magellan* from McCullough, *Truman*, 654–54, and www.goldcoast-railroad.org/magellan.htm.

54 *At no point would Truman's staff*: Murphy Hopkins OH, 12.

54 *"It is surprising"*: Albert Z. Carr letter to Matt, September 22, 1948, "1948, Campaign Trip, September 23, California—Major [address] (Los Angeles)" folder, Papers of Clark Clifford, HSTL.

54 *"Never use two words"*: McCullough, *Truman*, 665–66.

55 *Elsey had boarded*: Elsey Hopkins OH, 50–51; Elsey, *An Unplanned Life*, 166–67.

56 *"carnival shills"*: Quoted in Clifford, *Counsel*, 227.

56 *"Truman was entertainment"*: Author interview with Elsey.

56 *"In this sense"*: Charles Murphy oral history interview, May 2, 1963, HSTL.

57 *"It was a real ordeal"*: Clark Clifford oral history interview, July 26, 1971, HSTL 273.

57 *Clifford woke in cold sweats*: Ibid.

57 *Spared the stress*: Samuel Rosenman oral history interview, April 23, 1967, HSTL, 84.

58 *Not everyone agreed*: McCullough, *Truman*, 666.

58 *Even Clifford later conceded*: Hechler, *Working*, 93.

59 *"Perhaps the best way to describe"*: William J. Bray, "Recollections of the 1948 Campaign," undated, "Campaign Material, 1948" folder, Papers of Clark Clifford, HSTL.

59 *His memo won Elsey*: Elsey, *An Unplanned Life*, 173.

59 *Crossing out a paragraph*: Draft of State of the Union message with Truman notations, January 2, 1949, "1949 January 5, State of the Union—drafts (folder 4)" folder, Papers of George M. Elsey, HSTL.

60 *"The circumstances"*: George Elsey memorandum to Clark Clifford, November 16, 1948, "State of the Union [Address, January 5,] 1949—Departmental Memos [1 of 3]" folder, Papers of Clark Clifford, HSTL.

60 *"Today we find"*: "State-1" Outline for Inaugural Address, undated, "Inaugural Address, January 20, 1949 [2 of 4]" folder, Papers of Clark Clifford, HSTL.

61 *Enter Benjamin Hardy*: Clifford, *Counsel*, 249.

61 *"This is the way"*: Ben Hardy memo to Mr. Russell, November 23, 1948, "1949 January 20, Inaugural Address correspondence" folder, Papers of George M. Elsey, HSTL.

61 *On December 15*: George Elsey typed recollection of the genesis of Point Four, September 12, 1963, "Personal Correspondence File; Hardy, Benjamin" folder, Papers of George M. Elsey, HSTL.

61 *Grouped with the three familiar*: Ibid.

62 *"H.S.T." was "All for point 4"*: January 14, 1949, draft of Inaugural Address with Elsey

cover note and annotations, "1949 January 20, Inaugural Address" folder, Papers of George M. Elsey, HSTL.

62 *This was a reference*: William Safire, *Safire's New Political Dictionary* (New York: Random House, 1993), 338.

62 *"I'll announce it"*: Elsey, *An Unplanned Life*, 176.

62 *The 1949 inaugural*: McCullough, *Truman*, 724.

62 *Point Four was*: As quoted in "Press Comment on Truman Speech Is Mostly Favorable," by the Associated Press, January 21, 1949, "Inaugural Address, January 20, 1949 [4 of 4]" folder, Papers of Clark Clifford, HSTL.

62 *When it finally became*: Harry S. Truman, *Years of Trial and Hope: 1946–1952* (Garden City, NY: Doubleday & Co., 1956), 234–39.

63 *After the inauguration*: Elsey, *An Unplanned Life*, 177–79.

63 *Clifford was contemplating*: Clifford, *Counsel*, 257–58.

63 *"As far as I could see"*: Stephen J. Spingarn oral history interview, March 24, 1967, HSTL, 810–15.

63 *By the time*: Elsey, *An Unplanned Life*, 185.

63 *"Clifford's interest"*: Ibid., 180.

64 *"It would be difficult"*: Harry Truman letter to Clark Clifford, January 27, 1951, "Correspondence with Harry S. Truman, 1950–1953" folder, Papers of Clark Clifford, HSTL.

64 *"For ease of"*: Author interview with Elsey.

64 *Murphy was "the pivot"*: James L. Sundquist, "The Last Truly Anonymous White House Aide," *The Washington Post*, September 1, 1983.

64 *did not "share Clifford's pretense"*: Elsey, *An Unplanned Life*, 185.

65 *Murphy and Elsey started working*: The account of the drafting of the July 19, 1950, speech comes from George Elsey, memorandum for file regarding preparation of July 19, 1950, address on Korea, undated, "Korea—Radio address on Korea, July 19, 1950" folder, Papers of George M. Elsey, HSTL.

66 *"So the staff"*: Elsey, *An Unplanned Life*, 204.

66 *What Truman did not know*: Ibid., 205; Hechler, *Working*, 179.

66 *"I wasn't going"*: Elsey, *An Unplanned Life*, 205.

66 *his approval rating*: Polling data adapted from the Gallup Poll and compiled by Gerhard Peters for the University of California Santa Barbara's American Presidency Project.

66 *Truman and his staff finished*: Hechler, *Working*, 181–82.

67 *At 10:23 pm*: Elsey, *An Unplanned Life*, 206.

67 *A little over a week*: Ibid., 207.

67 *In June 1951*: Kenneth Hechler letter to his parents, July 26, 1951, "HST—Personal" folder, Papers of Kenneth Hechler, HSTL.

68 *"improvements in the mechanical"*: Charles Murphy memorandum to the president, September 13, 1950, "Truman—memos to and from the President, 1947–52 (folder 5) [of 5]" folder, Papers of Charles S. Murphy, HSTL.

68 *"He was a little suspicious"*: Hechler, *Working*, 215.

68 *On January 19, 1953*: Kenneth Hechler oral interview history, November 29, 1985, HSTL, 185–87.

3. "SOMETIMES YOU SURE GET TIRED OF ALL THIS CLACKETY-CLACK"

69 *The news electrified*: Emmet John Hughes, *The Ordeal of Power: A Political Memoir of the Eisenhower Years* (New York: Dell, 1963), 88.

69 *President Dwight Eisenhower*: Ibid.

69 *"Ever since 1946"*: Ibid.

70 *"Granted that Dulles"*: Sherman Adams, *Firsthand Report: The Story of the Eisenhower Administration* (New York: Popular Library, 1962), 114–15.

70 *"It is difficult"*: Chip Bohlen letter to Emmet Hughes, March 9, 1953, " 'Chance for Peace,' April 16, 1953 (4)" folder, Harlow, Bryce N.: Records, 1953–61, Dwight Eisenhower Library.

70 *"All this resolves"*: Emmet Hughes memorandum to Dwight D. Eisenhower, March 10, 1953, " 'Chance for Peace,' April 16, 1953 (4)" folder, Harlow, Bryce N.: Records, 1953–61, Dwight Eisenhower Library.

70 *Hughes leaned initially*: Hughes, *Ordeal*, 89–90.

70 *"I now came"*: Ibid., 89.

71 *"Emmet was a loner"*: Author interview with Robert Kieve.

71 *"a dashing fellow"*: Author interview with Arthur M. Schlesinger, Jr.

71 *Hughes "has been no help"*: Robert, Ferrell, ed., *The Eisenhower Diaries* (New York: W. W. Norton, 1981), 225.

71 *Late one afternoon*: Except where noted, the Hughes-Eisenhower Oval Office meeting is from Hughes, *Ordeal*, 90.

71 *an F-86 Sabre*: Robert Kieve, "How One President's Speeches Were Prepared," an undated standard talk he gives—copy provided to the author.

72 *There was little new*: Stephen Ambrose, *Eisenhower: Soldier and President* (New York: Simon & Schuster, 1990), 325.

72 *who less than twenty-four hours earlier*: Hughes, *Ordeal*, 92.

72 *"All right then"*: Ibid.

73 *New Soviet premier*: Harrison Salisbury, "Malenkov Offers to Settle Tensions by Peaceful Means," *New York Times*, March 16, 1953; Harry Schwartz, "Soviet 'Peace Offensives' Elaborately Staged," *New York Times*, March 22, 1953.

73 *Dulles did not buy*: Hughes, *Ordeal*, 95–96.

73 *"clearly indicated that"*: Handwritten letter to Emmet Hughes, April 10, 1953, Harlow, Bryce N.: Records, 1953–61, "Chance for Peace," April 16, 1953 (1) folder, Dwight Eisenhower Library.

73 *To protect the speech*: Hughes, *Ordeal*, 94.

74 *Hughes was summoned*: Ibid., 97–98.

74 *Arriving in Washington*: Adams, *Firsthand Report*, 325.

75 *Word later reached*: Ibid., 102.

75 *"a planned stage"*: "Text of Secretary Dulles' Address to U.S. Newspaper Editors," *New York Times*, April 19, 1953.

75 *more than "a few months"*: Hughes, *Ordeal*, 11.

75 *privately he told*: William Bragg Ewald, Jr., *Eisenhower the President* (Englewood Cliffs, NJ: Prentice-Hall, 1981), 228.

75 *Around the time that*: Adams, *Firsthand Report*, 114.

75 *One Gallup poll*: Joseph and Stewart Alsop, "Matter of Fact . . ." *Washington Post*, September 9, 1953.

76 *"I keep telling you fellows"*: Hughes, *Ordeal*, 115.

76 *He had a skin pigmentation*: Arthur Larson, *Eisenhower: The President Nobody Knew* (New York: Charles Scribner's Sons, 1968), 164–65.

76 *"His real role"*: Author interview with Kieve.

77 *He had brought the device*: Kevin McCann Columbia University oral history interview, December 21, 1966, Dwight Eisenhower Library, 81.

77 *He eventually did*: Larson, *Eisenhower*, 165; Arthur Larson typed journal notes, "Eisenhower Book Research Notes (1)" folder, Larson, Arthur: Papers, 1932–93, Dwight Eisenhower Library.

77 *"The patent purpose"*: James Lambie letter to Claude Robinson, June 9, 1953, "Candor and United Nations Speech 12/8/53 (1)" folder, Eisenhower, Papers as President, Speech Series, Dwight Eisenhower Library.

77 *C. D. Jackson's next set*: John Lear, "Ike and the Peaceful Atom," *The Reporter*, January 12, 1956.

77 *"to give our people"*: Dwight Eisenhower letter to Swede Hazlett, December 24, 1953, "DDE Diary December 1953 (1)" folder, Eisenhower, Papers as President, DDE Diary Series, Dwight Eisenhower Library.

77 *Jackson was losing hope*: Lear, "Ike and the Peaceful Atom."

78 *"The hope"*: Ferrell, ed., *Eisenhower Diaries*, 262.

78 *"The whole world"*: August 24, 1953, 3d Draft of speech on atomic energy, "Candor and United Nations Speech 12/8/53 (11)" folder, Eisenhower, Papers as President, Speech Series, Dwight Eisenhower Library.

78 *"I am afraid"*: C. D. Jackson memorandum to R. Gordon Arenson, September 2, 1953, "Candor and United Nations Speech 12/8/53 (10)" folder, Eisenhower, Papers as President, Speech Series, Dwight Eisenhower Library.

78 *"C. D. Jackson asks me"*: James Lambie memorandum to R. Gordon Arneson et al., September 28, 1953, "Candor and United Nations Speech 12/8/53 (8)" folder, Eisenhower, Papers as President, Speech Series, Dwight Eisenhower Library.

79 *"The speech should"*: C. D. Jackson memo to Dwight Eisenhower, October 2, 1953, "Operation 'Candor' (1)" folder, Eisenhower, Papers as President, Administration Files, Dwight Eisenhower Library.

79 *The next day*: Carol Gelderman, *All the Presidents' Words: The Bully Pulpit and the Creation of the Virtual Presidency* (New York: Walker & Co., 1997), 48.

79 *Jackson called Cutler*: Ibid., 48.

79 *Dulles and other State Department officials*: "Summary of Discussion of State Draft of Part of Presidential Speech," October 19, 1953, "Atoms for Peace—Evolution (7)" folder, Jackson, C. D.: Papers, 1931–67, Dwight Eisenhower Library.

79 *"The specific and simple terms"*: John Foster Dulles memorandum to Dwight Eisenhower, October 23, 1953, "Operation 'Candor' (1)" folder, Eisenhower, Papers as President, Administration Files, Dwight Eisenhower Library.

79 *"Big meeting in Foster"*: November 25, 1953 (Wednesday), Jackson log, "Log-1953 (5)" folder, Jackson, C. D. Papers, 1931–67, Dwight Eisenhower Library.

79 *"Real problem is"*: November 27, 1953 (Friday), Jackson log, "Log-1953 (5)" folder, Jackson, C. D.: Papers, 1931–67, Dwight Eisenhower Library.

80 *"as quickly as possible"*: Draft of "The Safety of the Republic," undated, "Atoms for Peace—Evolution (7)" folder, Jackson, C. D.: Papers, 1931–67, Dwight Eisenhower Library.

80 *As they made final tweaks*: Adams, *Firsthand Report*, 118–19.

80 *"You can't sit there"*: C. D. Jackson daily log, December 4, 1953–December 8, 1953, "Log-1953 (5)" folder, Jackson, C. D.: Papers, 1931–67, Dwight Eisenhower Library.

81 *The work continued*: Lear, "Ike and the Peaceful Atom."

81 *Uninterrupted as he spoke*: Ambrose, *Eisenhower*, 342–43.

81 *Eisenhower's proposal was met*: Ibid., 343.

82 *He was "short"*: Author interview with Stephen Benedict.

82 *Where Hughes was tall*: Author interview with William Bragg Ewald; author interview with Benedict.

82 *"In manner they were"*: Author interview with Kieve.

82 *"His greatest aversion"*: Hughes, *Ordeal*, 24–25.

82 *"The president must understate"*: Bryce Harlow Columbia University oral history interview, May 1, 1968, Dwight Eisenhower Library, 113.

82 *"He wanted the word"*: Author interview with Ewald.

82 *Harlow's writing and editing style*: Larson, *Eisenhower*, 150.

83 *"He tries to sound"*: Arthur Larson journal notes, January, 1958, "Eisenhower Book VI. Writer & Speaker (2)" folder, Larson, Arthur: Papers, 1932–93, Dwight Eisenhower Library.

83 *"ardent Republican"*: Author interview with Ewald.

83 *"He is really not"*: Arthur Larson journal notes, May 29, 1956, "Eisenhower Book III. Politics" folder, Larson, Arthur: Papers, 1932–93, Dwight Eisenhower Library.

83 *"Frankly, I don't care"*: Larson, *Eisenhower*, 35.

83 *"Try to write your way"*: Ewald, *Eisenhower*, 153.

83 *Harlow and other aides*: Ibid., 154.

84 *"almost devoid of politics"*: Bryce Harlow note to Dwight Eisenhower, September 17, 1954, "Speeches—September 23, 1954—Hollywood Bowl Speech (2)" folder, Harlow, Bryce N.: Records, 1953–61, Dwight Eisenhower Library.

84 *White House lobbyist Jack Martin*: Ewald, *Eisenhower*, 154–55.

84 *"By golly"*: Ibid., 158.

84 *"I don't see how"*: Ibid.

85 *"I've just been eaten"*: Author interview with Ewald.

85 *"You know, Kevin"*: McCann Columbia OH, 1–2.

85 *Tall, gaunt, gray*: Ewald, *Eisenhower*, 146.

85 *McCann among all*: Author interview with Ewald.

85 *"Both Southern and Yankee"*: "Whimsical Ghost," *New York Times*, December 11, 1959.

85 *He liked to dictate*: Author interview with Kieve.

85 *"neither technically nor emotionally"*: C. D. Jackson letter to Henry R. Luce, April 11, 1956, "Log-1956 (2)" folder, Jackson, C.D.: Papers, 1931–67, Dwight Eisenhower Library.

86 *"I think that we do"*: Ibid.

86 *Jackson wrote Adams on April 20*: C. D. Jackson letter to Sherman Adams, April 20, 1956, "Adams, Governor Sherman (2)" folder, Jackson, C.D.: Papers, 1931–67, Dwight Eisenhower Library; C. D. Jackson letter to Henry Luce, April 21, 1956, "Log-1956 (2)" folder, Jackson, C.D.: Papers, 1931–67, Dwight Eisenhower Library.

86 *Larson quickly learned*: Larson, *Eisenhower*, 146–47.

86 *Eisenhower had a strong sense*: Ibid., 149.

86 *He cited Lincoln*: Arthur Larson journal notes, July 20, 1956, "Eisenhower Book I. Principles (1)" folder, Larson, Arthur: Papers, 1932–93, Dwight Eisenhower Library.

86 *His admonitions*: Kieve, "How One . . ."

87 *He tried to avoid*: Arthur Larson memorandum to Fred Fox, February 3, 1958, "Chronological: January, February, 1958" folder, Larson and Moos Files, Dwight Eisenhower Library.

87 *Writing speeches*: Larson, *Eisenhower*, 5, 148–49.

87 *"the best American English"*: Author interview with Benedict.

87 *He would substitute*: Larson, *Eisenhower*, 148.

87 *Larson also learned*: Ibid., 126–27.

88 *Larson tried formulation*: Ibid., 128.

88 *"As a matter of fact"*: Ibid., 124.

88 *The previous week*: C. D. Jackson log of conversation with Emmet Hughes, August 20,

1956, "Log-1956 (3)" folder, Jackson, C. D.: Papers, 1931–67, Dwight Eisenhower Library.

89 *"The text on civil rights"*: Hughes, *Ordeal*, 176.

89 *"An indictment"*: Ibid., 287–88.

89 *Eisenhower's "purpose"*: Ibid., 289, 297–98.

90 *Working on his memoirs*: Ewald, *Eisenhower*, 224–25.

90 *"My position is desperate"*: Arthur Larson typed journal notes, October 1, 1957, and onward, "Eisenhower Book III. Politics" folder, Larson, Arthur: Papers, 1932–93, Dwight Eisenhower Library.

90 *Eisenhower did not personally*: Larson, *Eisenhower*, 157.

90 *Larson drew upon*: Ibid., 158.

91 *Larson put together*: 1958 Speech Schedule, "Memorandum Book October 1957 #2" folder, Larson, Arthur: Papers, 1932–93, Dwight Eisenhower Library.

91 *"In my long hours"*: Larson, *Eisenhower*, 151.

91 *"I had quite a few items"*: Larson journal, November 4, 1957, and November 5, 1957, "Eisenhower Book VI. Writer & Speaker (2)" folder, Larson, Arthur: Papers, 1932–93, Dwight Eisenhower Library.

91 *Three days later*: Larson journal, November 8, 1957, "Eisenhower Book VI. Writer & Speaker (2)" folder, Larson, Arthur: Papers, 1932–93, Dwight Eisenhower Library.

91 *he might pull out foot-long*: Larson, *Eisenhower*, 181.

92 *The son of a minister*: Morrow biographical information from the White House Historical Society: www.whitehousehistory.org/05/subs/05_c17.html.

92 *"correct in conduct"*: E. Frederic Morrow, *Black Man in the White House* (New York: Coward-McCann, 1963), 17.

92 *"It's a great day"*: McCann Columbia OH, 83.

92 *"This opportunity of service"*: Morrow, *Black Man*, 183–84.

92 *"that it has been decided"*: Ibid., 182–83.

92 *"This is an anxious . . . slight stroke"*: Ibid., 188.

92 *On the afternoon of November 25*: Ambrose, *Eisenhower*, 455.

93 *"The process of preparing"*: Larson typed journal notes, December 12, 1957, "Memorandum Book December 1957" folder, Larson, Arthur: Papers, 1932–93, Dwight Eisenhower Library.

93 *"Adams, with great tenderness"*: Ibid.

93 *"it is very embarrassing"*: Frederic Morrow diary, December 31, 1957, "Diary—E. Frederic Morrow (4)" folder, Papers of E. Frederic Morrow, Dwight Eisenhower Library.

93 *"The performance"*: Frederic Morrow diary, January 7, 1958, "Diary—E. Frederic Morrow (4)" folder, Papers of E. Frederic Morrow, Dwight Eisenhower Library.

93 *"Don't tell the damn staff"*: Larson typed journal notes, January 1, 1958, "Memorandum Book December 1957" folder, Larson, Arthur: Papers, 1932–93, Dwight Eisenhower Library.

94 *On January 9*: Larson, *Eisenhower*, 176–77.

94 *"When the President"*: Arthur Krock, "Some Reassurance and a Personal Triumph," *New York Times*, January 10, 1958.

94 *"extremely well, clear"*: Jackson daily log, January 14, 1958, "Log-1958 (1)" folder, Jackson, C. D.: Papers, 1931–67, Dwight Eisenhower Library.

94 *For example, Stephen Hess*: Author interview with Stephen Hess.

94 *When Larson "confided"*: Morrow, *Black Man*, 202.

94 *Morrow asked out . . . attend the ceremony*: Ibid., 275.

95 *"By the way, Malcolm"*: Malcolm Moos Columbia University oral history interview, November 2, 1972, 33.

95   *The president and Malcolm Moos*: Ibid., 33–34; William McGaffin and Robert Gruenberg, "Ike's Historic 1961 Warning," *Chicago Daily News*, April 14, 1969.

95   *"I am going to be"*: "Bull Mooser," *Time*, September 22, 1958.

95   *From 1954 to 1958*: "Moos, Malcolm C(harles)," *Current Biography 1968*, 268.

95   *"you'd think that"*: Ralph Williams Dwight Eisenhower Library oral history interview, June 3, 1988, 17.

95   *"an energetic mixture"*: "Bull Mooser."

95   *"no better than"*: Quoted in *Current Biography 1968*.

95   *"The excitement in town"*: "Random Notes in Washington: Strong Words, a Ghostly Ring," *New York Times*, October 27, 1958.

96   *During the Little Rock crisis*: Moos Columbia OH, 29.

96   *"an insane notion"*: Ibid., 14.

96   *"He liked to have a draft"*: Ibid., 12.

96   *"Usually his first brush"*: Ralph Williams letter to Martin Teasley, October 28, 1986, "Letters 1985–88" folder, Williams, Ralph E.: Papers, 1958–60, Dwight Eisenhower Library.

97   *In later years he joked*: Author interview with Hess.

97   *A Texas native*: Williams OH, 5, 12–14.

97   *"We're carpenters"*: Moos Columbia OH, 27.

97   *Data points*: Ibid., 34.

97   *"the problem of militarism"*: Ralph Williams memo to file, October 31, 1960, "Chronological (1)" folder, Williams, Ralph E.: Papers, 1958–60, Dwight Eisenhower Library.

98   *"there must be a balance"*: James, McPherson, and Alan Brinkley, gen. eds. *Days of Destiny: Crossroads in American History* (London: DK Publishing, 2001), 364.

98   *Eisenhower had spent his two terms*: Ibid., 365, 370n.

99   *It warned*: Douglas Brinkley, "Eisenhower," *American Heritage Magazine* (September 2001).

99   *"military-industrial-congressional"*: Michael Waldman, *My Fellow Americans: The Most Important Speeches of America's Presidents, From George Washington to George W. Bush* (Naperville, IL: Sourcebooks mediaFusion, 2003), 153.

99   *"I think you've got"*: Moos Columbia OH, 35.

99   *"give a 'farewell address'"*: Brinkley, "Eisenhower."

99   *"will be remembered"*: Walter Lippmann, "Eisenhower's Farewell Warning," *Washington Post*, January 19, 1961.

99   *"There is an interesting development"*: Bryce Harlow memo for Dwight Eisenhower and Richard Nixon, March 17, 1961, "Harlow, Bryce, 1961 (3)" folder, Eisenhower Papers, Post-Presidential, Dwight Eisenhower Library.

4. THE AGE OF SORENSEN

101   *The two quiet . . . nature of the position*: Theodore C. Sorensen, *Kennedy* (New York: Harper & Row, 1965), 11–12.

101   *"not a Harvard man"*: William Lee Miller, "Ted Sorensen of Nebraska," *The Reporter*, February 13, 1964.

102   *Sorensen's father*: "First Man Out," *Time*, January 24, 1964.

102   *His mother*: Robert Dallek, *An Unfinished Life: John F. Kennedy, 1917–1963* (New York: Back Bay Books, 2003), 179–80.

102   *The couple had met*: Michael R. Beschloss, *The Crisis Years: Kennedy and Khrushchev, 1960–1963* (New York: Edward Burlingame Books, 1991), 126.

102 *Young Ted*: Aleksandr Fursenko, and Timothy Naftali, *One Hell of a Gamble: Khrushchev, Castro and Kennedy, 1958–1964* (New York: W. W. Norton, 1997), 322.

102 *"that mid-western Unitarianism"*: Miller, "Ted Sorensen of Nebraska."

102 *Ted's older brother*: Ibid.

102 *C. A. Sorensen offered his son*: "Two for the New Show," *Time*, November 21, 1960.

103 *He had a fierce commitment*: Miller, "Ted Sorensen of Nebraska."

103 *"I arrived in Washington"*: Don Walton, "A Life in the Arena," *Lincoln Journal Star*, September 25, 2005.

103 *"Jack wouldn't hire"*: Sorensen, *Kennedy*, 11.

103 *"You couldn't write speeches"*: Ibid., 31.

103 *By 1954, Sorensen was*: Ibid., 59.

103 *Sorensen built up a card file*: "Kennedy's Top Adviser," *New York Times*, July 5, 1960.

103 *"Those three and a half years"*: Author interview with Theodore C. Sorensen,

104 *"When Jack is wounded"*: "Kennedy's Top Adviser."

104 *"my intellectual blood bank"*: Richard J. Tofel, *Sounding the Trumpet: The Making of John F. Kennedy's Inaugural Address* (Chicago: Ivan R. Dee, 2005), 16.

104 *"self-sufficient, taut"*: Richard N. Goodwin, *Remembering America: A Voice from the Sixties* (New York: Harper & Row, 1989), 71.

104 *"Even to this day"*: Author interview with Richard N. Goodwin.

104 *"Abrupt, cold, short"*: Walton, "A Life in the Arena."

104 *"Underneath the appearance"*: Arthur M. Schlesinger, Jr., *A Thousand Days: John F. Kennedy in the White House* (Boston: Houghton Mifflin, 1965), 208.

104 *The abstemious Sorensen*: Thurston Clarke, *Ask Not: The Inauguration of John F. Kennedy and the Speech That Changed America* (New York: Henry Holt & Co., 2005), 66.

104 *Sorensen even picked up*: Sorensen, *Kennedy*, 30.

104 *"Of Sorensen and Kennedy"*: Schlesinger, *A Thousand Days*, 208.

105 *"Make it the shortest"*: Sorensen handwritten notes, undated, "Memoranda, Speech materials + correspondence, 12/10/60–5/23/61 + Undated" folder, Theodore C. Sorensen Papers, JFK Library.

105 *"My conclusion"*: Sorensen, *Kennedy*, 240.

105 *As JFK's closest adviser*: Ibid., 229–30.

105 *They chatted*: Author interview with Myer Feldman.

105 *emerging after three hours*: Clarke, *Ask Not*, 26.

105 *Feldman read it*: Ibid., 26–27.

105 *a "stream of thoughts"*: Tofel, *Sounding*, 41.

105 *In 2006, Feldman*: Author interview with Feldman.

106 *"The President-Elect has asked"*: Telegram, Ted Sorensen to Dr. Allan Nevins et al., December 23, 1960, "Inaugural Address, 1/20/61, Memoranda, Speech materials + correspondence, 12/10/60–5/23/61 + Undated" folder, Theodore C. Sorensen Papers, Box 62, JFK Library.

106 *He got at least five*: Tofel, *Sounding*, 50.

106 *On the down side*: Sorensen, *Kennedy*, 234; Tofel, *Sounding*, 51.

106 *The president-elect flew*: The account of the flight to Palm Beach comes from Evelyn Lincoln, *My Twelve Years with John F. Kennedy* (New York: David McKay Co., 1965), 219; Clarke, *Ask Not*, 27–37; Tofel, *Sounding*, 64–66.

106 *"So let the word"*: All quotations from six-page draft are from "Inaugural Address, 1/20/61" folder, President's Office Files, Papers of President Kennedy, JFK Library.

107 *Sorensen borrowed liberally*: Tofel, *Sounding*, 61–62.

107 *Using Sorensen's draft*: Ibid., 64. Tofel's book also contains the first published transcription of Evelyn Kennedy's shorthand notes of Kennedy's dictation.

107 *Like other timeless sentiments*: Clarke, *Ask Not*, 78.

108 *He had tried different riffs*: Schlesinger, *A Thousand Days*, 4n; Sorensen, *Kennedy*, 241.

108 *The inaugural address had other*: Sorensen, *Kennedy*, 241.

109 *"It isn't all that important"*: Author interview with Sorensen.

109 *Kennedy spent a week*: Clarke, *Ask Not*, 38.

109 *He scribbled*: Schlesinger, *A Thousand Days*, 162; Clarke, *Ask Not*, 42–43.

109 *On the evening of January 11*: Ernest Gruening telegram to John F. Kennedy, January 11, 1961, "Inaugural Address, 1/20/61, Memoranda, Speech materials + correspondence, 12/10/60–5/23/61 + Undated" folder, Theodore C. Sorensen Papers, JFK Library.

109 *Once in the air*: Hugh Sidey, "He Asked Me to Listen to the Debate," *Time*, November 14, 1983.

110 *"It's tough"*: As quoted at Tofel, *Sounding*, 69, and Clarke *Ask Not*, 95–96.

110 *Sidey was stunned*: Clarke, *Ask Not*, 95.

110 *Lippmann, lunching with Sorensen*: Schlesinger, *A Thousand Days*, 163.

110 *Civil rights aides*: Undated "CHANGES IN INAUGURAL SPEECH—TO BE READ AND AP-PROVED BY SENATOR," "Inaugural Address, 1/20/61" folder, President's Office Files, Papers of President Kennedy, JFK Library; for authorship of suggestions, see Tofel, *Sounding*, 74.

111 *Asked forty-five years later*: Author interview with Sorensen.

111 *the marble pillars*: "A Brief Construction History of the Capitol," Office of the Architect of the Capitol, www.aoc.gov/cc/capitol/capitol_construction.cfm.

112 *"Someone—was it Falkland?"*: Sorensen, *Kennedy*, 62.

112 *"could do as well for him"*: Schlesinger, *A Thousand Days*, 690.

112 *"Words were regarded"*: Sorensen, *Kennedy*, 60–61.

112 *"The inaugural was a special occasion"*: Author interview with Sorensen.

113 *He felt that his voice*: Schlesinger, *A Thousand Days*, 690.

113 *"JFK used to tease me"*: Author interview with Arthur M. Schlesinger, Jr.

113 *"when the form of words"*: Author interview with Feldman.

113 *"not solely for reasons"*: Sorensen, *Kennedy*, 61.

113 *"He believed in retaining"*: Ibid., 511.

113 *As an editor*: Schlesinger, *A Thousand Days*, 690.

113 *Schlesinger gave him a draft*: Author interview with Schlesinger; marked-up draft of Nobel Prize Winners Dinner remarks, "Remarks for the President; Remarks at Nobel Prize Winners Dinner, 4/29/62" folder, Arthur M. Schlesinger Jr. Papers, JFK Library.

114 *"They all have a point"*: Arthur M. Schlesinger Jr. Journal, March 16, 1961.

114 *"Active government"*: Arthur Schlesinger memorandum for the president, March 16, 1961, "Schlesinger, Arthur M., 3/61–4/61" folder, Papers of President Kennedy, President's Office Files, JFK Library.

114 *"All this shows"*: Arthur Schlesinger memorandum for the president, November 21, 1961, "Future Presidential Speeches 1962, memoranda, 10/19/61–3/31/62" folder, Theodore C. Sorensen Papers, JFK Library.

115 *"I know that everyone"*: Theodore C. Sorensen JFK Library oral history interview, April 6, 1964, 1.

115 *"In one stroke"*: Schlesinger journal, June 7, 1961.

115 *JFK decided to use*: Arthur M. Schlesinger, Jr., *Robert Kennedy and His Times* (Boston: Houghton Mifflin, 1978), 474.

115 *"If we don't want Russia"*: Fursenko and Naftali, *One Hell*, 97.

115 *This was not uncommon*: Sorensen, *Kennedy*, 550–51.

116 *It was, he once explained*: Schlesinger journal, September 16, 1961.

116 *"The boldness and strength"*: Sorensen JFK Library OH, 48.

116 *A Philadelphia native*: Douglas Martin, "Myer Feldman, 92, Adviser to President Kennedy, Dies," *New York Times*, March 3, 2007.

116 *He met Kennedy*: Author interview with Feldman.

116 *Feldman directed research*: Sorensen, *Kennedy*, 176.

116 *"Ted Sorensen and I"*: Author interview with Feldman.

116 *"the White House's anonymous"*: Quoted in Martin, "Myer Feldman, 92, Adviser."

117 *In the late 1950s*: Goodwin, *Remembering*, 43–63.

117 *"I wish you"*: Ibid., 65.

117 *Goodwin had been the latest*: Sorensen, *Kennedy* 117.

117 *"Some, especially in those early"*: Schlesinger, *A Thousand Days*, 193.

117 *Goodwin, riding*: Goodwin, *Remembering*, 108–09.

118 Alianza *was fine*: Schlesinger, *A Thousand Days*, 193–94; Goodwin, *Remembering*, 108–09.

118 *(later, at the insistence)*: Schlesinger, *A Thousand Days*, 194.

118 *"I learned a lot from Ted"*: Goodwin, *Remembering*, 71.

118 *"Goodwin and Sorensen did not get along"*: Author interview with Feldman.

118 *When, just before the administration*: Goodwin, *Remembering*, 138–39.

119 *He was interested neither*: Ibid., 139.

119 *"You know how we do things"*: Ibid.

119 *"I was saddened"*: Ibid., 211.

119 *"Kennedy seemed very sincere"*: Arthur M. Schlesinger, Jr., *A Life in the 20th Century: Innocent Beginnings, 1917–1950* (Boston: Houghton Mifflin, 2000), 378.

120 *(After which he had received)*: Schlesinger, *A Thousand Days*, 285.

120 *"Arthur has minimal"*: Joseph Kraft, "Kennedy's Working Staff" *Harper's Magazine* (February 1963).

120 *In 1952, Stevenson had dispatched*: Author interview with Schlesinger.

120 *Rosenman thought the speeches*: Samuel Rosenman oral history interview, Columbia University, 1960, FDR Library, 182.

120 *"I learned a lesson"*: Author interview with Schlesinger.

120 *"As usual, I was overwhelmed"*: Schlesinger journal, September 22, 1962.

121 *After a meeting . . . "when he sees that"*: Schlesinger journal, January 14, 1962.

121 *Kennedy used the "weave" . . . "That's what I am doing now"*: Schlesinger journal, March 31, 1962; Schlesinger, *A Thousand Days*, 614–15.

122 *Walter Lippman told Bundy*: Schlesinger journal, March 31, 1962.

122 *At the Justice Department*: Beschloss, *Crisis Years*, 6.

122 *Cuba was also a public*: Sorensen, *Kennedy*, 668; Schlesinger, *A Thousand Days*, 798–99.

122 *In addition, Khrushchev*: Sorensen, *Kennedy*, 667.

123 *"what we're going to do* anyway": Ernest R. May, and Philip D. Zelikow, eds. *The Kennedy Tapes: Inside the White House During the Cuban Missile Crisis* (Cambridge, MA: Belknap Press, 1997), 71.

124 *"Each of us changed"*: Sorensen, *Kennedy*, 680.

124 *"Having some pride"*: Sorensen JFK Library OH, 51.

124 *"inescapable commitment"*: Beschloss, *Crisis Years*, 454.

125 *"I had to admit"*: Sorensen JFK Library OH, 51.

125 *"Inasmuch as no one"*: Laurence Chang and Peter Kornbluh, eds., *The Cuban Missile Crisis, 1962: A National Security Archive Documents Reader* (New York: New Press, 1992), 133.

125 *"This morning"*: Beschloss, *Crisis Years*, 454.

125 *That night the Ex Comm*: Sorensen, *Kennedy*, 692.

125 *He retired to his office*: Ibid.

125 *"combination of my legal background"*: Author interview with Sorensen.

126 *"As the concrete answers" . . . writing a draft*: Sorensen, *Kennedy*, 692–93.

126 *The group debated*: May and Zelikow, eds., *Kennedy Tapes*, 195.

126 *"Is this a 'nuclear quarantine'"*: Tentative agenda of NSC meeting, October 21, 1962, "Radio and Television Report to the American People on the Soviet Arms Buildup in Cuba—10/22/62" folder, Papers of President Kennedy, President's Office Files, JFK Library.

126 *Rusk questioned*: May and Zelikow, eds., *Kennedy Tapes*, 209.

127 *A passage that acknowledged*: Beschloss, *Crisis Years*, 484n.

127 *"someday go"*: Ibid., 485n.

127 *"appropriate action"*: 10/21/62 TCS—3rd Draft of Kennedy speech to nation, "Radio and Television Report to the American People on the Soviet Arms Buildup in Cuba—10/22/62" folder, Papers of President Kennedy, President's Office Files, JFK Library.

127 *"Do not become"*: Ibid.

127 *"The Russians are going to make"*: May and Zelikow, eds., *Kennedy Tapes*, 225.

128 *"From the start"*: Beschloss, *Crisis Years*, 470.

128 *JFK and his advisers*: May and Zelikow, eds., *Kennedy Tapes*, 225.

128 *Five minutes before*: Beschloss, *Crisis Years*, 482–83.

130 *"You can tell the president"*: Richard Reeves, *President Kennedy: Profile of Power* (New York: Simon & Schuster, 1993), 511.

130 *"What do I tell them?"*: Ibid., 476–77.

130 *"the most important speech"*: Ibid., 511–12.

131 *He also dug up material*: Sorensen, *Kennedy*, 730.

131 *seventeen typed pages*: TCS—6/6/63 AU Notes, "American University Commencement 6/10/63; 6/6/63–7/12/63 + Undated" folder, Theodore C. Sorensen Papers, JFK Library.

131 *"The clamor of conflicting"*: "American University Notes," June 6, 1963, "American University Commencement 6/10/63; 6/6/63–7/12/63 + Undated" folder, Theodore C. Sorensen Papers, JFK Library.

131 *"a small but select"*: McGeorge Bundy, Memorandum for the record, dictated June 13, 7:30 p.m., "[McGB memoranda for the record, July 1963–December, 1962, 1963: July–February]" folder, McGeorge Bundy Personal Papers, JFK Library.

131 *Not in the loop*: Dallek, *An Unfinished Life*, 618; Sorensen, *Kennedy*, 730.

131 *"did not want [his] new policy"*: Sorensen, *Kennedy*, 730–31.

131 *"was evidently to take"*: Schlesinger, *A Thousand Days*, 418.

132 *"I suppose that"*: Schlesinger journal, June 16, 1963.

132 *Though the president had discussed*: Sorensen JFK Library OH, 73.

133 *"Public cant"*: Dallek, *An Unfinished Life*, 621.

133 *Ten days later*: Schlesinger, *A Thousand Days*, 910.

133 *The Western European reaction*: United States Information Agency memorandum to McGeorge Bundy, June 12, 1963, "American University Commencement 6/10/63; 6/6/63–7/12/63 + Undated" folder, Theodore C. Sorensen Papers, JFK Library.

134 *Schlesinger later asked*: Schlesinger journal, July 28, 1963.

134 *The criticism that Schlesinger*: Schlesinger, *A Thousand Days*, 714.

134 *"It is clear"*: Schlesinger journal, August 6, 1962.

134 *The relationship between leadership*: Sorensen, *Kennedy*, 494.

135 *"I must confess"*: Schlesinger journal, May 8, 1963.

135 *"People forget this"*: Schlesinger journal, October 17, 1961.

135 *JFK liked to quote*: Schlesinger, *A Thousand Days*, 720.

135 *Even before the Birmingham confrontation*: Reeves, *Profile*, 515–16; Dallek, *An Unfinished Life*, 603; Edwin Guthman and Jeffrey Shulman, eds., *Robert Kennedy in His Own Words*:

The Unpublished Recollections of the Kennedy Years (New York: Bantam Books, 1988), 175–76.

135 *In fact, there was no draft*: Sorensen, *Kennedy*, 495.

136 *"We better give"*: Author interview with Sorensen.

136 *"C'mon Burke"*: Reeves, *Profile*, 521.

136 *At 7:40 pm*: Guthman and Shulman, eds., *Robert Kennedy*, 200.

136 *"For the first time"*: Sorensen, *Kennedy*, 495.

136 *"The speech was good"*: Guthman and Shulman, eds., *Robert Kennedy*, 200–1.

137 *"Yes—and look"*: Schlesinger journal, June 16, 1963.

137 *"He is deeply"*: Ibid.

137 *He had honed the skill*: Sorensen, *Kennedy*, 331.

137 *"text deviate"*: Ibid., 186.

138 *For the only time*: Sorensen, *Kennedy*, 526.

139 *In West Berlin, 300,000*: Beschloss, *Crisis Years*, 275.

139 *Almost two years later*: Arthur J. Olsen, "President Hailed by Over a Million in Visit to Berlin," *New York Times*, June 27, 1963.

139 *Before JFK left Washington*: Beschloss, *Crisis Years*, 605.

139 *"What was the proud boast"*: Reeves, *Profile*, citing O'Donnell's *Johnny We Hardly Knew Ye*, at 739, n536.

139 *"So there we were"*: Beschloss, *Crisis Years*, 605.

139 *"Ish bin ein"*: Handwritten notes for the speech, "Remarks at the Signing of the Golden Book at Rudolph Wildeplatz, Berlin, Germany, 6/26/63" folder, Papers of President Kennedy, President's Office Files, JFK Library.

139 *West Berlin mayor*: Gerald Strober and Deborah Strober, eds., *"Let Us Begin Anew": An Oral History of the Kennedy Presidency* (New York: HarperCollins, 1993), 371; Willy Brandt, *People and Politics: The Years 1960–1975* (New York: Little, Brown, 1978), 73.

139 *"You think this is any good?"*: Reeves, *Profile*, 535.

140 *"I think that went"*: Lochner at www.cnn.com/SPECIALS/cold.war/episodes/09/reflections/.

140 *"If I told them . . . another Hitler?"*: Dallek, *An Unfinished Life*, 624–25.

141 *"Fortunately the crowd"*: Beschloss, *Crisis Years*, 606n.

141 *"to be opened"*: Sorensen, *Kennedy*, 601.

141 *Around 10:45 am*: Ibid., 749.

141 *"It's easier for Kennedy"*: "Kennedy a 'Puppet' in 1960, Nixon says," *New York Times*, June 19, 1962.

142 *"Along with so many others"*: As quoted in Clarke, *Ask Not*, 8.

142 *"Sorensen knew Kennedy's mind"*: Author interview with Feldman.

142 *"I always felt"*: Author interview with Goodwin.

142 *"A few days before"*: Schlesinger journal, March 27, 1964.

143 *"I maintain"*: Author interview with Sorensen.

143 *"If I was writing a speech"*: Author interview with Goodwin.

5. "NOW THAT'S WHAT I CALL A NEWS LEAD"

145 *"The president is dead"*: Jack Valenti LBJ Library oral history interview, October 18, 1969, LBJ Library, 6. This account differs slightly from Valenti's recollection in his White House memoir *A Very Human President* and his autobiography, *This Time, This Place*, where he has Cliff Alexander saying, "The vice-president wants you and wants you now. I've been looking for you," then adding softly, after a hesitation, "The president is dead, you know."

145 *Cliff Carter and Valenti*: Valenti OH interview, and from Jack Valenti, *A Very Human President* (New York: W. W. Norton, 1976), 31–35.

145 *At 12:42 . . . "to have been wounded"*: "L.B.J.'s Young Man 'In Charge of Everything,'" *Time*, October 29, 1965; on the club not being integrated, see Lauren Reinlie, "New Campus Club Caters to Faculty, Staff," *Daily Texan*, October 17, 2002, and E. Ernest Goldstein LBJ Library oral history interview, December 9, 1968, LBJ Library, 16–17.

146 *The call*: Nathan Diebenow, "Party Rebuilding," *Lone Star Iconoclast*, November 26, 2006.

146 *"I'm here"*: "L.B.J.'s Young Man 'In Charge of Everything'"; the time of the swearing-in comes from the President's Daily Diary, November 22, 1963, LBJ Library.

146 *"This is a sad time"*: Marked-up, typed speaking card, November 22, 1963, "11.22.63 Remarks of President upon arrival at Andrews Air Force Base" folder, Statements of Lyndon Baines Johnson, LBJ Library.

146 *Johnson scrawled*: Ibid.

146 *At Andrews*: Horace Busby, *The Thirty-First of March* (New York: Farrar, Straus & Giroux, 2005), 159–60.

146 *He wanted the speech*: Walter Heller, "Notes on Meeting with President Johnson, 7:40 p.m., Saturday, November 23, 1963," contained in Arthur M. Schlesinger, Jr.'s journal.

147 *"I didn't think"*: Michael R. Beschloss, ed., *Taking Charge: The Johnson White House Tapes, 1963–1964* (New York: Simon & Schuster, 1997), 40–41.

147 *"the strong can be just"*: November 25, 1963, John Kenneth Galbraith letter to the president and attached speech draft, JFK Library.

147 *a French chateau–style*: "Ormes & the Man," *Time*, November 17, 1961.

147 *"corned it up"*: Schlesinger journal.

147 *"He is very hurt"*: Beschloss, ed., *Taking Charge*, 82.

147 *"This is of course"*: Schlesinger journal.

147 *Sorensen did not see*: Ibid., Stewart Alsop, "Johnson Takes Over: The Untold Story," *Saturday Evening Post*, February 15, 1964.

148 *On the car ride . . . they agreed*: Alsop, "Johnson Takes Over."

148 *"We spent"*: Beschloss, ed., *Taking Charge*, 82.

148 *"All I have ever"*: "TCS—11/26/63" draft of speech, "11.27.63 Remarks of the President Before a Joint Session of Congress, House Chamber—Capitol" Folder I, Statements of Lyndon Baines Johnson, LBJ Library.

148 *"—and I who cannot"*: Marked-up version of ibid.

148 *One of the speech's signature*: Horace Busby note to President Johnson and speech draft, November 26, 1963, "11.27.63 Remarks of the President Before a Joint Session of Congress, House Chamber—Capitol" Folder I, Statements of Lyndon Baines Johnson, LBJ Library.

149 *"He's got good sentence"*: Beschloss, ed., *Taking Charge*, 280.

149 *"The two roles"*: Richard N. Goodwin, *Remembering America: A Voice from the Sixties* (New York: Harper & Row, 1989), 268.

149 *He later advised*: Harry McPherson, *A Political Education: A Washington Memoir* (Austin: University of Texas Press, 1995), 327.

149 *"Almost from the outset"*: Jack Valenti LBJ Library oral history interview, July 12, 1972, LBJ Library, 3.

150 *"Nor were any of my"*: Goodwin, *Remembering*, 275.

150 *"It was great"*: Author interview with Richard N. Goodwin.

150 *Goodwin sifted*: Goodwin, *Remembering*, 253.

150 *"There's no question"*: Author interview with Jack Valenti.

151 *"I have had a lot"*: "Transcript of Johnson's Assessment in TV Interview of His First 100 Days in Office," *New York Times*, March 16, 1964.

151 *Johnson had been "badgering"*: Robert Dallek, *Flawed Giant: Lyndon Johnson and His Times, 1961–1973* (New York: Oxford University Press, 1998), 80–81.

151 *"Men deceive themselves"*: "Elucidator," *Time*, September 27, 1937.

152 *"fragment of rhetorical stuffing"*: Goodwin, *Remembering*, 272.

152 *"It was evident"*: Jack Valenti OH, July 12, 1972, LBJ Library, 4.

152 *"fondling and caressing"*: Ibid.

152 *"The country was alive"*: Goodwin, *Remembering*, 273.

153 *"It ought to do just fine"*: Ibid., 278.

153 *"I can tell you"*: Beschloss, ed., *Taking Charge*, 404, 404n.

153 *To drive home his point*: Ibid., 404n.

154 *"Doug, I want you"*: Douglass Cater LBJ Library oral history interview, April 29, 1969, LBJ Library, 7.

154 *The following February*: Ibid., 8–9.

154 *"Nothing compares"*: Quoted in Jack Valenti, *This Time, This Place* (New York: Harmony Books, 2007), 170.

154 *He told people*: Author interview with Ervin Duggan.

154 *"because I was from the South"*: Ibid.

155 *"this approach . . . this campaign"*: Horace Busby memorandum to the president, September 9, 1964, "Memos to President—October 1964" folder, Office Files of Horace Busby, LBJ Library.

155 *"Too often there is"*: W. J. Jorden memorandum to Douglass Cater, with Cater cover note to the president, September 18, 1964, "Memos to the President, September–November 1964 folder," Office Files of S. Douglass Cater, LBJ Library.

155 *"Tell Goodwin"*: Ken Hechler, "Ex-White House Speech Writers Go Down Memory Lane," *Sunday Gazette-Mail*, October 13, 1985.

155 *"The Great Society"*: "JOHN STEINBECK MATERIAL FOR READING AT THE INAUGURATION," undated, "1.20.65 The President's Inaugural Address folder," Statements of Lyndon Baines Johnson, LBJ Library.

156 *Goodwin included that phrase*: Valenti, *A Very Human President*, 65–66.

156 *"fell flat on his face"*: Robert Hardesty, "Searching for a News Lead: Writing Speeches for LBJ," unpublished text.

156 *"the drop outs"*: John Steinbeck letter to Jack Valenti, April 20, 1964, "Speech Material—John Steinbeck [1964] folder," Personal Papers of Jack Valenti, AC-84-57, LBJ Library.

156 *"It makes a lovely picture"*: John Steinbeck letter to Jack Valenti, May 19, 1964, "Speech Material—John Steinbeck [1964]" folder, Personal Papers of Jack Valenti, AC-84-57, LBJ Library.

156 *Goodwin had drafted*: Goodwin, *Remembering*, 355.

157 *The 1965 State of the Union*: Ibid., 364.

157 *"It will be difficult"*: Bill Moyers memo to the president, February 9, 1965, "Memos to the President and Others [1/64–10/65]" folder, Office Files of Bill Moyers, 1965, LBJ Library.

157 *a North Vietnamese attack two days earlier*: Seymour Topping, "Seven G.I.'s Slain in Vietcong Raid: 80 Are Wounded," *New York Times*, February 7, 1965.

157 *"I have some concerns"*: Horace Busby memo to the president, February 27, 1965, "Memos to the President—February 1965" folder, Office Files of Horace Busby, LBJ Library.

157 *They were confronted*: Dan Carter, *The Politics of Rage: George Wallace, the Origins of the New Conservatism, and the Transformation of American Politics* (New York: Simon & Schuster, 1995), 247–49.

158 *"Well, governor"*: Goodwin, *Remembering*, 321.

158 *"was like an avalanche"*: Author interview with Valenti.

158 *"What do you" . . . would tell the press*: Goodwin, *Remembering*, 323.

159 *"The hell you did"*: Ibid., 325–27. Valenti disputed this version of events, maintaining that he and Johnson selected Goodwin on the evening of Sunday, March 14, and assigned him the speech then. Johnson too, in his memoirs, says that a first draft was waiting for him in the morning. Goodwin sources his account of the Johnson-Valenti morning scene to Moyers, who in turn claims no knowledge of it. (Garth Pauley, *LBJ's American Promise: The 1965 Voting Rights Address* [College Station: Texas A&M University Press, 2007], 91–92.)

159 *"I thought you might"*: Ibid., 329.

159 *"There was, uniquely"*: Ibid., 327.

159 *Goodwin borrowed*: Pauley, *LBJ's American Promise*, 93–94.

159 *"Although I had written"*: Goodwin, *Remembering*, 329.

159 *Valenti and especially Moyers*: Pauley, *LBJ's American Promise*, 95.

160 *When Goodwin finished*: Goodwin, *Remembering*, 328.

160 *"I almost died"*: Robert Mann, *The Walls of Jericho: Lyndon Johnson, Hubert Humphrey, Richard Russell, and the Struggle for Civil Rights* (New York: Harcourt Brace, 1996), 461.

160 *"It flowed naturally"*: Author interview with Goodwin.

161 *Martin Luther King, Jr., told aides*: Goodwin, *Remembering*, 310.

161 *"Perhaps more than any"*: E. Frederic Morrow letter to the president, March 17, 1965, "Voting Rights—3-15-65" folder, Office Files of Horace Busby, LBJ Library.

161 *"He talked about what"*: Jack Valenti memo to the president, March 16, 1965, "3.15.65 Special Message to the Congress. The American Promise" folder 1 of 2, Statements of Lyndon Baines Johnson, LBJ Library.

161 *"Remember those assistants"*: Hardesty, "Searching for a News Lead."

162 *"Most of the stuff"*: Goodwin, *Remembering*, 418.

162 *Johnson reacted predictably*: Ibid., 420–21.

162 *"that lay somewhere"*: Valenti, *A Very Human President*, 11.

163 *He would only be gone*: Valenti LBJ Library OH, October 18, 1969, LBJ Library, 6.

163 *"Johnson chose me"*: Author interview with Valenti.

163 *Valenti lived in the White House*: Valenti, *This Time, This Place*, 166.

163 *"With his small, flashing"*: "Inside the White House," *Newsweek*, March 1, 1965.

163 *His brief ranged*: Goodwin, *Remembering*, 336.

163 *"He would seek"*: Author interview with Harry McPherson.

163 *At twenty-nine, the youngest*: Dallek, *Flawed Giant*, 68.

163 *He was a true believer*: "L.B.J.'s Man for the Press," *Life*, September 10, 1965.

163 *He drank only*: "L.B.J.'s Young Man 'In Charge of Everything.'"

163 *"I remember the sheer presence"*: Quoted in Eve Berliner, "The Moral Core of Bill Moyers," undated, www.evesmag.com.

164 *"The care of human life"*: "L.B.J.'s Young Man 'In Charge of Everything.'"

164 *He once gave Goodwin*: Goodwin, *Remembering*, 388–89.

164 *"Perhaps Moyers's"*: Patrick Anderson, "The No. 2 Texan in the White House," *New York Times Magazine*, April 3, 1966.

164 *Joseph Califano*: Joseph A. Califano, Jr., *The Triumph and Tragedy of Lyndon Johnson: The White House Years* (College Station: Texas A&M University, 2000), 12.

164 *When Johnson telephoned*: Ibid., 25, 168.

164 *"It was a very activist"*: Author interview with Joseph Califano.

164 *By 1967 he kept*: Califano, *Triumph*, 179.

164 *"Califano handled the domestic"*: George Christian, *The President Steps Down* (New York: Macmillan Company, 1970), 13.

165 *"You know what he thought"*: Author interview with Califano.

165 *"Rose Garden Rubbish"*: Peter Benchley LBJ Library oral history interview, November 20, 1968, LBJ Library, 17.

165 *In 1965, Busby asked*: Robert Hardesty LBJ Library oral history interview, March 26, 1969, LBJ Library, 2.

165 *"They were really running"*: Author interview with Califano.

165 *One night at eleven*: Author interview with Robert Hardesty.

166 *They would write individually*: Hardesty OH, LBJ Library, 4.

166 *Waking in the middle of the night*: Ibid., 22.

166 *After a particularly stressful day*: Author interview with Califano.

166 *"Brevity was the cardinal rule"*: Hardesty, "Searching for a News Lead."

166 *Califano and Harry McPherson*: Author interview with Califano.

166 *Ben Wattenberg, a Bronx native*: Ben Wattenberg LBJ Library oral history interview, November 23, 1968, LBJ Library, 26–27.

167 *"I'm going to go home"*: Hardesty, "Searching for a News Lead."

167 *There were three ways*: Ibid.

167 *"Can't you add something"*: Douglass Cater LBJ Library oral history interview, May 26, 1974, LBJ Library, 5.

167 *"Therefore. That's an important"*: Author interview with McPherson.

167 *"In an activist administration"*: Author interview with Duggan.

167 *The president convened*: Dallek, *Flawed Giant*, 275.

168 *"What the U.S. is doing"*: Horace Busby memo to the president, July 21, 1965, "Vietnam" folder, Office Files of Horace Busby, LBJ Library.

168 *He "could see"*: Doris Kearns Goodwin, *Lyndon Johnson and the American Dream* (New York: St. Martin's Press, 1976), 282.

168 *"People can take almost"*: John Steinbeck letter to Jack Valenti, July 22, 1965, "Speech Material—John Steinbeck [1965]" folder, Personal Papers of Jack Valenti, AC-84–57, LBJ Library.

168 *It was not a chip Johnson*: Califano, *Triumph*, 117; Valenti, *A Very Human President*, 192.

169 *A ceaseless week*: Goodwin, *Remembering*, 423.

169 *but not Goodwin, with whom Johnson*: Dallek, *Flawed Giant*, 301.

169 *The speech was "getting there"*: Califano, *Triumph*, 118.

169 *At day's end*: Goodwin, *Remembering*, 423–24.

169 *"It was just too much"*: Califano, *Triumph*, 117–18.

170 *"At forty yards" . . . "would love it"*: John Steinbeck letter to Jack Valenti, January 7, 1966, "Speech Material—John Steinbeck [1966]" folder, Personal Papers of Jack Valenti; AC-84–57, LBJ Library.

170 *"thoroughly investigated"*: Jack Valenti letter to John Steinbeck, January 22, 1966, "Speech Material—John Steinbeck [1966]" folder, Personal Papers of Jack Valenti; AC-84–57, LBJ Library.

170 *"We have to, simply"*: Dallek, *Flawed Giant*, 348.

170 *Valenti pressed Johnson*: Author interview with Valenti; Valenti, *A Very Human President*, 217–19.

170 *"I must confess"*: Valenti, *A Very Human President*, 217–19.

170 *"He never felt comfortable"*: Author interview with Valenti.

171 *"Why didn't Johnson do a better job?"*: Author interview with McPherson.

171 *"What he was trying"*: Harry McPherson oral history interview, January 16, 1969, LBJ Library, 14.

171 *Bob Hardesty was dining at home*: Except where noted, the account of the drafting of the March 16, 1966, Goddard Trophy speech comes from Hardesty, "Searching for a News Lead."

172 *"There is more chance"*: Carroll Kilpatrick, "LBJ Vows Landing on Moon by '70," *The Washington Post*, March 17, 1966.

172 *The initial luster of the moon*: Deborah Cadbury, *Space Race: The Epic Battle Between America and the Soviet Union for Dominion of Space* (New York: HarperCollins, 2006), 273–74; Charles Murray, and Catherine Bly Cox, *Apollo: The Race to the Moon* (New York: Simon & Schuster, 1989), 161.

172 *Shortly before he was to speak*: Evert Clark, "President Reaffirms Goal of Moon Landing in 60's," *New York Times*, March 17, 1966.

172 *"because of budget cuts"*: Ibid.

173 *That very night*: Cadbury, *Space Race*, 298.

173 *"You damned speechwriters"*: Hardesty, "Searching for a News Lead."

173 *"Holy God"*: Ibid.

173 *"had solved a speechwriting problem"*: Will Sparks, *"Who Talked to the President Last?"* (New York: W. W. Norton, 1971), 56–57.

174 *Looking for a news lead*: Hardesty, "Searching for a News Lead."

174 *"I choose not"*: Valenti, *This Time, This Place*, 274.

174 *"I guess I just didn't"*: Ibid., 278.

174 *He had known Johnson*: Dallek, *Flawed Giant*, 298.

175 *"When the president blew up"*: Author interview with Hardesty.

175 *"Looking at the fact"*: Charles Maguire LBJ Library oral history interview, July 8, 1969, LBJ Library, 37–38.

175 *"were really dreadful"*: Ben Wattenberg LBJ Library oral history interview, November 23, 1968, LBJ Library, 17.

175 *"The material that is"*: Robert Kintner memo, May 17, 1966, "Robert Kintner Memos 5.16.6 to 5.19.66" folder, Office Files of Robert Kintner, LBJ Library.

175 *"As you know"*: Robert Kintner memo to Robert Hardesty and Will Sparks, July 5, 1966, "Chronological—July, 1966 A–P" folder, Office Files of Robert Kintner, LBJ Library.

176 *"always angry"*: Robert Kintner LBJ Library oral history interview, July 13, 1972, LBJ Library, 29.

176 *"McPherson is one of the few"*: Valenti, *A Very Human President*, 54.

176 *"after you've worked"*: Dallek, *Flawed Giant*, 227.

176 *The writers were doing their job*: Charles Maguire, memo to Robert Kintner, March 31, 1967, "Office Files of Robert Kintner. 3.1.67–3.31.67" folder, Office Files of Robert Kintner, LBJ Library.

176 *"There shouldn't be quite"*: Peter Benchley LBJ Library oral history interview, November 20, 1968, LBJ Library, 31.

176 *"All right, damn it"*: Ibid., 32.

177 *"movie star handsome"*: Author interview with Harry Middleton.

177 *"I was the least competent"*: "A Celebration of the Life of Peter Benchley," April 30, 2006, privately produced DVD with video clips, including Benchley recounting his days in the Johnson White House.

177 *"He is somewhat"*: Robert Kintner memo to the president, February 22, 1967, "Chronological—Feb. 1967—Pres-Z" folder, Office Files of Robert Kintner, LBJ Library.

177 *He could be funny*: Liz Carpenter, *Presidential Humor* (Albany, TX: Bright Sky Press, 2006), 9; author interview with Middleton.

177 *Writing a toast*: "A Celebration of the Life of Peter Benchley."

177 *"I was convinced"*: Author interview with McPherson.

177 *One night in 1968*: Except where noted, the story of Benchley's "firing" comes from the author's interview with Middleton.

178 *"He didn't get paid"*: Author interview with Califano.

178 *"I don't remember that"*: Author interview with McPherson.

178 *Lady Bird would say*: Author interview with Middleton.

179 *"He is one of the last spellbinders"*: Maguire OH, LBJ Library 22.

179 *"I always considered"*: Author interview with Hardesty.

179 *"I want to get my hand"*: Author interview with Duggan.

180 *"No matter how much"*: Kintner OH, LBJ Library, 1.

180 *"He waved his arms"*: Roy Reed, "A New Presidential Style: That Was 'the Real Johnson,' His Old Friends Say," *New York Times*, November 18, 1967.

180 *"pretty darned effective"*: Ibid.

180 *Goddammit, Johnson said*: Author interview with Hardesty.

180 *He never used*: Harry Middleton, *LBJ: The White House Years* (New York: Harry N. Abrams, 1990), 200.

180 *"I think he was especially"*: McPherson OH, LBJ Library, 21.

181 *"And so, my friends"*: Except where noted, the entire account of January 14 comes from Horace Busby, *The Thirty-First of March*, 172–76.

182 *"to read, think, and come up"*: Ibid., 17–19.

182 *Square-faced and quiet*: "Johnson Takes Over."

182 *A heavy smoker*: Busby, *The Thirty-First*, xvi.

182 *Middleton, who not only went on*: Author interview with Middleton.

182 *"You feel each other"*: Busby, *The Thirty-First*, xiii.

182 *"Ultimately, I had fitted"*: Horace Busby LBJ Library oral history interview, April 23, 1981, LBJ Library, 29.

183 *One morning in June 1964*: Valenti, *A Very Human President*, 118–19.

183 *In October 1967*: Busby, *The Thirty-First*, 197–98.

183 *"This is a hell of a note"*: Ibid., 199.

183 *"It just didn't fit"*: Califano, *Triumph*, 269.

184 *"We're not going to let"*: Author interview with Califano.

184 *He preferred to focus*: Author interview with McPherson.

184 *He brought up the subject at Sunday*: Busby, *The Thirty-First*, 210.

184 *"Congress and I"*: McPherson, *A Political Education*, 428.

185 *"Now, I don't want to say"*: Ibid., 433–37.

185 *"That's OK"*: Ibid., 432–38.

185 *"write out for me"*: Busby, *The Thirty-First*, 12.

185 *"You and I"*: Ibid., 192.

185 *"You'd better keep this"*: Ibid., 207.

185 *"If this happens"*: Ibid., 223.

186 *Even as Johnson was still*: All reactions from undated memoranda, "Reactions to Speech" folder, Office Files of Harry Middleton, LBJ Library.

186 *According to Humphrey's autobiography*: Hubert H. Humphrey, *The Education of a Public Man: My Life in Politics* (New York: Doubleday, 1976), 267.

187 *"Afterwards, there were bottles"*: Charles Maguire LBJ Library oral history interview, August 19, 1969, LBJ Library, 15.

187 *The revelry was halted*: Ibid., 17.

6. "CONCERN FOR IMAGE MUST RANK WITH CONCERN FOR SUBSTANCE"

188 *Richard Nixon and Raymond Price*: Raymond Price, *With Nixon* (New York: Viking Press, 1977), 49.

188 *"Only the short ones"*: Ibid., 42.

188 *Nixon had drawn ideas*: Ibid., 43–48.

190 *He read the remarks prepared*: William Safire, *Before the Fall: An Inside View of the Pre-Watergate White House* (Garden City, NY: Doubleday & Co., 1975), 124.

190 *Watching with the rest of the staff*: Ibid.

190 *"opportunist"*: Author interview with William Safire.

190 *Safire had a playful*: Ibid.

190 *he served as a mentor*: Author interview with Lee Huebner.

190 *"I would like to have been"*: Safire, *Before the Fall*, 14.

191 *Nixon next flew on*: William Safire diary, February 27, 1969, Folder 6, "Trips with the President, European Tour, notes, 1969. 'Nixon Diary' notes," Papers of William Safire, Box 108, Library of Congress.

191 *"You could feel the strain"*: William Safire letter to Rowland Evans, March 19, 1971, "Trips with the President, European Tour, Freeman, John, 1971," Papers of William Safire, Box 108, Folder 2, Library of Congress; Safire, *Before the Fall*, 126.

191 *"They say there's a new Nixon"*: Safire, *Before the Fall*, 126.

191 *"That was one of the kindest"*: Ibid.

191 *"That was your crack"*: Safire diary, February 27, 1969.

191 *It was as close*: Ibid.

192 *"He is constantly competing"*: Ibid.

192 *Nixon's statements for the trip*: Safire, *Before the Fall*, 124.

192 *Incredible, the stuff*: Safire diary, February 27, 1969.

192 *With Bob Haldeman, he discussed*: H. R. Haldeman memo to James Keogh and Henry Kissinger, April 28, 1969, "Talking Papers 1970" folder, WHSF Haldeman, Nixon Presidential Materials, Archives II.

192 *"found his own medium"*: William Safire memo to the President, March 20, 1969, Folder 12, " 'Nixon Diary,' Chron. File, 1969 1/2," Papers of William Safire, Box 20, Library of Congress.

192 *"President Roosevelt could never"*: Ibid.

193 *a "workaholic student"*: Author interview with Patrick Buchanan.

193 *"You could trust"*: Author interview with Safire.

193 *"He was more comfortable"*: Author interview with Raymond K. Price.

193 *"My staff was a little"*: James Keogh, *President Nixon and the Press* (New York: Funk & Wagnalls, 1972), 52.

193 *"ornaments he would hang"*: Author interview with Huebner.

194 *"Whenever he was able"*: Keogh, *President Nixon*, 53.

194 *"Anecdotal material"*: White House tapes conversation 483-4, April 20, 1971, Nixon Presidential Materials, Archives II.

194 *An April 14 meeting*: William Safire diary, April 14, 1969, Folder 12, " 'Nixon Diary,' Chron. File, 1969 1/2," Papers of William Safire, Box 20, Library of Congress.

194 *"Nixon was a reflective man"*: Safire, *Before the Fall*, 603.

194 *"It was merely Rose Mary Woods and me"*: Author interview with Buchanan.

195 *"to bring it to the concrete"*: Ibid.

195 *Lee Huebner had met*: Author interview with Huebner.

195 *"Lee was our best guy"*: Author interview with Price.

195 *"I was the utility"*: Author interview with William Gavin.

195 *His arrival on the campaign*: Safire, *Before the Fall*, 59.

195 *"Richard Nixon realized"*: Ibid., 135.

196 *"Sometimes he would have"*: Author interview with Safire.

196 *"It is open season"*: "First Draft/Buchanan" of June 4, 1969, Air Force Academy speech,

Folder 5, "Air Force Academy, Colorado Springs Trip and Commencement Speech, 1969 2/10," Papers of William Safire, Box 65, Library of Congress.

196 *Not wholly satisfied*: Safire, *Before the Fall*, 136.

196 *"The time is ripe"*: Bill Safire memo to the President (via Keogh), May 28, 1969, Folder 5, "Air Force Academy, Colorado Springs Trip and Commencement Speech, 1969 2/10," Papers of William Safire, Box 65, Library of Congress.

197 *"That may seem odd"*: Safire, *Before the Fall*, 137.

197 *Nixon resurrected much of Buchanan's original text*: Buchanan's recollection is that Safire wrote the first draft and that Nixon then called Buchanan in to revise it. "He said it was too soft," Buchanan recalled. It is possible that the president brought Buchanan back in to re-toughen the Safire-Kissinger drafts. (Author interview with Buchanan.)

197 *"Patriotism is considered"*: "Excerpts from President's Speech at the Air Force Academy on Military Critics," *New York Times*, June 5, 1969.

197 *"He did indeed weigh"*: Author interview with Safire.

197 *"He would use that"*: Author interview with Price.

197 *"The other writers knew"*: Safire, *Before the Fall*, 69.

197 *Here was "Nixon at his"*: John Osborne, *The Nixon Watch* (New York: Liveright, 1970), 81.

198 *"the cries of outrage"*: Safire, *Before the Fall*, 141.

198 *"The accurate term"*: Pat Buchanan memorandum for the president, June 6, 1969, private papers of Patrick Buchanan.

198 *"Put yourself"*: Safire, *Before the Fall*, 141.

198 *was "a fanatic"*: William Safire diary, June 5, 1969, Folder 13, " 'Nixon Diary' Chron. File, 1969 2/2," Papers of William Safire, Box 20, Library of Congress.

198 *He scolded . . . "forget 'em!"*: Ibid.

199 *"Since the advent"*: Richard Nixon, *RN: The Memoirs of Richard Nixon* (New York: Grosset & Dunlap, 1978), 354.

199 *"The President is very much"*: Talking Paper, "Re: Meeting with Keogh," September 2, 1969, "Talking Papers 1969" folder, WHSF Haldeman, Nixon Presidential Materials, Archives II.

199 *"What he is looking for"*: Talking Paper, "*NOTE*: To be attached to the first Talking Paper in the KEOGH Folder," September 9, 1969, "Talking Papers 1969" folder, WHSF Haldeman, Nixon Presidential Materials, Archives II.

199 *"It was natural for him"*: Author interview with Price.

200 *"The President says he likes"*: William Safire diary, September 12, 1969, Folder 13, " 'Nixon Diary' Chron. File, 1969 2/2," Papers of William Safire, Box 20, Library of Congress.

200 *The president made sure*: Safire, *Before the Fall*, 172.

200 *"Don't get rattled"*: Nixon, *RN*, 403.

201 *"For perhaps three or four"*: Safire, *Before the Fall*, 533.

201 *"They can't defeat us"*: Nixon, *RN*, 404.

201 *As Nixon worked in solitude*: Ibid.

201 *Senate Republican leader Hugh Scott*: "Massive Pullout in '70 'Possible,' Ford Says," *The Washington Post*, November 3, 1969.

201 *"The 30-minute address"*: "President Polishes Vietnam Address," *The Washington Post*, November 3, 1969.

201 *"Big problem building"*: H. R. Haldeman, *The Haldeman Diaries: Inside the Nixon White House* (New York: Berkley Books, 1995), 122–23.

201 *On October 24, Nixon retreated*: Nixon, *RN*, 408–09.

202 *In the 1968 campaign*: William Safire, *Safire's New Political Dictionary* (New York: Random House, 1993), 708–9.

202 *He later told Safire*: Safire, *Before the Fall*, 174–75.

202 *"The baby's just"*: Nixon, *RN*, 409.

202 *"right down the hall"*: Safire, *Before the Fall*, 176.

202 *"Not many people"*: Ibid., 176–77.

203 *"detailed, building a case"*: Ibid., 174.

203 *"He was a logical student"*: Author interview with Huebner.

203 *" 'Let me make one thing' "*: Author interview with Gavin.

203 *"The most significant characteristic"*: "Talking Paper," June 29, 1970, "Talking Papers 1970" folder, WHSF Haldeman, Nixon Presidential Materials, Archives II.

204 *"Nothing of a substantial nature"*: David Greenberg, *Nixon's Shadow: The History of an Image* (New York: W. W. Norton, 2003), 145.

204 *"There wasn't a thing new"*: Ibid.

204 *"They talked as if"*: Nixon, *RN*, 410.

204 *"Then a plea"*: Haldeman, *Diaries*, 125.

204 *"Very few speeches"*: Nixon, *RN*, 409–10.

204 *"Nixon always had a feeling"*: Safire, *Before the Fall*, 309.

205 *" 'Bring us together' "*: Ibid.

205 *Nixon called Safire on November 4*: Ibid., 177.

205 *"We have got to discuss"*: H. R. Haldeman memo to James Keogh, November 7, 1969, "Talking Papers 1970" folder, WHSF Haldeman, Nixon Presidential Materials, Archives II.

206 *"they were produced under"*: Jim Keogh memo to Bob Haldeman, November 10, 1969, "Talking Papers 1970" folder, WHSF Haldeman, Nixon Presidential Materials, Archives II.

206 *they were oriented more toward*: Author interviews with Price and Huebner.

206 *"Feels our people"*: Haldeman, *Diaries*, 134.

206 *"I know how you and Ray"*: William Safire diary, October 7, 1971, Folder 4, " 'Nixon Diary' Chron. File 1971 2/2," Papers of William Safire, Box 21, Library of Congress.

207 *Safire "is too damn smart"*: White House tapes conversation 594–4, July 28, 1971, Nixon Presidential Materials, Archives II.

207 *"it repels him"*: White House tapes conversation 536-16, July 31, 1971, Nixon Presidential Materials, Archives II.

207 *"The President has the feeling"*: Talking Paper "Re: Speech Writers," December 15, 1969, "Talking Papers 1970" folder, WHSF Haldeman, Nixon Presidential Materials, Archives II.

207 *Preparation for the 1970 State of the Union*: Keogh, *President Nixon*, 50.

207 *"Why do we have"*: William Gavin, "His Heart's Abundance: Notes of a Nixon Speechwriter," *Presidential Studies Quarterly* (June 2001).

207 *"Led to a new harangue"*: Haldeman, *Diaries*, 142–43.

207 *Powered by White House*: Author interview with Price.

208 *"All this hemming"*: Haldeman, *Diaries*, 145.

208 *By Wednesday*: Haldeman, *Diaries*, 145; Keogh, *President Nixon*, 50–51.

208 *He wrote notes*: Richard Reeves, *President Nixon: Alone in the White House* (New York: Simon & Schuster, 2001), 161.

208 *Nixon returned to the White House*: Haldeman, *Diaries*, 146; Reeves, *Alone*, 162; Keogh, *President Nixon*, 51.

209 *It was a public relations triumph*: Reeves, *Alone*, 194.

209 *But the seeds were already*: Ibid., 192.

209 *The arguments were not new*: Ibid., 197–204.

209 *"This was not the time"*: Safire, *Before the Fall*, 183.

209 *"and said marry this"*: Author interview with Buchanan.

210 *They went through eight drafts*: Safire, *Before the Fall*, 183; Reeves, *Alone*, 205; Haldeman, *Diaries*, 189.

210 *"Doesn't this fly"*: Safire, *Before the Fall*, 187

210 *"The speech gave"*: Ibid., 183.

210 *drained "the venom"*: Price, *With Nixon*, 160.

210 *The National Security Council had tried*: Al Haig memo to Bob Haldeman, re "Foreign Policy Writer," April 3, 1970, "Talking Papers 1970" folder, WHSF Haldeman, Nixon Presidential Materials, Archives II.

211 *"My monthly question"*: H. R. Haldeman memo to General Haig, May 5, 1970, "Talking Papers 1970" folder, WHSF Haldeman, Nixon Presidential Materials, Archives II.

211 *"It is getting kind of"*: H. R. Haldeman memo to General Haig, September 14, 1970, "Talking Papers 1970" folder, WHSF Haldeman, Nixon Presidential Materials, Archives II.

211 *"I hate to keep"*: H. R. Haldeman memo to General Haig, October 1, 1970, "Talking Papers 1970" folder, WHSF Haldeman, Nixon Presidential Materials, Archives II.

211 *"The first draft"*: "Talking Paper—General Haig," Re: "Speeches," October 24, 1970, "Talking Papers 1970" folder, WHSF Haldeman, Nixon Presidential Materials, Archives II.

211 *"My speech & idea group"*: Reeves, *Alone*, 22.

211 *" 'the little things' "*: Alexander P. Butterfield memo to Robert Finch et al., February 6, 1971, Folder 1, "Anecdotes + 'Color Reports Miscellaneous, 1970–71 1/2," Papers of William Safire, Box 29, Library of Congress.

211 *One was John Andrews*: Author interview with John Andrews.

212 *"He would come reliably"*: Author interview with Noel Koch.

212 *"Which wasn't particularly"*: Author interview with Andrews.

212 *"He's got a sense"*: White House tapes conversation 457-1, February 24, 1971, Nixon Presidential Materials, Archives II.

212 *"Tell everyone"*: John Ehrlichman, *Witness to Power* (New York: Simon & Schuster, 1982), 268.

212 *"We've been searching"*: Price, *With Nixon*, 196.

212 *Nixon had awakened*: William Safire diary, January 24, 1971, Folder 3, " 'Nixon Diary' Chron. file 1971 1/2," Papers of William Safire, Box 21, Library of Congress.

213 *On January 19*: Larry Higby memo to William Safire et al., January 19, 1971, Folder 4, "State of the Union messages, 1971 Address, 1970–71, Memoranda," Papers of William Safire, Box 103, Library of Congress.

213 *"Somebody is using your name"*: William Safire memo to Larry Higby, January 20, 1971, Folder 4, "State of the Union messages, 1971 Address, 1970–71, Memoranda," Papers of William Safire, Box 103, Library of Congress.

213 *"Nevertheless, Safire sent*: William Safire memo to Larry Higby, January 21, 1971, Folder 4, "State of the Union messages, 1971 Address, 1970–71, Memoranda," Papers of William Safire, Box 103, Library of Congress.

213 *"How'd you feel"*: William Safire diary, January 24, 1971.

214 *Discussion in mid-November*: Haldeman, *Diaries*, 455–57.

214 *Noel Koch wrote a "barn-burner"*: Author interview with Noel Koch

214 *"Joe six-pack"*: Author interview with Aram Bakshian.

214 *"In one breath"*: Safire, *Before the Fall*, 36.

215 *"It's not simply writing"*: White house tapes conversation 15–196, December 2, 1971, Nixon Presidential Materials, Archives II.

215 *"cooped up"*: Safire, *Before the Fall*, 333.

215 *"I may decide to go"*: White House tapes conversation 15-196, December 2, 1971, Nixon Presidential Materials, Archives II.

215 *"He's really concerned"*: Haldeman diary unabridged CD-ROM edition, January 11, 1972, Nixon Presidential Materials, Archives II.

215 *"This has to be"*: Except where noted, the account of the drafting of the January 25, 1972, Vietnam speech comes from Safire, *Before the Fall*, 398–407.

216 *"All the way through"*: White House tapes conversation 649–1, January 17, 1972, Nixon Presidential Materials, Archives II.

216 *"I dunno"*: Safire, *Before the Fall*, 528.

216 *He hoped to use*: Author interview with Huebner.

217 *"We were"*: Safire, *Before the Fall*, 405.

217 *"Isn't that for the president"*: Ibid., 407.

217 *"It was the usual tirade"*: Haldeman diary unabridged CD-ROM edition, April 12, 1972, Nixon Presidential Materials, Archives II.

217 *"The littler you were"*: Author interview with Huebner.

218 *After dinner that night*: Ibid.

218 *What Huebner did not find out*: Ibid.

218 *"That popped my eyes"*: Author interview with Andrews.

219 *"Don't worry"*: David Gergen, *Eyewitness to Power: The Essence of Leadership, Nixon to Clinton* (New York: Simon & Schuster, 2000), 27.

219 *a former reporter named*: Aram Bakshian oral history interview, University of Virginia, Miller Center of Public Affairs, January 14, 2002, 6.

219 *"brilliant, eccentric"*: Author interview with Peter Robinson,

219 *a great, boisterous laugh*: Author interview with Koch.

219 *"Gergen was a very smooth"*: Author interview with Andrews.

219 *"H & Buchanan—Safire a conservative?"*: Reeves, *Alone*, 569.

220 *"You want to say goodbye"*: William Safire, *Before the Fall: An Inside View of the Pre-Watergate White House* (New Brunswick, NJ: Transaction Publishers, 2005), Preface, xvi.

220 *To hell with it*: Ibid., 7.

220 *"We have a cancer"*: White House tapes conversation 886-8, March 21, 1973, Nixon Presidential Materials, Archives II.

220 *"Had I gone in"*: Safire, *Before the Fall, An Inside View of the Pre-Watergate White House* (New Brunswick. Transaction Publishers, 2005, from the Preface to the Transaction Edition), xvi.

220 *"We are now forced"*: Nixon, *RN*, 803.

220 *Price reluctantly sent*: Price, *With Nixon*, 97.

221 *"Anyone who is not guilty"*: Nixon, *RN*, 836.

221 *On April 15*: Ibid., 834.

221 *Price would remain*: Gergen, *Eyewitness*, 68.

221 *"Look, if we went"*: Stanley Kutler, ed., *Abuse of Power: The New Nixon Tapes* (New York: Free Press, 1997), 350–51.

221 *"Tell him make it"*: Ibid., 351.

222 *"Oh, hell"*: Ibid., 380.

222 *Talk of resignation*: Price, *With Nixon*, 100–01.

222 *"Maybe I should resign"*: Ibid., 101. In his memoir, Nixon recalls saying to Price: "Ray, you are the most honest, cool, objective man I know. If you feel that I should resign, I am ready to do so. You won't have to tell me. You should just put it in the next draft" (*RN*, 849).

222 *Price turned around*: Price, *With Nixon*, 101–02.

222 *Price was relieved when*: Ibid., 103.

223 *Kissinger told Andrews that the key idea*: Author interview with Andrews.
224 *"constant contrition"*: Bill Safire memo for the president, July 12, 1973, Folder 5, "Watergate, memoranda and notes, 1973," Papers of William Safire, Box 115, Library of Congress.
224 *"The great lesson of Watergate"*: Ibid.
225 *a "thoughtful speech"*: William Safire, *"Lessons of Watergate," New York Times*, August 20, 1973.
226 *"Journalists are always saying"*: Author interview with Huebner.
226 *"I was not effective"*: Author interview with Andrews.
226 *"Emotions ran high"*: John Coyne, *Fall In and Cheer* (New York: Doubleday & Co., 1979), 39.
226 *A few minutes before 6:30 pm*: Price, *With Nixon*, 323.
227 *"We need a resignation speech"*: Ibid., 324.
227 *"want Price to write"*: Nixon, *RN*, 1057.
227 *Price started working*: Price, *With Nixon*, 327–28; Bob Woodward, and Carl Bernstein, *The Final Days* (New York: Simon & Schuster, 1976), 378.
227 *As he wrote*: Price, *With Nixon*, 328–29.
227 *Buchanan banged his clenched*: Woodward and Bernstein, *Final Days*, 340.
227 *Saturday brought word*: Price, *With Nixon*, 330–32; author interview with Price.
228 *Nixon had viewed*: Woodward and Bernstein, *Final Days*, 37–38.
228 *The two men met on Sunday*: Price, *With Nixon*, 332–33.
228 *Sitting in his Executive Office Building*: Nixon, *RN*, 1067.
228 *"As I believe you know"*: Price, *With Nixon*, 339–40.
228 *They worked down the hall*: Ibid., 341.
229 *"We wander from office"*: Coyne, *Fall In and Cheer*, 31.
229 *Safire wandered through*: Price, *With Nixon*, 346–47.
229 *"Look"*: Author interview with John Coyne.

7. "GO BACK AND GIVE ME *ONE* SPEECH, NOT *TWO* SPEECHES"

230 *As the Nixon administration*: Author interview with Robert Orben,
230 *And Ford was scheduled*: Gerald Ford, *A Time to Heal: The Autobiography of Gerald R. Ford* (New York: Harper & Row, 1979), 25.
230 *On the afternoon of August 5*: The account of Orben and Hartmann on August 5 and Orben's first meeting with Ford are drawn from the author's interview with Orben.
231 *"Let me assure"*: Ford, *A Time*, 119.
231 *Watching the news*: Author interview with Orben.
232 *"How much time"*: Robert T. Hartmann, *Palace Politics: An Inside Account of the Ford Years* (New York: McGraw-Hill, 1980), 151.
232 *That appointment*: Ford, *A Time*, 118.
232 *"brusque"*: Ibid., 1.
232 *He proudly kept*: John Hersey, *The President: A minute-by-minute account of a week in the life of Gerald Ford* (New York: Alfred A. Knopf, 1975), 116.
232 *"Beneath that was a very"*: Author interview with Jack Marsh.
232 *"Bob Hartmann may have"*: Sally Quinn, "The In (Fighting), Out (Bursts), Up (Swings), Down (Slides), and Other Times of R. T. Hartmann, Presidential Adviser," *The Washington Post*, November 24, 1974.
233 *"Sweet Ol' Bob"*: Alexander M. Haig, Jr., *Inner Circles: How America Changed the World* (New York: Warner Books, 1992), 511.

233 *"suspicious of everyone"*: Ford, *A Time*, 6.

233 *"You don't suspect"*: Ibid., 148.

233 *"an uncanny ability"*: Ibid., 32.

233 *At three o'clock*: Hartmann, *Palace Politics*, 153.

233 *"The Bible upon which"*: Hartmann makes no mention of this potential opening in his *Palace Politics*. That account has him writing the notes and then typing up the speech almost in its final form. The typed page with the opening verse from the Bible is in Hartmann's "8/9/74—Oath of Office" folder in the Gerald R. Ford Library. It makes no sense that he would write out the whole speech and then make a fresh start; rather, it seems safe to assume that the Bible opening was an aborted first go.

233 *"It is difficult"*: Hartmann, *Palace Politics*, 160n.

234 *"didn't struggle"*: Ibid., 154, 159.

234 *after almost eight hundred days*: "Time for Healing," *Time*, August 19, 1974.

234 *Arriving late*: John Coyne, *Fall In and Cheer* (New York: Doubleday & Co., 1979), 102.

235 *Newly minted*: Fred Barnes, "Nixon Holdovers, Ford Aides at Odds," *Washington Star*, August 30, 1974.

235 *Orben would ask if*: Author interview with Orben.

235 *Another new speechwriter*: Hartmann, *Palace Politics*, 106.

235 *"an older man"*: Coyne, *Fall In*, 90.

235 *At Christmastime*: Note from Paul Theis to the White House Telephone Operators, undated, "Dec. 1974 (2)" folder, Theis and Orben Files, Gerald Ford Library.

236 *"Hiya fellas!"*: Author interview with John Casserly.

236 *The other new scribe*: Author interview with Kaye Pullen,

236 *"is the best of the old speechwriters"*: Robert Hartmann memo to President Ford, December 9, 1974, "Editorial and speechwriting staff—reorganization" folder, Hartmann Papers, Gerald Ford Library.

236 *The Atlantic City reference*: John Robert Greene, *The Presidency of Gerald R. Ford* (Lawrence: University Press of Kansas, 1995), 13.

236 *Bakshian liked the fact*: Aram Bakshian oral history interview, University of Virginia, Miller Center of Public Affairs, January 14, 2002, 8.

237 *"Ford was not oratorical"*: Author interview with Marsh.

237 *"His approach to a speech"*: Hartmann, *Palace Politics*, 384.

237 *"Ford, he told us"*: Coyne, *Fall In*, 90.

237 *"Kids in college today"*: Hartmann, *Palace Politics*, 218.

238 *The press called the OMB*: Carol Gelderman, *All the President's Words: The Bully Pulpit and the Creation of the Virtual Presidency* (New York: Walker & Co., 1997), 126–27.

238 *"The Praetorian pattern"*: Hartmann, *Palace Politics*, 219.

238 *Ford held his first presidential*: Ford, *A Time*, 158.

238 *"Mr. President, you'll have to expect"*: Ibid., 161.

239 *"What's the rush"*: Hartmann, *Palace Politics*, 264.

239 *St. John's*: Ford, *A Time*, 175; Hartmann, *Palace Politics*, 266.

239 *In New York City*: Author interview with Orben.

240 *" 'Surprise', 'stunning' pardon"*: Weekend News Review, September 9, 1974, "9/8/74 Pardon Statement" folder, Hartmann Papers, Gerald Ford Library.

240 *"asshole"*: Barry Werth, *31 Days* (New York: Doubleday, 2006), 20.

240 *Bridling when Haig continued*: Hartmann, *Palace Politics*, 274.

240 *Haig thought Hartmann was*: Quinn, "The In (Fighting), Out (Bursts) . . ."

240 *Anti-Haig items started*: Ford, *A Time*, 185.

240 *"I guess this goes back"*: Hersey, *The President*, 87.

240 *"Throughout my political career"*: Ford, *A Time*, 185.

241 *"You'll have to let me"*: Haig, *Inner Circles*, 515–16.

241 *Hartmann showed up*: Hartmann, *Palace Politics*, 274.

241 *"that nobody could say"*: John Osborne, *White House Watch: The Ford Years* (Washington, DC: New Republic Books, 1977), 21.

241 *The idea had sprung*: Hartmann, *Palace Politics*, 297.

242 *Ford and his advisers hoped*: Ibid., 296–97.

242 *There were substantive problems*: "White House Issues Slew of Corrections Making Comments of Ford Inoperative," *Wall Street Journal*, October 11, 1974; E. W. Kenworthy, "Ford Energy Plan: Conversion of Oil-Fired Plants to Coal Held Unrealistic by Experts," *New York Times*, October 16, 1974.

242 *Part of the problem*: Rowland Evans and Robert Novak, "Mr. Ford's Economic Program: Born Out of Chaos," *The Washington Post*, October 12, 1974.

242 *"One area in which"*: Donald Rumsfeld memo to President Ford, October 15, 1974, "Staff Secretary Files—White House Operations—Staffing—Presidential Speeches" folder, Jones, Jerry Files, Gerald Ford Library.

243 *"the Ford presidency is never"*: Ron Nessen, *It Sure Looks Different from the Inside* (Chicago: Playboy Press, 1978), 80.

243 *"This is the most ideal"*: Bob Mead memo to Ron Nessen, January 7, 1975, "10/1/74–2/28/75" folder, Subject File Speeches, Gerald Ford Library.

243 *Nessen thought it was*: Nessen, *It Sure*, 81.

244 *"Tonight, if I might"*: 1/11/75 draft of 1/13/75 fireside address, undated, "1.15.75 State of the Union (4)" folder, Hartmann Papers, Gerald Ford Library.

244 *That evening the president*: Nessen, *It Sure*, 82–83.

245 *Once again Rumsfeld, Nessen*: Ibid., 84.

245 *Ford's assessment was*: Ford, *A Time*, 232.

245 *"it seems to me"*: Ron Nessen memo to Paul Theis, January 10, 1975, "State of the Union 1.10.75–1.14.75" folder, SP 2-4.1975, Gerald Ford Library.

245 *"There is no vision"*: Ken Cole memo to Paul Theis, January 10, 1975, "State of the Union 1.10.75–1.14.75" folder, SP 2-4.1975, Gerald Ford Library.

245 *Ford, wearing a blazer*: Nessen, *It Sure*, 84–85.

245 *"Go back"*: Ford, *A Time*, 233.

246 *"It was a long"*: Ibid.

246 *"Now, I want to speak"*: Ibid., 232.

246 *"The President's main problem"*: Robert Orben memo to Bob Hartmann, undated, "Orben, Robert (2)" folder, Hartmann files, Gerald Ford Library.

247 *Ford allowed John Hersey*: Hersey, *The President*, 29–30.

247 *"I am still profoundly"*: Ibid.

247 *"He rarely took the time"*: Hartmann, *Palace Politics*, 384.

248 *"I feel like a man"*: John J. Casserly, *The Ford White House: The Diary of a Speechwriter* (Boulder: Colorado Associated University Press, 1977), 52.

248 *Casserly and David Gergen*: Ibid., 56; David Gergen, *Eyewitness to Power: The Essence of Leadership, Nixon to Clinton* (New York: Simon & Schuster, 2000), 114.

248 *Orben, who thought working*: Author interview with Orben.

249 *"On the House floor"*: Patrick Butler, oral history interview by John Syers, June 27, 1985, "Butler, Pat" folder, William Syers Papers, Gerald Ford Library.

249 *Butler, twenty-five, had watched*: Ibid.

249 *"pick-up team quality"*: Author interview with Patrick Butler.

249 *As the 1976 presidential campaign*: Ibid.

250 *"I had the feeling"*: Bakshian UVA OH, 14.

250 *"We've got a morale problem"*: Paul Theis memo to Robert T. Hartmann, September 18, 1975, "Sept. 1975 (2)" folder, Theis and Orben Files, Gerald Ford Library.

251 *"The speechwriting staff is not"*: Casserly, *Ford White House*, 158.

251 *"Mess privileges were invaluable"*: Author interview with Butler.

251 *Rumsfeld and Cheney had summoned*: Gergen, *Eyewitness*, 114.

251 *Gergen met with Ford*: Aldo Beckman, "Ford Writers 'Blocked' by Inner-Circle Feuding," *Chicago Tribune*, October 13, 1975.

251 *"The president himself is bored"*: Ibid.

251 *Hartmann set Theis*: Paul Theis memo to Robert T. Hartmann, October 13, 1975, "Theis, Paul" folder, Hartmann Papers, Gerald Ford Library.

251 *Gergen's draft included*: Gergen, *Eyewitness*, 115.

252 *Three days later*: Ford, *A Time*, 326–27.

252 *By the summer of 1975*: James Reston, "Anybody *Not* Named George," *New York Times*, September 14, 1975.

252 *The next morning*: Robert Hartmann memo to the president, March 16, 1976, "Editorial and speechwriting staff—reorganization" folder, Hartmann Papers, Gerald Ford Library.

252 *"I have nothing at all"*: Hartmann, *Palace Politics*, 394.

253 *"People will clap"*: Author interview with Orben.

253 *In early October*: Osborne, *White House Watch*, 262.

253 *"An image of an"*: Handwritten note from the president to Robert Hartmann, undated, "1.19.76 SOTU memo to the president" folder, Hartmann Papers, Gerald Ford Library.

254 *"Mr. President"*: Hartmann, *Palace Politics*, 388.

254 *"In case you get back"*: Handwritten note from the president to Robert Hartmann, undated, "1.19.76 SOTU memo to the president" folder, Hartmann Papers, Gerald Ford Library.

254 *When Ford called a staff meeting*: Hartmann, *Palace Politics*, 390.

254 *"It soon became clear"*: Ibid.

255 *"it is too big"*: First draft of State of the Union with president's comments, January 12, 1976, "1.19.76 SOTU president's comments" folder, Hartmann Papers, Gerald Ford Library.

255 *Hartmann worked all of Wednesday*: Osborne, *White House Watch*, 265. Hartmann has a slightly streamlined timeline in *Palace Politics*, but I have utilized the Osborne timeline for a couple of reasons. First, it appears that Hartmann was a main source of Osborne's contemporary account: Osborne quotes Hartmann, acknowledges Hartmann as a source for the piece ("According to a source who could be none other than Hartmann, though I'm not supposed to say so"), and acknowledges in an end note that he was "accused of excessive reliance upon Bob Hartmann"; second, Hartmann's *Palace Politics* timeline has a weekend-to-Wednesday gap.

255 *Cheney had dismissed*: Gergen, *Eyewitness*, 132.

255 *"Roman Numeral Two"*: Author interview with Orben.

255 *The president was not expecting*: Ford, *A Time*, 350. Gergen's account has Cheney asking Ford for permission to produce a second draft (132), but Ford's firsthand account is presumably more authoritative than Gergen's secondhand.

255 *He took the two speeches*: Osborne, *White House Watch*, 265.

255 *"Go through theirs"*: Hartmann, *Palace Politics*, 391.

255 *Ford "was unwilling"*: Hartmann, Robert, oral history interview by Chase Haddix, April 9, 1991, "Hartmann, Robert—Interview with Chase Haddix" folder, Composite Oral History Accessions, Gerald Ford Library, 6.

256 *The showdown came*: Ford, *A Time*, 350; Osborne, *White House Watch*, 266.

256 *"Damn it"*: Ford, *A Time*, 350.

256 *Hartmann took charge*: Osborne, *White House Watch*, 266–67.

256 *Cheney, who had promised*: Hartmann, *Palace Politics*, 394.

256 *"Insofar as I was anything"*: Author interview with David Boorstin.

257 *And while Ford publicly predicted*: "Hoping to Win by Working on the Job," *Time*, January 12, 1976.

257 *Jimmy Carter had emerged*: Christopher Lydon, "Jimmy Carter's Dark-Horse Campaign Adds Gains in New England to Those in the South and Iowa," *New York Times*, November 3, 1975.

257 *Orben hired Al Parsons*: Robert T. Hartmann draft memo to the president, March 16, 1976, "Editorial and speechwriting staff—reorganization" folder, Hartmann Papers, Gerald Ford Library.

257 *He won a narrow victory*: Ford, *A Time*, 375.

258 *"If we consider our goal"*: Bob Orben memo to Robert T. Hartmann, March 26, 1976, "Orben, Robert (2)" folder, Hartmann files, Gerald Ford Library.

258 *"In show business"*: Author interview with Orben.

258 *Butler had not checked*: Author interview with Butler.

259 *Reagan swept all three primaries*: Ford, *A Time*, 389.

259 *"Very, very important"*: President note to Hartmann, June 1, 1976, "7.1–5.76 Bicentennial Speeches (2)" folder, Hartmann Papers, Gerald Ford Library.

259 *"It will be possible"*: Robert T. Hartmann memo to the president, June 8, 1976, "7.1–5.76 Bicentennial Speeches—President's notebook 2nd copy (1)" folder, Hartmann Papers, Gerald Ford Library.

260 *"What I'm going to say next"*: David Hume Kennerly, *Shooter* (New York: Newsweek Books, 1979), 213.

260 *One critic*: Author interview with Craig Smith.

261 *"Jimmy Carter's open espousal"*: Kenneth A. Briggs, "Carter's Evangelism Putting Religion into Politics for First Time Since '60," *New York Times*, April 11, 1976.

261 *"Righteous Ford"*: Kurt Ritter and Martin J. Medhurst, eds., *Presidential Speechwriting: From the New Deal to the Reagan Revolution and Beyond* (College Station: Texas A&M University Press, 2003), 151, 163.

261 *Hartmann had received*: Memo, Jim Connor to Doug Smith, June 24, 1976, Hartmann Papers, Box 185, 7.1–5.76 Bicentennial Speeches—president's notebook (1), Gerald Ford Library.

261 *"Excellent"*: Robert Hartmann memo to the president with Ford markings, June 8, 1976, "7.1–5.76 Bicentennial Speeches (3)" folder, Hartmann Papers, Gerald Ford Library.

262 *"To me it was a lot"*: Hartmann, *Palace Politics*, 400–01.

262 *"The lesson of the Bicentennial"*: Robert Hartmann memo to the president, July 13, 1976, "President" folder, Hartmann Files, Gerald Ford Library.

263 *He attached a list*: Hartmann, *Palace Politics*, 400–01; memo, Robert T. Hartmann to the president, July 13, 1976, "President" folder, Hartmann Files, Gerald Ford Library.

263 *"Since 1956"*: Ford handwritten note, August 9, 1976, "8.19.76—Republican Nomination Acceptance Speech (4)" folder, Hartmann Papers, Gerald Ford Library.

263 *What the speech needed*: Hartmann, *Palace Politics*, 401.

263 *"to reassert America's leadership"*: David Boorstin memo to Robert Hartmann, August 9, 1976, "8.19.76—Republican Nomination Acceptance Speech (4)" folder, Hartmann Papers, Gerald Ford Library.

263 *Charles McCall*: Charles McCall memo to Robert Hartmann, August 9, 1976, "8.19.76—Republican Nomination Acceptance Speech (4)" folder, Hartmann Papers, Gerald Ford Library.

263 *"take the unprecedented step"*: Craig Smith memo to Robert Hartmann, August 6, 1976, "8.19.76—Republican Nomination Acceptance Speech (4)" folder, Hartmann Papers, Gerald Ford Library.

263 *Hartmann thought this last*: Hartmann, *Palace Politics*, 401.

263 *Ford had rehearsed*: Ford, *A Time*, 404–05.

264 *Jack Marsh*: Author interview with Marsh.

264 *"And I will tell you"*: Ford, *A Time*, 405.

264 *"fine craftsmanship is always"*: Pat Butler memo to Robert Hartmann, August 24, 1976, "Campaign speeches and debates—speechwriters recommendations" folder, Hartmann Files, Gerald Ford Library.

264 *"a limited number"*: David Boorstin memo to Robert Hartmann, August 24, 1976, "Campaign speeches and debates—speechwriters recommendations" folder, Hartmann Files, Gerald Ford Library.

264 *George Denison*: George Denison memo to Robert Hartmann, August 24, 1976, "Campaign speeches and debates—speechwriters recommendations" folder, Hartmann Files, Gerald Ford Library.

264 *"one major speech a week"*: Bob Orben memo to Robert T. Hartmann, August 24, 1976, "Campaign speeches and debates—speechwriters recommendations" folder, Hartmann Files, Gerald Ford Library.

265 *"As I recall"*: Author interview with Butler.

265 *"Ford was in real control"*: Syers-Butler OH.

266 *Ford was scheduled to speak*: Author interview with Butler.

267 *"You're on such a treadmill"*: Author interview with Orben.

8. "DON'T GIVE ANY EXPLANATION. JUST SAY I CANCELLED

THE DAMN SPEECH"

268 *Patrick Anderson*: "Waltzing into Office," *Time*, January 31, 1977.

268 *his precise, right-slanting handwriting*: Handwritten inaugural draft, undated, "[Inaugural Speech Drafts—Notes and Suggestions] [1]" folder, Office of Staff Secretary, Jimmy Carter Library.

268 *Carter had written*: Ibid.

268 *He was rearranging*: "Waltzing into Office."

268 *"Carter thinks in lists"*: James Fallows, "The Passionless Presidency," *The Atlantic* (May 1979).

269 *"prepare simple* list": Handwritten note from Carter to Jim Fallows, undated, "Speeches—Preparation of (Guidance) 1/1/77–5/31/80" folder, Speechwriters, Subject File, Jimmy Carter Library.

269 *"only a few sentences"*: "Waltzing into Office."

269 *touched him "most of all"*: Jimmy Carter, *Keeping Faith: Memoirs of a President* (Fayetteville: University of Arkansas Press, 1995), 21.

269 *"over and over"*: Rosalyn Carter, *First Lady from Plains* (Boston: Houghton Mifflin, 1984), 4.

269 *"In simplistic terms"*: Jerry Rafshoon memo to Jimmy Carter, re: "Inaugural Address," January 4, 1977, "[Inaugural Speech Drafts—Notes and Suggestions] [2]" folder, Office of Staff Secretary, Jimmy Carter Library.

269 *The president-elect sent a draft*: James Fallows oral history interview, November 14, 1978, Jimmy Carter Library, 11.
269 *wearing a three-piece business*: James Wooten, "A Moralistic Speech: Nation's Spiritual Lineage Is Stressed—New Leader Pays Tribute to Ford," *New York Times*, January 21, 1977.
269 *Carter had been warned*: Carter, *Keeping Faith*, 22.
270 *"With his sense of the moment"*: Hedrick Smith, "A Call to the American Spirit," *New York Times*, January 21, 1977.
270 *"The more familiar"*: Jim Fallows memo to the president, re: "Two Questions on Speechwriting," January 21, 1977, "Speeches—Preparation of (Guidance) 1/1/77–5/31/80" folder, Speechwriters, Subject File, Jimmy Carter Library.
270 *"it was clear to me"*: Fallows OH, 6.
270 *"tall, slim, boyish-looking"*: Martin Schram, "Wondering Why Carter Remains Speechless," *Newsday*, December 11, 1977.
270 *"boyish-faced"*: James T. Wooten, "Carter Led a 'Writers Collective,'" *New York Times*, January 22, 1978.
270 *"Fallows is bright"*: William Greider, "The Seductions of White House Powers," *Washington Post*, March 20, 1977.
271 *Jerry Doolittle had worked*: Author interview with Jerry Doolittle,
271 *The only member*: Author interview with Achsah Nesmith,
271 *"He looked hurt"*: Achsah Nesmith typed notes, starting "The President's speechmaking and his speeches," undated, "In-House—[Memos and Drafts, 3/8/77–6/8/79]" folder, Speechwriters, Nesmith, Jimmy Carter Library.
271 *"were—for the most part"*: Author interview with Hendrik Hertzberg,
272 *it was the Carters' first*: Donnie Radcliffe, "Carter and Congress: Leaving Them Laughing," *The Washington Post*, January 27, 1977.
272 *The mantle*: Author interview with Doolittle.
272 *"Oh shit"*: Ibid.
272 *"In an evening where"*: Radcliffe, "Carter and Congress: Leaving Them Laughing."
272 *Doolittle received plaudits*: Author interview with Doolittle.
273 *"Jim, Very poor"*: Jim Fallows memo to the president, with Jimmy Carter handwritten reply on it, January 25, 1977, "Memoranda: Fallows, Jim, 1/21/77–5/20/77" folder, Jody Powell Papers, Jimmy Carter Library.
273 *"Working people understand"*: Fallows, "The Passionless Presidency."
273 *The president was wearing a beige*: "Warm Words from Jimmy Cardigan," *Time*, February 14, 1977.
273 *"the most memorable symbol"*: Ibid.
274 *"Brzezinski tended"*: Carter speechwriters oral history interview, December 3 and 4, 1981, University of Virginia, Miller Center for Public Affairs, on file at Jimmy Carter Library, 22.
274 *"President Carter has concluded"*: David Binder, "President to Ask Broader System of U.S. Alliances," *New York Times*, May 22, 1977.
274 *"Carter seemed to me"*: Author interview with Doolittle.
275 *"In the past"*: Jerry Doolittle memo to Jim Fallows, undated, "Speechwriters, [5/3/77–5/27/77]" folder, Saar and Sandage, Jimmy Carter Library.
275 *"as the end result"*: Author interview with Hertzberg.
276 *"obvious intensity and feeling"*: "Plain Talk About America's Global Role," *Time*, June 6, 1977.
276 *"President Carter has left many"*: Murrey Marder, "Test of Carter's 'Feel Good' Foreign Policy Is Workability," *The Washington Post*, May 24, 1977.
276 *"the reality of the military"*: "A Great Debate," editorial, *The Washington Post*, June 12, 1977.
277 *"All the recent policy statements"*: Achsah Nesmith memorandum to the president, July 15,

1977, "[Chronology]—Green Chrons—[7/1/77–9/28/77]" folder, Speechwriters, Fallows, Jimmy Carter Library.

277 *"scheduling complaint"*: Jim Fallows cover note to Rick, July 18, 1977, "[Chronology]—Green Chrons—[7/1/77–9/28/77]" folder, Speechwriters, Fallows, Jimmy Carter Library.

277 *"You can arrange"*: Author interview with Nesmith.

277 *"He did not particularly"*: Author interview with Hertzberg.

277 *"The President believes"*: James T. Wooten, "The President as Orator: His Deliberate Style Appears to Run Counter to Inspiration," *New York Times*, January 26, 1978.

278 *But his ad-libbed remarks*: Jim Fallows memo to the president, October 25, 1977, "[Chronology]—Green Chrons—[10/1/77–12/28/77]" folder, Speechwriters, Fallows, Jimmy Carter Library.

278 *"Carter, on Six-State Trip"*: James T. Wooten, "Carter, on Six-State Trip, Defends Policies, But Avoids the Jobs Bill," *New York Times*, October 22, 1977.

278 *"As you know"*: Jim Fallows memo to the president, October 25, 1977.

278 *"While Arthur Ashe"*: Jerry Doolittle memo to the president, October 25, 1977, "Speeches—Preparation of (Guidance) 1/1/77–5/31/80" folder, Speechwriters, Subject File, Box 28, Jimmy Carter Library.

279 *"There's a real aversion"*: Schram, "Wondering Why Carter Remains Speechless."

279 *Richard Goodwin*: Fallows OH, 11.

279 *"In the unwritten book"*: Hugh Sidey, "The Trouble with Loose Lingo," *Time*, November 21, 1977.

279 *"The talk around town"*: Nicholas von Hoffman, "Carter's Energy Speech: A Fumbling Attempt to Rally the Nation," *Washington Post*, November 16, 1977.

280 *The speech marked a turning point*: Fallows OH, 11.

280 *"There is a silver lining"*: Jim Fallows note, undated "Speeches—Preparation of (Guidance) 1/1/77–5/31/80" folder, Speechwriters, Subject File, Jimmy Carter Library.

280 *"From time to time"*: Jerry Doolittle oral history interview, December 25, 1978, Jimmy Carter Library, 3–4.

280 *"Morale in this department"*: Hendrik Hertzberg unpublished diary.

280 *"the President will be judged"*: Jim Fallows memo to Jody Powell, December 2, 1977, "Speechwriters, [Chronology]—Green Chrons—[10/1/77–12/28/77]" folder, Fallows, Jimmy Carter Library.

281 *"That is part of the difficulty"*: Schram, "Wondering Why Carter Remains Speechless."

281 *He drafted it in consultation*: Hertzberg diary; Curtis Wilkie, "Zbig Brzezinski: That Spells Clout," *Boston Globe*, January 15, 1978; Hendrik Hertzberg oral history interview, December 10, 1980, Jimmy Carter Library, 15–16.

282 *"The idea of me sitting"*: Hertzberg diary.

282 *The next day*: Wilkie, "Zbig Brzezinski: That Spells Clout."

282 *Hertzberg eventually conceded*: Hertzberg OH, 15–16.

282 *"Your speech"*: Hertzberg diary.

282 *"We were kind of allied"*: Author interview with Hertzberg.

282 *The speechwriters eventually*: Speechwriters OH, 49.

282 *Two days after Hertzberg's run-in*: Hertzberg diary.

283 *"I worry"*: Ibid.

283 *"Every reforming President"*: Rick Hertzberg memo to Jim Fallows, January 5, 1978, " 'Beloved Community,' 1/3/78–1/5/78" folder, Speechwriters, Subject File, Jimmy Carter Library.

284 *"needs a lot of work"*: Handwritten note from President Carter to Jim Fallows, undated, "State of the Union [Address], 1978, "Beloved Community" [2]" folder, Speechwriters, Subject File, Jimmy Carter Library.

284 *Fallows had put in thematic*: Hertzberg diary.

284 *"Whenever he edited"*: Fallows, "The Passionless Presidency."

284 *"If you sent a speech"*: Author interview with Bernie Aronson.

284 *"He distrusted rhetoric"*: Author interview with Nesmith.

284 *"yes, he capitalized" . . . At one point*: Hertzberg diary.

285 *coming so soon after Vietnam*: Edwin Warner, "That Troublesome Panama Canal Treaty," *Time*, October 31, 1977.

285 *"We bought it"*: "Panama Theatrics," *Time*, April 26, 1976.

285 *"He asked me to make it"*: Jim Fallows note to the First Lady, January 27, 1978, "2/1/78–Fireside Chat No. 4 (Panama Canal), File No. 2 [3]" folder, Speechwriters, Chron. Files, Jimmy Carter Library.

285 *"Having made 20"*: Jimmy Carter handwritten note to Jim Fallows, January 30, 1978, "Panama Canal Fireside Chat, [2/1/78] [1]" folder, Office of Staff Secretary, Jimmy Carter Library.

286 *"That made me almost uniquely"*: Fallows OH, 12.

286 *"He hated it"*: Ibid.

287 *"One of our biggest problems"*: Hertzberg diary.

287 *Rafshoon later recounted*: Gerald Rafshoon oral history interview, September 12, 1979, Jimmy Carter Library, 1.

287 *"developing the themes"*: Martin Tolchin, "Carter Selects Rafshoon to Take Long-Range Message to the Public," *New York Times*, May 19, 1978.

287 *The speechwriters solicited ideas*: Jim Fallows memo to the president, May 23, 1978, "6/7/78—Naval Academy Speech [1]" folder, Speechwriters, Chron. Files, Jimmy Carter Library; Rick Hertzberg et al. memo to the president, May 26, 1978, "6/7/78—Naval Academy Speech [2]" folder, Speechwriters, Chron. Files, Jimmy Carter Library.

288 *On Thursday, June 1*: Carter's daily diary, on file at the Jimmy Carter Library and online at the library's Web site, has Carter meeting Doolittle from 9:35 am to 9:40 am on June 1.

288 *There was a misperception*: Author interview with Doolittle.

288 *"spell out more clearly"*: Carter, *Keeping Faith*, 235.

288 *Carter gave Doolittle a ten-page*: Hertzberg diary; author interview with Doolittle.

288 *He again numbered and wrote*: Handwritten drafts of the speech and notes for the speech, undated, "[Annapolis Speech] [6/7/78] [1]" folder, Office of Staff Secretary, and "[Annapolis Speech] [6/7/78] [3]" folder, Office of Staff Secretary, Jimmy Carter Library.

289 *On Wednesday, June 7*: Terence Smith, "Carter Calls on Soviet to End Confrontation or Risk 'Graver' Strain," *New York Times*, June 8, 1978.

289 *"And now—war!"*: Fallows OH, 11.

290 *"It had an obvious break"*: Fallows, "The Passionless Presidency."

290 *"Mr. Carter's speech"*: Bernard Gwertzman, "Carter on Soviet: An Ambiguous Message," *New York Times*, June 8, 1978.

290 *"Two Different Speeches"*: Murrey Marder, "Two Different Speeches," *The Washington Post*, June 8, 1978.

290 *"should not be subjected to"*: Robert G. Kaiser and Walter Pincus, "Carter as Speechwriter: Limiting Split," *The Washington Post*, June 8, 1978.

290 *"It is precisely"*: Jim Fallows memo to Jerry Rafshoon, June 8, 1978, "Speeches—Preparation of (Guidance) 1/1/77–5/31/80" folder, Speechwriters, Subject File, Jimmy Carter Library.

291 *Fallows sent Carter a letter*: Jim Fallows letter to the president, June 21, 1978, "Administrative Matters—Speech Writing Office [1978]" folder, Rafshoon Files, Jimmy Carter Library.

291 *"I had always been interested"*: Fallows OH, 1.

291 *"The mistake was in failing"*: James Fallows, "The Passionless Presidency II: More from Inside Jimmy Carter's White House," *Atlantic Monthly* (June 1979).

291 *"It is precisely because"*: Jim Fallows letter to Colman McCarthy, September 8, 1978, "[Chronology]—Green Chrons—[7/3/78–12/4/78]" folder, Speechwriters, Fallows, Jimmy Carter Library.

291 *He did not, Fallows told*: Jim Fallows memo to Jody Powell and Rex Granum, August 16, 1978, "Administrative Matters—Speech Writing Office [1978]" folder, Rafshoon Files, Box 22, Jimmy Carter Library.

291 *Fallows made his first trip*: Hertzberg Diary.

292 *"If Jimmy Carter looks out"*: Hugh Sidey, "The Sweet Fruits of Success," *Time*, September 25, 1978.

292 *"Jim wrote a very good speech"*: Hertzberg diary.

293 *The first planning meeting*: Martin Tolchin, "Birth of 'New Foundation': Slogan Almost Discarded," *New York Times*, January 25, 1979.

293 *The writers assembled*: Ibid.

293 *Hertzberg—who had pressed*: Hertzberg diary.

293 *"Can't we do better"*: Author interview with Walter Shapiro.

293 *Fallows was leaving, however*: Tolchin, "Birth of 'New Foundation.'"

293 *Bernie Aronson*: Curtis Wilkie, "Purge Is Denied in Shakeup of White House Speechwriters," *Boston Globe*, November 22, 1978.

294 *Doolittle was shown*: Ibid.

294 *"We need to get"*: Robert Shrum, "Jerry Rafshoon's Ministry of Propaganda," *New Times*, July 10, 1978.

294 *"I've had it with"*: Greg Schneiders note to Jerry Rafshoon, undated, "Administrative Matters—Speech Writing Office [1978]" folder, Rafshoon Files, Jimmy Carter Library.

294 *"volatile . . . hostile, suspicious"*: Patrick H. Caddell memo to the president, December 14, 1978, "State of the Union [Address], 1979 [1]" folder, Speechwriters, Subject File, Jimmy Carter Library.

294 *Carter read the first draft*: Memo to Jerry, Greg, January 2, 1979, "[1/2/79–1/9/79]" folder, Speechwriters, Saar and Sandage, Jimmy Carter Library; Tolchin, "Birth of 'New Foundation.'"

294 *They met for thirty-seven minutes*: Daily Diary of the President, January 2, 1979, Jimmy Carter Library.

294 *"The New Foundation does"*: Hertzberg diary.

294 *Hertzberg had lunched*: Speechwriters OH, 39.

294 *"The idea of a 'new foundation'"*: William Safire, "The New Foundation," *New York Times*, January 25, 1979.

296 *Once, in an attempt*: Hertzberg, *Politics*, 55.

296 *"He regarded the whole process"*: Speechwriters OH, 11.

296 *"My personal guess is"*: Gordon Stewart oral history interview, February 6, 1981, Jimmy Carter Library, 9–10.

296 *"It was a bad scene"*: Hertzberg OH, 6–7.

297 *"For certain aspects"*: Fallows, "The Passionless Presidency."

297 *"It was very, very accurate"*: Author interview with Hertzberg.

297 *"We all have to make"*: Hertzberg diary.

297 *"Do not begin"*: Jimmy Carter, handwritten note to "Jerry & speechwriters," May 3, 1979, "Administrative Matters—Speech Writing Office 1979 [1]" folder, Rafshoon Files, Jimmy Carter Library.

297 *Gordon Stewart*: Author interview with Gordon Stewart.

298 *By mid-May 1979*: Data from the Gallup Poll, compiled by Gerhard Peters for the American Presidency Project—www.presidency.ucsb.edu/index.php.

298 *He trailed*: "He Can Catch Fire," *Time*, May 7, 1979.

298 *The revolution had caused*: "Drive Now, Freeze Later?" *Time*, May 14, 1979.

298 *"In politics—or at least"*: Jerry Rafshoon memo to the president, undated, re: "Style," "Memoranda from Jerry Rafshoon—June, July & August, 1979" folder, Rafshoon Files, Jimmy Carter Library.

299 *His senior advisers had discussed*: Martin Schram, "Color the White House Blue," *Washington Post*, July 1, 1979.

299 *"members are literally afraid"*: " 'Nothing Else Has So Frustrated the American People'" (text of June 28, 1979, Eizenstat memo to Carter), *Washington Post*, July 7, 1979.

299 *"Back home everything is"*: Hertzberg diary.

299 *"Since you left for Japan"*: " 'Nothing Else Has So Frustrated the American People.'"

299 *"The mood in the country"*: Achsah Nesmith et al. memo to Jerry Rafshoon/Rick Hertzberg, June 29, 1979, "Energy, 7/5/79, 6/1/79–7/31/79" folder, Speechwriters, Subject File, Jimmy Carter Library.

300 *Carter returned to Washington*: Speechwriters OH, 62–76; Hertzberg diary.

300 *including a 2:30 pm gathering*: Daily Diary of the President, July 2, 1979, Jimmy Carter Library.

300 *had to be alert not to get*: Hertzberg diary.

300 *It would be his fifth speech*: Michael Waldman, *My Fellow Americans: The Most Important Speeches of America's Presidents, From George Washington to George W. Bush* (Naperville, IL: Sourcebooks mediaFusion, 2003), 238.

300 *"The president will address"*: Hertzberg diary.

300 *"I was just feeling"*: Speechwriters OH, 62.

301 *In a fifteen-minute conference call*: Daily Diary of the President, July 4, 1979, Jimmy Carter Library.

301 *with Hertzberg having dismantled*: Speechwriters OH, 62–76; Hertzberg diary; Hendrick Hertzberg, *Politics: Observations and Arguments, 1966–2004* (New York: Penguin Books, 2005), 61.

301 *"Don't give any explanation"*: Hertzberg diary.

301 *"almost lost control"*: Jimmy Carter oral history interview, University of Virginia, Carter Presidency Project, November 29, 1982, 63.

301 *"I felt a remarkable sense"*: Carter, *Keeping Faith*, 120–21.

301 *"President Carter has reached"*: Tom Wicker, "Carter on the Precipice," *New York Times*, July 10, 1979.

301 *"He said he had a lot"*: Martin Schram and Edward Walsh, "Carter Sees Need to Do Better Job, Counter 'Malaise,'" *Washington Post*, July 10, 1979.

301 *"We were off"*: Speechwriters OH, 75.

302 *"For the last several days"*: Jerry Rafshoon memo to the president, July 10, 1979, "7/15/79—Address to the Nation—Energy/Crisis of Confidence [1]" folder, Speechwriters, Chron. File, Jimmy Carter Library.

302 *Caddell, who had produced*: Waldman, *My Fellow Americans*, 238.

302 *Rumors were spreading*: Speechwriters OH, 66.

302 *Eizenstat argued that*: Hertzberg, *Politics*, 61; speechwriters OH, 72.

302 *Hertzberg worried*: Speechwriters OH, 70.

302 *Stewart kept baiting Eizenstat*: Author interview with Stewart; speechwriters OH, 70.

303 *"made it possible"*: Author interview with Stewart.

303 *Concluding the meeting*: Ibid.

303 *Before joining*: Stewart OH; author interview with Stewart.

303 *Listening to Carter rehearse*: Author interview with Stewart.

304 *"The rhythm of his speech"*: David S. Broder, "After 30 Months, Self-Criticism, Sense of Purpose," *The Washington Post*, July 16, 1979.

305 *The White House received*: Hertzberg, *Politics*, 60.

305 *Carter thought it*: Carter OH, 63.

305 *"On an individual basis"*: "Carter's Great Purge," *Time*, July 30, 1979.

305 *then Caddell used it*: Waldman, *My Fellow Americans*, 238.

305 *"Of all the problems"*: Alonzo McDonald oral history interview, University of Virginia, Miller Center of Public Affairs, March 13–14, 1981, 18.

306 *"Rather, He & I"*: Rick Hertzberg memo to the president with Carter notations, October 7, 1979," "10/20/79—Remarks—Dedication of Kennedy Library, Boston, MA [1]" folder, Speechwriters, Chron. File, Jimmy Carter Library.

306 *Carter sat on a dais*: "The President and the Phantom," *Time*, October 29, 1979.

306 *It was a speech*: Author interview with Hertzberg.

306 *He told Hertzberg*: Speechwriters OH, 11.

306 *"In a press conference"*: Draft A-3 of Kennedy Library speech, with Carter edits, October 16, 1979, "10/20/79—Remarks—Dedication of Kennedy Library, Boston, MA [2]" folder, Speechwriters, Chron. File, Jimmy Carter Library.

307 *"I wish I'd put that"*: Author interview with Hertzberg.

307 *On February 26, 1980*: Adam Clymer, "Reagan Easily Defeats Bush and Baker in New Hampshire," *New York Times*, February 27, 1980.

308 *"We won with"*: Author interview with Nesmith.

308 *"As the first major"*: Hendrick Smith, "Key Victories for Favorites; Carter and Reagan Gain Formidable Advantages," *New York Times*, March 19, 1980.

308 *Hertzberg was jarred awake*: The account of the failed hostage rescue is drawn from Hertzberg diary and Hertzberg, *Politics*, 67–68.

309 *"In reality"*: Hertzberg, *Politics*, 138.

309 *"a great man"*: Ibid.

309 *"All the political dinners"*: Speechwriters OH, 92.

310 *"Chris is no Sorensen"*: Rick Hertzberg memo to Alonzo McDonald, October 4, 1979, "Administrative File—1979, MM, 9/1/79–12/31/79" folder, Speechwriters, Admin. File, Jimmy Carter Library.

310 *They would send*: Speechwriters OH, 92.

310 *"We write the words"*: Rick Hertzberg memo to Hamilton Jordan, October 1, 1980, "Oct 1–3, 1980" folder, Donated Historical Materials, Hertzberg Collection, Chron. Files, Jimmy Carter Library.

310 *The final: New York Times*: Adam Clymer, "Reagan and Carter Stand Nearly Even in Last Polls," *New York Times*, November 3, 1980.

310 *"There was no longer"*: Speechwriters OH, 101–02.

310 *It was, Stewart recalled*: Author interview with Stewart.

311 *"Rick—not bad"*: Hertzberg, *Politics*, 138.

9. THE MUSKETEERS

312 *He drew lines*: Author interview with Landon Parvin.

312 *When a sentence*: Speech cards for first inaugural, White House Office of Records Management (hereafter WHORM): SP100 begin-01299, Ronald Reagan Library.

312 *Reagan had handed*: Richard Reeves, *President Reagan: Triumph of Imagination* (New York: Simon & Schuster, 2005, cited hereafter as Reeves), 4.

313 *He wanted themes*: Lou Cannon, *President Reagan: The Role of a Lifetime* (New York: Touchstone, 1992, cited hereafter, as Cannon), 97.

313 *"This ceremony itself"*: Reeves, 4–5.

313 *"As God watches over us"*: Cannon, 97.

314 *"My Pledge"*: Ibid., 98.

314 *When Khachigian asked*: Ibid., 99.

314 *His edits tightened*: Speech cards for first inaugural, WHORM: SP100 begin-01299, Ronald Reagan Library.

315 *"Ronald Reagan has a sense"*: Cannon, 99–100.

315 *where they would remain undisturbed*: The inaugural file at the Ronald Reagan Library has a letter dated January 29, 1985, saying: "Attached are the speech cards from the 1981 Inaugural address. They were in the President's Bible." (January 29, 1985, note to David regarding the cards, WHORM: SP100 begin-01299, Ronald Reagan Library.)

315 *It was a working weekend*: Ronald Reagan, *The Reagan Diaries* (New York: HarperCollins, 2007), 4. Reagan's handwritten draft is dated February 14, while in his diary he specifies working on it on February 15 (he describes his February 14 activities as "desk work").

315 *Writing in his rounded, cramped*: Reagan handwritten draft, February 14, 1981, "Address to Joint Session/Economy/(Khachigian) 02/18/1981 Chronological Drafts Final" folders, Speechwriting, White House Office of: Speech Drafts, 1981–1989, Ronald Reagan Library.

316 *"We will fill in"*: Ken Khachigian memo to Ronald Reagan with Reagan notation, and attached draft, February 17, 1981, "Address to Joint Session/Economy/(Khachigian) 02/18/1981 Chronological Draft Final" folders, Speechwriting, White House Office of: Speech Drafts, 1981–1989, Ronald Reagan Library.

316 *"This was the big night"*: Reagan Diaries, 5.

316 *In the senior staff meeting*: Handwritten note marked "Senior Staff," "Senior Staff Meetings [Notes] (January 1981–March 1981)" folder, Khachigian, Kenneth L.: Files, 1981, Ronald Reagan Library.

316 *The following day*: Cannon, 118.

316 *"I can still see it all"*: Author interview with Mari Maseng-Will.

317 *"It's time for Ken to go away"*: Invitation to Ken Khachigian farewell, "Ken Khachigian File," Dolan, Anthony "Tony" R.: Files, 1981–1989, Ronald Reagan Library.

317 *In mid-June*: David Gergen, *Eyewitness to Power: The Essence of Leadership, Nixon to Clinton* (New York: Simon & Schuster, 2000), 179.

317 *Gergen had helped*: Ibid., 163.

317 *"Reagan-bopper"*: Author interview with Anthony Dolan.

317 *"Join the SDS"*: Peter Robinson, *How Ronald Reagan Changed My Life* (New York: HarperCollins, 2003), 212.

317 *"industrial cigar-haze"*: Author interview with Parvin.

318 *"Tony was able to flesh out"*: Author interview with Josh Gilder.

318 *"We considered ourselves"*: Author interview with Dana Rohrabacher.

319 *"We took periodic heat"*: Gergen, *Eyewitness*, 242.

319 *"the wild-eyed, mean dog"*: Juan Williams, "Writers of Speeches for President Claim Force Is with Him," *Washington Post*, March 29, 1983.

319 *the senior staff often tried*: Landon Parvin, oral history exit interview, November 23, 1983, Ronald Reagan Library.

319 *The State and Defense department had each*: Cannon, 302.

320 *the senior staff in October had asked*: Aram Bakshian oral history interview, University of Virginia, Miller Center of Public Affairs, January 14, 2002, 57–58.

320 *"Today was the big day"*: *Reagan Diaries*, 50.

321 *"West Europeans Are Enthusiastic"*: John Vinocur, "West Europeans Are Enthusiastic," *New York Times*, November 19, 1981.

321 *"In the Reagan administration"*: Author interview with Dolan.

321 *A Californian*: Robinson, *How Ronald Reagan*, 213.

321 *and had worked as a press aide*: William Ken Muir, *The Bully Pulpit: The Presidential Leadership of Ronald Reagan* (San Francisco: Institute for Contemporary Studies, 1992), 30.

321 *He would walk*: Author interview with Peter Robinson; Robinson, *How Ronald Reagan*, 213.

321 *Another time he brought*: Author interview with Maseng-Will.

321 *"very much a flower child"*: Author interview with Dolan.

321 *"He once merged"*: Bakshian UVA OH, 33.

322 *"The amusing thing"*: Author interview with Robinson.

322 *He was central casting's idea*: Muir, *Bully Pulpit*, 23.

322 *"bleeding heart conservative"*: Peggy Noonan, *What I Saw at the Revolution: A Political Life in the Reagan Era* (New York: Random House, 2003), 34.

322 *"Green Beret in the Reagan Revolution"*: Gerald M. Boyd, "Hot and Angry Words from the Wordsmiths," *New York Times*, June 12, 1986.

322 *An ardent proponent*: Muir, *Bully Pulpit*, 23.

322 *"You know what I think?"*: Author interview with Bentley Elliot.

323 *He was orderly and precise*: Author interview with Parvin.

323 *Bakshian refused to give up*: Author interview with Bakshian.

323 *"spiced his words"*: Author interview with Elliott.

323 *"That was a pleasant discovery"*: Aram Bakshian, oral history exit interview, August 9, 1983, Ronald Reagan Library.

323 *In his office in the old*: Author interview with Bakshian.

323 *An Air Florida 737*: David Shribman, "A Deafening Roar and Then Icy Silence," *New York Times*, January 14, 1982.

323 *"It just made sense"*: Author interview with Bakshian. Dolan disputes Bakshian's account. He recalls the idea for including Skutnik coming from either himself or an aide to Elizabeth Dole, the director of public liaison, as a mass editing session of the speech was breaking up. Skutnik first appears in a January 22 State of the Union draft marked as having been edited by Bakshian. Dolan maintains that this was an edit of a draft that already had Skutnik. Separate Dolan-only January 22 drafts do not have Skutnik. (Author interview with Dolan; drafts in WHORM SP 230-82 057188-057211 and Dolan's files at the Reagan Library.)

324 *"The best thing"*: Author interview with Bakshian.

324 *"I wonder if I'll ever"*: *Reagan Diaries*, 65.

324 *"tried to return"*: Aram Bakshian memo to the president and draft of speech to Parliament, May 14, 1982, "Address to Parliament: 'The Future of Freedom' (Bakshian) 06/08/1982" folders, Speechwriting, White House Office of: Speech Drafts, 1981–89, Ronald Reagan Library.

324 *the president was unhappy*: "Ash Heap of History: President Reagan's Westminster Address 20 Years Later," speech by Anthony Dolan at the Heritage Foundation, June 3, 2002; text available online at www.reagansheritage.org/html/reagan_panel_dolan.shtml.

324 *Dolan's ongoing feuds*: Author interview with Dolan.

325 *"in the councils"*: Draft of speech with Reagan edits, "Address to Parliament: 'The Future of Freedom' (Bakshian) 06/08/1982" folders, Speechwriting, White House Office of: Speech Drafts, 1981–89, Ronald Reagan Library.

325 *"The reason Reagan"*: Author interview with Dolan.

325 *He viewed the job*: Muir, *Bully Pulpit*, 78.

325 *Oh, replied Dolan*: Author interview with Dolan.

326 *one of "democracy's shrines"*: Speech insert with 3 pm note from Bill Clark, "Address to Parliament: 'The Future of Freedom' (Bakshian) 06/08/1982" folders, Speechwriting, White House Office of: Speech Drafts, 1981–1989, Ronald Reagan Library.

326 *"regimes planted by bayonets"*: Michael Waldman, *My Fellow Americans: The Most Important Speeches of America's Presidents, From George Washington to George W. Bush* (Naperville, IL: Sourcebooks mediaFusion, 2003), 252.

326 *"Soviet Says"*: John F. Burns, "Soviet Says Crusade by Reagan May Risk Global Catastrophe," *New York Times*, June 10, 1982.

326 *"It was a bad week"*: "In Moscow, Maybes Amid the Nos," *Time*, June 21, 1982.

326 *Reading the "indignant cables"*: Dolan, "Ash Heap of History: President Reagan's Westminster Address 20 Years Later."

327 *including the National Council of Churches*: Frank Warner, "The Battle of Evil Empire" (originally "New World Order") *The Morning Call*, March 5, 2000.

327 *the Synagogue Council of America had*: Francis X. Clines, "Reagan Denounces Ideology of Soviet as 'Focus of Evil,'" *New York Times*, March 9, 1983.

327 *"on the B-list"*: Bakshian UVA OH, 47.

327 *Dolan and Rohrabacher went*: Warner, "The Battle of Evil Empire."

327 *"The human conscience"*: Muir, *Bully Pulpit*, 78.

327 *Back came the Soviet Union*: Draft of National Association of Evangelicals address with president's edits, March 5, 1983, Ronald Reagan Library.

328 *"the State Department would have"*: Author interview with Bakshian.

328 *"Bud, we've got to go over this"*: Gergen, *Eyewitness*, 242–43.

328 *"on orders of the West Wing"*: Author interview with Dolan.

329 *"Reagan Denounces Ideology"*: Clines, "Reagan Denounces Ideology of Soviet as 'Focus of Evil.'"

329 *This was not mere good luck*: Author interview with Dolan.

329 *"What is the world to think"*: Anthony Lewis, "Onward, Christian Soldiers," *New York Times*, March 10, 1983.

329 *"The president has every right"*: Bill Peterson, "Reagan's Use of Moral Language to Explain Policies Draws Fire," *Washington Post*, March 23, 1983.

329 *"not presidential"*: Williams, "Writers of Speeches for President Claim Force Is with Him."

329 *"The President knows"*: Ibid.

330 *"I hate to admit it"*: Gergen, *Eyewitness*, 242–43.

330 *"Out of it came"*: *Reagan Diaries*, 130.

330 *Some friends dated the wish*: Reeves, 141–42.

331 *"Let's do it"*: Cannon, 326–31.

331 *"lunacy"*: Ibid., 331.

331 *"We've got to take this out!"*: Reeves, 143.

331 *Secretary of Defense Caspar Weinberger*: Cannon, 332.

331 *"Much of it was to change"*: *Reagan Diaries*, 139.

332 *"I guess it was O.K."*: Ibid., 139–40.

332 *"The Reagan White House was"*: Except where noted, the account of Reagan's talk with the National Federation of Business and Professional Women's Clubs comes from the author's interview with Maseng-Will.

333 *"There's going to be girls"*: Ibid.

333 *Usually when he spoke*: Steven R. Weisman, "Reagan's Joke Sours His Apology to Women," *New York Times*, August 4, 1983.

333 *"very degrading"*: Ibid.

333 *the businesswomen were "wonderful"*: Reagan Diaries, 172.

334 *He did not want to be*: Bakshian exit interview.

334 *"There were many tussles"*: Author interview with Elliott.

334 *"When Aram Bakshian left"*: Dave Gergen memo to Jim Baker and Mike Deaver, October 18, 1983, "[White House Staff Memoranda] Communications (1)" Baker, James A. III: Files, 1981–1985, Ronald Reagan Library.

335 *"Everyone in the White House"*: Author interview with Maseng-Will.

335 *They were also aided*: Author interview with Elliott.

335 *Peggy Noonan was at work*: Peggy Noonan, oral history exit interview, June 18, 1986, Ronald Reagan Library.

335 *A partisan stuck*: Noonan, What I Saw, 32–33.

335 *She would keep it*: Noonan exit interview.

335 *"I guess everyone gets a president"*: Noonan, What I Saw, 34.

336 *"tall and blonde"*: Muir, Bully Pulpit, 26.

336 *"a personality that's larger"*: Author interview with Maseng-Will.

336 *"The rub is"*: Ben Elliott memo to the president, February 23, 1984, Darman, Richard G.: Files, 1981–1984, Box 2, Ronald Reagan Library.

336 *Noonan got the formal offer*: Noonan exit interview.

336 *"I wasn't sure why"*: Ben Elliott memo to Michael K. Deaver, March 16, 1984, Darman, Richard G.: Files, 1981–1984, Box 2, Ronald Reagan Library.

336 *Deaver had a good relationship*: Cannon, 53, 433.

336 *she had opposed Noonan's hiring*: Richard Darman, Who's in Control? Polar Poltics and the Sensible Center (New York: Simon & Schuster, 1996), 191.

336 *Noonan started at the White House*: Noonan exit interview.

337 *"It was a wonderful paradox"*: Author interview with Dolan.

337 *He huddled*: Anthony R. Dolan memo to Richard Darman, undated, Darman, Richard G.: Files, 1981–1984, Box 2, Ronald Reagan Library.

337 *"After that"*: Author interview with Dolan.

338 *"I hired you to write"*: Noonan, What I Saw, 83.

338 *"a little paralyzed"*: Noonan exit interview.

338 *a condition not helped*: Noonan, What I Saw, 84.

338 *She paced*: Ibid., 84–85.

338 *It took fifteen drafts*: Noonan exit interview.

338 *By Noonan's estimate*: Noonan, What I Saw, 75.

338 *"like sending a beautiful"*: Ibid., 76.

338 *"It was really awful"*: Noonan exit interview.

338 *"It was controversial"*: Muir, Bully Pulpit, 37.

339 *The "boom" of the cannon*: Noonan, What I Saw, 88–89.

339 *"I have not incorporated"*: Peggy Noonan memo to Ben Elliott, May 30, 1984, "Pointe du Hoc Address, Normandy, 06/06/1984 (Noonan)(White) (1)(2)" folders, Speechwriting, White House Office of: Speech Drafts, 1981–89, Ronald Reagan Library.

339 *She and Bud McFarlane*: Noonan, What I Saw, 90.

339 *"I prefer 'borne'"*: Peggy Noonan memo to Ben Elliott, May 30, 1984, "Pointe du Hoc Address, Normandy, 06/06/1984 (Noonan)(White) (1)(2)" folders, Speechwriting, White House Office of: Speech Drafts, 1981–89, Ronald Reagan Library.

339 *"But they'll be there"*: Noonan, What I Saw, 86–87.

340 *There had been a fight*: Cannon, 483.

340 *Sitting in her New York apartment*: Noonan exit interview.

340 *"You know, a while ago"*: Noonan, What I Saw, 66–67.

340 *"The senior staff"*: Author interview with Rohrabacher.

341 *"Listen"*: Noonan, *What I Saw*, 230.

341 *"The single greatest mistake"*: Anthony R. Dolan memo to Donald Regan, January 14, 1985, Ronald Reagan Files, Ronald Reagan Library.

342 *and then spent two years studying*: Robinson, *How Ronald Reagan*, 9.

342 *He was an unlikely Reaganaut*: Author interview with Gilder.

342 *"When you're writing"*: Robinson, *How Ronald Reagan*, 64.

342 *Gilder's first assignment*: Author interview with Gilder.

343 *"You pretty quickly understood"*: Ibid.

343 *"Speeches could be yanked"*: Author interview with Dolan.

343 *Surrounding Regan were*: Walter Shapiro, with Margaret Garrard Warner and Thomas M. DeFrank, "Of Mice and Metaphors," *Newsweek*, February 1, 1986.

343 *Noonan and Elliott wanted his speech*: Muir, *Bully Pulpit*, 95–96.

343 *"One of the things"*: Noonan exit interview.

344 *"One odd thing"*: Noonan, *What I Saw*, 218.

344 *"I speak as a friend"*: The complete text of the original Noonan draft of the speech is printed in Muir, *Bully Pulpit*, 213–22.

344 *"It was all unauthorized"*: Noonan, *What I Saw*, 217–18.

344 *"There were times"*: Lesley Stahl, *Reporting Live* (New York: Simon & Schuster, 1999), 230.

345 *"Within a speech you knew"*: Author interview with Gilder.

345 *"Reagan was much more relaxed"*: Author interview with Buchanan.

345 *Buchanan—who did not know*: Stahl, *Reporting*, 231.

345 *"The draft which has been circulated"*: Noonan, *What I Saw*, 218–19.

345 *"We in the United States feel"*: Ibid., 220–21.

346 *"Speech writers aren't supposed to"*: Lou Cannon, "Reagan Aides Clash Over Europe Speech," *Washington Post*, April 30, 1985.

346 *Reagan ended up giving*: Stahl, *Reporting*, 231.

346 *"potentially serious problem"*: Patrick J. Buchanan memo to the Chief of Staff, December 9, 1985, Thomas, W. Dennis Files, OA14157, Box 2 of 7, Ronald Reagan Library.

347 *The pre-summit speech*: Bernard Weinraub, "State of the Union Prompts Debate in White House," *New York Times*, January 28, 1986.

347 *"infantile hopes"*: "Bolshoi," *Washington Times*, November 15, 1985.

347 *"Now, admittedly"*: Patrick J. Buchanan memo to the Chief of Staff, December 9, 1985, Thomas, W. Dennis Files, OA14157, Box 2 of 7, Ronald Reagan Library.

347 *"It didn't meet the specs"*: Shapiro et al., "Of Mice and Metaphors."

347 *"America is back!"*: Draft Revised, January 17, 1986, 11:00 am, WHORM: SP-230-86 (379864), Ronald Reagan Library.

347 *"I believe the President"*: January 15, 1986, 2:00 pm State of the Union draft with Ben covering note, WHORM: SP-230-86 (379864), Ronald Reagan Library.

347 *Buchanan called Regan*: Weinraub, "State of the Union Prompts Debate in White House."

347 *"This speech doesn't read"*: John A. Svahn memo to Ben Elliott, January 17, 1986, WHORM: SP-230-86 (379864), Ronald Reagan Library.

348 *"kudos. You have done"*: John A. Svahn memo to Ben Elliott, with Elliott note in the upper-right-hand corner, January 17, 1986, WHORM: SP-230-86 (379864), Ronald Reagan Library.

348 *The two sides "have resorted"*: Weinraub, "State of the Union Prompts Debate in White House."

348 *"the very tone"*: Shapiro et al., "Of Mice and Metaphors."

348 *"where we're going"*: January 17, 1986, 11:00 am draft of State of the Union with presidential edits, WHORM: SP-230-86 (379864), Ronald Reagan Library.

348 *"Sir, the* Challenger": Reeves, 306–07.

348 *Reagan, standing by the fireplace*: Author interview with Patrick Buchanan.

349 *"handle the horror"*: Noonan, *What I Saw*, 253–55.

349 *"Did you see"*: Ibid., 255.

349 *Noonan was depressed*: Ibid., 255–57.

349 *Pollster Richard Wirthlin*: Ibid., 282.

349 *Some of the speeches*: Author interview with Rohrabacher.

350 *"It was a non sequitur"*: Ibid.

350 *"his voice was hot"*: Noonan, *What I Saw*, 284.

350 *"had surfaced on almost all"*: "Reagan's Speechwriter Says He Was Dismissed in Dispute," *New York Times,* June 10, 1986.

350 *though one of Regan's aides*: Cannon, 178n.

350 *"Every time Ben fought"*: Peggy Noonan, "The Ben Elliott Story: What I Saw at the Funeral," *Wall Street Journal,* June 14, 2004.

350 *"There's no doubt about it"*: Author interview with Buchanan.

351 *"Mr. President, it's a great honor"*: Cannon, 177.

351 *He told Noonan*: Noonan, *What I Saw*, 293.

351 *Elliott later told Lou Cannon*: Cannon, 177n.

351 *"A photo with the speechwriters"*: *Reagan Diaries*, 413.

351 *In early 2006*: Author interview with Parvin.

351 *"The Groundhog saw his shadow!"*: *Reagan Diaries*, 472–73.

351 *He got another phone call*: Author interview with Parvin; Cannon, 734.

352 *"There were shades of Watergate"*: Author interview with Parvin.

352 *Parvin started consulting*: Cannon, 734.

352 *At day's end*: Author interview with Parvin.

352 *"At one point Tower"*: Ibid.

352 *Parvin's biggest problem*: Ibid.

353 *"If the President had to add"*: Author interview with Rohrabacher.

353 *"That's just the natural progression"*: Author interview with Bakshian.

353 *"Our wedding anniversary"*: *Reagan Diaries*, 480.

354 *Robinson's first stop*: Robinson, *How Ronald Reagan*, 95–96; Peter Robinson, "Tearing Down That Wall," *Weekly Standard,* June 23, 1997.

354 *That night, Robinson dined*: Robinson, *How Ronald Reagan*, 97.

354 *Discussion covered an array*: Peter Robinson typed final notes of Berlin Trip, undated, "Remarks: Brandenburg Gate, West Berlin, Germany 06/12/1987 (1)-(3)" folders, Robinson, Peter M.: Files, 1983–1988, Ronald Reagan Library.

354 *"Then one man raised an arm"*: Robinson, *How Ronald Reagan*, 97–98.

355 *"If the Russians are willing"*: Peter Robinson typed final notes of Berlin Trip.

355 *"represented a sudden illumination"*: Author interview with Robinson.

355 *Dolan held a war council*: Author interviews with Dolan and Rohrabacher.

355 *"We knew that there would be"*: Author interview with Rohrabacher.

356 *The speechwriters all worked*: Author interviews with Robinson and Rohrabacher.

356 *The following Monday*: Robinson, *How Ronald Reagan*, 100.

356 *"Well, there's that passage"*: Ibid.

357 *"One day, this ugly wall"*: Robinson, *How Ronald Reagan*, 101.

357 *"We still believe"*: WHORM: SP1150 501964 (1 of 9), Ronald Reagan Library.

357 *They asked*: Author interview with Tom Griscom.

357 *the line "unpresidential"*: Kenneth T. Walsh, "Seizing the Moment; Memorable presidential speeches are few and far between . . ." *U.S. News & World Report,* June 10, 2007.

357 *Progress has been made*: Author interview with Griscom.

358 *Reagan could hear anger*: Cannon, 774.

358 *"science fiction nightmare"*: Author interview with Gilder.

359 *much to the irritation of others*: Author interview with Maseng-Will.

359 *a "tone poem aimed at"*: Peggy Noonan letter to Ronald Reagan, undated, WHORM: SP-1314 (589277) (8 of 8), Ronald Reagan Library.

359 *"They love you, Mr. President"*: Ibid.

360 *"a sort of Jim Cagney"*: Author interview with Maseng-Will.

360 *She spent a week working*: Peggy Noonan handwritten note to Mari Maseng, January 1, 1989, WHORM: SP-1314 (589277) (8 of 8), Ronald Reagan Library.

360 *"The attempt to elicit"*: Noonan, *What I Saw*, 334.

360 *As technicians bustled around*: Author interview with Maseng-Will.

360 *"What is he doing?"*: Peggy Noonan, *When Character Was King: A Story of Ronald Reagan* (New York: Viking Penguin, 2001), 313.

361 *"Reagan at the time shared"*: Cannon, 90.

361 *"When I look back now"*: Author interview with Elliott.

361 *The true believers "help Reagan"*: Robinson, *How Ronald Reagan*, 216.

10. "I'M NOT GOING TO DANCE ON THE BERLIN WALL"

362 *"Know where I want to go"*: Peggy Noonan. *What I Saw at the Revolution: A Political Life in the Reagan Era* (New York: Random House, 2003), 299–300.

362 *He sent a list of words*: Ibid., 304.

362 *Senior campaign officials resisted*: Ibid., 314.

363 *Darman had his own reasons*: Richard Darman, *Who's in Control? Polar Politics and the Sensible Center* (New York: Simon & Schuster, 1996), 191–92.

363 *He met with his speechwriters*: Marlin Fitzwater places this meeting on Bush's first full day in office, but Bush's daily diary has no such meeting; other participants place the meeting later in the term. (Martin J. Medhurst, ed., *The Rhetorical Presidency of George Bush* [College Station: Texas A&M University Press, 2006], 5.)

363 *He gave the writers*: Craig D'Ooge, "History's Wordsmiths; LC's New CD Introduced by Presidential Speechwriters," Library of Congress, *Information Bulletin*, January 22, 1996; author interview with Mary Kate Cary.

363 *I would rather quote Yogi*: Author interview with Curt Smith.

364 *Eisenhower, he said, and Mark Twain*: Author interview with Cary.

364 *"The president detested anything"*: Author interview with Mark Davis.

364 *Bush told them a story*: Author interviews with Smith and Cary.

364 *"No problem"*: Fitzwater quoted in Medhurst, ed., *Rhetorical Presidency*, 5–6.

364 *"He felt that he would be judged"*: Author interview with David Demarest.

364 *Davis asked Bush once*: Author interview with Davis.

365 *Demarest had concluded that*: Author interview with Demarest.

365 *A foreign policy speech would often*: Author interview with Davis.

365 *Davis's turn of mind*: Author interview with Chriss Winston.

365 *"I'm not going to have"*: Ibid.

366 *"the guy you want to be captain"*: Author interview with Ken Askew.

366 *"He had a real writing gift"*: Author interview with Demarest.

367 *"a bunch of bullshit"*: Ibid.

367 *"very important because"*: Author interview with Mari Maseng-Will.

367 *Similarly, Bush's writers' access*: Author interview with Davis; David Demarest memo to Rose Zamaria, April 11, 1989, "Memos—Rose Zamaria 2/89–8/92" folder,

Speechwriting, White House Office of, Administrative Files, George Bush Library.

367 *"There never seems to be enough"*: Demarest memo to Rose Zamaria, April 11, 1989, "Memos—Rose Zamaria 2/89–8/92" folder, Speechwriting, White House Office of, Administrative Files, George Bush Library.

367 *"It was a signal"*: Author interview with Davis.

368 *"Are they important"*: Bernard Weinraub, "Washington Talk; White House," *New York Times*, April 7, 1989.

368 *But Bush kept editing that section*: Author interviews with Winston and Davis.

368 *Chriss Winston watched the speech*: Author interview with Winston.

369 *He swallowed hard*: Bernard Weinraub, "Bush Joins in the Grief Over Iowa," *New York Times*, April 25, 1989.

369 *"I kept rehearsing"*: George Bush, *All the Best, George Bush: My Life in Letters and Other Writings* (New York, Scribner, 1999), 423.

370 *Davis worked on the speech*: Author interviews with Davis and Demarest.

370 *"The President is speaking"*: Bob Simon memo to Ed McNally, June 26, 1989, "Documents 6201–6250" folder, Open P2/P5 documents, George Bush Library.

371 *Solidarity leader Lech Walesa*: George Bush and Brent Scowcroft, *A World Transformed* (New York: Vintage Books, 1999), 122.

371 *The crowd started a chant in Polish*: Author interview with Winston.

371 *At that moment he was sitting*: Author interview with Smith.

372 *There was concern*: Author interview with Davis.

372 *College basketball star Len Bias's*: Author interview with Demarest.

372 *a* Washington Post–*ABC News poll*: "The President's Paradox; Survey Finds Bush Well-Liked But Public Uneasy About Slow Start," *The Washington Post*, May 29, 1989.

372 *The speechwriters and Demarest were*: Author interviews with Davis, Winston, and Demarest.

372 *The drug prop first appeared*: Rough draft of drug speech, fifth draft, August 17, 1989, "Presidential Address on Drugs 9/5/89 [3]" folder, Speechwriting, White House Office of, Speech File Backup Files, Chron. Files, 1989–1993, George Bush Library.

372 *The request had meanwhile reached*: Michael Isikoff, "Drug Buy Set Up for Bush Speech," *The Washington Post*, September 22, 1989.

372 *"Any possibility of you moving"*: Ibid.; "Youth Is Arrested for Selling Crack That Bush Displayed," Associated Press in *New York Times*, September 27, 1989.

373 *That same day, Davis produced*: Drafts 10 and 10A of the drug speech, September 1, 1989, "Presidential Address on drugs 9/5/89 [2]" folder, Speechwriting, White House Office of, Speech File Backup Files, Chron. Files, 1989–1993, George Bush Library.

373 *"Jim: Isn't this a small response"*: Shirley Green memo to Jim Cicconi, September 7, 1989, "Case No. 02138 to No. 048329c4" folder, with September 7 Cicconi note to the president and September 6 Cicconi memo to the president, WHORM: SP series, George Bush Library.

374 *"White House speech-writers"*: Isikoff, "Drug Buy Set Up for Bush Speech."

374 *"I keep hearing the critics"*: Bush, *All the Best*, 441–442.

374 *He was at his desk*: Bush and Scowcroft, *A World Transformed*, 148–49.

375 *"Listen, Marlin"*: Marlin Fitzwater, *Call the Briefing! Reagan and Bush, Sam and Helen: A Decade with Presidents and the Press* (New York: Times Books, 1995), 261–62.

375 *They settled on an informal press*: Bush and Scowcroft, *A World Transformed*, 149.

375 *"Set forth below is a five-point plan"*: Edward McNally memo to David Demarest, November 10, 1989, "Documents 6251–6300" folder, Open P2/P5 documents, George Bush Library.

375 *The speechwriters would keep on urging*: Author interviews with Davis and Lange.
376 *"has the atmosphere of"*: "Memorandum of Telephone Conversation" between President Bush and Chancellor Helmut Kohl, November 10, 1989, 3:29–3:47 pm, available online at http://bushlibrary.tamu.edu/research/pdfs/telcon11-10-89.pdf.
376 *Days passed with little*: Bush and Scowcroft, *A World Transformed*, 149.
376 *House Democratic leader Richard Gephardt*: CNN interview of Bush in September and October 1997, available online at www.cnn.com/SPECIALS/cold.war/episodes/23/interviews/bush/.
376 *"In spite of the Congressional posturing"*: "Memorandum of Telephone Conversation" between President Bush and Chancellor Helmut Kohl, November 17, 1989, 7:55–8:15 am, Box FOIA 99-0393-F Box 1/1, George Bush Library.
377 *"they didn't buy it for a minute"*: Author interview with Davis.
377 *"Please re-do"*: President Bush note to Curt Smith, November 29, 1989, private papers of Curt Smith.
377 *"An old Indian proverb says"*: Draft five of Bush speech on the USS *Forrestal*, November 29, 1989, private papers of Curt Smith.
378 *Winston got a call*: Author interview with Winston.
378 *The speechwriters and Bush*: The account of the speechwriters' cocktails with Bush comes from author interviews with Winston, Smith, and Davis, and from Curt Smith, *Windows on the White House: The Story of Presidential Libraries* (South Bend: Diamond Communications, 1997), 206.
379 *On the morning of June 26*: Darman, *Who's in Control?*, 261–62.
379 *Darman wrote a two-sentence statement*: Ibid.
379 *Fitzwater was given the statement*: Doro Bush Koch, *My Father, My President: A Personal Account of the Life of George Bush* (New York: Warner Books, 2006), 325–26; author interview with Demarest.
379 *Demarest was in the West Wing*: Author interview with Demarest.
379 *"I wish I had never said"*: Koch, *My Father*, 327.
380 *"I was appalled"*: Medhurst, *Bully Pulpit*, 8.
380 *Bush hit a bucket*: Bush and Scowcroft, *A World Transformed*, 302.
380 *Some time after 8 pm*: Author interview with Lange.
381 *The speechwriters wanted to compare*: Author interview with Winston.
381 *the "speech should be about"*: Richard G. Darman note for President and speech outline, August 31, 1990, "Address to Joint Session of Congress 9/11/90 [2]" folder, Speechwriting, White House Office of, Speech File Draft Files, George Bush Library.
381 *the phrase "new world order"*: Ibid.
381 *"William Safire traces"*: Safire, *Safire's New Political Dictionary*, 495–96.
382 *"If he's not Winston Churchill"*: Author interview with Davis.
382 *Bush's edits on the speech*: Draft 3 of September 11, 1990, joint session speech, undated, "9/11/90 Address to the Nation on Persian Gulf Crisis, D.C., Case No. 172735SS [1]" folder, WHORM [c.f.] SP717, George Bush Library.
383 *Watching Bush deliver the speech*: Author interview with Davis.
383 *"The U.N. speech also"*: Edward E. McNally memo to the President and speech draft, September 28, 1990, "United Nations General Assembly Address 10/1/90 [1]" folder, Speechwriting, White House Office of, Speech File Draft Files, George Bush Library.
384 *Someone came up came up with*: Author interview with Winston.
384 *"There's a story"*: Bush, *All the Best*, 480.
384 *"We had a total mixed message"*: Author interview with Demarest.
384 *The speechwriters wrote a half-dozen*: Author interview with Winston; William Safire, "Mr. Bush Hires a Writer," *New York Times*, February 11, 1991.

385 *F-15 Eagle fighter jets*: Andrew Rosenthal, "Visiting U.S. Troops in the Desert, President Talks Tough About Iraq," *New York Times*, November 23, 1990.

385 *With the day's remarks*: Author interview with Demarest.

385 *"Dave, what are you trying"*: Ibid.

385 *"I think of Lt. Mary Danko"*: Reading cards for speech to Air Force personnel, SP740-04, TR090 [3], Thanksgiving Greeting to Air Force, Dhahran Airport, Saudi Arabia, 11/22/90, Case No. 195607SS Scanned, George Bush Library.

386 *Once again, he cut more*: Author interview with Demarest.

386 *"You all bring back thoughts"*: Reading cards for speech on USS *Nassau*, SP740-01, TR090, Thanksgiving Day Church Service, USS *Nassau*, Saudi Arabia, 11/22/90, Case No. 195467SS Scanned, George Bush Library.

386 *"It started to dawn on me"*: Author interview with Demarest.

386 *"The debate has become simplified"*: Bush, *All the Best*, 503.

387 *"There is no way to describe"*: Ibid., 503–04.

387 *And he had McGroarty sitting*: Koch, *My Father*, 349.

387 *"As a young man"*: McGroarty 4:40 pm draft of Gulf War speech, January 15, 1991, "1/16/91 Address to the Nation—Persian Gulf War, (War Began), Case No. 207102 to Case No. 22916" folder, WHORM: SP747, George Bush Library.

388 *"I am about to go to bed"*: Bush, *All the Best*, 504.

388 *The University of Michigan had been one*: Neil A. Lewis, "Friends of Free Speech Now Consider Its Limits," *New York Times*, June 29, 1990.

388 *"The speech to Michigan graduates"*: Maureen Dowd, "Bush Sees Threat to Flow of Ideas on U.S. Campuses," *New York Times*, May 5, 1991.

388 *"People were concerned about the PC bit"*: Aileen Hefferren, "Putting Words in the President's Mouth," *Washington City Paper*, June 21, 1991.

389 *"George Bush and his people"*: Ibid.

389 *Snow brought energy and good cheer*: John Podhoretz, *Hell of a Ride: Backstage at the White House Follies, 1989–1993* (New York: Simon & Schuster, 1993), 71.

389 *"It went too far"*: John E. Yang, "For Bush's Speech, a New Word Order," *Washington Post*, June 22, 1991.

389 *"Prodded by a new chief"*: Kenneth T. Walsh and David Gergen, "Bush's Campaign Tuneup," *U.S. News & World Report*, June 24, 1991.

389 *There were ominous signs*: Podhoretz, *Hell*, 71–72.

389 *"Chicken Kiev"*: William Safire, "Putin's Chicken Kiev," *New York Times*, December 6, 2004.

389 *The paper devoted*: John E. Yang, "President Assails Silencing of Unpopular Views," *Washington Post*, May 5, 1991.

390 *"President Bush today hailed"*: John E. Yang, "Bush Hails 'Power of Free Enterprise,'" *Washington Post*, May 5, 1991.

390 *The speechwriters lunched with Bush*: The account of the luncheon comes from "Meeting with the President; November 20, 1991, 12 Noon–1:20 P.M.," a memo to file by a speechwriting intern, private papers of Curt Smith.

391 *The next day, November 21*: American Presidency Project, adapted from the Gallup Poll by Gerhard Peters. Bush's is available at www.presidency.ucsb.edu/data/popularity .php? pres=41&sort=time&direct=ASC&Submit=DISPLAY.

391 *"I know many of you"*: Tony Snow memo to Speechwriters and Researchers, November 27, 1991, "Memorandum Economic," folder, Speech Writing, Office of, Snow, Tony: Files, George Bush Library.

392 *"Now, look, I have to be careful"*: Smith, *Windows*, 209.

392 *"Because that's the Bush"*: Author interview with Smith.

Notes

392 *When Grant and Demarest met*: Author interview with Cary.

392 *"I remember seeing the look"*: Ibid.

393 *Demarest meanwhile*: Author interview with Demarest.

393 *Bush did not cry*: Smith, *Windows*, 210.

394 *"chaos"*: Author interview with Andrew Ferguson.

394 *"French Breakfast Roll Man"*: Podhoretz, *Hell*, 71.

394 *"a significant number of things"*: Ann Devroy, "Skinner May Seek Shake-Up; Communications Office Seen as Failing Bush," *Washington Post*, January 8, 1992.

394 *Starting with the State of the Union address*: Podhoretz, *Hell*, 199.

394 *"In one of history's most painful paradoxes"*: John Greenwald, "Why We're So Gloomy," *Time*, January 13, 1992.

394 *The speechwriters prepared remarks*: Author interview with Smith.

395 *The State of the Union address was*: Podhoretz, *Hell*, 71–72.

395 *Peggy Noonan was summoned*: Carol Gelderman, *All the President's Words: The Bully Pulpit and the Creation of the Virtual Presidency* (New York: Walker & Co., 1997), 152.

395 *"Rarely had a speech"*: Ann Devroy, "A Declaration of Political War on the Democrats," *The Washington Post*, January 29, 1992.

395 *Noonan was among those*: Fitzwater, *Call the Briefing!*, 324–25.

395 *"He ad-libbed significantly"*: Michele Nix memo to David Demarest et al., February 21, 1992, "Documents 6251–6300" folder, Open P2/P5 documents, George Bush Library.

395 *"The President, Mrs. Bush"*: Dan McGroarty memo to Writers/Researchers, March 2, 1992, "Memorandum Economic," folder, Speech Writing, Office of, Snow, Tony: Files, George Bush Library.

396 *"a comically hangdog"*: Podhoretz, *Hell*, 200.

396 *"very studious, very methodical"*: Author interview with Ken Askew.

396 *Ferguson was told . . . scant attention*: Podhoretz, *Hell*, 199–201.

397 *Demarest was driving in to work*: Author interview with Demarest.

397 *"So in short"*: Ibid.

397 *"a deep-think piece"*: Andrew Rosenthal, "Bush Tries to Shift to Active Style on Domestic Policy," *New York Times*, May 10, 1992.

397 *It acknowledged that racism existed*: Michael Kranish and Peter G. Gosselin, "Aides Split Over Bush Urban Plan," *Boston Globe*, May 17, 1992.

397 *He showed it to Demarest*: Tony Snow memo to Samuel K. Skinner, May 12, 1992, "[Snow—Memos 2/92–1/93]" folder, Speech Writing, Office of, Snow, Tony: Files, George Bush Library.

397 *It was the approach*: Author interview with Demarest.

398 *"What I want from you"*: Podhoretz, *Hell*, 196.

398 *"This is absolutely ludicrous"*: Ann Devroy, "Bush Communications Chief Named; Critics Call Kentucky Friend Chicken Official Too Inexperienced," *Washington Post*, July 9, 1992.

398 *A friend faxed Provost*: Author interview with Steve Provost.

398 *"Provost came from a totally"*: Author interview with Ferguson.

398 *In some instances*: Author interview with Provost.

399 *"When you're in the bubble"*: Ibid.

400 *"My problem, very frankly"*: Medhurst, *Bully Pulpit*, 34.

400 *"The answer, before you change"*: George H. W. Bush letter to Curt Smith et al., June 14, 1993, private papers of Curt Smith.

547

11. "NO, NO, NO, THIS IS A SPEECH—I JUST WANT TO TALK TO PEOPLE"

402 *Vice President–elect Al Gore's head*: George Stephanopoulos, *All Too Human: A Political Education* (Boston: Back Bay Books, 2000), 115.

402 *Work on the speech had begun*: Michael Waldman, *POTUS Speaks: Finding the Words That Defined the Clinton Presidency* (New York: Simon & Schuster, 2000), 20, 27, 30, and 32.

402 *"Our job was to capture"*: Ibid., 30.

403 *They produced at least twenty*: Author interview with David Kusnet.

403 *Kusnet, adapting a slogan*: Waldman, *POTUS Speaks*, 32.

403 *From the late Father Timothy Healy*: Ibid., 35.

403 *"This capital, like every capital"*: Ibid., 33.

403 *Clinton and his staff had decamped*: Ibid., 33–37.

403 *"He's never met a sentence"*: Hillary Rodham Clinton, *Living History* (New York: Simon & Schuster, 2003), 122.

403 *"Clinton never knew exactly"*: Stephanopoulos, *All Too Human*, 200.

404 *"Bill Clinton was equal"*: "Taking Command with a Call to Change," *Time*, February 1, 1993.

404 *a "B+"*: William Safire, "Clinton's Forced Spring," *New York Times*, January 21, 1993.

404 *"Even at their moment of triumph"*: R. W. Apple, Jr., "A Change of Power, But Barely a Break in Stride," *New York Times*, January 21, 1993.

404 *The hope was that the initial*: John F. Harris, *The Survivor: Bill Clinton in the White House* (New York: Random House, 2005), 29.

404 *"ambitious, wide-ranging"*: Waldman, *POTUS Speaks*, 40.

405 *Only occasionally*: Harris, *Survivor*, 19–20.

405 *Clinton's advisers were split*: Ibid., 21, 29.

405 *"Was the budget to be sold"*: Waldman, *POTUS Speaks*, 40–41.

405 *"You know, I never"*: Jeff Shesol, remarks at the Anschutz Lecture, Princeton University, April 22, 2002.

406 *"No one looked"*: Author interview with Kusnet.

406 *"string of cursive 'u's"*: Author interview with Jeff Shesol.

406 *The deadline for getting*: Stephanopoulos, *All Too Human*, 136.

406 *Clinton, Stephanopoulos, and the senior staff*: Ibid., 137.

406 *The reviews were not good*: Author interview with Ted Sorensen.

406 *"You mean"*: Stephanopoulos, *All Too Human*, 137.

406 *"What's bungee jumping?"*: Safire, "Bunjee Jumping," *New York Times*, April 4, 1993.

407 *"one of the worst speeches"*: Margaret Carlson, " . . . And Then Came Carrot Cake," *Time*, March 1, 1993.

407 *The stock market fell*: Allen R. Myerson, "Dow Off 82.94 As Most Stocks Take a Beating," *New York Times*, February 17, 1993.

407 *Thomas "Mack" McLarty*: Waldman, *POTUS Speaks*, 41.

407 *"Hey Gene"*: Carlson, ". . . And Then Came Carrot Cake."

407 *On Wednesday morning*: Waldman, *POTUS Speaks*, 42.

407 *When Clinton arrived*: Carlson, ". . . And Then Came Carrot Cake."

407 *"We never received anything"*: Carol Gelderman, *All the President's Words: The Bully Pulpit and the Creation of the Virtual Presidency* (New York: Walker & Co., 1997), 161.

407 *"lawmakers stir and respond"*: Waldman, *POTUS Speaks*, 43–44.

408 *"The job of the speechwriters"*: Author interview with Antony Blinken,

408 *a "very structured, disciplined form"*: Author interview with Don Baer,

408 *"It's when he gets up there"*: Author interview with Terry Edmonds,

409 *Clinton's speechwriters would eventually*: Ibid.

409 *"that's the way the cookie crumbles"*: Author interview with Jordan Tamagni.

409 *Returning to the White House*: Carlson, ". . . And Then Came Carrot Cake."

409 *"a tremendous writer"*: Author interview with Baer.

409 *Speeches are written by*: Author interview with Jeremy Rosner,

410 *"The reason for doing this"*: Author interview with Anthony Lake,

410 *Rosner sent several drafts*: The entire account of the February 26, 1993, American University speech is drawn from the author's interview with Rosner.

411 *Rosner felt calmer*: Ibid.

412 *"pedestrian"*: Bob Woodward, *The Agenda: Inside the Clinton White House* (New York: Simon & Schuster, 1994), 317.

412 *The Clintons do not like*: Haynes Johnson and David Broder. *The System: The American Way of Politics at the Breaking Point* (Boston: Little Brown, xxxx), 1996, 21–22.

412 *Rosner said that*: Author interview with Rosner.

412 *Rosner and Dreyer were close friends*: Ibid.

412 *With his ponytail*: Johnson and Broder, *System*, 23.

412 *When the president's senior aides*: Stephanopoulos, *All Too Human*, 199.

412 *Clinton wrote all over it*: Johnson and Broder, *System*, 28.

413 *"And [Clinton] said, 'No,'"*: Author interview with Rosner.

413 *"everyone becomes the speechwriter"*: Johnson and Broder, *System*, 28.

413 *Rehearsal extended past 8 pm*: Stephanopoulos, *All Too Human*, 200.

413 *At the rostrum*: Johnson and Broder, *System*, 4–6.

413 *"just sort of whipped back"*: Bill Clinton, *My Life* (New York: Alfred A. Knopf, 2004), 548.

414 *After the longest seven minutes*: Johnson and Broder, *System*, 9.

414 *Clinton's approval rating*: The American Presidency Project has presidential polling data on its Web site, adapted from the Gallup Poll by Gerhard Peters. Clinton's is available at www.presidency.ucsb.edu/data/popularity.php?pres=42&sort=time&direct=ASC&Submit=DISPLAY.

414 *"He gave a thoroughly"*: Maureen Dowd, "Reporter's Notebook; Props and Fuzzy Anecdotes in a Sober, Grown-Up Talk," *New York Times*, September 23, 1993.

414 *"Members of Congress"*: Clifford Krauss, "Reaction; Congress Praises President's Plan But Is Wary of Taxes and Costs," *New York Times*, September 23, 1993.

415 *spending around $100 million*: Neil A. Lewis, "Vast Sum Spent to Sway Health Plan," *New York Times*, July 22, 1994.

415 *It seemed a political*: Harris, *Survivor*, 110–11.

415 *a scant five weeks before*: Ibid., 118.

415 *Carolyn Curiel*: Michael Waldman, *My Fellow Americans: The Most Important Speeches of America's Presidents, From George Washington to George W. Bush* (Naperville, IL: Sourcebooks mediaFusion, 2003), 285–86; William Safire, *Lend Me Your Ears: Great Speeches in American History* (New York: W. W. Norton, 1997), 538–39.

415 *"MLK didn't die"*: Waldman, *My Fellow Americans*, 288.

416 *"The Memphis speech was a hymn"*: Clinton, *My Life*, 560.

417 *I understand that you're not*: Author interview with Baer.

417 *"nice Jewish boy"*: Ibid.

417 *"I don't think [Clinton] liked"*: Ibid.

418 *Part of the problem*: Author interview with Kusnet.

418 *"If you were running against"*: Ibid.

418 *"It was meatball surgery"*: Author interview with Baer.

418 *"There are few voices"*: Author interview with Kusnet.

419 *The line had come to Baer*: Author interview with Baer.

419 *Rosner and Liu had learned to speak*: Author interview with Rosner.

419 *The three writers had an extended session*: Author interview with Eric Liu.
420 *The president hosted a dinner*: Author interviews with Baer and Rosner.
420 *Baer, Rosner, and Liu spent days*: Author interviews with Rosner and Baer.
421 *"He both liked rhetoric"*: Author interview with Tom Malinowski.
421 *"WORDS, WORDS, WORDS"*: Paul Glastris, "Immortal Words," *Washington Monthly*, July–August 2007.
421 *It was a line*: Author interview with Rosner.
421 *"You're going to lose the Senate"*: Dick Morris, *Behind the Oval Office: Getting Reelected Against All Odds* (Los Angeles: Renaissance Books, 1999), 16–17.
421 *Morris and Clinton went back*: Ibid., 42–69.
422 *The two man's relationship*: Harris, *Survivor*, 163, 168.
422 *"You can say things"*: Author interview with Dick Morris.
422 *"When he spoke"*: Waldman, *POTUS Speaks*, 75.
422 *The electorate saw Clinton*: Harris, *Survivor*, 149–50.
423 *"an unfamiliar frequency"*: Stephanopoulos, *All Too Human*, 329.
423 *"Just in case what"*: Morris, *Behind*, 16.
423 *Clinton maintained an air*: Harris, *Survivor*, 153.
423 *"This could be liberating"*: Don Baer, "Clinton's State of the Union Helped Turn Around Loss of Congress," *Politico.com*, January 22, 2007.
423 *"You saw I gave your statement"*: Morris, *Behind*, 83.
423 *"Party leaders wonder"*: Michael Duffy, "Getting Out the Wrecking Ball," *Time*, December 19, 1994.
423 *Clinton now retreated in gloom*: Harris, *Survivor*, 154.
423 *"Triangulate"*: Morris, *Behind*, 80.
424 *Morris faxed suggestions*: Harris, *Survivor*, 165.
424 *That December, he started meeting*: Morris, *Behind*, 348.
424 *"beachhead"*: Author interview with Jonathan Prince.
424 *Clinton was not the flip-flopper*: Morris, *Behind*, 84.
424 *Morris was in Paris*: Ibid., 87.
424 *"Who came up with this language?"*: Stephanopoulos, *All Too Human*, 336–37.
424 *"Immaculate Conception"*: Morris, *Behind*, 87.
425 *"Just about everybody"*: Michael Duffy, "The 12-Minute Makeover," *Time*, December 26, 1994.
425 *"A democracy also needs"*: Anthony Lewis, "Leading from Behind," *New York Times*, December 19, 1994.
425 *the question was should it be*: Baer, "Clinton's State of the Union."
425 *"did not regard the people"*: Harris, *Survivor*, 163.
426 *"These white guys"*: Ibid., 160.
426 *The president had commissioned*: Morris, *Behind*, 93.
426 *a "green monster"*: Author interview with Morris.
427 *chewing on an unlit cigar*: Morris, *Behind*, 90.
427 *writing the new line*: Author interview with Baer.
427 *"Here, listen to this"*: Baer, "Clinton's State of the Union."
427 *"You couldn't see the planets"*: Author interview with Baer.
427 *A line about "tax cuts"*: Stephanopoulos, *All Too Human*, 336.
427 *"It's your speech, Bill"*: Harris, Survivor, 160.
427 *That's weird*: Stephanopoulos, *All Too Human*, 336.
427 *"It was coming down"*: Baer, "Clinton's State of the Union."
427 *Baer's recollection is*: Author interview with Baer.
428 *"Theirs was the standard"*: Author interview with Morris.

428 *That night, Clinton sent a copy*: Baer, "Clinton's State of the Union."

428 *He never came down*: Author interview with Baer.

428 *"by turns conciliatory"*: Todd S. Purdum, "Clinton, with Bow to G.O.P., Reaffirms His Themes of '92 and Asks New Cooperation," *New York Times*, January 25, 1995.

429 *It was, in effect, two speeches*: Harris, *Survivor*, 160; Morris, *Behind*, 95.

429 *"In those final thirty minutes"*: Morris, *Behind*, 95.

429 *"who hoped for signs"*: R. W. Apple, Jr., "A Deflated Presidency," *New York Times*, January 25, 1995.

429 *Baer was at the White House*: Baer, "Clinton's State of the Union."

430 *"Every presidential event"*: Stephanopoulos, *All Too Human*, 337–38.

430 *"I get up there"*: Morris, *Behind*, 97.

430 *"As Newt Gingrich was orchestrating"*: Stephanopoulos, *All Too Human*, 338.

430 *In January 1995, Hillary Clinton*: Morris, *Behind*, 348.

430 *"Our ratings"*: Ibid., 369–71.

431 *"Be sure all White House staff"*: Ibid., 371.

431 *Liberals like Ickes*: Harris, *Survivor*, 170–71.

431 *And while he was no liberal*: Morris, *Behind*, 98.

431 *He would kick off*: Stephanopoulos, *All Too Human*, 338.

432 *Harold Ickes called Baer*: Author interview with Baer.

432 *Morris had one more idea*: Morris, *Behind*, 121.

432 *"That's odd"*: Waldman, *POTUS Speaks*, 80.

433 *"Mr. Clinton for the first time in months"*: Steven A. Holmes, "Clinton Defines the Limits of Compromise with G.O.P.," *New York Times*, April 8, 1995.

433 *Baer had argued unsuccessfully*: Author interview with Baer.

434 *Chris Matthews*: Ibid.

434 *When the presidential party*: Ibid.

435 *"style in the absence of all style"*: Author interview with Tamagni.

435 *"zoot suits"*: Waldman, *POTUS Speaks*, 141.

435 *He was cocky*: Author interview with Edmonds.

435 *No one had called*: Author interview with Baer.

435 *Prince's first clear memory*: Author interview with Prince.

436 *Curiel produced a first draft*: Author interview with Baer.

436 *Prince specialized*: Author interview with Prince.

436 *Typically, Clinton had edited*: Marked-up reading copy of April 23, 1995, speech, William J. Clinton Library Web site.

436 *"It was the first time"*: Author interview with Morris.

437 *"It changed dramatically"*: Author interview with Prince.

437 *When new speechwriters joined*: Author interviews with Jeff Shesol and June Shih.

437 *"Often the speeches were written"*: Author interview with Baer.

438 *and he was an aspiring poet*: Author interview with Edmonds.

438 *"Every time you write"*: Waldman, *POTUS Speaks*, 173.

438 *Morris polled everything*: Ibid., 94, 100.

438 *"that their values"*: Ibid., 99.

438 *"I would write the sound bite"*: Author interview with Morris.

439 *"In contrast to the stately"*: Waldman, *POTUS Speaks*, 107.

439 *"the past thirty years"*: Author interview with Waldman. Stephanopoulos, who opposed the "era" line, wrote that Morris's draft only contained the end of big government, and that he and his allies added the "every man for himself" line. Waldman's account credits Morris with the complete line, as does Baer. Morris does not recall. (Stephanopoulos, *All Too Human*, 412; author interviews with Baer and Morris.)

440 *In the summer of 1996*: Waldman, *POTUS Speaks*, 127.

440 *"coincidence"*: Author interview with Morris.

440 *The speechwriters expected*: Waldman, *POTUS Speaks*, 108.

440 *"the death of liberalism"*: Stephanopoulos, *All Too Human*, 412.

440 *"Clinton Embraces GOP Themes"*: Ann Devroy, "Clinton Embraces GOP Themes in Setting Agenda," *The Washington Post*, January 24, 1996.

440 *"House Republicans are muttering"*: Richard Stengel, "What Clinton Is Doing Right," *Time*, February 5, 1996.

441 *"that we had won some battles"*: Stephanopoulos, *All Too Human*, 412.

441 *"The reason lies in the"*: Morris, *Behind*, 207.

441 *Clinton often spoke extemporaneously*: Author interview with Morris.

441 *"we polled it and it blew up"*: Ibid.

441 *After his speeches*: Waldman, *POTUS Speaks*, 142.

442 *He opened the folder*: Author interview with Prince.

442 *"I loved your speech"*: Ibid.

444 *"like a basketball team"*: Waldman, *POTUS Speaks*, 190.

444 *A major speech would start*: Author interview with Baer.

444 *"would be a far-reaching attempt"*: Waldman, *POTUS Speaks*, 190–91.

444 *Waldman would have to finish*: Ibid., 196.

444 *On January 21, Jeff Shesol*: The details of Jeff Shesol's hiring come from the author's interview with Shesol.

445 *"Now the speech has to be"*: Waldman, *POTUS Speaks*, 202, 207.

445 *Don't use the word "millennium"*: Author interview with Tamagni.

446 *"What should we do with the surplus?"*: Waldman, *POTUS Speaks*, 207.

446 *"The notion that President Clinton"*: Author interview with Lowell Weiss.

446 *In the spectator seats*: Waldman, *POTUS Speaks*, 207.

446 *"What is usually a gladiator's"*: Alessandra Stanley, "If Only for an Hour, Playing by the Time-Honored Rules," *New York Times*, January 28, 1998.

446 *Waldman was standing*: Author interview with Blinken.

446 *A year earlier he had introduced*: Waldman, *POTUS Speaks*, 161.

447 *Congressional Republicans had raised*: Francis X. Clines and Jeff Gerth, "Subpoenas Sent as Clinton Denies Reports of an Affair with Aide at the White House," *New York Times*, January 22, 1998.

447 *"white noise"*: Author interview with Shesol.

447 *so the closest the speechwriters came*: Author interview with Weiss.

447 *"slip up mid-paragraph"*: Waldman, *POTUS Speaks*, 219.

447 *"Part of the strategy"*: Author interview with Paul Glastris,

447 *"I was wrong"*: Peter Baker, *The Breach: Inside the Impeachment and Trial of William Jefferson Clinton* (New York: Scribner, 2000), 32.

448 *Paul Begala*: Harris, *Survivor*, 342.

448 *"I have fallen short"*: Baker, *Breach*, 24–25.

448 *"People don't care about you"*: Harris, *Survivor*, 343.

448 *"It's your speech, Bill"*: Ibid., 344.

449 *reading a text that he had written*: Waldman, *POTUS Speaks*, 232.

449 *Starr hoped to so appall*: Harris, *Survivor*, 350.

450 *As the 1999 State of the Union speech*: Author interview with Josh Gottheimer.

450 *Always aware that he was considered*: Waldman, *POTUS Speaks*, 255.

450 *"Without once uttering"*: John M. Broder, "By Day and Night, an Argument for Survival," *New York Times*, January 20, 1999.

451 *Candidate Clinton had made this*: Harris, *Survivor*, 44.

451 *"muddling through"*: Ibid., 51, 195–202.

451 *Tom Malinowski*: Author interview with Tom Malinowski.

451 *he would amuse himself*: Author interview with Paul Orzulak.

452 *"If you think about the tools"*: Author interview with Malinowski.

452 *"I will not"*: Except where noted, the account of the March 24, 1999, Kosovo speech comes from the author's interview with Malinowski.

452 *"If the TelePrompTer had failed"*: Author interview with David Halperin.

452 *"The implication of that"*: Author interview with Malinowski.

453 *"In his televised speech tonight"*: R. W. Apple, Jr., "A Fresh Set of Goals," *New York Times*, March 25, 1999.

453 *The underlying assumption*: Harris, *Survivor*, 368.

453 *"Mr. Clinton's aides said"*: Steven Lee Myers, "Serb Forces in Kosovo Under Attack as Weather Clears," *New York Times*, April 6, 1999.

453 *"I'm not saying"*: Author interview with Malinowski.

454 *Berger recommended that*: Harris, *Survivor*, 374–75.

454 *He and Paul Glastris*: Author interviews with Glastris and Shesol.

454 *It was originally conceived*: Ibid.

454 *"No, no, no"*: Author interview with Shesol.

454 *He kept asking for more detail*: Jeff Shesol, remarks at the Anschutz Lecture, Princeton University, April 22, 2002.

455 *"What happened to salmonella?"*: Ibid.

455 *Edmonds was in his office*: Author interviews with John Pollack and Edmonds.

12. "THE TROIKA"

456 *"Did you see that?"*: The account of the McConnell-Cheney meeting comes from author interview with John McConnell.

456 *Matthew Scully was in his office*: Author interview with Matthew Scully.

457 *Michael Gerson, the director*: Michael Gerson, "The View from the Top," *Newsweek*, August 21–28, 2006; Michael Gerson, *Heroic Conservatism: Why Republicans Need to Embrace American's Ideals (And Why They Deserve to Fail if They Don't)* (New York: Harper One, 2007), 67–68.

457 *but not before he had written*: Robert Draper, *Dead Certain: The Presidency of George W. Bush* (New York: Free Press, 2007), 140.

457 *"They're evacuating this building"*: David Frum, *The Right Man: An Inside Account of the Bush White House* (New York: Random House, 2005), 113–15.

457 *"We're just a couple of blocks"*: Ibid., 116–17, 120.

458 *Scully had wandered north*: Author interview with Scully.

458 *"was trying to crack the whip"*: Ibid.

458 *On speakerphone*: Author interviews with Scully and McConnell.

458 *They sent their text to Gerson*: Frum, *Right Man*, 120.

459 *"Our mission is reassurance"*: Bob Woodward, *Bush at War* (New York: Simon & Schuster, 2002), 30.

459 *Hughes's pastor had e-mailed her*: Karen Hughes, *Ten Minutes from Normal* (New York: Viking, 2004), 244.

459 *Standing between the White House*: Author interview with McConnell.

459 *At some point*: Michael Gerson interview on ABC News's *Nightline*, December 19, 2002.

459 *"You need to get a good translation"*: Hughes, *Ten Minutes*, 244.

459 *And he tweaked the phrase*: Woodward, *Bush at War*, 30.

460 *"unequal to the moment"*: Gerson, *Heroic Conservatism*, 69.

460 *"stiff and small"*: Gerson, "The View from the Top."

460 *"At the center of the speech"*: Frum, *Right Man*, 126–27, 133.

460 *Gerson drove in before dawn*: Gerson, *Heroic Conservatism*, 70.

460 *"the troika"*: Matthew Scully, "Present at the Creation," *The Atlantic* (September 2007).

460 *"owlish" appearance*: D. T. Max, "The Making of the Speech," *New York Times*, October 7, 2001.

460 *"One of his great talents"*: Author interview with McConnell.

461 *Gerson was born in Belmont*: Michael Gerson appearance on *Q&A*, C-SPAN, January 7, 2007.

461 *"I've read your stuff"*: Jeffrey Goldberg, "The Believer," *The New Yorker*, February 13 and 20, 2006.

461 *"an infectious confidence"*: Gerson on *Q&A*.

462 *"When you bring the West Texas"*: Goldberg, "The Believer."

462 *He might chew on a pen*: Frum, *Right Man*, 25.

462 *In Austin, in April 1999*: Author interview with Scully.

462 *"the best writer"*: Author interview with McConnell.

462 *He "is the most interesting"*: George Will, "A Conservative Case for Animal Rights," *Newsweek*, July 18, 2005.

463 *"I love the history"*: Author interview with McConnell.

463 *"Imagine a typical all-American"*: Author interview with Joe Shattan.

463 *"In his hands moral and religious"*: Scully, "Present at the Creation."

463 *McConnell had a capacity for producing*: Author interview with Scully.

463 *"Usually when you're a speechwriter"*: Gerson *Q&A*.

464 *The president made one apparent*: Author interview with Scully.

464 *"It is no small goal"*: R. W. Apple, Jr., "President Seems to Gain Legitimacy," *New York Times*, September 16, 2001.

464 *"final victory over terrorism"*: Dana Milbank and Dan Balz, "Bush Negotiates a Rhetorical Minefield," *Washington Post*, September 20, 2001.

464 *"I'm sure that the man"*: Author interview with Scully.

464 *He teared up*: Gerson on *Nightline*.

464 *"I hadn't expected that"*: Gerson on *Q&A*.

464 *During the transition, a standard e-mail*: Author interview with John Gibson.

465 *"an extremely odd experience"*: Ibid.

465 *The Bush crowd ran things*: Ibid.

465 *"Good soul."*: Author interview with McConnell.

466 *"America is united and strong"*: Dan Balz and Bob Woodward, "A Presidency Defined in One Speech," *Washington Post*, February 2, 2002.

466 *"If we've done something"*: Max, "The Making of the Speech."

466 *"I want it by 7"*: Balz and Woodward, "A Presidency Defined in One Speech."

466 *set up in McConnell's office*: Author interview with McConnell.

466 *"Darkness. Light"*: Scully, "Present at the Creation." Scully is sure the notes are from their meeting with Bush on September 13, and thinks that he and his colleagues may have started writing that day, but he is not certain. Contemporaneous press accounts have the work starting on Monday, September 17. (Author interview with Scully.)

467 *They worked quickly*: Max, "The Making of the Speech."

467 *"We were all Americans after 9/11"*: Author interview with Tom Malinowski.

467 *After a hesitant performance*: Milbank and Balz, "Bush Negotiates a Rhetorical Minefield," September 20, 2001.

467 *Malinowski tried to help*: Author interview with Malinowski; copy of suggested remarks provided by Malinowski.

468 *Gibson passed on*: Author interview with Malinowski.

468 *"There's nothing wrong"*: Ibid.

468 *and it was in by 8 pm*: Hughes, *Ten Minutes*, 257.

468 *The writers suggested including*: Max, "The Making of the Speech."

468 *"I don't want to quote anyone!"*: Draper, *Dead Certain*, 154.

468 *"This is what my presidency is about"*: Balz and Woodward, "A Presidency Defined in One Speech."

468 *Rice walked in*: Max, "The Making of the Speech."

468 *As Gerson pulled into his driveway*: Balz and Woodward, "A Presidency Defined in One Speech."

468 *"You all have smiles on your faces"*: Max, "The Making of the Speech."

468 *He was feeling loose*: Author interview with Scully.

469 *"Isn't that kind"*: Draper, *Dead Certain*, 153; author interview with Scully.

469 *"Let's call the Congress"*: Max, "The Making of the Speech."

469 *There had been some discussion*: Ibid.

469 *but Bush generally preferred*: Author interview with Scully.

469 *Rove had argued for*: Max, "The Making of the Speech."

469 *He would notice if*: Author interview with McConnell.

469 *"Karl is a very serious"*: Gerson on *Q&A*.

469 *Bush ambled into the family theatre*: Max, "The Making of the Speech."

469 *"What is this stuff?"*: Scully, "Present at the Creation."

469 *He again made fun*: Author interview with Scully.

469 *"This crisis found us"*: Matthew Scully, "Building a Better State of the Union," *New York Times*, February 2, 2005.

469 *"I probably rejected"*: Hughes, *Ten Minutes*, 259.

469 *He inserted "After all"*: Max, "The Making of the Speech."

469 *He came to the end of the speech*: Author interview with Scully.

470 *Donald Rumsfeld was concerned*: Balz and Woodward, "A Presidency Defined in One Speech."

470 *Bush had a second practice*: Author interview with Scully.

470 *"The Capitol looked as if"*: Dana Milbank, "On Fortress Capitol Hill, United Roars of Approval," *The Washington Post*, September 21, 2001.

470 *As Laura Bush walked to her seat*: Alison Mitchell, "Joint Congress Turned into a Showcase of Courage and Resolve," *New York Times*, September 21, 2001.

471 *This was an example*: Scully, "Present at the Creation."

471 *"This is the great irony"*: Author interview with Malinowski.

471 *Secretary of State Colin Powell:*: Balz and Woodward, "A Presidency Defined in One Speech."

471 *using another Hughes line*: Max, "The Making of the Speech."

472 *"a little bit of a Hallmark touch."*: Author interview with Scully.

472 *The "mission" line*: Scully, "Present at the Creation."

472 *"I have never"*: Gerson, *Heroic Conservatism*, 79.

472 *"understood the importance of speechwriting"*: Author interview with Scully.

472 *"The President wants"*: Gerson on *Nightline*.

472 *"He would often say"*: Author interview with Noam Neusner.

472 *Bush "would always say"*: Author interview with Scully.

473 *"He'll say, 'Yeah the speech?'"*: Author interview with McConnell.

473 *"It's just words, isn't it"*: Ibid.

473 *Do not start sentences with the word*: Ibid.

473 *"He was very clear"*: Author interview with Neusner.

473 *"cram-ins"*: Author interview with Scully.

474 *"Bush decided that the United States"*: Frum, *Right Man*, 231.

474 *During the 2000 campaign*: John Lancaster, "In Saddam's Future, a Harder U.S. Line," *The Washington Post*, June 3, 2000.

474 *"No one envisioned"*: Peter Baker, "Conflicts Shaped Two Presidencies," *Washington Post*, December 31, 2006.

474 *As early as February 2001*: Alan Sipress and Dan Balz, "Bush Signals Escalation in Response to Hussein," *The Washington Post*, February 17, 2001.

475 *"his determination to dig"*: Frum, *Right Man*, 26.

475 *In the initial hours and days*: Woodward, *Bush at War*, 49.

475 *"Here's an assignment"*: Frum, *Right Man*, 224.

475 *Frum was an odd choice*: Ibid., 3–4, 43.

475 *"a highly coscnientious person"*: Scully, "Present at the Creation."

475 *The case could not merely be*: Frum, *Right Man*, 234–35.

475 *"terror organizations and the terror states"*: Ibid., 234–37.

476 *In early January, Bush huddled*: Ibid., 223.

476 *"back room of a cheap restaurant"*: Scully, "Building a Better State of the Union."

476 *McConnell, who kept a supply*: Author interview with McConnell.

477 *"There was this unspoken sense of relief"*: Ibid.

477 *Throughout their collaboration*: Author interview with Scully.

477 *"Education speeches in particular"*: Scully, "Present at the Creation."

477 *Gerson summed up the feeling*: Author interview with Scully.

477 *To Frum's surprise*: Frum, *Right Man*, 236.

477 *The topic of weapons*: Bob Woodward, *Plan of Attack* (New York: Simon & Schuster, 2004), 87.

478 *"I hate hatred"*: Scully, "Present at the Creation."

478 *The three discussed it*: Author interview with McConnell.

478 *"The testosterone talk"*: Tony Karon, "Tough Talking Bush Rattles Friend and Foe," *Time*, February 2, 2002.

478 *"He is using his war popularity"*: Charles Krauthammer, "Redefining the War," *Washington Post*, February 1, 2002.

479 *Frum resigned*: Frum, *Right Man*, 267.

479 *Her e-mail had been forwarded*: Timothy Noah, "David Frum's Axis of Evil; Authorial Vanity Strikes the Bush White House," *Slate*, February 5, 2002.

479 *"the non-negotiable demands"*: Draper, *Dead Certain*, 180–81.

480 *Domestically, it kicked off*: Peter Eisner, and Knut Royce, *The Italian Letter: How the Bush Administration Used a Fake Letter to Build the Case for War in Iraq* (New York: Rodale, 2007), 98–104.

480 *Scully, who had taken a leave*: Author interview with Scully.

480 *"I'm not totally there yet"*: Michael Isikoff, and David Corn, *Hubris: The Inside Story of Spin, Scandal, and the Selling of the Iraq War* (New York: Crown Publishers, 2006), 85.

480 *"a reputation for pushing evidence"*: Ibid., 85–86.

480 *Joseph faxed Gibson*: Ibid., 86.

481 *There had been intense debate*: Draper, *Dead Certain*, 181–82.

481 *Gibson had worked on this*: Isikoff and Corn, *Hubris*, 143.

481 *The following day, the CIA sent*: Eisner and Royce, *Italian Letter*, 107.

482 *and others*: Dana Milbank and Walter Pincus, "Bush Aides Disclose Warnings from CIA," *Washington Post*, July 23, 2003; Woodward, *Plan of Attack*, 201.

482 *"Remove the sentence because"*: Report on the U.S. Intelligence Community's Prewar Intelligence Assessments on Iraq, U.S. Senate Select Committee on Intelligence, 55–56.

482 *"should not be a fact witness"*: Ibid., 56.

482 *"You need to take this"*: Woodward, *Plan of Attack*, 97.

482 *". . . More on why"*: Report on the U.S. Intelligence Committee's Prewar Intelligence Assessments on Iraq, 55–57.

482 *Gerson and Gibson wanted to include*: Isikoff and Corn, *Hubris*, 143.

483 *It was a Gerson creation*: Ibid., 35, 42.

483 *"These findings seemed very credible"*: Author interview with Scully.

484 *"this will be checked"*: Ibid.

484 *"We had stuff taken out"*: Author interview with McConnell.

484 *"I know that we often did overstate"*: Author interview with Scully.

484 *They felt that "it was more cautious"*: Ibid.

484 *Say where the evidence comes from*: Isikoff and Corn, *Hubris*, 171.

485 *Secretary of State Colin Powell, reviewing*: Scully, "Building a Better State of the Union."

485 *Hadley and Gerson both later said*: Eisner and Royce, *Italian Letter*, 115.

485 *Tenet was given a hard copy*: Report on the U.S. Intelligence Community's Prewar Intelligence Assessment on Iraq, 64.

485 *"The final conclusion was"*: Author interview with McConnell.

486 *McConnell was in bed*: Ibid.

486 *Karen Hughes was at home*: Mike Allen, "Comforting Words as a Matter of Faith," *Washington Post*, February 3, 2003.

487 *In fact, he had not been to*: Michael R. Gordon and Bernard E. Trainor, "Iraqi Leader, in Frantic Flights, Eluded U.S. Strikes," *New York Times*, March 12, 2006.

487 *According to the advocacy group*: Douglas Jehl and Eric Schmitt, "Errors Are Seen in Early Attacks on Iraqi Leaders," *New York Times*, June 13, 2004.

487 *"one of the most audacious moments"*: Elisabeth Bumiller, "Keepers of Bush Image Lift Stagecraft to New Heights," *New York Times*, May 16, 2003.

487 *Gerson came in with a copy*: Scully, "Present at the Creation."

487 *"These are beautiful sentences"*: Ibid.

488 *Rumsfeld told Bob Woodward*: Woodward, *State of Denial*, 186.

488 *But according to Scully*: Author interview with Scully.

488 *Sforza spent several days*: Bumiller, "Keepers of Bush Image Lift Stagecraft to New Heights."

488 *"Scott was simply reporting to us"*: Author interview with Scully.

488 *"That was the first time"*: Author interview with McConnell.

488 *"Mr. President, the first reports"*: Baker, "Conflicts Shaped Two Presidencies."

489 *"There was no false confidence"*: Author interview with Scully.

489 *Bush put on a white cowboy hat*: Ibid.

489 *"I want this to be the freedom"*: William Safire, "Bush's 'Freedom Speech,'" *New York Times*, January 21, 2005.

489 *"The future of America"*: Woodward, *State of Denial*, 371.

489 *"a belief in the power and importance"*: Gerson on *Q&A*.

489 *On the morning of December 17*: The account of Gerson's heart attack comes from ibid.; and from Gerson, *Heroic Conservatism*, 222.

490 *"I told you that budget was too extreme"*: Goldberg, "The Believer."

490 *"I'm not calling to see"*: Safire, "Bush's 'Freedom Speech.'"

490 *"he was really asking"*: Gerson on *Q&A*.

490 *He and McConnell wrote the speech*: Author interview with McConnell.

490 *"I can't wait"*: Woodward, *State of Denial*, 377–78.

490 *"No longer running for anything"*: Nancy Gibbs, "Celebration and Dissent," *Time*, January 24, 2005.

491 *"among the top five"*: Safire, "Bush's 'Freedom Speech.'"

491 *"The inaugural address itself"*: Peggy Noonan, "Way Too Much God; Was the President's Speech a Case of 'Mission Inebriation'?" *Wall Street Journal*, January 21, 2005.

491 *"It is for historians"*: Todd S. Purdum, "The President's Speech Focuses on Ideals, Not the Details," *New York Times*, January 21, 2005.

491 *"White House officials said yesterday"*: Dan Balz and Jim VandeHei, "Bush Speech Not a Sign of Policy Shift, Officials Say," *Washington Post*, January 22, 2005.

492 *"Two and a half years after"*: Peter Baker, "As Democracy Push Falters, Bush Feels Like a 'Dissident,'" *Washington Post*, August 20, 2007.

492 *"You're not the only dissident"*: Ibid.

492 *"I'm a worrier"*: Goldberg, "The Believer."

492 *McConnell turned down*: Author interview with McConnell.

493 *"The man whose words helped"*: Chuck Raasch, "Bush's Wordsmith Leaves with Vivid 9/11 Memories," *USA Today*, July 13, 2006.

493 *"author of nearly of all"*: Peter Baker, "Top Bush Speech Writer to Step Down," *Washington Post*, June 14, 2006.

493 *Typical was a December 2002*: Scully, "Present at the Creation"; Gerson on *Nightline*.

494 *"I wasn't out there"*: Peter Baker, "Bush's Muse Stands Accused," *Washington Post*, August 11, 2007.

494 *"For me, the poignancy"*: Bruce Reed, "Honor Among Scribes; A Vegan Speechwriter Pens the Juiciest Hatchet Job of the Bush Era," *Slate*, August 11, 2007.

Acknowledgments

This book would not have been possible without the always patient, often enthusiastic support of countless presidential speechwriters and other aides. More than ninety White House aides spared their time (over 127 hours) and memories, many in multiple interview sessions, most on the record, all generous with their support. Many appear in these pages. Some are members of the Judson Welliver Society, whose meetings inspired this history. They are too numerous to name here, but all made valuable contributions to this work—and for them I have the deepest gratitude and appreciation. In particular, I would like to give special thanks to Hendrik Hertzberg, William Safire, and Curt Smith for sharing or granting me access to their personal papers and for their generous support of this project.

Our national system of presidential libraries, administered by the National Archives, remains a remarkable resource for veteran historians and amateurs alike. Research for this book took me to nine presidential libraries (ten, as the Archives II in College Park, Maryland, is now considered a branch of the Richard Nixon Library) as well as the Library of Congress. I collected nearly 30,000 pages of documents. The staffs at these libraries have been friendly, helpful, and insightful. In particular, I would like to thank Bob Clark and the staff at the FDR Library in Hyde Park, New York; Randy Sowell and the staff at the Truman Library in Independence, Missouri; Dwight Strandberg and the staff at the Eisenhower Library in Abilene, Kansas; the staff at the JFK Library in Boston, Massachusetts; Sarah Haldeman and the staff at the LBJ Library in Austin, Texas; the staff who handle the Nixon materials at Archives II in College Park, Maryland; William McNitt and the staff at the Ford Library in Ann Arbor, Michigan; Albert Nason and the staff at the Carter Library in Atlanta, Georgia; Diane Barrie and Mike Duggan at the Reagan Library in Simi Valley, California; and Chris Pembelton at the Bush Library in College Station, Texas.

Gathering this material was made much easier by grants from several organizations. Specifically, I owe a debt of thanks to the Franklin and Eleanor Roosevelt Institute, the Harry S. Truman Library Institute, the John F. Kennedy Library Foundation, the George Bush Presidential Library Foundation, and the White House Historical Association for their grants supporting this project.

I have been fortunate in trying to pull all of this material together in a coherent manner to have the support and assistance of a wide array of people. Key in this effort was Alice Mayhew, my editor at Simon & Schuster, whose guidance regarding structure and pacing gave this book shape and flow, and whose keen line edits have improved the writing immeasurably. Her fellow editor Roger Labrie was also invaluable in shepherding the various chapters into readable form, ready with both wise suggestions and the strategic pat on the back.

Robert Dallek, John A. Farrell, and Charles Lewis all provided early support for this project, for which I am grateful. Linda Killian and the staff at the Boston University Washington Journalism Center have been helpful throughout. I would especially like to thank Mason McAllister, who aided me in numerous ways, always cheerfully and tirelessly. Jamie Hammon, Sara Hatch, and Katie Stevenson each volunteered their time and help with research, expecting (and receiving) little in the way of compensation save my lasting gratitude and amazed appreciation. Jack Harris and Beka Sturges also made an invaluable contribution.

Others contributed in important non-literary ways. Randy Brown, Rob Pegoraro, and Bob Vanasse acted as my personal technical support team, for which I am grateful. OnTrack Data Recovery performed a historically impossible feat—saving Nixon and Carter. Brian and Joslyn Schaefer and Jennifer Crow housed me on my travels. Numerous other friends and family contributed through their ongoing patience, good humor, and offers to read.

My agent, Andrew Wylie, has a deserved reputation as the best in the business, and he has been a great help not only to me but to my family in trying times. For that, and especially for taking an early interest in this book, I am most grateful.

In the end, an undertaking like this one can only be as successful in print as it is at home. I owe more than I can express to my extraordinary parents. My enduring regret is that my father, Arthur Schlesinger, will not read this book, though he saw very rough drafts of the Roosevelt and Truman chapters. In many ways, this work is the product of thirty-five years of his love, support, and guidance, along with that of my wonderful mother, Alexandra Schlesinger, who has read draft after draft with tireless enthusiasm.

Most of all, I owe thanks to my wondrous wife, Francesca Schlesinger. She has given unstinting support throughout this project, sharing the highs, steadying the lows, and not letting the swings back and forth unsettle her. She has carefully read each chapter and provided her perceptive and honest reactions. I marvel at my remarkable luck to have her as a companion and best friend through life.

Robert Emmet Kennedy Schlesinger
Alexandria, Virginia
*September 19, 2007**

*Happy birthday, Peter!

Index

Aaron, David, 281–82
abortion, 328–29, 344, 390–91, 461
Abshire, David, 352
Acheson, Dean, 44, 46, 172, 247
Adams, Sherman, 70, 74, 85, 86, 88, 91
Adenauer, Konrad, 141
Afghanistan, 307, 321–22, 467, 468, 469, 475, 476, 479, 491
African Americans, 87–88, 89, 90, 91–92, 93, 94, 96, 102–3, 110–11, 132, 134–38, 157–62, 187, 396–97, 438, 454
Age of Roosevelt (Schlesinger), 120
Agnew, Spiro T., 202, 222, 226, 233, 236
Air Florida Flight 737 crash (1982), 323–24
Alcorn, Meade, 96
al Qaeda, 467, 468, 470, 471, 475–76
Alsop, Joseph, 78
Alsop, Stewart, 78
Ambrose, Stephen, 81, 420
American Society of Newspaper Editors, 49, 72, 115, 411, 431–33
America the Vincible (Hughes), 90
Anderson, John, 310, 367
Anderson, Patrick, 268, 269
Andrews, John, 211–12, 218, 223, 226
Apple, R. W., Jr., 404, 429, 453, 464
Armey, Richard, 470
Aronson, Bernie, 284, 293–95, 296
Ash, Roy, 242
Ashe, Arthur, 278
Askew, Ken, 396
Austria, 72, 369

Baer, Don, 408, 409, 417, 418, 419–20, 423, 427, 429, 430, 431, 432, 433, 434, 435, 437, 444
Baker, Howard, 357
Baker, James A., III, 318, 319, 334, 335n, 341, 343, 345, 352, 361, 398, 399, 451
Baker, Peter, 492
Bakshian, Aram, 219, 236, 250, 319–20, 321, 323–24, 328, 334, 342, 353
Ball, George, 167
Balz, Dan, 464
Bancroft, George, 2
"Bang!" papers, 76, 77–78
Barkley, Alben, 52
Barnes, Ben, 145–46
Barnes, Julius H., 12
Baroody, William, 254, 261
Bartlett, Dan, 459, 462
Batt, William, 53, 54–55
Bay of Pigs invasion (1961), 114–15, 120, 122, 123, 223
Begala, Paul, 405, 407, 409, 431, 448
Begin, Menachem, 291–92
Bell, David, 54, 65
Bell, Griffin, 305
Benchley, Peter, 175, 176, 177–78
Benedict, Stephen, 76n, 82, 87
Benjamin, Daniel, 437
Bennett, Henry, 63
Bennett, Robert, 173
Benson, Ezra Taft, 76
Berger, Sandy, 409, 410, 419, 452, 454
Berle, Adolph, 13
Berlin Blockade, 127, 138
Berlin Wall, 138–41, 191, 354–58, 374–78, 383
Bernstein, Carl, 225–26
Berra, Yogi, 363
Beschloss, Michael, 128, 139, 141
Bias, Len, 372
Bible, 154, 163, 212, 233, 270, 315, 390, 436, 459–60, 486

Biddle, Anthony, 20
Biddle, Francis, 28
Biffle, Les, 40
Bill of Rights, 388
bin Laden, Usama, 467, 470
Blair, Tony, 455
Blessey, Stephanie, 371
Blinken, Tony, 408, 437, 446
Blumenthal, Richard, 208
Bohlen, Charles E. "Chip," 70, 115, 172
Bolling, Richard, 180
Bolten, Joshua, 456, 490
Boorstin, Daniel, 256, 259, 261
Boorstin, David, 256–57, 259, 263, 264, 266
Bowles, Erskine, 430, 442
Brady, Dorothy, 25
Brady, Jim, 351
Brady, Nicholas, 379
Branch, Taylor, 403, 407
Brandt, Willy, 139, 140
Bray, William, 59
Brezhnev, Leonid, 298–99, 320
Broder, David, 305, 412, 413
Brownell, Herbert, 76
Browning, Robert, 111
Brown v. Board of Education, 88
Brzezinski, Zbigniew, 274, 275, 281–82,
    288, 290, 410
Buchanan, Patrick, 192, 193, 194–95, 196,
    197, 198, 208, 209–10, 219–20, 221,
    225n, 226, 227, 228, 235, 312, 322,
    345, 346, 347, 348, 349, 350, 351,
    391, 406
Buckley, William F., Jr., 317
Bullitt, William, 13, 19–20
Bundy, McGeorge, 121, 122, 123, 126, 131,
    139, 141, 162
Burger, Warren, 198–99
Busby, Horace "Buzz," 148, 155, 157, 158–59,
    162, 165, 168, 181–83, 185–86
Bush, Barbara, 395, 426n
Bush, George H. W., 362–401
    advisers of, 364, 367–68, 393–94, 395,
        398, 399
    approval ratings of, 388, 391, 394
    "Chicken Kiev" speech of (1992), 389
    as CIA director, 252
    collapse of communism and, 369–72,
        374–78, 381, 383, 394
    concession speech of (1992), 399–400
    "dead cat" speech of, 384–85
    diary of, 369, 384, 388
    domestic policies of, 363, 369, 372–74,
        379–80, 382, 383–85, 388–91,
        394–99, 404

drug policy of, 372–74
economic policies of, 363, 369, 379–80,
    383–85, 390, 394, 404
editorial revisions by, 368, 377, 381, 382,
    385–86, 387, 391n, 392–93, 399–400
emotionalism of, 368–69, 392–93
European tours of (1989), 369–72
extemporaneous remarks of, 371–72,
    381, 394, 395
foreign policy of, 369–72, 374–83, 384,
    385–88, 394, 451
George W. Bush advised by, 467, 472,
    474, 488
Gulf War policy of, 366, 380–83, 385–88,
    474, 476
"kinder, gentler" quote of, 362
Malta speech of, 377–78, 382
"new world order" phrase of, 381–82,
    383, 387
oratorical skills of, 362–65, 369, 382–83,
    390–91, 408n
Panama invasion ordered by (1989),
    378–79
Pearl Harbor anniversary speech of
    (1991), 392–93
presidential campaign of (1980), 318, 366
presidential campaign of (1988), 362,
    363, 366, 369
presidential campaign of (1992), 386,
    388, 391, 394–99
press coverage of, 367, 369, 373–76,
    378–80, 388–90, 394, 395, 398
"read my lips" quote of, 363, 379–80
Reagan compared with, 363, 364, 365,
    367, 373, 380, 381, 382, 391
as Republican Party leader, 379–80,
    383–84, 391
speechwriters of, 322, 342, 361,
    362–401, 491
State of the Union addresses of, 394,
    395, 426n
style of, 362–66, 370–72, 374–78, 380,
    382, 389, 390–91, 394, 395, 400–401,
    408n, 472
tax policy of, 363, 369, 379–80, 383–85
television broadcasts of, 373–74, 380–83
Thanksgiving Day speeches of, 385–86,
    393
"thousand points of light" phrase of,
    362–63
typed notes of, 377, 382, 391n
University of Michigan speech of
    (1992), 388–90
as veteran combat pilot, 368–69,
    377–78, 385–86, 392–93

Bush, George H. W. *(cont.)*
  as vice president, 318, 331, 348, 359, 361, 364
Bush, George W., 456–94
  advisers of, 465n, 466, 467, 468–69, 472, 473–74, 477–78, 480–86, 488
  aircraft carrier speech of (2003), 487–88
  "Axis of Evil" speech (2002), 475–79
  Bush Doctrine of, 479
  Columbia disaster speech of (2003), 486
  congressional address of (2001), 465–72
  editorial revisions by, 458–59, 465–74
  extemporaneous remarks of, 481
  foreign policy of, 464–65, 474–86, 490–92
  George H. W. Bush as adviser to, 467, 472, 474, 488
  as governor of Texas, 423, 461
  gubernatorial campaign of (1994), 423
  Iraq War policy of, 474–89, 491
  National Cathedral speech of (2001), 460, 463–64
  oratorical skills of, 408n, 459–60
  presidential campaign of (2000), 455, 474
  presidential campaign of (2004), 489
  press coverage of, 464, 467, 470, 478–79, 480, 483, 487–88, 490, 491–92, 493
  second inaugural address of (2005), 489, 490–92
  September 11th Oval Office speech of, 26, 456–60, 467, 469, 486
  speechwriters of, 26, 32n, 456–94
  State of the Union addresses of, 42n, 96n, 474–79, 483–86
  style of, 408n, 461–62, 465–74, 487–89, 491–92
  television broadcasts of, 459–60, 481, 487–88
  "Troika" speechwriting team of, 460–65, 476–77, 478, 480, 488–89, 492–94
  UN Security Council speech of (2002), 479–83
  "weapons of mass destruction" warning of, 474–86
Bush, Laura, 470–71
Butler, London, 297
Butler, Patrick, 249–50, 253, 258–59, 264, 265–66
Butterfield, Alexander, 218, 223
Buzhardt, Fred, 227
Byrd, Robert, 187

Caddell, Pat, 283n, 294, 302, 305, 308, 310
Caffrey, Mary, 80
Califano, Joseph, 164–65, 166, 169, 177–78, 183–84, 434n

Cambodia, 209, 210–11, 219, 247, 409
Cannon, James, 254
Cannon, Lou, 315, 350, 351, 361
Caplan, Tommy, 403
Carey, Hugh, 271, 303
Carlucci, Frank, 366
Carpenter, Liz, 145, 146, 177
Carr, Albert Z. "Bob," 54
Carter, Billy, 272, 292
Carter, Cliff, 145
Carter, Jimmy, 268–311
  advisers of, 270, 274, 281–82, 287–93, 299–304, 308–9, 410
  approval ratings of, 298, 305, 395
  "Beloved Community" phrase of, 283–84
  cabinet appointments of, 164, 270, 274, 305
  Camp David Accords of (1978), 291–93
  Clinton compared with, 405–6
  Democratic National Convention speech of (1980), 309
  domestic policies of, 273–74, 277–80, 282–84, 293–96, 298–305
  economic policies of, 294–95, 298
  editorial revisions by, 268–73, 274, 284, 288–89, 297
  energy policy of, 273–74, 277–80, 294–95, 298, 299–305
  European tour of (1977), 281–82
  extemporaneous remarks of, 277–79, 285–86, 309
  farewell address of (1981), 310–11
  "fireside chats" of, 273–74, 285, 299
  foreign policy of, 274–77, 278, 281–82, 284–93, 298–99, 310–11, 320, 410
  "Georgia mafia" of, 272, 282–83
  gubernatorial campaign of (1966), 271
  inaugural address of (1977), 269–70
  "inordinate fear" quote of, 275–76
  in Iran hostage crisis, 307, 308–9, 375
  Los Angeles Bar Association speech of (1978), 286–87
  "malaise" speech of, 301–5
  memoirs of, 288
  "moral equivalent of war" phrase of, 279
  Naval Academy speech of (1978), 287–90, 302
  "New Foundation" phrase of, 293–96
  "New Spirit" phrase of, 284
  Notre Dame speech of (1977), 274–77, 278, 288
  nuclear policy of, 278, 289, 298–99, 310–11, 320
  oratorical skills of, 271, 277–79, 284, 285–86, 303–4, 309

personality of, 268–69, 272–73, 461
presidential campaign of (1976), 257,
    261, 263, 264, 266–67, 280, 304
presidential campaign of (1980), 298,
    306, 307–10, 312, 317
press coverage of, 270, 272, 273, 274,
    275, 276, 277, 278, 279–80, 289,
    290, 292, 294, 296, 297, 300, 301,
    305
religious convictions of, 261, 461
Soviet policy of, 274–77, 278, 288–90,
    298–99, 307
speechwriters of, 267, 268–311, 405–6,
    410, 493
State of the Union addresses of, 282–84,
    293–97, 310
style of, 268–73, 277–80, 284, 285–87,
    297, 298, 302–5, 309, 310–11
television broadcasts of, 273–74,
    279–80, 299–300, 302–5
at Vienna summit, 298–99
Wake Forest speech of (1978), 288
Washington Press Club speech of
    (1977), 272–73
Carter, Rosalynn, 261, 285, 289
Casey, William, 317
Casserly, Jack, 235–36, 248, 250, 251, 253
Castro, Fidel, 114–15, 122
Cater, Douglass, 154, 155, 167, 187
Central Intelligence Agency (CIA), 122,
    123, 126, 227, 252, 480–83, 487
Chambers, Whittaker, 318, 325
Chase, Stuart, 6
Cheney, Dick, 245, 250, 251, 252–53, 256,
    264, 266, 267, 352, 456, 463, 465n,
    470, 481, 493
Chew, David, 343
Chiang Kai-shek, 156
China, 66, 72, 118n, 130, 156, 183, 253–54,
    452
Christian, George, 164, 183
Churchill, Winston S., 22, 24, 33, 73–74,
    75, 182, 326, 382
Cicconi, James, 370, 373
civil rights movement, 87–88, 89, 90, 96,
    102–3, 110–11, 132, 134–38, 157–62,
    187
Civil War, U.S., 2, 466
Cizik, Richard, 327
Clark, Ramsey, 187
Clark, William, 325, 331
Clarke, Richard, 456
Clay, Lucius, 139
Clifford, Clark, 4, 33–34, 36, 37, 38–43, 44,
    45, 46, 47, 48–49, 51, 56, 57, 58, 59,

60, 61, 63–65, 67, 71, 97, 149, 169,
    184–85, 267, 301
Clines, Francis X., 329
Clinton, Bill, 402–55
    advisers of, 402–11, 412, 417–19, 421–33,
        437–39, 445, 447, 448, 450, 451–55
    American University speech of (1993),
        410–11
    approval ratings of, 423
    Balkans policy of, 450–54
    Carter compared with, 405–6
    as centrist ("New Democrat"), 402,
        405, 418, 423–25, 428, 430, 431,
        438–41
    D-Day anniversary speech of (1994),
        419–21
    Democratic National Convention
        speech of (2000), 454–55
    domestic policies of, 404–9, 412–17,
        421–35, 438–41, 443
    economic policies of, 404–9, 413,
        424–25, 443
    editorial revisions by, 402–4, 407,
        410–11, 424, 427, 450, 451, 454–55
    "era of big government" phrase of, 438–41
    extemporaneous remarks of, 407–8,
        410–11, 425–26, 429, 432, 441–42
    FDR memorial speech of (1995), 433–34
    foreign policy of, 408, 409–11, 450–54,
        465, 474
    as governor of Arkansas, 405, 406, 421
    health care program of, 412–15, 422
    impeachment of, 447, 449–50, 461
    inaugural address of (1993), 402–4
    Lewinsky scandal and, 442–50, 454
    memoirs of, 413, 416–17
    Memphis speech of, 415–17, 420
    "New Covenant" phrase of, 428
    Oklahoma City bombing speech of
        (1995), 435–37
    oratorical skills of, 404, 405–11, 413,
        428–29, 446, 450
    Oval Office speech of (1993), 404–7
    "Pile of Vetoes" speech of, 431, 432–33,
        438
    polls used by, 417, 424, 426, 429,
        430–31, 438, 441
    presidential campaign of (1992), 394,
        399, 405, 418
    presidential campaign of (1996), 431,
        440, 441–42
    press coverage of, 404, 406, 407, 414,
        428, 433, 434–36, 439–41, 444, 446,
        447, 450, 453, 461
    "putting people first" slogan of, 405

Clinton, Bill *(cont.)*
  Republican opposition to, 421–35,
    438–41, 447, 449–50, 452, 461
  speechwriters of, 4, 402–55, 464–65,
    471, 480
  State of the Union addresses of, 404,
    407–9, 415, 425–29, 430, 438–41,
    443–46, 448, 449–50
  style of, 402–9, 417–21, 436–37, 438,
    440–41, 478
  television broadcasts of, 451, 452–53
  "triangulation" strategy of, 423–25
Clinton, Hillary, 403, 407, 409, 412, 414,
    422, 424, 426, 427, 430, 435, 443,
    446, 448, 449
Cohen, Ben, 15, 21
Colby, William, 252
Cold War, 42–47, 69–81, 97–100, 127, 133,
    138–41, 143, 274–75, 288–90,
    317–30, 343–47, 369–72, 374–78,
    381, 383, 411, 416, 420, 450
Cole, Ken, 245
Colson, Charles, 222, 461
Columbus, Christopher, 33
communism, 35, 42–47, 63, 65–66, 69–71,
    83, 96, 115, 117–18, 119, 274–77,
    295n, 369–72, 374–78, 381, 383,
    394, 416, 467
Connally, John, 183, 196
Conner, Caryl, 294
Connor, James, 257
Constitution, U.S., 10n, 135, 136, 228, 233,
    313, 388, 435n, 450n
Contract with America, 421–35
Conway, Rose, 36, 39
Coolidge, Calvin, 2, 3, 42n
Cooper, Gary, 382
Corcoran, Tom, 15, 17, 18, 21, 47
Corn, David, 480
Cousins, Norman, 99, 129–30
Cox, Archibald, 223, 225
Coyne, John, 226, 229, 235, 236, 237, 250
Coyne, Walter, 175
Crittenden, Danielle, 457
Croisant, Eugene, 394
Cuba, 114–15, 117–18, 120, 122–29, 156,
    223, 274
Cuban Missile Crisis (1962), 122–29
Curiel, Carolyn, 415, 418, 436, 437–38
Cutler, Robert, 75, 79

Daley, Richard J., 186
Dallek, Robert, 110n, 133, 151, 153n
Daniels, Jonathan, 49
Danko, Mary, 385–86

Darman, Richard, 319, 335–36, 338, 343,
    345, 361, 363, 379, 381, 395
Davis, Mark, 364–68, 373, 376–77, 381–82
Dawson, Thomas, 343
D-Day (Ambrose), 420
Dean, John, 220, 221, 222, 223
Deaver, Michael, 265, 313, 334, 336, 337,
    338, 341
Defense Department, U.S., 70, 72–73,
    79–80, 319–20, 338
Demarest, David, 364, 367, 370, 372, 375,
    380, 385–86, 387n, 389, 392, 393,
    394, 396, 397, 400–401
Democratic National Committee (DNC),
    50, 53, 54–55, 165
Democratic national conventions, 3, 5–9,
    51–52, 108, 155, 187, 309, 454–55
Denison, George, 264
Dewey, Thomas E., 58–59, 96
Diamond, Martin, 261
Dillon, Douglas, 106, 126
Dobrosielski, Marian, 134
Dolan, Anthony, 317–18, 319, 321, 324–25,
    326, 327, 329, 330, 337, 341–42, 343,
    355–56, 406–7
Dole, Elizabeth, 332, 334, 367
Dole, Robert, 219, 322, 429, 438, 441, 442,
    461
Doolittle, Jerry, 271, 272–75, 285–86, 288
Downton, Dorothy, 255
Dreyer, David, 405, 407, 412, 413
Drug Enforcement Agency (DEA), 369–72
Duberstein, Ken, 358
Duggan, Ervin, 154, 179
Dukakis, Michael, 363, 402
Dulles, Allen, 73, 115
Dulles, John Foster, 70, 72–73, 75, 79–80, 81

Eagleburger, Lawrence, 210
East Germany, 138–41, 356, 358, 374–78,
    383
Eastwood, Clint, 342, 363
Edmonds, Terry, 408–9, 438, 454, 455
Ehrlichman, John, 192, 198, 212, 217, 221,
    222, 223
Eisenhower, Dwight D., 69–100
  anticommunism of, 69–71, 83, 96
  "Atoms for Peace" speech of (1953),
    77–81, 98
  "Chance for Peace" speech of (1953),
    74–75
  civil rights as viewed by, 87–88, 89, 90,
    96, 135, 161
  in congressional campaign (1954),
    83–85, 96

.

in congressional campaign (1958), 95–97
Cuban policy of, 114, 117–18
domestic policies of, 87–88
editorial revisions by, 86–87, 96–97
farewell address of (1961), 95, 97–100, 129
foreign policy of, 69–81, 87n, 89, 90, 97–100, 114, 117–18
Hollywood Bowl speech of (1954), 83–84
ill health of, 74, 92–94
Korean policy of, 90, 98
"military-industrial complex" warning of, 98–100
military spending criticized by, 71–75, 97–100
nuclear policy of, 71–81, 129
"Operation Candor" approach of, 75–81
personality of, 84–85
personal secretaries of, 80, 92
presidential campaign of (1952), 70, 83, 90, 95, 96
presidential campaign of (1956), 88–89, 103
press coverage of, 86, 89, 94, 95–96
as Republican Party leader, 58, 83–84, 88–89, 95–97
second inaugural address of (1957), 89
Soviet policy of, 69–81, 90, 97–100
speechwriters of, 68, 69–100, 161, 164, 165
State of the Union addresses of, 93–94, 97–98
style of, 76–77, 83–88, 90–91, 96–97, 135, 284, 364
television broadcasts of, 76–77, 79, 90–91
Eisenhower, Milton, 74, 96
Eizenstat, Stuart, 282–83, 284, 287, 294–95, 299, 300, 302
Eliot, T. S., 440–41
Elizabeth II, Queen of England, 192
Elliott, Bentley, 322, 334, 335, 337, 338, 342, 343, 347–48, 349, 350–51, 355, 361
Ellsberg, Daniel, 223
Elsey, George, 32–33, 37, 40–43, 45, 46–47, 49, 51, 54–55, 56, 59, 60, 61, 62, 63–64, 65, 67, 97
Elz, Dieter, 354
Elz, Ingeborg, 354, 355
Emancipation Proclamation, 378
Emanuel, Rahm, 445, 448
Erwin, Frank, 145–46
Europe, Eastern, 267, 326, 369–72, 374–78, 383
see also specific countries

Europe, Western, 133–34, 137, 138–41, 191, 276–77, 320–21, 331, 343–46
see also specific countries
Ewald, William Bragg, 82, 83, 85

Fahrenkopf, Frank, 365
Fallows, James, 267, 268–71, 273, 275, 278, 279, 280–86, 288, 289, 290–94, 297, 493
Farewell Address (Washington), 1, 95, 100
Feldman, Myer "Mike," 105–6, 108, 113, 116, 118–19, 142, 147, 148–49
Ferguson, Andrew, 394, 396, 398, 399
Fitzwater, Marlin, 352, 374–75, 378, 395, 397
Flanigan, Peter, 198
Foley, Tom, 379
Ford, Betty, 253, 264
Ford, Gerald R., 230–67
advisers of, 230–37, 240–67
Bicentennial speeches of, 253, 258–59, 261–63, 267
as congressional leader, 232, 249
domestic policies of, 237–38, 241–50, 251, 265–66
economic program of, 241–42, 244, 251, 265–66
editorial revisions by, 243–47, 251
"fireside chat" of (1975), 243–45
foreign policy of, 201, 247, 263, 265, 266, 267, 285
Gridiron Club speech of (1968), 231
"national nightmare" quote of, 233–34
Nixon compared with, 233, 236, 243
Nixon pardoned by, 238–40, 243, 267
Nixon's resignation and, 230–32
Ohio State speech of (1974), 237–38
oratorical skills of, 246–48, 249, 253, 260–61, 263–64
personality of, 236–39, 254–55
presidential campaign of (1976), 249–50, 252, 253, 254, 257–59, 261, 262, 263–67, 285
press coverage of, 231, 234–35, 238, 239–40, 242, 247, 251, 261, 263, 265
Republican National Convention speech of (1976), 232, 249, 262, 263–64, 267
as Republican Party leader, 232, 241, 249, 252, 253, 256–57, 262
Southern Baptist Convention speech of (1976), 260–61
speechwriters of, 230–67, 314, 317, 319, 323, 338, 352, 367n
State of the Union addresses of, 243, 245–47, 253–56

Ford, Gerald R. *(cont.)*
style of, 236–38, 243–49, 260–61, 263–65
swearing-in ceremony of (1974), 231–34
television broadcasts of, 243–45, 252
Truman compared with, 246, 247, 267
Valley Forge speech of (1976), 259, 262
as vice president, 230–32
Vietnam policy of, 201, 247
"whip inflation now" program of, 241–42
Fortas, Abe, 147, 169
Foster, Vince, 443
France, 20, 21, 133–34, 190, 337–40,
419–21, 482
Frankfurter, Felix, 13, 117
Freedman, Tom, 441
Freeman, John, 191
Freeman, Orville, 186
Friedman, Milton, 235, 242, 247, 249, 253,
254–55, 256
Friendly, Al, 308
From, Al, 428
Frum, Danielle Crittenden, 457
Frum, David, 457–58, 459, 460, 462,
474–76, 477, 479
Fulbright, William J., 198
Furness, Betty, 177

Galbraith, John Kenneth, 106, 107, 109,
119, 142
Gallagher, Cornelius, 187
Gallup, George, 20
Garment, Leonard, 195, 198
Gates, Robert, 370
Gavin, William, 195, 200, 203
Gephardt, Richard, 376, 379, 405
Gergen, David, 219, 225–26, 234–35, 248,
251–52, 255, 256, 261, 266, 317, 319,
328, 329–30, 334, 389, 412, 417
Germany, 19–20, 32, 138–41, 190, 191–92,
343, 354–58, 374–78, 381, 383, 475,
476
Gerson, Michael, 32n, 457, 458, 459, 460–63,
466, 467, 468, 469, 472, 473n, 475,
476–77, 478, 479, 480, 481–82, 483,
485, 486, 489–90, 492–94
Gettysburg Address, 2n, 105, 166, 314n, 338
Gibson, John, 464–65, 467–68, 471, 480,
481, 482
Gilder, Josh, 318, 342–45, 347, 348, 356,
357n, 358, 361
Gingrich, Newt, 96n, 384, 421–35
Ginsburg, David, 6
Giuliani, Rudolph, 417, 470–71
Glastris, Paul, 447, 454, 455
Goethe, Johann Wolfgang von, 191

Goldberg, Arthur, 106
Goldman, Eric, 151
Goldwater, Barry, 152n, 231, 313
Goldwin, Robert, 244
Good Society, The (Lippmann), 151–52
Goodwin, Doris Kearns, 168
Goodwin, Richard N., 104, 108, 116–19,
120, 142, 143, 147, 149–53, 155–57,
158, 159–61, 162, 164, 168–69, 174,
279, 402
Gorbachev, Mikhail, 346, 353–54, 355, 357,
358, 377
Gore, Al, 402, 413, 417, 428, 430, 454, 455,
472n
Gottheimer, Josh, 454
Graham, Billy, 188, 199
Graham, Katharine, 142, 147, 148
Graham, Wallace, 56
Grant, Mary Kate, 363, 366, 392–93, 400–401
Granum, Rex, 301
Great Britain, 20, 22, 23, 24–25, 28, 32, 42,
132, 190, 191, 192, 324–26, 327, 482,
484, 485–86, 487n
Great Depression, 9–10, 14, 15, 16–19, 27,
151–52, 394
Greenspan, Alan, 244, 245, 255, 256
Griscom, Tom, 355n, 356n, 357, 395
Gromyko, Andrei, 128, 282
Gruening, Ernest, 109
Gulf War, 366, 380–83, 385–88, 474, 476

Haass, Richard, 380
Hadley, Stephen, 465, 478, 481–82, 483,
484, 485
Haig, Alexander, 211, 226–27, 228, 240–41
Haldeman, H. R., 191, 192, 194, 196, 198,
199, 200, 201, 202, 203–7, 208, 211,
212, 215, 216, 217, 219–21, 226, 250
Haley, Alex, 288
Halperin, David, 452
Hamilton, Alexander, 1
Hardesty, Robert, 161, 165–67, 171–74,
175–76
Harding, Warren G., 2–3, 108
Hardy, Benjamin, 60, 61, 63
Harkin, Tom, 418
Harlow, Bryce, 81–85, 99
Harriman, Averell, 67, 287
Harris, John F., 425
Hart, Gary, 409, 412
Hartley, Muriel, 227
Hartmann, Robert, 230, 231–35, 236, 237,
238–42, 243, 244, 245–49, 250, 251–66
Hassett, William, 66–67
Healy, Timothy, 403

Hechler, Kenneth, 44, 55n, 65, 67–68
Heller, Walter, 146–47
Helms, Jesse, 417
Henry, Patrick, 254
Hernreich, Nancy, 424
Hersey, John, 240, 247
Hertzberg, Hendrik "Rick," 271–72, 274,
    275, 280, 281–83, 284, 287, 292–93,
    296–97, 299, 301–2, 303, 305–9, 310,
    311, 329, 367n, 472n
Hesbergh, Theodore, 261
Hess, Stephen, 94, 97
Higby, Larry, 213, 215
Higgins, Anne, 335
High, Stanley, 16–17, 18, 21
"High Flight" (Magee), 349
Hinchliffe, Beth, 400–401
Hinckley, John, Jr., 316
Hirohito, Emperor of Japan, 34
Hirschberg, Vera, 219
Hitler, Adolf, 141, 381
Hobby, Oveta Culp, 76
Holmes, Oliver Wendell, 107–8
Hoover, Herbert, 4, 58, 102
Hoover, J. Edgar, 47, 218
Hopkins, Harry L., 21–24, 25, 26, 27,
    28–29, 33, 163
Howard, George, 469–70
Howe, Louis McHenry, 8–9, 12, 13, 14, 21,
    22
Huebner, Lee, 193–94, 195, 203, 217–18,
    219, 225–26
Hughes, Emmet, 69, 70–73, 74, 75, 81, 82,
    86, 88–90, 149, 165
Hughes, Karen, 458, 459, 465–66, 468–69,
    471, 472, 479, 484, 486, 487
Hull, Cordell, 9, 14
Humes, Jamie, 194, 195
Hummelsine, Carl, 45
Humphrey, George, 76
Humphrey, Hubert, 119, 186–87, 189n,
    231, 257, 309
Hunt, E. Howard, 220
Hunt, James, 417
Huntley, Chet, 198
Hussein, Saddam, 380–83, 385–88, 474–89
Hutcheson, Rick, 277

Ickes, Harold, 429, 430, 431, 432, 434
Intermediate Nuclear Forces Treaty (1987),
    320n, 353–54, 358
Iowa, USS, explosion on (1989), 368–69
Iran, 63, 298, 307, 308–9, 351–53, 375, 445,
    475–76, 478–79
Iran-Contra scandal, 351–53, 445

Iran hostage crisis, 307, 308–9, 375
Iraq, 366, 380–83, 385–88, 474–89, 491
Iraq War, 474–89, 491
Isikoff, Michael, 374, 480
Israel, 116, 291–93
Italy, 21, 32, 124, 125, 190, 191–92, 475, 476

Jackson, Andrew, 1–2, 284
Jackson, C. D., 69–70, 73, 75, 78, 79–80,
    86, 88–89, 94
Jackson, Jesse, 446
Jackson, Keith, 373
Jagoda, Barry, 273
Japan, 26–27, 28, 32, 34, 66, 299, 475, 476,
    487n
Jefferson, Thomas, 113–14, 163–64,
    313–14, 363
Jensen, Paul, 293
Johnson, Andrew, 2
Johnson, Haynes, 412, 413
Johnson, Hugh, 9–10, 13, 21
Johnson, Lady Bird, 145, 178–79, 183
Johnson, Lyndon B., 145–87
    advisers of, 148–49, 162–64, 167–68,
        169, 170, 174–77, 181–85
    budget of, 172–74
    cabinet appointments of, 64, 65, 67, 167
    civil rights legislation of, 157–62, 187
    as "courthouse square politician,"
        178–81
    as Democratic Party leader, 149, 444
    domestic policies of, 151–64, 165, 167,
        168, 171, 183–84, 441
    editorial revisions by, 149, 159–62, 164,
        166
    extemporaneous remarks of, 150–51,
        178–81
    FDR compared with, 151, 155
    foreign policy of, 152n, 156–57, 162,
        167–71, 284
    "Great Society" phrase of, 151–53
    Great Society programs of, 151–56,
        163–64, 165, 167, 168, 174n,
        183–84, 208, 388
    "guns and butter" speech of (1966),
        168–69, 171, 183
    inaugural address of (1965), 155, 157
    JFK assassination and, 145–48
    JFK compared with, 150, 155, 159,
        175–76, 180
    memoirs of, 182
    "my fellow Americans" phrase of, 364
    Nixon compared with, 191, 192
    personality of, 149–51, 157–58, 162,
        166, 169, 174–83

Johnson, Lyndon B. *(cont.)*
  presidential campaign of (1964), 152n,
    155, 156–57, 183, 187, 188
  press conferences of, 168, 180–81
  press coverage of, 152, 153, 161, 163,
    167, 168, 171–74, 176, 179, 180–81,
    187
  "rule of four" of, 166
  second term declined by (1968), 181–87,
    191, 257n
  space program of, 171–73
  speechwriters of, 142, 145–87, 279, 406,
    437
  State of the Union addresses of, 148,
    157, 168–69, 171, 181–87
  style of, 146, 148, 150–51, 154–55,
    159–62, 165, 166, 175–83
  swearing-in ceremony of (1963), 145,
    146
  television broadcasts of, 151, 170,
    179–81
  as Texas politician, 147, 150, 154,
    162–63, 166, 178–81
  Truman compared with, 179, 183–84
  University of Kentucky speech of
    (1965), 157
  University of Michigan speech of
    (1964), 152–53
  as vice president, 111, 123, 139, 145–46
  Vietnam policy of, 152n, 156–57,
    167–71, 183–87
  "we shall overcome" phrase used by,
    160–61
  written messages of, 165–67
Johnson, Michael, 257
Joint Chiefs of Staff, U.S., 79–80, 115, 126,
  131, 330–32, 451
Jones, Joseph, 44, 45
Jones, Paula, 442, 443, 444–45, 448–49
Jordan, Hamilton, 281, 287, 294–95, 297,
  300, 301
Jorden, W. J. "Bill," 155
Joseph, Robert, 480, 484n
Joulwan, George, 227
Judge, Clark, 361, 408n
Judson Welliver Society, 321, 406–7, 472n

Katzenbach, Nicholas, 135–36
Kayle, Milton, 45
Kaysen, Carl, 130–31
Kean, Thomas, 398
Kendall, Amos, 1
Kennan, George, 287
Kennedy, Caroline, 106, 130
Kennedy, Edward M., 298, 306, 307, 309

Kennedy, Jacqueline, 109, 145, 146
Kennedy, John F., 100–144
  advisers of, 105–11, 109, 114–29, 163,
    267
  Alliance for Progress policy of, 117–18,
    119, 152
  American University speech of (1963),
    130–34, 135, 140, 411
  America's Cup speech of (1962), 112n
  anticommunism of, 115, 117–18, 133,
    138–41
  "ask not" passage of, 105–9
  assassination of, 141, 145–48, 306–7
  Bay of Pigs invasion ordered by (1961),
    114–15, 120, 122, 123, 223
  Berlin speech of (1963), 138–41,
    191–92, 345, 354
  bureaucracy circumvented by, 115–16,
    120–21, 129, 131–32
  cabinet appointments of, 65, 106, 116,
    123, 126–27, 132
  as Catholic, 101, 103, 118, 261
  civil rights movement supported by,
    110–11, 132, 134–38
  correspondence of, 124–25, 130, 133
  in Cuban Missile Crisis (1962), 122–29
  Cuban policy of, 114–15, 120, 122–29
  Democratic National Convention
    speech of (1960), 108
  domestic policies of, 110–11, 116, 123,
    129, 134–38
  editorial revisions by, 102, 109–10,
    113–14, 116, 119, 121, 141–44,
    202n, 427n
  extemporaneous remarks of, 136–41
  FDR compared with, 13, 105, 110, 114,
    121, 142
  foreign policy of, 98–99, 100, 111,
    117–18, 119, 120–34, 138–41
  "Ich bin ein Berliner" phrase of, 139–41,
    191–92, 345
  inaugural address of (1961), 100,
    104–13, 122, 131, 141n, 142–43,
    188, 189–90, 269, 427n, 491
  Latin American policy of, 117–18, 119,
    120, 121, 127
  LBJ compared with, 150, 155, 159,
    175–76, 180
  liberalism of, 101–2, 103, 119, 134–35
  "missile gap" allegations of, 98–99
  New Frontier policies of, 108, 151, 208,
    283, 293
  Nixon compared with, 111, 141–42,
    188, 189–92, 197, 223
  nuclear policy of, 122–34

nuclear test ban treaty of, 129–34
oratorical skills of, 111, 113, 136–41
presidential campaign of (1960), 97,
    104–5, 116, 117–18, 119, 137,
    141–42, 264
press conferences of, 114, 122–23, 306
press coverage of, 103–4, 109–10, 114,
    121, 122–23, 126, 128, 137, 141–42,
    306
public educated by, 114, 130, 133–36
Pulitzer Prize awarded to, 110, 119
Republican opposition to, 117–18
reputation of, 141–44, 148, 175–76,
    306–7
Senate campaign of (1952), 101–2
Soviet relations of, 110, 115, 122–34,
    138, 140–41, 143
space program of, 138, 171
speechwriters of, 4, 100–144, 147, 148,
    149, 150, 159, 279, 402, 406, 427n
State of the Union addresses of, 109,
    121, 138
style of, 13, 101–2, 111–13, 131–32,
    136–44, 148, 150, 155, 159, 175–76,
    180, 188, 359, 382, 390, 438, 491
television broadcasts of, 108, 135,
    136–37, 180
Truman compared with, 129, 134
University of California speech of
    (1962), 121–22
as vice-presidential candidate (1956),
    103
at Vienna summit (1961), 115–16, 135
Kennedy, Joseph P., Sr., 102, 103, 117, 121
Kennedy, Robert F., 115, 120, 122, 123,
    135, 136, 137, 139, 184, 192, 444
Kennedy or Nixon: Does It Make Any Dif-
    ference? (Schlesinger), 119, 120
Kennerly, David Hume, 260
Keogh, James, 192, 194, 195, 198, 199, 200,
    205, 206, 207, 211
Kerry, John F., 489
Keyes, Paul, 188–89
Khachigian, Ken, 226–27, 312–14, 315,
    316, 317, 367n
Khomeini, Ayatollah Ruholla, 298
Khrushchev, Nikita, 112, 115–16, 124–25,
    129–30, 132, 140n
Kieve, Robert, 71, 76–77, 82
Kilberg, Bobbie, 379
Killian, James, 99
King, Martin Luther, Jr., 161, 403, 415–16,
    420
King, Rodney, 396–97
Kingon, Al, 343

Kintner, Robert, 174–76, 177, 178, 179
Kissinger, Henry, 188, 189, 192, 196, 197,
    206, 207, 209–10, 211, 212, 216–17,
    218, 223, 252, 275, 276–77, 410
Kleindienst, Richard, 221
Koch, Noel, 212, 214, 314
Kohl, Helmut, 376
Koppel, Ted, 308
Korean War, 65–67, 90, 98, 156, 176,
    183–84, 274
Kornblum, John, 354, 357
Kosovo, 451–54
Kraemer, Sven, 328
Krauthammer, Charles, 479
Kristol, Irving, 259, 261
Kross, Anna, 152
Kusnet, David, 402, 403, 405, 406, 409,
    412, 418–19, 437
Kuwait, 380–83, 385–88

labor unions, 37–40, 47, 57, 58, 214,
    241–42, 361
Lake, Anthony, 210–11, 409, 410, 411, 412,
    419, 452
Lambie, James, 77, 78
Lamm, Richard, 367
Landis, Jim, 103
Lange, Mark, 367, 380, 400–401
Langlie, Arthur, 88
Larson, Arthur, 83, 86, 87–88, 89, 90–94,
    165
Latin America, 117–18, 119, 120, 121, 127,
    206
Lawrence, Bill, 204
Leach, James, 365
LeHand, Marguerite "Missy," 15, 17, 19
Lenin, V. I., 358
Levi, Edward, 263
Lewinsky, Monica, 442–50, 454
Lewis, Ann, 440
Lewis, Anthony, 329, 425
Lewis, C. S., 327
Lewis, John, 283
Lewis, Neil A., 388
Libby, I. Lewis "Scooter," 456, 483
Lincoln, Abraham, 2, 22, 62, 86, 105, 106,
    166, 188, 313–14, 316, 338, 378,
    391n
Lincoln, Evelyn, 107, 109
Lindley, Ernest K., 15
Lindsay, John, 303
Lippmann, Walter, 99, 109, 110, 122,
    151–52
Little, Rich, 322
Liu, Eric, 419–20, 437

Lloyd, David, 54, 59, 60, 65
Lochner, Robert, 140
Long, Russell, 187
Lord, Winston, 206n, 210, 211
Lott, Trent, 422
Luce, Henry, 86

MacArthur, Douglas, 28, 65–67, 85, 87, 487
Macaulay, Thomas, 163
McAuliffe, Christa, 348
McCain, John, Jr., 209
McCall, Charles, 263
McCann, Kevin, 77, 85–86, 88
McCarthy, Colman, 291
McCarthy, Eugene, 184, 257n
McCarthy, Joseph, 83, 96, 101, 275
McConnell, John, 32n, 456, 457–58, 459,
    460, 461, 462, 463, 466, 467, 473,
    476–77, 478, 479, 483, 484, 485–86,
    488, 493
McCord, James, 220
McCormack, John, 187
McCrum, Marie, 80
McCullough, David, 38, 62
McCurry, Mike, 438
McDonald, Alonzo, 305
McFarlane, Robert "Bud," 328, 330–31,
    339, 346
McGroarty, Dan, 366, 387, 395–96, 399,
    400–401
McGurn, William, 492–93
McHugh, Frank, 313
McLarty, Thomas "Mack," 407
McLaughlin, Ann, 367
McLaughlin, John, 235
MacLeish, Archibald, 21
McNally, Ed, 366–67, 370–71, 375, 383,
    385, 400–401
McNamara, Robert, 123, 131, 165, 167,
    186
McNulty, Jack, 175
McPherson, Harry, 113n, 163, 166, 167,
    171, 176, 177, 178, 181n, 184–85
Madison, James, 1
Magee, John Gillespie, 349
Magnuson, Warren, 109
Maguire, Charles, 175, 179, 187
Malenkov, Georgi, 73, 77
Malinowski, Tom, 421, 451–54, 467–68,
    471
Mansfield, Mike, 187, 198
Marsh, Jack, 232, 237, 261, 264
Marshall, Burke, 136
Marshall, George C., 53, 83, 96
Marshall Plan, 60–63, 129, 263

Martin, Christina, 399
Martin, Jack, 84
Martin, Louis, 110–11
Marx, Karl, 326
Maseng, Mari, 316, 322, 326, 332–33, 335,
    336, 360, 367
Matthews, Chris, 309–10, 434
Mead, Bob, 243
Meany, George, 214
Meese, Ed, 341
"Men behind the Guns, The" (Rooney),
    368
Mencken, H. L., 3, 95
Menino, Thomas, 418
Meyer, Karl, 118
"Mice," 343, 346–47, 349, 361
Michel, Bob, 99, 235
Middle East, 116, 291–92, 381, 394, 474,
    489, 491
Middleton, Harry, 175, 177, 178
Milbank, Dana, 464
Milford, James, 372–73
Miller, Emma Guffey, 52
Miller, William Lee, 102
Milosevic, Slobodan, 452–54
Mitchell, George, 376, 379
Mitchell, John, 222
Mizell, Wilmer "Vinegar Bend," 249
Mohammad Reza Pahlavi, shah of Iran,
    298, 307
Moley, Raymond, 6–7, 8, 9–12, 14–16, 17,
    18, 21, 23n, 71, 89, 110
Molotov, Vyacheslav, 75
Mondale, Walter, 292, 293–94, 299, 301,
    302, 341, 402, 409
Monnet, Jean, 25
Montgomery, Robert, 76–77
Moore, Dick, 211
Moore, Henson, 396, 397
Moos, Malcolm, 85n, 91, 95–97
Moran, Robert, 457
Morison, Samuel Eliot, 63
Morris, Dick, 421–33, 436n, 438, 439, 440,
    441
Morrow, Frederic, 91–92, 93, 94, 161
Morse, Brad, 99
Morse, Wayne, 40
Moyers, Bill, 145–46, 149, 152–53, 154,
    159–60, 162, 163–64, 165, 168–69,
    175, 176, 293
Moynihan, Daniel Patrick, 188, 276, 295n
Mudd, Roger, 307
Muir, William, 322, 336
Murphy, Charles, 41, 47–49, 51, 54, 56, 63,
    64–65, 68, 71

Murphy, Daniel, 331
Murphy, George, 231
Mutual Contempt (Shesol), 444

Nader, Ralph, 270, 309
National Security Council (NSC), 114–15,
    123–29, 192, 210–11, 217, 252, 281,
    282, 308, 319–20, 324, 325, 328, 339,
    346–47, 357, 381, 382, 409–10, 411,
    419, 421, 456, 464–65, 480
Nazism, 19–20, 32, 343, 381, 475, 476
Nesmith, Achsah, 270n, 271, 277, 284,
    307–8
Nessen, Ron, 235n, 243, 244, 245
Neusner, Noam, 472
Neustadt, Richard, 41, 65
"New Deal for America, A" (Chase), 6
Nix, Michele, 395
Nixon, Richard M., 188–234
    advisers of, 188–92, 204, 410
    Air Force Academy speech of (1969),
        195–99
    Canadian Parliament speech of (1972),
        217–18
    "Checkers speech" of (1952), 192
    conservatism of, 194–99, 201–5, 214,
        219–20
    domestic policies of, 195, 212–14
    editorial revisions by, 197, 199–210,
        215, 216
    European tour of (1969), 190–92
    extemporaneous remarks of, 190, 191,
        192–93, 214, 229
    FDR compared with, 188, 192–93, 213
    Ford compared with, 233, 236, 243
    foreign policy of, 189, 191–92, 195–99,
        200, 201–5, 206, 209–12, 215–17,
        222, 275, 410
    "I am not a crook" quote of, 225
    impeachment proceedings against,
        226–27, 228
    inaugural address of (1969), 188–90,
        195, 228
    JFK compared with, 111, 141–42, 188,
        189–92, 197, 223
    LBJ compared with, 191, 192
    liberal opposition to, 196, 198, 201,
        204–5
    memoirs of, 204
    "New American Revolution" phrase of,
        212–13
    Nixon Doctrine of, 203, 210
    pardon of, 238–40, 243, 267
    personality of, 193, 197–200, 221–23,
        226, 228, 461
    presidential campaign of (1960), 97,
        104–5, 116, 119, 141–42, 190, 192,
        264
    presidential campaign of (1968), 184,
        189n, 195
    presidential campaign of (1972), 219
    press conferences of, 192, 194
    press coverage of, 15, 191, 192, 194,
        197–98, 201, 204, 209, 213, 223,
        226–27, 231
    as Republican Party leader, 195–96
    resignation of, 222, 227–34, 240
    secret tapes of, 220, 223, 225, 226,
        227–28
    "silent majority" phrase of, 201–5,
        212–13, 214
    Silent Majority speech of (1969), 201–5,
        212–13
    Soviet policy of, 189, 197, 198, 218
    speechwriters of, 188–229, 312, 314,
        323, 345, 367n, 409, 410
    State of the Union addresses of, 207–9,
        212–13, 215–17, 445
    style of, 188, 190, 191–94, 196–97,
        199–200, 203–6, 209–10, 212, 214,
        215–19, 221–23, 228–29
    television broadcasts of, 189n, 192,
        201–5, 213, 216
    as vice president, 192
    Vietnam policy of, 195, 196, 198–99,
        200, 201–5, 209–11, 215–16, 218,
        219
    Watergate scandal of, 220–34, 240, 241,
        243, 294, 301, 352, 445, 461
Nixon, Tricia, 204
Noonan, Peggy, 137n, 195, 335–46,
    348–49, 350, 351, 359–60, 362, 363,
    367, 395, 420, 491
Noriega, Manuel, 378–79
Norris, George, 102
North American Free Trade Agreement
    (NAFTA), 410, 415
North Atlantic Treaty Organization
    (NATO), 60, 210, 241, 331, 451–54
North Korea, 157, 478–79
Novak, Robert, 479
nuclear weapons, 71–81, 97–100, 122–34,
    196–97, 278, 289, 298–99, 310–11,
    320–21, 327, 330–32, 353–54, 358,
    416
Nugent, Luci Johnson, 185–86

O'Brien, Larry, 148, 186
O'Donnell, Kenneth, 139
O'Neill, Paul, 238, 254

Orben, Robert, 230–31, 235, 239–40, 246–49, 253, 256, 257, 258, 264–65, 267
Ordeal of Power, The (Hughes), 89–90
Osborne, John, 197–98, 241

Pace, Frank, 66
Paine, Thomas, 255
Panama, 149, 263, 278, 281, 284–86, 378–79
Panetta, Leon, 405, 430, 431
Parsons, Al, 257
Parvin, Landon, 318, 319n, 322–23, 334, 342, 351–53
"Passionless Presidency, The" (Fallows), 297
Pataki, George, 470–71
Peale, Norman Vincent, 199
Pearl Harbor attack (1941), 26–27, 39, 125, 126, 392–93
Penn, Mark, 438
Penny, Don, 263–64
Pericles, 105, 106
Perot, H. Ross, 399
Persons, Wilton J., 85
Pierce, Samuel, 365
Podesta, John, 445
Podhoretz, John, 396
Poindexter, John, 348
Poland, 19–20, 326, 369, 370–71, 374, 487n
Polk, James K., 2, 134
Polke, James, 139
Pollack, John, 455
Porter, Roger, 396
Powell, Colin, 352, 356n, 357, 451, 465n, 468, 471, 481, 484, 485
Powell, Jody, 271, 280, 287, 297, 300, 301, 308
Price, Raymond, 188, 192, 193, 194, 195, 197, 199–200, 205–8, 209, 210, 211, 213, 215, 219, 220–23, 226–29
Prince, Jonathan, 408n, 430n, 435, 436, 437, 438, 442, 446
Profiles in Courage (Kennedy), 102, 110, 202n
Provost, Steve, 398–400
Pucinski, Roman, 187
Pullen, Frances "Kaye," 236, 250, 253
Pulliam, Eugene, 187

Qaddafi, Muammar al-, 320–21
Quayle, Dan, 462, 463, 479
Quigg, Philip, 210
Quinn, Jack, 430
Quinn, Sally, 232–33

Rackleff, Robert, 293
Rafshoon, Gerald, 269, 273, 283n, 287, 290, 294–98, 299, 300, 301, 302

Rather, Dan, 226, 336
Rayburn, Sam, 40, 52
Reagan, Nancy, 27n, 315, 324, 336, 351–52, 353
Reagan, Ronald, 312–61
  advisers of, 312, 317–25, 328, 334–53
  "America is back" phrase of, 347, 348
  anticommunism of, 276, 313, 317–30, 343–48, 354–59
  assassination attempt against (1981), 316–17, 320; 351
  Berlin Wall speech of (1987), 354–58
  big government opposed by, 313, 314
  Bitburg Cemetery speech of (1985), 343
  British Parliament addressed by (1982), 324–26, 327, 346
  Challenger disaster speech of (1986), 348, 486
  conservative support for, 276, 313, 314, 317–30, 341–48, 350, 355–57, 360–61
  D-Day anniversary ("Pointe du Hoc") speech of (1984), 337–40, 391, 419, 420
  diary of, 315n, 320–21, 324, 333–34, 351, 353
  domestic policies of, 313, 314, 315–16, 319, 322, 328–29, 330, 333, 342, 380, 404n, 406
  economic policies of, 315–16, 322, 330, 342, 380, 404n, 406
  editorial revisions by, 312–15, 325, 353
  European Parliament speech of (1985), 343–46
  "Evil Empire" speech of (1982), 325–30, 344
  extemporaneous remarks of, 333–34
  farewell speech of (1989), 359–60
  foreign policy of, 318–21, 324–47, 351–58
  as former actor, 312–13, 330, 340–41, 361
  at Geneva summit (1985), 346–47
  George H. W. Bush compared with, 363, 364, 365, 367, 373, 380, 381, 382, 391
  as GE spokesman, 312–13
  "Gipper" quote of, 340–41
  as governor of California, 313
  as "Great Communicator," 360–61
  gubernatorial campaign of (1966), 321
  inaugural address of (1981), 312–15
  in Iran-Contra scandal, 351–53, 445
  "message of the day" approach of, 265
  Moscow University speech of (1988), 358–59

National Press Club speech of (1981), 319–21

nuclear policy of, 320–21, 330–32, 353–54

oratorical skills of, 312–15, 340–41, 360–61, 364, 408n

pragmatist support for, 318–19, 324–25, 328–29, 361

presidential campaign of (1976), 252, 253, 257, 258, 259, 263, 285, 321

presidential campaign of (1980), 308, 309–10, 312, 317, 318, 322

presidential campaign of (1984), 324, 338, 340, 341

press coverage of, 265, 321, 326, 329–30, 333–36, 345, 347, 348, 350

at Reykjavik summit (1986), 353–54

Soviet policy of, 320–21, 324–32, 337, 339, 343–48, 353–54

speech cards used by, 312–13, 364

"The Speech" of, 312–13, 316, 317

speechwriters of, 137n, 265, 312–61, 365, 367n, 380, 381, 395, 418, 491

"Star Wars" program of, 330–32, 353

State of the Union addresses of, 323–24, 347, 349–50, 445

style of, 13, 27n, 180, 265, 312–16, 323–24, 340–48, 351–61, 363, 364, 408n, 418, 487

symbolism used by, 27n, 313–15, 323–24, 354–58, 487

television broadcasts of, 327, 331–32, 340, 353

at Vienna summit (1985), 353

Reed, Bruce, 407, 424, 428, 431, 437, 438, 443–44, 494

Regan, Donald, 341–42, 343, 345, 347–48, 349–50, 351, 361

Reich, Robert, 405

Reinsch, Leonard, 36

Republican Looks at His Party, A (Larson), 86

Republican National Committee (RNC), 285

Republican national conventions, 3, 88–89, 95, 108, 195, 262, 263–64, 313, 338

Reynaud, Paul, 21

Rice, Condoleezza, 371, 456, 458, 465, 466, 468, 470, 477–78, 481, 482, 483

Richardson, Elliott, 225

Richberg, Donald, 13, 18, 21

Rich Nations and the Poor Nations, The (Ward), 153

Ridgway, Matthew, 67

Robinson, Claude, 77

Robinson, Peter, 322, 342, 354–57, 361

Rockefeller, Nelson, 190, 252

Rogers, William, 217

Rohrabacher, Dana, 318, 319n, 340–41, 342, 350, 353, 355

Rooney, John Jerome, 368

Roosevelt, Eleanor, 5, 12, 27, 119

Roosevelt, Elliott, 5

Roosevelt, Franklin D., 5–30
  advisers of, 21–30
  annual congressional message of (1934), 16n
  annual congressional message of (1936), 16
  "arsenal of democracy" phrase of, 25
  "Brains Trust" of, 6, 7, 13
  death of, 28, 31, 433–34
  Democratic National Convention speech of (1932), 5–9
  Democratic National Convention speech of (1936), 17–18
  as Democratic Party leader, 9–10, 21
  editorial revisions by, 4, 10–12, 15–19, 24, 25–27, 38, 110, 121, 427
  "fear itself" quote of, 12
  "fireside chats" of, 14, 20, 25, 29, 36, 90, 92–93, 114, 213, 273–74
  first inaugural address of (1933), 10–12, 14, 188
  "Four Freedoms" speech of (1941), 25–26
  Great Depression policies of, 9–10, 14, 15, 16–19, 27, 151–52, 394
  gubernatorial campaign of (1928), 5–6, 7
  "infamy" quote of, 26–27
  LBJ compared with, 151, 155
  legacy of, 433–34, 441
  "new deal" phrase of, 6–7, 11–12, 59–60, 151, 283, 293
  New Deal policies of, 6–7, 11–12, 13, 14, 15, 16–19, 21, 35, 48, 59–60, 61, 95, 151–52, 208, 242, 249–50, 283, 293
  Nixon compared with, 188, 192–93, 213
  Pearl Harbor speech of (1941), 26–27, 126, 475
  personal secretaries of, 15, 17, 19
  presidential campaign of (1932), 5–10, 17, 31
  presidential campaign of (1936), 16, 17–18, 21
  presidential campaign of (1940), 22
  presidential campaign of (1944), 28
  press coverage of, 15, 17
  radio broadcasts of, 4, 12–13, 20, 213, 273–74

Roosevelt, Franklin D. *(cont.)*
  "rendezvous with destiny" phrase of, 17
  second inaugural address of (1937), 18–19
  speechwriters of, 5–32, 71, 120, 142, 161, 192–93, 223, 427
  State of the Union address of (1941), 24–26
  style of, 4, 12–13, 14, 18–19, 25–27, 29–30, 31, 32, 35–36, 38, 114, 151, 155, 192–93, 261, 468
  Truman compared with, 31, 32, 35–36, 38, 60, 62
  wartime inauguration of (1945), 105
  wartime leadership of, 19–28, 32, 381
Roosevelt, Sara, 5
Roosevelt, Theodore, 6, 95, 105, 134, 188, 229, 284
Rosenman, Dorothy, 5, 16
Rosenman, Samuel, 5–6, 7, 8, 9, 12, 16, 17, 18, 21, 22, 23–24, 25, 27–28, 29, 31–32, 33, 34–37, 39, 40, 41–42, 46, 51, 57, 71, 120, 142, 149, 165, 192–93, 213
Rosner, Jeremy, 407, 409, 410–11, 412, 413, 419–20, 421
Ross, Charlie, 33, 35, 38, 48–49, 58
Rostow, Walt, 130–31
Rove, Karl, 460n, 466, 469, 471, 472, 483
Rowe, James, 47
Rubin, Robert, 405
Ruckelshaus, William, 225
Rumsfeld, Donald, 241, 242–44, 245, 246–47, 250–51, 252, 267, 465n, 470, 487–88
Rusk, Dean, 106, 115, 123, 126–27, 131, 141, 162, 172, 184, 287
Russell, Francis, 61
Russell, Richard, 187, 213

Sadat, Anwar, 291–92
Safire, William, 29, 190–92, 193, 194, 195–97, 202–7, 208, 209, 210, 211, 213, 214, 215–16, 217, 219–20, 224, 295, 381, 384n, 389, 404, 406, 491
Salinger, Pierre, 109, 126, 148
SALT treaties, 278, 289, 298–99
Sanders, Barefoot, 187
Schlesinger, Arthur M., Jr., 104, 112n, 113, 115, 116, 119–22, 130–31, 133, 134, 135, 137, 142–43, 147, 151, 158, 166n, 283n, 402, 406–7, 434n, 445
Schlesinger, James, 252
Schneiders, Greg, 294–95, 296
Schoen, Doug, 430
Schoen, William, 175

Schram, Martin, 281
Schultze, Charles, 173
Schwarzkopf, Norman, 385
Schweiker, Richard, 365
Scott, Hugh, 201
Scowcroft, Brent, 252, 370, 374, 378, 380, 393
Scully, Matthew, 32n, 456–57, 458, 459, 460, 461, 462–63, 470, 471–73, 474, 475, 476–77, 478, 479, 480, 483, 484, 486, 488–89, 492, 493–94
Seaton, Fred, 82–83
Secret Service, U.S., 85n, 146, 220, 372, 399, 411, 441, 457
September 11, 2001 terrorist attacks, 26, 436n, 456–60, 463–72, 475, 477, 479, 483, 486, 493
Serbia, 450–54
Sevareid, Eric, 204
Seward, William, 2
Sforza, Scott, 488
Shakespeare, William, 12, 135
Shalala, Donna, 438
Shapiro, Walter, 293, 348n
Shattan, Joseph, 463, 479
Sheehan, Michael, 436
Sherwood, Robert Emmet, 22–24, 25, 28, 29, 33, 35–36, 120
Shesol, Jeff, 405–6, 444, 445, 447, 454–55
Shipley, David, 431, 437–38
Short, Joe, 66, 67
Shrum, Robert, 269, 448
Shultz, George, 331, 345
Sidey, Hugh, 109–10, 153, 182, 279, 292
Simon, Bob, 370–71
Simon, William, 242, 248
Sirica, John, 220
Skelton, Red, 231, 240
Skinner, Samuel, 393–94, 395, 397, 398
Skutnik, Lenny, 323–24
Small, Karna, 349
Smith, Bedell, 74
Smith, Craig, 260–61, 262
Smith, Curt, 364n, 365–66, 371–72, 377, 378–79, 382n, 391n, 392, 399, 400–401
Smith, Griffin, 271
Smith, Howard K., 198
Snow, Anthony, 388–89, 391–92, 395, 397, 406–7, 458
Snyder, John, 35, 39
Sorensen, Annis Chaikin, 102
Sorensen, C. A., 102
Sorensen, Theodore C. "Ted," 101–29, 141–44

Sorensen, Tom, 102, 131
Soviet Union, 41, 42–47, 49, 50, 60, 63,
    65–66, 69–81, 90, 97–100, 110, 115,
    122–34, 138, 140–41, 143, 171–72,
    189, 197, 198, 218, 267, 274–77, 278,
    288–90, 298–99, 307, 320–21,
    324–32, 337, 339, 343–48, 353–54
Sparks, Will, 165–67, 175–76
Speakes, Larry, 348, 349, 352
Spencer, Stuart, 352
Sperling, Gene, 405, 407, 408, 437, 443–44,
    455
Spingarn, Stephen, 41, 63
Sputnik launch (1957), 90, 98, 275
Squier, Bob, 432
Srebenica massacre (1995), 451
Stahl, Lesley, 344, 375
Stalin, Joseph, 33, 50, 69–71, 73
Starr, Kenneth, 444–49
State Department, U.S., 14, 21, 23, 44,
    45–46, 61–62, 70, 72–73, 74, 75,
    79–80, 119, 131–32, 155, 192, 290,
    319–20, 322, 328, 344–46, 356n,
    357, 358, 371
Steelman, John, 39, 40
Stein, Ben, 227, 229
Stein, Herbert, 227
Steinbeck, John, 155–56, 168, 170
Stephanopoulos, George, 402, 403, 404,
    405, 406–7, 413, 414, 423, 424, 427,
    430, 431, 433, 440, 441
Stevenson, Adlai, 103, 106, 107, 109, 113,
    119, 126, 147
Stewart, Gordon, 296, 297, 300, 301–4,
    310
Stone, Alan, 418, 437
Storing, Herbert, 261
Straub, Bruno, 371
Strauss, Lewis, 79, 80
Sundquist, James, 64
Sununu, John, 370, 379, 389, 393–94
Supreme Court, U.S., 13, 18, 63, 87–88,
    147n, 198–99, 226, 442, 443, 455
Svahn, Jack, 347–48
Swing, Raymond Gram, 22

Taft, Robert A., 50, 58
Taliban, 467, 468, 475
Tamagni, Jordan, 408n, 409, 435, 438, 445
Taylor, Maxwell, 123, 131
Teeter, Bob, 394, 395, 398
Temple, Larry, 186, 187
Tenet, George, 465n, 482, 485
Tennyson, Alfred Lord, 381
terHorst, Jerald, 235, 239

Theis, Paul, 235, 236, 241–42, 247, 248,
    250–51, 253
Thomas, Albert, 145
Thomas, Dennis, 343
Thoreau, Henry David, 12
Thurmond, Strom, 51, 322
Tower, John, 352
Treptow, Martin, 314–15
Truman, Bess, 56
Truman, Harry S., 31–68
    advisers of, 31–42, 46, 51, 247
    anticommunism of, 63, 65–66
    approval ratings of, 66
    Congress addressed by (1946), 37–40
    "credo" formulation of, 46–47
    Democratic National Convention
        speech of (1948), 51–52
    as Democratic Party leader, 47, 48,
        50–59, 68, 83, 95, 430
    domestic policies of, 34–40, 49, 51,
        52–60, 62, 134, 151, 183–84, 284
    economic policies of, 37–38, 49, 52–53,
        54
    editorial revisions by, 38–40, 44–45
    extemporaneous remarks of, 48–50,
        53–59, 179, 193n
    "fair deal" phrase of, 59–60, 151
    Fair Deal programs of, 59–60, 62, 151,
        183–84, 208
    FDR compared with, 31, 32, 35–36, 38,
        60, 62
    Ford compared with, 246, 247, 267
    foreign policy of, 33, 34–35, 41, 42–47,
        49, 50, 54, 59, 60–63, 65–67, 129,
        183–84, 247, 263
    HST compared with, 192–93
    inaugural address of (1949), 59, 60–63,
        491
    JFK compared with, 129, 134
    Korean policy of, 65–67, 183–84
    labor relations of, 37–40, 47, 57, 58
    LBJ compared with, 179, 183–84
    MacArthur dismissed by (1951), 66–67
    Marshall Plan of, 60, 61–63, 129, 263
    "Missouri English" of, 44–45
    oratorical skills of, 36, 44–45, 48–50,
        67–68, 179
    personality of, 38–39
    "Point Four" policy of, 61–63, 129
    at Potsdam Conference (1945), 33, 34
    presidential campaign of (1948), 47–59,
        65, 267
    press coverage of, 49, 51, 52, 56–57, 59,
        60, 62, 66, 67
    radio broadcasts of, 49, 54, 66–67

Truman, Harry S. *(cont.)*
  Republican opposition to, 47, 48, 49, 50,
    51, 52–59, 95
  Soviet policy of, 41, 42–47, 49, 50, 60,
    63, 65–66
  speechwriters of, 4, 31–68, 129, 169,
    406, 418n
  State of the Union addresses of, 42–49,
    59–60, 64, 246
  style of, 31–32, 35–36, 38–42, 44–45,
    48–50, 53–59, 95, 179, 193, 284, 477,
    491
  television broadcasts of, 49, 52, 62, 67–68
  Truman Doctrine of, 43–47
  UN Conference addressed by (1945),
    31, 33
  vice-presidential campaign of (1944), 36
  whistle-stop campaign of, 49–50, 53–59
Truman, Margaret, 38n, 43n, 56
Tugwell, Rex, 13, 21
Tully, Grace, 19, 25, 26
Turner, Stansfield, 287–88
Tutwiler, Margaret, 399
Twain, Mark, 6, 364
Twenty-fifth Amendment, 233

United Nations, 31, 33, 38, 60, 66, 78,
    80–81, 126, 206, 211, 263, 383,
    386–87, 412, 479–83

Valenti, Jack, 145, 146, 149–50, 152, 155,
    156, 158, 159–63, 165, 168, 169,
    170–71, 172, 174, 176, 179, 183–84
Vance, Cyrus, 274, 275, 282, 288, 289–90
Vandenberg, Arthur, 42, 384
Van Doren, Charles, 117
Vardaman, James K., 33–34, 38–39
Vidal, Gore, 91
Vietnam War, 152n, 156–57, 167–71,
    183–87, 195, 196, 198–99, 200,
    201–5, 209–11, 215–16, 218, 219,
    247, 271, 276, 285, 421
von Hoffman, Nicholas, 279–80
Voting Rights Act (1965), 158–62

Waldman, Michael, 402–3, 404, 405, 406n,
    407–8, 418n, 422, 432, 433, 437–39,
    440, 443–44, 445, 446, 447, 454
Walesa, Lech, 371, 375
Wallace, George, 134–36, 157–58
Wallace, Henry, 62
Walsh, Kenneth, 389
Walters, Logan, 470
Ward, Barbara, 153

Warren, Earl, 87, 111
Washington, George, 1, 95, 100, 233, 262,
    313–14
Watergate scandal, 220–34, 240, 241, 243,
    294, 301, 352, 445, 461
Watson, Jack, 300
Watson, Marvin, 186, 187
Wattenberg, Ben, 166, 175, 177
Webb, James, 171–72
Weber, Max, 291
Wehner, Pete, 456–57
Weinberger, Caspar, 320n, 331, 366
Weiss, Lowell, 446
Welles, Sumner, 21
Welliver, Judson, 2–3
Wells, H. G., 202
Welsh, Ed, 172
West Germany, 138–41, 190, 191–92,
    354–58, 374–78, 383
What I Saw at the Revolution (Noonan),
    338
White, Theodore, 104
White, William Allen, 23
Whitewater investigation, 443, 444
Whitman, Ann, 80, 81, 92
Why England Slept (Kennedy), 102
Wicker, Tom, 301
Wiley, Mary Margaret, 162–63
Wilkie, Carter, 418, 437
Will, George, 326
Williams, Ralph, 97–98
Wilson, Charles, 73, 79
Wilson, Edith, 27
Wilson, Harold, 191
Wilson, Woodrow, 6, 27, 62, 126, 134, 188,
    202–3, 269, 284, 464
Winston, Chriss, 365–66, 368–69, 371, 381,
    384–85
Wirthlin, Richard, 349–50, 352
Witness (Chambers), 318, 325
Wofford, Harris, 110–11
Woods, Rose Mary, 191–92, 194, 204, 217
Woodward, Bob, 225–26, 488
World War I, 38, 102, 126, 202, 464
World War II, 19–28, 32, 33, 34, 48, 63,
    102, 274, 313, 337–40, 392–93,
    419–21, 475, 487n
Wurzburger, Walter S., 329

Yugoslavia, 450–54

Ziegler, Ron, 211, 219, 221, 223
Zoellick, Robert, 399
Zumwalt, Elmo, 288

Illustration Credits

About the Author

Robert Schlesinger teaches political journalism at the Boston University Washington Journalism Center. His work has appeared in *The Washington Monthly, Salon.com, The Weekly Standard, People*, and the *Boston Globe Magazine*. He lives with his wife and dog in Alexandria, Virginia.